SECOND EDITION, Excel 2007 Update

MANAGEMENT SCIENCE
The Art of Modeling with Spreadsheets

STEPHEN G. POWELL

Dartmouth College

KENNETH R. BAKER

Dartmouth College

WILEY

John Wiley & Sons, Ltd.

PUBLISHER   *Susan Elbe*
EXECUTIVE EDITOR   *Beth Lang Golub*
SENIOR PRODUCTION EDITOR   *Nicole Repasky*
SENIOR MARKETING MANAGER   *Amy Scholz*
ASSISTANT MARKETING MANAGER   *Carly DeCandia*
SENIOR DESIGNER   *Hope Miller*
SENIOR MEDIA EDITOR   *Allie K. Morris*
SENIOR EDITORIAL ASSISTANT   *Maria Guarascio*
PRODUCTION MANAGEMENT SERVICES   *Thomson Digital*
COVER DESIGN   *David Levy*

This book was set in Times Ten by Thomson Press and printed and bound by Courier/Westford. The cover was printed by Phoenix Color.

This book is printed on acid free paper. ∞

ISBN-13: 978-0-470-39376-5

Printed in the United States of America

10   9   8   7   6   5   4   3   2   1

To Becky and Judy,
for all their encouragement and support

Brief Contents

Table of Contents

* Optional Sections

Preface

This is a book for business analysts about *modeling*. A *model* is a simplified representation of a situation or problem, and *modeling* is the process of building, refining, and analyzing that representation for greater insight and improved decision making. Some models are so common that they are thought of as routine instruments rather than models. A budget, a cash flow projection, or a business plan may have many uses, but each one is a model. In addition, many sophisticated models are embedded in software. Option pricing models, credit scoring models, or inventory models are key components of important decision support systems. Beyond these types, we encounter many customized models, built by the millions of people who routinely use spreadsheet software to analyze business situations. This group includes consultants, venture capitalists, marketing analysts, and operations specialists. Almost anyone who uses spreadsheets in business has been involved with models and can benefit from formal training in the use of models.

Models also play a central role in management education. A short list of models that nearly every business student encounters would include cash flow models, stock price models, option pricing models, product life cycle models, market diffusion models, order quantity models, and project scheduling models. For the management student, a basic ability to model in spreadsheets can be a powerful tool for acquiring a deeper understanding of the various functional areas of business. But to fully understand the implications of these models, a student needs to appreciate what a model is and how to learn from it. Our book provides that knowledge.

For many years, modeling was performed primarily by highly trained specialists using mainframe computers. Consequently, even a simple model was costly and frequently required a long development time. The assumptions and results often seemed impenetrable to business managers because they were removed from the modeling process. This situation has changed radically with the advent of personal computers and electronic spreadsheets. Now, managers and analysts can build their own models and produce their own analyses. This new kind of modeling is known as *end-user modeling*. Now that virtually every analyst has access to a powerful computer, the out-of-pocket costs of modeling have become negligible. The major cost now is the analyst's *time*: time to define the problem, gather data, build and debug a model, and use the model to support the decision process. For this time to be well spent, the analyst must be efficient and effective in the modeling process. This book is designed to improve modeling *efficiency* by focusing on the most important tasks and tools and by suggesting how to avoid unproductive steps in the modeling effort. This book is also designed to improve modeling *effectiveness* by covering the most relevant analytic methods and emphasizing procedures that lead to the deepest business insights.

WHY THIS BOOK?

One of our reasons for writing this book was the conviction that many analysts were not being appropriately educated as modelers. Business students tend to receive strong training in management science but little training in practical modeling. They often receive inadequate training, as well, in using spreadsheets for modeling. In most educational programs, the emphasis is on *models*, rather than on *modeling*. That is, the curriculum covers a number of classical models that have proven useful in management education or in business. Although studying the classics may be valuable for a number of reasons (and our book covers a number of the classics), studying models does not provide the full range of skills needed to build models for new situations.

We also have met many analysts who view modeling essentially as a matter of having strong spreadsheet skills. But spreadsheet skills are not sufficient. The spreadsheet is only one tool in the creative, open-ended problem-solving process we call modeling. Modeling is both a technical discipline and a *craft*. The craft aspects of the process have largely been overlooked in the education of business analysts. Our purpose is to provide both the technical knowledge and the craft skills needed to develop real expertise in business modeling. In this book, therefore, we cover the three skill areas that a business analyst needs to become an effective modeler:

- spreadsheet engineering
- management science
- modeling craft

NEW IN THE SECOND EDITION

In the time that has elapsed since the first edition of this book was published, we have had the opportunity to discuss it with numerous readers and teachers. The second edition offers us an opportunity to make the book easier to use and to broaden its appeal. The key changes in the second edition include:

- Additional coverage of management science
  To provide instructors with more options, we have added depth to our coverage of forecasting, decision analysis, and optimization. In addition, each chapter contains some advanced material in a designated section.

- Broader coverage of Excel
  To create an integrated treatment of spreadsheet topics, we have added a chapter that covers the skills every reader should have, as well as a chapter that covers some of the skills used by experts.

- Shorter chapters
  To make the book more flexible as a textbook, we have devoted three separate chapters to data analysis, regression, and forecasting; four chapters to optimization topics; and two chapters to simulation.

- Additional exercises and cases
  We have added exercises to the chapters and extended the set of cases. We have also added elementary exercises to provide practice for less experienced students.

NEW IN THE UPDATE EDITION

The Second Edition was written to be compatible with Excel 2003, which was the prevalent version of Excel at the time the Second Edition was published. This Update Edition is compatible with Excel 2007. The major changes occur in Chapters 3, 4, and 7, which illustrate a number of specific Excel skills. Some changes occur in other chapters, but most of those involve minor changes to sequences of commands. The topic coverage is essentially unchanged.

In principle, two students could work side by side in a course, one using the Second Edition and relying on Excel 2003, the other using the Update Edition and relying on Excel 2007. They should be able to learn the same skills, as both versions of the book are self-contained.

In some cases, our software vendors have produced new versions of their software to work with Excel 2007. Students using the Second Edition should download software from the CD included with the book. Students using the Update Edition should download software from the websites listed in the book's insert.

TO THE READER

Modeling, like painting or singing, cannot be learned entirely from a book. However, a book can establish principles, provide examples, and offer additional practice. We suggest that the reader take an *active learning* attitude toward this book. This means working to internalize the skills taught here by tackling as many new problems as possible. It also means applying these skills to everyday situations in other classes or on the job. Modeling expertise (as opposed to modeling appreciation) can be acquired only by *doing* modeling. There is no substitute for experience.

The book is organized into five parts:

- Spreadsheet modeling in the context of problem solving (Chapters 1–4)
- Spreadsheet engineering (Chapters 5 and 6)
- Data analysis and statistics (Chapters 7–9)
- Optimization (Chapters 10–13)
- Decision analysis and simulation (Chapters 14–16)

Our table of contents provides details on the topic coverage in the various chapters, and in Chapter 1, we provide a diagram of the prerequisite logic among the chapters. Several chapters contain advanced material in sections marked with (*). Students can find Spreadsheet files for all models presented in the text on the website at www.wiley.com/college/powell.

TO THE TEACHER

It is far easier to teach technical skills in Excel or in management science than it is to teach modeling. Nonetheless, modeling skills *can* be taught successfully, and a variety of effective approaches are available. Feedback from users of our book and from reviewers of the first edition suggests that there are almost as many course designs as there are instructors for this subject. Our book does not represent an idealized version of our own course; rather, it is intended to be a versatile resource that can support a selection of topics in management science, spreadsheet engineering, and modeling craft.

At the book's website, www.wiley.com/college/powell, we provide some teaching tips and describe our views on the different ways that this material can be delivered successfully in a graduate or undergraduate course. All spreadsheet files for all models in the text as well as PowerPoint slides created by Alan Olinsky at Bryant University can be found on the site as well. In addition, we provide some sample syllabi to suggest the course designs that other instructors have delivered with the help of this book.

SOFTWARE ACCOMPANYING THE TEXT

Users of this text have access to the following software applications which can be downloaded by following the procedures given in the book's insert.

- *Premium Solver for Education*
- *Crystal Ball 7 Student Edition*
- *TreePlan*
- *Spreadsheet Professional*
- *Sensitivity Toolkit*

Users of this book can download the spreadsheets referred to in the text from the Student Companion Site at www.wiley.com/college/powell.

Premium Solver is used for linear and nonlinear optimization, which is the topic of Chapters 10–13, and is revisited briefly in Chapter 16.

Crystal Ball is used for Monte Carlo simulation, which is the topic of Chapter 15. Its OptQuest package is used for optimization in simulation models, which is covered in Chapter 16, and its CB Predictor package is used for Forecasting, as illustrated in Chapter 9.

TreePlan is used for decision analysis, the subject of Chapter 14.

Spreadsheet Professional is an add-in for Excel that automates error checking. It is introduced in Chapter 5.

The *Sensitivity Toolkit* is an Excel add-in that provides the capability to perform four types of sensitivity analysis:

Data Sensitivity

Tornado Chart

Solver Sensitivity

Crystal Ball Sensitivity

These tools are covered in Chapters 6, 10, and 15.

ACKNOWLEDGMENTS

A book such as this evolves over many years of teaching and research. Our ideas have been influenced by our students and by other teachers, not all of whom we can acknowledge here. Our students at Dartmouth's Tuck School of Business have participated in many of our teaching experiments and improved our courses through their inimitable feedback. Without the collaborative spirit our students bring to their education, we could not have developed our ideas as we have.

As in the first edition, we wish to mention the many excellent teachers and writers whose ideas we have adapted. We acknowledge Don Plane, Cliff Ragsdale, and Wayne Winston for their pioneering work in teaching management science with spreadsheets and the later influence of Tom Grossman, Peter Bell, Zeger Degraeve, and Erhan Erkut on our work.

The first edition benefited from careful reviews from the following reviewers: Jerry Allison (University of Central Oklahoma), Jonathan Caulkins (Carnegie-Mellon University), Jean-Louis Goffin (McGill University), Roger Grinde (University of New Hampshire), Tom Grossman (University of Calgary), Raymond Hill (Air Force Institute of Technology), Alan Johnson (United States Military Academy), Prafulla Joglekar (LaSalle University), Tarja Joro (University of Alberta), Ron Klimberg (Saint Joseph's University), Larry Leblanc (Vanderbilt University), Jerry May (University of Pittsburgh), Jim Morris (University of Wisconsin), Jim Mote (RPI), Chuck Noon (University of Tennessee), Tava Olsen (Washington University), Fred Raafat (San Diego State University), Gary Reeves (University of South Carolina), Moshe Rosenwein (Columbia University), David Schilling (Ohio State University), Linus Schrage (University of Chicago), Donald Simmons (Ithaca College), George Steiner (McMaster University), Stephen Thorpe (Drexel University).

Additional feedback and help on the second edition came from: R. Kim Craft (Southern Utah University), Joan Donohue (University of South Carolina), Steve Ford (University of the South), Phillip Fry (Boise State University), Li Guodong (Maryville University), LeRoy Honeycutt (Gardner-Webb University), Rich Kilgore (St. Louis University), Frank Krzystofiak (University at Buffalo SUNY), Shailesh Kulkarni (University of North Texas), Dale Lehman (Alaska Pacific University), Vedran Lelas (Plymouth State University), David Walter Little (High Point University), Leo Lopes (University of Arizona), Alvin J. Martinez (University of Puerto Rico, Rio Piedras), Jacquelynne McLellan (Frostburg State University), Ajay Mishra (Binghamton University SUNY), Shimon Y. Nof (Purdue University),

Manuel Nunez (University of Connecticut), Alan Olinsky (Bryant University), Tava Olsen (Washington University), Susan Palocsay (James Madison University), Ganga P. Ramdas (Lincoln University), B. Madhu Rao (Bowling Green State University), Jim Robison (Sonoma State University), Christopher M. Rump (Bowling Green State University), Thomas Sandman (California State University, Sacramento), Sergei Savin (Columbia University), Daniel Shimshak (University of Massachusetts Boston), Minghe Sun (University of Texas at San Antonio), David Tufte (Southern Utah University).

Beth Golub of John Wiley & Sons encouraged us to write this book for years and has been a supportive influence since we began. We appreciate the extensive network she has continually tapped for feedback and her initial willingness to support us in writing a new kind of textbook.

SGP

KRB

About The Authors

Steve Powell is a Professor at the Tuck School of Business at Dartmouth College. His primary research interest lies in modeling production and service processes, but he has also been active in research in energy economics, marketing, and operations. At Tuck, he has developed a variety of courses in management science, including the core Decision Science course and electives in the Art of Modeling, Business Process Redesign, and Applications of Simulation. He originated the Teacher's Forum column in *Interfaces*, and has written a number of articles on teaching modeling to practitioners. He is the Academic Director of the annual INFORMS Teaching of Management Science Workshops. In 2001 he was awarded the INFORMS Prize for the Teaching of Operations Research/Management Science Practice.

Ken Baker is a faculty member at Dartmouth College. He is currently Nathaniel Leverone Professor of Management at the Tuck School of Business and also Adjunct Professor at the Thayer School of Engineering. At Dartmouth, he has taught courses relating to Management Science, Manufacturing Management, and Environmental Management. He is the author of two other textbooks, *Elements of Sequencing and Scheduling* and *Optimization Modeling with Spreadsheets*, in addition to a variety of technical articles. He has served as Tuck School's Associate Dean and directed the Tuck School's management development programs in the manufacturing area. He is an INFORMS Fellow as well as a Fellow of the Manufacturing and Service Operations Management (MSOM) Society.

1 Introduction

1.1 MODELS AND MODELING

Modeling is the process of creating a simplified representation of reality and working with this representation in order to understand or control some aspect of the world. While this book is devoted to *mathematical* models, modeling itself is a ubiquitous human activity. In fact, it seems to be one of just a few fundamental ways in which we humans understand our environment.

As an example, a map is one of the most common models we encounter. Maps are models because they simplify reality by leaving out most geographic details in order to highlight the important features we need. A state road map, for example, shows major roads but not minor ones, gives rough locations of cities but not individual addresses, and so on. The map we choose must be appropriate for the need we have: a long trip across several states requires a regional map, while a trip across town requires a detailed street map. In the same way, a good model must be appropriate for the specific uses intended for it. A complex model of the economy is probably not appropriate for pricing an individual product. Similarly, a back-of-the-envelope calculation is likely to be inappropriate for acquiring a multibillion-dollar company.

Models take many different forms: mental, visual, physical, mathematical, and spreadsheet, to name a few. We use mental models constantly to understand the world and to predict the outcomes of our actions. Mental models are informal, but they do allow us to make a quick judgment about the desirability of a particular proposal. For example, mental models come into play in a hiring decision. One manager has a mental model that suggests that hiring older workers is not a good idea because they are slow to adopt new ways; another manager has a mental model that suggests hiring older workers is a good idea because they bring valuable experience to the job. We are often unaware of our own mental models, yet they can have a strong influence on the actions we take, especially when they are the primary basis for decision making.

While everyone uses mental models, some people routinely use other kinds of models in their professional lives. Visual models include maps, as we mentioned earlier. Organization charts are also visual models. They may represent reporting relationships, reveal the locus of authority, suggest major channels of communication, and identify responsibility for personnel decisions. Visual models are used in various sports, when a coach sketches the playing area and represents team members and opponents as X's and O's. Most players probably don't realize that they are using a model for the purposes of understanding and communication.

Physical models are used extensively in engineering to assist in the design of airplanes, ships, and buildings. They are also used in science, as, for example, in depicting the spatial arrangement of amino acids in the DNA helix or the makeup of a chemical compound. Architects use physical models to show how a proposed building fits within its surroundings.

Mathematical models take many forms and are used throughout science, engineering, and public policy. For instance, a groundwater model helps determine where flooding is most likely to occur, population models predict the spread of infectious disease, and exposure-assessment models forecast the impact of toxic spills. In other settings, traffic-flow models predict the buildup of highway congestion,

1

fault-tree models help reveal the causes of an accident, and reliability models suggest when equipment may need replacement. Mathematical models can be extremely powerful, especially when they give clear insights into the forces driving a particular outcome.

1.1.1 Why Study Modeling?

What are the benefits of building and using formal models, as opposed to relying on mental models or just "gut feel?" The primary purpose of modeling is to generate *insight*, by which we mean an improved understanding of the situation or problem at hand. While mathematical models consist of numbers and symbols, the real benefit of using them is to make better *decisions*. Better decisions are most often the result of improved understanding, not just the numbers themselves.

Thus, we study modeling primarily because it improves our thinking skills. Modeling is a discipline that provides a structure for problem solving. The fundamental elements of a model—such as parameters, decisions, and outcomes—are useful concepts in all problem solving. Modeling provides examples of clear and logical analysis and helps raise the level of our thinking.

Modeling also helps improve our quantitative reasoning skills. Building a model demands care with units and with orders of magnitude, and it teaches the importance of numeracy. Many people are cautious about quantitative analysis because they do not trust their own quantitative skills. In the best cases, a well-structured modeling experience can help such people overcome their fears, build solid quantitative skills, and improve their performance in a business world that demands (and rewards) these skills.

Any model is a laboratory in which we can experiment and learn. An effective modeler needs to develop an open, inquiring frame of mind to go along with the necessary technical skills. Just as a scientist uses the laboratory to test ideas, hypotheses, and theories, a business analyst can use a model to test the implications of alternative courses of action and develop not only a recommended decision but, equally important, the rationale for why that decision is preferred. The easy-to-understand rationale behind the recommendation often comes from insights the analyst has discovered while testing a model.

1.1.2 Models in Business

Given the widespread use of mathematical models in science and engineering, it is not surprising to find that they are also widely used in the business world. We refer to people who routinely build and analyze formal models in their professional lives as **business analysts**. In our years of training managers and management students, we have found that strong modeling skills are particularly important for consultants, as well as for financial analysts, marketing researchers, entrepreneurs, and others who face challenging business decisions of real economic consequence. Practicing business analysts and students intending to become business analysts are the intended audience for this book.

Just as there are many types of models in science, engineering, public policy, and other domains outside of business, many different types of models are used in business. We distinguish here four model types that exemplify different levels of interaction with and participation by the people who use the models:

- **One-time decision models**
- **Decision-support models**
- **Models embedded in computer systems**
- **Models used in business education**

Many of the models business analysts create are used in one-time decision problems. A corporate valuation model, for example, might be used intensively during merger negotiations but never thereafter. In other situations, a one-time model might be created to evaluate the profit impact of a promotion campaign, or to help select a health insurance provider, or to structure the terms of a supply contract. One-time models are usually built by decision makers themselves, frequently under time pressure. Managerial judgment is often used as a substitute for empirical data in such models, owing to time constraints and data limitations. Most importantly, this type of model involves the user intensively, because the model is usually tailored to a particular decision-making need. One major benefit of studying modeling is to gain skills in building and using one-time models effectively.

Decision-support systems are computer systems that tie together models, data, analysis tools, and presentation tools into a single integrated package. These systems are intended for repeated use, either by executives themselves or by their analytic staff. Decision-support systems are used in research and development planning at pharmaceutical firms, pricing decisions at oil companies, and product-line profitability analysis at manufacturing firms, to cite just a few examples. Decision-support systems are usually built and maintained by information systems personnel, but they represent the routine use of what were once one-time decision models. After a one-time model becomes established, it can be adapted for broader and more frequent use in the organization. Thus, the models within decision-support systems may initially be developed by managers and business analysts, but later streamlined by information systems staff for a less intensive level of human interaction. An additional benefit of studying modeling is to recognize possible improvements in the design and operation of decision-support systems.

Embedded models are those contained within computer systems that perform routine, repeated tasks with little or no human involvement. Many inventory replenishment decisions are made by automated computer systems. Loan payments on auto leases or prices for stock options are also determined by automated systems. Routine real estate appraisals may also be largely automated. In these cases, the models themselves are somewhat hidden in the software. Many users of embedded models are not aware of the underlying models; they simply assume that the "system" knows how to make the right calculations. An ancillary benefit of studying modeling is to become more aware, and perhaps more questioning, of these embedded models.

1.1.3 Models in Business Education

Models are useful not only in the business world, but also in the academic world where business analysts are educated. The modern business curriculum is heavily dependent on models for delivering basic concepts as well as for providing numerical results. An introductory course in Finance might include an option-pricing model, a cash-management model, and the classic portfolio model. A basic Marketing course might include demand curves for pricing analysis, a diffusion model for new-product penetration, and clustering models for market segmentation. In Operations Management, we might encounter inventory models for stock control, allocation models for scheduling production, and the newsvendor model for trading off shortage and surplus outcomes. Both micro- and macroeconomics are taught almost exclusively through models. Aggregate supply-and-demand curves are models, as are production functions.

Most of the models used in education are highly simplified, or *stylized*, in order to preserve clarity. Stylized models are frequently used to provide insight into qualitative phenomena, not necessarily to calculate precise numerical results. In this book, we frequently use models from business education as examples, so that we can combine learning about business with learning about models. In fact, the tools presented in this book can be used throughout the curriculum to better understand the various functional areas of business.

1.1.4 Benefits of Business Models

Modeling can benefit business decision making in a variety of ways.

- Modeling allows us to make inexpensive errors. Wind-tunnel tests are used in airplane design partly because if every potential wing design had to be built into a full-scale aircraft and flown by a pilot, we would lose far too many pilots. In a similar way, we can propose ideas and test them in a model, without having to suffer the consequences of bad ideas in the real world.

- Modeling allows us to explore the impossible. Many companies have policies, procedures, or habits that prevent them from making certain choices. Sometimes these habits prevent them from discovering better ways of doing business. Modeling can be used to explore these "impossible" alternatives and to help convince the skeptics to try a different approach.

- Modeling can improve business intuition. As we have said, a model is a laboratory in which we perform experiments. We can usually learn faster from laboratory experiments than from experience in the real world. With a model, we can try thousands of combinations that would take many years to test in the real world. We can also try extreme ideas that would be too risky to test in the real world. And we can learn about how the world works by simulating a hundred years of experience, all in a few minutes.

- Modeling provides information in a timely manner. For example, while a survey could be used to determine the potential demand for a product, effective modeling can often give useful bounds on the likely range of demand in far less time.

- Finally, modeling can reduce costs. Data collection is often expensive and time-consuming. An effective modeler may be able to provide the same level of information at much lower cost.

Even among those who do not build models, skill in working with models is very important. Most business students eventually find themselves on a team charged with recommending a course of action. If these teams do not build models themselves, they often work with internal or external consultants who do. Experience in building and analyzing models is, in our minds, the best training for working effectively on problem-solving teams. People who have not actually built a few models themselves often accept model results blindly or become intimidated by the modeling process. A well-trained analyst not only appreciates the power of modeling but also remains skeptical of models as panaceas.

We believe that modeling skills are useful to a very broad range of business-people, from junior analysts without a business degree to senior vice presidents who do their own analysis. Many recent graduates have only a superficial knowledge of these tools because their education emphasized passive consumption of other people's models rather than active model building. Thus, there is considerable potential even among master's-level graduates to improve their modeling skills so that they can become more capable of carrying out independent analyses of important decisions. The only absolute prerequisite for using this book and enhancing that skill is a desire to use logical, analytic methods to reach a higher level of understanding in the decision-making world.

1.2   THE ROLE OF SPREADSHEETS

Because spreadsheets are the principal vehicle for modeling in business, spreadsheet models are the major type we deal with in this book. Spreadsheet models are also mathematical models, but, for many people, spreadsheet mathematics is more accessible than algebra or calculus. Spreadsheet models do have limitations, of course, but they allow us to build more detailed and more complex models than traditional mathematics allows. They also have the advantage of being pervasive in business analysis. Finally, the spreadsheet format corresponds nicely to the form of accounting statements that are used for business communication; in fact, the word "spreadsheet" originates in accounting and only recently has come to mean the electronic spreadsheet.

It has been said that the spreadsheet is the *second best* way to do many kinds of analysis and is therefore the *best* way to do most modeling. In other words, for any one modeling task, a more powerful, flexible, and sophisticated software tool is almost certainly available. In this sense, the spreadsheet is the Swiss Army knife of business analysis. Most business analysts lack the time, money, and knowledge to learn and use a different software tool for each problem that arises, just as most of us cannot afford to carry around a complete toolbox to handle the occasional screw we need to tighten. The practical alternative is to use the spreadsheet (and occasionally one of its sophisticated add-ins) to perform most modeling tasks. An effective modeler will, of course, have a sense for the limitations of a spreadsheet and will know when to use a more powerful tool.

Despite its limitations, the electronic spreadsheet represents a breakthrough technology for practical modeling. Prior to the 1980s, modeling was performed only by specialists using demanding software on expensive hardware. This meant that only the most critical business problems could be analyzed using models, because only these problems justified the large budgets and long time commitments required to build, debug, and apply the models of the day. This situation has changed dramatically in the past 15 years or so. First the personal computer, then the spreadsheet, and recently the arrival of add-ins for specialized analyses have put tremendous analytical power at the hands of anyone who can afford a laptop and some training. In fact, we believe the 1990s will come to be seen as the dawn of the "end-user modeling" era. End-user modelers are analysts who are not specialists in modeling, but who can create an effective spreadsheet and manipulate it for insight. The problems that end-user modelers can solve are typically not the multibillion-dollar, multiyear variety; those are still the preserve of functional-area specialists and sophisticated computer scientists. Rather, the end user can apply modeling effectively to hundreds of important but smaller-scale situations that in the past would not have benefited from this approach. We provide many illustrations throughout this book.

Spreadsheet skills themselves are now in high demand in many jobs, although experts in Excel may not be skilled modelers. In our recent survey of MBAs from the Tuck School of Business (available at http://mba.tuck.dartmouth.edu/spreadsheet/), we found that 77 percent said that spreadsheets were either "very important" or "critical" in their work. Good training in spreadsheet modeling, in what we call **spreadsheet engineering**, is valuable because it can dramatically improve both the efficiency and effectiveness with which the analyst uses spreadsheets.

1.2.1 Risks of Spreadsheet Use

Countless companies and individuals rely on spreadsheets every day. Most users assume their spreadsheet models are error-free. However, the available evidence suggests just the opposite: many, perhaps most, spreadsheets contain internal errors, and more errors are introduced as these spreadsheets are used and modified. Given this evidence, and the tremendous risks of relying on flawed spreadsheet models, it is critically important to learn how to create spreadsheets that are as close to error-free as possible and to use spreadsheets in a disciplined way to avoid mistakes.

It is rare to read press reports on problems arising from erroneous spreadsheets. Most companies do not readily admit to these kinds of mistakes. However, the few reports that have surfaced are instructive. The European Spreadsheet Risks Interest Group (EUSPRIG) maintains a website (http://www.eusprig.org/stories.htm) that currently documents dozens of verified stories about spreadsheet errors that have had a quantifiable impact on the organization. Here is just a small sample:

- Some candidates for police officer jobs are told they passed the test when in fact they have failed. Reason: improper sorting of the spreadsheet.
- An energy company overcharges consumers between $200 million and $1 billion. Reason: careless naming of spreadsheet files.
- A think-tank reports that only 11 percent of a local population has at least a bachelor's degree when in fact the figure is 20 percent. Reason: a copy-and-paste error in a spreadsheet.
- Misstated earnings lead the stock price of an online retailer to fall 25 percent in a day and the CEO to resign. Reason: a single erroneous numerical input in a spreadsheet.
- A school loses £30,000 because its budget is underestimated. Reason: numbers entered as text in a spreadsheet.
- The Business Council reports that its members forecast slow growth for the coming year when their outlook is actually quite optimistic. Reason: the spreadsheet shifted, so the wrong numbers appeared in the wrong columns.
- Benefits of unbundling telecommunication services are understated by $50 million. Reason: incorrect references in a spreadsheet formula.

These cases suggest that spreadsheets can lead to costly errors in a variety of ways. But are spreadsheets themselves properly *built* in the first place? Apparently not, at least according to the evidence cited by Ray Panko. He summarizes the results of seven field audits involving 367 real-world spreadsheets. Overall, 24 percent were found to contain material errors. Considering only the more recent studies, 91 percent of the 54 spreadsheets tested contained errors, presumably because our ability to find errors has improved.[1] This evidence serves notice that errors in spreadsheets are rampant and insidious.

Why are errors in spreadsheets so common? Traditional computer programming, which is much older than spreadsheet programming and carried out largely by trained professionals, typically uses elaborate and formalized development methods. One aspect of these methods is **code inspection**, which involves a line-by-line audit of finished computer code by a separate team from the one that originally created the code. A typical code inspection finds errors in 5 percent of the lines of code written (and tested) by professional programmers. If this error rate characterizes professional programmers, how much more prevalent are errors among end-user programmers building spreadsheets?

Despite this evidence, very few corporations (and even fewer individuals) employ even the most basic design and inspection procedures. These procedures take time and effort, whereas one of the great appeals of spreadsheet modeling is that it is quick and easy for business analysts who are not professional programmers. But this ease of use is a delusion if the spreadsheets that result contain significant errors.

Drawing on various field studies, Panko offers the following summary of the current state of spreadsheet model building.

> Overall, these studies show that many spreadsheets are large, complex, important, and affect many people. Yet [spreadsheet] development tends to be quite informal, and even trivial controls such as cell protection are not used in most cases. In [traditional] programming, code inspection and data testing are needed to reduce error rates after a module is developed. Yet code inspection is very infrequent [in spreadsheet programming], and while data testing is done, it lacks such rigors as the use of out-of-bounds data. *In general, end-user development in spreadsheeting seems to resemble programming practice in the 1950s and 1960s.*[2] [emphasis added], p.19.

[1]Panko, R. "What We Know about Spreadsheet Errors," *Journal of End User Computing* 10, (Spring 1998): 15–21.
[2]Ibid.

1.2.2 Challenges for Spreadsheet Users

Spreadsheets represent the ubiquitous software platform of business. Millions of spreadsheet models are used each day to make decisions involving billions of dollars, and thousands of new spreadsheets come into being each day. Given this usage pattern, we might think that spreadsheet engineering is a well-developed discipline and that expertise in spreadsheet modeling can be found in just about any company. Amazingly, the opposite is true.

What is the current state of spreadsheet use by end-user modelers? The evidence available from audits of existing spreadsheets, laboratory experiments, surveys of end users, and field visits suggests that, despite widespread use, the quality with which spreadsheets are engineered generally remains poor. There are four major problem areas:

- End-user spreadsheets frequently have major bugs.

- End users are overconfident about the quality of their own spreadsheets.

- The process that end users employ to create their spreadsheets is inefficient at best and chaotic at worst.

- End users fail to employ the most productive methods for generating insights from their spreadsheets.

We mentioned previously the research studies that have attempted to determine the error rate in existing spreadsheets. These studies range over many companies and many industries. The methods used in these studies differ as well. One major shortcoming of these studies is that only certain types of errors can be identified. In particular, careful audits can uncover errors in specific cells but cannot reveal conceptual errors in the modeling behind the spreadsheet. We might wonder, for example, how many existing spreadsheets were designed to solve the wrong problem. Nevertheless, an estimated error rate of 90 percent is noteworthy. It seems fair to conclude that most spreadsheets in actual use contain bugs.

Our own auditing research, conducted as part of the Spreadsheet Engineering Research Project (http://mba.tuck.dartmouth.edu/spreadsheet/), suggests that errors in individual cells may be only the tip of the iceberg. We have found that a substantial majority of spreadsheets in use contain at least one error. However, some of these errors do not materially change the overall results of the model. But many of the spreadsheets we have studied involve a very high degree of complexity, even when the underlying problem being modeled is rather simple. Complexity arises in many ways:

- Individual cell formulas that are excessively long and involved

- Poorly designed worksheets that are difficult to navigate and understand

- Poorly organized workbooks whose underlying structure is concealed

Spreadsheets that are overly complex and difficult for anyone other than the designer to use, even if they are technically correct, may be the cause of some of the costly mistakes attributed to spreadsheets.

Laboratory experiments have uncovered another disturbing fact about spreadsheet modeling: end users appear to be overconfident about the likelihood of errors in their own spreadsheets. In these experiments, undergraduate volunteers were asked to build a spreadsheet for a well-defined problem. After they were done, the volunteers were given time to review and audit their models. Finally, they were asked to evaluate the likelihood that their model contained one or more bugs. While 18 percent of the subjects thought their models had one or more bugs, the actual proportion proved to be 80 percent. That is, 80 percent of these spreadsheets actually had bugs but only about 18 percent of those who built them suspected they had bugs. This finding of overconfidence is consistent with the findings of other studies: people tend to underestimate the possibility that they might make mistakes. Unfortunately, this overconfidence translates directly into a casual attitude toward spreadsheet design and ultimately into a disturbingly high error rate among spreadsheets in actual use.

Our observations and research into how end users actually construct spreadsheets suggest that the process is often inefficient:

- End users typically do not plan their spreadsheets. Instead, they build them live at the keyboard and are drawn into endless rework. (In our survey of MBA graduates, we found that about 20 percent sketched a spreadsheet on paper first, whereas about 50 percent started by entering data and formulas directly into the computer.)

- End users do not use a conscious prototyping approach, which involves building a series of models starting with the simplest and gradually adding complexity.

- End users rarely spend time debugging their models, unless the model performs in such a counterintuitive manner that it demands intervention.

- End users almost never subject their spreadsheets to review by another person. In general, end users appear to trust that the model they *thought* they had built is actually the model they see on their screens, despite the fact that spreadsheets show only numbers, not the relationships behind the numbers.

- Finally, many end users, even some who are experts in Excel, do not consistently use tools that can help generate the insights that make modeling worthwhile. Excel's Data Table and Goal Seek tools, to cite just two examples, are overlooked by the majority of end users. Without these tools, the end user either fails to ask questions that can provide telling insights, or else wastes time generating results that could be found more easily.

The evidence is strong that the existing state of spreadsheet design and use is generally inadequate. This is one reason we devote a significant portion of this book to spreadsheet engineering. Only with a solid foundation in spreadsheet engineering can the business analyst effectively generate real insights from spreadsheet models.

1.2.3 Background Knowledge for Spreadsheet Modeling

Many people new to modeling fear it because modeling reminds them of painful experiences with mathematics. We do not wish to downplay the essentially mathematical nature of modeling, even modeling using spreadsheets. However, an effective modeler does not need to know any really advanced math. Knowledge of basic algebra (including functions such as the quadratic, exponential, and logarithmic), simple logic (as expressed in an IF statement or the MAX function), and basic probability (distributions and sampling, for example) will usually suffice. When we find it necessary to use any higher math in this book, we provide explanations. But our focus here is less on the mathematical details of models than on the creative process of constructing and using models.

We assume throughout this book that the reader has a basic familiarity with Excel. This includes the ability to build a simple spreadsheet, enter and format text and data, use formulas and simple functions such as SUM, construct graphs, and so on. We do not assume the reader is an expert in Excel, nor do we assume knowledge of the advanced tools we cover, such as Solver and Crystal Ball. We have found that, in many situations, advanced Excel skills are not required for building effective models. And we believe that the main purpose of modeling is to improve the insight of the modeler. Thus, it is appropriate for a modeler with only basic Excel skills to build a model using only basic tools, and it is appropriate for a modeler with advanced skills to draw on advanced tools when needed. We have also found that too much skill in Excel can sometimes distract from the essential modeling tasks, which are almost always more about finding a simple and effective representation of the problem at hand than about finding some Excel trick.

For easy reference we have included two chapters that deal specifically with Excel. In Chapter 3 we give an overview of Excel, from the basics of entering text and data to charting. Chapter 4 presents some advanced Excel skills that are particularly useful to modelers, including range names, advanced formulas and functions, macros, and Visual Basic. We expect most readers to already know Excel to some degree, and to use these chapters as needed to hone specific skills. We believe that, by working through the examples in the book, the reader's Excel skills will improve naturally and painlessly, just as ours have improved over years of building models and teaching modeling to students whose Excel skills often exceeded ours.

1.3 THE REAL WORLD AND THE MODEL WORLD

We stated at the outset that modeling provides a structure for problem solving. It does this through a process of abstraction, in which the essence of the problem is captured in a simplified form. Because of this abstraction process, modeling does not come naturally to most people but must be learned. Because it does not come naturally, it can appear to be artificial and counterintuitive, causing many students of modeling to become uncomfortable with the process. This section attempts to reduce that discomfort by placing modeling in the context of problem solving in the real world.

A model is an abstraction, or simplification, of the real world. It is a laboratory—an artificial environment—in which we can experiment and test ideas without the costs and risks of experimenting with real systems and organizations. Figure 1.1 is a schematic showing how modeling creates an artificial world. We begin in the real world, usually with a messy problem to solve. If we determine that modeling is an appropriate tool, we then move across an invisible boundary into the model world.

In order to move into the model world, we abstract the essential features of the real world, leaving behind all the inessential detail and complexity. We then construct our laboratory by combining our abstractions with specific assumptions and building a model of the essential aspects of the real world. This is the process of **model formulation**. It is an exercise in simplifying the actual situation and capturing its

FIGURE 1.1 The Real World and the Model World

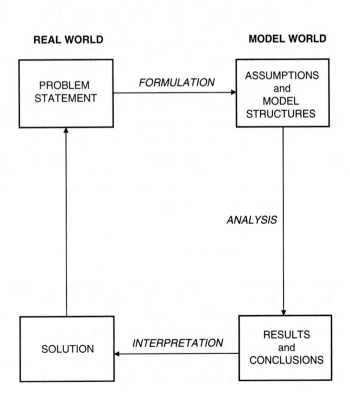

essence, with a specific purpose in mind. The model formulation process typically forces us to confront four features of a model:

- Decisions
- Outcomes
- Structure
- Data

Decisions refers to possible choices, or courses of action, that we might take. These would be controllable variables, such as quantities to buy, manufacture, spend, or sell. (By contrast, uncontrollable variables such as tax rates or the cost of materials are not decision variables.) **Outcomes** refers to the consequences of the decisions— the performance measures we use to evaluate the results of taking action. Examples might include profit, cost, or efficiency. **Structure** refers to the logic and the mathematics that link the elements of our model together. A simple example might be the equation $P = R - C$, in which profit is calculated as the difference between revenue and cost. Another example might be the relationship $F = I + P - S$, in which final inventory is calculated from initial inventory, production, and shipments. Finally, **data** refers to specific numerical assumptions. That may mean actual observations of the real world (often called "raw" or "empirical" data), or it may mean estimates of uncontrollable variables in the problem's environment. Examples might include the interest rate on borrowed funds, the production capacity of a manufacturing facility, or the first-quarter sales for a new product.

Once it is built, we can use the model to test ideas and evaluate solutions. This is a process of **analysis**, in which we apply logic, often with the support of software, to take us from our assumptions and abstractions to a set of derived conclusions. Unlike model formulation, which tends to be mostly an art, analysis is much more of a science. It relies on mathematics and reason in order to explore the implications of our assumptions. This exploration process leads, hopefully, to insights about the problem confronting us. Sometimes, these insights involve an understanding of why one solution is beneficial and another is not; at other times, the insights involve understanding the sources of risk in a particular solution. In another situation, the insights involve identifying the decisions that are most critical to a good result, or identifying the inputs that have the strongest influence on a particular outcome. In each instance, it is crucial to understand that these insights are derived from the *model* world and not from the *real* world. Whether they apply to the real world is another matter entirely and requires managerial judgment.

To make the model insights useful, we must first translate them into the terms of the real world and then communicate them to the actual decision makers involved. Only then do *model* insights turn into useful *managerial* insights. And only then can we begin the process of evaluating solutions in terms of their impact on the real world. This is a process of **interpretation**, and here again, the process is an art. Good modelers can move smoothly back and forth between the model world and the real world, deriving crisp insights from the model, and translating the insights, modifying them as needed, to account for real-world complexities not captured in the model world.

This schematic description of the modeling process highlights some of the reasons it can be a challenge to incorporate modeling into problem solving. Powerful in competent hands, modeling is also somewhat esoteric. It involves deliberate abstraction and simplification of a situation, which appears to many people as a counterproductive exercise. Modeling requires a willingness to temporarily set aside much of the richness of the real world and to operate in the refined and artificial world of models and model insights. It also requires confidence that whatever insights arise in the model world can be translated into useful ideas in the real world. In addition, it requires an ability to mix art with science in order to exploit the modeling process to its full potential. Until we have some experience with this process, we may be resistant and skeptical. And it is always easy to criticize a model as being too simple. Good models are as simple as they can possibly be. But this very simplicity can appear to be a fatal flaw to skeptics. Nevertheless, modeling is one of the most powerful tools in the problem solver's tool kit, simply because there is no more practical way to arrive at the insights modeling can provide.

1.4 LESSONS FROM EXPERT AND NOVICE MODELERS

Perhaps the best way to become a good modeler is to serve an apprenticeship under an expert. Unfortunately, such opportunities are rare. Moreover, experts in all fields find it difficult to express their expertise or to teach it. While narrow, **technical** skills are relatively easy to teach (e.g., how to use the NPV function in Excel), expertise consists largely of **craft** skills that are more difficult to teach (e.g., what to include and exclude from the model). In the arts, there is a tradition of studio training, where a teacher poses artistic challenges to students and then coaches them as they work through the problems on their own. This is one way for students to acquire some of the difficult-to-articulate craft skills of the master. There is no comparable tradition in the mathematical fields; in fact, there is a long-standing belief that modeling cannot be taught but must simply be acquired by experience.

One way to improve modeling skills is to understand what expert and novice modelers actually do when they build and use models. From closely observing experts, we can attempt to articulate a set of modeling best practices. From observing novices we can understand the reasons for their relatively lower level of modeling accomplishment: the blind alleys, counterproductive behaviors, misperceptions, and cognitive limitations that keep them from attaining expert performance. In this section we summarize research studies on both expert and novice modelers.

1.4.1 Expert Modelers

An alternative to an apprenticeship under an expert is to study experts in a laboratory setting. Tom Willemain did this in a series of experiments with 12 expert modelers. He gave each expert a short problem description as it would come from a client and observed the subject working for one hour on the problem. The subjects were asked to think out loud so that their thought processes could be recorded. Willemain's results concerning the "first hour in the life of a model" are highly suggestive of some of the ingredients of good modeling practice.[3]

Willemain was interested in determining the issues to which expert modelers devote attention as they formulate their models. He identified five topics important to modelers:

- Problem context
- Model structure
- Model realization
- Model assessment
- Model implementation

Problem context refers to the situation from which the modeler's problem arises, including the client, the client's view of the problem, and any available facts about the problem. In this activity, the modeler tries to understand the problem statement as provided by the client and to understand the messy situation out of which the problem arises.

Model structure refers to actually building the model itself, including issues such as what type of model to use, where to break the problem into subproblems, and

[3]Thomas R. Willemain, "Insights on Modeling from a Dozen Experts," *Operations Research* 42, No. 2 (1994): 213–222; "Model Formulation: What Experts Think About and When," *Operations Research* 43, No. 6 (1995): 916–932.

how to choose parameters and relationships. In Figure 1.1, this would be the process of moving into the model world, making abstractions and assumptions, and creating an actual model.

Model realization refers to the more detailed activities of fitting the model to available data and calculating results. Here, the focus is on whether the general model structure can actually be implemented with the available data and whether the type of model under development will generate the hoped-for kinds of results. This topic corresponds to the analysis process in Figure 1.1.

Model assessment includes evaluating the model's correctness, feasibility, and acceptability to the client. Determining the correctness of a model involves finding whether the model assumptions correspond well enough to reality. Feasibility refers to whether the client has the resources to implement the developed model, whether sufficient data are available, and whether the model itself will perform as desired. Client acceptability refers to whether the client will understand the model and its results and whether the results will be useful to the client. In this phase, we can imagine the modeler looking from the model world back into the real world and trying to anticipate whether the model under construction will meet the needs of the client.

Finally, **model implementation** refers to working with the client to derive value from the model. This corresponds to the interpretation activity in Figure 1.1.

One of Willemain's interesting observations about his experts was that they frequently switched their attention among these five topics. That is, they did not follow a sequential problem-solving process, but rather moved quickly among the various phases—at one moment considering the problem statement, at another considering whether the necessary data would be available, and at yet another thinking through whether the client could understand and use the model. A second significant finding was that model structure, presumably the heart of a modeler's work, received a relatively small amount of attention (about 60 percent of the effort) when compared to the other four topics. Finally, it turned out that experts often alternated their attention between model structure and model assessment. That is, they would propose some element of model structure and quickly turn to evaluating its impact on model correctness, feasibility, and acceptability. Willemain suggests that the experts treat model structuring as the central task, or backbone, of their work, but they often branch off to examine related issues (data availability, client acceptance, and so on), eventually returning to the central task. In effect, model structuring becomes an organizing principle, or mental focus, around which the related activities can be arrayed.

The overall picture that emerges from this research is one in which craft skills are as essential to the effective modeler as technical skills. An effective modeler must understand the problem context, including the client, or modeling will fail. Similarly, a model that is technically correct but does not provide information the client can use, or does not gain the trust of the client, represents only wasted effort. Experts approach modeling with a general process in mind, but they move fairly quickly among the different activities, creating, testing, and revising constantly as they go. The experts appear to be comfortable with a high degree of ambiguity as they approach the task of structuring a model. They do not rush to a solution, but patiently build tentative models and test them, always being ready to revise and improve.

1.4.2 Novice Modelers

Novices have been studied in many domains, from solving physics problems to playing golf. In general, novice problem solvers can be expected to show certain kinds of counterproductive behaviors. One is that they focus on just one approach to a problem and devote all their time to it, while experts are likely to try many different approaches. Novices also do not evaluate their performance as frequently or as critically as expert problem solvers do. Finally, novices tend to attempt to solve a problem using only the information given in that problem, while experts are more likely to draw on experience with other problems for useful analogies or tools.

In an attempt to better understand how our own students model problems, we conducted an experiment similar in most respects to Willemain's experiment with experts.[4] We audiotaped 28 MBA students while they worked through four ill-structured modeling problems. Thus, this experiment did not focus on building a spreadsheet model for a well-defined problem, as might be assigned in a course for homework, but rather on formulating an approach to an ill-structured problem of the kind that consultants typically encounter. (Some of these problems will be presented in Chapter 2.) The students were given 30 minutes to work on each problem. The task was to begin developing a model that could ultimately be used for forecasting or for analysis of a decision.

We observed five behaviors in our subjects that are not typical of experts and that limit their modeling effectiveness:

- Overreliance on given numerical data
- Use of shortcuts to an answer
- Insufficient use of abstract variables and relationships
- Ineffective self-regulation
- Overuse of brainstorming relative to structured problem solving

In the study, some of the problems included extensive tables of numerical data. In these problems, many subjects devoted their time to examining the data rather than building a general model structure. Having data at hand seemed to block these students from the abstraction process required for effective modeling. In other problems, very little data was provided, and in these cases, some students attempted to "solve" the problem by performing calculations on the given numbers. Again, the data seemed to block the abstraction process. Many subjects complained about the lack of data in problems in which little was given, seeming to believe that data alone could lead to a solution. In general, then, our subjects appear to rely more on data than do experts, who build general model structures and only tangentially ask whether data exist or could be acquired to refine or operationalize their model structures.

Another problematic behavior we observed in our subjects was taking a shortcut to an answer. Where experts would consider various aspects of a problem and try out several different approaches, some students rushed to a conclusion. Some would simply rely on intuition to decide that the proposal they were to evaluate was a good or bad idea. Others would use back-of-the-envelope calculations to come to a conclusion. Still others would claim that the answer could be found by collecting data, or performing marketing research, or asking experts in the industry. (We call this behavior "invoking a magic wand.") All of these approaches seem to avoid the assigned task, which was to structure a *model* for analyzing the problem, not to come to a conclusion.

Expert problem solvers generally use abstract variables and relationships in the early stages of modeling a problem. We saw very little of this in our subjects, who appeared to think predominantly in concrete terms, often using specific numbers. Expert modelers tend to be well trained in formal mathematics, and they naturally think in terms of variables and relationships. Our subjects were generally less well trained in mathematics but tended to have extensive experience with spreadsheets. Their approach to spreadsheet modeling involved minimal abstraction and maximal reliance on numbers. Our subjects did not often write down variables and functions, but they fairly often sketched or talked about a spreadsheet in terms of its row and column headings.

[4]Stephen G. Powell and Thomas R. Willemain, "How Novices Formulate Models. Part I: Qualitative Insights and Implications for Teaching," *Journal of the Operational Research Society*, forthcoming 2007; Thomas R. Willemain and Stephen G. Powell, "How Novices Formulate Models. Part II: A Quantitative Description of Behavior," *Journal of the Operational Research Society*, forthcoming 2007.

As we noted earlier, experts pause frequently during problem solving to evaluate the approach they are taking. They are also willing to try another approach if the current one seems unproductive. By contrast, many of our subjects did little self-evaluation during the experiment. Some focused more on the problem we had given them as a business problem than a modeling problem. So the special features that a model brings to analyzing a situation seemed lost on them. Without a clear goal, a typical subject would launch into a discussion of all the factors that might conceivably influence the problem. Only rarely did we observe a subject stopping and asking whether progress was being made toward a *model*.

Finally, the predominant problem-solving strategy we observed our subjects using could be described as unstructured problem exploration. For example, they would list issues in a rambling and unstructured manner, as if they were brainstorming, without attempting to organize their thoughts in a form that would support modeling. Structured problem solving, as used by experts, seeks to impose an organized plan on the modeling process.

In general our subjects failed to think in modeling terms—that is, by deciding what the outcome of the modeling process was to be and working backwards through variables and assumptions and relationships to the beginning. Instead, they explored a variety of (usually) unrelated aspects of the problem in a discursive manner.

What can a business analyst who wants to improve modeling skills learn from this research? First, expertise takes time and practice to acquire, and the novice should not expect to perform like an expert overnight. However, some expert behaviors are worth imitating from the start. Don't look for quick answers to the problem at hand, and don't expect the data to answer the problem for you. Rather, use what you know to build a logical structure of relationships. Use whatever language you are most comfortable with (algebra, a spreadsheet, a sketch), but work to develop your ability to abstract the essential features of the situation from the details and the numbers. Keep an open mind, try different approaches, and evaluate your work often. Most important, look for opportunities to use modeling, and constantly upgrade both your technical and craft skills.

1.5   ORGANIZATION OF THE BOOK

This book is organized around the three skills we believe business analysts most need in their modeling work:

- Spreadsheet engineering
- Modeling craft
- Management science and statistics

Spreadsheet engineering deals with how to design, build, test, and perform analysis with a spreadsheet model. Modeling craft refers to the nontechnical but critical skills that an expert modeler employs, such as abstracting the essential features of a situation in a model, debugging a model effectively, and translating model results into managerial insights. Management science covers optimization and simulation. Along with statistics, a basic knowledge of these tools is important for the well-rounded analyst. Figure 1.2 provides an overview of the organization of the book.

The heart of this book is the material on building spreadsheet models and using them to analyze decisions. However, before the analyst can build spreadsheet models successfully, certain broader skills are needed. Therefore, we begin in Chapter 2 with a discussion of the various contexts in which modeling is carried out and the role that modeling plays in a structured problem-solving process. We also introduce in this chapter the craft aspects of modeling—the tricks of the trade that experienced and successful modelers employ. These are not Excel tricks, but rather approaches to dealing with the ambiguities of analysis using models. Chapters 3 and 4 provide the basic and advanced Excel skills needed by effective modelers. Chapters 5 and 6 provide the essential tools of spreadsheet engineering. Along with Chapters 1 and 2,

FIGURE 1.2 Outline of the Book

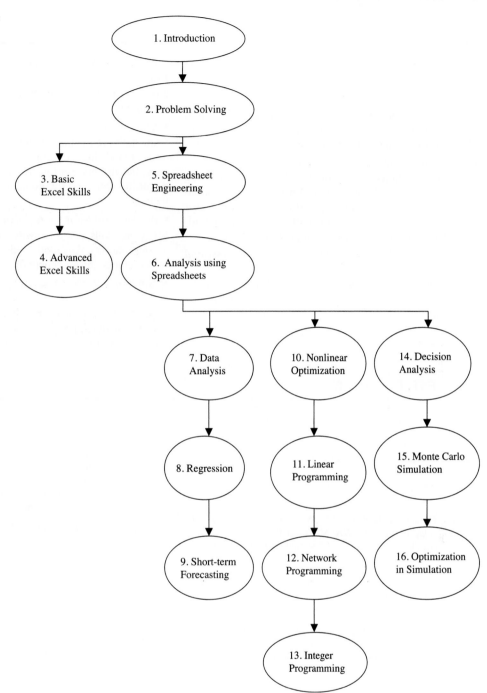

these chapters should be studied by all readers. Chapter 5 provides guidelines for designing effective spreadsheets and workbooks, while Chapter 6 provides an overview of various tools available for analyzing spreadsheet models. Chapters 7 through 16 cover the advanced tools of the management scientist and their spreadsheet implementations. Chapters 7–9 deal with data analysis, regression, and forecasting. Chapters 10–13 explore optimization, and Chapters 15 and 16 cover simulation. Numerous examples throughout the text illustrate good modeling technique, and most chapters contain exercises for practice. Many of these exercises relate to a set of case problems, which are included at the end of the book. These problems provide an opportunity to gain experience with realistic modeling problems that build on concepts in different chapters.

1.6 SUMMARY

The following statements summarize the principles on which this book is based.

• *Modeling is a necessary skill for every business analyst.*
Models are encountered frequently in business education and in the business world. Furthermore, analysts are capable of formulating their own models.

• *Spreadsheets are the modeling platform of choice.*
The wide acceptance and flexibility of the spreadsheet make it the modeling platform of choice for most business situations. Since familiarity with spreadsheets is required for almost everyone in business, the basis for learning spreadsheet-based modeling is already in place.

• *Basic spreadsheet modeling skills are an essential foundation.*
While basic knowledge about spreadsheets is usually assumed in business, spreadsheet skills and spreadsheet modeling skills are not the same. Effective education in business modeling begins with training in how to use a spreadsheet to build and analyze models.

• *End-user modeling is cost-effective.*
In an ever-growing range of situations, well-trained business analysts can build their own models without relying on consultants or experts.

• *Craft skills are essential to the effective modeler.*
Craft skills are the mark of an expert in any field. The craft skills of modeling must gradually be refined through experience, but the process can be expedited by identifying and discussing them and by providing opportunities to practice their use.

• *Analysts can learn the required modeling skills.*
Modeling skills do not involve complex mathematics or arcane concepts. Any motivated analyst can learn the basics of good modeling and apply this knowledge on the job.

• *Management science/statistics are important advanced tools.*
Extensive knowledge of these tools is not required of most business analysts; however, solid knowledge of the fundamentals can turn an average modeler into a power modeler.

SUGGESTED READINGS

Many books are available on Excel, although most of them cover its vast array of features without isolating those of particular relevance for the business analyst. In the chapters on Excel, we provide several references to books and other materials for learning basic Excel skills. A working business analyst should probably own at least one Excel guide as a reference book. Two such references are:

Stinson, C., and M. Dodge. 2003. *Microsoft Excel Version 2003 Inside Out*. Bellingham, WA: Microsoft Press.
Walkenbach, J. 2003. *Excel 2003 Bible*. New York: John Wiley and Sons.

Several textbooks present the tools of management science using spreadsheets. We recommend these for a more detailed treatment of management science than we provide here.

Ragsdale, C. 2001. *Spreadsheet Modeling and Decision Analysis*. 4th ed. Cincinnati: South-Western.
Winston, W., and C. Albright. 2004. *Practical Management Science*. 2d ed. Pacific Grove, CA: Duxbury.

The standard reference on the mathematics of management science is:

Hillier, F., and G. Lieberman. 2004. *Introduction to Operations Research*. 8th ed. Oakland, CA: McGraw-Hill.

While this text does not rely on spreadsheets, it does provide in a relatively accessible form the methods behind much of the management science we present in this book.

The following two references are more narrowly focused books that apply spreadsheet modeling to specific business disciplines.

Benninga, S. 2000. *Financial Modeling*. 2d ed. Cambridge, MA: MIT Press.
Lilien, G., and A. Rangaswamy. 2004. *Marketing Engineering*. State College, PA: Decision Pro.

Finally, for stimulating books on modeling and problem solving, we recommend:

Casti, J. 1997. *Would-be Worlds: How Simulation Is Changing the Frontiers of Science*. New York: John Wiley and Sons.
Koomey, J. D. 2001. *Turning Numbers into Knowledge: Mastering the Art of Problem Solving*. Oakland, CA: Analytics Press.
Starfield, A., K. Smith, and A. Bleloch. 1990. *How to Model It*. New York: McGraw-Hill.

2 Modeling in a Problem-Solving Framework

2.1 INTRODUCTION

Modeling is an approach that helps us develop a better understanding of business situations. As a result, it helps us make better decisions. Thus, we don't view modeling as an end in itself, but rather as part of the broader process of business decision making. In this chapter, we discuss how modeling contributes to that broader process. We refer to the decision-making process generically as a **problem-solving** process, although specific instances could involve making forecasts, evaluating business opportunities, or allocating resources.

Any successful problem-solving process begins with recognition of a problem and ends with implementation of a proposed solution. All the work that comes between these two points is the problem-solving process. In some cases, this process is highly structured and planned, perhaps involving a large team working over several months; in other cases, it is informal and unstructured, perhaps involving only one person for a couple of hours. Modeling is just one of many tools or strategies that can be used within problem solving. An effective problem solver knows when and how to use modeling effectively within the broader context of problem solving.

Modelers can play different roles in the problem-solving process. Primarily, these roles are:

- End user
- Team member
- Independent consultant

When the entire team consists of one person, then problem owner (or client) and modeler are one and the same. We refer to this role as the **end-user** modeler. The end user is often a small-business owner or an entrepreneur, who has no staff and no budget for consultants. In large firms, many managers are also end users at times, when there is no time to brief the staff or bring in consultants, or when the problem is too sensitive to share with anyone else. The end user carries out all of the activities in modeling: identifying a problem worthy of attention, developing a model, using the model to develop insights and practical solutions, and implementing the results. There is an enormous untapped potential for end-user modeling, because there are so many relatively small problems for which modeling can provide insight, and because there are so many end users who have (or can acquire) the spreadsheet and modeling skills necessary to develop useful models.

In addition to the end-user role, modelers are often assigned to the role of **team member** on an internal committee or task force. In many cases, the problem-solving process may have begun before the committee was formed, and the modeler may or may not have been part of that process. Although chosen for expertise in modeling, the team-member modeler's role also requires good interpersonal and communication skills. A critical part of the work is communicating with nonmodelers on the team about the assumptions that go into the model and the intuition behind the model's results. Of course, the team-member modeler must also have the necessary technical skills to apply modeling successfully, but communication skills are more important for the team-member than for the end-user modeler.

A third role for the modeler is that of **independent consultant**. This role differs from the role of team member because there is usually a client—someone who identifies the problem and ultimately manages the implementation of any solution. The role of consultant modeler also requires excellent communication and interpersonal skills. Despite being an organizational outsider, the consultant modeler must understand the client's problem deeply and translate the client's understanding of the problem into modeling terms. This role also requires the ability to translate model insights back into a language the client can understand, so that the client can implement a solution.

As we build our formal modeling skills we need to have an overall concept of the problem-solving process and where modeling fits into that process. Thus, we begin this chapter by describing a widely used problem-solving process and the role that formal modeling plays in this process.

Influence charts, which are the second topic in this chapter, help to bridge the gap between a qualitative understanding of a fuzzy problem and a formal model with numbers and equations. Influence charts help the modeler construct a logical structure within which to represent the parameters, relationships, and outcomes of a model without excessive detail or precision. They are an essential tool for both novice and expert modelers.

The final topic of the chapter is the craft of modeling. The technical side of modeling concerns the specific and well-defined tasks necessary to build a model, such as how to use an IF statement. The craft side of modeling, on the other hand, represents the artistry that experts bring to bear. Craft skills are harder to learn than technical skills, but they are just as important for successful modeling. We describe some of the most important craft skills and discuss the role these skills play in modeling. The modeling cases that appear later in the book provide opportunities to practice these skills in ill-structured problem situations.

2.2 THE PROBLEM-SOLVING PROCESS

While problem solving is an almost universal aspect of life, very few individuals follow a structured approach to it. This could indicate that effective problem solving is instinctive and intuitive and that the only way to improve in this area is through experience. We do not, however, subscribe to this point of view. In our experience, some degree of conscious attention to the process pays off in improved results and efficiency, even for experienced modelers and managers. This is especially true for problem-solving teams, where intuitive methods often fail because what is intuitive to one member makes no sense to another. While the end-user modeler can perhaps get by with shortcuts, team members and independent consultants are more effective when they carefully manage the problem-solving process.

The problem-solving process is often described as a sequential, step-by-step procedure. While this makes for easy description, there is, in fact, no simple plan that represents the universal problem-solving process. Moreover, when people look back on their own problem-solving activities, they tend to remember more structure than was really there. Thus, a sequential description of problem solving should not be taken literally. As we described in the previous chapter, even modeling experts appear to jump around from one aspect of a problem to another as they attempt to formulate models. Any process must be flexible enough to accommodate different work styles, unexpected discoveries and disappointments, and inevitable fluctuations in effort and creativity. The process we discuss later in this chapter helps focus attention on some of the critical aspects of effective problem solving, without providing a straitjacket that will cramp a problem solver's style. Our description comes from what experts tell us, from what we observe in our students, and from what we have experienced in our own problem solving.

2.2.1 Some Key Terms

We begin by making an important distinction between a **problem** and a **mess**. On the one hand, a mess is a morass of unsettling symptoms, causes, data, pressures, shortfalls, and opportunities. A problem, on the other hand, is a well-defined situation that is capable of resolution. Why is the concept of a mess important in problem solving? Simply because problems do not come to us fully defined and labeled. Rather, we operate in a world full of confusion: causes and effects are muddled, data exist but there is little relevant information, problematic shortfalls or inadequacies appear alongside attractive opportunities, and so on. Where are the problems in this mess? Identifying a problem in the mess is itself a creative act that will do much to determine the quality of any solutions we propose. In most situations, a number of problems could be extracted from a given mess. Which one we choose depends on our understanding of the situation and on our insight into where analysis and action could be most effective. Our first piece of advice on problem solving, then, is to recognize that defining the problem to be solved is a critical step in the process—one that deserves considerable attention.

One way to focus attention on the problem definition is to use a problem statement of the form "In what ways might …" Imagine the situation facing a manufacturing company whose costs are rising sharply due to increasing wages. Here are some possible problem statements the company could use:

- In what ways might we increase the productivity of our workforce?
- In what ways might we reduce the labor content of our products?
- In what ways might we shift our manufacturing to lower-cost regions?
- In what ways might we increase revenues to keep pace with costs?
- In what ways might we change our product line to maintain profit margins?

This is just a sample of the problem statements that could apply to a given situation. It should be obvious that the approach taken to resolving the "problem" will be very different depending on which of these statements is adopted. Our advice is to pay close attention to the problem definition, take any problem definition as tentative, and prepare to alter it if evidence suggests that a different problem statement would be more effective.

The appropriate problem-solving approach depends, of course, on the problem at hand. Some problems are simple and require only a rudimentary approach, while others are complex and require a much more elaborate and thought-out process. It is useful to distinguish **well-structured** from **ill-structured problems**.

Well-structured problems have the following characteristics:

- The objectives of the analysis are clear.
- The assumptions that must be made are obvious.
- All the necessary data are readily available.
- The logical structure behind the analysis is well understood.

Algebra problems are typically well-structured problems. Consider this problem: Solve the following system of equations for X and Y:

$$3X + 4Y = 18$$
$$9X + Y = 21$$

The solution to this problem consists of the values $X = 2$, $Y = 3$. Not only can we easily demonstrate that these values actually do solve the problem, but we can prove that this is the only solution to the problem. Once we have found these values for X and Y, there is nothing more to be said about the problem.

By contrast, in a typical ill-structured problem, to varying degrees, the objectives, assumptions, data, and structure of the problem are all unclear. Here are several examples of ill-defined problems:

- Should the Red Cross institute a policy of paying for blood donations?
- Should Boeing's next major commercial airliner be a small supersonic jet or a slower jumbo jet?
- Should an advertiser spend more money on the creative aspects of an ad campaign or on the delivery of the ad?
- How much should a midcareer executive save out of current income toward retirement?

Unlike well-structured problems, ill-structured problems require *exploration* more than *solution*. Exploring a problem involves formulating hypotheses, making assumptions, building simple models, and deriving tentative conclusions, all with an inquiring mind and in a spirit of discovery. Problem exploration is a more creative and open-ended process than problem solving. It often reveals aspects of the problem that are not obvious at first glance. These discoveries can become useful insights.

At any stage in the problem-solving process, there are two quite different styles of thinking: **divergent** and **convergent**. Divergent thinking stresses generating ideas over evaluating ideas. It involves thinking in different directions or searching for a variety of answers to questions that may have many right answers. Brainstorming, in which the evaluation process is strictly prohibited, promotes divergent thinking and allows many ideas to flourish at the same time, even ideas that contradict each other. Convergent thinking, on the other hand, is directed toward achieving a goal, a single solution, answer, or result. It involves trying to find the one best answer. In convergent thinking, the emphasis shifts from idea generation to evaluation: Which of these ideas leads to the best outcomes? In many cases, this evaluation is carried out using a model.

Why is this distinction between divergent and convergent thinking useful? One reason is that some individuals naturally prefer, enjoy, or are skilled at one or the other type of thinking. When working as end users, these individuals should be conscious of their preference or skill and take steps to ensure that they devote sufficient time and energy to the other approach. Good evaluators need to encourage themselves to generate more ideas; good idea generators need to encourage themselves to test their ideas thoroughly. Since end users do it all, they must ensure that the balance between divergent and convergent thinking is appropriate throughout the problem-solving process.

An understanding of these concepts is just as important to members of a problem-solving team. In this situation, members can afford to specialize in their preferred thought process: idea generators can take a lead role in that phase, while strong evaluators can take a lead role when that becomes the primary activity of the group. But people need to understand their own strengths and the strengths of others on the team and need to appreciate that the other types make an important contribution. Finally, teams work best when they are aware of which type of thinking they are stressing at each point in the process. It is disruptive and inefficient to have one member of a team evaluating ideas during a brainstorming session; it is just as disruptive to have someone offering great new ideas during the preparation of the final presentation to the client.

2.2.2 The Six-Stage Problem-Solving Process

We now describe a six-stage problem-solving process (Figure 2.1) that begins with a mess and ends with implementation of a solution. This process can be used to solve (or explore) almost any problem, from the most well structured to the most ill structured. Since not all problem solving involves the use of formal models, we first describe the

FIGURE 2.1 The Creative
Problem-Solving Process
Source: After Couger, *Creative
Problem Solving and
Opportunity Finding*

Exploring the mess
  Divergent phase
    Search mess for problems and opportunities.
  Convergent phase
    Accept a challenge and undertake systematic efforts to respond to it.

Searching for information
  Divergent phase
    Gather data, impressions, feelings, observations; examine the situation from many
    different viewpoints.
  Convergent phase
    Identify the most important information.

Identifying a problem
  Divergent phase
    Generate many different potential problem statements.
  Convergent phase
    Choose a working problem statement.

Searching for solutions
  Divergent phase
    Develop many different alternatives and possibilities for solutions.
  Convergent phase
    Select one or a few ideas that seem most promising.

Evaluating solutions
  Divergent phase
    Formulate criteria for reviewing and evaluating ideas.
  Convergent phase
    Select the most important criteria. Use the criteria to evaluate, strengthen, and
    refine ideas.

Implementing a solution
  Divergent phase
    Consider possible sources of assistance and resistance to proposed solution.
    Identify implementation steps and required resources.
  Convergent phase
    Prepare the most promising solution for implementation.

process in its most general form. Subsequently, we discuss how formal modeling fits within this overall framework. Throughout this section, we illustrate the stages of the process with the following example.

EXAMPLE
Invivo Diagnostics

Invivo Diagnostics is a $300M pharmaceutical company built on the strength of a single product that accounts for over 75 percent of revenues. In 18 months, the patent for this product will expire, and the CEO wants to explore ways to plug the expected $100–$200M revenue gap as revenues from this product decline. ∎

The six stages in the problem-solving process are:

- Exploring the mess
- Searching for information
- Identifying a problem
- Searching for solutions
- Evaluating solutions
- Implementing a solution

Divergent thinking tends to predominate early in this process, while convergent thinking comes to dominate later on, but there is a role for each type of thinking in every stage of the process.

Stage 1: Exploring the Mess   As we have said, problems do not appear to us in the form of well-posed problem statements. Rather, we find ourselves in various messes, out of which problems occasionally emerge. It often takes a special effort to rise above the press of day-to-day activities and begin a problem-solving process. In this sense, the most important aspect of this phase may be more psychological than intellectual. The divergent thinking in this phase involves being open to the flow of problems and opportunities in the environment; the convergent phase distills a specific problem out of the mess. During this phase, we ask questions such as the following:

- What problems (or opportunities) do we face?
- Where is there a gap between the current situation and the desired one?
- What are our stated and unstated goals?

This stage will be complete when we have produced a satisfactory description of the situation and when we have identified (although not necessarily gathered) the key facts and data.

In the Invivo example, management in the pharmaceutical company is well aware that one drug has provided the bulk of their profits over the past decade. Nevertheless, most of their day-to-day attention is devoted to tactical issues, such as resolving conflicts with suppliers or allocating R&D funds to the development of new drugs. As the date approaches on which their major drug loses its patent protection and alternative drugs can begin to compete, the managers gradually shift attention to the situation facing them. While the threat is obvious, the problem is not well defined. Each member of management probably explores this mess individually, in an informal way. They might make rough estimates of the magnitude of the threat (how much will profits fall when the patent expires?), and they might consider alternatives to improve outcomes (should we institute a cost-cutting program in manufacturing?). Eventually, management as a whole realizes the importance of the issue and creates a task force to address it. All of this activity comes under the heading of *exploring the mess.*

Stage 2: Searching for Information   Here we mean information in the broadest sense: opinions, raw data, impressions, published literature, and so on. In this phase we cast about widely for any and all information that might shed light on what the problem really is. Examining the situation from many different points of view is an important aspect of this phase. We might survey similar companies to determine how they approach related problems. We might search the literature for related academic research. The search itself at this stage is divergent. Eventually, we begin to get a sense that some of the information is more relevant, or contains suggestions for solutions, or might otherwise be particularly useful. This is the convergent part of this phase. In this stage, we should expect to be using diagnostic skills, prioritizing, and constructing diagrams or charts. During this phase, we ask questions such as the following:

- What are the symptoms and causes?
- What measures of effectiveness seem appropriate?
- What actions are available?

This stage will be complete when we have found and organized relevant information for the situation at hand and when we have made some initial hypotheses about the source of the problem and potential solutions.

The task force at Invivo holds several meetings to get to know each other and to get organized. They also hire a consultant to gather information and to bring an outside perspective to the discussion. The CEO charges the group to "find a strategy to deal with the patent situation;" the task force recognizes, however, that this is not a problem statement, but only a vague indication of senior management's discomfort about the future of the company. The consultant, meanwhile, begins interviewing key managers inside the firm and gathering information externally. She collects information on general trends in the pharmaceutical industry as well as case studies on the transition off patent for other drugs. A rough picture emerges of the rate at which generics have invaded a market once patent protection has been lost. She also collects specific information on strategies that other market-dominating firms have used to limit their losses during similar transitions. The consultant interviews economists specializing in industry structure. Inside the firm, she interviews the scientists who develop new drugs, and she begins to formulate a picture of how the firm's portfolio of new drugs will contribute to future revenues. If the problem-solving process is to work well here, a broad search for information must precede any effort to close in on a specific problem that can be resolved. However, even while this search goes on, the members of the task force are beginning to form opinions as to the real problem they face and the solutions they prefer.

Stage 3: Identifying a Problem In the divergent portion of this phase, we might pose four or five candidate problem statements and try them on for size. We will eventually choose one of these statements, perhaps somewhat refined, as our working problem statement. As mentioned before, there is a significant benefit for any problem-solving group to have an unambiguous statement of the problem they are solving. This is not to say that we can't modify or even replace one problem statement with another if the evidence suggests this is necessary. All problem statements should be viewed as tentative, although as time passes, the cost and risk of changing the problem statement increase. In this stage, we should be asking whether the situation fits a standard problem type, or whether we should be breaking the problem into subproblems. During this phase, we ask questions such as the following:

- Which is the most important problem in this situation?
- Is this problem like others we have dealt with?
- What are the consequences of a broad versus narrow problem statement?

This stage will be complete when we have produced a working problem statement.

The consultant to Invivo holds a series of meetings with the task force to present and discuss her preliminary research. The group now has a shared understanding of the financial state of their own firm, as well as a general idea of the state of the industry. They discuss how other firms fared when major drugs came off patent and what strategies were used to smooth the transition. At this point, the consultant leads an effort to define a problem statement that can serve as an organizing theme for the future efforts of the task force. In the discussion that ensues, two major points of view emerge. One group focuses on preserving the revenue-generating power of the patent drug as long as possible. They ask whether it would be possible to extend the patent, slow the introduction of generic competitors, or perhaps make an alliance with competitors that would share the profits from this category of drugs without significantly reducing its revenues. The other group focuses on a different issue: how to generate more revenue from other drugs now in the development pipeline. They ask whether the firm should increase its R&D spending, narrow its efforts to just the most promising drugs, or look for quicker ways to get regulatory approval. The consultant recognizes that no one is looking at reducing costs or shrinking the firm as possible strategies.

The task force has reached a critical stage in the problem-solving process. How they define the problem here will determine in large measure the solutions they eventually recommend. The consultant, recognizing this, makes an effort to have the group debate a wide range of problem statements. Here are some candidate problem statements they may consider:

- In what ways might we slow the decline in revenues from our patented drug?
- In what ways might we increase the chances of success of R&D on new products?
- In what ways might we increase market share for our existing products?

- In what ways might we resize the firm to match declining profits?
- In what ways might we develop more products with the same investment?
- In what ways might we partner with other firms?

Eventually, the task force comes to the conclusion that protecting the revenues from the existing drug is both difficult and risky. The most effective strategy probably involves developing a portfolio of new drugs as quickly and effectively as possible. Accordingly, they adopt the problem statement: "In what ways might we reduce the time to market for the six drugs currently under development?"

Stage 4: Searching for Solutions Again, there is a divergent aspect to this phase, in which a deliberately open-ended process searches for good, even radical, solutions. Brainstorming or other creativity-enhancing techniques might be particularly useful, since the team has a well-considered problem statement to serve as a focal point for the creation of solutions. Prior to this point, it is premature to consider solutions. It can even be dangerous to do so, since superficially appealing solutions often gain support on their own, even if they solve the wrong problem. The convergent part of this phase involves a tentative selection of the most promising candidate solutions. The selection process must be tentative at this point, because criteria have not yet been established for a careful comparison of solutions. Nonetheless, there are costs to considering too many solutions, so some pruning is often necessary. During this phase, we ask questions such as the following:

- What decisions are open to us?
- What solutions have been tried in similar situations?
- How are the various candidate solutions linked to outcomes of interest?

This stage will be complete when we have produced a list of potential solutions and perhaps a list of advantages and disadvantages for each one.

Having decided to focus their efforts on improving the R&D process, the task force at Invivo first forms a subcommittee composed mainly of scientists from the R&D division, along with a few business experts. The consultant conducts extensive interviews within the R&D group to uncover inefficiencies and possible ways to improve the process of bringing drugs to market. The subcommittee eventually develops a list of potential solutions, along with an evaluation of their advantages and disadvantages. Three areas for potential improvement stand out:

- Hire outside firms to conduct clinical trials and develop applications for Food and Drug Administration (FDA) approvals. This will speed up the approval process, although it will also increase costs.
- Invest a higher percentage of the R&D budget in drugs with the most promise of winning FDA approval. This should reduce the time required for the most promising drugs to reach the market, but it may also reduce the number of drugs that do so.
- Focus the drug portfolio on drugs in the same medical category. This should help develop an expertise in just one or two medical specialties, rather than spreading efforts over many technical areas and markets.

Stage 5: Evaluating Solutions This stage can be considered the culmination of the process, as it is here that a preferred solution emerges. Any evaluation of the candidate solutions developed in the previous phase requires a set of criteria with which to compare solutions. Usually, many criteria could be relevant to the outcome; some divergent thinking is useful in this phase to ensure that all relevant criteria, even those that are not obvious, are considered. Once the most important criteria are identified, the various solutions can be evaluated and compared on each criterion. This can lead directly to a preferred alternative. More often, this process leads to changes—and improvements—in the solutions themselves. Often, an aspect of one solution can be grafted onto another solution, or a particularly negative aspect of a generally attractive solution can be removed once the weakness has been recognized. So this phase, while generally stressing convergent thinking, still involves considerable creativity. During this phase, we ask questions such as the following:

- How does this solution impact each of the criteria?
- What factors within our control could improve the outcomes?
- What factors outside our control could alter the outcomes?

This stage will be complete when we have produced a recommended course of action, along with a justification that supports it.

During this phase, the Invivo task force develops a set of criteria with which to evaluate each of the previously proposed solutions. The overall goal is to ensure that the firm remains profitable into the future, even as the main drug goes off patent and its revenues are lost. However, it is difficult to anticipate how any one solution will impact profits directly. For example, how much additional profit will the firm realize if it saves two months in the development process for a particular drug? For this reason, each solution is measured against many criteria, and the results are synthesized by the task force. Here are some of the criteria they develop:

- R&D cost reduction
- Increase in market share
- Months of development time saved
- Increase in probability of FDA approval

After extensive discussion, the task force finally decides that the one most critical area for improvement is how R&D funds are allocated over time. In the past, the firm has generally been very slow to cancel development of any particular drug. Each drug has the passionate support of the scientists working on it, and the commitment of this group to its own drug has superseded the business judgment needed to recognize that other drug-development teams can make better use of scarce R&D resources. With a more business-oriented allocation process, fewer drugs will be developed, but each will get increased R&D funding. Hopefully, more drugs will then come to market quickly.

Stage 6: Implementing a Solution This stage is included to remind us that a solution is useless if it cannot be implemented. Political resistance, departures from established tradition, and high personal cost or risk are some of the many reasons apparently rational solutions do not get implemented in real organizations. In the divergent portion of this phase, the problem-solving team identifies potential sources of resistance and support. As this phase proceeds and specific implementation plans for the proposed solution are developed, the thinking style turns from divergent toward convergent. In this stage, we should expect to perform change management and focus on communication. During this phase, we ask questions such as the following:

- What are the barriers to successful implementation?
- Where will there be support and motivation, or resistance and conflict?
- Are the resources available for successful implementation?

This stage will be complete when we have produced an implementation plan and executed enough of it to begin evaluating how well it is succeeding.

To implement its plan, the task force at Invivo must first convince senior management to support its recommended solution. The consultant has a major role to play here in developing an effective presentation and in convincing both scientists and executives that this solution will work. The task force's role ends when it has won approval and has appointed a new committee to manage the implementation of the new R&D budget allocation process. Of course, the problem-solving process does not really end here, as the new committee must carry the plan forward, monitor its impacts, modify it as needed, and solve a new set of problems as they arise. To this extent, no problem-solving process ever really ends; it just flows into a subsequent process.

Every successful problem-solving effort starts with a mess and concludes with an implemented solution. Sometimes the cycle will be repeated more than once, so that the implementation itself creates a new situation and paves the way for follow-on problems to be identified. Nevertheless, the process passes through the stages we have outlined here. Knowledge of these stages is helpful in planning the overall tasks and resources, allocating effort, and setting expectations about progress. Within each stage, an awareness of the contributions from divergent and convergent thinking is helpful in balancing the need for creativity with the need for closure.

It is worth repeating that only rarely are these six stages followed in a strict sequence. Most problem-solving processes move back and forth from one stage to another, perhaps rethinking the problem statement while evaluating solutions, or returning to an information-gathering mode while searching for solutions. As in any creative endeavor, it is important for a problem-solving team (or individual) to remain flexible. That means remaining open to discoveries and to evidence that past work needs to be rethought.

2.2.3 Mental Models and Formal Models

The problem-solving process described earlier is generic in that it does not specifically address how formal modeling is used within the overall framework. Informal modeling, often called *mental modeling*, goes on constantly during problem solving. That is, problem solvers construct quick, informal mental models at many different points in the process. For example, when a potential solution is proposed, everyone on the team runs that idea through a mental model to get a quick first impression of its attractiveness. As an example, consider the following question:

> Would a tax on carbon emissions in developed countries significantly reduce global warming?

What mental models do you use to evaluate this question? How do you think a tax would affect actual emissions of carbon? What effect would it have on economic growth and quality of life? How would developing countries react to such a policy, and what would be the long-term impact on global temperature? Usually, when we consider questions like this, we use mental models to link causes (the tax) with their effects (changes in global temperature).

Mental models help us to relate cause and effect, but often in a highly simplified and incomplete way. Mental models also help us to determine what might be feasible in a given situation, but our idea of what is possible is often circumscribed by our personal experiences. Finally, mental models are always influenced by our preferences for certain outcomes over others, although those preferences may not be acknowledged or even understood. One source of confusion and debate on topics such as global warming is that we all use different mental models, based on different assumptions and preferences for outcomes, and we have limited means of sharing those models because they are informal and hidden from view. So, while mental models may be useful, even necessary, they can also be extremely limiting. A common pitfall is to reject an unusual idea because it appears at first to be unworkable. Effective divergent thinking can help overcome this pitfall and allow unusual ideas to persist long enough to get a thorough hearing. But in some circumstances, mental models are simply not robust enough to provide sufficient insight, and formal models are called for.

Formal models (see Figure 2.1) provide the same kind of information as mental models. In essence, they link causes to effects and help us evaluate potential solutions. Once a set of potential solutions and a set of criteria have been identified, a formal model can be used to measure how well each solution performs according to the criteria. Formal models are undoubtedly costlier and more time-consuming to build than mental models, but they have the great advantage of making our assumptions, logic, and preferences explicit and open to debate.

Mental models were used extensively during the problem-solving process in our pharmaceutical company example. Every member of the task force was experienced in the industry, so each of them had developed mental models to think through the implications of the various proposals. For example, they each had some idea of the development and testing protocols for new drugs, the current process used to allocate R&D funds, and the profit streams new drugs typically generate. Using this experience, they were able to make rough, qualitative assessments of the impact the new R&D-allocation process would have on new-drug success, as well as the profit impact of introducing fewer drugs sooner. However, given the complexity of the drug-development process and the interaction of the various competing companies in the market, mental models would simply not support quantitative estimates of the overall profit impact of the proposed solution.

How could Invivo use formal modeling in its problem-solving process? With a formal model, it could track the progress of each of the six drugs through the various stages of development. One of the key assumptions it needs to agree on is how the new R&D process affects the completion time and probability of success at each stage. They would probably want to add to this basic model a module that projects the introduction of competing products in each medical category. This requires discussion and agreement on a set of assumptions about the plans of their competitors. Finally, they can complete the model by adding a financial component to determine their profits under any scenario. Taken as a whole, this model projects a stream of new-drug introductions by the firm and its competitors, then determines the price and market share for each drug, and ultimately calculates the resulting profits. Unlike mental models, a formal model built along these lines can help analyze whether the firm will be able to generate enough revenues from new drugs to offset the loss in revenues from its blockbuster drug.

2.3   INFLUENCE CHARTS

As we have pointed out, model building and analysis are used within the broader context of problem solving. To be successful, this process must begin with recognition of a problem and end with implementation of a solution. At a minimum, modeling should help in evaluating alternative solutions, but it also can provide the analyst with an enhanced intuitive understanding of the problem and the forces at work within it.

A key challenge modelers face in the problem-solving process is how to translate an initial, vague understanding of a problem into a concrete model. A mathematical model, of course, requires specific numerical inputs and outputs along with the precise relationships that connect them. Many modelers make the mistake of plunging into the details of a model before they think through the role the model will play in the overall process. We recommend a different approach, using the power of visualization to develop a broad understanding of the critical inputs, outputs, and relationships in a chart before building an initial model. An **influence chart** is a simple diagram that shows what outcome variables the model will generate and how these outputs are calculated from the necessary inputs. Influence charts are not designed to provide numerical results or insights into which particular solutions are desirable. Rather, they can help to bring clarity to the initial stages of the model formulation process.

Influence charts are particularly powerful in the early, conceptual stages of a modeling effort. They encourage the modeler or modeling team to focus on major choices, such as what to include and what to exclude from the model, rather than on details that may ultimately turn out to be unimportant. Influence charts provide a high-level view of the entire model that can be comprehended at one glance. This high-level perspective, in turn, supports modeling in teams by facilitating communication among team members. As a result, areas of agreement and disagreement among team members surface early. Influence charts can also be highly effective in communicating the essence of the modeling approach to clients.

Influence charts are flexible, so they support the frequent revision that effective modeling requires. We often encourage our student teams to devote the first hour in the life of a model to working out an influence chart. In addition, we ask them not to turn on the computer until all members of the team agree that their chart represents a suitable initial description of their model.

2.3.1 A First Example

To illustrate how influence charts are built, we begin with a highly simplified example.

EXAMPLE
A Pricing Decision

Determine the price we should set for our product so as to generate the highest possible profit this coming year.

∎

Since our plan will ultimately be measured by its profitability, we define Profit as the outcome measure and enclose it in a hexagon to distinguish it from other variables in the chart (Figure 2.2a). Next we ask what we need to know to determine Profit. The major components of Profit, Total Revenue and Total Cost, are drawn as variables enclosed in circles to the left of Profit and connected to it by arrows (Figure 2.2b). These arrows identify which variables are required to calculate the outcome. Next, Total Cost is determined by Fixed Cost and Variable Cost, which are drawn to the left of Total Cost (Figure 2.2c). Variable Cost in turn is the product of Quantity Sold and Unit Cost (Figure 2.2d). Now we turn to Total Revenue, which is the product of Quantity Sold and Price. We add Price and enclose it in a box to show it is our decision variable (Figure 2.2e). Finally, Price Elasticity, along with the price we set, determines Quantity Sold, so in Figure 2.2f, we add the Price Elasticity variable and an arrow from Price to Quantity Sold.

Traditionally, influence charts are built from right to left, using diagrammatic conventions that distinguish the roles of different types of variables (Figure 2.3). For example, we use hexagons to represent outputs and boxes to represent decisions, as indicated in our example. We also use circles to represent other variables. As we complete the layout, we can identify certain of the variables as inputs. These are shown in the diagram as triangles. Later, we will also use double circles to represent variables that are random.

While this is a highly simplified example, its development does involve a number of modeling choices. For example, we can see in the influence chart that Fixed Cost is assumed to be a known quantity, because there are no variables that are needed to determine Fixed Cost. In another situation, we might face a set of choices as to which production technology to choose for the coming year. In that case, Fixed Cost would not be known but would be influenced by our technology choices, and the chart would have to reflect those complexities. Another modeling choice is evident in how Quantity Sold is determined. In our chart, both Price and Price Elasticity influence Quantity Sold. This reflects our modeling judgment that we face a price-dependent market. In many situations, we might assume instead that Sales are independent of Price, at least within a reasonable range of prices. One final modeling decision is evident in our chart: because Quantity Sold determines Revenue, we are assuming

FIGURE 2.2a Start the Influence Chart with the Objective (Profit)

Profit

FIGURE 2.2b Decompose Profit into Total Revenue and Total Cost

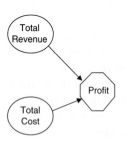

FIGURE 2.2c Decompose Total Cost into Variable Cost and Fixed Cost

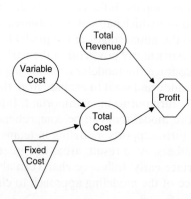

FIGURE 2.2d Decompose Variable Cost into Quantity Sold and Unit Cost

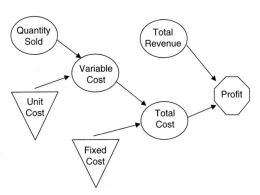

that production and sales are simultaneous. If, on the other hand, it were our practice to produce to stock and to sell from inventory, we would need to modify the chart to reflect this practice. This example illustrates that influence charts help the modeler make explicit decisions about what is included in the model and how the variables interact to determine the output.

2.3.2 An Income Statement as an Influence Chart

An income statement is a standard accounting framework that is widely used for reporting on the past performance of a company. The bottom line in an income statement is Retained Earnings, which is roughly the difference between revenue and costs, adjusted for taxes and dividends. A simple income statement is shown in the form of an influence chart in Figure 2.4.

If our purpose were simply to record the historical performance of a company, then the relationships depicted in Figure 2.4 would be sufficient. Moreover, the related spreadsheet would consist entirely of numbers; no formulas would be needed

FIGURE 2.2e Decompose Total Revenue into Quantity Sold and Price

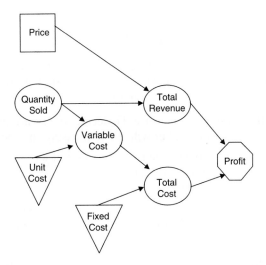

FIGURE 2.2f Decompose Quantity Sold into Price and Price Elasticity

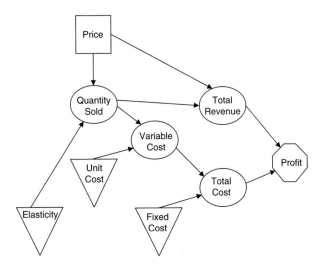

FIGURE 2.3 Symbols Used in Influence Charts

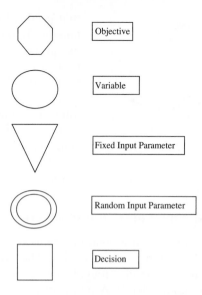

because all variables are already determined. However, Figure 2.4 would be inadequate if our purpose were to make projections into the future because it reveals nothing about how critical variables such as Sales Revenue and Cost of Goods Sold will be determined. (A projected income statement is known as a *pro forma* income statement; the Latin phrase *pro forma* literally means "as a formality," but the meaning in accounting is "provided in advance.") In other words, Figure 2.4 represents only a static accounting framework and not a *model* of the future. To convert a static income statement into a model, we need to determine how underlying variables such as Quantity Sold evolve over time. In a simple model, we could assume that Unit Cost and Price are constant and that Quantity Sold is determined by Initial Sales and Sales Growth Rate. Figure 2.5 shows an influence chart for this model.

Even in this case, where accounting rules determine much of the model structure, an influence chart is useful for depicting the underlying forces that drive the results.

2.3.3 Principles for Building Influence Charts

An influence chart is not a technical flowchart that must conform perfectly to a rigid set of rules. Rather, it is a somewhat free-form visual aid for thinking conceptually about a model. We offer the following guidelines for constructing such charts:

- Start with the outcome measure. To decide which variable this is, ask what single variable the decision maker will use to measure the success of a plan of action.

- Decompose the outcome measure into a small set of variables that determine it *directly*. Each of these influencing variables should be independent of the others, and together they should be sufficient to determine the result.

- Take each variable in turn and repeat this process of decomposition. For each variable, ask, "What do I need to know to determine... ?"

- Identify input data and decisions as they arise.

- Make sure that each variable appears only once in the diagram.

- Highlight special types of elements with consistent symbols. For example, we use squares for decision variables and double circles for random variables, but any consistent code will work.

FIGURE 2.4 Influence Chart for a Static Income Statement

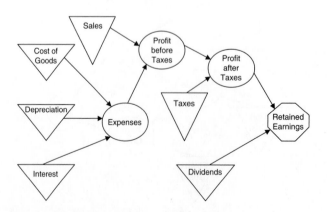

FIGURE 2.5 Influence Chart for an Income Statement Model

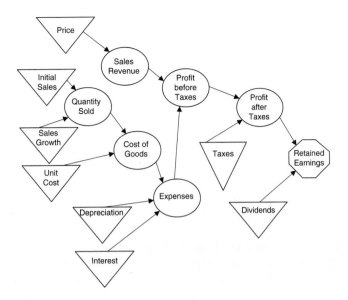

The most common error in drawing influence charts is to draw an arrow from the output back to the decisions. The thinking here seems to be that the outcome will be used to determine the best decisions. Remember, however, that an influence chart is simply a *description* of how we will calculate outcomes for *any* set of decisions and other parameters. It is not intended to be used to find the best decisions. That is a separate process, requiring an actual model, not simply a diagram.

2.3.4 Two Additional Examples

In this section, we present two detailed exercises in building influence charts for unstructured problems. Read each case and draw an influence chart before proceeding. We will then describe the process of building an influence chart and discuss some of our modeling choices. Keep in mind, however, that there is no one correct diagram, just as there is no one correct model.

EXAMPLE
The S.S. Kuniang

In the early 1980s, New England Electric System (NEES) was deciding how much to bid for the salvage rights to a grounded ship, the S.S. *Kuniang*.[1] If the bid was successful, the ship could be repaired and outfitted to haul coal for the company's power-generation stations. But the value of doing so depended on the outcome of a U.S. Coast Guard judgment about the salvage value of the ship. The Coast Guard's judgment involved an obscure law regarding domestic shipping in coastal waters. If the judgment indicated a low salvage value, and if NEES submitted the winning bid, then NEES would be able to use the ship for its shipping needs. If the judgment was high, the ship would be considered too costly for use in domestic shipping. The Coast Guard's judgment would not be known until after the winning bid was chosen, so there was considerable risk associated with submitting a bid. If the bid were to fail, NEES could purchase either a new ship or a tug/barge combination, both of which were relatively expensive alternatives. One of the major issues was that the higher the bid, the more likely that NEES would win. NEES judged that a bid of $2 million would definitely not win, whereas a bid of $12 million definitely would. Any bid in between was possible. ∎

The goal here is to select an amount to bid for the S.S. *Kuniang* that will allow NEES to supply coal to its plants in the most economical way. We assume that the amount of coal to be shipped is fixed and that NEES will either use the *Kuniang* or buy a new ship or a tug/barge combination. That is, we explicitly rule out the possibility that NEES can avoid meeting the demand for shipped coal. We further assume that

[1]D. E. Bell, "Bidding for the S.S. *Kuniang*," *Interfaces* 14 (1984): 17–23.

FIGURE 2.6 S.S. *Kuniang*
Influence Chart

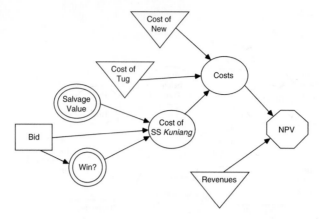

the outcome measure is the Net Present Value (NPV) of profits from this shipping operation over an appropriate time period (in the case of a ship, perhaps 20 years).

Our influence chart starts with an outcome measure for NPV and two influences: Costs and Revenues (Figure 2.6). Since the revenues are independent of the ship chosen, that part of the diagram does not need to be developed further. The costs incurred in coal shipping depend on which option is chosen. Apparently, NEES can always buy a new ship or a tug/barge combination, and it may have the option to buy the *Kuniang* if its bid wins. The costs of the *Kuniang* are the essential part of the model. These costs are dependent on the salvage value set by the Coast Guard, which is unpredictable and is therefore shown as a random variable (a double circle). The cost is also influenced by the size of the bid and by whether it wins the auction. In Figure 2.6, we have shown the outcome of the auction as the random variable "Win?" We have in mind a simple model in which the probability of winning increases as our bid increases. But this is an area of the diagram where further elaboration could be productive. We could, for example, add modules for the bids of our competitors. We could also add a module for the auction process itself. Whether to add further detail is always the modeler's judgment. But this simple influence chart is sufficiently detailed to support the building of a prototype model.

One additional point to notice here is that the numerical information in the problem statement, which places some limits on reasonable bids, plays no role at all in constructing the influence chart. In fact, we routinely ignore all available numerical data when we build influence charts because the goal is to develop a problem *structure*, not to solve the problem. Problem structure is not influenced by the values of parameters. This principle conflicts with another that many of us learned in early math classes, which was to use all the given data to solve the problem. This may be an appropriate problem-solving heuristic for simple math problems in school, but it is not necessarily helpful in structuring real business decisions.

EXAMPLE
Automobile Leasing

During the 1990s, leasing grew to 40 percent of new-car sales. Nowadays, the most popular leases are for expensive or midrange vehicles and terms of 24 or 36 months. The most common form of leasing is the closed-end lease, where the monthly payment is based on three factors:

• *Capitalized Cost*: the purchase price for the car, net of trade-ins, fees, discounts, and dealer-installed options.

• *Residual Value*: the value of the vehicle at the end of the lease, specified by the leasing company (the "lessor") in the contract. The customer has the right to purchase the vehicle at this price at the end of the lease.

• *Money Factor*, or *Rate*: the interest rate charged by the leasing company.

A lower residual value results in higher monthly payments. Therefore, a leasing company with the highest residual value usually has the lowest, and most competitive, monthly payment. However, if the actual end-of-lease market value is lower than the contract residual value, the customer is likely to return the car to the lessor. The lessor then typically sells the vehicle, usually at auction, and realizes a "residual loss."

On the other hand, if the actual end-of-lease market value is greater than the contract residual, the customer is more likely to purchase the vehicle. By then selling the vehicle for the prevailing market value, the customer in essence receives a rebate for the higher monthly payments. (Of course, the customer may also decide to keep the car.) When customers exercise their purchase option, the lessor loses the opportunity to realize "residual gains." ∎

The primary challenge for companies offering a closed-end lease is to select the residual value of the vehicle. Intelligent selection means offering competitive monthly payments on the front end without ignoring the risk of residual losses on the back end. In approaching this problem from a modeling perspective, the first task is to find ways to cut it down to size. After all, any leasing company offers leases on dozens of vehicles at any one time. Furthermore, unless it is just starting to do business, the company has an existing portfolio of hundreds of leases on its books, and the risk characteristics of this portfolio may influence the terms offered on new leases. We can become overwhelmed by complexity if we start by trying to model the entire problem. It is vital in modeling an ill-structured problem of this type to start simple and add complexity sparingly.

One reasonable approach is to develop an influence chart for a specific lease on a single type of vehicle. Once a prototype model based on this diagram is tested and proved, we can expand on it by bringing in excluded aspects of the problem.

An example will make the problem more concrete. Consider new Honda Accord models, which sell for $25,000. Also consider only three-year leases, and assume the money rate is fixed at 5 percent. Given these assumptions, our goal is to determine the best contract residual value (CRV) for a single lease on this single class of vehicles.

The CRV is clearly our decision variable. How will we determine whether we have made a good choice? Once we have chosen the CRV (and the other terms of the lease), we will offer it to the leasing market. Some number of customers will purchase our lease and pay us the monthly lease payments for three years. (A few will default during this period, but we ignore that factor in our initial prototype.) Our monthly lease revenues will be the product of the monthly payment and the number of leases sold. The monthly payment, in turn, will depend on the term, the money factor, and the CRV.

At the end of three years, all our leases will expire. Some customers will buy their vehicles at the CRV; others will return their vehicles and take a new lease with us; still others will return their vehicles and not purchase another lease with us. (We ignore the value of follow-on leases in our initial prototype.) When all is said and done, we will have made some level of profit. Profit, then, is our outcome measure, and it is influenced by three factors: lease revenues, our cost of borrowing (to pay for new vehicles), and the residual value of vehicles at the end of the lease (Figure 2.7).

So far, this is a rather straightforward influence chart. But two parts of it deserve additional attention. First, what determines how many leases are sold? Presumably,

FIGURE 2.7 National Leasing Influence Chart

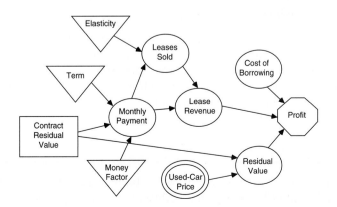

customers are sensitive to the monthly payment, and that influence is shown in the diagram, but what else influences volume? One simple approach is to assume a value for demand elasticity: volume increases (or decreases) by x percent when our monthly payments decrease (or increase) by 1 percent. This relationship is sufficient to generate some realistic aspects of the lease market—namely, a decline in volume with increasing payments—and it may be sufficient for a prototype model. But it does not explicitly include any information about our competitor's monthly payments. In particular, the elasticity is probably different when our payments are above the competition than when they are below. This may be a fertile area for refinement in later prototypes.

We should also consider what factors determine the residual value of the vehicle to the leasing company. When a lease expires, the contract allows the customer to purchase the vehicle for the CRV or to return it to the leasing company. The customer's decision at this point is crucial to determining the profitability of the lease. If used-car prices are high relative to the CRV, it is in the customer's interest to buy the car at the CRV and then sell it for the higher market price. But if used-car prices are low, customers will tend to return their leased vehicles and buy a cheaper equivalent used car. In this case, the leasing company will have to sell the vehicle at the low market price. And, of course, some customers will lease a new vehicle regardless of used-car prices, and some may not behave in an economically rational manner at all. Should we include all of these factors in our influence chart?

One approach would be to assume that all vehicles will be purchased if used-car prices exceed the CRV, and none will be purchased if the reverse holds. But how do we know how much used cars will be worth three years from now? In our chart, we model used-car prices as a random variable—for example, a normal distribution with a mean of $15,000 and a standard deviation of $2,000. Alternatively, we might assume that this class of vehicles loses a random amount of its value each year, where the annual loss is uniformly distributed between 8 and 12 percent. This slightly more detailed model will also generate a distribution of values three years from now. In further refinements of the chart, we might expand on these ideas and model the fundamental determinants of used-car values: new-vehicle quality, the macro economy, and so on. In any case, a random value for used-car prices captures one of the essential features of this problem—namely, the uncertainty surrounding residual losses and residual gains. This influence chart is probably sufficiently detailed to support construction of a prototype model. Working with this model will help us discover whether we have captured the essential trade-offs in the problem.

As we have stressed before, the influence chart documents the simplifying assumptions made during the modeling process. Here are some of the critical assumptions embodied in Figure 2.7:

- One vehicle/one lease term
- No lease defaults
- No follow-on leases
- Rational behavior of customers at lease end
- Random used-car prices

We recommend that the modeler or one member of the modeling team record each assumption as it is made during the process of developing an influence chart. This is useful for two reasons. First, it focuses attention and discussion on assumptions as they are being made. Second, each assumption should be viewed as a potential area for later refinement of the model.

2.4   CRAFT SKILLS FOR MODELING

Successful modelers can draw on both technical and craft skills in their work. **Technical skill** refers to the ability to carry out specific, narrow, well-defined tasks in the modeling process. This includes, for example, calculating present values, or linking balance sheets and income statements correctly, or identifying a tail probability in the results of a simulation model. Proper use of technical skill leads to a correct result and allows little room for creativity. In contrast, **craft skill** does not lead to a single correct result and does require creativity. Some examples of craft skill are making useful simplifications in a complex problem, designing a prototype, or brainstorming ways to increase demand for a new product. Craft skills develop slowly, over time and with experience, whereas technical skills can be learned at one pass. In playing the piano, technical skill is developed by practicing scales, while real craft is needed to interpret the music while playing it. Craft skills are harder to describe and teach than technical skills, but they are just as important to successful modeling. In fact, it is the high level of craft skill that distinguishes the expert modeler from the journeyman. In this section, we describe some of the most important craft skills and discuss the role that these skills play in modeling. The modeling cases that appear later in the book provide opportunities to practice these skills in ill-structured problem situations.

Craft skills are rarely discussed in books on spreadsheets or management science. One reason may be the common perception that modeling is an art that cannot be taught, only learned through long experience. Another reason may be that expert modelers, like experts in all fields, are largely unconscious of their own craft skills. There is also no well-accepted theory or classification for the craft skills in modeling. Nevertheless, we have found that awareness of these skills is essential to the successful development of truly skilled modelers. We commonly encounter highly skilled spreadsheet users whose craft skills are weak. As a consequence, they cannot successfully employ modeling in new and ill-structured situations. On the other hand, we rarely encounter analysts with good craft skills who cannot learn enough Excel to become good modelers. Furthermore, craft skills *can* be learned, despite the impediments we have cited. The first step in this process is to identify the skills themselves so that the modeler-in-training can begin to develop an awareness of modeling on a higher level than the merely technical.

It is helpful to classify craft skills into useful rules of thumb, or **modeling heuristics**. In general, a heuristic is an approach, a strategy, or a trick that has often proved effective in a given situation. A widely cited example from general problem solving is to write down everything we know about a problem. Heuristics are thought to be one of the most common ways humans deal with the complexities of the world around them, so it should not be surprising to find that modelers have their own. A modeling heuristic is a rule of thumb that experienced modelers use to help them overcome the inevitable difficulties that arise in modeling. We believe that novices can improve their modeling abilities by observing how these heuristics are used in a number of different situations. However, the only way to acquire these skills is to practice them on new problems.

In this section, we describe eight fundamental heuristics and illustrate how they can be used in practice. For the novice modeler, our purpose here is to raise awareness of the role these skills play so that they can be called on routinely in modeling work. With practice and refinement they can become as familiar as technical skills. Implementing these ideas will lead to a stronger personal tool kit of modeling skills. The modeling cases provide an opportunity to begin practicing these skills. In fact, we initiate that process in this chapter.

Throughout this section, we will refer to four modeling cases that describe ill-structured problems. One involves assisting a friend in planning for retirement, another deals with determining how many draft TV commercials to commission, the third requires evaluating the feasibility of towing icebergs to Kuwait for drinking water, and the fourth involves determining the profitability of a new production process. Short synopses of these cases are given here, while the complete versions can be found in the collection of modeling cases at the end of the book. Before proceeding any further, it would be helpful to read these synopses and give some thought to how to model them.

EXAMPLE
Retirement Planning

The client currently is 46 years old, with an income of about $126,000 per year. His goal is to retire between ages 62 and 67 and to have enough savings to live comfortably in about the same fashion he does now (with some money available for expanded travel). The client's accumulated savings for retirement total $137,000. His employer contributes around $10,000 per year into the retirement fund, while he has been contributing $7,500. How much should he be saving?   ∎

EXAMPLE
Draft TV Commercials

The client directs TV advertising for a large corporation. His budget for a single ad campaign is typically around $10 million. Under current procedures, a single TV advertisement is commissioned for about $500,000, and the remainder of the budget is spent on airing the ad. The client is considering a new approach, in which two or more draft commercials (at about the same cost) would be commissioned from different agencies. The best of these drafts would then be aired using the remainder of the budget. Is this new plan more effective than the old procedure?   ∎

EXAMPLE
Icebergs for Kuwait

Drinking water is in short supply in Kuwait and is therefore very expensive. One suggested remedy is to tow icebergs from Antarctica to Kuwait (a distance of about 9,600 kilometers) and melt them for freshwater. The volume of an iceberg ranges from about 500,000 cubic meters to more than 10 million cubic meters. Theoretical analysis suggests that an idealized spherical iceberg would lose about 0.2 meter of radius per day during transport, although this amount increases with the speed of towing and the distance from the pole. Fuel costs for towboats depend on the size of the boat, the speed, and the volume of the iceberg being towed. Would it be cost-effective to tow icebergs to Kuwait for freshwater, and, if so, how should this be done?   ∎

EXAMPLE
The Racquetball Racket

A new and cheaper process has been invented for manufacturing racquetballs. The new ball is bouncier but less durable than the major brand. Unit variable costs of production for the new process will run about $0.52, while the current process costs $0.95. A new plant would cost between $4 million and $6 million. We have 14 years of data on the number of racquetball players in the United States, the average retail price of balls, and the number of balls sold. The number of players is expected to increase about 10 percent per year for 10 years and then level off. In a recent survey, 200 players were asked to use both balls over several months, and their preferences were assessed at several different prices for the new ball. What is the net present value of an investment in a new plant to manufacture balls using this new process? What is the best price for the new ball, and how might the competitor react to introduction of a new ball?   ∎

2.4.1 Simplify the Problem

Without a doubt, the most important heuristic in all modeling is to *simplify*. Simplification is the very essence of modeling. We should never criticize a model for being simple, only for being too simple for the purposes at hand. Remember: a model that is too simple can often be modified to better suit the desired purposes.

A model that is more complex than necessary, however, already represents a waste of some modeling effort. Worse yet, a model may be so complex that it cannot be simplified effectively. It is, in fact, much harder to detect when a model is more complex than needed than it is to detect when a model is too simple. Overly simple models make us uncomfortable and motivate us to improve them; overly complex models may simply confuse and overwhelm us.

In discussing the importance of simplicity in models, Michael Pidd offers the following aphorism: [2] "Model simple, think complicated." By this, he reminds us that models are not independent of their users. So the right question to ask about a model is not whether the model by itself is adequate, but whether the user can discover helpful insights with the model. Simple models can support rigorous, critical thinking on the part of the user. Simple models are also more transparent and therefore easier to understand and apply. Users (and their managers) are more likely to trust simple

[2]Michael Pidd, *Tools for Thinking: Modelling in Management Science* (Chichester: John Wiley and Sons, 1996), p. 95.

models and implement the recommendations that are developed from their analysis. A modeling team will find that a simple model facilitates communication within the team, while only the modeling experts may understand a complex model.

There is no more useful tool in the modeler's kit than "keeping it simple." Thus, we try to cut away all complexity that is not essential. Never stop asking whether any particular aspect of a model is necessary for achieving the goals at hand. Novice modelers are often amazed at the simplicity of experts' models, particularly the simplicity of an expert's *first* model. Two other heuristics we will discuss later, decomposition and prototyping, are themselves powerful tools for keeping models simple.

How does one go about simplifying situations for modeling? One approach is to focus on the connections between the key decisions and the outcomes that result from those decisions. Then, ask what central trade-offs make these decisions difficult and build a model to explore those trade-offs. In the Retirement Planning case, for example, increasing one's savings rate reduces current disposable income but increases one's assets at retirement. If that trade-off makes the problem difficult, focus the modeling effort on that issue and leave out anything that seems peripheral.

In the Draft TV Commercials case, money spent on creative work will increase the quality of the advertisement, while money spent on buying airtime will increase the number of consumers who see the advertisement. If the budget is limited, there is an inevitable trade-off between spending money on creative work and spending money on airtime. Focus the modeling effort on illuminating this trade-off.

In the Icebergs for Kuwait case, we know that large icebergs will provide more water, but they may take longer and cost more to transport. Small icebergs provide less water but may be more efficient to move. Here is an essential trade-off to capture in the model.

The goal in the Racquetball Racket case is not to make a highly accurate forecast of profits from the venture, but rather, to understand the risks introduced by various factors such as the competitor's response to our entry. This argues for a simple but highly flexible model. Obviously, the pricing decision will be a key one. A high price may provide attractive margins but also limit our market share. On the other hand, a low price may provide a large market share but leave us with very tight margins. The relationship between price and profitability is one important aspect of the problem, but it helps to keep this relationship simple because we are interested in understanding how it is affected by the competitive response.

Simplification by its nature involves making assumptions. Boldness and self-confidence in making assumptions is a mark of an experienced modeler. Many modelers, however, make assumptions but do not recognize that they are doing so. For example, in the Racquetball Racket case, many student modelers assume that sales will immediately reach a steady state. But if they don't realize this is an assumption, they miss the opportunity to test the sensitivity of their results to it. Thus, it is important both to make assumptions and to recognize them as they are being made. Every assumption should be revisited at some point in the analysis, to see if an alternative assumption would substantially change the results or provide new insights.

This discussion is summarized well by Morgan and Henrion:

> There are some models, especially some science and engineering models, that are large or complex because they need to be. But many more are large or complex because their authors gave too little thought to why and how they were being built and how they would be used.[3]

2.4.2 Break the Problem into Modules

One of the fundamental ways to approach any type of problem solving is to decompose the problem into simpler components. The decomposition approach is basic to Western science and, some would say, to Western thought itself.

---

[3]M. G. Morgan and M. Henrion, *Uncertainty: A Guide to Dealing with Uncertainty in Quantitative Risk and Policy Analysis* (Cambridge, UK: Cambridge University Press, 1992), p. 289.

The challenge, of course, is to know where to draw the lines; that is, which are the most productive components to create? One approach is to divide the problem into components that are as *independent* of each other as possible.

In the Retirement Planning case, it is natural to decompose the problem into a working-life module and a retirement module. Within the working-life module, we will want to keep track of salary and other income as well as accumulating retirement assets. In the retirement module, we will follow the accumulated assets as they are drawn down for consumption. We may also track certain aspects of consumption, such as travel expenses. These modules are nearly independent: the only necessary connection is that the final assets from the working-life module become the initial assets in the retirement module.

In the Draft TV Commercials case, one module can be devoted to determining the quality of the advertisement that is ultimately aired, while another can be devoted to determining the impact of a budget for airing an advertisement of a given quality. These modules are largely independent: the quality of the advertisement chosen depends on the distribution of quality in the population from which advertisements are drawn, as well as on the number of drafts purchased. Meanwhile, the impact of a given budget in creating audience impressions depends on the size of the budget and the quality of the ad being aired. This latter module requires some assumption about the influence of incremental advertising dollars on incremental impact. The simplest assumption would be that impact is proportional to advertising spending, although we might expect diminishing returns to set in eventually.

In the Icebergs for Kuwait case, a productive approach would be to create three modules. The first determines the supply of icebergs at the edge of the ice cap in Antarctica (by size, shape, etc.). The second module determines how large the iceberg is when it arrives in Kuwait, given its size and shape at the start of the trip, the speed at which it is towed, melting rates, and other factors. Finally, the third module converts the iceberg into a certain quantity of drinking water and a corresponding economic value.

In the Racquetball Racket case, a typical decomposition is to determine annual dollar sales of our ball by multiplying the number of users by the average number of balls purchased per year. The number purchasing our ball is the total number of users multiplied by our share of the market. Our share, in turn, is a function of our price and quality relative to the competitor's price and quality. There are, of course, other ways to decompose sales: by geographic region, by age of buyer, by product type, and so on. Choosing among these methods in a given situation depends on two things: how effective it is to build a model of one component and how easy it is to extend the model for one component to cover all the other components.

Why does the decomposition heuristic work? The great advantage of decomposing a problem is that the components are simpler to deal with than the whole. In addition, the process provides a natural structure for the analysis, thereby allowing the analyst to focus effort on one area at a time. Finally, this heuristic naturally leads us to think in terms of modules, and from there, it is a short step to discover the *interchangeability* of modules. For example, we can change our approach to modeling market share in the Racquetball Racket case without changing any other module. This leads us naturally to another powerful heuristic: *prototyping*.

2.4.3 Build a Prototype and Refine It

A **prototype** is just a working model. A prototype of a new car, for example, is a working model of the car, built to test design concepts prior to high-volume manufacturing. A prototype of a computer program is a working model that can be used to test whether the program works as intended. It can also be used to test the reactions of the users, who may not be able to specify their needs in the abstract but may discover their needs through experimenting with the prototype. A prototype of a model (in our sense) is nothing more than a working version of a model. As a working model, it should take data and inputs from the user and produce key outputs in response. However, the prototype is very likely to need further refinements, since

FIGURE 2.8   Sketch of
Results for the Retirement
Planning Case

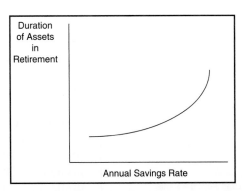

FIGURE 2.8   Sketch of
Results for the Retirement
Planning Case

there will probably be gaps between its current performance and the desired results. These gaps describe the tasks that remain, either in terms of interaction with the user or in terms of analysis yet to be done, if the prototype is to be elevated to a finished model. Prototyping is an essential part of an effective modeling approach, especially when modeling is performed under tight limits on the available time and budget.

What would a prototype for the Retirement Planning case look like? In this case, the essential concern is to explore the relationship between working life savings and retirement assets. We might take as our objective the number of years that we can live off our retirement assets before they are exhausted. In order to estimate this result, it will be useful to simplify at the start some of the many complexities of the problem. For a first prototype, we could make the following assumptions:

- Income grows at a constant rate during the working years.
- The savings rate is a constant percentage of annual income in the working years.
- Retirement assets provide a fixed rate of return.
- The retirement date is fixed.
- Postretirement consumption is a fixed percentage of income in the final year of work.

Using these assumptions, we can rather easily build a model that accomplishes the following tasks:

- Project our income (at some assumed growth rate) from the present to retirement.
- Calculate our retirement contributions (given a constant savings rate).
- Accumulate our retirement assets (at some assumed rate of return).
- Project our assets as they are drawn down during retirement (at the assumed consumption rate).
- Determine the year in which they are exhausted.

This simple model allows us to create a plot that shows how long our assets last as a function of our savings rate (Figure 2.8). If that relationship is the essential summary of our analysis, we have completed our first prototype. We can now test the model, varying decisions and parameters in an attempt to gain insight into the problem. Eventually, we may want to build a refined model, if the first prototype proves inadequate in some way.

In an initial approach to the Draft TV Commercials problem, we might avoid the complexities of sampling from a population of potential drafts and simply assume that advertisement quality increases with the number of draft ads, but with diminishing returns. We might implement this relationship using a power function:

$$Quality = a(Number\,of\,drafts)^b$$

We might also assume that the total budget is fixed and that each draft advertisement costs a fixed percentage of the budget. It follows that each additional draft advertisement reduces the budget available for airing by the same amount. If we assume that the total impact created by an advertisement is the product of the quality of the advertisement (in impressions per dollar spent on airing) and the airing budget, we have the basis for a prototype. From this simple model, we can plot a graph that relates the total number of impressions created to the number of draft advertisements (Figure 2.9).

FIGURE 2.9 Sketch of Results for the Draft TV Commercials Case

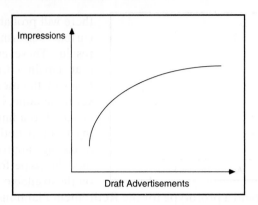

Are we content with this first prototype? Probably not. Assuming that we have or can acquire some data on the variability of ad quality, we might later refine the portion of the model in which the quality of the best draft is determined. Sampling from a distribution of ad quality will give us the average quality of the best advertisement as a function of the number of drafts. We expect this function to have the same concave shape as the power function in our first prototype. But it will be better in at least two ways: first, it more closely resembles the actual process by which the best advertisement is created; second, it allows us to test the sensitivity of the results (total impressions created) to the variability in the distribution of quality.

A prototype for the Icebergs for Kuwait problem could be a model for the radial shrinking of a spherical iceberg of fixed initial size being towed at constant speed from the ice pack to Kuwait. If we calculate the final volume of the iceberg and multiply by the price of water, then we can compute an initial estimate of the value of the project.

This is the information the client wants, so our simple model is a legitimate prototype. Is this approach highly simplified? Of course it is. But the model's simplicity is its strength, not its weakness. If we have built our prototype quickly, we have time left over to refine it. Rather than having a number of separate pieces to integrate, we can work with one unified model.

Before refining this model, we would want to use it to explore the problem. For example, we would want to test the sensitivity of the final cost to the initial size of the iceberg, the towing speed, and the size of the boat. These tests will give us ideas not only about the ultimate results the model will generate, but also about where improvements might be warranted. We might, for example, want to test towing strategies that involve changes in speed over the trip. On the other hand, perhaps the weakest part of the model is the assumption that the iceberg is spherical and melts with a constant radius. Does the submerged portion of an iceberg melt faster or slower than the visible part? Does the ratio of these parts change with size? Every assumption is an opportunity to improve the analysis. The trick to effective prototyping is to find those improvements that lead to significant improvements in the results, not merely to a more elegant, more complex, or more "realistic" model.

In the Racquetball Racket case, the objective is to help the client make a go/no-go decision. A highly accurate forecast of the NPV is not necessarily required, especially if the estimated NPV is clearly positive or negative. Thus, a prototype should give us a first, rough estimate of project NPV. It will move us closer to that goal if we assume that

- our competitor will price at its current level,
- our price and our competitor's price both remain constant over the life of the product,
- no third competitor will enter, and
- total demand for balls will grow at a constant percentage rate, independent of prices.

The only remaining component involves our market share, which we could model as an S-shaped function of our price. The following function is useful in this context:

$$Share = b + (a - b)(Price^c/(d + Price^c))$$

We can use the market research data to help us determine plausible values for the parameters a, b, c, and d. With this module in place, we have a full prototype, because the model can generate an NPV for any price we choose. With the model, we

FIGURE 2.10 Sketch of Results for the Racquetball Racket Case

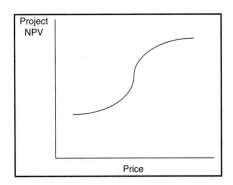

can develop a chart showing how project NPV varies with our price and whether there is a price we can charge at which the project looks attractive (Figure 2.10). Once again, we are not done with the analysis. These results are only the first in what will most likely be a long sequence of estimates for project NPV, but this prototype supports the next stage in the analysis, which involves testing the sensitivity of our results to our assumptions.

In general, how do we know when we have a completed prototype? If we have

- decomposed the problem into modules,
- built at least a simple model for every module, and
- coordinated the modules so that they work together to generate results in the form we think the client wants,

then we have a prototype. If we cannot provide at least a tentative answer to the client's major questions, we don't have a prototype. If one or more modules are missing, we don't have a prototype. But once our ideas come together in a working model, the event marks a key milestone, for then the emphasis will shift from creation to refinement, in collaboration with the client.

The cyclic nature of prototyping is worth some elaboration. Many people think that prototyping involves building one model after another until we are satisfied that we have the final model, and *then* carrying out the analysis. This is a fundamental misconception. It is essential to use each successive prototype to answer the managerial questions in the problem before refining the model further. This discipline helps keep the modeler's attention on the *problem*, and not exclusively on the model or the modeling process. One reason modelers sometimes hesitate to use prototypes in this way is that they are embarrassed by the shortcomings of their early models and don't want to see them being used "for real." But it is only in this way that a modeler can see the value of each successive refinement.

Why is prototyping such a powerful idea? One reason is that a prototype keeps the entire problem in the mind of the modeler. It is impossible to perfect a module in isolation because it has value only as part of the entire model. In most situations, we cannot know how well a module works until it is integrated with the others, so it is vital to build prototypes in which every major component is represented. Prototyping also helps avoid the seduction of modeling for its own sake. Remember that the task is to provide management with *insight*. Modeling is merely a means to that end. One way to maintain focus on the managerial question at hand is to use a series of prototypes to generate tentative answers to the client's questions. By using each model to provide an answer and by performing sensitivity analysis on each model, the focus will remain, appropriately, on the problem rather than on the model.

Prototyping is a particularly critical tool for novice modelers, who often struggle psychologically with the vagaries of the creative process. Many of our students have never struggled as hard as they do in modeling ill-structured problems. Some of them suffer from all the symptoms of depression when they have worked for a week and feel they have nothing to show for it. For these students, as for most modelers, having a working prototype, *no matter how primitive*, is a great psychological boost. Once we have a prototype, we have not only a tentative answer for the client, but also a road map for future work.

Finally, prototyping is an essential tool for the practicing analyst who operates under severe time constraints. Once a prototype is up and running, the analyst should ask this question: Where would my model benefit most from additional work? Or, to put it more precisely: Where should I focus my efforts to most improve the quality of my advice to the client? This is an impossible question to answer in the abstract. But with a prototype and some skill in sensitivity analysis, we can get a fair idea of which modules or which components within a given module have the biggest impact on the results. Thus, the prototype is itself a necessary tool in the analyst's efforts to use time effectively.

2.4.4 Sketch Graphs of Key Relationships

One of the reasons modeling is so difficult for many people is that it appears to be highly abstract or mathematical, and they cannot find a way to express their thoughts in these terms. Most people have good intuitions about the modeling challenges they face, but they lack the skills to represent those intuitions in a useful way. The ability to change representation systems is one of the powerful heuristics that experts suggest for general problem solving. Good problem solvers can look at a problem from many angles—inventing analogies, drawing pictures, hypothesizing relationships, or perhaps carrying out suggestive physical experiments.

Novice modelers rarely use drawings or sketches to represent their understanding of a problem. They haven't discovered that visual depictions of models are often much easier to work with than verbal or mathematical ones. When it comes to creating a relationship between variables, sketching a graph is a very useful first step.

The inability to visualize the relation between variables is a common stumbling block in modeling. Ask a manager whether the relation between advertising and sales is linear or concave, and you may get a puzzled look. Yet if we draw coordinate axes and label the horizontal axis "Advertising," and the vertical "Sales," most anyone will say the graph slopes up and probably "bends over" at some point. So the *intuition* for a concave relation in this case is widely shared; what many people lack is a representation system within which they can express their intuition. Such people lack the mathematical sophistication to select a plausible family of functions to represent a given graphical relation.

Here is another example of the power of visualization. When one of our students is completely stuck about how to start a modeling problem, we might draw a simple diagram (Figure 2.11) consisting of a box with one arrow coming in from the top and another going out to the right. Along with the drawing, we'll say that the way we see the problem, we have some decisions to make (arrow going into box), then the future will evolve in some way (inside the box), and in the end, we'll have some outcomes (arrow going out of box). The model we need to build is going to transform alternative decisions into outcomes we can evaluate. This simple picture does wonders—it focuses the novice on three key issues:

- What *decisions* do we have?
- How will we evaluate *outcomes*?
- What system of *relationships* connects the decisions to the outcomes?

To an experienced modeler, this picture would seem trivial. To a struggling novice, however, it can be a revelation. Somehow, the picture itself is far more powerful than an equivalent verbal or algebraic description.

Why does this visualization heuristic work? We suspect one reason has to do with the power of looking at a problem from different viewpoints. Somehow, changing how we look at a problem often helps us overcome a sense of being stuck, of having no useful knowledge about a particular issue. (Novice modelers usually are able to sketch a graph for a relation, even when they say they know nothing about the mathematical function involved.)

Visualization probably works by *externalizing* the analysis—that is, by moving the focal point of analysis from inside the mind to an external artifact

FIGURE 2.11 Visualization of the Modeling Process

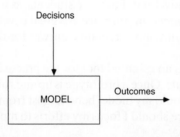

Decisions

Outcomes

MODEL

FIGURE 2.12 Useful Functions for Modeling

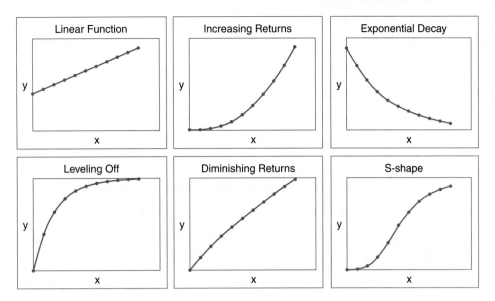

(such as a graph or equation). This is clearly essential for modeling in groups, where thoughts in the mind cannot be debated unless they are represented outside the mind. But it is also crucial for the solo modeler, because it is far easier to test and refine an external artifact than an inchoate idea in the mind.

Sketching graphs is also a powerful heuristic because there is only a small set of possible relations between two variables that are useful in a typical modeling problem, and common sense can rule out most of them. The most often used is the simple straight line (with either positive or negative slope). In the spirit of prototyping, we often suggest that the *first* relation we would propose between *any* variables is a linear one. Build a working prototype first and gain some experience with it. Come back later and refine the linear relation if theory or intuition suggests a more complex relation and if model testing suggests that the results will be sensitive to this relation.

In order to make full use of this heuristic, the modeler also needs to know a few useful families of functions. Here is a basic list. (These families are also depicted in Figure 2.12.)

- Linear function, showing constant returns (positive or negative), $y = a + bx$.
- Power function with increasing returns, $y = ax^b$ with $(b > 1)$.
- Exponential function, representing decline and decay, $y = ae^{-bx}$.
- Exponential function, representing leveling off at an asymptote, $y = a(1 - e^{-bx})$.
- Power function, with diminishing returns, $y = ax^b$ with $(b < 1)$.
- The S-shaped curve, for rapid, then slowing growth, $y = b + (a - b)(x^c/(d + x^c))$.

This use of graphs to select a family of curves to represent a relation is closely related to the parameterization heuristic discussed next.

2.4.5 Identify Parameters and Perform Sensitivity Analysis

We have seen that sketching a graph is a powerful way to express one's intuitions about the relationship between two variables. (The idea could be extended to three variables, although it gets more complicated.) But there is no direct way as yet to enter a sketch into a spreadsheet. Some explicit formula must be created to stand for the sketch in the model itself. This could take the form of a traditional mathematical function, for example:

$$D5 = \$A\$1 + \$A\$2^*D4$$

or it could be a complex combination of spreadsheet functions, for example:

D5= IF(D2-D1 > $E$4,VLOOKUP(E7,Data,3),VLOOKUP(E7,Data,2))).

In either case, the relations involve input numbers, and these parameters play an essential role in spreadsheet modeling and analysis.

For example, we might hypothesize that there is a downward-sloping relation between the quantity we sell and the price we can charge. This assumption is consistent with the linear demand curve

$$Price = a - b \times (Quantity)$$

and also with the constant-elasticity demand curve

$$Price = a \times (Quantity)^b (b < 1)$$

In each of these functions, the symbols a and b are parameters that stand for as-yet-undetermined numbers. Each of these functions represents a *family* of relations having the common property of sloping downward; the linear family declines at a constant rate, while the constant-elasticity family declines at a decreasing rate. When we implement one of these families in a spreadsheet model, we choose particular values of the parameters; that is, we select one from among the family of curves. Rarely will we know the values of these parameters exactly. This is where sensitivity analysis comes in. With sensitivity analysis, we can determine plausible ranges for the parameters and test the impact of changing parameter values on model outputs. In fact, we will recommend in Chapter 6 that testing the sensitivity of the critical outputs to model parameters is an essential step in any modeling activity. One reason we can be creative in the functional relationships we put in our models is that we have confidence that we can eventually test our results with respect both to the functions we have used and to the parameters that drive those functions.

Parameterization plays a key role in one of our favorite short modeling problems, called *Hot and Thirsty*.[4] The goal is to model the temperature of a warm beer as it cools over time in a refrigerator. Common sense leads to a difference equation of the form

$$T_{t+1} = T_t - Heat\ loss\ over\ the\ interval\ (t, t+1)$$

where T_t represents the temperature of the beer at time t. What factors influence the heat loss? Clearly, the type of beer may be relevant, as are the material used in its container, the shape of the container, the humidity of the refrigerator, how frequently it is opened, and so on. So many factors influence heat loss that one might think the only feasible approach is to gather data on all of them, a daunting task. However, there is an easier way.

A little understanding of thermodynamics (or some experience with refrigerators) will suggest that heat loss is proportional to the temperature difference between the beer and the air in the refrigerator, with the constant of proportionality depending on all the factors cited above; that is:

$$T_{t+1} = T_t - k \times (T_t - T_{fridge})$$

If, for the moment, we assume some arbitrary value for the constant of proportionality k, it is straightforward to build a spreadsheet model for this relation. Then, as we choose different values of the parameter k, we can graph different decline curves for the temperature (see Figure 2.13). It is surprising but true that we can use common sense and a little experience with beer to determine plausible values for k within a rather narrow range, just based on the time it takes to cool to refrigerator temperature. We could also determine k rather accurately by cooling a beer for, say, 15 minutes and then determining its temperature. We can then use the family of curves in Figure 2.13 to read off the value of k that gives us this temperature.

---

[4]A. Starfield, K. Smith, and A. Bleloch, *How to Model It* (New York: McGraw-Hill, 1990), 54–69.

FIGURE 2.13 Temperature of Beer over Time

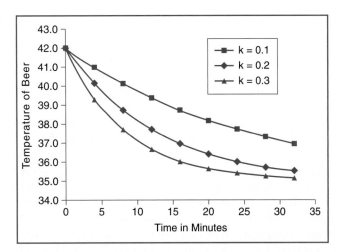

This looks like sleight of hand, as if we were manufacturing knowledge out of ignorance. After all, we know that k depends on a long list of factors, none of which is known in this problem. Yet here we lump all these influences into a single number. What really has happened is that we have used intuition and common sense to build a structure (or model) that is more general than needed for the immediate purpose, and then we have specialized it to the case at hand by varying the single number k. We have also saved a lot of effort by building a model structure before we tried to collect data, because, using this approach, we never have to know the type of beer, its container, or anything about the refrigerator.

Why is parameterization such a powerful heuristic? We believe its power comes, as the previous example suggests, from our ability to select one from a family of curves by using sensitivity analysis. Parameterization also reduces the vagueness in relation to a single dimension, which itself is a great simplification. Then, if we can find ways (such as the graphical approach described earlier) to display the implications of a particular choice for the parameter, we can bring to bear our usually considerable intuition about the problem. So the power of parameterization, in part, lies in building links between our rational knowledge and our intuition.

2.4.6 Separate the Creation of Ideas from Their Evaluation

Jim Evans, who has written extensively on the role of creativity in management science, points out in his book *Creative Thinking*[5] that one of the important emotional blocks to creativity is the tendency to judge ideas before they receive an adequate hearing. Many modelers we have worked with show a marked *preference* for judging ideas over generating them, especially if generating ideas means coming up with wild notions that probably will not work. But some wild notions actually do work, and others spark the mind to generate additional creative solutions. It is, therefore, essential to have methods available that help *quiet the critical voice* during the most creative phases of the problem-solving process.

The "quiet the critic" heuristic is based on the distinction, discussed earlier, between divergent and convergent thinking. Divergent thinking involves generating alternative problem statements, approaches, and possible solutions, with a minimum of evaluation. Convergent thinking, on the other hand, involves the rational analysis of these alternatives, with the goal of choosing the best (and rejecting the rest). Each stage of the problem-solving process involves both divergent and convergent thinking. However, it is generally most effective to stress divergent types of thinking early in the modeling process and to gradually shift to more convergent thinking as the model and analysis take shape.

[5]James R. Evans, *Creative Thinking* (Cincinnati: South-Western, 1991).

The quintessential divergent-thinking process is **brainstorming**, in which a group generates as many ideas on an issue as possible, without any critical evaluation. The most effective brainstorming sessions involve a facilitator, who can set the ground rules and remind participants not to criticize the ideas of others. The purpose of not criticizing ideas is to prevent premature selection of obvious or mundane approaches to a problem. Some participants always seem to have difficulty refraining from evaluating their own ideas or those of others during such a session. It is often equally difficult for them to show overt enthusiasm for ideas, from whatever source. Fostering a climate in which ideas are celebrated, regardless of their source or their apparent usefulness, should be a goal of modeling teams and individuals.

It's difficult to appreciate the power of brainstorming without seeing it in action. We recall a class session in which we were analyzing the problem of how to configure a highway tunnel to accommodate the maximum traffic volume. We had determined the optimal speed and heading for cars to follow, but were stuck on how to ensure that drivers would actually follow our solution. We then had a short brainstorming session focused on how to accomplish this. Among many other creative ideas, one student suggested installing rows of lights in the tunnel that would blink on and off at a speed set by the traffic engineers to guide drivers to the correct speed. This student was from another country, and the other students' first reaction was that this solution must be something she had seen in use in her home country. Once they began to realize it was not a known solution but something she had invented on the spot, they were more willing to think of alternatives beyond their own experience.

Why does this heuristic work? Apparently, our educational systems encourage students to criticize their own ideas and those of others, but not to create ideas or to appreciate their own and others' creative ideas. This imbalance can be so extreme that an open-ended project such as modeling becomes overwhelming because the pitfalls of every approach seem so clear to the modeler. When the critical faculty is so strong, the modeler needs reassurance that mistakes and blind alleys are a necessary part of the creative process. By finding ways to "quiet the critic," the novice modeler gains time to find a solution that eventually will stand up to their own scrutiny and to the scrutiny of others.

2.4.7 Work Backward from the Desired Answer

Most modeling projects proceed from the ground up: make assumptions, gather data, build a prototype, and so on. This is a reasonable approach in many ways, and to some extent, there is no alternative. But the bottom-up approach can lead to difficulties, especially in the hands of creative individuals. Creative exploration of a problem with a succession of models sometimes leaves the modeling team in a quandary about which approach among many to take and which results to show the client.

One way to break through this dilemma is to *work backward from the desired answer*. That is, imagine the *form* the answer will take, and then work backward from that point to select the model and analysis necessary to generate the chosen form of answer. An example will clarify this point.

It is clear in the Retirement Planning case that the client wants to know how his savings during his working life will influence his retirement years. But there are many ways to measure the quality of retirement living; which ones are best suited to this client? Would he like to know his asset level at retirement, or the number of years his assets will hold out, or the maximum amount he can afford to spend if he lives to 75, or the probability of running out of money before he is 90? Before we can focus our modeling, we must have an answer (even a tentative one) to this question. We also need to know how the client thinks about his savings decision—in terms of a constant percentage of his income or a constant dollar amount, or perhaps a percentage rising at a certain rate. Until we settle this question, we are also not ready to think about how we are going to present our results. If, after sufficient thought, we decide we want to show the client how his final assets depend

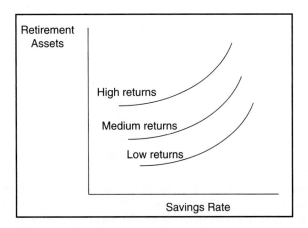

FIGURE 2.14 Sketch of Results for Retirement Analysis

on his (constant percentage) savings rate and how this relationship itself depends on the returns he can earn on his assets, we can sketch the chart shown in Figure 2.14. Notice that we do not need a model, nor do we need any data, to sketch this chart because it is only an illustration. But the chart has considerable value because it focuses our modeling effort on a clear end product.

We sometimes facetiously call this the "PowerPoint heuristic." Here's the idea: most decision makers are very busy, so they cannot sit through a long-winded presentation. In fact, we like to imagine that our client is so busy that we have to condense our entire presentation to *one* PowerPoint slide. If that's all we have, that one slide must contain the essential message we have to deliver. What is that message? Is it a number, a table, a chart, a procedure, a recommendation? Sketching out what that one slide might look like involves making decisions about the critical outputs, thus focusing the modeling effort on the essential message.

The power of this heuristic lies not just in being able to organize one's thoughts at the end of a modeling effort, but also in organizing the work itself by asking periodically: What will our final results look like?

2.4.8 Focus on Model Structure, not on Data Collection

As we mentioned in Chapter 1, novice modelers often spend a high proportion of their time searching for and analyzing *data*. Expert modelers, however, spend most of their time working on the *structure* of their models. This contrast has significant implications for the appropriate conduct of a modeling project.

Why do novices emphasize data analysis over model structure? This attitude appears to be based on three beliefs. First, novices assume that the available data are an accurate indicator of the information needed in the modeling process. Second, they believe that obtaining data moves the process forward in a productive direction. Third, they believe that the available data will ultimately improve the quality of the recommendations developed as a result of modeling. From these beliefs, it seems to follow logically that data collection and analysis should be an important and early activity in any modeling project. But these beliefs are not supported by experience. As Mosteller, Fienberg, and Rourke state it, "Although we often hear that data speak for themselves, their voices can be soft and sly."[6]

Novice modelers tend to accept, without critical screening, any data provided to them. By contrast, expert modelers know that most data contain hidden biases and errors. Perhaps the biggest single problem with empirical information is that it reports on the *past*, whereas modeling looks to the *future*. Even if we have accurate data on the growth in sales over the past 10 years, can we be sure next year's growth will follow the same pattern? Other common sources of biases and errors in empirical data include:

- *Sampling error* (e.g., a phone survey does not contact the homeless)
- *Differences in purpose* (e.g., accounting profits do not correspond to economic profits)

[6]Frederick Mosteller, Stephen E. Fienberg, and Robert E. K. Rourke, as quoted in Jonathan G. Koomey, *Turning Numbers into Knowledge* (Oakland, CA: Analytics Press, 2001), p. 86.

- *Masking* (e.g., actual sales may not reflect underlying customer demand)
- *Inappropriateness* (e.g., growth rates on one product may not predict those on another)
- *Definitional differences* (e.g., demand histories do not reveal price elasticity)

Experts look at all data skeptically, asking where the information came from and who gathered it (and with what motivations). They try to determine all the ways in which it may be flawed for the purpose they have in mind. Even when high-quality data are available, the modeler must use judgment before incorporating the data into a model. Sometimes, good judgment involves discarding parts of the data as irrelevant or misleading; sometimes it involves choosing how to summarize the data (whether to use the average or the worst case, for example). Experts, then, are much more skeptical than novices about the accuracy and appropriateness of data, and therefore more skeptical about the usefulness of data in a modeling effort.

While novices believe that collecting data will move the modeling process forward beneficially, they seldom recognize that data collection can also be distracting and limiting. For example, if the corporate database records sales by industry and by company size, most likely a model for sales will relate it to these two driving variables, rather than to less readily available, but perhaps more important, factors. A better model results in most cases if it is built up from first principles, without being overly influenced by the available data.

The Racquetball Racket case provides another example of how the availability of data can limit modeling creativity. The market research firm has given us information on the percentage of people who would buy our ball at various prices. They present the data in the form of a ratio of our competitor's price to our price. Does this imply that we should use the price *ratio* as the driving variable in our model of market share? The implication of such an approach would be that consumers do not react to the actual level of prices but only to relative prices. In other words, our share would be the same if we charged $5 and the competition $10, or if we charged $1 to their $2. Is this a plausible model, or might consumers react instead to the *difference* in prices? If we focus first on the data as presented, we may not even recognize the relevance of this question.

Thus, experts first build an appropriate model structure and use data to refine that model. The principle, in essence, is to let the model tell us what data we need rather than letting the data dictate our model.

Novice modelers often think they cannot build a useful model without acquiring good data first. Worse, they often feel that collecting good data, or at least better data than they currently have, is necessary before they even begin to *think* about a model. In either case, their premise is that data hold the key to a successful analysis. Some companies foster this attitude by emphasizing "data-driven decision making." A popular textbook even offers the advice that "one of the *first jobs* of an analyst is to gather exactly the *right data* and summarize the data appropriately." [Emphases added.] But how can a modeler identify the right data before building an initial model within which these questions can be answered? Most important, how can the modeler know what data will have the biggest impact on the ultimate recommendations that flow out of the modeling process? As Clifford Stoll says: "Minds think with ideas, not information. No amount of data, bandwidth, or processing power can substitute for inspired thought."[7]

Inexperienced modelers appear to believe that the quality of a model's recommendations depends critically on the quality of the model's data. But the managerial recommendations that evolve from modeling and analysis are often driven far more by the structure of the model than by the specific parameters in it. Therefore, it is imperative to get the model structure right, but it may be quite acceptable to work with rough parameter estimates. Once the modeling process has

[7]As quoted in Jonathan G. Koomey, *Turning Numbers into Knowledge: Mastering the Art of Problem Solving.* (Oakland, CA: Analytics Press, 2001), p. 101.

begun and a prototype provides us a basis for determining which data would be desirable, we can address the question of whether rough parameter estimates will work. The precision needed for the numerical inputs can be determined only through testing the model itself. This is an additional benefit from sensitivity analysis, beyond the plausibility tests that we mentioned earlier. Sensitivity tools can help identify which parameters require precise values—that is, the ones for which data analysis would be most beneficial. Experts, then, focus on getting model structure right and on acquiring only data that they anticipate will materially affect their conclusions.

Based on our observations of expert modelers, we believe that data collection should rarely be the main concern in modeling. It is quite possible to build models, analyze models, and draw insights from models without relying on data analysis or statistical methods at all. In fact, we endorse that approach as a first cut. Data collection should ideally be undertaken only after a model-based determination has been made as to precisely which data are needed and with what level of precision. We have come to this point of view after observing problem-solving teams waste large amounts of precious time and effort on poorly conceived data collection expeditions, and observing novice modelers in a research setting become distracted from model structuring by the lack of data or by an excess of data. This is not to say that data collection is irrelevant; there are circumstances in which empirical data have a major impact on the quality of model-based recommendations. However, most business analysis takes place under a fairly severe time constraint. In such circumstances, modelers seldom have the luxury to search for the best possible data. Sometimes, we can find only data that were collected for other purposes and may not be tailored to our needs. At other times, very little data are available at all. Nevertheless, we must remember that *modeling* is central, not data.

2.5 SUMMARY

Effective modeling takes place within a larger problem-solving process. Modeling can be useful both in finding a good solution and in facilitating communication as the solution is developed, refined, and implemented. Therefore, it is important to recognize the larger context in which modeling occurs. We organize the problem-solving process into six stages.

1. Exploring the mess
2. Searching for information
3. Defining the problem
4. Searching for solutions
5. Evaluating solutions
6. Implementing a solution

Although it's convenient to describe these stages as if they were separate and occurred in a strict sequence, that is seldom the case. In fact, we can't always identify the specific activities at each stage until after the fact. Nevertheless, every implemented solution comes about through some version of this problem-solving process. Generally speaking, the bigger the problem at hand or the larger the team working on it, the more important it is to use a structured problem-solving process.

Mental modeling is an essential tool in problem solving. A mental model allows us to trace the consequences of a course of action without actually implementing it. In that way, mental models save us the time and cost, not to mention the occasionally disastrous consequences, of actually trying out alternative solutions to a problem.

Formal models provide the same kind of benefits as mental models. A formal model is a laboratory within which we can search for the best solution, without incurring the time and cost of trial-and-error approaches. Formal models are costlier and more time-consuming to build than mental models, but they have the great advantage that they make our assumptions, logic, and preferences explicit. They also allow us to search among many more solutions than would otherwise be possible. Finally, an effective formal model can help communicate the reasoning behind a solution and in that way help to motivate an individual or organization to act.

Influence charts offer the modeler a bridge between an ill-structured problem and a formal model. A formal model is usually precise and quantitative, but an influence chart is conceptual, abstract, and nonnumerical. It helps the modeler decide what is to be included in the model and what is to be excluded. It also helps focus attention on outputs, inputs, and the logic that connects them. Finally, it helps a modeler or modeling team to surface and recognize the assumptions behind the model and its limitations.

Modeling heuristics are rules of thumb that help in the design and use of models. They enhance pure technical skill by enabling us to invent models for new and unfamiliar situations. They also play a major role in the craft of modeling. Our list of modeling heuristics includes:

1. Simplify the problem.
2. Break the problem into modules.
3. Build a prototype and refine it.
4. Sketch graphs of key relationships.

5. Identify parameters and perform sensitivity analysis.

6. Separate the creation of ideas from their evaluation.

7. Work backward from the desired answer.

8. Focus on model structure, not on data collection.

Some of the items on the list are useful to help a modeling effort get off to a good start. If we think in terms of the chronological steps in a typical modeling project, the last heuristic may be the first one to apply: focus first on structuring a model rather than on obtaining data. The first model ought to be simple. It should be guided mainly by the desire to capture an essential trade-off in the problem. Simplification, by its nature, involves making assumptions about the problem, and these should be explicit. In any stage of model development, there should be a companion phase in which those assumptions are subjected to sensitivity analysis so that we can determine which ones need refinement. Devising a model structure made up of modules enables us to focus on the components of the model as a means of overcoming complexity in the overall problem. An ideal structure contains independent modules and allows interchangeable substitutes for the original module.

In building an initial model structure, we might start with visual representations, such as diagrams or graphs, for the inputs and also for the outputs. Visualizing the outputs, in the sense of working backward, keeps us focused on the precise requirements of the problem. Then, in order to convert graphical representations to mathematical representations, we might want to draw on a small family of familiar functions, specifying parameters as needed. Parameters used in this way are numerical assumptions, and, as with structural assumptions, they deserve sensitivity analysis. Sensitivity testing will tell us which parameters or which functional relationships are most critical to the ultimate outcomes.

Some of the heuristics on our list may be applied repeatedly during a modeling project. Developing a good model is a multistep process involving successive refinement. We start with a first prototype, and we test it to determine how well it addresses the problem. This testing may suggest we do some data collection, and it might stimulate our thinking about enrichments to the model. At various stages in the process, especially when the project is team-based, we may need some creative input from brainstorming activity. However, with the repeated cycles of model enhancement and model testing, we will have compiled some analysis, perhaps overly simple, that we can bring to bear on the problem. As we improve the model, we continually add to our store of knowledge and insight about the problem, so that at every stage in the process, we have an answer for the client and a sense of whether our analysis is adequate. Prototyping thus creates an important dialogue with the client and helps assure that the focus remains on the problem rather than the model.

SUGGESTED READINGS

For more information on problem solving and creativity, consult the following books:

Adams, J. L. 2001. *Conceptual Blockbusting*. Reading, MA: Addison-Wesley.

Couger, J. D. 1995. *Creative Problem Solving and Opportunity Finding*. Danvers, MA: Boyd & Fraser.

Evans, J. R. 1991. *Creative Thinking*. Cincinnati: South-Western.

Very little has been written on the craft aspects of modeling, whether in business or science. The original work on heuristics in problem solving is the following:

Polya, G. 1971. *How to Solve It*. Princeton, NJ: Princeton University Press.

This little classic, which is still in print 60 years after it was written, is focused on problem solving in mathematics, but it still provides worthwhile reading.

Two more recent books that discuss some of the ideas in this chapter are:

Pidd, M. 1996. *Tools for Thinking: Modelling in Management Science*. Chichester: John Wiley and Sons.

Koomey, J. G. 2001. *Turning Numbers into Knowledge: Mastering the Art of Problem Solving*. Oakland, CA: Analytics Press.

The following classic articles are still relevant after many years and remain worth reading:

Geoffrion, A. M. 1976. "The Purpose of Mathematical Programming Is Insight, Not Numbers." *Interfaces* 7, 81–92.

Little, J. D. C. 1970. "Models and Managers: The Concept of a Decision Calculus." *Management Science* 16, B466–B485.

Morris, W. T. 1967. "On the Art of Modeling." *Management Science* 13, B707–717.

Urban, G. L. 1974. "Building Models for Decision Makers." *Interfaces* 4, 1–11.

EXERCISES

PROBLEM FORMULATION

The four short cases we have analyzed in this chapter (Retirement Planning, Draft TV Commercials, Icebergs for Kuwait, and Racquetball Racket) are reproduced with full details toward the end of this book. For each of these cases, prepare for building a model by reading the full case and answering the following questions.

1. Explore the mess by answering the following questions:

(a) What do we know?

(b) What can we assume?

(c) What could the results look like?

(d) What information can be brought to bear?

(e) What can we ask the client?

(f) Are there any similar situations or problems?

2. Formulate one or more problem statements.

3. What are the decisions, outcomes, and relationships in the problem?

4. Draw an influence chart for the problem.

5. In what ways could we simplify the problem?

6. What modules will we need to build?

7. What are the key relationships in the problem? Draw their graphs.

8. What are the parameters of the problem?

INFLUENCE CHARTS

Draw influence charts for each of the following problems.

1. The Boeing Company faces a critical strategic choice in its competition with Airbus Industries for the long-haul flight segment: should it design and build a super-747 model that can carry 550 passengers at speeds around 350 mph, or a plane that can fly at 95 percent of the speed of sound but carry only about 350 passengers? As a member of Boeing's Planning Group, your task is to build a model to investigate the trade-offs involved in this decision.

2. The Red Cross provides about 40 percent of the replacement blood supply for the United States. The available donor base has been shrinking for years, and although increased advertising has kept Red Cross supplies adequate, the time is approaching when demand will outstrip supply. For many years, the Red Cross has refused to pay donors for blood, because to do so would "put the blood supply of the country at risk." However, Red Cross management has begun to consider changing its policy. Evaluate the impacts of a policy under which the Red Cross would pay each of its donors a set fee.

3. Your client is the planning office of a major university. Part of the job of the planning office is to forecast the annual donations of alumni through the university's long-established giving program. Until now, the forecast has been made subjectively. The client wants you to develop a more objective approach. The Planning Office can make data available for the past 10 years that shows for each alumni class in that year:

- The number of living alumni in the class
- The number of givers

- Total direct donations from the class
- Other gifts for the class (e.g., employer matching)

4. Congress is considering a new law that will grant amnesty to the roughly 11 million illegal aliens in the United States. Under this law, anyone who has entered the country illegally in the past can apply for permanent residence status and a green card, which conveys the right to work. This law, if passed, can be expected to have significant impacts on industries that currently rely on illegal workers (such as hospitality, meat packing, and construction). It may also have impacts on wages, school enrollments, healthcare costs, and the future rate of illegal immigration.

5. A major pharmaceutical manufacturer is facing a difficult decision concerning one of its hearing-enhancement products. The product has been on the market less than two years, and reports have recently begun to come in that the product may cause serious hearing loss in certain users. The number and severity of these reports are not sufficiently high to warrant a recall order from the FDA, but if the reports continue this could eventually happen. In the meantime, management is considering issuing a voluntary recall to limit the potential damages. However, any such recall will probably destroy the future market for this product, which may be entirely safe, and it will also hurt sales of all other products sold by this company and depress its stock price.

SKETCHING GRAPHS

Sketch graphs for the relationships described in each of the following problems and select one or more of the families of functions discussed in Section 4 to represent it.

1. The relationship between the effectiveness of a new drug and the amount spent on R&D.

2. The relationship between the cost of manufacturing a product and the cumulative quantity produced.

3. The relationship between the time it takes to complete a project and the number of people assigned to work on it.

4. The relationship between the probability the FDA will approve a given drug and the number of patients enrolled in the clinical trials of the drug.

5. The relationship between the sales of a given brand of cereal in a grocery store and the amount of shelf space devoted to displaying it.

3   Basic Excel Skills

3.1   INTRODUCTION

Excel may be the most versatile software program ever created. It is used daily by millions of people in every conceivable walk of life. Some of its users are simply adding up short columns of numbers, while others are creating sophisticated applications in which Excel is performing complex numerical calculations while interacting with several other software systems. With such a versatile and flexible tool, it is difficult for any user to determine just which of the thousands of features in Excel are really worth knowing. In this chapter, we describe the basic Excel skills we think are important for every business analyst.

This chapter is not intended to serve as a beginner's tutorial on Excel. Those who are new to Excel and who need a tutorial should work through a book or a CD, or take an online course. Several of these are listed in the suggested readings. Those who have a working knowledge of Excel will find in this chapter some reminders about familiar tools and perhaps pointers to some new ones as well. We have found that many experienced users have never taken the time to explore Excel systematically, so their skills are deep in some areas but shallow in others. We recommend that you skim this chapter for Excel features that are new to you and add them to your skill set. A few minutes spent in learning how to use Excel more efficiently, even if you are an experienced user, can pay dividends in the future every time you build a spreadsheet model.

3.2   EXCEL PREREQUISITES

What spreadsheet skills are prerequisites for an analyst who would like to learn to *model* in Excel? The most basic skill, and one that doesn't show up in the books, is the ability to *learn by trial and error*. Few successful users of software learn primarily from manuals or help facilities. Most have learned to scan the menus and search in a partly random, partly intelligent fashion for the tool they need and to experiment freely, knowing that (almost) nothing they do cannot be undone. In fact, the Undo command is one of the most important features in Excel!

Getting down to Excel, the first necessary skill is to be able to *navigate* around a worksheet and between worksheets in a workbook. This includes moving the cursor, scrolling, using the Home and End keys, and so on. Even the novice modeler needs to *enter text* and *enter data* and to choose the *format* of these entries. It is handy to be able to change the font name, style, and size; to use bold and italics; and to color a cell or its contents. The ability to *edit* the contents of a cell is important. Other necessary skills include *inserting* and *deleting* rows or columns and entire worksheets; *cutting, copying,* and *pasting*; *printing*; and *drawing charts*.

Skillful use of *formulas* and *functions* separates the novice spreadsheet user from the advanced user. To create formulas effectively, users must understand both *relative cell addressing* and *absolute cell addressing*. Excel has innumerable built-in functions that can drastically simplify calculations. Some of the most useful are SUM,

FIGURE 3.1 Office
Building Spreadsheet

	A	B	C	D	E	F	G
1	Office Building						
2							
3	Parameters	Rate of increase	Year 1	Year 2	Year 3	Year 4	Year 5
4	Building cost per sq ft		$80.00				
5	Size of building		180,000				
6	Rent per sq ft	5%	$15.00	15.75	16.54	17.36	18.23
7	Operating expense per sq ft	6%	$1.20	1.27	1.35	1.43	1.51
8	Vacancy rate	-4%	30%	0.26	0.22	0.18	0.14
9	Percent financed		85%				
10	Mortgage rate		12%				
11	Sale multiple		12				
12	Cost of capital		10%				
13							
14			Year 1	Year 2	Year 3	Year 4	Year 5
15	Cash Flow						
16		Gross income	1,890,000	2,097,900	2,321,865	2,562,982	2,822,406
17		Operating expense	216,000	228,960	242,698	257,259	272,695
18		Net operating income	1,674,000	1,868,940	2,079,167	2,305,722	2,549,710
19		Interest cost	$1,464,720	$1,464,720	$1,464,720	$1,464,720	$1,464,720
20		Before-tax cash flow	$209,280	$404,220	$614,447	$841,002	$1,084,990
21							
22		Down payment (at time 0)	$2,160,000				
23		Sale price					$30,596,526
24		Mortgage cost					$12,240,000
25		End of year cash flows	$209,280	$404,220	$614,447	$841,002	$19,441,516
26							
27	NPV	$11,472,032					

IF, MAX, MIN, AVERAGE, and NPV. The Insert Function window not only lists all the available functions by category, but also specifies the syntax of each function, explaining what inputs each requires and in what order.

Beyond these basic tools, Excel contains literally hundreds of specialized features. Few modelers use more than several dozens of these routinely, and even fewer can remember all of them between uses. It is *not* necessary to master all of these specialized tools in order to succeed at modeling.

We will use a simple spreadsheet model as an example throughout this chapter. The reader should open this model and use it to test out the features described below. The spreadsheet itself is shown in Figure 3.1[*].

EXAMPLE
Office Building Planning

Potential investors in an office building construction project have asked us to evaluate this opportunity. Our task is to predict the after-tax cash flows resulting from constructing and operating this proposed office building over a five-year period. At a planned size of 180,000 square feet, the expected construction cost is $80 per square foot. The investors plan to take out a mortgage for 85 percent of the cost of the building (paying the remainder in cash), and they have been guaranteed a rate of 12 percent for a term of 30 years. The owners must also pay for the cost of operating the building, which includes taxes, insurance, maintenance, and certain utilities. They assume that the average operating cost per square foot will be $1.20. They have also estimated that they can charge a rental rate of $15 per square foot, with an occupancy rate of 70 percent. The cost of capital is 10 percent. Rents in the future are expected to grow 5 percent per year, while operating expenses grow 6 percent and the occupancy rate drops 4 percentage points yearly as the building ages. The owners plan to sell the building at the end of the fifth year for 12 times the final year's net operating income. ∎

3.3 THE EXCEL WINDOW

Each Excel file is called a *workbook*. A workbook consists of a number of individual *worksheets*. We will use the word "spreadsheet" to refer to both workbooks and worksheets.

The basic spreadsheet layout consists of a grid of rows and columns of cells (see Figure 3.2). The rows are labeled with numbers and the columns are labeled with letters. The maximum number of rows in a single worksheet is 1,048,576; the maximum number of columns is 16,384. The address of a cell corresponds to its column and row label—for example, C3 or AB567.

[*]To download spreadsheets for this chapter, go to the Student Companion Site at www.wiley.com/college/powell.

FIGURE 3.2 Features of the Excel Window

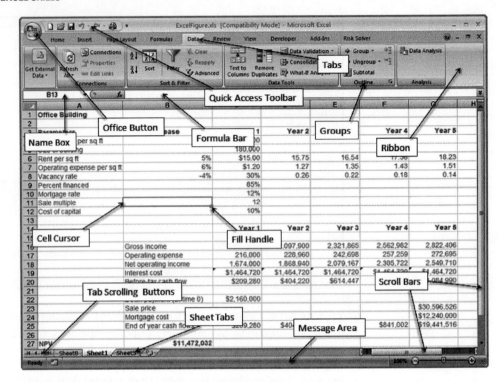

Excel displays on the computer screen a portion of this grid surrounded by other information. Some of the important features of the Excel window are described here and noted in Figure 3.2.

Office Button The Office Button, which is located at the upper left corner of the window, provides access to the most commonly used commands such as New, Open, Close; Save, Save As; and Print. It also provides access to Excel Options.

Quick Access Toolbar Just to the right of the Office Button is the Quick Access Toolbar. This toolbar provides a set of icons that provide shortcuts to frequently used commands. You can customize this toolbar by selecting the downward pointing arrow to the right of the icons.

Tabs The main Excel commands are organized across the top row into the following *tabs*:

- Home
- Insert
- Page Layout
- Formulas
- Data
- Review
- View
- Add-ins

Additional tabs may, under certain conditions, appear to the right of the eight listed above.

Ribbons and Groups Each tab gives access to a *ribbon* in which *commands* are organized into *groups*. For example, the Home tab has the following groups of commands:

- Clipboard
- Font
- Alignment
- Number
- Styles
- Cells
- Editing

The Font group includes the following commands:

- Font
- Font size (increase and decrease)
- Bold, italics, underline
- Borders
- Fill color
- Font color

In addition, the Font group includes a small downward-pointing arrow icon ($\searrow$) that opens the Format Cells window.

Message Area   When Excel performs lengthy calculations, a message will appear in this area giving information on the progress of the procedure.

Scroll Bars   These bars allow the user to change the portion of the spreadsheet displayed on the screen.

Sheet Tabs   These tabs allow the user to select which worksheet is displayed. The selection allows the user to move from sheet to sheet within a workbook.

Tab-Scrolling Buttons   These small triangles allow the display of different tabs in workbooks where not all of the tabs are visible at once.

Name Box   This box displays the cell address where the cursor is located, as well as the list of any named ranges. (Named ranges are covered in Chapter 4.)

Formula Bar   This box displays the contents of the cell where the cursor is located, whether a number, formula, or text. This is usually the area in which the user enters information into a cell.

Mouse Cursor   The location of the cursor is shown with an open cross symbol.

Cell Cursor   When a cell has been selected, it is outlined with a dark border. When a range of cells has been selected, it is colored blue and outlined with a dark border.

Fill Handle   At the lower right-hand corner of the cell border is a cross that can be selected for copying the contents of the cell to adjacent cells. When this cross is selected, the mouse cursor changes to a darkened cross.

3.4   CONFIGURING EXCEL

Many users are not aware that they can control the look and behavior of their spreadsheets by setting certain parameters. Select Office Button▶Excel Options, and a window appears with nine tabs listed in a column on the left (see Figure 3.3).

FIGURE 3.3   The Excel
Options Window

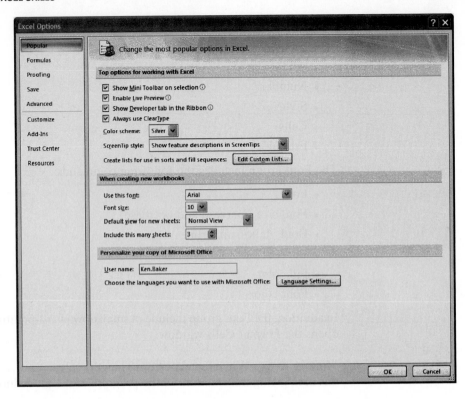

Except where noted below, most of the choices provided on these tabs can safely be
left at their default values.

Popular Tab   Select an appropriate font and font size.

Formulas Tab   In most uses, it is preferable to have the spreadsheet calculate all
formula cells each time a change is made to any cell. This updating occurs if
`Automatic Calculation` is selected under `Calculation` options. On occasion,
it is useful to turn this feature off. To do so, check `Manual Calculation`. When the
manual calculation option is chosen, the spreadsheet can be recalculated at any time
by pressing F9, but it will not recalculate automatically when a cell is changed. The
message "Calculate" will appear in the Message area when a cell has been changed
but the spreadsheet has not been recalculated.

When a spreadsheet contains simultaneous relationships, calculations cannot
be made in the usual manner. This situation typically generates an error message
warning of a *circular reference*. This error message is useful because circular
references usually occur when there is a mistake in the logic. However, there are
circumstances where a circular reference is sensible (for example, when linking
income statement and balance sheet models). In these cases, it is necessary to specify
a number of iterations to calculate the desired values. Check the box labeled `Enable`
`iterative calculation` to implement an iterative approach.

Under `Error Checking` check the box labeled `Enable background error`
`checking`. Check all nine `Error checking rules`.

Proofing Tab   Select the preferred options for the AutoCorrect feature in Excel.

Save Tab   Check the box labeled `Save AutoRecovery information` so that Excel
will automatically save your spreadsheets as often as specified.

Advanced Tab   Under `Editing` options, check the boxes labeled `Enable fill`
`handle and cell drag and drop`, and `Allow editing directly in cells`.

Under Cut, copy, and paste, check the boxes labeled Show Paste Options buttons and Show Insert Options buttons.

Customize Tab   Customize the Quick Access Toolbar. Experienced Excel users will recognize that they use some commands quite frequently and instead of hunting for the commands in the ribbon, they can place the corresponding icon in the Quick Access Toolbar for convenience.

Add-ins Tab: View and manage add-ins.

Trust Center Tab: Information on privacy and security.

Resources Tab: Access to software updates and other information.

3.5   MANIPULATING WINDOWS AND SHEETS

Since most workbooks contain far more information than can be displayed on a computer screen, it is important to know how to display the most useful portion of the worksheet. The Zoom level (or magnification) of the worksheet can be set with a slider located at the lower right corner of the Excel window (see Figure 3.2). Alternatively, click on the 100% button to the left of the slider and the Zoom window opens (Figure 3.4). This window allows you to choose a preset or custom level of magnification. (The Zoom window can also be opened by selecting View▶ Zoom▶Zoom.)

The View▶Window command makes it possible to simultaneously display more than one worksheet on the screen. These sheets may be from the same workbook or from different workbooks. This command can be particularly useful when we are building formulas in one sheet using cells located in another. Select Window▶ New Window to add a spreadsheet window, and then resize the new window and select the sheets to display, as in Figure 3.5.

Excel provides an option to split the screen horizontally, vertically, or both in order to display two sets of rows or columns in the same spreadsheet. If, for example, we wish to enter formulas in row 100 that reference cells in rows 1–10, we highlight row 10 and select View▶Window▶Split. Excel will open a second pane of rows with its own scroll bar, splitting the window horizontally. We can then display row 100 in the bottom pane while displaying rows 1–10 in the upper pane. The window can also be split vertically by highlighting a column. The window can even be split both horizontally and vertically by highlighting a cell. Figure 3.6 shows the worksheet split both horizontally and vertically at cell B13. (The screen can also be split by dragging the horizontal or vertical split bars, which are located just above and to the right of the row and column scroll bars, respectively.)

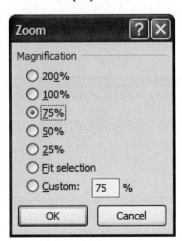

FIGURE 3.4   The Zoom Window

3.6   NAVIGATION

There are several ways to move the display from one portion of a spreadsheet to another. The horizontal and vertical scroll bars move the display of the portion of the entire spreadsheet that contains cell entries left and right or up and down,

FIGURE 3.5   Two Excel Windows Displayed Simultaneously

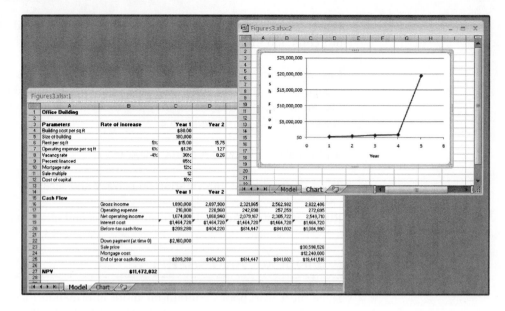

respectively. However, the scroll bars cannot move the display to blank areas. This can be done by clicking on the scroll arrows above and below the vertical scroll bar and to the left and right of the horizontal scroll bar. We can also shift the display by clicking on a cell and highlighting a range that extends outside the display area.

The display area also can be moved by using the arrow keys ($\uparrow \downarrow \leftarrow \rightarrow$). If we hold one of these keys down, the cursor moves in the direction indicated until it reaches the limit of the display area, at which point the display shifts to keep the cursor on the screen. The Page Up and Page Down keys also shift the display up or down by a fixed number of rows. These keys are useful for quickly scanning the contents of a spreadsheet. (Other more complex ways of navigating a spreadsheet are covered in Chapter 4.)

Another way to navigate around a spreadsheet is to type a cell address into the Name Box (just above column A). When we press the Enter key, the cursor moves to the cell address we have entered and the display shifts to accommodate the

FIGURE 3.6   Using Split Screen to Fix Row and Column Headings

	A	B	C	D	E	F	G
1	Office Building						
2							
3	Parameters	Rate of increase	Year 1	Year 2	Year 3	Year 4	Year 5
4	Building cost per sq ft		$80.00				
5	Size of building		180,000				
6	Rent per sq ft	5%	$15.00	15.75	16.54	17.36	18.23
7	Operating expense per sq ft	6%	$1.20	1.27	1.35	1.43	1.51
8	Vacancy rate	-4%	30%	0.26	0.22	0.18	0.14
9	Percent financed		85%				
10	Mortgage rate		12%				
11	Sale multiple		12				
12	Cost of capital		10%				
13							
14			Year 1	Year 2	Year 3	Year 4	Year 5
15	Cash Flow						
16		Gross income	1,890,000	2,097,900	2,321,865	2,562,982	2,822,406
17		Operating expense	216,000	228,960	242,698	257,259	272,695
18		Net operating income	1,674,000	1,868,940	2,079,167	2,305,722	2,549,710
19		Interest cost	$1,464,720	$1,464,720	$1,464,720	$1,464,720	$1,464,720
20		Before-tax cash flow	$209,280	$404,220	$614,447	$841,002	$1,084,990
21							
22		Down payment (at time 0)	$2,160,000				
23		Sale price					$30,596,526
24		Mortgage cost					$12,240,000
25		End of year cash flows	$209,280	$404,220	$614,447	$841,002	$19,441,516
26							
27	NPV		$11,472,032				

change. (If we use Names for cells or ranges of cells, they will appear in this box, and we can click on them to move the cursor. Range Names are covered in Chapter 4.) We can also use the Home▶Editing▶Find & Select▶Go To command to shift the cursor and display within a worksheet or to another worksheet.

3.7   SELECTING CELLS

There are many ways to select some or all of the cells in a spreadsheet. Here are the essentials. (More specialized methods are covered in Chapter 4.)

Selecting All Cells in a Worksheet   Click on the box immediately to the left of column A and above row 1.

Selecting a Column or a Row   Click on a single column label or a row label (for example, A or 1). To select several adjacent columns or rows, click on the first label and drag the cursor to the last label.

Selecting Rectangular Ranges   Any rectangular range of cells can be selected by selecting one of its four corner cells and dragging the cursor across to the diagonal corner. The same effect can be achieved by selecting a corner, dragging across the columns to the opposite corner and then across the rows to the diagonal corner, or vice versa.

Selecting Noncontiguous Ranges   To select two distinct rectangles of cells, select the first range, hold down the Control key, and select the second range. This method can be used to select three or more ranges as well.

3.8   ENTERING TEXT AND DATA

Information typed into a cell appears in two places: in the cell itself and in the formula bar. After we have clicked on Enter, we can edit the contents of the cell either by moving the cursor to the formula bar or by double-clicking on the cell and editing directly in the cell.

When we type letters into a cell, Excel automatically understands that the contents are text, and it left-justifies the contents in the cell. When we type in numbers, it recognizes the contents as numerical and right-justifies the contents.

To copy the contents of one cell to adjacent cells, we can either drag the Fill handle (the solid square at the lower right corner of the selected cell) over the adjacent cells, or else use Home▶Editing▶Fill▶Down (or Right, Up, Left).

FIGURE 3.7   The Series Window

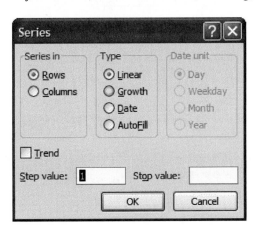

We often need to enter a series of numbers or dates. Examples include the numbers of successive customers (1, 2, 3, 4, . . .) or successive quarters in a year (Q1, Q2, Q3, . . .). Excel provides several ways to enter these series quickly. The Home▶Editing▶Fill▶Series command will enter various kinds of series (see Figure 3.7). The same effect can be accomplished by entering the first two cell entries, highlighting them, and copying to the rest of the range using the Fill handle. Excel can usually guess the pattern correctly. For example, enter 1 and 2 in one column. Highlight the two cells. Fill down to the next eight cells using the Fill handle, and the remainder of the series (3, 4, 5, 6, 7, 8, 9, 10) will appear. To enter the numbers between 10 and 50 in steps of 5, enter 10 and 15 in adjacent cells and fill down until 50 is reached.

3.9 EDITING CELLS

There are several ways to edit the information in cells. Here are the most useful alternatives:

Formula Bar The simplest way to edit is to click on the Formula bar. A vertical cursor will appear in the Formula bar, and information can be entered or modified using all the normal Windows typing options. If the selected cell is not empty, its contents will appear in the Formula bar. Clicking on the text there will make the editing cursor appear.

Double-Click A handy alternative approach is to double-click on a cell, or equivalently, to press the F2 key. This allows editing in the cell itself. If the selected cell is not empty, any cells referred to in the formula will be highlighted in color, a useful debugging device. See Figure 3.8, where we have double-clicked on cell E19 and the formula in the cell is displayed. The four cell references used to calculate the result in cell E19 (C4, C5, C9, and C10) are highlighted in color, and a border with the matching color is drawn around each of those cells. Finally, the function used in the formula (ISPMT) is displayed below the cell, along with its arguments. If we click on the function name, the Help page for that function will appear.

We can modify the cell contents by inserting the vertical cursor where it is needed and typing directly into the cell or by moving the vertical cursor to the Formula bar and typing there. Alternatively, we can alter any cell reference in a formula by dragging the highlighted outline to another location. This option provides a visual device for editing, which is convenient when the formula is based on distinctive reference patterns.

Insert Function An alternative for editing a formula is Insert Function (the f_x icon to the left of the Formula bar). If we click on this icon when the cursor is on a cell that does not contain a function, it will bring up the Insert Function window, which lists all available functions. If a specific function is then selected, it will be entered into the

FIGURE 3.8 Double-Clicking on a Cell Containing a Formula

	A	B	C	D	E	F	G
1	Office Building						
2							
3	Parameters	Rate of increase	Year 1	Year 2	Year 3	Year 4	Year 5
4	Building cost per sq ft		$80.00				
5	Size of building		180,000				
6	Rent per sq ft	5%	$15.00	15.75	16.54	17.36	18.23
7	Operating expense per sq ft	6%	$1.20	1.27	1.35	1.43	1.51
8	Vacancy rate	-4%	30%	0.26	0.22	0.18	0.14
9	Percent financed		85%				
10	Mortgage rate		12%				
11	Sale multiple		12				
12	Cost of capital		10%				
13							
14			Year 1	Year 2	Year 3	Year 4	Year 5
15	Cash Flow						
16		Gross income	1,890,000	2,097,900	2,321,865	2,562,982	2,822,406
17		Operating expense	216,000	228,960	242,698	257,259	272,695
18		Net operating income	1,674,000	1,868,940	2,079,167	2,305,722	2,549,710
19		Interest cost	$1,464,720	$1,464,720	=-12*ISPMT($C$10/12,1,360,$C$9*$C$4*$C$5)		
20		Before-tax cash flow	$209,280	$404,220	ISPMT(rate, per, nper, pv) 02		$1,084,990
21							
22		Down payment (at time 0)	$2,160,000				
23		Sale price					$30,596,526
24		Mortgage cost					$12,240,000
25		End of year cash flows	$209,280	$404,220	$614,447	$841,002	$19,441,516
26							
27	NPV		$11,472,032				
28							

formula, and its own window will appear, which facilitates entering the inputs properly. If we click on the f_x icon when the cursor is on a cell that already contains a function, it will bring up the corresponding function window, allowing the definition of the function to be verified or the arguments of the function to be revised. (More information on functions can be found in Section 3.12.)

Absolute and Relative Cell References   A relative reference to cell C3 is simply "C3," whereas an absolute reference is $C$3. These types of references are useful primarily to make copying of complex formulas easy and reliable. Rather than typing in the appropriate dollar signs, it can be easier to enter all addresses in relative form (without dollar signs), highlight one or more addresses, and then press F4 repeatedly until the desired combination of absolute and relative references appears. (More information on formulas can be found in Section 3.11.)

3.10   FORMATTING

We can change individual column widths and row heights by moving the vertical or horizontal lines between the column and row labels. Widths or heights common to multiple columns or rows can be set using the Home▶Cells▶Format▶Cell Size▶Row Height/Column Width commands after highlighting the appropriate rows or columns. Alternatively, change one column width or one row height after highlighting the appropriate columns or rows.

Any range of cells can be formatted by highlighting the range and then selecting Home▶Cells▶Format▶Format Cells (or by selecting Home▶Font▶ ). This opens a window with the following six tabs (see Figure 3.9):

Number   Choose a type of formatting—for example, Currency or Date—and specify parameters such as the number of decimal places displayed.

Alignment   Align text horizontally and vertically, and choose `Wrap Text` to fit long text labels into cells.

FIGURE 3.9   The Format Cells Window

Font   Specify font, size, color, and superscript or subscript for the cell contents.

Border   Set various borders around a range of cells.

Fill   Set a background pattern or a color shade for the cell (but not its contents).

Protection   Lock or hide cells for safety.

Many of these options are also available on the Home ribbon. The most frequently used icons on this ribbon are Increase Decimal and Decrease Decimal, which change the number of decimals displayed in selected cells by one decimal place each time they are clicked.

3.11   BASIC FORMULAS

Formulas in Excel provide the basic mechanism for entering the relationships in a model. In modeling terms, every cell in a spreadsheet that involves a formula is either an output of the model or an intermediate calculation needed to calculate an output.

With very few exceptions, well-written formulas contain no numbers, only cell references. Although it is often permissible to use numbers that never change in a formula, like the value 24 for the number of hours in a day, it is dangerous to embed parameters that may change in formulas. (In Chapter 5 we will see that isolating parameters is a feature of well-built spreadsheets.) Because formulas are built up from the values in other cells, they are written in terms of references to the contents of those cells.

Excel uses the following symbols for the basic arithmetic operations:

- Addition $+$
- Subtraction $-$
- Multiplication $*$
- Division $/$
- Raise to a power $^\wedge$

Excel formulas start with the equal sign ($=$) and are evaluated from left to right. However, arithmetic operations will be carried out in a specified order unless parentheses are used to control the calculation order. The basic arithmetic operations are calculated in the following order:

- Negation (as in -1)
- Exponentiation ($^\wedge$)
- Multiplication and division ($*$ and $/$)
- Addition and subtraction ($+$ and $-$)

If a formula involves both multiplication and division (or both addition and subtraction), the leftmost of these operations is performed first.

Here are some examples that show how the calculation order and the use of parentheses can determine the outcome of a calculation.

- $2 + 3/10 = 2.3$
- $(2 + 3)/10 = 0.5$
- $(2 + 3)/10^\wedge 2 = 0.05$
- $(2 + 3)/(10^\wedge 2) = 0.05$
- $2 + 3/10^\wedge 2 = 2.03$

It is generally a good practice to use parentheses to make the meaning of a calculation clear and to ensure that it is calculated correctly.

When a formula is to be entered into just one cell, the references to its inputs can simply specify column and row, as for example, (D2+D3)/D5. The cell reference D2 is an example of a **relative reference**. If the formula above was entered in cell E3, then the reference to cell D2 would be interpreted by Excel as referring to the cell one column to the left and one row above the current cell. That is, the cell reference is interpreted *relative to the current cell*. Likewise, from cell E3, a reference to J14 is interpreted as a reference to the cell 5 columns to the right and 11 rows down.

Many spreadsheets are built by copying formulas from one cell to a range of cells. For example, row 18 in the Office Building spreadsheet (Net Operating Income) requires subtracting Operating Income from Gross Income each year. Thus the formula entered into cell C18 (C16–C17) is the same formula that we need in the following years, cells D18:G18. We can fill these four cells efficiently by entering the formula once in cell C18 and then copying it to the other cells. Because Excel interprets the cell addresses C16 and C17 relative to the current cell, when we copy the formula, it continues to apply correctly.

However, this same procedure will not work for row 17, in which we calculate Operating Expense. The Operating Expense for Year 1 is the size of the building in square feet (C5) times the cost per square foot (C7). Thus we could calculate the correct value in C17 using the formula C5*C7. But the Operating Expense in the next year, Year 2, is not calculated in the same way. The size of the building is fixed for all time in C5, but the cost per square foot grows each year as given in cells D7:G7. So the correct formula in cell D17 is C5*D7. In other words, one of the addresses in the original formula (C5) needs to remain fixed, while the other (C7) needs to shift from year to year. Clearly, we need a way to write a cell address so that Excel will interpret it not in a relative fashion but as fixed. This is done using dollar signs before the column letter and row number, as in $C$5. The first dollar sign fixes the column during copying; the second dollar sign fixes the row. So, if we write the original formula in cell C17 as $C$5*C7, which does not change the value in C17, we can then copy it across the row correctly. The reference to the size of the building in C5 will remain fixed, and the reference to the cost will change as needed. Addresses with fixed columns or rows are known as **absolute addresses**. Examine all the formulas in the Office Building spreadsheet to see how relative and absolute addresses are used to make copying easy.

3.12 BASIC FUNCTIONS

Excel provides hundreds of built-in functions for calculating almost anything. No matter how complex or unusual the calculation we have in mind, Excel almost always has a function (or perhaps several functions) that can accomplish the task. Using Excel functions presents three challenges:

- Identifying the appropriate function or functions
- Using the function correctly
- Testing that the results match what was intended.

An efficient way to locate useful functions is to open the Insert Function window by clicking f_x next to the formula bar. (The Insert Function window can also be accessed from the Formulas ribbon.) Figure 3.10 shows the Insert Function window with the category Financial selected. The drop-down menu displays a list of function categories. The major categories are as follows:

- Most Recently Used
- All

FIGURE 3.10 The Insert
Function Window

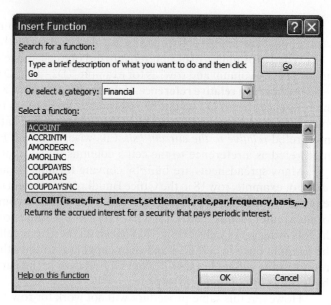

- Financial
- Date & Time
- Math & Trig
- Statistical
- Lookup & Reference
- Database
- Text
- Logical
- Information

To find a function, first identify the category it is likely to fall into, and then scan the alphabetical list of functions in this category. Each time a function is highlighted, the Insert Function window displays a brief description of the function and its inputs. For example, in Figure 3.11 we have highlighted the financial function ISMPT. The window displays its inputs (rate, per, nper, pv) and gives a short description: Returns the interest paid during a specific period of an investment.

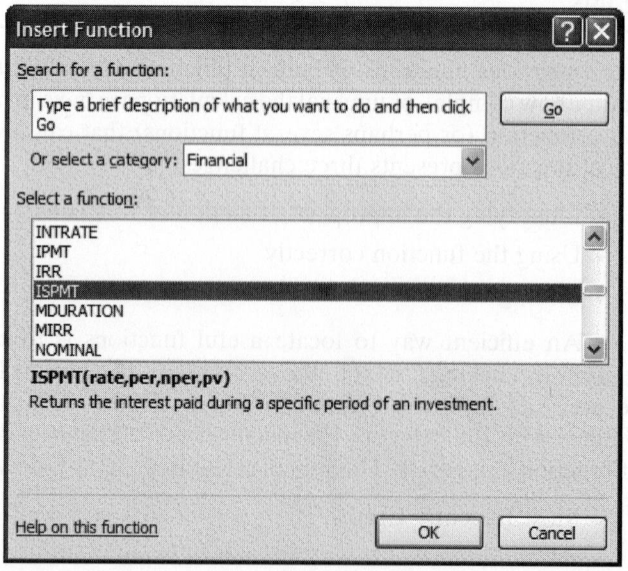

FIGURE 3.11 The ISPMT
Function

FIGURE 3.12 The Function Arguments Window for the ISMPT Function

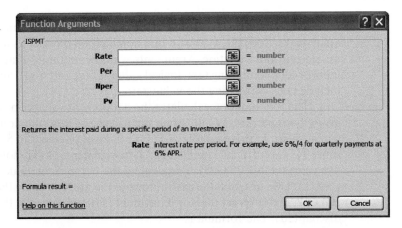

At this point, click on OK and the Function Arguments window opens (Figure 3.12). This window displays a reference box for each of the arguments of the function (four in this case). We can either enter numbers directly in these boxes or (better) enter cell addresses (click on the icon at the right end of the box and identify the inputs by selecting them in the spreadsheet). The Function Arguments window shows the numerical value of each input as it is entered, and when enough inputs are entered, the window shows the value of the function. This allows us to see if we are getting plausible results before entering the function in the spreadsheet. (Help on this specific function is also available directly from the link at the bottom of this window.) Figure 3.13 shows the Function Arguments window with all four inputs entered and the result calculated (−122,060). Click on OK and the function will be entered in the cell we are editing.

Business analysts make heavy use of just a few of the hundreds of functions in Excel. We will describe six of the most important of these functions here. Other useful functions are described in Chapter 4.

The SUM function is used to add a set of numbers. Its arguments can simply be a list of cell references. For example, SUM(C1, C3, C5) adds the contents of the three cells listed, where the cell references are set off by commas. Alternatively, SUM(C1:C5) adds the contents of the cells in the range C1:C5. The SUM function can also be used to add a list of noncontiguous ranges, for example, SUM(C1:C5, D2:D6, E3:E7).

The MAX and MIN functions are used to find the largest and smallest values in a range. Thus MAX(1, 3, 5) yields 5, and MIN(C1:C5) calculates the smallest value in the range C1:C5.

The AVERAGE function calculates the average of the values in a range. The range can be in a column, in a row, or in an array (a rectangular range extending over

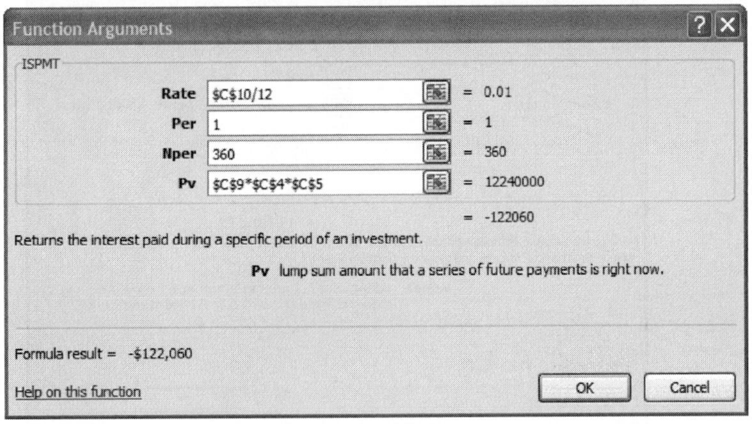

FIGURE 3.13 The ISMPT Function Evaluated

multiple columns and/or rows). If we are averaging a column of data that contains empty cells, does the AVERAGE function include those cells in the calculation? Click on Help in the Function Arguments window and note that the AVERAGE function ignores cells containing text, logical values (True or False), and empty cells, but does include cells containing the value zero.

The NPV function calculates the net present value of a stream of payments at a given discount rate. We illustrate the use of the NPV function in the Office Building spreadsheet. In this example, we make a down payment of $2,160,000 at the present time, the *start* of Year 1 (cell C22). Then we receive cash inflows at the *end* of the next five years (cells C25:G25). To calculate the net present value of this set of payments (cell B27), we discount the cash inflows to the present, using the discount rate given in cell C12, and subtract the down payment (since it occurs at the present time, it is not discounted). The formula is

$$NPV(C12,C25:G25)-C22$$

The Function Arguments window (Figure 3.14) shows the cell addresses of the arguments of the NPV function as well as their numerical values. It also shows the resulting value of the NPV calculation ($13,632,032.03), as well as the value of the entire formula ($11,472,032).

It is important to remember that the NPV function discounts the first payment in a stream of payments. Thus in the Office Building example, we discounted the cash inflow in Year 1 because according to the model, it comes in at the *end* of the year and the date of the evaluation is the *beginning* of the year. If, instead, the first cash inflow occurred at the beginning of the year, at the same time as the down payment, we would discount with the NPV function starting with Year 2 and add the undiscounted cash inflow from Year 1.

The IF function is used to perform a logical test and calculate one value if the test is true and another if it is false. The syntax for the IF function is

$$IF(logical\ test,\ value\text{-}if\text{-}true,\ value\text{-}if\text{-}false)$$

The first argument, the logical test, is an expression that Excel can evaluate as TRUE or FALSE. For example, the expression $100 > 0$ evaluates as TRUE, while $100 > 200$ evaluates as FALSE. (For practice, go to the Office Building spreadsheet and enter the formula $= C4 > 0$ in an empty cell. The result should be TRUE. The formula $= E16 > 5,000,000$ should be FALSE.)

If the logical test in an IF statement is TRUE, the *second* argument (value-if-true) is calculated and placed in the cell. If the logical test is FALSE, the *third* argument (value-if-false) is calculated and placed in the cell. For example, IF $(100 > 0, 25, 50)$ evaluates as 25, and IF $(100 < 0, 25, 50)$ evaluates as 50. Each of the three arguments in

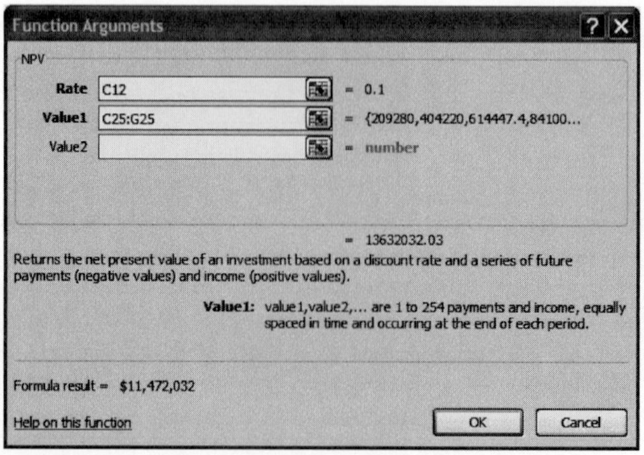

FIGURE 3.14 The NPV Function

an IF function can be as complex as needed, as long as Excel can evaluate the logical test as TRUE or FALSE. So we could write the following function to choose one of two column sums, depending on the relative values of two other cells:

$$IF(D36 > G76, SUM(A1:A100), SUM(B1:B100))$$

This example illustrates the **nesting of functions**. Nesting involves using one function within another. So in the example above, we have nested two SUM functions within an IF function. Excel imposes no practical limit on the number of functions that can be nested. However, nested functions can become complex and difficult to debug. It is good practice to calculate the components of a complex nested function separately to ensure that the logic is correct before bringing them together. And remember that future users of the model will appreciate documentation of formulas like the following one, whose meaning is not transparent:

$$IF(D345 < I87, OFFSET(G118, MAX(I87:J129) - I86), -H45)$$

3.13   CHARTING

Charting is an essential skill for the business analyst, because model results can often best be understood in graphical terms. Excel provides tools that automate much of the detailed work involved in developing a chart. Charts are created by selecting the Insert tab and the Charts group.

The first step in creating a chart is to highlight the relevant data on the spreadsheet. Then select Insert▶Charts. Next select the type of chart (Column, Line, Pie, Bar, Area, Scatter, or Other Charts). A window then opens showing a variety of ways to depict that type of chart. Select one of these and Excel will plot the data in that format.

Note that when Excel displays a chart, it adds three Chart Tools tabs to the ribbon (Design, Layout, and Format). These tabs also appear whenever an existing chart is selected. The Design tab includes the following groups:

- Type
- Data
- Chart Layouts
- Chart Styles
- Location

The Type group allows a change in the chart type or saves the current chart as a template. The Data group allows data rows and columns to be swapped or the data range to be modified. Chart Layouts includes a variety of chart layouts for titles, axes, and so on. Chart Styles offers a variety of colors and shades. Finally, the Location group helps move the chart to a desired location.

We illustrate two types of frequently used charts: **line charts** and **scatter charts**. The data involve advertising and sales over the past 11 years, as given in the table. A line chart allows us to see how Advertising and Sales have changed over the past 11 years, while a scatter chart allows us to see whether Advertising and Sales are related to each other.

Year	Advertising	Sales
1995	56	600
1996	56	630

1997	59	662
1998	60	695
1999	61	729
2000	61	766
2002	65	844
2003	69	886
2004	68	931
2005	67	977

To create a line chart for Advertising and Sales over time, highlight all the data in the spreadsheet (including the column headings) and select Insert▶Chart. Choose the Line chart type and the 2D-Line subtype that shows each data point (Line with Markers), as shown in Figure 3.15. This chart is problematic because the years have been plotted as a data series rather than the X-axis values. To correct this, and to ensure that Years are on the horizontal axis, select Design▶Data▶Select Data. Under Legend Entries (Series) highlight Year and click on Remove. Also, under Horizontal (Category) Axis Labels click on Edit and enter the range for years: C5:C15. Click on OK and the chart will appear as in Figure 3.16. Clearly, Sales have increased steadily over this period. A close look reveals that the same is true for Advertising.

We can continue to refine this chart, using the options under Chart Layouts and Chart Styles. Our final version, shown in Figure 3.17, has an overall title, a Y-axis label, and a key showing the exact values for each data point. This is just one of the 11 predefined options under Chart Layouts.

FIGURE 3.15 Initial Line Chart for Advertising and Sales

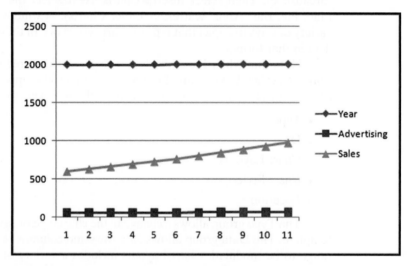

FIGURE 3.16 Entering Years as X-Axis Labels

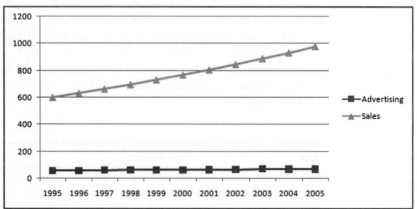

FIGURE 3.17 Final Line Chart for Advertising and Sales

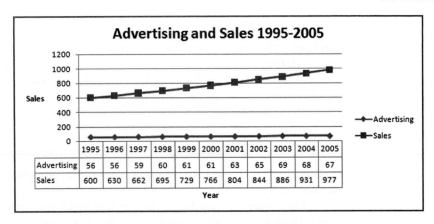

FIGURE 3.18 Initial Scatter Chart for Advertising and Sales

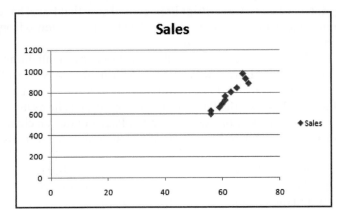

To create a scatter chart, highlight just the Advertising and Sales data and select Insert▶Chart▶Scatter▶Scatter with only Markers. The result is shown in Figure 3.18. This graph is correct, but it does not display the data in the clearest fashion because the axis scales are inappropriate. We change the horizontal axis scale by right-clicking in the Chart Area, selecting Format Chart Axis, and setting the minimum value under Axis Options to 50. Repeat this process for the vertical axis, setting the minimum to 500 and the maximum to 1,000. The improved chart is shown in Figure 3.19.

FIGURE 3.19 Final Scatter Chart for Advertising and Sales

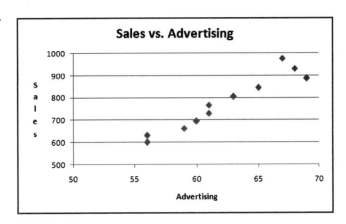

This chart conveys a different message from the line chart. Here, we see that higher levels of Advertising seem to be associated with higher levels of Sales, which perhaps suggests that Advertising is effective in increasing Sales. But the relationship may be influenced by other factors, since the scatter plot is not a straight line.

3.14　PRINTING

Printing in Excel is similar to printing in any Office application, with a few exceptions we discuss here.

First, many spreadsheets contain too much information to print on a single page. Depending on the column width and row height, Excel will select a range of cells to print on each page. Open the Office Building spreadsheet and select Office Button▶Print▶Print Preview. Excel displays the spreadsheet as it will look when printed. Click on Close Print Preview and note that Excel has divided the spreadsheet into pages with heavy dotted lines. The first page extends from A1 to E52, the second page from A53 to E104, and so on.

We can select certain cells for printing by highlighting the relevant range and selecting Page Layout▶Page Setup▶Print Area▶Set Print Area.

We display the Page Setup window by selecting Page Layout▶Page Setup ↘. Figure 3.20 shows the Page Setup window, which allows us to control other aspects of the printed page. For example, on the Page tab we can change the orientation of the printed spreadsheet from Portrait to Landscape. We can also change the scaling on this tab. A particularly useful option here is the button that fits a worksheet to a specified number of pages. Quite often, the number of pages is set to 1 for a scaled snapshot of the entire worksheet. On the Margins tab, we can alter the top, bottom, left, and right margins and the location of the contents on the page. Using the Header/Footer tab, we can enter text that will appear on every printed page, such as a page number or the name of the author of the workbook. Moreover, on the Sheet tab we can control whether gridlines and row and column headings will appear on the printed spreadsheet.

FIGURE 3.20　The Page Setup Window

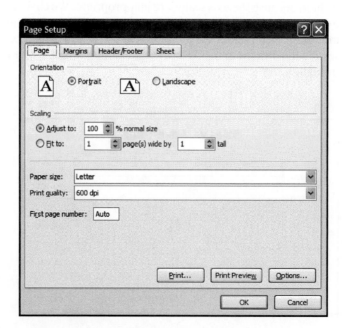

FIGURE 3.21 The Excel
Help Window

3.15   HELP OPTIONS

A great deal of useful information is available in Excel Help, which is opened by either pressing F1 or clicking on the question mark icon in the upper right corner of the spreadsheet (Figure 3.21).

Excel also offers access to targeted Help topics in a variety of specific situations. For example, some dialog boxes show a question mark at the right-hand end of the title bar. Click on the question mark and Excel opens the Help window for the operation controlled by the window. In other windows, there is a special link to Help. For example, the Insert Function window has a link to Help on this function, which opens the Help window for the function highlighted.

3.16   SUMMARY

Excel is both a highly versatile and a highly complex computer application. Not only can it be used for routine calculation, but it can also be used for complex decision support tasks. Each user must determine how many of the thousands of Excel features are needed on the job. This chapter presents the basic Excel skills every business analyst should have.

This chapter covers these basic features of Excel:

- The Excel window
- Configuring Excel
- Manipulating windows and sheets

- Navigation
- Selecting cells
- Entering text and data
- Editing cells
- Formatting
- Basic formulas
- Basic functions
- Charting
- Printing
- Help

SUGGESTED READINGS

Books

- Jacobs, K. 2007. *Microsoft Office Excel 2007: The L Line, The Express Line to Learning.* New York: John Wiley and Sons.

This book covers the fundamentals of Excel as well as some advanced features, such as macros and data analysis.

- Reding, E. and L. Wermers. 2007. *Microsoft Office Excel 2007—Illustrated Introductory.* Cambridge, MA: Course Technology.

This is an elementary workbook. Chapters A through E are essential. The remaining chapters are quite advanced and can be omitted by the beginner.

- Reding, E. and L. Wermers. 2007. *Microsoft Excel 2007—Illustrated Complete.* Cambridge, MA: Course Technology.

This book contains the previous one. Its additional chapters make it a handy reference manual.

Compact Disk

- Taylor, A. J. HAMISH. 2002. *Excel Essentials: Using Microsoft Excel for Data Analysis and Decision Making.* Pacific Grove, CA: Duxbury Press.

This CD focuses on Excel skills useful in analyzing business problems. It consists of nine modules, starting with Excel menus and moving through more advanced topics, including Solver, graphing, regression, and pivot table.

Online Programs

Online courses in Excel 2007 are available from the following sources:

- ElementK: www.elementk.com
- CustomGuide: www.customguide.com
- Microsoft Office Online: http://office.microsoft.com
- RemoteCourse: http://www.remotecourse.com

4 Advanced Excel Skills

4.1 INTRODUCTION

Excel is a software application of almost unlimited depth and complexity. There is no way to count the number of features it offers, but they must run into the thousands, if not tens of thousands. Fortunately, most business analysts do not need to become experts in all aspects of Excel, but they often find that they need to develop expertise in a few specialized domains within Excel. Which domains are relevant depends on the job they perform as well as on their level of interest in Excel and spreadsheet modeling generally.

The previous chapter presented the Excel features we believe the great majority of business analysts should know. Even there our coverage was not exhaustive. For example, every analyst should know the basics of cell formatting, but only a few will need to learn and retain all the various ways to customize formats in a workbook.

In this chapter, we pursue several specialized topics in more depth. These are features of Excel that intermediate and advanced spreadsheet modelers use to make their work more efficient, to make their spreadsheets easier to use, or to make them more powerful. We suggest that novice modelers skip this chapter until they have developed at least a basic familiarity with the skills covered in Chapter 3. More advanced users can skim this chapter, focusing on topics of particular interest or relevance to their work.

The chapter covers the following topics:

- Keyboard shortcuts
- Controls
- Cell comments
- Naming cells and ranges
- Advanced formulas and functions
- Recording macros and using Visual Basic for Applications (VBA)

4.2 KEYBOARD SHORTCUTS

Most users of Windows are familiar with using the keyboard as an alternative to selecting commands or tools with the mouse. In Word, for example, using only the mouse to copy and paste a portion of text requires highlighting the text, selecting the Copy icon from the Home tab, clicking on the new location for the text, and selecting the Paste icon from the Home tab. Alternatively, and possibly more quickly, we can replace the first selection with the keystroke combination Ctrl + C and the second selection with the keystroke combination Ctrl + V. These keystroke combinations are examples of **keyboard shortcuts**. Since Ctrl + C and Crtl + V can be executed with two fingers of the left hand, we can keep the right hand on the mouse and use both hands almost simultaneously. (Most keyboard shortcuts are not case sensitive, so upper and lower cases give the same results.)

Excel shares many keyboard shortcuts with other Windows applications. For example, we can use Ctrl + C and Ctrl + V in Excel to copy and paste the contents of individual cells or ranges of cells just as we copy text in Word. Other shortcuts for familiar actions include

Ctrl + N	Office Button▶New
Ctrl + O	Office Button▶Open
Ctrl + S	Office Button▶Save
Ctrl + P	Office Button▶Print
Ctrl + X	Home▶Clipboard▶Cut
Ctrl + F	Home▶Editing▶Find & Select▶Find
Ctrl + H	Home▶Editing▶Find & Select▶Replace
Ctrl + G	Home▶Editing▶Find & Select▶Go To

These familiar shortcuts are only a small sample of the shortcuts available in Excel. Most of these use the special keys labeled F1–F12, Ctrl, Alt, or Shift. Here is a further sample:

Format cells	Ctrl + 1
Display Help	F1
Insert new worksheet	Shift + F11
Move cursor to cell A1	Ctrl + Home
Display the Find and Replace dialog box	Shift + F5
Switch to the next nonadjacent selection to the left	Ctrl + Left Arrow

In Figure 4.1 we list for handy reference some of the most useful of these keyboard shortcuts. (An exhaustive list is available under Help: search on "keyboard shortcuts" and select the topic `Excel shortcut and function keys`.) We recommend scanning this list for shortcuts that may have been forgotten or new ones for operations that have become routine. Whenever we regularly encounter a tedious and slow operation, it makes sense to search for a keyboard shortcut to save time.

4.3 CONTROLS

Excel controls allow the user to change the contents or behavior of a spreadsheet without interacting directly with individual cells. Controls such as boxes and buttons are familiar because they appear frequently in commonly used windows in the Excel user interface. Among the Excel Options, for example, the window for Formula options uses a button to select a Workbook Calculation mode (only one of the three available choices is allowed) and a check box (on or off) to Enable Iterative Calculation.

Controls can be inserted into a spreadsheet to assist users in choosing parameter inputs and to assist the analyst in performing sensitivity analysis. The controls available are displayed by selecting Developer▶Controls▶Insert, as in Figure 4.2. (If the Developer tab does not appear, choose Office Button▶Excel Options▶ Popular and check the box `Show Developer Tab in the Ribbon`.) Each icon can be identified by holding the cursor above it. For example, the fourth icon in the top row (under Form Controls) is the Spin Button icon.

To place a control on a spreadsheet requires a sequence of steps. First, click on the desired control icon from the toolbar. Using the cursor, which now appears as a cross, drag and drop the control to the desired location in the spreadsheet. In doing so, use the cursor to set the size of the control as well as its location. With the control

FIGURE 4.1 Useful
Keyboard Shortcuts

For moving and scrolling	
Ctrl + arrow key	Move to the edge of the current data region
Home	Move to the beginning of the row
Ctrl + Home	Move to the beginning of the worksheet (A1)
Ctrl + End	Move to the bottom-right corner of the used area of the worksheet
PgDn	Move down one screen
PgUp	Move up one screen
Alt + PgDn	Move one screen to the right
Alt + PgUp	Move one screen to the left
F5	Display the Go To dialog box
For entering data on a worksheet	
Alt + Enter	Opens a new workbook, if one is already open
Shift + Enter	Complete a cell entry and move up one cell
Tab	Complete a cell entry and move to the right cell
Shift + Tab	Complete a cell entry and move to the left cell
Ctrl + Delete	Delete text to the end of the line
Shift + F2	Edit a cell comment
Ctrl + D	Fill down (a selected column of cells with the content of the first cell)
Ctrl + R	Fill to the right (a selected row of cells with the content of the first cell)
Ctrl + F3	Open the Define Name dialog box
For working in cells or the formula bar	
Ctrl + Shift + Enter	Enter a formula as an array formula
F2	Edit the active cell
F3	Open the Paste Name window
Shift + F3	Open the Insert Function (or Function Arguments) window
F9	Calculate all sheets in all open workbooks
Ctrl + Alt + F9	Calculate all worksheets in the active workbook
Shift + F9	Calculate the active worksheet
Ctrl + ;(semicolon)	Enter the current date
Ctrl + Shift + :(colon)	Enter the current time
Ctrl+ ~	Display all formulas
For inserting, deleting, and copying selection	
Ctrl + C	Copy the selection
Ctrl + X	Cut the selection
Ctrl + V	Paste the selection
Delete	Clear the contents of the selection
Ctrl + - (hyphen)	Delete (dialog box)
Ctrl + Z	Undo the last action
Ctrl + Shift + Plus sign	Insert (dialog box)
For selecting cells, columns, or rows	
Shift + arrow key	Extend the selection by one cell
Ctrl + Shift + arrow key	Extend the selection to the last nonblank cell in the same column or row
Ctrl + space bar	Select the entire column
Ctrl + A	Select the entire worksheet
For working with worksheets and macros	
Shift + F11	Insert a new worksheet
Alt + F8	Display the Macro dialog box
Alt + F11	Display the Visual Basic Editor (VBE)
Ctrl + PgDn	Move to the next sheet in the workbook
Ctrl + PgUp	Move to the previous sheet in the workbook
Miscellaneous	
Ctrl + S	Save an active workbook
Ctrl + N	Open new workbook
Ctrl + O	Open an existing workbook
Shift + F5 or Ctrl + F	Display the Find dialog box
Ctrl + H	Display the Replace dialog box
Note: In most cases, these shortcuts are not case sensitive.	

FIGURE 4.2 Form Controls Window

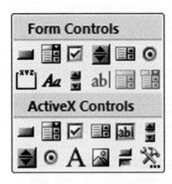

highlighted, right click and choose Format Control (or click Developer▶Controls▶Properties) and edit the inputs in this window to make the control work as desired. In some cases, preparations will involve entering input data for the control in a special section of the spreadsheet.

As an illustration, we demonstrate how the List Box and Spin Button controls work in a version of the Office Building model from Figure 3.1. (Other controls work in a similar fashion.) Figure 4.3 shows a version of the Office Building spreadsheet to which we have added a control panel in cells A2:B13. The purpose of the control panel is to make it easy to select two parameters: the building cost in cell C20 and the sale multiple in cell C27. The building cost is controlled by a List Box and the sale multiple by a Spin Button.

We input the List Box first. Imagine that we have three quotes from construction companies for the cost per square foot for the building: $78.50, $80.00, and $83.75. Because the building will be built by one of these three companies, we know that the cost will be one of these three numbers. Therefore, we do not want any numbers other than these three entered into cell C20, so we place a List Box on the spreadsheet that offers these three numbers as options.

In preparation for the construction of the List Box, enter the three allowable input parameters into a spare location in the spreadsheet such as F3:F5. Next, choose Developer▶Controls▶Insert and click on the List Box icon under Form Controls (not the one under ActiveX Controls). On the spreadsheet, select cell B4 to place the control there. With the List Box highlighted, right click and choose Format Control, then select the Control tab in the Format Control window, and enter F3:F5 for the Input range and F6 for the CellLink. These choices ensure that the options shown in the box come from F3:F5, and the result (1, 2, or 3) appears in F6. Finally, enter the formula =INDEX(F3:F5,F6) in A4 and revise cell C20 to reference A4.

We can test the control by selecting any one of the three inputs in the list box and verifying that the value in cell C20 changes appropriately. We can see that the ultimate NPV (displayed for convenience in cell A13) changes very little as the building costs change.

To install the Spin Button for the sales multiple, repeat the same procedure. From the Forms Control toolbar, click on the Spin Button icon and place it on cell B9.

FIGURE 4.3 Use of Controls

	A	B	C	D	E	F	G
1	Control panel						
2						Cost quotes	
3	Choose building costs	78.50				78.50	
4		$80.00				80.00	
5		83.75				83.75	
6						2	
7							
8	Sale multiple						
9		12	▲				
10							
11			▼				
12	NPV						
13		$11,472,032					
14							
15							
16							
17	Office Building						
18							
19	Parameters	Rate of increase	2002	2003	2004	2005	2006
20	Building cost per sq ft		$80.00				
21	Size of building		180,000				
22	Rent per sq ft	5%	$15.00	15.75	16.54	17.36	18.23
23	Operating expense per sq ft	6%	$1.20	1.27	1.35	1.43	1.51
24	Vacancy rate	-4%	30%	0.26	0.22	0.18	0.14
25	Percent financed		85%				
26	Mortgage rate		12%				
27	Sale multiple		12				
28	Cost of capital		10%				
29							
30			2002	2003	2004	2005	2006

With the Spin Button highlighted, right click and choose Format Control, select the Control tab, and change `Current value` to 12, `Minimum value` to 5, `Maximum value` to 15, and `Incremental change` to 1. Then change the Cell link to A9. These choices allow the sales multiple to be any integer from 5 to 15, and the result appears in A9. Finally, revise cell C27 to reference A9. By clicking on the up and down arrows in the Spin Button, we can see that the NPV for this investment ranges from a low of about $400,000 to a high of $16 million over the allowable range for the sales multiple (with the cost quote at $80), indicating a high degree of sensitivity.

EXCEL TIP *Using Controls*	1. Open the Control toolbar on the screen (Developer▶Controls▶Insert).
	2. Select the desired control icon (under Form Controls).
	3. Click on the desired location for placement.
	4. Click on Controls▶Properties (or right-click on the icon and select Format Control...).
	5. Edit properties as needed.

4.4   CELL COMMENTS

With few exceptions, the spreadsheets we have seen in actual use are poorly documented. Most practicing analysts have experienced the frustration of trying to understand a complex formula or a model design six months after they built it, or two years after someone else built it. But while everyone agrees that spreadsheets should be documented, almost no one does it. The reason seems to be that most forms of documentation are too time-consuming. Cell comments are one easy way to document the details behind a cell or range of cells.

Inserting Comments   To insert a comment in a particular cell, highlight the cell and choose Review▶Comments▶New Comment. This opens a comment window to the side of the cell, linked to the cell by an arrow. The comment contains the user's name as a default. It also places a red triangle in the upper right corner of the cell, which is the indicator that the cell contains a comment.

The location or size of a comment can be changed after it is highlighted (by clicking on its border). It is good practice to size the comment box so that is does not extend beyond the contents and to place it on the spreadsheet where it will be visible but not cover up other important cells. Figure 4.4 shows a comment entered in cell C12 and sized to fit a blank portion of the spreadsheet.

Displaying Comments   All of the comments in a workbook can be displayed by choosing Review▶Comments▶Show All Comments. This command toggles back and forth between showing all of the comments and showing none of them. The command Show/Hide Comment applies only to the selected cell.

Editing Comments   Edit the comment by placing the cursor anywhere within the comment box. All the usual Excel text editing features can be used inside comment boxes.

Deleting Comments   To delete a comment, click on Review▶Comments▶ Delete. Another way to access these commands is to select a cell with a comment and then right-click. The menu that appears will contain the commands that manage cell comments.

Copying Comments   When a cell containing a comment is copied, the contents and the comment are both copied to the new cell. To copy *just* the comment in a cell, copy

FIGURE 4.4 Cell Comment

	A	B	C	D	E	F	G
1	Office Building						
2							
3	Parameters	Rate of increase	2002	2003	2004	2005	2006
4	Building cost per sq ft		$80.00				
5	Size of building		180,000				
6	Rent per sq ft	5%	$15.00	15.75	16.54	17.36	18.23
7	Operating expense per sq ft	6%	$1.20	1.27	1.35	1.43	1.51
8	Vacancy rate	-4%	30%	0.26	0.22	0.18	0.14
9	Percent financed		85%				
10	Mortgage rate		12%	This is the discount rate used			
11	Sale multiple		12	on all projects in this class.			
12	Cost of capital		10%				
13							
14				2002	2003	2004	2005	2006
15	Cash Flow						
16		Gross income	1,890,000	2,097,900	2,321,865	2,562,982	2,822,406
17		Operating expense	216,000	228,960	242,698	257,259	272,695
18		Net operating income	1,674,000	1,868,940	2,079,167	2,305,722	2,549,710
19		Interest cost	$1,464,720	$1,464,720	$1,464,720	$1,464,720	$1,464,720
20		Before-tax cash flow	$209,280	$404,220	$614,447	$841,002	$1,084,990
21							
22		Down payment (at time 0)	$2,160,000				
23		Sale price					$30,596,526
24		Mortgage cost					$12,240,000
25		End of year cash flows	$209,280	$404,220	$614,447	$841,002	$19,441,516
26							
27	NPV	$11,472,032					

the source cell, and then highlight the destination cell. Next, select Home▶ Clipboard▶Paste▶Paste Special, selecting Comments and clicking OK.

Printing Comments Comments on the spreadsheet will be printed just as they appear on the screen. If the comments are extensive, we may want to print them in one place. Print all comments at the end of the worksheet by choosing Page Layout▶Page Setup ↘ Sheet tab and selecting Comments: At end of sheet from the pull-down menu.

4.5 NAMING CELLS AND RANGES

Individual cells and ranges of cells can be given names, and these names can be used in formulas to make them more readable. Named ranges are also used occasionally in other contexts, such as identifying a database for filtering or specifying input data for a Pivot Table (see Chapter 7). The use of range names is highly recommended in corporate settings for models that are used by many people. However, for the solo modeler, it is an open question whether the additional complexity of range names justifies their use.

Some examples of the use of range names will make their advantages clear. Here is a typical formula from a financial spreadsheet written in the standard manner, with cell addresses:

$$D20 = D13 + D14 + D15$$

Here is the same formula when written using range names:

Total_Expenses = Cost_of_Goods_Sold + Depreciation + Interest

Here are two equivalent formulas for calculating the actual quantity of a product sold depending on whether demand is more or less than the quantity available:

D14 = IF(D13 > D10, D10, D13)

Sales = IF(Demand > Quantity_Available, Quantity_Available, Demand)

In both of these cases, the formulas with range names are easy to read and easy to test against the underlying logic of the situation. In other words, when we see that Interest is included in the calculation of Total Expenses, we can mentally check whether this is the correct accounting treatment of interest costs. It is more difficult to do so when we see that D20 includes D15. Similarly, we can read and verify the logic of the IF statement more easily when it is written using range names than when it involves cell references.

However, there are some drawbacks to using range names. The most obvious is that entering range names takes time away from other work. Another drawback is that we must verify that each range name actually points to the correct cell or range. For example, it is not enough to check that Interest is *conceptually* part of Total Expenses; we must also verify that the range name "Interest" actually points to the cell where interest is calculated. Range names introduce an additional layer of complexity in a model, even as they simplify the look of formulas. Perhaps the best argument for their use is that they make a model more understandable for new users. Thus, if a model is expected to have a long lifetime and to be used and modified by a number of other users, range names are probably a worthwhile investment.

The simplest way to define a range name for a single cell is to place the cursor on that cell and note that the address of the cell appears in the Name box above column A. Click in the Name box and enter the name of the cell there. For example, place the cursor on cell C4 in the Office Building workbook, and its cell address appears in the Name box. Type "Building_cost" in the box and press Enter. (*Note*: Range names cannot contain blanks, so one common approach is to use the underscore character to turn a multiword name into a single word.) Now whenever we highlight cell C4, its range name appears in the Name box. When range names have been entered for all the parameters in cells B4:C12, we can click on the down arrow at the side of the Name box, and a list of all range names will appear. Highlight one of those names and the cursor will move to the named cell.

An alternative means for entering range names is to choose Formulas▶ Defined Names▶Define Name. This opens the New Name window, as shown in Figure 4.5. The cell address of the cursor appears in the lower portion of the window. Note that the cell address for this range name includes the sheet name (followed by an exclamation point) and an absolute reference to the cell location ($C$4). To enter the range name Size for cell B5, place the cursor on cell B5, choose Formulas▶Defined Names▶Define Name, and type "Size" in the upper box. Now when the cursor is placed on B5, "Size" will appear in the Name box. In the New Name window, the user has an option to select the scope of the name, determining whether it applies to the workbook or just to the worksheet. The default is workbook scope, which is the most common use because it avoids confusion. Note that when names are entered in the Name box, they are automatically assigned workbook scope.

Entering a name for a cell does not automatically change cell references in existing formulas to name references. For example, the original formula in cell D6, $C$6*(1+$B$6), does not change when we later assign range names to cells B6 and C6. We can rewrite this formula, however, using the range names, as Rent*(1+Rent_ growth). Similarly, we can rewrite the formula in E6 as D6*(1+Rent_growth) and copy this formula to the two cells to the right (because Rent_growth is specified by an absolute address). Alternatively, to insert newly created range names into existing formulas, we can highlight the range D6:G6 and select Formulas▶ Defined Names▶Define Name▶Apply Names... Then we select Rent_growth from the list of range names and click OK. When we look at the formulas in cells D6:G6, we will see that $B$6 has been replaced by its range name.

In the worksheet corresponding to Figure 4.6, we have entered range names for all the input parameters and

FIGURE 4.5 New Name Window

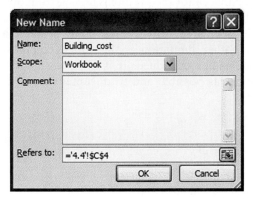

FIGURE 4.6 Documenting Range Names with the Paste List Command

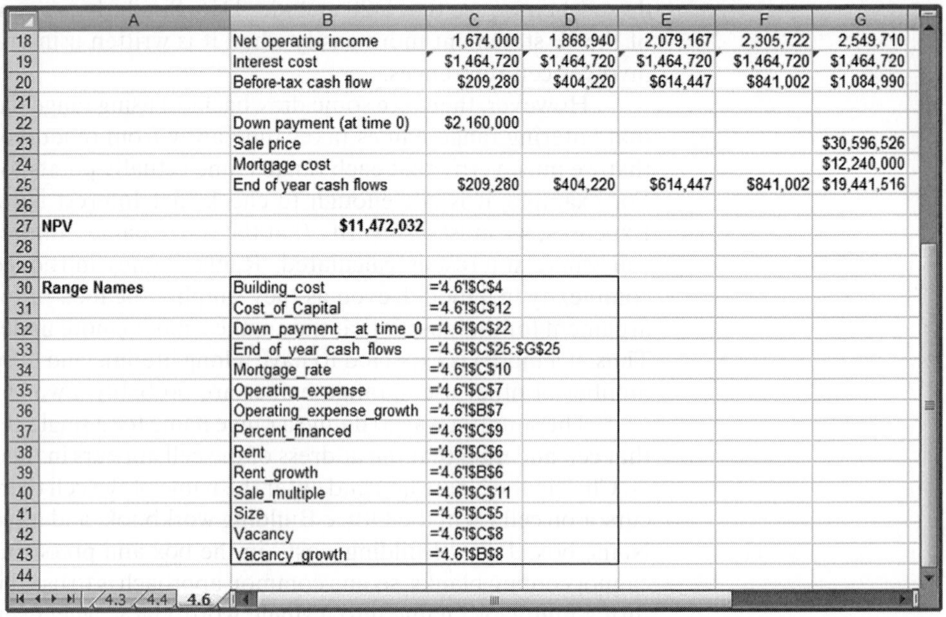

	A	B	C	D	E	F	G
18		Net operating income	1,674,000	1,868,940	2,079,167	2,305,722	2,549,710
19		Interest cost	$1,464,720	$1,464,720	$1,464,720	$1,464,720	$1,464,720
20		Before-tax cash flow	$209,280	$404,220	$614,447	$841,002	$1,084,990
21							
22		Down payment (at time 0)	$2,160,000				
23		Sale price					$30,596,526
24		Mortgage cost					$12,240,000
25		End of year cash flows	$209,280	$404,220	$614,447	$841,002	$19,441,516
26							
27	NPV	$11,472,032					
28							
29							
30	Range Names	Building_cost	='4.6'!$C$4				
31		Cost_of_Capital	='4.6'!$C$12				
32		Down_payment__at_time_0	='4.6'!$C$22				
33		End_of_year_cash_flows	='4.6'!$C$25:$G$25				
34		Mortgage_rate	='4.6'!$C$10				
35		Operating_expense	='4.6'!$C$7				
36		Operating_expense_growth	='4.6'!$B$7				
37		Percent_financed	='4.6'!$C$9				
38		Rent	='4.6'!$C$6				
39		Rent_growth	='4.6'!$B$6				
40		Sale_multiple	='4.6'!$C$11				
41		Size	='4.6'!$C$5				
42		Vacancy	='4.6'!$C$8				
43		Vacancy_growth	='4.6'!$B$8				
44							

for many of the formulas. Examine this worksheet carefully to see how range names are used and how they improve the readability of formulas. Note that the formula for NPV in cell B27 reads

```
NPV(Cost_of_capital,End_of_year_cash_flows) – Down_payment_at_time_0
```

The range names Cost_of_capital and Down_payment_at_time_0 each refer to a single cell. However, the range name End_of_year_cash_flows refers to the range C25:G25. Range names can refer to ranges of any size and dimension and can be used in formulas and functions as long as the range itself is appropriate.

Range names often need to be edited, deleted, or redefined. All of these operations can be carried out in the Name Manager window. Another useful option within that window creates a table of names in the spreadsheet. To do this, move the cursor to an unused area of the spreadsheet. Choose Formulas ▶ Defined Names ▶ Use in formula, and then select `Paste Names ...` and `Paste List`. Figure 4.6 shows the range names and their cell addresses pasted into cells B30:C43. This is one way to document range names and to make them easier to check. Note, however, that if we redefine the location of a range name, this list will *not* be updated automatically.

There are many more options for using range names; for more information refer to the references at the end of the chapter. But a warning is in order: range names are not a panacea for the problems arising from obscure and undocumented formulas. One limitation of range names is that in most cases copying and pasting formulas is easier with a mixture of relative and absolute addresses than it is using range names. Another limitation is the added complexity and possibilities for error that range names introduce. It is always a good idea to keep individual formulas as simple as possible and to document any formula whose logic is not self-explanatory.

EXCEL TIP ***Advantages and Disadvantages***

Advantages

- Formulas are easier to understand.
- Useful in Pivot Table and other applications.

of Range Names | *Disadvantages*

- May reference incorrect cells or ranges.
- Adds complexity to spreadsheet.
- Requires additional effort.
- Complicates copying.

∎

1.6 ADVANCED FORMULAS AND FUNCTIONS

Sophisticated use of formulas and functions is a mark of an expert Excel modeler. Unfortunately, there are so many different ways to use these tools that no book can communicate them all. The exhaustive lists of functions that are commonly provided in Excel manuals are a useful reference, once the user knows what function to look up. But users who don't know the basics of creating complex formulas often cannot use such references effectively. In this section, we present some of the tools of advanced formulas and functions:

- R1C1 references
- Mixed addresses
- Nesting calculations
- Parameterization
- Advanced functions

1.6.1 R1C1 Reference Style

Most Excel users are familiar with the column-and-row style of cell references. Thus, D16 and $D$16 are two different ways to refer to the contents of the cell in the fourth column and 16th row. Although familiar, this system has some disadvantages. One is that the columns after column Z are designated AA, AB, and so on. Another is that when we copy a formula that employs a relative address, the relative cell reference changes in each successive cell. Thus, a formula like $C$6*(1+D6), when copied to the right, becomes $C$6*(1+E6), $C$6*(1+F6), $C$6*(1+G6), and so on, which makes debugging a challenge.

Excel makes available a different way to reference cell addresses that corrects some of these problems. In the **R1C1 style**, the columns are numbered from 1 to 16,384. Absolute cell references simply specify the row and column of the cell, as in R16C4 for D16. Relative references specify the number of rows above or below the current cell and the number of columns left or right of the current cell. For example, the relative address R[1]C[1] refers to the cell one row below the current cell and one column to the right. The address R[−1]C[−1] refers to the cell one row above and one column to the left. To refer to the cell one row above and in the same column, we simply use R[−1]C. To refer to the cell in the same row and one column to the right, we use RC[1].

To get an idea of what this style of cell references looks like in practice, open the Office Building model (Figure 1.4). The formula in cell C16, $C$5*C6*(1-C8), involves both absolute and relative addresses. It is constructed to allow copying to cells D16:G16. Now turn on the R1C1 reference style by selecting Office Button▶Excel Options▶Formulas. Then, under Working with formulas, check the box R1C1 reference style. The same formula now appears in the following way:

$$R5C3*R[-10]C*(1 - R[-8]C)$$

Instead of the absolute reference $C$5, we have the absolute reference R5C3. Instead of the relative reference C6, we have the relative reference R[−10]C. And instead of the relative reference C8, we have R[−8]C. Note that this formula can also be copied across the row. The biggest difference between these two approaches is that in the R1C1 style *all* the formulas from C16 to G16 are identical. This makes debugging a model much simpler. In fact, all of the formulas in this worksheet that are copied across the columns are identical (see rows 6–9, 16–20, and 25).

Since Excel allows us to switch back and forth from one style of addressing to the other, there is no reason not to use the system that is most convenient at the moment. Some modelers use the R1C1 style when developing their models but switch to the normal style when the model is complete. In this way, they enjoy the benefits of the more logical and more easily debugged R1C1 style without imposing this less well known style on users.

4.6.2   Mixed Addresses

We discussed in Chapter 3 using absolute and relative addresses like $C$5 and C5 to make the copy–paste operation easier. We can think of the dollar signs in absolute addresses as fixing the column and the row of the address during copying. Often, we wish to fix both column and row, but there are circumstances in which we want to fix just one. We do this with **mixed addresses**. In a mixed address, either the column is fixed and not the row, as in $C5, or the row is fixed and not the column, as in C$5.

Here is an example of a situation in which mixed addresses are useful. Refer to the workbook in Figure 4.7. In column B, we have input data on sales covering 12 months from January to December. In column C, we want to calculate cumulative sales from January to the current month. Can we enter a formula for cumulative sales in cell C2 that we can copy for the remaining 11 months? Each month we need a formula that sums the cells in column B from January (row 2) down to the current row. This can be accomplished with the formula SUM($B$2:$B2). Note that the absolute address $B$2 fixes the starting value for the sum, and the mixed address $B2 allows the row (but not the column) of the ending value to change as we copy. Enter this formula in cell C2; the result is 145 as expected. Then copy it down to row 13 and verify that it calculates the cumulative sales as required. The formula for December (C13), for example, becomes SUM($B$2:$B13).

Entering the dollar signs in cell addresses can be tedious, especially when using mixed addresses. The function key F4 is a useful hotkey in this situation. When editing a formula, place the cursor on a relative cell reference. Press F4 once and both dollar signs are added; press again, and only the column dollar sign appears; press a third time, and only the row dollar sign appears; press a fourth time and the original relative reference appears (with no dollar signs).

4.6.3   Nesting Calculations

We have seen before that Excel allows calculations within formulas, such as in

$$\mathtt{IF((D16+D17)>(E2/F7), F9*F10, G9*G10)}$$

FIGURE 4.7   Using Mixed Addresses in Copying

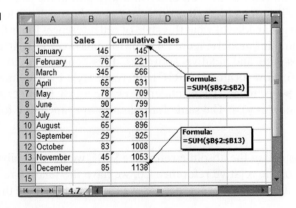

Excel also allows functions to be used within other functions. This is referred to as **nesting**. So, for example, we could nest a SUM function within an IF function:

$$IF(SUM(A1:A10) > 0, F9*F10, G9*G10)$$

In fact, we can nest functions as many times as we like (in most cases), as long as the resulting calculations can be performed by the functions themselves. For example, we can nest IF functions within IF functions (although there is a limit of seven IFs in one formula), as in

$$IF(D2 > D3, G7, IF(B2 > B3, G8, G9))$$

Or we can nest several different functions:

$$MIN(MAX(D4:D10), SUM(E4:E10), MIN(F4:F10))$$

We demonstrate other ways to nest functions in the discussion of advanced functions.

4.6.4 Parameterization

We discussed in Chapter 2 the importance in effective modeling of well-parameterized functions, and we provided a set of useful mathematical functions for this purpose. A well-parameterized function is one that represents the relationship between two or more variables accurately, with parameters that have a natural meaning in the problem being modeled. For example, a linear function is a natural way to represent a supply contract in which a fixed charge is incurred for every order placed and a variable charge is incurred for every unit ordered. In this case, the slope of the linear function represents the variable charge and the intercept the fixed charge. When we vary either of these parameters during sensitivity analysis, the results are likely to be meaningful because the parameters themselves have a natural meaning.

Most relationships can be parameterized in alternative ways. Choosing the best parameterization for the problem at hand is part of the art of modeling. For example, a demand relationship between the price of a product and the quantity demanded could be modeled using the constant-elasticity function

$$Q = aP^b$$

In this function, the parameter b measures the *percentage* change in quantity that results from a *percentage* change in price.

An alternative is the linear relationship

$$Q = c - dP$$

The parameter d here represents the *unit* change in quantity for a *unit* change in price.

Yet another demand function might be used in a situation in which there is a reference price in the market, perhaps set by our major competitor's price. If we set our price above the reference price, we face one demand curve; if we price below the reference price, we face another demand curve. One way to model this is with an IF function, such as

$$Q = IF(Our\ Price > Reference, a - bP, c - dP)$$

These three functions represent three equally useful ways to relate demand to price. Which one works best in a given situation depends on the shape of the relationship we wish to create and on the parameters we wish to vary in sensitivity analysis.

Another application of parameterization is to create flexible functions for situations that are encountered often. A consulting company repeatedly found itself forecasting the market penetration of new products over time. After experimenting with many different parameterizations of the relationship between market share and time for new products, it settled on one that required four inputs: the initial share (*IShare*), the final share (*FShare*), the year in which share first starts to grow

FIGURE 4.8 A Flexible
Four-Parameter Function for
Market Share Growth

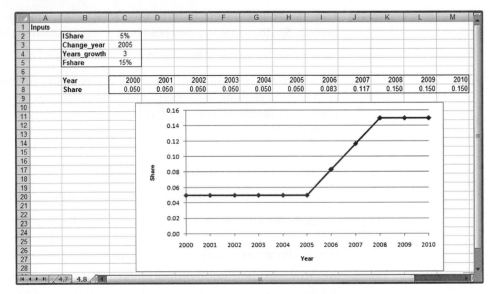

(*Change_year*), and the number of years of growth (*Years_growth*). The function takes the following form:

$$Share\ in\ current\ year = IF(Current\ year < Change\_year, IShare,$$
$$IF(Current\_year > Change\_year + Years\_growth, FShare,$$
$$IShare + (Current\_year - Change\_year)^*((FShare - Ishare)/Years\_growth))$$

Before the *Change_year*, share is constant at *IShare*. After share has reached its limit (at *Change_year+ Years_growth*), it is constant at *FShare*. In between, the share is calculated by adding to *IShare* the annual growth ((*FShare−Ishare*)/*Years_growth*) times the number of years since *Change_year* (or *Current_year−Change_year*). Figure 4.8 shows a typical output from this function. Change any of the four input parameters and see how the function adjusts to show linear growth from *IShare* to *FShare*.

When we undertake sensitivity analysis with this function, we can easily vary the four parameters that appear explicitly: *IShare*, *FShare*, *Change_year*, and *Years_ growth*. However, we cannot perform sensitivity analysis on parameters that appear implicitly, such as the *growth rate* of share. If the growth rate is an important parameter, we might want to create a different parameterization of this relationship in which this parameter appears explicitly. Here is an example of such a function:

$$Share\ in\ current\ year = IF(Current\ year < Change\_year, IShare,$$
$$IF(Current\_year > Change\_year + Years\_growth,$$
$$IShare^*(1 + Growth\_rate)^\wedge Years\_growth,$$
$$IShare^*(1 + Growth\_rate)^\wedge (Current\_year - Change\_year))$$

Neither of these alternatives is a simple function. If we were building only a single model involving growth in share, we would probably not go to the trouble of creating and debugging such a flexible function. But in a situation where this relationship is needed routinely, it may well be worth the effort.

4.6.5 Advanced Functions

AND and OR The logical functions AND and OR can be used to detect the relationship between values in various cells in a spreadsheet as it changes during analysis. For example, in the Office Building model we can determine whether the building cost is above $100 and the NPV is above $10,000,000 by using

$$AND(C4>100, B27>10000000)$$

The logical functions take on only two values: TRUE and FALSE. Thus in this spreadsheet

$$\text{AND}(C4>100, B27>10000000) = \text{TRUE}$$

$$\text{OR}(C4<100, B27<10000000) = \text{FALSE}$$

These functions can also be used to set flags, which are cells that warn the user when spreadsheet values are outside normal or acceptable ranges. (Flags are covered in more detail in Chapter 5.)

Truth tables are helpful for understanding how these logical functions operate. For example, the AND function is only true when *both* conditions are true, as shown in the table below.

Truth Table for AND

		Condition 1	
		True	False
	True	True	False
Condition 2			
	False	False	False

The OR function, by contrast, is true if one or the other or both conditions are true, as shown in the following table.

Truth Table for OR

		Condition 1	
		True	False
	True	True	True
Condition 2			
	False	True	False

Logical functions are particularly useful in combination with the IF function. When the logical test in an IF function depends on two conditions being true, such as D3>10 and D4<5, we could use two IF functions:

    IF(D3>10, IF(D4<5, value_if_true, value-if-false), value-if-false)

or we can simplify using AND:

    IF(AND(D3>10, D4<5), value_if_true, value-if-false).

If the logical condition were true if one or the other or both conditions were true, we would use the OR function:

    IF(OR(D3>10, D4<5), value_if_true, value-if-false).

SUMIF and COUNTIF   Two functions closely related to the IF function are SUMIF and COUNTIF. SUMIF adds all the cells in a range that satisfy a specified condition, while COUNTIF counts all the cells in a range that satisfy a specified condition. (COUNTIF is related to the COUNT function, which counts all the cells in a range that contain numbers.)

For example, if the range from D1 to D5 contains the following values

26

19

33

14

21

then SUMIF(D1:D5, ''<20'')=33 and COUNTIF(D1:D5, ''<22'')=3. (Note that the condition in the SUMIF and COUNTIF functions is enclosed in quotes.)

VLOOKUP and HLOOKUP   The VLOOKUP (and HLOOKUP) functions are useful for capturing relationships based on tables. Suppliers, for example, typically offer discounts for larger order quantities. Here is an example of such a price schedule:

Order at least	Unit price
100	$39.50
200	38.00
300	37.00
400	36.00
500	35.00

We could capture this relationship using IF functions, but it would require nesting five IF functions. A simpler way is to use VLOOKUP, which takes three inputs: Lookup_value, Table_array, and Col_index_number. The Lookup_value is the value in the first column of the table. In this case, it is the order quantity for which we want to determine the price. The Table_array is the range in which the table is located. If the two columns of data in the above table were in cells C4:D8, the Table_array would be C4:D8. Finally, the Col_index_number is the number of the column in the table in which the result lies. In our example this is column 2. So

$$VLOOKUP(100, C4:D8, 2) = 39.50$$

and

$$VLOOKUP(425, C4:D8, 2) = 35.00$$

Note that the values in the first column of the table must be sorted, in either ascending or descending order. When the Lookup_value is not found in the first column, the VLOOKUP function finds the range in which it lies and chooses the next value in the table. Thus, all values above 400 but below 500 are treated as if they were 500. (Other options are available; see the Function Arguments window or Help.)

The HLOOKUP function performs the same function as the VLOOKUP function except that it is designed for horizontal tables.

INDEX, SMALL, and MATCH[*]   The following example shows how three specialized functions, INDEX, SMALL, and MATCH, can be used in combination to carry out a sophisticated sequence of calculations. The example arises in power generation, where a large set of power plants must be brought into production in order from lowest cost to highest. Figure 4.9 shows part of the data in a workbook that contains cost and capacity data for 50 plants. The plants are numbered from 1 to 50 in column B. Plant capacities and costs are given in columns C and D, respectively. Our goal is to determine cumulative capacity when we employ only a certain number of plants in order of cost. Thus, we want to know, for example, how much capacity we have if we use the 35 cheapest plants.

The first step is to rank the costs from lowest to highest. We do this in column F using the SMALL function. The SMALL function calculates the kth smallest value in a range. So SMALL($D$6:$D$55,B6) returns the smallest cost; SMALL($D$6:$D$55,B7) the second lowest cost, and so on. Next, we need to find the relative position of a ranked cost in the cost range. For example, the lowest cost is 0.5; which plant has that cost, the 10th lowest, or the 25th lowest? We answer these questions in column G using the MATCH function, which gives the relative position

[*]This example is due to Jay Goldman of Strategic Decisions Group.

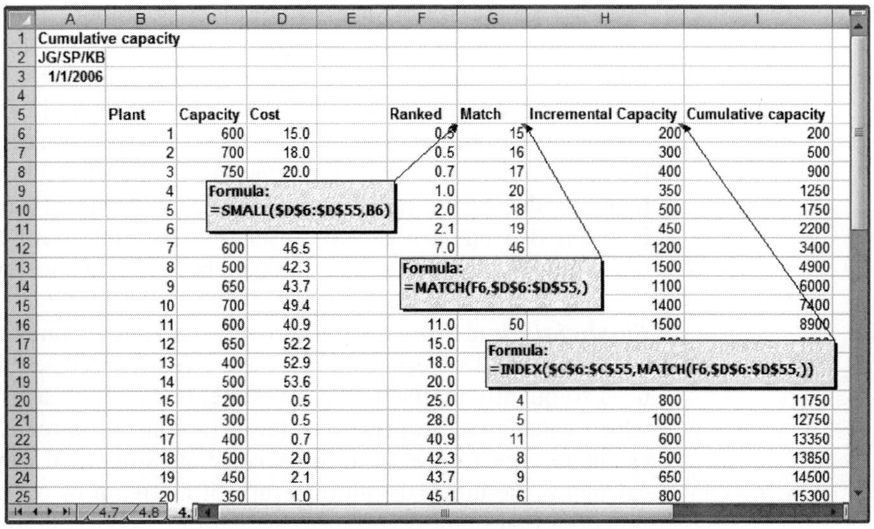

FIGURE 4.9   Using Nested
Functions

of an item in a sorted range. Thus MATCH(F6, $D$6:$D$55) = 15, which says that the lowest cost of 0.5, which appears in cell F6, is associated with the 15th plant. The next step is to determine the capacity of each plant as it appears in cost order. In other words, we know that the lowest cost plant is number 15; what is its capacity? We calculate this value using the INDEX function. The INDEX function gives the value at the intersection of a row and column index in a given range. So INDEX($C$6:$C$55, MATCH(F6, $D$6:$D$55,)) = 200. This function says, in effect, in the capacity range, find the value of the 15th entry. Column H thus gives the capacities of all the plants as they occur in cost order. Column I completes the calculation by adding up cumulative capacity. (Note that column G was included only for this explanation; it could be omitted from the final spreadsheet.)

Text and Date Functions   Excel offers a variety of functions for working with text and dates. These functions are often needed when working with information from databases. For example, if the first names of customers are in column A and the last names in column B, we can form their full names using the CONCATENATE function, which joins several text strings into one. Thus CONCATENATE("Sue", "Smith") = SueSmith. (To insert a space between the two names, we can use CONCATENATE("Sue", " ", "Smith")). Other useful text functions include EXACT, which compares two test strings, and LEFT, which returns a specified number of characters from the start of a string.

Date and time functions largely convert data from one format to another. Excel uses a date code in which years are numbered from 1900 to 9999. Thus if we enter the NOW function and format the cell as a date, the result is today's date, which happens to be 2/26/06. However, if we format it as a number, the result is 38774 in Excel's date code. Similarly, DATE(2006, 2, 26) = 2/26/06 as a date and 38774 as a number.

ROUND, CEILING, FLOOR, and INT   There are several ways to change the precision with which numbers are maintained in a spreadsheet. The CEILING function rounds up, and the FLOOR function rounds down, both to a given significance. The INT function rounds down to the nearest integer, and the ROUND function rounds to the specified number of digits. For example, ROUND(23.346,2) = 23.35. Note that these functions actually *change* the number that is stored in the cell, whereas formatting a cell does not change the number actually used in calculations. So we can format the number 23.346 to two digits and it will appear as 23.35, but any calculations based on this cell will use 23.346. By contrast, if we use ROUND(23.346,2), then both the display and the actual number are 23.35.

RAND* and *RANDBETWEEN Random numbers are often useful in modeling simple situations involving uncertainty (for more complex situations we use Crystal Ball, which is discussed in Chapters 15 and 16). The RAND() function returns a uniformly distributed random number between 0 and 1 each time the spreadsheet is calculated. To choose from a list of names randomly, we can create a random number for each student using this function and then sort students from the lowest to the highest value of the random number. RANDBETWEEN() returns a random number between two limits set by the user. For example, RANDBETWEEN(50,150) returns uniformly distributed random integers between 50 and 150.

Financial Functions Excel provides dozens of functions for financial calculations, some quite specialized. We have already discussed the NPV function, which is used frequently in evaluating investments. Some closely related functions are PV, which calculates the present value of a constant stream of payments; FV, which calculates the future value of a constant stream of payments; and IRR, which calculates the internal rate of return of a stream of payments. A couple of other functions that simplify complex calculations are PRICE, which calculates the price of a bond for given settlement date, redemption date, redemption value, rate and yield; and SYD, which gives the sum-of-years' digits depreciation for given cost, salvage value, life, and period.

4.7 RECORDING MACROS AND USING VBA[*]

Macros are small computer programs that automate frequently performed tasks. Macros are written in the Visual Basic for Applications language and stored in Visual Basic modules, so a deep understanding of macros requires knowledge of VBA. Fortunately, Excel provides a mechanism for creating macros simply by recording the steps involved, so many simple macros can be created by users who have little or no programming knowledge. We illustrate here how to *create* a macro by recording keystrokes, how to *edit* a macro using basic concepts from VBA so as to make it more powerful, and how to turn a macro into a *user-defined function*.

Any set of steps in Excel that an analyst repeats frequently is a good candidate for a macro. For example, some organizations require that every spreadsheet has a certain header and footer (containing date, author, and related information) and that the first several columns are formatted in a standard manner. To carry out these tasks manually might require 20–30 separate actions in Excel and take 10–15 minutes every time a new workbook must be created. If these actions can be captured in a macro, the entire sequence can be executed with one key combination that takes seconds to execute. Some firms provide such macros to employees as a way of ensuring compliance with corporate standards for good spreadsheet practice.

4.7.1 Recording a Macro

Financial analysts often need to calculate cumulative returns for a series of returns data over time. Consider, for example, the following daily returns on the stock of Apple Computer for December 2004. What is the cumulative return for each day, calculated from December 1?

Date	Daily Return
20041201	0.011
20041202	−0.038

[*]The assistance of Bob Burnham, Senior Research Computing Associate, Tuck School of Business at Dartmouth College, on this section is gratefully acknowledged.

20041203	−0.039
20041206	0.049
20041207	−0.044
20041208	0.006
20041209	0.011
20041210	0.018
20041213	−0.004
20041214	0.006
20041215	0.000
20041216	0.020
20041217	−0.024
20041220	−0.035
20041221	0.015
20041222	0.001
20041223	0.004
20041227	−0.013
20041228	0.016
20041229	0.004
20041230	0.006
20041231	−0.006

Since there is no single function in Excel for calculating cumulative returns, we need to proceed in steps. The first step is to add 1 to each return. Then we multiply these growth factors together over the period in question and subtract 1 from the total to calculate the cumulative return. For example, the cumulative return over the first two days is $(1 + 0.011)^*(1 − 0.038) − 1 = −0.027$. We have carried out this calculation in the workbook shown in Figure 4.10. The input data appear in columns A and B. In column C we have added 1 to each return; in column D we have multiplied the growth factors in column C. We use the PRODUCT function to do this; for example, the cumulative return from December 1 to December 31 is calculated in cell D25 using the formula PRODUCT($C$4:$C25)−1.

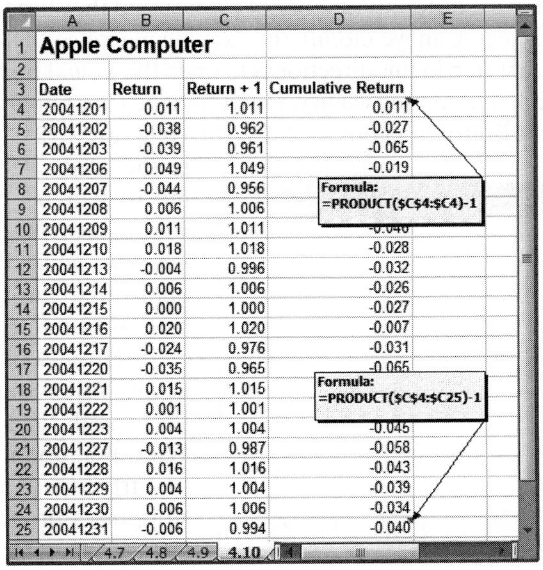

FIGURE 4.10 Calculating Cumulative Returns in Excel

There are several shortcomings to the procedure we have described. One is that we have to repeat these steps every times we want to calculate a cumulative return, which could be dozens of times a day. Second, we have to clutter up our spreadsheet with intermediate calculations in column C. Instead, we can use a macro to solve the first problem and a user-defined function to solve the second.

The first step in creating a macro is to document the steps that must be executed to create the desired outcome. Calculating cumulative returns for every period given a column of returns requires four steps:

Step 1: In the cell to the right of the first return, write a formula that adds 1 to the first return (e.g., =B4+1).

Step 2: Copy this formula down to the last time period.

Step 3: In the next column over, write a formula that calculates the cumulative return (e.g., =PRODUCT($C$4:$C4)-1).

Step 4: Copy this formula down to the last time period.

This procedure will work for the data in our example, but if we want our macro to be more useful, we should anticipate that the columns to the right of the returns data may in some instances not be empty. If this is the case, our first step should be to insert two blank columns to the right of the returns data.

To record a macro for this process, display the Returns data sheet. Then turn on the Macro Recorder, which is a device that will record every action performed on a workbook until the Recorder is turned off. The Recorder is turned on by selecting Developer▶Code▶Record Macro. This opens the window shown in Figure 4.11. Give the macro a descriptive name (such as Compound_growth), store it in This Workbook, and assign it a shortcut key that is not normally used (such as "a"). Click on OK and notice that the Stop Recording button has replaced the Record Macro button in the Code group. Next, proceed carefully through the steps outlined above. Then click on the Stop Recording button. Check that the macro works correctly by invoking it using Ctrl + a after deleting the contents of columns C and D. (It might be wise to make a copy of the worksheet beforehand.) The results should be the same as those obtained earlier by manual calculation.

4.7.2 Editing a Macro

The macro we have created is very efficient for calculating cumulative returns as long as the data are located in the range B4:B25. But we should expect to face situations in which we have a different number of returns and they are located somewhere else in the spreadsheet. Can we modify the existing macro so that it works more generally?

The first step in this direction is to open the Visual Basic Editor (VBE) and view the code that was created when we recorded the Compound_growth macro. Open the Visual Basic Editor by choosing Alt-F11 (see Figure 4.12). The large pane on the right is the **Code window**. The code for the macro can be viewed and edited here. The pane on the left is the **Project Explorer window**, which lists all the open workbooks and can be used to locate all the macros in a workbook.

Three toolbars are commonly used in the VBE: Standard, Edit, and Debug. The Standard toolbar allows for the usual Windows operations (Save, Help, and so on), but it also allows running and stopping a program as well as displaying various information in the Editor (such as

FIGURE 4.11 Record Macro Window

FIGURE 4.12 Visual Basic Editor

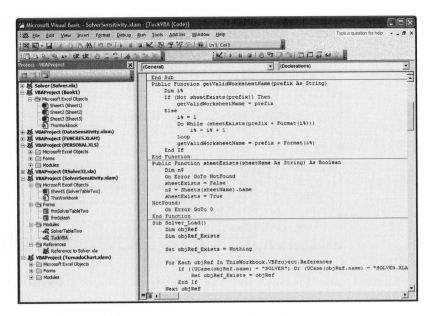

the Properties window or the Object browser). The Edit toolbar is helpful for working with the code itself. It has useful icons for indenting text, adding comments, and so on. Finally, the Debug toolbar makes it possible to run the program in steps and to add a watch window to keep track of variables during code execution.

The actual code for the Compound_ growth macro is shown in Figure 4.13. The first line of the macro starts with the word Sub followed by the name of the macro: Compound_growth(). The last line of the macro is EndSub. The second line of the code begins with a single quote ('); this is a comment line and is not executed by the code. The remainder of the code is reproduced below, along with a brief explanation of what each line accomplishes.

Columns("C:D").Select	select columns C and D
Selection.Insert shift:=xlToRight	insert two columns
Range("C4").Select	select C4
ActiveCell.FormulaR1C1 = "=RC[−1]+1"	enter formula = B4+1
Range("C4").Select	select C4
Selection.Copy	copy C4
Range("C5:C25").Select	select C5:C25
ActiveSheet.Paste	paste to C5:C25
Range("D4").Select	select D4
Application.CutCopyMode = False	exit copy mode
ActiveCell.FormulaR1C1 = "= PRODUCT(R4C3:RC3)−1"	enter formula = PRODUCT($C$4:$C4) −1
Range("D4").Select	select D4
Selection.AutoFill Destination:= Range("D4:D25"), Type:=xlFillDefault	autofill to D4:D25
Range("D4:D25").Select	select D4:D25

FIGURE 4.13 Compound Growth Macro as Recorded

The major task in making this macro more general is to replace the references to specific cell locations with generic locations, to be specified by the user. The edited code for this more powerful macro is given in Figure 4.14. Comments have been added to this code to help explain the various changes.

The first part of the code uses Dim (Dimension) statements to create names for three ranges: userdata, plusOneRng, and cumRetRng. The first range, userdata, will be set by the user, who must highlight the range of returns before running this macro. The plusOneRng will contain the returns plus one; the cumRetRng will contain the cumulative returns.

The second block of code inserts two blank columns to the right of the returns data. The line ActiveSheet.Columns(userdata.Column + 1).Select highlights the column to the right of the returns data. The line Selection.Insert shift:=xlToLeft, which occurs twice, inserts a blank column.

The next block of code gives the names plusOneRng and cumRetRng to the first and second columns, respectively, to the right of the returns data.

The fourth block of code creates the column of returns with 1 added. First the range plusOneRng is selected. Then the formula RC[-1]+1 is used to add one to the return one cell to the left. Then this formula is copied to the bottom of the range.

FIGURE 4.14 Compound Growth Macro as Edited

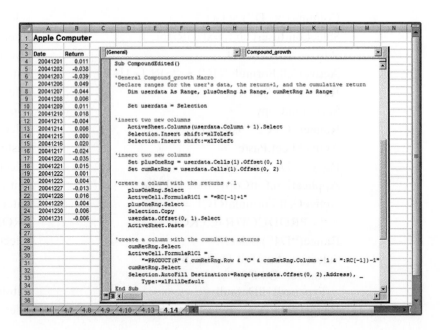

The fifth and final block of code calculates the cumulative returns. First the range cumRetRng is selected. Then the PRODUCT formula is entered. Finally, the formula is copied to the bottom of the range.

Test this macro by first highlighting the range B4:B25, then choosing Developer▸Code▸Macros (or Alt+F8), highlighting CompoundEdited, and selecting Run. The results should be identical to those obtained earlier. Now delete these results, highlight just the range B10:B20, and repeat the macro. This should add returns in columns C and D starting in 12/09 and running to 12/23. This demonstrates the increased generality of this version of the macro.

Most of the lines of code that appeared in the original macro have been changed in the edited version. Nonetheless, the overall flow of the logic as established in the recorded macro carries over to the edited version. It is usually the case that recorded macros are narrow in their scope and often contain superfluous details. With some knowledge of VBA, it is possible to edit these templates and make them both more general and more efficient.

4.7.3 Creating a User-Defined Function

The macros we have created to this point are powerful tools for analysts who frequently work with cumulative returns. Nevertheless, they still have limitations. One is simply that they require the use of macros, which are not familiar to the majority of Excel users. Another limitation is that we have to clutter the spreadsheet with intermediate calculations. It would be preferable if Excel itself had a built-in function for calculating cumulative returns. Then we could simply enter this function into any cell where it was needed, anywhere in a spreadsheet. Although Excel does not have such a function, we can create one in VBA.

There are two types of VBA programs: Sub procedures and Function procedures. Both perform actions in Excel. The macros we have created are examples of Sub procedures. A Function procedure differs from a Sub procedure in that it can return a value. The user-defined function we wish to create will return the cumulative return for a specified range of returns data. Figure 4.15 shows such a program written in VBA.

A user-defined function begins with the words Public Function, the function name (CumulativeReturn), and the type of inputs it accepts. Here our function requires one input: a range called "Returns." The next two lines create a variable called "cell" (a range) and another called TotalRet, a real number. Then the variable TotalRet is set to the value 1# (1# is equivalent to 1.0).

FIGURE 4.15 User-defined Function for Cumulative Return

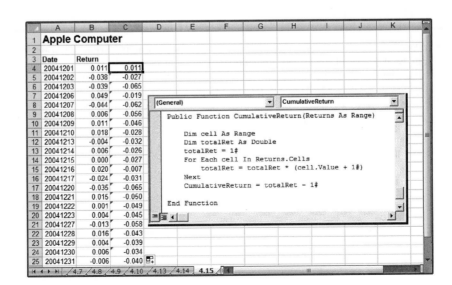

The core of this function is a For ... Next loop. This loop takes each cell in the range Returns, adds 1, and multiplies by the current value of TotalRet. When we subtract 1 from the final value of TotalRet, we have the cumulative return over the range, which is assigned to the function value, CumulativeReturn.

How can this function be used in a spreadsheet? First, we can confirm that the function is available in a given spreadsheet by opening the Insert Function window and selecting User-defined functions. Then we can use the function just as we use any other Excel function. In the worksheet corresponding to Figure 4.15, we have entered the function CumulativeReturn($B$4:$B4) in cell C4. Then we copy that function down the column. The results are identical to those we have found using macros.

User-defined functions are preferable to macros in many ways. They are easier to use for those unfamiliar with macros. They can be used to calculate just the needed results without adding anything extraneous to the spreadsheet. And they can be made highly general.

We have not attempted to give a comprehensive overview of VBA in this section, but rather to convey a sense of what can be accomplished using macros and VBA. For those who spend a high percentage of their work life using Excel, many of whom create elaborate spreadsheets and perform highly repetitive tasks, macros and VBA represent the next frontier in power and efficiency.

4.8   SUMMARY

This chapter covers selected Excel features that are used by intermediate and advanced modelers to make their work with spreadsheets more efficient or to make their spreadsheets more powerful.

The chapter covered the following topics:

- Keyboard shortcuts
- Controls
- Cell comments
- Naming cells and ranges
- Advanced formulas and functions
- Recording macros and using Visual Basic for Applications

Keyboard shortcuts can make interacting with Excel easier and quicker. Controls and cell comments make spreadsheets easier to understand and easier to work with. Named ranges are generally used by sophisticated modelers to make formulas easier to read and less prone to error.

All Excel modelers must know how to create simple formulas, but some models require more advanced use of formulas. We show how to nest functions to create powerful formulas in a single cell and how to create reusable formulas using flexible parameterizations.

SUGGESTED READINGS

An interactive Excel tutorial that covers many of the topics in this chapter can be downloaded at no cost from http://www.kelley.iu.edu/albrightbooks/#Tutorial.

There are a number of excellent advanced books on Excel. Here are some of our favorites.

ALBRIGHT, S. C. 2007. *VBA for Modelers*. Belmont CA: Duxbury.
GROSS, D., F. AKAIWA, and K. NORDQUIST. 2006. *Succeeding in Business with Microsoft Excel 2003*. Boston MA:, Thomson Learning.

ROMAN, S. 2002. *Writing Excel Macros with VBA*. 2nd ed., Sebastopol CA: O'Reilly.
SENGUPTA, C. 2004. *Financial Modeling Using Excel and VBA*. Hoboken NJ: John Wiley and Sons.
WINSTON, W. 2004. *Microsoft Excel Data Analysis and Business Modeling*. 2nd ed. Redmond, WA: Microsoft Press.

5 Spreadsheet Engineering

5.1 INTRODUCTION

Builders of ships, bridges, and skyscrapers all spend considerable time and money planning the structure before they order concrete and steel. Even the builder of a modest house starts with blueprints and a plan of activities. Without detailed planning, complex structures cannot be built efficiently, and they sometimes fail in use. The same is true of spreadsheet models. Spreadsheets can be as important to a business as bridges are to a road network. If a business relies on a spreadsheet, the business should devote sufficient resources to ensuring that the spreadsheet is suitably *engineered*.

Advance planning can speed up the process of implementing a complex design. Some years ago, the auto industry learned that investing more resources in pre-production activities saved a great deal of time and money when a new car was being prepared for manufacturing. One of the major sources of efficiency in this case was avoiding cycles of rework and redesign. Without good planning, the need for design improvements is detected only after implementation has begun, and much of the implementation effort is wasted. The same is true of spreadsheet models: extra time spent in planning can actually *reduce* the overall time required to perform a spreadsheet analysis.

Sometimes, at the outset, it seems as if a spreadsheet project will be fairly straightforward. The flexibility of the spreadsheet environment seduces us into believing that we can jump right in and start entering formulas. Then, as we move further into the process of building the spreadsheet, it turns out that the project is a bit more complicated than it seemed at first. We encounter new user requirements, or we discover obscure logical cases. We redesign the spreadsheet on the fly, preserving some parts of the original design and reworking others. The smooth logical flow of the original spreadsheet gets disrupted. Rather quickly, a simple task becomes complicated, driven by a cycle of unanticipated needs followed by rework and additional testing. Before long, we face a spreadsheet containing "spaghetti logic," and as a result, we have reason to worry that the spreadsheet contains errors.

In addition to speeding up the design process, advance planning can help the designer avoid critical errors in a design. A mistake in the design of a building or bridge can cause it to collapse; a bug in a spreadsheet can lead to poor decisions and substantial monetary losses. As we pointed out in Chapter 1, research suggests that many spreadsheets actually in use contain hidden errors. Learning how to avoid bugs is an essential aspect of spreadsheet modeling. Many analysts spend 80 percent of their time building (and fixing) models, and only 20 percent using them for analysis. With good design skills, this ratio can be reversed, so that analysts can spend the majority of their effort improving actual decisions.

In this chapter, we offer guidelines for the engineering of spreadsheets. Our motivation is to improve both the efficiency and the effectiveness with which spreadsheets are created. An *efficient* design process uses the minimum time and effort to achieve results. An *effective* process achieves results that meet the users' requirements. Although spreadsheet modeling is a creative process, and thus cannot be reduced to a simple recipe, every spreadsheet passes through a predictable series of stages. Accordingly, we organize our guidelines around these phases:

- Designing
- Building
- Testing

In this chapter, and several later chapters, we draw on the following example to illustrate our precepts and methods.

EXAMPLE
The Advertising Budget Decision

As product-marketing manager, one of our jobs is to prepare recommendations to the Executive Committee as to how advertising expenditures should be allocated. Last year's advertising budget of $40,000 was spent in equal increments over the four quarters. Initial expectations are that we will repeat this plan in the coming year. However, the committee would like to know whether some other allocation would be advantageous and whether the total budget should be changed.

Our product sells for $40 and costs us $25 to produce. Sales in the past have been seasonal, and our consultants have estimated seasonal adjustment factors for unit sales as follows:

Q1 90%	Q3 80%
Q2 110%	Q4 120%

(A seasonal adjustment factor measures the percentage of average quarterly demand experienced in a given quarter.)

In addition to production costs, we must take into account the cost of the sales force (projected to be $34,000 over the year, allocated as follows: Q1 and Q2, $8,000 each; Q3 and Q4, $9,000 each), the cost of advertising itself, and overhead (typically around 15 percent of revenues).

Quarterly unit sales seem to run around 4,000 units when advertising is around $10,000. Clearly, advertising will increase sales, but there are limits to its impact. Our consultants several years ago estimated the relationship between advertising and sales. Converting that relationship to current conditions gives the following formula:

$$Unit\ sales = 35 \times seasonal\ factor \times \sqrt{(3,000 + Advertising)}$$

∎

Although this problem is not ill structured in the terms we discussed in Chapter 2, it is still good practice to begin the process of building a spreadsheet model by drawing an influence chart. The key output measure is Profit, which decomposes readily into Revenue and Cost (see Figure 5.1). Revenue depends on

FIGURE 5.1 Influence Chart for the Advertising Budget Problem

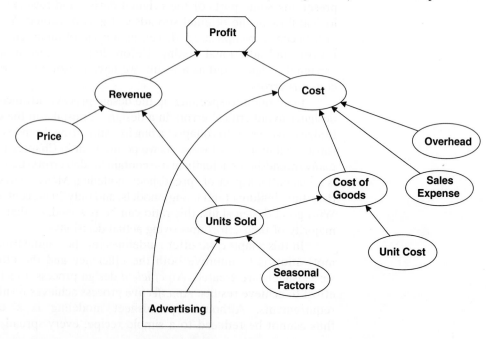

Price and Units Sold, while Cost depends on Overhead, Sales Expense, and Cost of Goods. The Cost of Goods depends on the Unit Cost and Units Sold. Finally, Units Sold depends on the Seasonal Factors and Advertising.

Drawing the influence chart helps us to clearly identify outputs (Profit) and decisions (Advertising). It also helps lay bare the essential relationships that connect the two. Finally, it should help us to recognize assumptions as we make them. Two assumptions in particular may be relevant later: one is that units sold are identical to units produced, so we ignore the timing of production and inventory; the second is that price is considered a parameter, not a decision variable, and it does not influence unit sales.

5.2   DESIGNING A SPREADSHEET

The essential first step in developing any spreadsheet model is to *design* it. In this section we offer some tips on good design practices for single-worksheet models. In the next section we discuss how to design an effective workbook composed of interconnected worksheets. We begin with eight guidelines for designing a worksheet.

5.2.1   Sketch the Spreadsheet

Carpenters have the saying, "Measure twice, cut once." That is, since planning is inexpensive and miscut wood is useless, plan carefully to avoid waste and rework. A similar piece of advice applies to spreadsheets: careful planning tends to result in far less time spent correcting mistakes.

Turn the computer *off* and *think* for a while before hitting any keys. This advice may seem harsh at the start, but we have seen many modelers create a spreadsheet in a flurry of keystrokes, only to discover at some later point that their design is flawed and in need of wholesale revision. To those who are relatively new to spreadsheet modeling, we recommend beginning with a sketch of their spreadsheet before entering anything into the computer. We also believe this is a good first step for experienced modelers. A sketch should show the physical layout of major elements and should contain at least a rough indication of the flow of calculations. Instead of laboriously writing out formulas with cell addresses, we use variable names to indicate how calculations will be performed. For example, we might write: *Profit = Total Revenue – Total Cost*. In order to show the logic for calculating unsold goods, we might write: IF(*Stock > Demand, Stock – Demand*, 0). The acid test for whether a sketch is sufficiently detailed is whether someone else could build a spreadsheet from it without any significant redesign.

An influence chart often provides a useful starting point for a spreadsheet design, as we illustrated earlier. The process of constructing an influence chart helps to identify the key outputs and inputs, as well as the logic that connects them. These are all critical ingredients in the spreadsheet model, but a spreadsheet provides a somewhat different view. For one thing, a spreadsheet has to be populated with numbers, while an influence chart involves only the *names* of parameters, variables, and relationships. Also, the physical design of the spreadsheet is usually different from that of the influence chart. Whereas an influence chart begins with outputs and works back to inputs, a spreadsheet typically starts with inputs and works toward outputs.

For the Advertising Budget example, a sketch of the spreadsheet might include four major sections (Parameters, Decisions, Outputs, and Calculations), row headings for the entries in the Calculations section, and a brief indication of how each row in the model will be calculated. For example, we could note the equation, *Gross Margin = Revenue – Cost of Goods*. Figure 5.2 shows an initial sketch along these lines. In this sketch we have not listed each of the parameters or the values of the decision variables. Nor have we shown specific cell addresses. The level of detail that

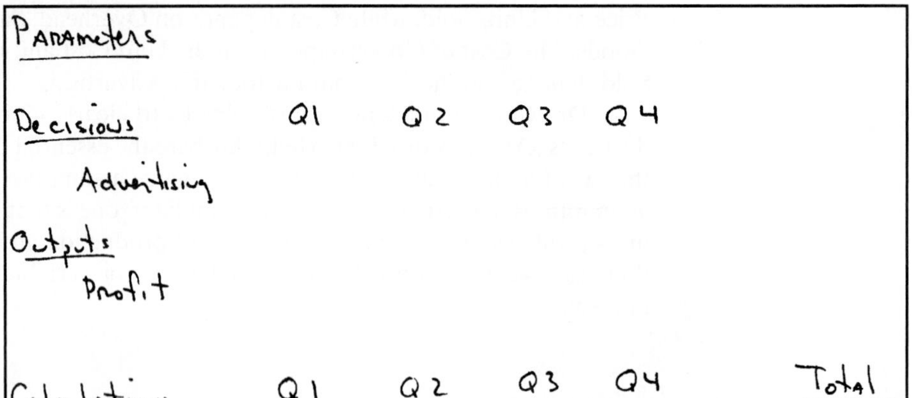

FIGURE 5.2 Sketch of Spreadsheet for the Advertising Budget Problem

is appropriate for a sketch depends on the complexity of the problem and the preferences of the designer.

The normal logical flow would require calculations to precede outputs. Why have we placed calculations at the bottom of the spreadsheet? The reason has to do with the use we envision for the model. We expect to vary some of the decision variables, and we'll want to know the consequences for the output measure. Since we want to see the effects of varying decisions on the output, it makes sense to place these items close together in the spreadsheet. In addition, we may also want to alter one or more of the input parameters and revisit the relationship between decisions and output. Therefore, it also makes sense to have inputs in close proximity to output and decisions. The one part of the spreadsheet we won't be examining or altering, once we've tested it, is the set of calculations. Therefore, we place the calculations in a secondary location.

Part of the thinking process, then, is anticipating what use will be made of the model. We will return to this point later, but for now, the planning process should take this into consideration when the model structure is sketched.

5.2.2 Organize the Spreadsheet into Modules

Modules bring together groups of similar items, and they separate unlike items. Modularization is a basic principle of good design and a useful first step in organizing information. In spreadsheets, this means separating data, decision variables, outcome measures, and detailed calculations. If an influence chart has been constructed, as

FIGURE 5.3 The Advertising Budget Spreadsheet

	A	B	C	D	E	F	G	H	I	J
1	**Advertising Budget Model**									
2	SGP/KRB									
3	1/1/2006									
4										
5	PARAMETERS									
6				Q1	Q2	Q3	Q4			Notes
7		Price	$40.00							Current price
8		Cost	$25.00							Accounting
9		Seasonal		0.9	1.1	0.8	1.2			Data analysis
10		OHD rate	0.15							Accounting
11		Sales Parameters								
12			35							Consultants
13			3000							
14		Sales Expense		8000	8000	9000	9000			Consultants
15		Ad Budget	$40,000							Current budget
16										
17	DECISIONS							Total		
18		Ad Expenditures		$10,000	$10,000	$10,000	$10,000	$40,000		sum
19										
20	OUTPUTS									
21		Profit	$69,662							
22										
23	CALCULATIONS									
24		Quarter		Q1	Q2	Q3	Q4	Total		
25		Seasonal		0.9	1.1	0.8	1.2			
26										
27		Units Sold		3592	4390	3192	4789	15962		given formula
28		Revenue		143662	175587	127700	191549	638498		price*units
29		Cost of Goods		89789	109742	79812	119718	399061		cost*units
30		Gross Margin		53873	65845	47887	71831	239437		subtraction
31										
32		Sales Expense		8000	8000	9000	9000	34000		given
33		Advertising		10000	10000	10000	10000	40000		decisions
34		Overhead		21549	26338	19155	28732	95775		rate*revenue
35		Total Fixed Cost		39549	44338	38155	47732	169775		sum
36										
37		Profit		14324	21507	9732	24099	69662		GM -TFC
38		Profit Margin		9.97%	12.25%	7.62%	12.58%	10.91%		pct of revenue
39										

discussed in Chapter 2, then a lot of this work will already have been done. An influence chart will have identified the outcome measure (or measures) of major interest as well as the data and decisions that make up the inputs. Most importantly, the influence chart will also have organized the major steps in the calculations required to produce the outputs.

Along with grouping and separating, the next step is to consider the flow of information in the model—that is, to specify which information will need to pass from one group to another. Data and decisions will serve as inputs to some of the calculations, and a small number of the calculations will eventually be highlighted as outputs. After these key linkages are identified, the additional development of one module can go on somewhat independently of modifications in other modules. Keep in mind that formulas should generally reference cells located above and to the left.

Figure 5.3[*] displays our spreadsheet for the Advertising Budget example. Following the layout in our initial sketch, we use four modules and surround each one with a border for clarity. The detailed calculations are simple enough to include in a single block, but even here, we use blank lines to separate gross margin, costs, and profits. We highlight values of decision variables (the quarterly advertising expenditures) and the output measure (annual profit) with color shading. Models that are more complex may, of course, contain many more modules and require layouts that are more elaborate.

As planned, the modules for parameters, decisions, and outputs are in close proximity. Therefore, we can change the value of an input and immediately see the impact on the output in the same Excel window.

5.2.3 Start Small

Do not attempt to build a complex spreadsheet all at once. Isolate one part of the problem or one module of the spreadsheet; then design, build, and test that one part.

---

[*]To download spreadsheets for this chapter, go to the Student Companion Site at www.wiley.com/college/powell.

Once that part of the model is in good shape, go on to the next one. By making (and correcting) many little mistakes in each module, and thus keeping the mistakes local if they occur, it is possible to avoid making really large and complex mistakes that require much more effort to detect and correct.

If we were building a model to cover 100 customers, it would make sense to start with a model for one customer, or perhaps a few customers. If the model structure is the same or similar for each of the customers, it should be easy to replicate this initial building block. Then, when the basic building block is working, the model can be expanded to include the remaining customers. Similarly, if we were building a complex model to cover 12 months, we would start by building a model for the first month; then we would expand it to 2 months and ultimately to all 12.

In the Advertising Budget example, we start by creating the Parameters and Decisions modules, because those simply organize and display the information we have gathered. Since we do not know at the outset what values we will ultimately choose for the decision variables, we enter convenient values (last year's expenditures of $10,000 each quarter seem appropriate), simply to hold a place and to assist us in debugging the logic of the spreadsheet. When we begin work on the financial logic, we focus on the first quarter. Only when the profit in the first quarter has been calculated successfully should we move on to the rest of the year. (Recursive formulas, which use a previous value to calculate the current value, facilitate this process.)

5.2.4 Isolate Input Parameters

Place the numerical values of key parameters in a single location and separate them from calculations. This means that formulas contain only cell references, not numerical values. It also means that a parameter contained in several formulas appears only once as a numerical value in the spreadsheet, although it may appear several times as a cell reference in a formula.

Parameterization offers several advantages. First, placing parameters in a separate location makes it easy to identify them and change them. It also makes a particular scenario immediately visible. Parameterization ensures that changing a numerical value in one cell is sufficient to induce a change throughout the entire model. In addition, parameterization is required for effective sensitivity analysis, as we discuss in Chapter 6. Finally, it is relatively easy to document the assumptions behind parameters, or the sources from which they were derived, if those parameters appear in a single location.

In our audits of spreadsheets, we frequently observe a tendency to bury parameters in cell formulas and to replicate the same parameter in multiple cells. This makes identifying parameters difficult, because they are not immediately visible. It's also difficult to know whether all numerical values of a parameter have been changed each time an update is required. By contrast, the habit of using a single and separate location considerably streamlines the building and debugging of a spreadsheet.

In our sample spreadsheet, all the parameters are located in a single module (cells B6:G15). Notice, for example, that price is referenced in cells D28:G28. When price is changed in C7, it is automatically changed in these other cells as well.

5.2.5 Design for Use

While designing a spreadsheet, try to anticipate who will use it and what kinds of questions they will want to address. Make it easy to change parameters that can be expected to change often. Make it easy to find key outputs by collecting them in one place. Include graphs of the outputs to make it easier to learn from the spreadsheet.

In our example spreadsheet, we have anticipated that when we move into the analysis phase, we will primarily be changing one or more values in the Parameters module (or the Decisions module) and observing the effect on the key output, annual profits. That is why we have copied the value of profits from cell H37 to cell C21, where it can be read more conveniently. In a larger model, the outputs may be scattered over many locations in different worksheets. It is very helpful to gather them together and place them near the inputs so that the details of the model itself do not interfere with the process of analysis. We will have more to say about this principle when we discuss workbooks in the next section.

5.2.6 Keep It Simple

Just as good models should be simple, good spreadsheets should be as simple as possible while still getting the job done. Complex spreadsheets require more time and effort to build than simple ones, and they are *much* more difficult to debug. Some of our earlier guidelines, such as modularization and parameterization, help keep models simple.

Long formulas are a common symptom of overly complex spreadsheets. The most serious constraint on effective spreadsheet modeling is not computing power, but human brainpower. Therefore, there is little to be gained from minimizing the number of cells in a spreadsheet by writing a long formula in one cell. It is better to decompose a complex calculation into its intermediate steps and to display each step in a separate cell. This makes it easier to spot errors in the logic and to explain the spreadsheet calculations to others. Overall, it is a more efficient use of the combined human–computer team.

In the Advertising Budget example, we could calculate Gross Margin (cell D30) in a single row rather than use three rows to calculate its components (Units Sold, Revenue, and Cost of Goods). However, the detail helps in checking the logic, and it may eventually prove helpful during analysis. Later on, for example, we may decide that it would be more realistic to model sales as a function of price. Instead of modifying a complicated Gross Margin formula, we will find it easier to work with the formula for Units Sold.

5.2.7 Design for Communication

Spreadsheets are often used long after the builder ever thought they would be, and frequently by people who are not familiar with them. Logical design helps users understand what the spreadsheet is intended to accomplish and how to work with it effectively. The look and the layout of a spreadsheet often determine whether its developer or another user can understand it several months or years after it was built. Visual cues that reinforce the model's logic also pay dividends when the spreadsheet gets routine use in a decision-support role.

The use of informative labels and the incorporation of blank spaces can go a long way toward conveying the organization of a spreadsheet. The specialized formatting options in Excel (outlines, color, bold font, and so on) can also be used to highlight certain cell entries or ranges for quick visual recognition. This facilitates navigating around the spreadsheet, both when building the spreadsheet and when using it. However, formatting tools should be applied with care. If used to excess, formatting can confuse, obscure, and annoy rather than help. In our example spreadsheet, we use various formatting tools to improve readability, including bold font, borders, color shading, and capitalization. Within a team or an organization, or when creating a series of spreadsheets, it also helps to use these formatting tools consistently. For example, we use yellow shading and a border to designate cells that represent decision variables in virtually all of our spreadsheet models.

Sometimes large spreadsheets can be reorganized with the help of split windows. For example, if we were to display the Advertising Budget spreadsheet at normal size, it would not fit within one (laptop) window. As a result, the lower part of the Calculations module would drop out of view. If we wanted to preserve the top portion of the spreadsheet, but also view the quarterly profit levels and the profit-margin percentages, we could split the window vertically, as shown in Figure 5.4. (To split a screen, select a row or column and choose View▶Window▶Split.)

FIGURE 5.4 Split-Window Display in the Advertising Budget Spreadsheet

	A	B	C	D	E	F	G	H	I	J
1	Advertising Budget Model									
2	SGP/KRB									
3	1/1/2006									
4										
5	PARAMETERS									
6				Q1	Q2	Q3	Q4			Notes
7		Price	$40.00							Current price
8		Cost	$25.00							Accounting
9		Seasonal		0.9	1.1	0.8	1.2			Data analysis
10		OHD rate	0.15							Accounting
11		Sales Parameters								
12			35							Consultants
13			3000							
14		Sales Expense		8000	8000	9000	9000			Consultants
15		Ad Budget	$40,000							Current budget
16										
17	DECISIONS							Total		
18		Ad Expenditures		$10,000	$10,000	$10,000	$10,000	$40,000		sum
19										
20	OUTPUTS									
21		Profit	$69,662							
37		Profit		14324	21507	9732	24099	69662		GM -TFC
38		Profit Margin		9.97%	12.25%	7.62%	12.58%	10.91%		pct of revenue
39										

5.2.8 Document Important Data and Formulas

Spreadsheets have become widespread in the business world because they are easy to build and use. Originally, many analysts learned to build spreadsheets because their corporate information technology departments could not serve their needs in a timely fashion. One reason for the lack of a timely response is that information technology professionals use a careful and time-consuming design process for creating computing applications, including extensive documentation. Spreadsheet users rarely apply the same level of effort to their applications. The question, then, is: How can we preserve the benefits of using spreadsheets, while also gaining the benefits of a careful design process?

One answer to this question is to find *practical* ways to document a spreadsheet. Creating separate documentation or user manuals is often impractical. But it is neither difficult nor time consuming to record the source of each important parameter and explain each important calculation in the spreadsheet itself. A design sketch or influence chart of the spreadsheet provides documentation, in a fashion, for every important relationship in the model. Transferring this information to the actual spreadsheet helps preserve the underlying logic of the model and ultimately helps convey that logic to users of the spreadsheet.

In our example spreadsheet, we have documented both input parameters and the model logic in column J (refer to Figure 5.3). We have noted the source of each of the parameters: the accounting department, consultants, and so on. For each formula, we have provided a short explanation of the arithmetic, such as *Revenue = Price*Units*.

At the detailed level, we can provide documentation within individual cells by inserting cell comments. The command Review▶Comments▶New Comment brings up a small window in which we can describe the contents of the cell where the cursor is located. Figure 5.5 shows an example in which the Comment window explains that last year the budget was distributed equally among the quarters. The format of the comment is controlled by a selection from the Excel Options▶Advanced menu. In the Display Section within this menu are three buttons controlling the display of cell comments. A comment can be displayed permanently by clicking on Comments and indicators. Or we can click on Indicators only, in which case there will be a red triangle in the upper right-hand corner of the cell, but the comment will be displayed only when the cursor is placed within that cell. If we click on No Comments, then neither the comment nor the indicator will be visible at all.

Finally, it may be worth creating a separate module to list the assumptions in the model, particularly the structural simplifications adopted at the outset of the model-building process. In the Advertising Budget example, we assumed that production

	A	B	C	D	E	F	G	H	I	J
1	**Advertising Budget Model**									
2	SGP/KRB									
3	1/1/2006									
4										
5	PARAMETERS									
6				Q1	Q2	Q3	Q4			Notes
7		Price	$40.00							Current price
8		Cost	$25.00							Accounting
9		Seasonal		0.9	1.1	0.8	1.2			Data analysis
10		OHD rate	0.15							Accounting
11		Sales Parameters		The budget was split						
12			35	equally among the						Consultants
13			3000	quarters last year.						
14		Sales Expense		8000	8000	9000	9000			Consultants
15		Ad Budget	$40,000							Current budget
16										
17	DECISIONS							Total		
18		Ad Expenditures		$10,000	$10,000	$10,000	$10,000	$40,000		sum
19										
20	OUTPUTS									
21		Profit	$69,662							
22										
23	CALCULATIONS									
24		Quarter		Q1	Q2	Q3	Q4	Total		
25		Seasonal		0.9	1.1	0.8	1.2			
26										
27		Units Sold		3592	4390	3192	4789	15962		given formula
28		Revenue		143662	175587	127700	191549	638498		price*units
29		Cost of Goods		89789	109742	79812	119718	399061		cost*units
30		Gross Margin		53873	65845	47887	71831	239437		subtraction
31										
32		Sales Expense		8000	8000	9000	9000	34000		given
33		Advertising		10000	10000	10000	10000	40000		decisions
34		Overhead		21549	26338	19155	28732	95775		rate*revenue
35		Total Fixed Cost		39549	44338	38155	47732	169775		sum
36										
37		Profit		14324	21507	9732	24099	69662		GM -TFC
38		Profit Margin		9.97%	12.25%	7.62%	12.58%	10.91%		pct of revenue
39										

H ◄ ► H \ 5.3 ⟨ 5.4 ⟩ 5.5 ⟨ | ◄

quantities would be equal to demand quantities each quarter and that there would be no inventory. That is, we assumed that we could ignore the detailed timing problems that might arise in the supply chain when we attempt to meet demand directly from production. These assumptions will not be obvious to another user of the model but may significantly influence the results. Thus, they should be noted on the spreadsheet itself.

Workbooks offer additional options for effective documentation, as they do for most of the other guidelines. We now turn to the question of how to design workbooks effectively.

5.3   DESIGNING A WORKBOOK

Although many effective spreadsheet models use only a single worksheet, it is often desirable to use multiple worksheets in a workbook. In fact, the multisheet format can be exploited to better accomplish many of the goals discussed in the previous section, such as modularization and ease of use. Most of the design principles described above apply equally well to the design of workbooks. However, some additional issues arise, as we discuss below. (The Northern Museum model is available with the book. We recommend that the reader open this model and explore it before reading on.)

EXAMPLE
*Northern
Museum
Capital
Campaign*

The Northern Museum is a 115-year-old natural history museum located in northern New England. It houses extensive natural history, historical, and ethnological collections in a 20,000-square-foot building. It also houses a planetarium and weather station.

The physical plant of the Museum has grown increasingly inadequate for its programs and collections, and the Board has begun planning seriously for a major capital campaign. This campaign will attempt to raise several million dollars over a six-year period. In order to raise this money, the Board will have to authorize significant expenditures for consultants and other expenses. In a typical campaign, expenses exceed donations for at least the first two years. The Board is concerned that the campaign and ongoing revenue shortfalls from operations may have serious impacts on its endowment.

In order to better understand the financial implications of the capital campaign, the Board and the executive director asked the treasurer to construct a planning model. This model would link the short-term budgeting perspective the Board had traditionally taken to finances with a long-term planning perspective. It would allow the Board and the director to make explicit their assumptions about the future growth of the Museum in the context of the capital campaign and to evaluate the consequences of those assumptions on its financial health.

An early step in the process of developing this model was to construct an influence chart (Figure 5.6). This chart shows that a central purpose of the model was to track the evolution of the endowment and how it is influenced by both operating results and the capital campaign. The critical assumption that drives the model is that shortfalls between operating revenues and costs will be made up by withdrawals ("Drawdowns") from the endowment. This process had actually been going on at the Museum for several years, and the Board was concerned that expenses associated with the capital campaign not be allowed to reduce the endowment to a dangerous level before it could be built up from donations. ∎

5.3.1 Use Separate Worksheets to Group Similar Kinds of Information

Workbooks should be designed to make a model easy to understand and use. Individual worksheets should each have a well-defined purpose and be given descriptive names. They should also appear in a natural order. Assumptions, calculations, and results should be placed on separate worksheets whenever possible. This allows users to view assumptions and results without being distracted by the details of the calculations.

The Northern Museum workbook consists of 10 worksheets appearing in the following order.

Overview: Describes the purpose and assumptions behind the model

Instructions: Gives step-by-step instructions for using the model

Log of changes: Records the major changes made to the model over time

Guide to sheets: Shows the logical relationships among the worksheets and provides hyperlinks to navigate directly to any worksheet

Influence chart: Depicts the fundamental logic of the model itself

FIGURE 5.6 Influence Chart for Northern Museum Model

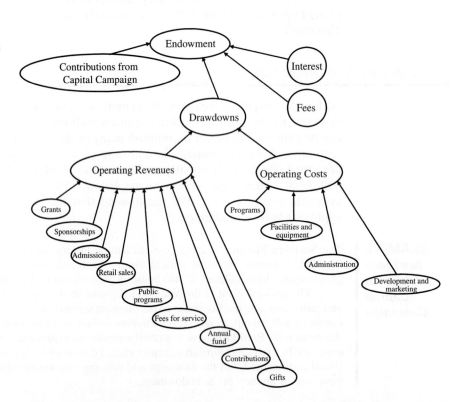

Assumptions: Provides some historical data and records assumptions used in the model

Long-term Model: Projects revenues, costs, endowment, and critical ratios from 2006 to 2016

Short-term results: Summarizes projections one and three years out in the same format as the Long-term Model worksheet

Historical data: Records historical data

Ratio charts: Provides graphical depiction of the ratios calculated in the Long-term Model worksheet

Figure 5.7 shows the Guide to sheets. This simple worksheet helps the user to understand the structure of the workbook and to determine which worksheets provide inputs to other sheets. For example, it shows that the Long-term Model sheet takes its inputs only from the Assumptions sheet. If we examine cell F30 in the Long-term Model sheet, we see that it references cell F30 on the Assumptions sheet (using the formula =Assumptions!F30). Note that a reference to a cell on another worksheet begins with the name of that worksheet followed by an exclamation mark. When using formulas that contain references to other worksheets, the references themselves begin to look complicated, and most users find it convenient to create these references by pointing and clicking. The complexity of multisheet references reinforces the importance of keeping formulas and worksheet names simple, so that someone examining the logic for the first time can follow the calculations. Another way to make formulas look simple is to use range names.

5.3.2 Design Workbooks for Ease of Navigation and Use

The purpose of a structured workbook is to facilitate understanding by users, so any form of structural help for finding their way around the workbook is beneficial. Using revealing names for individual worksheets is one helpful approach. (To change a worksheet name, double-click on the name tab at the bottom of the spreadsheet and edit the name, or right-click on the worksheet name and select Rename.)

The Northern Museum workbook illustrates a number of techniques for assisting with navigation and use. We pointed out previously that the worksheet named Guide to sheets (Figure 5.7) shows the logical relationships among the

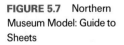

FIGURE 5.7 Northern Museum Model: Guide to Sheets

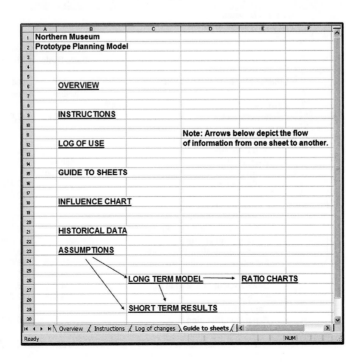

worksheets. It also provides an easy way to navigate to a particular worksheet. Each of the cells that displays a worksheet name also has a hyperlink, so that when the user clicks on the worksheet name, the display moves to the corresponding worksheet. (A hyperlink can be added to a cell by choosing Insert▶Links▶Hyperlink.) The Influence chart sheet also uses hyperlinks to take the user from a given variable such as Revenues to the exact location in the Long-term Model sheet where that variable is calculated (cell A26). Finally, the Long-term Model sheet illustrates another use of hyperlinks for navigation. The phrase `Return to Influence chart` appears near the upper left corner of the worksheet. This phrase is created using Word Art (Insert▶Text▶WordArt). A hyperlink can be associated with WordArt by highlighting the WordArt object and choosing Insert▶Links▶Hyperlink. Click on this phrase and Excel returns to the Influence chart sheet.

Another approach to navigation aids is to use buttons. A button is one of the Form Controls that can be selected from the Developer tab. Select Developer▶Controls▶Insert to display the menu of choices, as discussed in Chapter 4. For example, we can create a command button that will invoke a particular macro. (Macros are also covered in Chapter 4). In the Ratio charts sheet, we have created a Command Button called `Go to Guide`, whose purpose is to take the user back to the Guide to sheets. It calls on the following macro that was created using the Record Macro procedure (Developer▶Code▶Record Macro):

```
ActiveSheet.Shapes("CommandButton1").Select
Sheets("Guide to sheets").Select
ActiveSheet.Range("A1").Select
```

In worksheets with many rows it is often difficult to recognize the large-scale structure among all the details. The Excel Group and Outline option (Data▶Outline▶Group) can be used in these cases to help the user understand the structure and navigate to the desired location quickly. Grouping simply provides a display option in which the rows that provide details can be hidden in the display. Figure 5.8 shows how grouping is used in the Northern Museum Long-term Model sheet. The details behind the calculation of Revenues are grouped so that rows 10 to 25 are

FIGURE 5.8 Northern Museum Model: Outlining

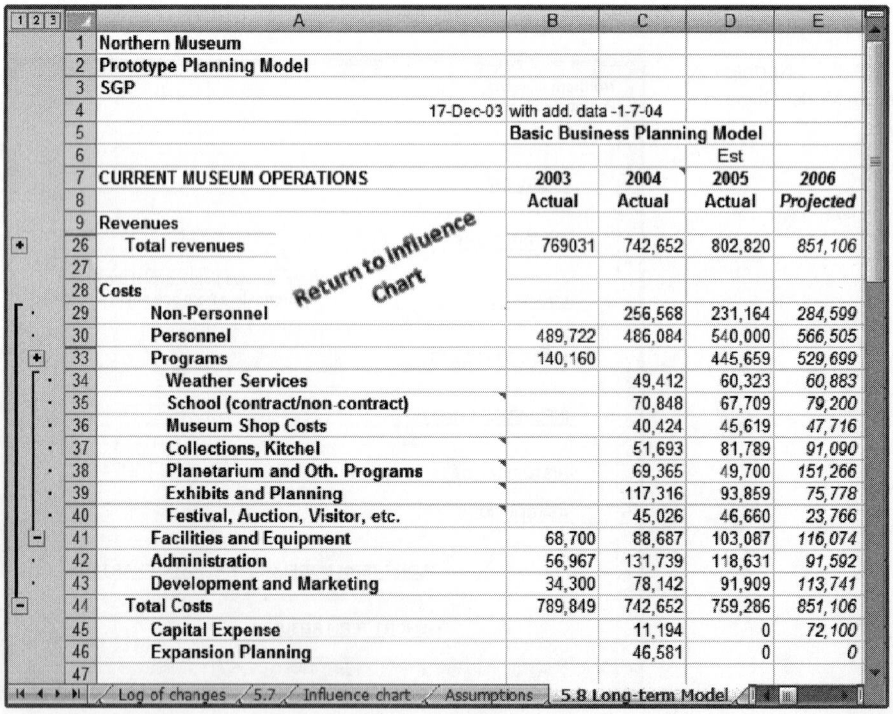

	A	B	C	D	E
1	Northern Museum				
2	Prototype Planning Model				
3	SGP				
4	17-Dec-03	with add. data -1-7-04			
5		Basic Business Planning Model			
6				Est	
7	CURRENT MUSEUM OPERATIONS	2003	2004	2005	2006
8		Actual	Actual	Actual	Projected
9	Revenues				
26	Total revenues	769031	742,652	802,820	851,106
27					
28	Costs				
29	Non-Personnel		256,568	231,164	284,599
30	Personnel	489,722	486,084	540,000	566,505
33	Programs	140,160		445,659	529,699
34	Weather Services		49,412	60,323	60,883
35	School (contract/non-contract)		70,848	67,709	79,200
36	Museum Shop Costs		40,424	45,619	47,716
37	Collections, Kitchel		51,693	81,789	91,090
38	Planetarium and Oth. Programs		69,365	49,700	151,266
39	Exhibits and Planning		117,316	93,859	75,778
40	Festival, Auction, Visitor, etc.		45,026	46,660	23,766
41	Facilities and Equipment	68,700	88,687	103,087	116,074
42	Administration	56,967	131,739	118,631	91,592
43	Development and Marketing	34,300	78,142	91,909	113,741
44	Total Costs	789,849	742,652	759,286	851,106
45	Capital Expense		11,194	0	72,100
46	Expansion Planning		46,581	0	0
47					

hidden. Similarly, the details under Personnel Costs have been grouped so that rows 31 and 32 are hidden. Other groupings have been created, but they are not active in the view shown in Figure 5.8. By selecting among the + and − symbols to the left of the worksheet, the user can tailor the display.

5.3.3 Design a Workbook as a Decision-Support System

Frequently, a spreadsheet evolves from a single use by its developer to repeated use by multiple users or a team. When this evolution takes place, the spreadsheet has become a decision-support system. A **decision-support system** is an integrated information system that provides data, analytics, and reporting capabilities over an extended period of time to multiple users. The Northern Museum model is a decision-support system because the Board and the executive director regularly use it to address a variety of budget and planning issues. In fact, one of the keys to its success is that it has helped the various interested parties at the Museum focus on a common way to think about and plan for the future.

Effective decision-support systems are designed to present information in a manner that is most useful to decision makers. Often, this means using graphs instead of tables of numbers, as in most Excel models. In the National Museum model, nine ratios are calculated in the Long-term Model sheet. These ratios indicate how the Museum is performing over time on important aspects of its operation, such as the ratio of general admission revenues to total expenditures (row 62). Museum professionals track this ratio carefully and compare it to the results of similar museums to understand the financial health of the operation. In order to make this information most useful, the tables in the Long-term Model sheet are displayed in the form of graphs in the Ratio charts sheet. While the treasurer, who is most familiar with the model, concentrates on the Assumptions and Long-term Model sheets, other users naturally concentrate on the graphical summaries in the Ratio graphs sheet.

If a workbook will be used by multiple users, it is important to protect the contents of the workbook from unwanted changes. In the Advertising Budget example, if we wanted to protect all the cells other than the decision variables, we would first lock all cells, then unlock the cells for the advertising allocation, and finally protect the entire worksheet. The details are as follows. First, we select the entire worksheet. Then, we select Home▶Font↘, choose the Protection tab, and check the box for Locked (Figure 5.9). Next, we repeat the process for the decision variables, first selecting the range C18:F18. Again, we select Home▶Font↘ and

FIGURE 5.9 The Protection Tab in the Format Cells Window

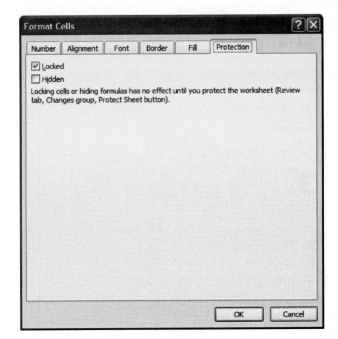

FIGURE 5.10 The Protect
Sheet Window

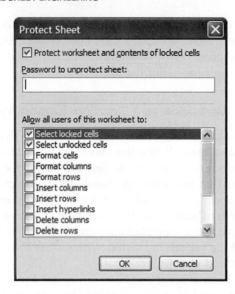

choose the Protection tab, but this time we uncheck the box for Locked. Finally, we
protect the entire worksheet, using Review▶Changes▶Protect Sheet. At the top of
the Protect Sheet window (Figure 5.10), we check the box for Protect worksheet.
In the lower window, there is a list of actions that can be allowed users. If we check
only the box for Select locked cells, then a user will be able to select and modify
only the decision variable cells. It will not be possible to select other cells. On the
other hand, if we check the boxes for Select locked cells and Select unlocked
cells, then the user will be able to select any of the locked cells (e.g., to verify a
formula) but will not be permitted to alter the contents of those cells.

It can also be useful to ensure that only legitimate values are used as inputs. This
process is called **data validation**, a technique that is highly recommended for workbooks available to multiple users over an extended period. To invoke data validation,
highlight the cells involved and click on Data▶Data Tools▶Data Validation. The
Data Validation window contains three tabs, as shown in Figure 5.11. On the first tab,
we can restrict the allowable inputs to a cell—for example, to require a number (as
opposed to text) and one that lies between certain minimum and maximum values. In
the Advertising Budget example, we require a user to enter a price that lies between
unit cost (cell C8) and $100. On the second tab, we have an option of creating an input
message that will appear whenever the cursor is placed on this cell. This message
functions like a cell comment. On the third tab, we can design an error alert for the
case of an invalid entry. An example for the Advertising Budget spreadsheet is shown

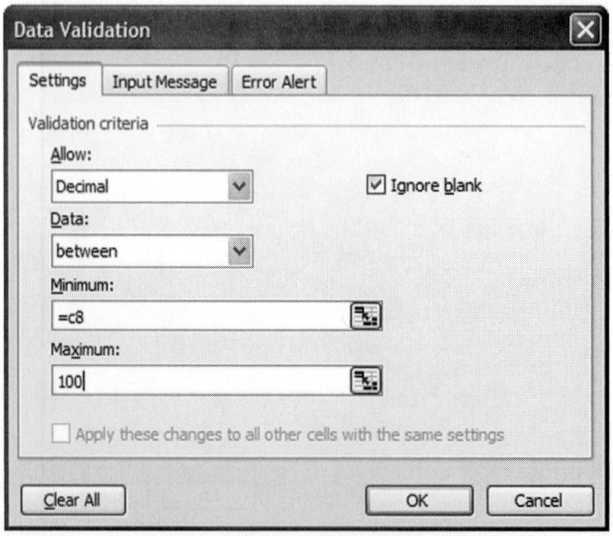

FIGURE 5.11 The Data
Validation Window

FIGURE 5.12 Error Alert
Produced by Data Validation

in Figure 5.12, which shows the error alert when we attempt to enter a price greater than $100 or less than the unit cost.

5.4 BUILDING A WORKBOOK

The second stage in creating a useful spreadsheet model is actually building it. Since most spreadsheet users do not consciously design their spreadsheets, they merge the designing and building processes. The usual result is that a great deal of time and energy are wasted fixing mistakes and redesigning a model that should have been designed once at the start.

A well-*designed* spreadsheet should be easy and quick to *build*. However, speed is not the only criterion here. Most bugs in spreadsheets are introduced during the building process. Therefore, learning to build spreadsheets without introducing errors is also vital. All of the guidelines in this section are designed to make the building process routine, repeatable, and error-free.

5.4.1 Follow a Plan

Having gone to the trouble of sketching the spreadsheet, we should follow the sketch when building. With a sufficiently detailed sketch, the building process itself becomes largely mechanical and therefore less prone to mistakes.

5.4.2 Build One Worksheet or Module at a Time

Rather than trying to build an entire workbook at one pass, it is usually more efficient to build a single worksheet or module and test it out before proceeding. For one thing, as we build the first module, we may discover that the design itself can be improved, so it is best to have made a limited investment in the original design before revising it. Another rationale for this advice is to localize the potential effects of an error. If we make an error, its effects are likely to be limited mainly to the module we're building. By staying focused on that module, we can fix errors early, before they infect other modules that we build later.

5.4.3 Predict the Outcome of Each Formula

For each formula entered, predict the numerical value expected from it before pressing the Enter key. Ask what order of magnitude to expect in the result, and give some thought to any outcomes that don't correspond to predictions. This discipline helps to uncover bugs: without a prediction, every numerical outcome tends to look plausible. At the same time, a prediction that is orders of magnitude different from the calculated number provides an opportunity for error. For example, if we predict $100,000 for annual revenue, and the calculated value comes to $100,000,000, then there is a flaw either in our intuition or in our formula. Either way, we can benefit: our intuition may be sharpened, or we may detect an error in need of fixing.

5.4.4 Copy and Paste Formulas Carefully

The Copy-and-Paste commands in Excel are not simply time-savers; they are also helpful in avoiding bugs. Instead of entering structurally similar formulas several times, we copy and paste a formula. Repetition can be a source of errors, and copying formulas can diminish the potential for this type of error. Careless copying is also a source of bugs. One of the most common errors is to select the wrong range for copying—for example, selecting one cell too few in copying a formula across a row. Recognizing this problem keeps us alert to the possibility of a copying error, and we are therefore more likely to avoid it.

5.4.5 Use Relative and Absolute Addressing to Simplify Copying

Efficient copying depends on skillful use of relative and absolute addressing. Remember that an address such as B7 is interpreted in a *relative* fashion in Excel: if the highlighted cell is A6, B7 is read as the cell one row down and one column to the right. When we include a cell with a relative address in a formula and then copy the formula, the cell address changes to preserve the relative position between the highlighted cell and the input cell. On the other hand, an *absolute* address, such as $B$6, refers to the cell B6 regardless of the location of the highlighted cell. When a formula with an absolute address is copied, the address remains $B$6. Absolute addresses are usually used when referring to a parameter, because the location of the parameter is fixed.

5.4.6 Use the Function Wizard to Ensure Correct Syntax

The button f_x on the standard toolbar brings up the Insert Function window, which contains a complete listing of all the functions built into Excel. It is not necessary to memorize the exact syntax of an occasionally used function, or to guess at the correct syntax, because help is available. For example, we might want to calculate the payment on a car loan once in a while, but it is difficult to memorize the exact form of the PMT function. Whenever this function is needed, click on the Insert Function button and select PMT. A window then appears that shows what inputs the function needs and in what order (see Figure 5.13). This window even calculates the value of the function when its inputs are specified, thus providing quick feedback on whether the results are as expected.

5.4.7 Use Range Names to Make Formulas Easy to Read

Any cell or range of cells in a spreadsheet can be given a name. This name can then be used in formulas to refer to the contents of the cell. If cell B6 is named VblCost, we can use either B6 or VblCost interchangeably in any formula. Obviously, it is easier to understand a formula that uses range names than one that uses cell addresses.

FIGURE 5.13 Function Arguments Window

Function Arguments

PMT

Rate	0.1	= 0.1
Nper	20	= 20
Pv	10000	= 10000
Fv		= number
Type		= number

= -1174.596248

Calculates the payment for a loan based on constant payments and a constant interest rate.

Rate is the interest rate per period for the loan. For example, use 6%/4 for quarterly payments at 6% APR.

Formula result =   ($1,174.60)

Help on this function   OK   Cancel

FIGURE 5.14 New Name Window

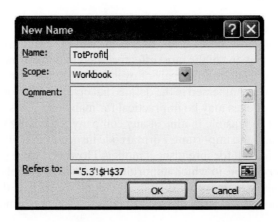

Formulas containing descriptive names are easier for the developer to debug and easier for new users to understand.

Range names require extra work to enter and maintain, so they may not be worth the effort in simple spreadsheets destined for one-time use. But in a spreadsheet that will become a permanent tool or be used by other analysts after the designer has moved on, it is a good idea to use range names to help subsequent users understand the details. Some firms require that all major spreadsheets use range names throughout.

We can assign a name to a cell or a range of cells by selecting Insert▶ Formulas▶Defined Names▶Define Name and specifying the relevant cell range (see Figure 5.14). For example, in the spreadsheet of Figure 5.3, we have assigned the name TotProfit to cell H37. This allows us to use the formula =TotProfit in C21, our main output cell. (To view all the range names in use, look in the pull-down window at the top of the spreadsheet, to the left of the formula window.) As a more ambitious example, we can assign the name Price to cell C7 and the name Sales to the range D27:G27 (by highlighting the four-cell range before defining the name). Then, the revenue formulas in cells D28:G28 can be entered as =Price*Sales. This makes the formulas easier to interpret and reduces the possibility for errors.

5.4.8 Choose Input Data to Make Errors Stand Out

Most modelers naturally use realistic values for input parameters as they build their spreadsheets. This has the advantage that the results look plausible, but it has the disadvantage that the results are difficult to check. For example, if the expected price is $25.99 and unit sales are 126,475, revenues will be calculated as $3,287,085.25. We could check this with a calculator, but it is not easy to check by eye. However, if we input arbitrary values of $10 for price and 100 for unit sales, we can easily check that our formula for revenue is correct if it shows a result of $1,000. Generally speaking, it saves time in the long run to input arbitrary but simple values for the input parameters (for example, 1, 10, and 100) during the initial building sequence. Once the spreadsheet has been debugged with these arbitrary values, it is then a simple matter to replace them with the actual input values.

5.5 TESTING A WORKBOOK

Even a carefully designed and built spreadsheet may contain errors. Errors can arise from incorrect references in formulas, from inaccurate copying and pasting, from lack of parameterization, and from a host of other sources. There is no recipe to follow for finding all bugs. When a bug is found late in the analysis phase, the user must backtrack to fix the bug *and* to repeat most or all of the previous analysis. This can be avoided by carefully testing the spreadsheet before using it for analysis.

The tips we offer here can help an end user test whether a model is correct. However, common sense and the experience of thousands of professional programmers suggest that one of the most effective ways to find errors in a model is to give it to an outsider to test. Another pair of eyes can often find errors that have eluded the builder, who is so immersed in the details that errors are no longer detectable. Finding another pair of eyes may be impractical for many end users who work on their own, but it should be feasible in almost any company, especially when the spreadsheet is large, complex, and important. Formal code inspection, as practiced by professionals, is rarely carried out for spreadsheet models. However, some sophisticated companies practice *peer review,* in which important spreadsheet models are examined in detail by individuals or teams other than the builders. We suspect this practice will become more common as the risks of spreadsheet errors become more widely appreciated.

5.5.1 Check That Numerical Results Look Plausible

The most important tool for keeping a spreadsheet error-free is a skeptical attitude. As we build the spreadsheet, we transform input parameters into a set of intermediate results that eventually lead to final outcomes. As these numbers gradually appear, it is important to check that they look reasonable. We offer three distinct ways to accomplish this:

- Make rough estimates.
- Check with a calculator.
- Test extreme cases.

Make Rough Estimates   In an earlier section, we recommended predicting the rough magnitude of the result of each formula before pressing Enter. This helps catch errors as they are made. Similarly, it is a good idea to scan the completed spreadsheet and to check that critical results are the correct order of magnitude. For example, in the Advertising Budget example, if we sell about 3,000 units in Q3 at $40 each, we should make about $120,000. This calculation can be made in our heads, and it helps to confirm that the value in cell F28 ($127,700) is probably accurate.

Check with a Calculator   A more formal approach to error detection is to check some portion of the spreadsheet on a calculator. Pick a typical column or row and check the entire sequence of calculations. Errors often occur in the last row or column due to problems in Copy-and-Paste operations, so check these areas, too.

Test Extreme Cases   If the logic behind a spreadsheet is correct, it should give logical results even with unrealistic assumptions. For example, if we set Price to $0, we should have zero revenues. Extreme cases such as this are useful for debugging because the correct results are easy to predict. Note, however, that just because a spreadsheet gives zero revenues when we set Price to $0 does not guarantee that the logic will be correct for all cases.

In the Advertising Budget example, if we price at cost, we should get a Gross Margin of zero. We can make this test by entering $25 for Price in C7 and then observing that Gross Margin in D30:G30 becomes zero. Testing extreme cases is one of the tools professional programmers use that end users can easily adopt as their own.

5.5.2 Check That Formulas Are Correct

Most spreadsheet errors occur in formulas. We can reduce the possibility of errors by making formulas short and using multiple cells to calculate a complex result. We can also reduce errors by using recursive formulas wherever possible, so that successive formulas in a row or column have the same form. Yet another good idea is to design the spreadsheet so that formulas use as inputs only cells that are above and to the left and are as close as possible. But having taken all these precautions, we still need to test that formulas are correct before beginning the analysis. We offer seven ways to perform this testing.

- Check visually.
- Display individual cell references.
- Display all formulas.
- Use the Auditing Tools.
- Use Error Checking.
- Use error traps.
- Use auditing software.

Check Visually Most end users check formulas one at a time, by highlighting each cell in a row or column in sequence and visually auditing the formula. This procedure can work fairly well, especially if the formulas are recursive so that many cell references change in a predictable way or do not change at all from cell to cell. A visual check also works best if range names are used. This method is extremely tedious, however, and tedious methods encourage carelessness. Several better methods are described in the following sections.

Display Individual Cell References Another way to check formulas is to use the cell-edit capability, invoked either by pressing the F2 key or by double-clicking on the cell of interest. This reveals the formula in the cell, displayed with color-coded cell references. Each cell that appears in the formula is highlighted by a selection border, which is color-coded to the cell reference in the formula. Often, the locations of the cell references in a formula give visual clues to whether a formula is correctly structured. When an error is found, it is often possible to drag a highlighted border to a different cell as a means of correcting the address in the formula. This method is preferred to scanning formulas because it provides stronger visual clues for locating logical errors.

Display All Formulas Another excellent device is to display all the formulas in the spreadsheet by holding down the Control key and pressing the tilde key (~) on the upper-left corner of the main keyboard (Control + ~). This displays all the spreadsheet formulas, as shown in Figure 5.15, making them easier to scan. Usually, successive formulas in a row or column have some consistent pattern. For example,

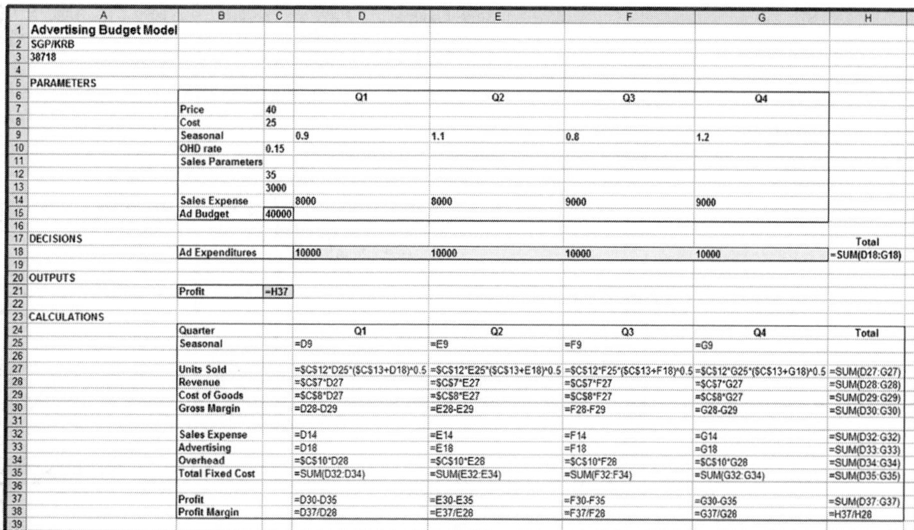

	A	B	C	D	E	F	G	H
1	**Advertising Budget Model**							
2	SGP/KRB							
3	38718							
4								
5	PARAMETERS							
6				Q1	Q2	Q3	Q4	
7		Price	40					
8		Cost	25					
9		Seasonal		0.9	1.1	0.8	1.2	
10		OHD rate	0.15					
11		Sales Parameters						
12			35					
13			3000					
14		Sales Expense		8000	8000	9000	9000	
15		Ad Budget	40000					
16								
17	DECISIONS							Total
18		Ad Expenditures		10000	10000	10000	10000	=SUM(D18:G18)
19								
20	OUTPUTS							
21		Profit	=H37					
22								
23	CALCULATIONS							
24		Quarter		Q1	Q2	Q3	Q4	Total
25		Seasonal		=D9	=E9	=F9	=G9	
26								
27		Units Sold		=$C$12*D25*($C$13+D18)^0.5	=$C$12*E25*($C$13+E18)^0.5	=$C$12*F25*($C$13+F18)^0.5	=$C$12*G25*($C$13+G18)^0.5	=SUM(D27:G27)
28		Revenue		=$C$7*D27	=$C$7*E27	=$C$7*F27	=$C$7*G27	=SUM(D28:G28)
29		Cost of Goods		=$C$8*D27	=$C$8*E27	=$C$8*F27	=$C$8*G27	=SUM(D29:G29)
30		Gross Margin		=D28-D29	=E28-E29	=F28-F29	=G28-G29	=SUM(D30:G30)
31								
32		Sales Expense		=D14	=E14	=F14	=G14	=SUM(D32:G32)
33		Advertising		=D18	=E18	=F18	=G18	=SUM(D33:G33)
34		Overhead		=$C$10*D28	=$C$10*E28	=$C$10*F28	=$C$10*G28	=SUM(D34:G34)
35		Total Fixed Cost		=SUM(D32:D34)	=SUM(E32:E34)	=SUM(F32:F34)	=SUM(G32:G34)	=SUM(D35:G35)
36								
37		Profit		=D30-D35	=E30-E35	=F30-F35	=G30-G35	=SUM(D37:G37)
38		Profit Margin		=D37/D28	=E37/E28	=F37/F28	=G37/G28	=H37/H28
39								

FIGURE 5.15 Displaying Formulas in the Advertising Budget Spreadsheet

one cell reference is absolute and does not change, while another is relative and changes from D28 to E28 to F28, and so on. If there is an error, it can often be detected as a break in a pattern. (Return the spreadsheet to its normal form by pressing Control + ~ again.)

In the spreadsheet for the Advertising Budget example, note the similar structure in the four formulas for Gross Margin in the range D30:G30. A copying error would show up as a break in the pattern here.

Use the Excel Auditing Tools Another useful and underutilized set of debugging tools in Excel is available on the ribbon under Formulas ▶ Formula Auditing. These options can be used to identify the cells used to calculate a given cell (its **predecessors**) or the cells it is used to calculate (its **dependents**). The `Trace Precedents` option draws colored arrows to the predecessors of a given cell. Invoking the `Trace Precedents` option again from this point will identify the predecessors of the predecessors, and so on, reaching backward into the logic of the calculations. The `Trace Dependents` option works similarly, but in the forward direction. The arrows convey a pattern of information flow, which should conform to the underlying logic of the model. For debugging purposes, the auditing tools can be used to display the information flows related to a group of cells. If these cells have a parallel or recursive structure, there should be a distinctive pattern in the arrows produced by the auditing tools. As with displaying formulas, bugs often show up as unexpected breaks in the pattern of these arrows.

In the spreadsheet for the Advertising Budget example, suppose we select cell H38. Next, we choose the option for `Trace Precedents` several times in succession. The cells that are used to calculate profit are highlighted, then their predecessors are highlighted, and so on, as shown in Figure 5.16. Again, an error in the formulas would show up as a break in these visual patterns. (Use the `Remove Arrows` option to erase the auditing arrows.)

FIGURE 5.16 Using the Auditing Toolbar in the Advertising Budget Spreadsheet

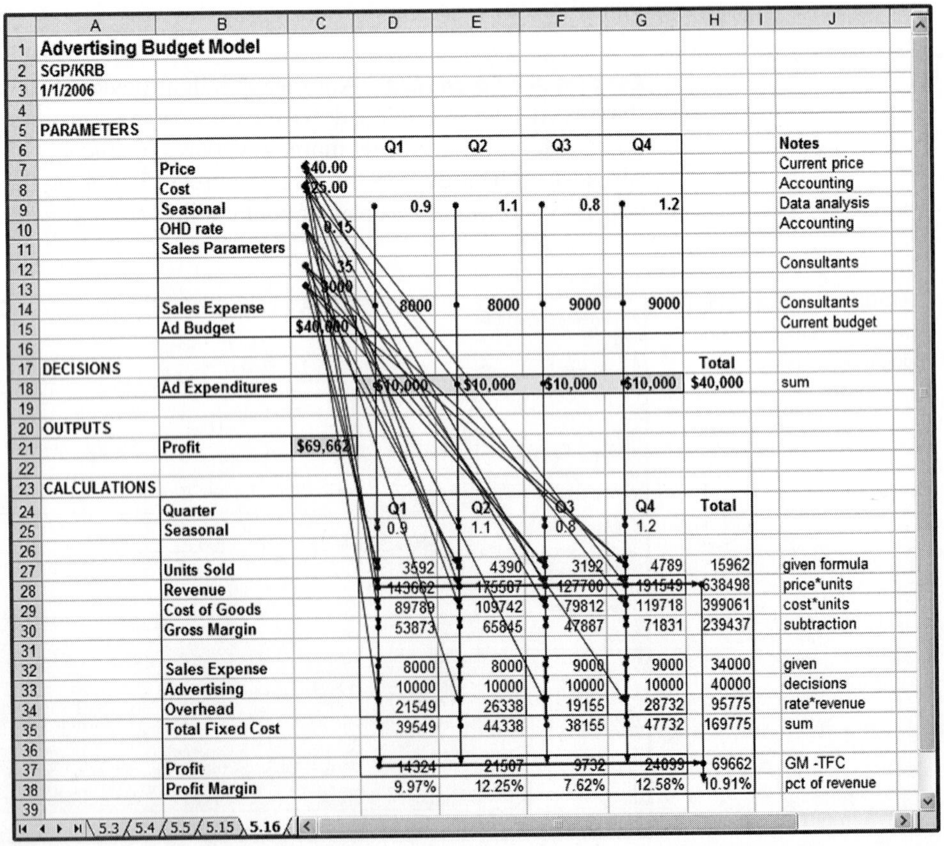

	A	B	C	D	E	F	G	H	I	J
1	Advertising Budget Model									
2	SGP/KRB									
3	1/1/2006									
4										
5	PARAMETERS									
6				Q1	Q2	Q3	Q4			Notes
7		Price	$40.00							Current price
8		Cost	$25.00							Accounting
9		Seasonal		0.9	1.1	0.8	1.2			Data analysis
10		OHD rate	0.15							Accounting
11		Sales Parameters								
12			35							Consultants
13			3000							
14		Sales Expense		8000	8000	9000	9000			Consultants
15		Ad Budget	$40,000							Current budget
16										
17	DECISIONS							Total		
18		Ad Expenditures		$10,000	$10,000	$10,000	$10,000	$40,000		sum
19										
20	OUTPUTS									
21		Profit	$69,662							
22										
23	CALCULATIONS									
24		Quarter		Q1	Q2	Q3	Q4	Total		
25		Seasonal		0.9	1.1	0.8	1.2			
26										
27		Units Sold		3592	4390	3192	4789	15962		given formula
28		Revenue		143662	175507	127700	191549	638498		price*units
29		Cost of Goods		89789	109742	79812	119718	399061		cost*units
30		Gross Margin		53873	65845	47887	71831	239437		subtraction
31										
32		Sales Expense		8000	8000	9000	9000	34000		given
33		Advertising		10000	10000	10000	10000	40000		decisions
34		Overhead		21549	26338	19155	28732	95775		rate*revenue
35		Total Fixed Cost		39549	44338	38155	47732	169775		sum
36										
37		Profit		14324	21507	9732	24099	69662		GM -TFC
38		Profit Margin		9.97%	12.25%	7.62%	12.58%	10.91%		pct of revenue
39										

FIGURE 5.17 The Error
Checking Window

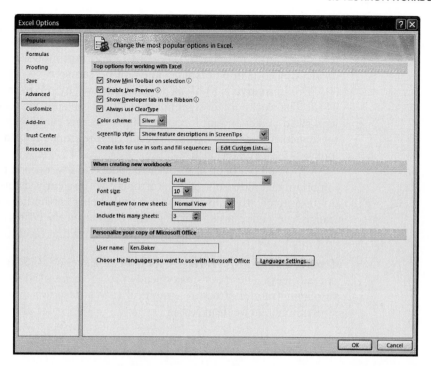

Use Excel Error Checking This is the spreadsheet equivalent of grammar checking in word processing. Error checking is managed from the Formulas tab of the Excel Options menu. The single check box under Error Checking (See Figure 5.17) chooses whether the tool is enabled or disabled. If it is enabled, then all cells that are identified as possibly containing an error are flagged with a colored triangle. (The color can be chosen under Error Checking.) The Error checking rules comprise a list of nine types of checks. Although the user can choose which of these rules to activate, we generally recommend keeping all nine boxes checked.

Three of these categories of possible errors seem to be most prevalent: formulas inconsistent with other formulas in the region, formulas which omit cells in a region, and formulas referring to empty cells. Inconsistent formulas are those that violate a pattern. For example, a recursive formula that is copied across a row but that changes its pattern of references to absolute addresses would be flagged under this category. Often, these potential errors are consciously designed into the spreadsheet, and although they are not errors, they are nonetheless indicative of poor programming practice. Formulas that omit cells in a region also violate an expected pattern. Finally, formulas that refer to empty cells are either wrong outright or at least indicate dangerous programming practice. While this Error Checking capability can highlight only certain well-defined categories of potential errors (and the user can determine which categories by using the check boxes), it is a useful tool—one that should be employed during the design and testing phases of spreadsheet construction.

Use ErrorTraps Error traps are formulas added to a spreadsheet that warn the user of potential errors. They can check for errors in input data or for errors in formulas.

A simple application is to check that row sums and column sums are consistent. For example, in cell H30 in the Advertising Budget spreadsheet we calculate total Gross Margin by adding up the four quarterly values for grow margin. But total Gross Margin can also be calculated by subtracting total Cost of Goods from total Revenue. If these two calculations do not give the same result, we have an error. An error trap can be set by entering an IF statement that checks the cells in question and returns a warning if an error occurs. For example, the statement

```
IF(SUM(D30:G30)<>(H28 - H29), "Warning: row and
         column totals do not match"," ")
```

returns the warning text when there is an error and returns a blank value otherwise.

The Long-term Model sheet of the Northern Museum workbook uses a different kind of error checking. In this situation there are two ways to calculate total costs, and both are of interest to important model users. One approach is to divide total costs into personnel and non-personnel costs. This is done in rows 29 and 30. The alternative is to break total costs down by programs, which is done in rows 34–40. The workbook designer decided that both approaches should be shown on the worksheet and even that inconsistent projections could be allowed. But to highlight these inconsistencies when they occur, the difference in total costs between the two methods is calculated in row 50.

Any number of error traps can be added to a workbook to improve its safety. It is important that the results of these error checks be clearly visible to the user. One way to do this is to create an overall error trap that checks whether *any one* of the individual traps is true, and returns a warning. This trap can be placed in a prominent place near the outputs, so a user will be unlikely to trust outputs that result from a model with errors.

Use Auditing Software A number of Excel add-ins are available for auditing spreadsheets. These add-ins typically provide a set of tools for detecting errors and displaying model structure graphically. We describe one such tool, Spreadsheet Professional, in Section 5.6.

5.5.3 Test That Model Performance Is Plausible

For many end users, the analysis phase begins while testing is still in progress. This is natural and perhaps unavoidable, although we have stressed the importance of taking a careful and structured approach to designing, building, and testing a spreadsheet *before* using it for analysis. However, if analysis begins before testing is complete, it is at least desirable to retain a skeptical attitude toward the early results from using the model. Many minor bugs come to light during analysis. More importantly, actually using the model can reveal major logical flaws. These types of errors, which usually cannot be uncovered by the most meticulous checking of formulas, can destroy the credibility of the entire modeling process.

If a spreadsheet model is logically sound and built without errors, it should react in a plausible manner to a range of input values. Thus, sensitivity testing, which we discuss in Chapter 6, can be a powerful way to uncover logical and mechanical errors. In our Advertising Budget example, if profit were to go *down* as we increased the price, we could be fairly sure we had a bug in the model. But even if we have confirmed that profits rise with price, would we expect that relationship to be linear or nonlinear? We can test our intuition and the model by calculating profit for a range of prices and graphing the results. In this model as it is currently built, that relationship is in fact linear. We might conclude that this is as we expected and intended. On the other hand, we might decide that demand should instead depend on price (which, in our model, it does not) and that the model needs further refinement.

5.6* AUDITING SOFTWARE: SPREADSHEET PROFESSIONAL

Spreadsheet Professional is an add-in to Excel that assists the end user in building, testing, documenting, and using spreadsheets. It is one of a number of software products that have appeared in recent years that offer tools for building error-free spreadsheets. Some of these tools are specialized to a particular industry or range of applications. Spreadsheet Professional, which is available with this book, is a generic tool that can be used in any application.

Spreadsheet Professional, like most software, contains many tools and options. Here, we outline the major options and illustrate by example how to use the most important ones. More details can be found by reading Spreadsheet Professional Help or visiting the website www.spreadsheetinnovations.com.

5.6.1 Building tools

Spreadsheet Professional offers five tools to assist in building spreadsheet models.

Standard format: Formats the first three columns of a new spreadsheet to accept row titles, units, and source.

Build bar: Simplifies entering and copying formulas by allowing the user to copy the formula and its format to any number of cells in one step.

Translation bar: Translates formulas into English equivalents.

Spreadsheet Painter: Colors cells according to whether they are inputs, formulas, or labels.

Spreadsheet Formula Tracer: Displays the antecedents of a cell to any depth required. For example, in Figure 5.18 we use the Formula Tracer to show the antecedents of Profit in the Advertising Budget model. This display shows the cell address, its label (if any), its numerical value, and its formula.

5.6.2 Testing Tools

Spreadsheet Professional provides two related error-checking tools. The Spreadsheet Checker tests cells one by one for violations of any of 25 test conditions. The Spreadsheet Reports tool runs a batch test looking for violations in the entire workbook (or any selected worksheets) and writes the results to another workbook.

FIGURE 5.18 The Formula Tracer in Spreadsheet Professional

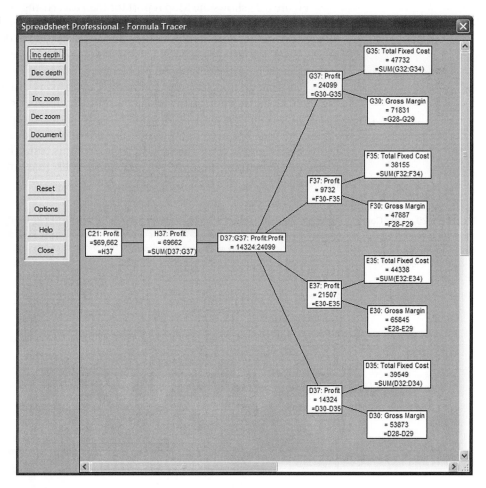

FIGURE 5.19 The Spreadsheet Checker in
Spreadsheet Professional

Figure 5.19 shows the results of selecting the Checker when cell C21 is highlighted in the Advertising Budget model. The window displays the contents of the cell (=H37) and notes that it violates the test condition Unused calculation. Click Continue, and the Checker lists any additional error conditions the current cell violates and then moves on to the next cell in which a violation occurs. Click Precedents, and it lists all the cells used to calculate the current cell and their contents.

Figure 5.20 shows the 25 test conditions Spreadsheet Professional can identify. (Navigate to this window by selecting from the Spreadsheet Professional toolbar Test▶Spreadsheet Test Reports tool▶Options▶Test options.) Note that many of these conditions represent poor spreadsheet engineering but are not necessarily errors in the sense of cells producing wrong results. However, it is good practice to allow Spreadsheet Professional to test for all of these conditions.

The Spreadsheet Reports tool provides eight distinct analyses of a given workbook (see Figure 5.21). The most useful are the Map report and the Calculation test report, one of which is produced for each sheet. The Map report displays the structure of a worksheet by denoting the contents of each cell as a Label (L), Number (N), or Formula (F). The Calculations test report lists all the cells that violate any of the 25 test conditions.

Figure 5.22 shows the Map report for the Advertising Budget model. This report is best used to identify copying errors. The symbol "<" is used to denote a formula cell that has been copied from the left; the symbol "∧" is used to denote a cell copied from above. Note, for instance, cells H27, H32, and H37. These cells break a pattern of cell copying in their rows and may be problematic.

The Calculation test report for the Advertising Budget model is shown in Figure 5.23. This report provides a count of the number of cells that violate each test condition along with their cell addresses. For example, under the condition Unused input value, it describes the condition and explains why it may be problematic, and it notes that cell C15 violates this test. This report can be used to focus the debugging activity on just those cells that are most likely to cause problems.

FIGURE 5.20 Error Conditions in Spreadsheet Professional

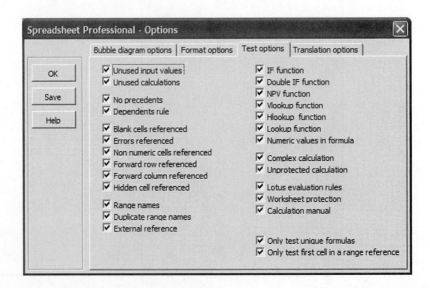

FIGURE 5.21 Report Selection Window in Spreadsheet Professional

5.6.3 Documenting Tools

Many of the reports that are created by the Spreadsheets Reports tool can be used to document a spreadsheet. The following eight reports are provided:

Summary: Provides background information on the workbook and its worksheets

Range names: Lists all range names and external references

FIGURE 5.22 Map Report for Advertising Budget

	A	B	C	D	E	F	G	H	I	J
1	L									
2	L									
3	N									
4										
5	L									
6				L	L	L	L			L
7		L	N							L
8		L	N							L
9		L		N	N	N	N			L
10		L	N							L
11		L								
12			N							L
13			N							
14		L		N	N	N	N			L
15		L	N							L
16										
17	L							L		
18		L		N	N	N	N	F		L
19		L		L		L				
20	L			L				L		
21		L	F		L	N		L		
22										
23	L									
24		L		L	L	L	L	L		
25		L		F	<	<	<			
26										
27		L		F	<	<	<	F		L
28		L		F	<	<	<	^		L
29		L		F	<	<	<	^		L
30		L		F	<	<	<	^		L
31										
32		L		F	<	<	<	F		L
33		L		F	<	<	<	^		L
34		L		F	<	<	<	^		L
35		L		F	<	<	<	^		L
36										
37		L		F	<	<	<	F		L
38		L		F	<	<	<	<		L
39										

FIGURE 5.23 Calculation Test Report for Advertising Budget

	A	B	
3	**Summary statistics**		
4	**Range analysed**	A1:K40	
5	**Number of numeric inputs**	20	
6	**Number of formulas**	56	
7	**Number of unique formulas**	22	
8	Unique cells are those that are not copies of the cell to their left.		
9	**Percentage of unique formulas**	39%	
10	**Number of labels**	63	
11			
12	**Potential errors summary**		
13	**Possible error condition**	**Frequency**	
14	Unused input value	1	
15	Unused calculation	10	
16	Forward row reference	1	
17	Forward column reference	1	
18	Numeric rule	1	
19			
20			
21	**Protection not enabled.**		
22	This sheet is not protected. Users can overwrite the		
23	contents of any cell even if the cell is locked.		
24	**Test notes.**		
25	Only unique cells have been tested.		
26	Remember to check cells that are a copy of the cells shown on this report.		
27			
28	Only the first cell in each range referenced by a formula has been tested.		
29			
30	**Unused input value**		
31	A number has been entered which is not used in any calculation. Potential errors to watch for:		
32	1. A calculation contains an incorrect reference.		
33	2. The writer of the spreadsheet may have forgotten that this input value exists and hard coded the value directly into subsequent calculations.		
34	C15		
35			
36	**Unused calculation**		
37	The results from this calculation are not used elsewhere on this worksheet Potential errors to watch for:		
38	1. The results should be used but there is an incorrect reference in a subsequent calculation.		
39	H18, C21, H27, H29:H30, H32:H35, D38		
40			

Maps: Codes cells as labels, numbers, or formulas (described above)

Translation of calculations: Translates calculations into English

Blank input worksheets: Provides a blank form for collecting all inputs

Current input values: Reports the current value of all inputs

General tests: Examines the workbook for problematic conditions, such as manual calculation

Calculation tests: Tests each formula for violations of 25 test conditions (described above)

5.6.4 Usage Tools

Spreadsheet Professional also provides several productivity tools. One is a sensitivity analysis tool, which is similar to the Data Sensitivity tool described in Chapter 6. Another is a breakeven tool, which is similar to Excel's Goal Seek tool, also described in Chapter 6. Finally, it provides the Spreadsheet Comparison tool, which allows a cell-by-cell comparison of two spreadsheets to find the differences.

5.7 SUMMARY

Spreadsheets are important throughout business, and important tools deserve careful engineering. Although spreadsheet modeling is not a science, we can enumerate a set of guidelines for designing, building, and testing our spreadsheets. Our guidelines have evolved from our observations working with both experienced and inexperienced model builders. These guidelines are designed to make the process of spreadsheet development both more efficient and more effective.

The available evidence suggests strongly that most spreadsheets in use contain errors and that their developers are overconfident about the reliability of their models. The implication is that we should be humble about our ability to develop spreadsheets that correctly implement the models we have conceived. Care and effort are required to build models successfully. Some useful lessons can be learned from professional programmers—most importantly, *be skeptical* and *test thoroughly*.

Here is a summary list of the guidelines given in this chapter.

Designing a Spreadsheet

1. Sketch the spreadsheet.
2. Organize the spreadsheet into modules.
3. Start small.
4. Isolate input parameters.
5. Design for use.
6. Keep it simple.
7. Design for communication.
8. Document important data and formulas.

Designing a Workbook

1. Use separate spreadsheets to group like information.
2. Design workbooks for ease of navigation and use.
3. Design a workbook as a decision support system.

Building a Workbook

1. Follow a plan.
2. Build one module at a time.
3. Predict the outcome of each formula.
4. Copy and Paste formulas carefully.
5. Use relative and absolute addressing to simplify copying.
6. Use the Function Wizard to ensure correct syntax.
7. Use range names to make formulas easy to read.
8. Choose input data to make errors stand out.

Testing a Workbook

1. Check that numerical results look plausible.
2. Check that formulas are correct.
3. Test that model performance is plausible.

SUGGESTED READINGS

The most thoughtful writing on spreadsheet design has appeared not in books but in journal articles. We list some useful articles here. More information can be found in references compiled in the Edwards and Panko articles.

Caine, D. J., and A. J. Robinson. 1993. "Spreadsheet Modeling: Guidelines for Model Development." *Management Decision* 31, 38–44.

Conway, D. G., and C. T. Ragsdale. 1997. "Modeling Optimization Problems in the Unstructured World of Spreadsheets." *Omega* 25, 313–322.

Edwards, J. S., P. N. Finlay, and J. M. Wilson. 2000. "The Role of OR Specialists in 'Do It Yourself' Spreadsheet Development." *European Journal of Operational Research* 127, 14–27.

Panko, R. R. 1999. "Applying Code Inspection to Spreadsheet Testing." *Journal of Management Information Systems* 16, 159–176.

The following short monographs and websites contain more detailed recommendations for best practices in spreadsheet design, building, and testing:

BPM Analytical. 2004. "Best Practice Spreadsheet Modelling Standards." http://www.bpmhome.com/bpm_standards.html.

Mailbarrow. Undated. "52 Ways to Prevent Spreadsheet Problems." http://www.mailbarrow.com/pdf/PreventingSpreadsheet- Problems_FULL_sample.pdf.

Raffensperger, J. F., 2002. "The Art of the Spreadsheet." http://www.SpreadsheetStyle.com.

Read, N., and J. Batson. 1999. "Spreadsheet Modeling Best Practice." http://www.eusprig.org/smbp.pdf.

EXERCISES

The following exercises refer to the cases in the back of this book. Read the case description carefully, sketch an appropriate spreadsheet on paper, then build and test a prototype model. The purpose of the model is specified in the question.

1. Refer to the XYZ Company case. Design a spreadsheet that will allow an analyst to predict the month in which the cash balance falls below zero, signaling a need to borrow money.

2. Refer to the Medical Supplies for Banjul case. Design a spreadsheet that will enable you to request the required funds from your team's finance officer, order supplies from the home office, and ensure dissemination of appropriate quantities to each village. Your final order to the home office should specify the number of packages required of each item.

3. Refer to the Reid's Raisins case. Design a spreadsheet that will allow the firm to project profit for base-case conditions; the open market grape price is $0.30.

4. Refer to the Big Rig Rental Company case. Design a spreadsheet that will allow the firm to determine the Net Present Value of cash flows over the five-year period.

5. Refer to the Flexible Insurance Coverage case. Design a spreadsheet that will allow an individual employee with estimated annual medical expenses of $400 to compare the total expenses under each plan.

6. Refer to the Snoey Software Company case. Design a spreadsheet that will determine the annual profit when the prices for the Educational, Large-Scale, and Professional versions are $100, $300, and $500, respectively.

7. Refer to the Cox Cable and Wire Company case. In the role of Meredith, design a spreadsheet with which to find a machine schedule and a corresponding inventory and shipment schedule that meets demand. What is the profit contribution of this schedule?

8. Refer to the BMW Company case. Design a spreadsheet that will allow the firm's managers to estimate what percentage of the firm's net income 10 years into the future will be devoted to disposal of vehicles, assuming there are no changes in trends and policies.

9. Refer to the ERP Decision case. Design a spreadsheet that will assist the Board in evaluating the net benefits of implementing the ERP system.

10. Refer to the Retirement Planning case. Review the problem statement and influence diagram that were generated for this case in conjunction with the corresponding exercise in Chapter 2. (If this has not yet been done, develop the problem statement and influence diagram as preliminary steps.) Design a spreadsheet to estimate the impact on Davidson's retirement of increasing his annual retirement savings by 10 percent.

11. Refer to the Draft TV Commercials case. Review the problem statement and influence diagram that were generated for this case in conjunction with the corresponding exercises in Chapter 2. (If this has not yet been done, develop the problem statement and influence diagram as preliminary steps.) Design a spreadsheet to determine the impact on ad quality of paying for three draft commercials.

12. Refer to the Icebergs for Kuwait case. Review the problem statement and influence diagram that were generated for this case in conjunction with the corresponding exercises in Chapter 2. (If this has not yet been done, develop the problem statement and influence diagram as preliminary steps.) Design a spreadsheet to estimate the economic value of the freshwater produced by towing the largest possible iceberg using the largest available boat.

13. Refer to the Racquetball Racket case. Review the problem statement and influence diagram that were generated for this case in conjunction with the corresponding exercises in Chapter 2. (If this has not yet been done, develop the problem statement and influence diagram as preliminary steps.) Design a spreadsheet to evaluate the Net Present Value of selling the new ball at $0.65, assuming the competitor does not change prices.

6 Analysis Using Spreadsheets

6.1 INTRODUCTION

In the previous chapter, we pointed out that spreadsheet models often play a critical role in business planning and analysis. Because of their importance, spreadsheets should not be created haphazardly. Instead, they should be carefully engineered. We recommended a process for designing, building, and testing a spreadsheet that is both efficient and effective. Not only does this process minimize the likelihood that the spreadsheet contains errors, but it also prepares the user to investigate the business questions at hand in the analytic phase of the modeling process. In this chapter we provide a structure for this investigation and present the essential Excel tools that support analysis. Advanced methods, and the Excel tools that go with them, are elaborated in later chapters.

We have found that, over time, most analysts develop their own informal approaches to the analytic phase of modeling. Many of us have favorite tools that we tend to rely on, even when they are not really adequate to the task. But it is difficult to develop a *complete* set of analytic tools simply through experience. An analyst who does not know a particular tool generally does not think to ask the business question that the tool helps answer. By the same token, an analyst with a complete analytic toolkit would be more likely to ask the right questions.

Although Excel itself has thousands of features, most of the analysis done with spreadsheets falls into one of the following five categories:

- Base-case analysis
- What-if analysis
- Breakeven analysis
- Optimization analysis
- Risk analysis

Within each of these categories, there are specific Excel tools—such as the Goal Seek tool—and add-ins—such as Crystal Ball and Solver—which can be used either to automate tedious calculations or to find powerful business insights that cannot be found any other way. Some of these tools are quite complex and will be given more complete treatment in later chapters. Here, we provide only a brief introduction to these tools so as to give the reader an overview of the process of spreadsheet analysis. By contrast, some of the other tools we describe in this chapter are extremely simple, yet they seem to be underutilized by the majority of analysts.

Once again, we draw on the Advertising Budget example, which was introduced in Chapter 5, to illustrate the different kinds of analysis. Here is a sample of the kinds of questions we answer in this chapter:

- If we follow last year's plan to spend the same amount on advertising in each quarter, how much profit can we expect to make?
- How much will profit change if our product costs turn out to be 10 percent higher or lower than we have assumed?
- If our product costs rise, at what point will profit reach zero?

- What is the maximum profit we can make with an advertising budget of $40,000?
- How likely is it that we will lose money if price and cost are uncertain?

6.2 BASE-CASE ANALYSIS

Almost every spreadsheet analysis involves measuring outcomes relative to some common point of comparison, or **base case**. Therefore, it's worth giving some thought to how the base case is chosen. A base case is often drawn from current policy or common practice, but many other alternatives are available. Where there is considerable uncertainty in the decision problem, it may be appropriate for the base case to depict the most likely scenario; in other circumstances, the worst case or the best case might be a good choice.

Sometimes, several base cases are used during the course of analysis. For example, we might start the analysis with a version of the model that takes last year's results as the base case. Later in the analysis, we might develop another base case using a proposed plan for the coming year. At either stage, the base case is the starting point from which an analyst can explore the model using the tools described in this chapter, and thereby gain insights into the corresponding business situation. The base case also sets the tone for presenting results to decision makers.

In the Advertising Budget example, most of the input parameters such as price and cost are forecasts for the coming year. These inputs would typically be based on previous experience, modified by our hunches as to what will be different in the coming year. But what values should we assume for the decision variables in the base case? Our ultimate goal is to find the best values for these decisions, but that is premature at this point. A natural alternative is to take last year's advertising expenditures ($10,000 in each quarter) as the base-case decisions, both because this is a simple plan and because initial indications point to a repeat for this year's decisions.

6.3 WHAT-IF ANALYSIS

Once a base case has been specified, the next step in analysis often involves nothing more sophisticated than varying one of the inputs to determine how the key outputs change. Assessing the change in outputs associated with a given change in inputs is called **what-if analysis**. The inputs may be *parameters*, in which case we are asking how sensitive our base-case results are to forecasting errors or other changes in input values. Alternatively, the inputs may be *decision variables*, in which case we are exploring whether changes in our decisions might improve our results, for a given set of parameters. Finally, there is another type of what-if analysis, in which we test the effect on the results of changing some aspect of our model's *structure*. For example, we might replace a linear relationship with a nonlinear one. In these three forms of analysis, the general idea is to alter an assumption and then trace the effect on the model's outputs.

We use the term **sensitivity analysis** interchangeably with the term *what-if analysis*. However, we are aware that sensitivity analysis sometimes conveys a distinct meaning. In the optimization models of Chapters 10–13, we use the term sensitivity analysis more narrowly to mean the effect of changing a parameter on the *optimal* outcome. (In optimization models, the term *what-if analysis* is seldom used.)

When we vary a *parameter*, we are implicitly asking what would happen if there were an unexpected change in that parameter or if our forecast of that parameter were wrong. That is, what if we had made a different numerical assumption at the outset, but everything else remained unchanged? This kind of questioning is important because the parameters in our model represent assumptions or forecasts about the environment for decision making. If the environment turns out to be different from what we had assumed, then it stands to reason that the results will also be different. What-if analysis measures that difference and helps us appreciate the potential importance of each numerical assumption.

In the Advertising Budget model, for example, if unit cost rises to $26 from $25, then annual profit drops to $53,700. In other words, an increase of 4 percent in the unit cost will reduce profit by nearly 23 percent. Thus, it would appear that profits are quite sensitive to unit cost, and in light of this insight, we may decide to monitor the market conditions that influence the material and labor components of cost.

When we vary a *decision variable*, we are changing inputs that we control. First, we'd like to know whether changing the value of a decision variable would lead to an improvement in the results. If we locate an improvement, we can then try to determine what value of the decision variable would result in the largest improvement. This kind of questioning is different from asking about a parameter, because we can act directly on what we learn. What-if analysis can thus lead us to better decisions.

In the Advertising Budget model, if we spend an additional $1,000 on advertising in the first quarter, then annual profit rises to $69,882. In other words, an increase of 10 percent in the advertising expenditure during Q1 will translate into an increase of roughly 0.3 percent in annual profit. Thus, profits seem quite insensitive to small changes in advertising expenditures in Q1, all else being equal. Nevertheless, we have identified a way to increase profits. We might guess that the small percentage change in profit reflects the fact that expenditures in the neighborhood of $10,000 are close to optimal, but we will have to gather more information before we are ready to draw conclusions about optimality.

In addition to testing the sensitivity of results to parameters and decision variables, there are situations in which we want to test the impact of some element of model structure. For example, we may have assumed that there is a linear relationship between price and sales. As part of what-if analysis, we might then ask whether a nonlinear demand relationship would materially alter our conclusions. As another example, we may have assumed that our competitors will not change their prices in the coming year. If we then determine that our own prices should increase substantially over that time, we might ask how our results would change if our competitors were to react by matching our price increases. These what-if questions are more complex than simple changes to a parameter or a decision variable because they involve alterations in the underlying structure of the model. Nonetheless, an important aspect of successful modeling is testing the sensitivity of results to key assumptions in the model's structure.

In the Advertising Budget model, the nonlinear relationship between advertising and sales plays a fundamental role. In the spirit of structural sensitivity analysis, we can ask how different our results would be if we were to replace this relationship with a linear one. For example, the linear relationship

$$Sales = 3,000 + 0.1(Advertising \times Seasonal\ Factor)$$

lies close to the nonlinear curve for advertising levels around $10,000. When we substitute this relationship into the base-case model, holding advertising constant at $10,000 each quarter, we find that profit changes only slightly, to $70,000. But in this model, if we then increase Q1 advertising by $1,000, we find that profit *decreases*, while in the base-case model it increases. Evidently, this structural assumption does have a significant impact on the desired levels of advertising.

We have illustrated what we might call a "one-at-a-time" form of what-if analysis, where we vary one input at a time, keeping other inputs unchanged. We could, of course, vary two or more inputs simultaneously, but these more complex experiments become increasingly difficult to interpret. In many cases, we can gain the necessary insights by varying the inputs one at a time.

It is important not to underestimate the power of this first step in analysis. Simple what-if exploration is one of the most effective ways to develop a deeper understanding of the model and the system it represents. It is also part of the debugging process, as we pointed out in the previous chapter. When what-if analysis reveals something unexpected, we may have found a useful insight or perhaps discovered a bug.

Predicting the outcome of a what-if test is an important part of the learning process. For example, in the Advertising Budget model, what would be the result of doubling the selling price? Would profits double as well? In the base case, with a price of $40, profits total $69,662. If we double the price, we find that profits increase to $612,386. Profits increase by much more than a factor of two when prices double. After a little thought, we should see the reasons. For one, costs do not increase in proportion to volume; for another, demand does not decline as price increases. Thus, the sensitivity test helps us to understand the nature of the cost structure—that it's not proportional—as well as one possible limitation of the model—that no link exists between demand and price.

6.3.1 Benchmarking

During what-if analysis, we repeatedly change inputs and observe the resulting change in outputs. This can get confusing unless we keep a record of the results in some organized fashion. One simple solution to this problem is to **benchmark** sensitivity results against the base case by keeping a record of the base-case outcome on the spreadsheet.

In the Advertising Budget spreadsheet, we benchmark the base-case profit of $69,662 on the spreadsheet in cell F21, as shown Figure 6.1[*]. Note that this cell contains the *number* $69,662, not a cell reference to profit in C21. We construct this entry by selecting C21 and choosing Home▶Clipboard▶Copy, then selecting F21 and choosing Home▶Clipboard▶Paste▶Paste Special with the option `Values`, as shown in Figure 6.2. With this design, the result of any new sensitivity test appears in C21, while the base-case value is maintained in F21. If we wish, we can add a cell to measure the difference in profit between the base case and the sensitivity test, or the percentage difference, if that is more useful.

FIGURE 6.1 The Advertising Budget Spreadsheet

	A	B	C	D	E	F	G	H	I	J
1	**Advertising Budget Model**									
2	SGP/KRB									
3	1/1/2006									
4										
5	PARAMETERS									
6				Q1	Q2	Q3	Q4			Notes
7		Price	$40.00							Current price
8		Cost	$25.00							Accounting
9		Seasonal		0.9	1.1	0.8	1.2			Data analysis
10		OHD rate	0.15							Accounting
11		Sales Parameters								
12			35							Consultants
13			3000							
14		Sales Expense		8000	8000	9000	9000			Consultants
15		Ad Budget	$40,000							Current budget
16										
17	DECISIONS							Total		
18		Ad Expenditures		$10,000	$10,000	$10,000	$10,000	$40,000		sum
19										
20	OUTPUTS									
21		Profit	$69,662		Base case	$69,662				
22										
23	CALCULATIONS									
24		Quarter		Q1	Q2	Q3	Q4	Total		
25		Seasonal		0.9	1.1	0.8	1.2			
26										
27		Units Sold		3592	4390	3192	4789	15962		given formula
28		Revenue		143662	175587	127700	191549	638498		price*units
29		Cost of Goods		89789	109742	79812	119718	399061		cost*units
30		Gross Margin		53873	65845	47887	71831	239437		subtraction
31										
32		Sales Expense		8000	8000	9000	9000	34000		given
33		Advertising		10000	10000	10000	10000	40000		decisions
34		Overhead		21549	26338	19155	28732	95775		rate*revenue
35		Total Fixed Cost		39549	44338	38155	47732	169775		sum
36										
37		Profit		14324	21507	9732	24099	69662		GM -TFC
38		Profit Margin		9.97%	12.25%	7.62%	12.58%	10.91%		pct of revenue
39										

Base case value of profit recorded as a fixed number.

6.1

---

[*]To download spreadsheets for this chapter, go to the Student Companion Site at www.wiley.com/college/powell.

6.3.2 Scenarios

Up to this point, we have viewed each parameter in our model as independent of all the others. But it is often the case that certain *sets* of parameters go together in some natural way. For example, in the airline industry during a recession, we might expect passenger miles to be low and interest rates also to be low. Thus, in using a model to forecast future airline profitability, we might want to analyze a recession, and to do so, we would choose low values for these two inputs. Furthermore, when we perform what-if analysis, we would vary both parameters up and down *together*, not independently.

In general, we can think of a **scenario** as a story about the future decision-making environment translated into its effects on several of the model's parameters. More specifically, a scenario is a set of parameters that describes an internally consistent view of the future. In our airline example, the story involves a recession and the impact the recession has on specific parameters affecting demand and investment. In the oil industry, a scenario might depict the breakup of the OPEC cartel and its impacts on production and exploration worldwide. In the semiconductor business, a scenario might involve a breakthrough in optical technology that leads to the first chip powered by light. To translate these stories into useful terms, we would have to determine how such events influence specific parameters in a coordinated fashion.

In the Advertising Budget example, we can construct an optimistic scenario in which prices are high ($50) and costs are low ($20), yielding a profit of $285,155. Similarly, we can construct a pessimistic scenario, in which prices are low ($35) and costs are high ($30), leading to a loss of $77,991. Each scenario tells a coherent story that has meaning to the decision makers and is implemented in the model through a set of two or more parameters. Excel's Scenario Manager provides a way to record the inputs and outputs of multiple scenarios. We select Data▶Data Tools▶What-If Analysis▶Scenario Manager and enter the first scenario by clicking on the Add button and entering the information required in the Add Scenario window and (after clicking OK) the Scenario Values window. Thereafter, we can use the Edit button to change the details, or the Add button to enter another scenario. Figure 6.3 shows the window for the Scenario Manager after the optimistic and pessimistic scenarios have been added. If we click on the Show button, the values corresponding to the selected scenario are placed in the spreadsheet. If we click on the Summary button, we obtain the summary table shown in Figure 6.4.

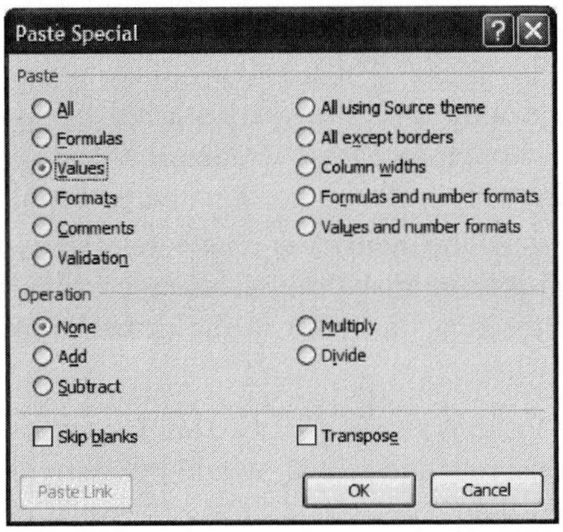

When scenarios involve a large number of parameters, it is convenient to switch from one set of parameters to another all at once. This can be accomplished using the Excel CHOOSE function. CHOOSE selects a value from a range based on an index number. The index number is the number of the scenario, and the range contains the inputs for a given parameter. This is illustrated in Figure 6.5. In cell C6 we enter the number of the scenario, 1, 2, or 3 in this case. In L7:N7 we enter the values for the price parameter for three scenarios: Optimistic (#1), Base Case (#2), and Pessimistic (#3).

FIGURE 6.2 The Paste Special Window

FIGURE 6.3 The Scenario Manager Window

FIGURE 6.4 The
Summary Produced by the
Scenario Manager

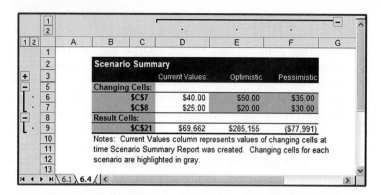

The CHOOSE function appears in cell C8, where the appropriate price is entered depending on the scenario chosen in C6. The appropriate value for cost is entered in cell C9 using the same approach. This method can be used to enter any number of parameters for a given scenario simply by changing the index number in cell C6.

As an application of scenario analysis, consider the Heineken Brewery case.[1] The modeling task in this case was to develop a forecast for Heineken profits over the five years 1999–2003. Because of uncertainty over the strategies that major players in the beer industry would pursue over this time period, no single base case was considered appropriate. Three scenarios were developed, as described in the following.

> *Business As Usual:* The industry avoids major price wars, and financial returns improve slightly. Heineken's performance is the same as in the late 1990s, and in the near future, the company makes two major acquisitions and some small ones. Heineken continues to globalize and augments its market share by 8 percent over the five years.
>
> *Price War:* The industry price wars started by Miller and Busch continue worldwide, dropping returns toward the cost of capital. Heineken's performance is stable but with weaker margins and no new acquisitions.
>
> *Market Discipline:* The industry consolidates and avoids price wars. Heineken improves gross margins through an aggressive mergers-and-acquisitions program. It becomes a leader in the drive for industry consolidation.

These alternative futures were then translated into appropriate sets of input parameters. For the Price War scenario, two adjustments were made to the Business As Usual assumptions: revenue growth would be 0 percent (rather than 2 percent), and 1 percent (rather than 3 percent) of revenue growth would come from acquisitions. In the Market Discipline scenario, growth by acquisitions was increased so that Heineken augments its market share by 15 percent.

The results of the Heineken scenario analysis are summarized below. To focus on just one result, we can see that equity per share is 19.3 guilders lower in the Price War scenario and 40.5 guilders higher in the Market Discipline scenario, relative to the Business As Usual scenario.

Result	Units	Price war	Business as usual	Market discipline
Average annual growth	Percentage	2.4	5.6	7.0
Average ROIC	Percentage	13.0	13.1	14.2
Company value	NLG Billion*	29.8	35.8	48.5
Equity value	NLG Billion	27.5	33.5	46.2
Equity value per share	NLG	87.6	106.9	147.4
Probability	Percentage	15.0	60.0	25.0

*Netherlands guilders

[1] T. Koller, M. Goedhart, and D. Wessels. *Valuation* (New York: John Wiley and Sons, 2005), 253.

FIGURE 6.5 Use of the CHOOSE Function to Implement Scenarios

Callout: Choose scenario inputs by inserting a number representing the column of the scenario.

Callout: Use Choose function to select parameters from L8:N8 as specified by scenario number in C6.

	A	B	C	D	E	F	G	H		K	L	M	N
1	Advertising Budget Model												
2	SGP/KRB												
3	1/1/2006												
4													
5	PARAMETERS									SCENARIOS	1	2	3
6		Scenario	1								Optimistic	Base Case	Pessimistic
7				Q1	Q2	Q3	Q4			Price	$50	$40	$35
8		Price	$50.00							Cost	$20	$25	$30
9		Cost	$20.00										
10		Seasonal		0.9	1.1	0.8	1.2						
11		OHD rate	0.15										
12		Sales Parameters											
13			35										
14			3000										
15		Sales Expense		8000	8000	9000							
16		Ad Budget	$40,000										
17													
18	DECISIONS							Total					
19		Ad Expenditures		$10,000	$10,000	$10,000	$10,000	$40,000					
20													
21	OUTPUTS												
22		Profit	$285,155		Base case	$69,662							
23													
24	CALCULATIONS												
25		Quarter		Q1	Q2	Q3	Q4	Total					
26		Seasonal		0.9	1.1	0.8	1.2						
27													
28		Units Sold		3592	4390	3192	4789	15962					
29		Revenue		179578	219484	159625	239437	798123					
30		Cost of Goods		71831	87794	63850	95775	319249					
31		Gross Margin		107747	131690	95775	143662	478874					
32													
33		Sales Expense		8000	8000	9000	9000	34000					
34		Advertising		10000	10000	10000	10000	40000					
35		Overhead		26937	32923	23944	35916	119718					
36		Total Fixed Cost		44937	50923	42944	54916	193718					
37													
38		Profit		62810	80768	52831	88747	285155					
39		Profit Margin		34.98%	36.80%	33.10%	37.06%	35.73%					
40													

Several aspects of this case are noteworthy. First, scenarios should describe the major events that could impact the company or individual in the future. The story told in each scenario should be believable and coherent, although credible scenarios are not necessarily highly likely. (In fact, one of the strengths of scenario analysis is to focus attention on important but unlikely futures.) Second, the description of each scenario must be sufficiently complete to suggest plausible values for all the input parameters. Often, the parameters of a business-as-usual scenario are set first, and the parameters of the other scenarios are selected as changes from the base values.

6.3.3 Data Sensitivity

Simple what-if analysis requires changing one input and observing the resulting value of the output. But we often wish to understand how the output varies over a *range* of inputs. We could type in a series of input values and record the outputs manually, but an automatic procedure would be more efficient.

The **Data Sensitivity** tool was created to automate simple what-if analysis. It recalculates the spreadsheet for a series of values of an input cell and tabulates the resulting values of an output cell. This allows the analyst to perform several related what-if tests in one pass rather than entering each input value and recording each corresponding output.

The Data Sensitivity tool is one module in the **Sensitivity Toolkit**, which is an Excel add-in that is available with this book. Once the Toolkit is installed, the Sensitivity Toolkit option will appear on the far right of the menu bar. Data Sensitivity and the other modules can be accessed from this menu.

We illustrate the use of the Data Sensitivity tool in the Advertising Budget model by showing how variations in unit cost affect profit. We first select Add-ins▸Sensitivity Toolkit▸Data Sensitivity. The first window that appears (Figure 6.6) provides a choice for Table Type, which we leave at the default of One-Way Table. We also enter the address of the Result Cell, C21, which is the output cell in our model.

After pressing the Next button, a second window appears (Figure 6.7) that asks for information on the input parameter. The Cell to Vary is C8, which contains the unit-cost parameter. The Input Type has two options: Begin, End, Increment and Begin, End, Num Obs (Number of Observations). We most often use the default choice of Begin, End, Increment. To create a table in which the unit cost varies

FIGURE 6.6 Initial Inputs for a One-way Data Sensitivity

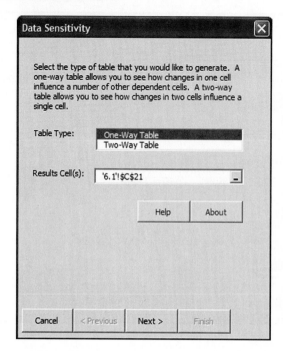

from $20 to $30 in steps of $1, we enter 20 for the First Value, 30 for Last Value, and 1 for Increment/N.

Figure 6.8 shows the output generated by the Data Sensitivity tool. A worksheet has been added to the workbook, and the first two columns on the sheet contain the table of what-if values. In effect, the what-if test has been repeated for each unit-cost value from $20 to $30 in steps of $1, and the results have been recorded in the table. In addition, the table is automatically converted to a graph, which can be edited at the user's discretion. As both the table and graph show, annual profits drop as the unit cost increases, and the cost-profit relationship is linear. We can also see that the breakeven value of the unit cost falls between $29 and $30, since profits cross from positive values to negative values somewhere in this interval.

Note that the Data Sensitivity tool requires that we provide a single cell address to reference the input being varied in a one-way table. The tool will work correctly only if the input has been placed in a single location. By contrast, if an input parameter had been embedded in several cells, the tool would have given incorrect answers when we tried to vary the input. Thus, the use of single and separate locations for parameters (or for decisions), which we advocated in Chapter 5, makes it possible to take advantage of the tool's capability.

We can also use the Data Sensitivity tool to analyze the sensitivity of an output to *two* inputs. This option gives rise to a two-way table, in contrast to the one-way sensitivity table illustrated in Figure 6.8. To demonstrate this feature, we build a table showing how profits are affected by both Q1 advertising and Q2 advertising. When we invoke the Data Sensitivity tool after using it for the one-way analysis, some of the values we specified remain visible. Thus, for example, the Result Cell remains C21 and does not need editing. In the Two-Way Inputs window, we ask for both cells to vary from $5,000 to $15,000 in steps of $1,000, giving rise to the table shown in Figure 6.9 (after some modest reformatting), which appears on another newly added worksheet. A quick check that helps us confirm our work is to look up the profit value in the table corresponding to advertising expenditures of $10,000 in both Q1 and Q2. In the center of the table, we see that this value is $69,662, as expected.

By studying Figure 6.9, we can make a quick comparison between the effect of additional spending in Q1 and the effect of

FIGURE 6.7 Parameter Inputs for a One-way Data Sensitivity

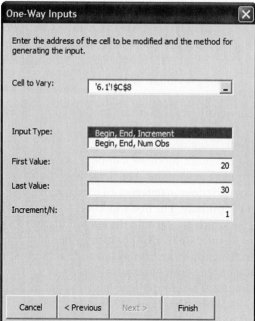

FIGURE 6.8 One-way Data Sensitivity: Profit as a Function of Cost

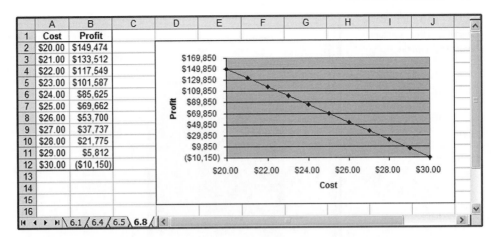

the same spending in Q2. As we can observe in the table, moving across a row generates more profit than moving the same distance down a column. This pattern tells us that we can gain more from spending additional dollars in Q2 than from the same additional dollars in Q1. This observation suggests that, starting with the base case, we could improve profits by shifting dollars from Q1 to Q2. We can also note from the table, or from the three-dimensional chart that automatically accompanies it, that the relationship between profits and advertising expenditures is not linear. Instead, profits show diminishing returns.

6.3.4 Tornado Charts

Another useful tool for sensitivity analysis is the **tornado chart**. In contrast to the information produced by the Data Sensitivity tool, which shows how sensitive an output is to one or perhaps two inputs, a tornado chart shows how sensitive the output is to several different inputs. Consequently, it shows us which parameters have a major impact on the results and which have little impact.

Tornado charts are created by changing input values one at a time and recording the variations in the output. The simplest approach is to vary each input by a fixed percentage of its base-case value, such as ±10 percent. For each parameter in turn, we increase the base-case value by 10 percent and record the output, then we decrease the base-case value by 10 percent and record the output. Next, we calculate the absolute difference between these two outcomes and display the results in the order of these differences.

The Sensitivity Toolkit contains a tool for generating tornado charts. For the Advertising Budget example, we select Add-ins▶Sensitivity Toolkit▶Tornado Chart and specify cell C21 as the `Result Cell`, just as we did when using the Data Sensitivity tool. Next, we designate the `Input Parameters` for the chart. Given the structure of our model (refer to Figure 6.1), we can simply enter the range C7:G15, since the tool will ignore blank cells and titles. However, it is also possible to enter a list of cells in the usual fashion, by holding down the Control key and pointing to each cell or cell range desired.

FIGURE 6.9 Two-way Data Sensitivity: Profit as a Function of Q1 and Q2 Advertising

	A	B	C	D	E	F	G	H	I	J	K	L
1	Profit: $D$18 by $E$18											
2												
3	Q1						Q2					
4			$5,000	$6,000	$7,000	$8,000	$9,000	$10,000	$11,000	$12,000	$13,000	$14,000	$15,000
5		$5,000	$64,180	$65,060	$65,838	$66,529	$67,145	$67,695	$68,187	$68,625	$69,017	$69,366	$69,676
6		$6,000	$64,718	$65,598	$66,376	$67,067	$67,683	$68,233	$68,725	$69,164	$69,555	$69,904	$70,214
7		$7,000	$65,173	$66,053	$66,831	$67,522	$68,138	$68,688	$69,179	$69,618	$70,010	$70,359	$70,669
8		$8,000	$65,557	$66,437	$67,215	$67,906	$68,522	$69,072	$69,563	$70,002	$70,394	$70,743	$71,053
9		$9,000	$65,879	$66,759	$67,537	$68,228	$68,844	$69,394	$69,885	$70,324	$70,716	$71,065	$71,375
10		$10,000	$66,147	$67,027	$67,805	$68,496	$69,112	$69,662	$70,153	$70,592	$70,984	$71,333	$71,643
11		$11,000	$66,367	$67,247	$68,025	$68,716	$69,332	$69,882	$70,374	$70,813	$71,204	$71,553	$71,863
12		$12,000	$66,544	$67,424	$68,203	$68,894	$69,510	$70,060	$70,551	$70,990	$71,382	$71,731	$72,040
13		$13,000	$66,683	$67,563	$68,341	$69,033	$69,648	$70,198	$70,690	$71,129	$71,520	$71,869	$72,179
14		$14,000	$66,787	$67,667	$68,445	$69,136	$69,752	$70,302	$70,793	$71,232	$71,624	$71,973	$72,283
15		$15,000	$66,858	$67,738	$68,517	$69,208	$69,824	$70,374	$70,865	$71,304	$71,696	$72,045	$72,354
16												

FIGURE 6.10 Tornado Chart Using the Constant Percentage Option

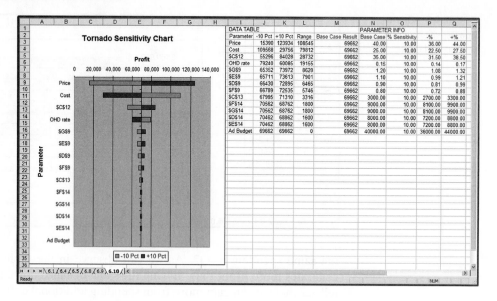

The Tornado Chart tool provides a choice of three options:

- Constant percentage
- Variable percentage
- Percentiles

Suppose we select `Constant Percentage` and click the `Next` button. In the Constant Inputs window, we enter 10. In this instance, we vary the following parameters by ±10 percent of their base-case values: price, unit cost, overhead percentage, two sales parameters, four seasonal factors, four quarterly sales expenses, and the advertising budget. The final step is to click `Finish`.

The tornado chart appears on a newly inserted worksheet, as shown in Figure 6.10. The horizontal axis at the top of the chart shows profits, and the bars in the chart show the changes in profit resulting from ±10 percent changes in each input. After calculating the values (which are recorded in the accompanying table on the same worksheet), the bars are sorted from largest to smallest for display in the diagram. Thus, the most sensitive inputs appear at the top, with the largest horizontal spans. The least sensitive inputs appear toward the bottom, with the smallest horizontal spans. Drawing the chart using horizontal bars, with the largest span at the top and the smallest at the bottom, suggests the shape of a tornado, hence the name. If some of the information in the chart seems unclear, details can usually be found in the accompanying table, which is constructed on the same worksheet by the Tornado Chart tool. In our example, we can see in the table that price has the biggest impact (a range of more than $108,000), with unit cost next (a range of nearly $80,000), and the other inputs far behind in impact on profit.

The standardization achieved by using a common percentage for the change in inputs (10 percent in our example) makes it easy to compare the results from one input to another, but it may also be misleading. A 10 percent range may be realistic for one parameter, while 20 percent is realistic for another and 5 percent for a third. The critical factor is the size of the forecast error or uncertainty for each parameter. If these ranges are significantly different, we should assign different percentages to different inputs. This can be accomplished using the Variable Percentage option in the Tornado Chart tool.

To illustrate the Variable Percentage option in the Advertising Budget example, suppose we limit ourselves to seven parameters: price, cost, four seasonal factors, and overhead rate. Suppose that, based on a detailed assessment of the uncertainty in these parameters, we choose to vary price by 5 percent, cost by 12 percent, seasonal factors by 8 percent, and overhead rate by 3 percent. Before invoking the tool, we must enter this information into our spreadsheet. A reliable way to do so is to

FIGURE 6.11 Tornado Chart Using the Variable Percentage Option

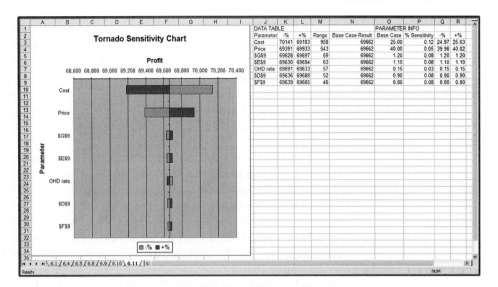

duplicate the range containing the input parameters in an unused region of the spreadsheet and then replace each parameter with the corresponding percentage. In this example, we can copy cells B6:G10 and paste into the range K6:P10. Then, we can replace the parameters we wish to vary with the corresponding percentages. (For more details on how to use these tools, click on the `Help` button on the first window under each option in the Sensitivity Toolkit.)

When we invoke the Tornado Chart tool, the `Result Cell` remains unchanged. For `Input Parameters`, we enter the range C7:G10 and select the `Variable Percentage` type of analysis. When we click on the `Next` button, we come to the Variable Inputs window, where we can enter the range L6:P10 and click `Finish`.

The resulting tornado chart is shown in Figure 6.11. As the results show, cost now has the biggest impact on profits, partly because it has a larger range of uncertainty than price.

Tornado charts are an extremely useful tool for determining quickly which parameters are most important in a model. Nevertheless, they have several drawbacks. We have already pointed out the potential pitfalls of assuming that every parameter varies by the same percentage of the base case. Models with significant nonlinearities present an additional pitfall. If the output is related to an input in a nonlinear fashion, the degree of sensitivity implied by a tornado chart may be misleading. An extreme example will make the point. Figure 6.10 suggests that profits are highly sensitive to costs. In particular, if costs increase by 10 percent, profit drops to around $30,000. This might suggest that cost increases alone could lead to losses. But suppose that costs are capped by a contract that specifies we will never pay more than $28 (at which value profits are still positive). Then cost increases cannot lead to losses, despite what the tornado chart suggests. In general, we must be cautious about drawing conclusions about the sensitivity of a model outside the range of the parameters tested in a tornado chart.

In Chapter 7, we discuss how to use confidence-interval information to guide the Variable Percentage analysis when some of our parameters are based on sample data. Later, in Chapter 15, we show how to use Monte Carlo simulation to fully account for uncertainty in spreadsheet models. There, we also explain how to use the Percentiles option in the Tornado Chart tool, and we show how a tornado chart can serve as a useful first step in simulation analysis.

6.4 BREAKEVEN ANALYSIS

Many managers and analysts throw up their hands in the face of uncertainty about critical parameters. If we ask a manager to directly estimate market share for a new product, the reply may be: "I have *no idea* what market share we'll capture." A powerful strategy in this situation is to reverse the sense of the question: instead of asking "What will our market share be?" ask, "How high does our market share have to get before we turn a profit?" The trick here is to look for a **breakeven**, or cutoff, level for a parameter—that is, a target value of the parameter at which some particularly interesting event occurs, such as reaching zero profits or making a 15 percent return on invested assets. Managers who cannot predict market share can often determine whether a particular breakeven share is likely to occur. This is why breakeven analysis is so powerful.

Even if we have no idea about the market share for the new product, we should be able to build a model that calculates profit given some *assumption* about market share. Once market share takes the role of a parameter in our model, we can use the Data Sensitivity tool to construct a graph of profit as a function of market share. Then, from the graph, we can find the breakeven market share quite accurately.

New capital investments are usually evaluated in terms of their net present value, but the appropriate discount rate to use is not always obvious. Rather than attempting to determine the appropriate discount rate precisely, we can take the breakeven approach and ask how high the discount rate would have to be in order for this project to have an NPV of zero. (The answer to this question is generally known as the **internal rate of return**.) If the answer is 28 percent, we can be confident that the project is a good investment. On the other hand, if breakeven occurs at 9 percent, we may want to do further research to establish whether the discount rate is clearly below this level.

FIGURE 6.12 The Goal Seek Window

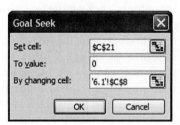

Breakeven values for parameters can be determined manually by repeatedly changing input values until the output reaches the desired target. This can often be done fairly quickly by an intelligent trial-and-error search in Excel. In the Advertising Budget model, suppose we want to find the breakeven cost to the nearest penny. Recall from

FIGURE 6.13 Using the Goal Seek Tool in the Advertising Budget Example

	A	B	C	D	E	F	G	H	I	J
1	**Advertising Budget Model**									
2	SGP/KRB									
3	1/1/2006									
4										
5	PARAMETERS									
6				Q1	Q2	Q3	Q4			Notes
7		Price	$40.00							Current price
8		Cost	$29.36							Accounting
9		Seasonal		0.9	1.1	0.8	1.2			Data analysis
10		OHD rate	0.15							Accounting
11		Sales Parameters								
12			35							Consultants
13			3000							
14		Sales Expense		8000	8000	9000	9000			Consultants
15		Ad Budget	$40,000							Current budget
16										
17	DECISIONS							Total		
18		Ad Expenditures		$10,000	$10,000	$10,000	$10,000	$40,000		sum
19										
20	OUTPUTS									
21		Profit	$0		Base case	$69,662				
22										
23	CALCULATIONS									
24		Quarter				Q3	Q4	Total		
25		Seasonal		0.9	1.1	0.8	1.2			
26										
27		Units Sold		3592	4390	3192	4789	15962		given formula
28		Revenue		143662	175587	127700	191549	638498		price*units
29		Cost of Goods		105463	128899	93745	140617	468724		cost*units
30		Gross Margin		38199	46688	33955	50932	169775		subtraction
31										
32		Sales Expense		8000	8000	9000	9000	34000		given
33		Advertising		10000	10000	10000	10000	40000		decisions
34		Overhead		21549	26338	19155	28732	95775		rate*revenue
35		Total Fixed Cost		39549	44338	38155	47732	169775		sum
36										
37		Profit		-1350	2350	-4200	3200	0		GM -TFC
38		Profit Margin		-0.94%	1.34%	-3.29%	1.67%	0.00%		pct of revenue
39										

‹ › ›|\ 6.1 ⟨ 6.4 ⟨ 6.5 ⟨ 6.8 ⟨ 6.9 ⟨ 6.10 ⟨ 6.11 ⟨ **6.13** ⟨ ‹

Figure 6.8 that profit goes to zero somewhere between $29 and $30. By repeating the search between these two costs in steps of $0.10, we can find the breakeven cost to the nearest dime. If we repeat the search once more, in steps of $0.01, we will obtain the value at the precision we seek.

Excel also provides a specialized tool called **Goal Seek** for performing this type of search. Three pieces of information are required: the output-cell address, the target level sought, and the input for which the search is conducted. To determine the breakeven cost in the Advertising Budget example, we select Data▶Data Tools▶What-If Analysis▶ Goal Seek. The Set Cell is Profit in C21; the To Value is the profit target of zero; and the Changing Cell is unit cost, in C7. With these three specifications, the Goal Seek window takes the form shown in Figure 6.12. The tool locates the desired unit cost as $29.36, and the corresponding results are displayed on the spreadsheet (see Figure 6.13). Choosing the OK button in the Goal Seek Status window preserves these values in the spreadsheet; choosing the Cancel button returns the spreadsheet to its base case.

Note that the Goal Seek tool searches for a prescribed level in the relation between a single output and a single input. Thus, it requires that the parameter or decision being varied resides in a single location, reinforcing one of the design principles we introduced in Chapter 5.

One warning should be added. If we invoke Goal Seek when there is more than one breakeven point, the value returned by the Goal Seek tool may depend on where we start. A simple example illustrates this feature. Suppose our model contains the formula $y = x^2 - 5x + 6$, and we want to find the value of x for which $y = 0$. If we set up this search on a spreadsheet and initially assign $x = 7$, then Goal Seek produces the result $x = 3$ as the desired value. However, if we initially assign $x = 1$, then Goal Seek returns the value $x = 2$. Thus, we may need to be alert to the possibility of more than one breakeven point, because Goal Seek can return only one value. If we suspect that there may be a second breakeven level, we may make a preliminary run with Data Sensitivity to see whether multiple breakeven points are a possibility.

6.5 OPTIMIZATION ANALYSIS

Another fundamental type of managerial question asks what decision variables achieve the best possible value of an output. In fact, we might claim that the fundamental management task is to make choices that result in optimal outputs. **Solver** is an important tool for this purpose. Solver is an add-in for Excel that makes it possible to optimize models with many decision variables and with constraints on the choice of decision variables. A basic version of Solver comes with Excel. A more powerful version is available with this book. Optimization is a complex subject, and we devote Chapters 10 to 13 to it and to the use of Solver. However, we can provide a glimpse of its power by demonstrating a simple application in the Advertising Budget example.

Suppose we wish to maximize total profits with an advertising budget of $40,000. We already know that, with equal expenditures in every quarter, annual profits come to $69,662. The question now is whether we can achieve a higher level

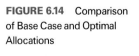

FIGURE 6.14 Comparison of Base Case and Optimal Allocations

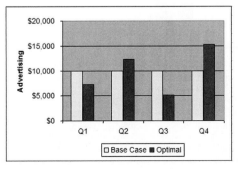

of annual profits. By using Solver we can find that a higher level is, in fact, attainable. An optimal reallocation of the budget produces annual profits of $71,447. The chart in Figure 6.14 compares the allocation of the budget in the base case with the optimal allocation. As we can see, the optimal allocation calls for greater expenditures in quarters Q2 and Q4 and for smaller expenditures in Q1 and Q3.

This is just one illustration of Solver's power. Among the many questions we could answer with Solver in the Advertising Budget example are these:

- What would be the impact of a requirement to spend at least $8,000 each quarter?
- What would be the marginal impact of increasing the budget?
- What is the optimal budget size?

Chapters 10–13 develop the techniques to answer these and a host of related questions for a variety of spreadsheet models.

6.6 SIMULATION AND RISK ANALYSIS

Uncertainty often plays an important role in analyzing a decision because with uncertainty comes risk. Until now, we have been exploring the relationship between the inputs and outputs of a spreadsheet model as if uncertainty were not at issue. However, risk is an inherent feature of all managerial decisions, so it is frequently an important aspect in modeling. In particular, we might want to recognize that some of the inputs are subject to uncertainty. In other words, we might want to associate probability models with some of the parameters. When we take that step, it makes sense to look at outputs the same way—with probability models. The use of probability models in this context is known as **risk analysis**.

One tool we use for risk analysis in spreadsheets is **Crystal Ball**, an add-in for Monte Carlo simulation that is available with this book. This tool allows us to generate a probability distribution for any output cell in a spreadsheet, given probability assumptions about some of the input cells. Simulation and risk analysis are the subjects of Chapters 15 and 16. Here, we simply illustrate how Crystal Ball can help us answer an important question about risk.

We return to the base case in the Advertising Budget example, in which we assumed equal expenditures of $10,000 for advertising each quarter. Our analysis, which assumed that all parameters are known exactly, showed an annual profit of $69,662. However, we might wonder about the distribution of profits if there's uncertainty about the unit price and the unit cost. Future prices depend on the number of competitors in our market, and future costs depend on the availability of raw materials. Since both the level of competition and raw material supply are uncertain, so, too, are the parameters for our price and cost. Suppose we assume that price is normally distributed with a mean of $40 and a standard deviation of $10, and that unit cost is equally likely to fall anywhere between $20 and $30. Given these

FIGURE 6.15 Distribution of Profits in the Advertising Budget Example

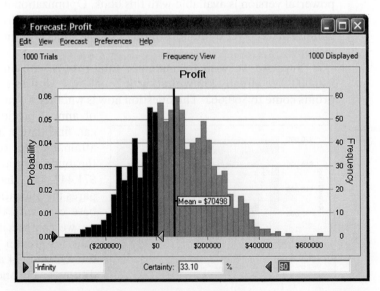

assumptions, what is the probability distribution of annual profits; specifically, what is the *average* profit? And how likely is it that profits will be *negative*?

Figure 6.15 shows the probability distribution for profits in the form of a histogram, derived from the assumptions we made about price and cost. The graph shows us that the estimated average profit is $70,498 under our assumptions. It also shows that the probability is about 33 percent that we will lose money. This exposure may cause us to reevaluate the desirability of the base-case plan.

Chapters 15 and 16 develop the techniques to address uncertain elements in the analysis, for a variety of spreadsheet models. There we show how to:

- Determine which inputs require probability models.
- Select appropriate probability models for those inputs.
- Configure Crystal Ball to generate a histogram for any output cell.

6.7 SUMMARY

The process of analyzing a spreadsheet model has several identifiable steps. The first step is to construct a base case, which becomes a key point of comparison for all of the subsequent analyses. The next step is what-if analysis: changing inputs and tracing the effects on one or more of the outputs. Early in the development of a spreadsheet, this step is an aid in debugging the model, as we mentioned in Chapter 5. Once the spreadsheet has been debugged and tested, what-if analysis helps us discover how sensitive an output is to one or more of the inputs. The Data Sensitivity tool helps us automate one-at-a-time sensitivity analysis. The information produced by this tool is also translated into a chart so that relationships can be portrayed visually.

A tornado chart provides another form of what-if analysis, treating several of the inputs at once. Scenario analysis can be used to analyze the outputs for a set of inputs that together tell a story. Whatever tool we use, probing for sensitivities helps provide useful insight to support management decisions. In the Advertising Budget example, our early probing revealed that profits respond in straight-line fashion to changes in the unit cost and that profits show diminishing returns to additional advertising expenditures.

A related step involves inverting the analysis, where we start with a target for a particular output and "back into" the input value that achieves that target level of performance. The most prominent form is breakeven analysis, which aims at a target of zero, but the concept can be applied to any target level. Excel provides the Goal Seek tool to automate the search for a single input value that achieves a desired output value. Breakeven analysis provides us with an early indication of risk: we can determine how much of a "cushion" there is in any one of our parameter forecasts. Should the actual value

turn out to be worse than our base-case assumption, breakeven analysis tells us how much of a difference we can tolerate before our output measure reaches a critical level. In the Advertising Budget example, we found that the $25 unit cost could grow to more than $29 before we would face negative profits.

The most ambitious forms of analysis are optimization and simulation. Optimization methods look for the best value of an output by searching through various combinations of the decisions. Simulation methods allow some of the inputs to be treated as probabilistic, tracing the implications for outputs. These two methods represent advanced techniques of modeling, and we devote several later chapters to them. In our analysis framework, they play the role of powerful tools capable of delivering further insights. In the Advertising Budget example, the insight obtained from optimization was that the allocation of advertising expenditures across the four quarters should not be equal, but rather should reflect the size of the seasonal factors. In fact, further optimization analysis reveals that the $40,000 budget itself is probably too small. A larger budget could increase profitability.

The progression from a base case to what-if and breakeven analysis, then to optimization and simulation analyses, represents a logical and increasingly sophisticated set of methods for *experimenting* with a spreadsheet model. This kind of experimentation provides the opportunity for the same kind of learning that a scientist derives from laboratory experiments. Indeed, the spreadsheet is an analyst's electronic laboratory, and in supporting management decisions with laboratory work, the analyst is serving as a *management scientist*. In the following chapters, we begin to develop the management scientist's advanced modeling tools.

EXERCISES

1. Refer to the XYZ Company case. From the corresponding exercise in Chapter 5, review the design of a spreadsheet that will allow an analyst to predict monthly cash needs and profitability for the first five months of the year.

a. In what month does the cash balance fall below zero, signaling a need to borrow money?

b. What is the profit, as a percentage of sales, in April?

c. Suppose the monthly increment in sales is 600—instead of 500, as in the base case. How does this change affect the answers in (a) and (b)? Construct a table to examine the month in which the cash balance disappears as a function of the monthly increment in sales.

d. Suppose the monthly increment in sales is 300—instead of 500, as in the base case. How does this change affect the answers in (a) and (b)? Construct a graph showing the profitability percentage in (b) as a function of the monthly increment in sales.

e. Starting with the base case, suppose that unit cost runs higher than originally thought. What level of unit cost will lead the firm to run out of cash by the end of March?

2. Refer to the Medical Supplies for Banjul case. Design a spreadsheet that will enable you to request the required funds from your team's finance officer, order supplies from the home office, and ensure dissemination of appropriate quantities to each village. Your final order to the home office should specify the number of packages required of each item.

a. The population figures will show that there are 3,000 children, 2,500 teenagers, 500 seniors, and 9,000 other adults in the population. If there were no stock on hand, what amount would be required for ordering supplies?

b. Using the parameters in (a), construct a graph showing how the amount required for the order would vary if the unit cost of a package of bandages rose by $0.25, $0.50, and so on, up to $3.00 per package.

c. Following up on (a), a check on stock shows an inventory of 124 packages of A-bandages, 16 packages of B-bandages, 82 packages of C-bandages, 72 rolls of tape, and 4 hearing aids. What amount will be required for ordering supplies?

3. Refer to the Reid's Raisins case. Design a spreadsheet that will allow the firm to determine how many grapes to buy under contract and how much to charge for the raisins they sell.

a. What is the profit projected for the base-case conditions, assuming a market price of $0.30 for the open-market grape price?

b. What is the breakeven value of the open-market grape price?

c. Construct a table showing how profit varies as a function of the price set for raisins. Cover a range from $1.80 to $2.80 in steps of $0.10.

d. Construct a tornado chart for the analysis in (a). List the relevant parameters in descending order of their impact on annual profit.

4. Refer to the Big Rig Rental Company case. Design a spreadsheet that will provide the owner with the five-year economic analysis requested.

a. What is the Net Present Value of the firm's cash flows over the five-year period?

b. Construct a tornado chart for the analysis in (a). List the relevant parameters in descending order of their impact on the Net Present Value.

c. What is the internal rate of return for the cash flows in (a)?

d. Construct a table to show how profit varies with the base rental rate, which is currently $1,000 per month.

5. Refer to the Flexible Insurance Coverage case. From the corresponding exercise in Chapter 5, review the design of a spreadsheet that will allow an individual employee to compare the annual expenses for each plan and thereby choose the cheapest alternative.

a. Consider the case of a single employee with estimated annual expenses of $400. What plan is the cheapest? What is the total annual cost associated with this plan?

b. For the analysis in (a), construct a table to show the best plan and the associated cost for annual expenses ranging from $100 to $1,200 in steps of $100.

c. Consider the case of a married employee with estimated annual expenses of $1,000 and an equal amount for the spouse. What plan is the cheapest? What is the total annual cost associated with this plan?

d. For the analysis in (c), construct a table to show the best plan and the associated cost for annual expenses ranging from $100 to $1,500 in steps of $100 for the employee, assuming that the employee's expenses and the spouse's expenses are the same.

e. For the analysis in (d), find the level of expenses at which the cost is the same under Plan 1 and Plan 2.

6. Refer to the Snoey Software Company case. Design a spreadsheet for the desired five-year economic analysis mentioned in the case.

a. Consider a recommendation that the prices for the Educational, Large-Scale, and Professional versions should be $75, $275, and $475, respectively. What annual profit would these prices achieve?

b. Construct three separate sensitivity analyses, starting from the base case in (a). For each analysis, vary the price above and below the base case, and find the best price for the version being analyzed. When these prices are used in combination, what annual profit is achieved?

c. For the pricing in (a), consider the set of prices that the five segments would be willing to pay for the three products. If each of these prices could vary by 15 percent, which one would have the greatest dollar impact on the annual profit?

7. Refer to the Cox Cable and Wire Company case. In the role of Meredith, design a spreadsheet that will evaluate the profitability of any particular production and delivery schedule.

a. Find a machine schedule and a corresponding inventory and shipment schedule that meets demand. What is the profitability of this schedule?

b. Suppose that material costs for both products were to rise by a specific percentage. At what percentage increase would profitability drop to zero?

c. Construct a table showing how profitability varies with changes in the selling price of Plastic reels. Repeat for Teflon reels. Which price has a greater effect on profitability?

8. Refer to the BMW Company case. From the corresponding exercise in Chapter 5, review the design of a spreadsheet that will allow BMW management to estimate the cost of disposal a decade into the future (i.e., in 1999) as a percentage of net income.

a. What percentage is predicted for 1999, assuming there are no changes in trends and policies?

b. How does the percentage change as a function of BMW's market share in 1999? (Consider a range from 5 to 8 percent.)

c. Construct a tornado chart for the analysis in (a). List the relevant parameters in descending order of their impact on the disposal cost.

d. Consider three scenarios, called Slow, Medium, and Fast, characterized by different landfill costs in 1999 (600, 1,200, and 1,800DM, respectively) and by different landfill percentages (60 percent, 50 percent, and 40 percent, respectively). For these scenarios, and assuming that incineration costs will run double landfill costs, construct a scenario table for BMW's disposal cost in 1999 and the percentage of its net income that this figure represents.

9. Refer to the ERP Decision case. Design a spreadsheet that will assist the Board in understanding the likely costs and benefits of implementing ERP.

a. Develop a base case. You may create any data you need for this purpose. Why is this base case appropriate for this situation?

b. How sensitive are the benefits of ERP in the base case to the efficiency gains?

c. Break the total benefits down into the contribution from efficiency gains, inventory turns, and CRM.

10. Refer to the Retirement Planning case. From the corresponding exercise in Chapter 5, review the design of a spreadsheet for this problem.

a. Develop a base case. You may create any data you need for this purpose. Why is this base case appropriate for this situation?

b. Perform an appropriate sensitivity analysis. Which parameters have the most significant impact on the results? Can you find applications for the Data Sensitivity, Tornado Chart, and Scenario Manager tools?

c. Identify applications of the Goal Seek tool in this situation. (For example, find the savings rate needed to ensure that assets do not run out before age 90.)

d. Identify potential applications of *optimization* in this case.

e. Identify potential applications of *simulation* in this case.

11. Refer to the Draft TV Commercials case. From the corresponding exercise in Chapter 5, review the design of a spreadsheet for this problem.

a. Develop a base case. You may create any data you need for this purpose. Why is this base case appropriate for this situation?

b. Perform an appropriate sensitivity analysis. Which parameters have the most significant impact on the results? Can you find applications for the Data Sensitivity, Tornado Chart, and Scenario Manager tools?

c. Identify applications of Goal Seek in this situation. (For example, what percentage of the overall budget should be devoted to draft commercials in order to achieve a preset target number of impressions?)

d. Identify potential applications of *optimization* in this case.

e. Identify potential applications of *simulation* in this case.

12. Refer to the Icebergs for Kuwait case. From the corresponding exercise in Chapter 5, review the design of a spreadsheet for this problem.

a. Develop a base case. You may create any data you need for this purpose. Why is this base case appropriate for this situation?

b. Perform an appropriate sensitivity analysis. Which parameters have the most significant impact on the results? Can you find applications for the Data Sensitivity, Tornado Chart, and Scenario Manager tools?

c. Identify applications of Goal Seek in this situation. (For example, how large an iceberg should they tow in order to break even at the current price for pure water?)

d. Identify potential applications of *optimization* in this case.

e. Identify potential applications of *simulation* in this case.

13. Refer to the Racquetball Racket case. From the corresponding exercise in Chapter 5, review the design of a spreadsheet for this problem.

a. Develop a base case. You may create any data you need for this purpose. Why is this base case appropriate for this situation?

b. Perform an appropriate sensitivity analysis. Which parameters have the most significant impact on the results? Can you find applications for the Data Sensitivity, Tornado Chart, and Scenario Manager tools?

c. Identify applications of Goal Seek in this situation. (For example, what percentage of the market must they achieve to break even on their investment?)

d. Identify potential applications of *optimization* in this case.

e. Identify potential applications of *simulation* in this case.

7   Data Analysis for Modeling

7.1   INTRODUCTION

In this chapter, we discuss the roles that data, data analysis, and statistics play in modeling, and we present a variety of relevant Excel tools. Data analysis and statistical techniques are used in many situations, not all of which are pertinent to the building of spreadsheet models for decision making. Since that is our focus in this book, we organize this chapter around tools that are most useful in the modeling context.

We emphasize that modeling is motivated by the existence of a problem to be resolved or a decision to be made. In the course of developing and testing a model for the purpose of shedding light on the problem, we may decide to collect empirical data to help determine either the value of a parameter or the structure of a relationship. However, the collection and analysis of that data is a means to an end, not a primary goal. Data analysis should be undertaken to improve the accuracy and usefulness of the conclusions drawn from the model, not to enhance the model for its own sake. In that sense, data analysis *supports* the modeling process, but modeling remains the primary focus.

Data analysis and statistical techniques are often used in contexts other than in modeling. Data analysis, for example, is often used to provide general background for managers. A marketing manager might ask for a report on company sales by geographic region and by product line—not to help make a specific decision, but simply to better understand the business environment. A credit card company might request a study to identify the predictors of overdue accounts, even though no specific decision is at hand. These uses of data analysis and statistical methods, while valuable in their own right, are not the focus of this chapter.

In Chapter 2, as part of our discussion of the craft of modeling, we recommended an emphasis on *structuring the model*, not on collecting data. Novice modelers generally place too much reliance on empirical data and fail to recognize biases, distractions, and irrelevancies in the data collection process. That is why we stress the importance of prototyping using readily available data, even roughly estimated data. Moreover, in Chapter 6, we noted the importance of using sensitivity analysis to determine which parameters have a significant impact on the results and may therefore be worthy of further refinement through data analysis.

We emphasize model structure over data analysis because we find that model structure almost always has a strong impact on the ultimate recommendations. Analysis of empirical data, by contrast, may or may not have such an impact. The modeling process itself, as described in earlier chapters, suggests what data to collect and how accurate these data must be for the purposes at hand.

As with the advanced techniques covered in later chapters, we have found that business analysts can themselves do much of the data analysis they need. To do so, they need an understanding of the fundamentals of data analysis and statistics. Most analysts will call on experts when their needs go beyond the fundamentals. With that in mind, our coverage in this chapter includes the basic methods for finding facts in databases: editing, searching, sorting, filtering, and tabulating. We then discuss sampling and making estimates of parameters using basic statistical techniques.

7.2 FINDING FACTS FROM DATABASES

One of the ways we encounter data is in the form of a database. For our purposes, a **database** is a table of information, with each row corresponding to a **record** in the database and each column corresponding to a **field** for the various records. For example, one record might correspond to a single customer order, and the fields might include the customer's name, items ordered, and total value of the order. Excel refers to a table of this type as a **list**. The first row of a list contains names for each of the fields. Each successive row contains one record. In this section, we cover some basic Excel commands that help us manipulate lists and thus seek out information in a given database. We consider commands that edit, search, sort, or filter information in a database, along with Pivot Table, which is used to build two- and three-way summary tables.

As examples, we'll work with three databases:

- Analgesics.xlsx, with data on retail sales of painkillers
- Applicants.xlsx, with data on MBA applicants from one year's pool
- Executives.xlsx, with data on executive compensation for a sample of companies

Figure 7.1 shows a portion of the Analgesics database. A second worksheet in the database provides definitions of the fields, in case the column titles are not self-explanatory. The information in the database describes more than 7,500 sales transactions for a variety of painkillers over a 10-week period at six different stores that form part of a retail chain. We might use this database to answer such questions as the following:

- What were the market shares of the various brands?
- What were weekly sales volumes at the different stores?

We use past tense here to emphasize that, although we are interested in projecting into the future, the data actually tell us something about the past.

FIGURE 7.1 First Portion of the Analgesics Database

	A	B	C	D	E	F	G	H
1	ID	ITEM	UPC	DESCRIPTION	SIZE	STORE	WEEK	SALES
2	1	6122741	2586610502	ALEVE CAPLETS	24 CT	101	383	0
3	2	6122741	2586610502	ALEVE CAPLETS	24 CT	101	384	0
4	3	6122741	2586610502	ALEVE CAPLETS	24 CT	101	385	0
5	4	6122741	2586610502	ALEVE CAPLETS	24 CT	101	386	0
6	5	6122741	2586610502	ALEVE CAPLETS	24 CT	101	387	0
7	6	6122741	2586610502	ALEVE CAPLETS	24 CT	101	388	0
8	7	6122741	2586610502	ALEVE CAPLETS	24 CT	101	389	0
9	8	6122741	2586610502	ALEVE CAPLETS	24 CT	101	390	0
10	9	6122741	2586610502	ALEVE CAPLETS	24 CT	101	391	0
11	10	6122741	2586610502	ALEVE CAPLETS	24 CT	101	392	0
12	11	6122741	2586610502	ALEVE CAPLETS	24 CT	103	383	0
13	12	6122741	2586610502	ALEVE CAPLETS	24 CT	103	384	0
14	13	6122741	2586610502	ALEVE CAPLETS	24 CT	103	385	0
15	14	6122741	2586610502	ALEVE CAPLETS	24 CT	103	386	0
16	15	6122741	2586610502	ALEVE CAPLETS	24 CT	103	387	0
17	16	6122741	2586610502	ALEVE CAPLETS	24 CT	103	388	0
18	17	6122741	2586610502	ALEVE CAPLETS	24 CT	103	389	0
19	18	6122741	2586610502	ALEVE CAPLETS	24 CT	103	390	0
20	19	6122741	2586610502	ALEVE CAPLETS	24 CT	103	391	0
21	20	6122741	2586610502	ALEVE CAPLETS	24 CT	103	392	0
22	21	6122751	2586610504	ALEVE CAPLETS	50 CT	102	383	0
23	22	6122751	2586610504	ALEVE CAPLETS	50 CT	102	384	0
24	23	6122751	2586610504	ALEVE CAPLETS	50 CT	102	385	0
25	24	6122751	2586610504	ALEVE CAPLETS	50 CT	102	386	0
26	25	6122751	2586610504	ALEVE CAPLETS	50 CT	102	387	0
27	26	6122751	2586610504	ALEVE CAPLETS	50 CT	102	388	0
28	27	6122751	2586610504	ALEVE CAPLETS	50 CT	102	389	0
29	28	6122751	2586610504	ALEVE CAPLETS	50 CT	102	390	0
30	29	6122751	2586610504	ALEVE CAPLETS	50 CT	102	391	0
31	30	6122751	2586610504	ALEVE CAPLETS	50 CT	102	392	0

FIGURE 7.2 First Portion
of the Applicants Database

	A	B	C	D	E	F	G	H	I
1	ID	ROUND	AGE	SEX	CITZ CODE	1ST CONTACT	JOB MONTHS	INDUSTRY	INDUSTRY DESC.
2	1	1	30	M	U	Email	84	260	Finan Serv-Diversified
3	2	1	29	M	U	Phone call	86	370	Government
4	3	1	27	M	U	Phone call	40	260	Finan Serv-Diversified
5	4	1	30	M	U	Email	48		
6	5	1	32	M	U	Home Page	85	290	Finan Serv-Invest Mgt/Research
7	6	1	26	M	U	Home Page	32	280	Finan Serv-Invest Bk/Brokerage
8	7	1	29	M	U	Phone call	60	10	Accounting
9	8	1	27	F	U		44	220	Entertainment/Leisure/Media
10	9	1	29	M	U	Phone call	66	40	Agribusiness
11	10	1	31	M	U	Letter	78	420	Nonprofit
12	11	1	27	M	U	Phone call	24	460	Retail
13	12	1	27	M	U	Phone call	51	370	Government
14	13	1	28	M	U		26	230	Environmental Services
15	14	1	30	M	U	Phone call	72	20	Advertising/Marketing Services
16	15	1	27	F	U	Phone call	48	420	Nonprofit
17	16	1	25	M	U	Home Page	31	260	Finan Serv-Diversified
18	17	1	24	F	U	Phone call	24	210	Energy/Utilities
19	18	1	28	M	U	Phone call	31	400	Law
20	19	1	27	M	N	Home Page	54	80	Construction
21	20	1	26	M	U	Letter	32	230	Environmental Services
22	21	1	24	M	U	World Wide Web	24	580	Other Services
23	22	1	27	M	U	Phone call	46	260	Finan Serv-Diversified
24	23	1	28	M	U	Home Page	50	160	Consumer Gds-Food/Beverage
25	24	1	28	M	U	Home Page	60	10	Accounting
26	25	1	29	M	U	Phone call	30	370	Government
27	26	1	27	M	U		48	120	Consulting-Strategy/Management
28	27	1	26	M	U	Phone call	36	260	Finan Serv-Diversified
29	28	1	28	F	U	Home Page	44	260	Finan Serv-Diversified
30	29	1	35	M	U	Phone call	146	220	Entertainment/Leisure/Media
31	30	1	27	M	U	World Wide Web	50	120	Consulting-Strategy/Management

Figure 7.2 shows a portion of the Applicants database. Again, a second worksheet provides a glossary for the field names. The information was collected on nearly 3,000 MBA applicants, showing the status of the applicant pool on a date early in the summer. We might use this database to answer such questions as the following:

- What proportion of the applicants had nonprofit work experience?
- What was the average GMAT score for accepted applicants?

Figure 7.3 shows a portion of the Executives database. The information constitutes a sample of 100 records from a publicly available survey of executive compensation. We might use this database to answer such questions as the following:

FIGURE 7.3 First Portion
of the Executives Database

	A	B	C	D	E	F	G	H	I
1	ID	EXECID	GENDER	SALARY	BONUS	OTHER	SHARES	CONAME	TICKER
2	2611	00006	MALE	683.462	412.768	0.000	207.828	ADC TELECOMMUNICATIONS INC	ADCT
3	4666	00029	MALE	750.000	1012.500	0.000	641.691	ALLTEL CORP	AT
4	2702	00074	MALE	875.000	1000.000	22.100	2234.402	ARROW ELECTRONICS INC	ARW
5	5562	00085	MALE	324.389	80.563	0.000	16632.050	ATMEL CORP	ATML
6	314	00111	MALE	750.000	825.000	294.770	183.031	BAXTER INTERNATIONAL INC	BAX
7	2766	00140	MALE	509.734	77.257	0.000	354.541	BOB EVANS FARMS	BOBE
8	2777	00152	MALE	700.000	317.665	0.000	39.928	KEYSPAN CORP	KSE
9	5588	00167	MALE	820.677	500.000	45.687	1208.415	CALLAWAY GOLF CO	ELY
10	516	00197	MALE	1350.000	1965.000	0.000		CHEVRON CORP	CHV
11	2962	00223	MALE	1000.000	0.000	0.000	255.198	CMS ENERGY CORP	CMS
12	2654	00246	MALE	1357.026	2162.508	91.721	1517.168	AFLAC INC	AFL
13	5865	00313	MALE	933.333	5554.350	300.034	6033.567	TRIARC COS INC -CL A	TRY
14	822	00315	MALE	771.018	463.200	0.000	224.861	EASTERN ENTERPRISES	EFU
15	9283	00393	MALE	1000.000	2750.000	143.698	643.966	FREEPRT MCMOR COP&GLD -CL B	FCX
16	5067	00398	MALE	205.000	0.000	56.891	9040.113	HUMANA INC	HUM
17	16384	00415	MALE	550.000	275.000	60.703	48.542	BARNES GROUP INC	B
18	1016	00418	MALE	620.000	952.468	0.000	334.430	GENUINE PARTS CO	GPC
19	10891	00474	MALE	410.004	400.000	0.000	1469.256	HORACE MANN EDUCATORS CORP	HMN
20	3296	00482	MALE	450.000	0.000	0.000	151.477	HUNT (JB) TRANSPRT SVCS INC	JBHT
21	3367	00522	MALE	750.000	0.000	46.067	740.528	KANSAS CITY SOUTHERN INDS	KSU
22	1329	00555	MALE	1185.577	3331.968	0.000	46497.711	LIMITED INC	LTD
23	4837	00563	MALE	1051.946	0.000	712.393	17308.998	LOEWS CORP	LTR
24	1459	00608	MALE	369.231	0.000	77.757	141.572	MCKESSON HBOC INC	MCK
25	1679	00705	MALE	730.769	0.000	159.776		OGDEN CORP	OG
26	5415	00731	MALE	800.000	10662.500	0.000	1185.531	PAINE WEBBER GROUP	PWJ
27	4903	00741	MALE	689.178	448.630	0.000	216.999	PPL CORP	PPL
28	9594	00749	MALE	990.000	698.465	128.496	1075.749	FORT JAMES CORP	FJ
29	586	00778	MALE	1000.000	8732.474	448.577	17500.746	CITIGROUP INC	C
30	10955	00791	MALE	773.085	975.000	0.000	4931.348	QUALCOMM INC	QCOM

FIGURE 7.4 Form for the Analgesics Database

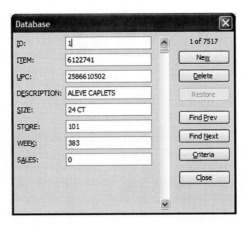

- What was the average salary among these executives?
- What proportion of compensation was due to annual bonuses?

These three databases contain what we might think of as "raw" data. That is, the databases were not necessarily compiled for the purpose of answering the questions we posed. They were likely built for other purposes, or in the hope that they might be generally helpful to unspecified users.

7.2.1 Searching and Editing

It is usually helpful to assign a range name to a list (see Chapter 4 for details on assigning range names). For example, we might assign the range name *Data* to our lists, so that we can easily select the entire database including column titles.

We can always search and edit a list directly, but Excel also provides a specialized tool for this purpose. To add this tool to the Quick Access Toolbar, choose Office Button▶Excel options▶Customize▶Choose commands from...▶ All Commands▶Form▶Add▶OK. With the database selected, we choose the Form icon on the Quick Access Toolbar. A window appears containing a form that is tailored to the structure of the database, as shown in Figure 7.4 for the Analgesics list. This form allows us to examine the records one at a time, using the Find Prev and Find Next buttons. We can also enter a record, using the New button, or delete a record, using the Delete button.

A simple way to search for a record in the database is to click on the form's Criteria button, type an identifying entry into one of the field windows, and then click on Find Next. A broader search of the entire database, which does not rely on the form, uses the Find command after the database has been selected. To access the Find command, choose Home▶Editing▶Find & Select▶Find. With this command, entries in the database can be edited from the Find and Replace window. One of the flexible aspects of the Find and Replace commands is the use of the symbols "?" and "*" to assist in these operations. The question mark stands for a single symbol, and the asterisk stands for any sequence of symbols.

> *Question*: In the Analgesics database, which transactions involve the brand Aleve?

The database contains entries for individual brands with tablets, caplets, gelcaps, and the like, each indicated in the Description field. For the purposes of investigating sales by brand name, we would like to combine all of these variations into a single descriptor for each brand. To accomplish this conversion, we use the Replace tab to locate Aleve* (where the asterisk stands for anything that may follow the brand name in the description of the item) and to designate the replacement as Aleve, as shown in Figure 7.5. By clicking on the Replace All option, we convert the

FIGURE 7.5 The Find and Replace Window

FIGURE 7.6 Replacing Compound Descriptions with a Simple Brand Name

	A	B	C	D	E	F	G	H	I
1	ID	ITEM	UPC	DESCRIPTION	SIZE	STORE	WEEK	SALES	UNITS
2	1	6122741	2586610502	Aleve	24	101	383	0	0
3	2	6122741	2586610502	Aleve	24	101	384	0	0
4	3	6122741	2586610502	Aleve	24	101	385	0	0
5	4	6122741	2586610502	Aleve	24	101	386	0	0
6	5	6122741	2586610502	Aleve	24	101	387	0	0
7	6	6122741	2586610502	Aleve	24	101	388	0	0
8	7	6122741	2586610502	Aleve	24	101	389	0	0
9	8	6122741	2586610502	Aleve	24	101	390	0	0
10	9	6122741	2586610502	Aleve	24	101	391	0	0
11	10	6122741	2586610502	Aleve	24	101	392	0	0
12	11	6122741	2586610502	Aleve	24	103	383	0	0
13	12	6122741	2586610502	Aleve	24	103	384	0	0
14	13	6122741	2586610502	Aleve	24	103	385	0	0
15	14	6122741	2586610502	Aleve	24	103	386	0	0
16	15	6122741	2586610502	Aleve	24	103	387	0	0
17	16	6122741	2586610502	Aleve	24	103	388	0	0
18	17	6122741	2586610502	Aleve	24	103	389	0	0
19	18	6122741	2586610502	Aleve	24	103	390	0	0
20	19	6122741	2586610502	Aleve	24	103	391	0	0
21	20	6122741	2586610502	Aleve	24	103	392	0	0
22	21	6122751	2586610504	Aleve	50	102	383	0	0
23	22	6122751	2586610504	Aleve	50	102	384	0	0
24	23	6122751	2586610504	Aleve	50	102	385	0	0
25	24	6122751	2586610504	Aleve	50	102	386	0	0
26	25	6122751	2586610504	Aleve	50	102	387	0	0
27	26	6122751	2586610504	Aleve	50	102	388	0	0
28	27	6122751	2586610504	Aleve	50	102	389	0	0
29	28	6122751	2586610504	Aleve	50	102	390	0	0
30	29	6122751	2586610504	Aleve	50	102	391	0	0

H ◀ ▶ H \ 7.1 \ 7.2 \ 7.3 \ 7.4 \ 7.5 \ **7.6** / | < |

description of all Aleve brand items to the same description, as shown in Figure 7.6. The Find command is indifferent to case (i.e., whether Aleve is in capital letters or lower case.) When we want to be more precise about capital letters, we can click on the Options button for more detailed specifications.

7.2.2 Sorting

The Sort command can be used not only for database sorting but also for sorting any contiguous set of rows and columns on a spreadsheet. It is found by choosing Home▶Editing▶Sort & Filter. We give an example using the Executives database and another using the Applicants database.

Question: In the Executives database, are there any duplicate records?

Suppose we wish to determine whether any executive (identified by the number in column B) is represented more than once in the sample. We begin by selecting the database. (Exploiting the range name, we do this by clicking the pull-down menu of range names, located directly above column A, and selecting the name Data.) Then, we choose Home▶Editing▶Sort & Filter▶Custom Sort, which opens the Sort window (Figure 7.7). This window has three pull-down windows: Column (to Sort by), Sort On, and Order. Here we sort by the EXECID field, sort on Values, and sort in the order A to Z (note that this field is entered as text, so it must be sorted in alphabetical order). When we click on OK, the sorting procedure is carried out,

FIGURE 7.7 The Sort Window

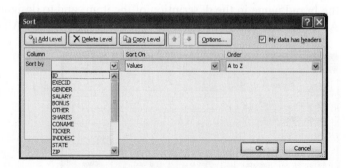

FIGURE 7.8 The Executives Database Sorted by the EXECID Field

	A	B	C	D	E	F	G	H	I
1	ID	EXECID	GENDER	SALARY	BONUS	OTHER	SHARES	CONAME	TICKER
2	2611	00006	MALE	683.462	412.768	0.000	207.828	ADC TELECOMMUNICATIONS INC	ADCT
3	4666	00029	MALE	750.000	1012.500	0.000	641.691	ALLTEL CORP	AT
4	2702	00074	MALE	875.000	1000.000	22.100	2234.402	ARROW ELECTRONICS INC	ARW
5	5562	00085	MALE	324.389	80.563	0.000	16632.050	ATMEL CORP	ATML
6	314	00111	MALE	750.000	825.000	294.770	183.031	BAXTER INTERNATIONAL INC	BAX
7	2766	00140	MALE	509.734	77.257	0.000	354.541	BOB EVANS FARMS	BOBE
8	2777	00152	MALE	700.000	317.665	0.000	39.928	KEYSPAN CORP	KSE
9	5588	00167	MALE	820.677	500.000	45.687	1208.415	CALLAWAY GOLF CO	ELY
10	516	00197	MALE	1350.000	1965.000	0.000		CHEVRON CORP	CHV
11	2962	00223	MALE	1000.000	0.000	0.000	255.198	CMS ENERGY CORP	CMS
12	2654	00246	MALE	1357.026	2162.508	91.721	1517.168	AFLAC INC	AFL
13	5865	00313	MALE	933.333	5554.350	300.034	6033.567	TRIARC COS INC -CL A	TRY
14	822	00315	MALE	771.018	463.200	0.000	224.861	EASTERN ENTERPRISES	EFU
15	9283	00393	MALE	1000.000	2750.000	143.698	643.966	FREEPRT MCMOR COP&GLD -CL B	FCX
16	5067	00398	MALE	205.000	0.000	56.891	9040.113	HUMANA INC	HUM
17	16384	00415	MALE	550.000	275.000	60.703	48.542	BARNES GROUP INC	B
18	1016	00418	MALE	620.000	952.468	0.000	334.430	GENUINE PARTS CO	GPC
19	10891	00474	MALE	410.004	400.000	0.000	1469.256	HORACE MANN EDUCATORS CORP	HMN
20	3296	00482	MALE	450.000	0.000	0.000	151.477	HUNT (JB) TRANSPRT SVCS INC	JBHT
21	3367	00522	MALE	750.000	0.000	46.067	740.528	KANSAS CITY SOUTHERN INDS	KSU
22	1329	00555	MALE	1185.577	3331.968	0.000	46497.711	LIMITED INC	LTD
23	4837	00563	MALE	1051.946	0.000	712.393	17308.998	LOEWS CORP	LTR
24	1459	00608	MALE	369.231	0.000	77.757	141.572	MCKESSON HBOC INC	MCK
25	1679	00705	MALE	730.769	0.000	159.776		OGDEN CORP	OG
26	5415	00731	MALE	800.000	10662.500	0.000	1185.531	PAINE WEBBER GROUP	PWJ
27	4903	00741	MALE	689.178	448.630	0.000	216.999	PPL CORP	PPL
28	9594	00749	MALE	990.000	698.465	128.496	1075.749	FORT JAMES CORP	FJ
29	586	00778	MALE	1000.000	8732.474	448.577	17500.746	CITIGROUP INC	C
30	10955	00791	MALE	773.085	975.000	0.000	4931.348	QUALCOMM INC	QCOM

⏮ ◀ ▶ ⏭ \ 7.1 / 7.2 / 7.3 / 7.4 / 7.5 / 7.6 / 7.7 \ **7.8** / |<

producing the results shown in Figure 7.8. Then, when we scan the ID numbers in the sorted list, we can see that no two adjacent entries match. Therefore, no executive appears twice in the list.

EXCEL TIP
The Sort Command

When we sort a list with column headings, we check the box `My data has headers` in the Sort window. If we need to sort by columns instead of by rows, we click on the Options button and choose `Sort left to right`. Note also that although the Sort operation can be reversed by the Undo command, it is often a good idea to save the data to a new worksheet before sorting, so that the sorted data can be saved and analyzed separately. ∎

Question: In the Applicants database, how does work experience vary among the applicants in successive rounds?

In the previous example, we chose one basis for sorting—the executive identification. Sometimes we want to sort on a second or third criterion. When two sort criteria are specified, ties on the first criterion are broken by the second; and when three sort criteria are specified, ties on the second criterion are broken by the third. To sort on additional criteria, click on `Add Level` in the Sort window. In the Applicants database, for example, we can sort first by Round, then by Industry, and finally by Job Months (see Figure 7.9 for the entries in the Sort window) to get a sense of how applications arrive over time from people in different industries and with different lengths of service in their current job. The first portion of the result appears

FIGURE 7.9 Sorting by Three Fields

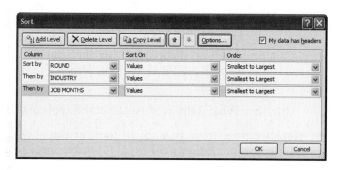

FIGURE 7.10 The Applicants Database Sorted by Round, Industry, and Job Months

	A	B	C	D	E	F	G	H	I
1	ID	ROUND	AGE	SEX	CITZ CODE	1ST CONTACT	JOB MONTHS	INDUSTRY	INDUSTRY DESC.
2	1637	1	25	M	U	Letter	22	10	Accounting
3	470	1	26	M	U	Letter	35	10	Accounting
4	91	1	26	F	U	Letter	36	10	Accounting
5	1694	1	27	M	U	Home Page	36	10	Accounting
6	1585	1	28	M	U	Phone call	37	10	Accounting
7	1638	1	27	M	U	Home Page	40	10	Accounting
8	392	1	24	F	U	Home Page	43	10	Accounting
9	1846	1	28	M	N	Phone call	44	10	Accounting
10	46	1	27	M	U	Phone call	45	10	Accounting
11	118	1	25	M	U	Phone call	48	10	Accounting
12	184	1	27	M	U	Test Score Tape (DNU)	48	10	Accounting
13	371	1	27	F	U	Phone call	48	10	Accounting
14	1793	1	27	F	U	Home Page	48	10	Accounting
15	1710	1	28	M	U	Phone call	49	10	Accounting
16	115	1	28	F	U	Phone call	56	10	Accounting
17	249	1	27	M	N	Home Page	56	10	Accounting
18	7	1	29	M	U	Phone call	60	10	Accounting
19	24	1	28	M	U	Home Page	60	10	Accounting
20	1906	1	29	M	U	Reapplicant	60	10	Accounting
21	1584	1	29	M	U	Phone call	66	10	Accounting
22	1626	1	29	M	U	Phone call	67	10	Accounting
23	504	1	29	M	U	Reapplicant	72	10	Accounting
24	1689	1	29	M	U	Home Page	75	10	Accounting
25	1518	1	29	M	N	Phone call	78	10	Accounting
26	1726	1	32	M	U	Email	82	10	Accounting
27	130	1	30	F	N	Phone call	100	10	Accounting
28	338	1	32	M	N	Email	102	10	Accounting
29	515	1	35	M	U	Reapplicant	120	10	Accounting
30	370	1	35	M	U	Home Page	144	10	Accounting

7.1 / 7.2 / 7.3 / 7.4 / 7.5 / 7.6 / 7.7 / 7.8 / 7.9 / 7.10 /

in Figure 7.10. Looking deeper into this worksheet, we might observe, for example, that the applicants with relatively fewer months in advertising tend to apply in the first two rounds.

7.2.3 Filtering

The Filtering capabilities in Excel allow us to probe a large database and extract a portion of it that deals with the specific records in which we are interested. We may simply want to view the extracted portion temporarily, or we may want to store it separately, for further analysis. As an illustration, we use the Applicants database.

> *Question:* In the Applicants database, what are the characteristics of the applicants from nonprofit organizations?

Suppose we want to view only the applicants who worked in nonprofit organizations. We first select the database and then choose Home▶Editing▶Sort & Filter▶Filter. This adds a list arrow to the title of each column. If we click on the Industry Description list arrow, we see a list of all the possible entries in this column, each one next to a checked box. The first step is to uncheck the box for Select All; this step removes all the checks. Then we can check Nonprofit, and we see the subset of the database that contains Nonprofit entries (Figure 7.11). Filtering does not actually extract any records: it merely hides rows that do not match the filter criteria. Thus, in Figure 7.11, we see that applicants from the Nonprofit sector appear in rows 11, 16, 87, 103, and so on. We can copy and paste this subset to a different sheet if we wish. Alternatively, to restore the view of the entire database, we can either check Select All using the list arrow again, or we can choose Home▶Editing▶Sort & Filter▶ Filter▶Clear. While we are viewing a filtered subset of the database, the triangle marking the list arrow we had used shows up with the Filter symbol. This is a reminder that the information on the screen is filtered.

> *Question:* What is the average age of the applicants from the nonprofit sector?

Here we don't merely want to look at the subset of applicants from the nonprofit sector, but rather we want to describe one aspect of their characteristics

FIGURE 7.11 Filtering the Applicants Database to Highlight Nonprofit Backgrounds

	A	B	C	D	E	F	G	H	I
1	ID	ROUND	AGE	SEX	CITZ CODE	1ST CONTACT	JOB MONTHS	INDUSTRY	INDUSTRY DESC.
11	10	1	31	M	U	Letter	78	420	Nonprofit
16	15	1	27	F	U	Phone call	48	420	Nonprofit
87	86	1	29	M	U	Test Score Tape (DNU)	4	420	Nonprofit
103	102	1	27	M	U	World Wide Web	30	420	Nonprofit
174	173	1	26	M	U	Home Page	37	420	Nonprofit
176	175	1	28	M	U	Phone call	60	420	Nonprofit
209	208	1	32	F	U	Home Page	108	420	Nonprofit
328	327	1	30	M	U	Phone call	62	420	Nonprofit
336	335	1	35	M	U	Phone call		420	Nonprofit
344	343	1	27	M	U	Phone call	44	420	Nonprofit
375	374	1	32	M	U	Home Page	88	420	Nonprofit
412	411	1	27	F	U	Phone call	48	420	Nonprofit
428	427	1	29	F	U	Phone call	62	420	Nonprofit
454	453	1	29	F	N	Test Score Tape (DNU)	56	420	Nonprofit
470	469	1	32	M	N	World Wide Web	61	420	Nonprofit
521	520	1	29	M	U	Home Page	72	420	Nonprofit
570	577	2	26	M	U	Test Score Tape (DNU)	26	420	Nonprofit
614	613	2	30	M	U	Home Page	6	420	Nonprofit
686	685	2	37	M	U	Letter	144	420	Nonprofit
748	747	2	28	F	U	Phone call	60	420	Nonprofit
825	824	2	29	M	N	Letter	58	420	Nonprofit
990	989	2	29	F	U	Phone call	67	420	Nonprofit
998	997	2	32	M	U	Reapplicant	98	420	Nonprofit
1120	1119	3	28	F	U	Phone call	35	420	Nonprofit
1172	1171	3	26	M	U	Home Page	36	420	Nonprofit
1184	1183	3	25	F	U	Phone call	38	420	Nonprofit
1202	1201	3	32	F	U	Email	84	420	Nonprofit
1229	1228	3	31	M	N	Home Page	15	420	Nonprofit

with a quantitative calculation. Intuitively, we might think of using the AVERAGE function. Suppose we place the cursor in cell U1, which lies immediately to the right of the database, and we enter the formula = AVERAGE (C2:C2917). The number that appears (28.97) is the average of the entire set of applicants. In other words, Excel's AVERAGE function does not adjust for the fact that we have done some filtering: it makes the calculation for the hidden cells as well as the visible cells. To make the calculation for just the visible cells, we move the cursor to cell V1 and enter the formula = SUBTOTAL (1,C2:C2917). This produces the desired value 29.48. The SUBTOTAL function ignores the hidden cells in its range.

The SUBTOTAL function is a general function that can be made to perform the calculations of one of Excel's more familiar functions, according to the first argument inside the parentheses. In our example, the argument 1 asks for the average value. The table below lists some of the most common functions that can be calculated with the SUBTOTAL function.

1	AVERAGE
2	COUNT
4	MAX
9	SUM

For a full list of the 11 functions that can be represented this way, invoke Help for the SUBTOTAL function.

One of the options on the arrow list is Number Filters. This allows us to use numerical criteria to sort a field. In a text field, the Text Filters option appears in the same place.

> *Question:* In the Applicants database, what are the ages of the oldest applicants?

For example, to find the 10 oldest applicants, we filter on Age and from its arrow list, we select Number Filters ▶ Top 10. The Top 10 AutoFilter window appears (see Figure 7.12). We could similarly create a list of the Top 10 percent by editing the Items entry in the right-hand window. By editing the middle window, we can restrict ourselves to the Top 5, or the Top 12, and so on, and by editing the left-hand window, we can obtain the Bottom 5, or the Bottom 15 percent, and so on.

> *Question:* Isolate the applicants who worked in either the Nonprofit or Government sectors.

FIGURE 7.12 The Top 10
Autofilter Window

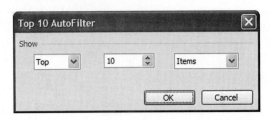

FIGURE 7.13 The Custom
Autofilter Window

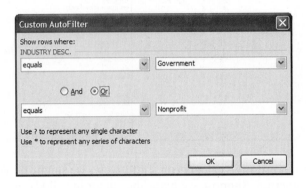

Another option under
`Number Filters` or `Text
Filters` is `Custom Filter`,
which allows us to filter data
using compound criteria. For
example, to isolate the applicants who worked in *either* the
Nonprofit or Government sectors, we select the Custom Filter
option and click the Or button in
the Custom AutoFilter window
to set up the appropriate logical
structure (see Figure 7.13).

Question: Isolate the
applicants who work-
ed in either the Non-
profit or Govern-
ment sectors and
had GMAT scores
above 700.

For more complicated compound criteria, we use the Custom filter on more
than one field. Suppose, for example, that we wish to isolate the applicants who
worked in either the Nonprofit or Government sectors and had GMAT scores above
700. We first filter the Industry Description field for Nonprofit and Government, and
then we filter the GMAT field for scores above 700. The result of these filtering steps
is shown in Figure 7.14.

7.2.4 Tabulating

Pivot Tables allow us to view summaries of the data in convenient tables, most often
in formats known as **cross-tabulation tables** or **cross-tabs**. To appreciate how pivot
tables work, we return to the Analgesics database and specifically to the edited
version where we combined all of the item descriptions into single-word brand names.
(The modified data are saved as a separate worksheet, with a new database name,
such as BrandData.) In what follows, we describe the construction of three pivot
tables, each an elaboration on the one before.

FIGURE 7.14 The Appli-
cants Database After
Filtering

	A ID	B ROUI	C A(	D St	E CITZ COI	F 1ST CONTACT	G JOB MONTI	H INDUSTR	I INDUSTRY DESC.	J DECISION	K GM.
13	12	1	27	M	U	Phone call	51	370	Government	Cancel Enrollment	760
26	25	1	29	M	U	Phone call	30	370	Government	Deny	750
103	102	1	27	M	U	World Wide Web	30	420	Nonprofit	Deny	750
122	121	1	28	M	U	Letter		370	Government	Wait List Deny	720
209	208	1	32	F	U	Home Page	108	420	Nonprofit	Deny	740
263	262	1	32	M	U	Home Page	97	370	Government	Deny	770
323	322	1	32	M	U	Letter	76	370	Government	Wait List Deny	710
412	411	1	27	F	U	Phone call	48	420	Nonprofit	Wait List Deny	710
578	577	2	26	M	U	Test Score Tape (DNU)	26	420	Nonprofit	Deny	730
769	768	2	29	M	U	Email	62	370	Government	Deny	730
863	862	2	30	M	U	World Wide Web	84	370	Government	Deny	750
1128	1127	3	31	M	U	Phone call	78	370	Government	Deny	730
1184	1183	3	25	F	U	Phone call	38	420	Nonprofit	Deny	710
1229	1228	3	31	M	N	Home Page	15	420	Nonprofit	Deny	740
1251	1250	3	28	M	U	Home Page	61	370	Government	Deny	780
1259	1258	3	30	F	N	Letter	86	370	Government	Deny	720
1322	1321	4	28	M	N	World Wide Web	61	370	Government	Deny	730
1497	1496	1	30	F	U	Phone call	82	370	Government	Withdraw before Decisior	770
1532	1531	1	26	F	U	Letter	50	370	Government	Withdraw after Decision	710
1561	1560	1	27	F	U	Phone call	48	420	Nonprofit	Deny	720
1574	1573	1	25	M	U	Email	38	420	Nonprofit	Deny	720
1609	1608	1	33	M	U	Phone call	115	420	Nonprofit	Withdraw after Decision	740
1654	1653	1	32	M	U	Home Page	98	370	Government	Enrolling	750
1809	1808	1	29	M	U	Phone call	24	370	Government	Deny	720
1834	1833	1	29	M	U	Home Page	63	370	Government	Wait List Deny	730
1844	1843	1	27	M	U	Home Page	46	420	Nonprofit	Withdraw after Decision	710
1846	1845	1	26	M	U	Home Page	38	420	Nonprofit	Deny	760
2101	2100	2	31	M	U	Phone call	48	420	Nonprofit	Wait List Deny	720
2113	2112	2	32	F	N	Test Score Tape (DNU)	89	370	Government	Deny	710
2116	2115	2	27	M	U	Phone call	60	370	Government	Wait List Deny	760
2199	2198	2	27	F	U	Home Page	48	420	Nonprofit	Wait List Deny	740
2200	2199	2	26	F	U	Email	28	370	Government	Deny	720

FIGURE 7.15   The Create
Pivot Table Window

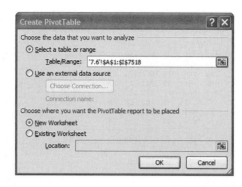

Question: What are total sales of painkillers, and how do they break down by brand name and by store?

First select the database and then choose   Insert▶Tables▶Pivot   Table▶ Pivot Table, which opens the Create Pivot-Table window (Figure 7.15). Place the Pivot Table report in a new worksheet and click OK. The new worksheet will have a template for the pivot table and a panel on the right (Pivot Table Field List) containing the field names (Figure 7.16).

FIGURE 7.16   The Pivot
Table Template

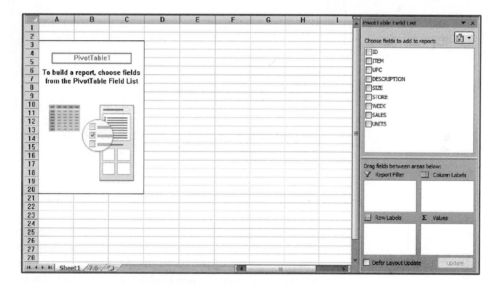

The Pivot Table Field List contains a drop-down menu that offers different layouts; we have shown the "stacked" layout in Figure 7.16. Next, drag the list item SALES to the Values box. A simple pivot table appears with the title Sum of SALES in cell A3 and the value 9432 in cell A4. (If a different title appears, such as Count of SALES, double-click on that name, and the Value Field Settings window appears, similar to the one in Figure 7.17. Select Sum in the main window of this option and click OK.) When the cursor is located on the pivot table (cells A3:A4), the Field List remains visible, otherwise it disappears.

FIGURE 7.17   The Value
Field Settings Window

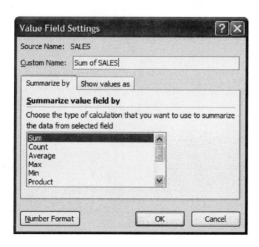

Extend the pivot table by dragging the list item DESCRIPTION to the Row Labels box. A more detailed pivot table appears in cells A3:B12, showing the breakdown of sales by brand name. Extend the pivot table again by dragging the list item STORE to the Column Labels box. The pivot table now shows a sales breakdown by both brand name and store, as shown in Figure 7.18.

Pivot tables can be modified easily after they are built. For example, we can use the filtering arrows in the row or column headings to limit our table to particular row and column entries. We can also edit the table using

FIGURE 7.18 Pivot Table
Showing Sales by Brand
Name and by Store Number

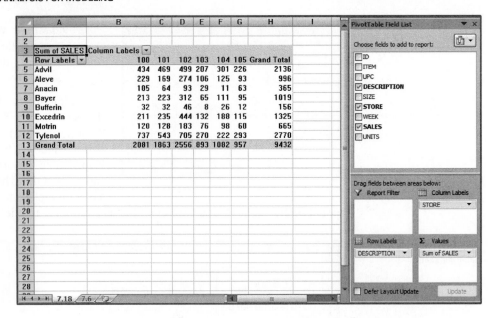

FIGURE 7.18 Pivot Table
Showing Sales by Brand
Name and by Store Number

the Pivot Table Field List. (If the Pivot Table template and Field List are not visible, click anywhere in a pivot table to display them.) We can, for example, substitute WEEK for STORE in the Column Labels box to obtain a breakdown of sales by brand and by week.

> *Question:* In the Applicants database, how does the average GMAT score vary according to the round in which the application is filed?

The admissions process operates on a rolling basis, with a series of five decision periods (rounds). In developing a strategy for round-by-round selections, it is helpful to know whether there are systematic differences among the rounds. To probe this topic, we return to the Applicants database and set up a pivot table. The pivot table shows average GMAT score broken down by ROUND. Figure 7.19 displays the result. Evidently, there is a trend toward lower GMAT scores during the course of the overall admission period.

FIGURE 7.19 Pivot Table
Showing Average GMAT
Scores by Round

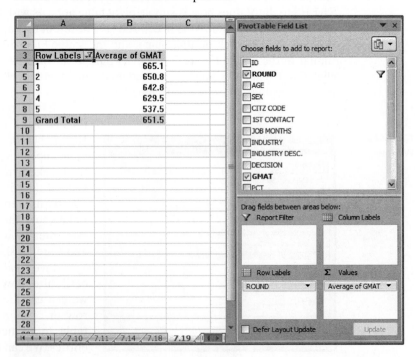

7.3   ANALYZING SAMPLE DATA

As explained earlier, our context for data analysis is determining parameters for our models. For example, we might want to determine the price parameter in the Advertising Budget model. If we have data on past prices—say, quarterly data for 10 years–we can expect to use this information to help determine the price parameter for next year. But next year's price could be different from any of the prices we have seen over the past 10 years. We think of the past data as a sample from some population of prices, just as next year's price is another sample, perhaps from the same or a related population.

We call the set of all possible values for a parameter the **population**. If we were to obtain data for the entire population, then we could build a comprehensive numerical picture of the parameter we are using in our model. Numerical features of populations are described by probability distributions, and, in modeling applications, we are often interested in three measures related to the probability distribution:

- The mean of the distribution
- The variance of the distribution
- A tail probability, or proportion, in the distribution

It is seldom the case, however, that we find ourselves with data covering an entire population. For one thing, the population may have infinite size, making it impossible to obtain all the data. But even with manageable populations, it may be prohibitively time-consuming or expensive to collect population data. Instead, we find ourselves working with information from a portion of the entire population; this portion is called the **sample**. In this situation, **statistics** are summary measures about the values in the sample, and the goal is to construct statistics that are representative of the overall population.

Terms Used in Sampling

Population: the set of all possible values of a parameter

Sample: a subset of the population

Statistic: a summary measure of sample values   ■

When we were analyzing the Analgesics database, we assumed implicitly that our data were complete. In other words, the database contains data on *all* sales for the given stores and time periods. By contrast, the Executives database obviously does not cover all executives; it is a sample of 100 records drawn from a larger population.

The analysis of sample data provides a basis for estimating each of the three measures that help to describe a population (mean, variance, and tail probability). Ideally, the sample data points are drawn from the population of interest. As a practical matter, this may not be possible, but we might have a situation where the population from which samples are drawn is considered to be equivalent to the population of interest. For example, if we are interested in modeling customer demand for *next* month, we may use data on demand in the *previous* 12 months. At some level, observations from six months ago cannot be considered samples from the population of future demand levels, but there may be enough stability in the demand process that we can consider future populations to be essentially equivalent to six-month-old populations. This is an area where judgment is a crucial element in model building.

Samples can be generated in different ways, and the sampling process can determine whether the data are valuable or not. The most common forms of sampling are convenience sampling and random sampling. As its name implies, **convenience sampling** refers to a situation where we have easy access to information about a particular subset of the population. However, a convenience sample may not be representative. Suppose an insurance company wants a sample of customers to estimate family incomes, and it happens that one of its staff members is about to process the forms for all of this month's new customers. Can we use the income data from this group of customers as a sample? It is certainly convenient, because the processing will be taking place in any event. But new customers tend to be younger than the set of all customers, and their incomes tend to be lower. Thus, if we use the convenience sample to estimate income, we will be working with a sample that is not representative.

By contrast, **random sampling** refers to a situation where all values in the population have an equal chance of appearing in the sample. We assume random sampling in our examples unless we specify otherwise, because it is the simplest form of representative sampling. As an example, suppose we wish to take a random sample of 100 applicants from our Applicants database. One quick way to do so is to enter random numbers into the cells of column U by entering the random number function RAND() in the range U2:U2917. Then, using Paste Special to preserve the numbers generated, copy and paste the random values into column V. Next, sort the database by the values in column V. The first 100 applicants make up the desired random sample.

Classical methods in statistics deal with situations involving a random sample of observations. The data points in the sample are drawn from a population that can be described by a probability distribution, but the parameters of that distribution are unknown. Sampling and the analysis of sample information produce statistical data regarding the sample. Statistical data can be used in two ways—**descriptive** and **inferential**. Descriptive statistics summarize information in the sample. They have a limited purpose: they simply give a numerical picture of the observations. Inferential statistics have a different orientation. They use the information in the sample to make inferences about the population and thereby become the basis for estimating model parameters. However, we have to recognize that this type of estimation is subject to two important kinds of errors. First, there is **systematic error**, which occurs if the sample is not representative of the population. We can avoid systematic error by taking some time to design the sampling process and making sure that no unwanted patterns or biases occur in the sample. Second, there is **sampling error** (sometimes called statistical error), which occurs because the sample is merely a subset of the entire population. Because the subset is hardly ever a perfect representation of the population, sampling error is inevitable. The effects of sampling error can be mitigated (e.g., by taking larger samples), but they cannot be avoided entirely.

Sampling error is influenced by two factors—the size of the sample and the amount of variation in the population. Obviously, we can't do much about the latter; it is the nature of the population that we want to learn about, and we have to work with the extent of variation in it, whatever it may be. For example, there may be great variation in executive compensation, or there may be limited variation in applicants' GMAT scores. Whatever the case, we have to accept the level of variation in the population when we are devising our samples. By contrast, we can do something about the size of the sample. The larger the sample, the more it resembles the entire population, and so the smaller the chance for sampling error to occur. Moreover, when we're working on a computer and can obtain data in electronic form, it is only slightly more difficult to manage a large sample than a small one. Thus, a large sample can mitigate the effect of sampling error, even if we cannot overcome it completely.

Recall from our earlier remarks that it is a good idea to do some sensitivity analysis before collecting data. One of the outcomes of sensitivity analysis is insight into how precisely we need to determine certain parameters. From that information, we can estimate how large a sample we really need. The convenience of collecting data aside, we may often find that we need only a small sample to achieve the precision we desire.

7.4 ESTIMATING PARAMETERS: POINT ESTIMATES

As introduced in Chapter 2, parameters are numerical inputs, or uncontrollable variables, in a model. Parameters can be natural constants, such as the speed of sound or the density of water. These are numerical values that we would want to look up in a reference book. Parameters can also be quantitative phenomena in our environment, such as overhead rates, lead times, or process yields. These are numerical values that we might want to estimate from empirical data. When we are building a deterministic model, where we assume that all elements in the model are known with certainty, we want to use the most accurate values possible for our parameters. For such models, we are most likely to be interested in a single value to represent each parameter. When we are building a probabilistic model, and some parameters are described by probability distributions, we often want to estimate the means and variances of those distributions. The information on which estimates are based may come from a database or from a specialized study organized explicitly for the purpose of obtaining estimates. In either case, we can use standard statistical techniques to provide the estimates we seek.

A **point estimate** produces a single number that becomes our "best guess" for the value of the parameter. We then use this estimate in our model as the parameter's value. Following standard practice, we assume that the given data represent a random sample of observations. The ith observation in the sample has the value x_i, and the sample size is n. Three summary statistics for the sample are the sample average, the sample variance, and the sample standard deviation.

The **sample average** is calculated as

$$\bar{x} = \frac{1}{n} \sum_{i=1}^{n} x_i \tag{7.1}$$

The **sample variance** is calculated as

$$s^2 = \sum_{i=1}^{n} \frac{(x_i - \bar{x})^2}{n - 1} \tag{7.2}$$

and its square root is the **sample standard deviation**

$$s = \sqrt{\sum_{i=1}^{n} \frac{(x_i - \bar{x})^2}{n - 1}} \tag{7.3}$$

The sample average is the point estimate of the population mean. For example, in a production model, we might want to represent the time required for a product's final assembly. We might collect data on the 10 most recent assemblies to estimate the final assembly time. If we take the sample average of these 10 observations, using (7.1), that calculation gives us a point estimate of the assembly time to use in our model. The sample average is an estimate of the mean assembly time in the population.

The sample variance is the point estimate of the population variance. Consider an investment model in which we need to estimate the variance of week-to-week changes in a particular stock index. By creating a historical sample of the index and tracking its weekly changes, we can compute the sample variance as a point estimate, using (7.2), for the purposes of our model. The sample variance is an estimate of the variance of weekly values of the stock index in the population.

For purposes of illustration, we use our sample in the Executives database to estimate an average salary. If we select Data▶Analysis▶Data Analysis, we see a window listing a collection of Excel-based statistical analyses. (If the Data Analysis tool does not appear on the Analysis menu, load it by selecting Office Button▶Excel

FIGURE 7.20 The Descriptive Statistics Window

FIGURE 7.21 Descriptive Statistics for Executive Salaries

	SALARY
Mean	679.13806
Standard Error	34.39584508
Median	682.356
Mode	750
Standard Deviation	343.9584508
Sample Variance	118307.4159
Kurtosis	1.147135395
Skewness	0.785424204
Range	1908.296
Minimum	91.704
Maximum	2000
Sum	67913.806
Count	100

options▶Add-ins▶Analysis Toolpak.) If we select Descriptive Statistics, we see another window for this specific tool (see Figure 7.20). We select D1:D101 as the input range (because column D contains salaries) and cell U1 as the output range. Excel detects nonnumerical data in cell D1 unless we check the box for Labels in first row. When we click OK, Excel produces a standard table of descriptive statistics based on our sample, as shown in Figure 7.21. Some of the entries in this table involve advanced material beyond our present coverage, but a few of the items are worth noting. The sample average is listed as the Mean, with a value of 679.138. This result indicates that the average salary in our sample was slightly more than \$679,000. The sample variance and the sample standard deviation are also shown as 118,307 and 343.9585, respectively. These calculations can also be made directly in a cell, using Excel's AVERAGE, VAR, and STDEV functions.

In some cases, we might be interested in **categorical**, or qualitative, information rather than numerical information. Examples might include good (versus defective) output items, in-the-money (versus worthless) stock options, or profitable (versus unprofitable) product introductions. We have two approaches for dealing with this kind of information. First, we can define the value x_i to be 1 or 0, according to whether the ith observation in the sample is, say, good or defective. Having created a quantitative measure out of the categorical information, we can use the above three formulas. A second approach is to use the proportion p observed in the sample as the summary statistic. Since this approach is often the most convenient, we treat the **sample proportion** as a fourth summary statistic of interest. We usually use p to denote the observed proportion in a sample. For example, we may be interested in the number of executives in our sample who received a bonus as part of their compensation. We can construct a small pivot table, based on column E in the Executives database, to verify that 81 of the 100 executives received bonuses that were larger than zero. Therefore, $p = 0.81$ is our sample proportion for positive bonuses. In the spirit of inferential statistics, the calculated proportion is an estimate of the proportion in the population.

7.5 ESTIMATING PARAMETERS: INTERVAL ESTIMATES

We can estimate parameters in two ways: with **point estimates** and with **interval estimates**. As we have seen, a point estimate is a single number that serves as the value of a parameter in our model. The interval estimate approach produces a range of values in which we are fairly sure that the parameter lies, in addition to a single-value point estimate. A range of values for a parameter allows us to perform sensitivity analysis in a systematic fashion, and it provides input for tornado charts or sensitivity tables, as described in Chapter 6.

7.5.1 Interval Estimates for the Mean

An interval estimate is expressed as the point estimate "plus or minus" some amount. In the case of our executive salaries, an interval estimate for the mean might be

$$679.138 \pm 58.525$$

In other words, the interval consists of a range on either side of the point estimate. The width of the range depends on how confident we wish to be at capturing the true value of the parameter. (Recall that, because of sampling error, the sample may not be perfectly representative of the population.) A wide range gives us considerable confidence that we've captured the true mean value, while a narrow range gives us less confidence.

We sometimes state an interval estimate in the form of a probability:

$$P(L \leq \mu \leq U) = 1 - \alpha$$

In this form, L and U represent the lower and upper limits of the interval, and $1 - \alpha$ (usually a large percentage) represents the **confidence level**. The symbol μ represents the true value of the parameter. The confidence level gives the long-run probability that the interval contains the true value of the parameter we're estimating. In other words, if we were to repeat the sampling process many times, about $(1 - \alpha)$ percent of our confidence intervals would contain the true value. However, given any one estimate, either the true value is within the confidence interval or it is not, with probability 1 or 0. In the case of our salary estimate, the interval estimate could be stated as

$$P(679 - 58 \leq \text{true mean salary} \leq 679 + 58) = 1 - \alpha$$

We discuss below how to determine the value of α.

To appreciate the reasoning that lies behind interval estimates, we return briefly to sampling theory. (See Appendix for background information on sampling theory.) Suppose, for the moment, that we are working with a population that is described by a normal probability model with mean μ and standard deviation σ. Imagine that we take repeated samples of n items from that population and calculate the sample average each time. How will this collection of sample averages be distributed? The answer is that the sample averages also follow a normal distribution, with a mean of μ and a variance of σ^2/n. As a specific illustration, suppose we start with a normal population with a mean of 100 and standard deviation of 10. In our experiment, we take samples of size 25 and calculate the sample average for each one. Figure 7.22

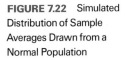

FIGURE 7.22 Simulated Distribution of Sample Averages Drawn from a Normal Population

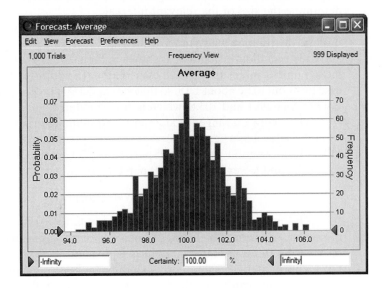

shows the sample averages in a histogram. Note that the histogram resembles the shape of a normal distribution and that, although most of the *population* lies between 70 and 130, the *sample averages* cluster in a much narrower range, from about 94 to 106. Sample averages show far less variability than the population they are drawn from because high outcomes in the sample tend to be balanced by low ones.

We use the term **standard error** to refer to the standard deviation of some function being used to provide an estimate. Here, the sample average (or sample mean) provides our estimate. Its standard deviation is called the **standard error of the mean**, defined as the square root of the variance of the sample average, or

$$\sigma_{\bar{x}} = \sigma/\sqrt{n}$$

We assume here that σ is known; later, we discuss how to proceed when it, too, must be estimated.

For a normal distribution, the *z*-**score** measures the number of standard deviations (in this case, standard deviations of the sample average) away from the mean. Here, the z-score corresponding to any particular sample average is the following:

$$z = \frac{\bar{x} - \mu}{\sigma_{\bar{x}}} = \frac{\bar{x} - \mu}{\sigma/\sqrt{n}} \tag{7.4}$$

The *z*-score tells us how many standard errors we are from the mean. For example, 90 percent of the sample averages will have *z*-scores between -1.64 and $+1.64$. In other words, they differ from μ by at most 1.64 standard errors. Stated another way, the chances that the sample average will fall no more than 1.64 standard errors from the true mean are 90 percent. In our example, the standard error is 2.0 ($\sigma/\sqrt{n} = 10/\sqrt{25} = 2.0$), so we expect 90 percent of the sample averages to fall between 96.72 and 103.28, which is confirmed in Figure 7.22.

Now imagine that we run the same experiment (calculating a sample average for a sample of size n), but without knowing the probability model that describes the original population. Even if the population does not follow a normal distribution, the sample averages will still follow a normal distribution with mean μ and variance σ^2/n, as long as n is sufficiently large. A value of $n > 30$ is considered large enough for the normal distribution to hold, but n can be a good deal smaller if the original population resembles the normal. (A value as small as $n = 6$ is large enough if the population is symmetric with a single peak.) Thus, for large samples, we can conclude that the chances are 90 percent that the sample average will fall no more than 1.64 standard errors from the true mean. The figure of 90 percent is the **confidence level**, and it helps determine the size of the relevant interval.

To continue our illustrative experiment, we take samples of size 25 from a uniform distribution with a range from 80 to 120. Again, we calculate sample averages and construct their histogram, as shown in Figure 7.23. As expected, the form of the histogram resembles the normal distribution. In addition, the standard error in this case turns out to be about 1.15, so that we expect 90 percent of the sample averages to fall between 96.1 and 103.8, which is confirmed in Figure 7.23.

To calculate a range for an interval estimate, then, we begin by expressing the confidence level as a percentage. A typical confidence level would be 90 percent, but other levels commonly used are 95 percent and 99 percent. Using (7.4), we can obtain the upper and lower limits of a 90 percent confidence interval for the mean:

$$\bar{x} \pm z(\sigma/\sqrt{n}) \tag{7.5}$$

The *z*-value in this formula corresponds to a tail probability of 0.05 in a normal distribution. (Including 90 percent of the area under a standard normal distribution in a particular interval is equivalent to 5 percent of the area in each tail.) The numerical value corresponding to a 90 percent confidence interval is $z = 1.64$, which can be verified using the Excel formula NORMSINV(0.95).

FIGURE 7.23 Simulated Distribution of Sample Averages Drawn from a Uniform Population

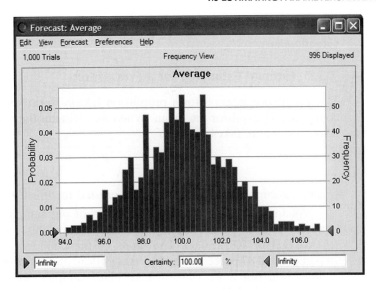

Excel's standard normal inverse function computes a z-value from a value of the cumulative distribution function (see Appendix). Because the confidence interval of 90 percent corresponds to 5 percent in each tail, the cumulative distribution function corresponds to 0.95 in this case. The Excel formula returns a value of approximately 1.645. Some common z-values are summarized in the table below:

confidence level	90%	95%	99%
z-value	1.645	1.960	2.576

■

We mentioned earlier that formula (7.5) for the interval estimate assumes that the standard deviation σ in the underlying population is known. But this will rarely be the case. When the standard deviation is not known, its value also must be estimated from the sample data. To do so, we replace σ by its point estimate, the sample standard deviation s, and then we can use (7.5), provided that our sample is larger than about $n = 30$. (When n is less than 30, other approaches are needed that are beyond the level of this book.) In the case of our sample of executive salaries, we have $s = 343.9585$. The form of a 90 percent confidence interval for the mean becomes

$$\bar{x} \pm z(s/\sqrt{n}) \tag{7.6}$$

Thus, our interval estimate for the population mean becomes

$$679.138 \pm 1.64(34.396) = 679.138 \pm 56.409$$

The 90 percent confidence interval for the true mean extends from \$622,729 to \$735,547. (In Excel's Descriptive Statistics tool, there is an option to calculate the half-width of the confidence interval and include it in the summary table. When Excel makes this calculation, it does not use the normal approximation mentioned earlier for sample sizes above 30, but instead uses a more precise formula. In the case of our example, the half-width is reported as 57.111, as compared to the approximate value of 56.409.)

Thinking back to our discussion of tornado charts in Chapter 6, an interval estimate calculated from (7.6) could provide a useful guideline for the high and low values of the parameter. If one of the parameters in our model is an executive's salary, then we can use \$679,138 as a point estimate; when we perform sensitivity analysis, we can use upper and lower limits of \$622,729 and \$735,547 to generate a tornado chart.

7.5.2 Interval Estimates for a Proportion

The confidence interval for a proportion takes a form very similar to that of the confidence interval for the mean. When we estimate the sample proportion p, the interval estimate takes the form

$$p \pm z\sqrt{\frac{p(1-p)}{n}} \tag{7.7}$$

Usually, a sample size of at least 50 is needed for this formula to be reliable.

As an example, recall that 81 percent of our sample of executives received bonuses. The 90 percent confidence interval for this estimate becomes $0.81 \pm 1.64(0.0392)$ or 0.81 ± 0.06. The limits of the confidence interval are therefore 75 percent and 87 percent. The true proportion, of course, either lies in this interval or does not. But if we were to take many samples, we would capture the true proportion with (7.7) about 90 percent of the time.

7.5.3 Sample-Size Determination

Formulas for interval estimates—such as (7.5), (7.6), and (7.7)—express the range of the interval as a function of the sample size n. To this point, we have started with a sample of size n and proceeded to calculate an interval estimate. However, if we know the precision we want, we can use this same relationship to calculate the minimum necessary sample size. For example, suppose we wish to estimate the mean of a sample to within a range of $\pm R$. We can manipulate (7.5) algebraically to obtain

$$n = (z\sigma/R)^2 \tag{7.8}$$

This formula applies to the conditions associated with (7.5): sampling from a normal distribution with a known variance. When the standard deviation is unknown, we simply substitute its estimate. But where do we find an estimate if we haven't yet taken the sample? The solution is to take a fairly small sample (say, 10 or 20) to get an initial estimate s of the standard deviation, and then use (7.8), with s in place of σ, to determine more precisely how large the sample size should be.

For example, if we take our entire sample of 100 executives, we estimate the standard deviation of salaries to be 343.958. If we wish to estimate the mean salary to within \$25,000 with 90 percent confidence, then the necessary sample size, from (7.8), must be

$$n = [(1.64)(343.958)/25]^2 = 509$$

Therefore, to produce an estimate with the desired precision, we need a sample more than five times as large as what we have. This assumes, of course, that our original estimate of the standard deviation is accurate.

The same reasoning applies to the case of estimating a proportion. Because the formula in (7.7) involves the sample size, we can solve for the minimum necessary sample size in terms of the proportion p. The algebra leads us to the following sample-size formula:

$$n = z^2 p(1-p)/R^2 \tag{7.9}$$

If we have only a rough idea of the unknown proportion p, we can use that value in the formula, but if we have absolutely no idea at all about p, we can still proceed. The term $p(1-p)$ is maximized when $p = 0.5$. So a conservative value would be obtained by substituting this value into (7.9) to obtain

$$n = (z/2)^2/R^2 \tag{7.10}$$

If we wish to estimate the proportion of executives who receive bonuses to within 0.02, at 90 percent confidence, then (7.9) tells us that we would need a sample size of 1,035, based on our estimate of the proportion p as 0.81. The more conservative formula in (7.10) prescribes a sample size of 1,681, using $p = 0.5$.

7.6 SUMMARY

Our premise in this chapter is that modeling is the central task; data collection and analysis support the modeling task where appropriate. Nevertheless, when early sensitivity testing indicates that certain parameters must be estimated precisely, we turn to data analysis for locating relevant information and for estimating model parameters.

The process of finding facts in data is aided by a facility with Excel and in particular with its database capabilities. As more data sets become available through public sources or on the Internet, it will become more valuable to be able to probe data sets quickly and intelligently. Excel provides an array of commands for searching, sorting, filtering, and tabulating data. Business analysts should be familiar with these tools in order to use data intelligently in spreadsheet modeling.

The basic numerical task involving data is to estimate model parameters. For this purpose, Excel provides statistically oriented tools that help make the process convenient. The Data Analysis tool for calculating descriptive statistics enables rapid construction of point estimates and interval estimates from raw data.

SUGGESTED READINGS

The popularity of spreadsheets, both in education and in industry, has influenced the writing of textbooks in several areas, including statistics. The list below contains textbooks on basic statistics, mostly with a classical treatment of the subject, except that they rely on a spreadsheet perspective.

Albright, S. C., W. L. Winston, and C. Zappe. 2006. *Data Analysis and Decision Making with Microsoft Excel*. 3rd ed. Mason, OH: South-Western.

Evans, J. R. 2007. *Statistics, Data Analysis, and Decision Modeling*. 3rd ed. Upper Saddle River, NJ: Prentice-Hall.

Levine, D. M., D. Stephan, T. C. Krehbiel, and M. L. Berenson. 2004. *Statistics for Managers using Microsoft Excel*. 4th ed. Upper Saddle River, NJ: Prentice-Hall.

Pelosi, M. K., and T. M. Sandifer. 2002. *Doing Statistics for Business with Excel*. 2nd ed. New York: John Wiley and Sons.

EXERCISES

1. The database Dish.xlsx contains a transaction history describing more than 4,000 purchases of detergent at a number of stores in a grocery chain over a period of several weeks.

a. Compile a pivot table that gives a tabulation of sales (in cases) by brand (Dove, Sunlight, and so on).

b. Compile a pivot table that gives a tabulation of sales broken down by brand and by week.

c. Compile a pivot table that gives a tabulation of sales broken down by brand, by week, and by store.

d. Compile a pivot table that gives a tabulation of the number of ounces purchased broken down by brand and by size of container. What is the sales volume in ounces for each brand?

2. The database Tissue.xlsx contains a transaction history describing more than 3,700 purchases of facial tissues at a number of stores in a grocery chain over a period of several weeks.

a. Compile a pivot table that gives a tabulation of the number of units sold by brand.

b. Compile a pivot table that gives a tabulation of sales units broken down by brand and by week.

c. Compile a pivot table that gives a tabulation of sales units broken down by brand, by week, and by store.

d. Compile a pivot table that gives a tabulation of sales units broken down by brand and by size of container. What is the sales volume in ounces for each brand?

3. The database Applicants.xlsx contains a description of an MBA applicant pool for an unspecified year in the 1990s. For each of the following requirements, create a separate worksheet and extract the data from the original database.

a. Among enrolling students, what is the average GMAT score? What is the average in the applicant pool as a whole?

b. How many in the applicant pool represented Financial Services in terms of job background? What was their average age? What was their average work experience (months)? What was their average GMAT score?

c. How many in the applicant pool represented Consulting in terms of job background? What was their average age? What was their average work experience (months)? What was their average GMAT score?

d. What proportion of the applicant pool had two or more degrees?

4. The database Population.xlsx contains data on the populations of the 50 states from 1990 to 1999. For each of the following requirements, create a separate worksheet and extract the data from the original database.

a. Sort the states by population in 1999, from highest to lowest.

b. Were the 10 states with the highest population the same in 1999 as in 1990?

c. Which state had the largest percentage increase in population from 1990 to 1999?

d. Which states had populations of more than 2 million or less than 1 million in 1995?

5. The database Executives.xlsx contains salary and company data on 100 executives. For each of the following requirements, create a separate worksheet and extract the data from the original database.

a. Among the top five executives in terms of Salary, how many work in the oil industry?

b. What is the total compensation (salary, bonus, and other) for each of the executives who rank in the top 10 on this dimension?

c. How many executives work for companies in California or New York and have sales less than 4,000?

d. How many executives who work for companies in California or New York have sales less than 4,000 or assets above 10,000?

6. The database Applicants.xlsx contains a description of an MBA applicant pool for an unspecified year in the 1990s. For each of the following requirements, create a separate worksheet and extract the data from the original database.

a. What percentage of the applicants were male?

b. How old was the youngest male applicant?

c. What was the GMAT score of the female with the highest score?

d. How many Economics majors are there among these applicants?

e. How many male Economics majors are there with Nonprofit experience?

f. How many males are there over the age of 28 who contacted the school with a phone call or letter?

7. Your company is changing its name, and you've been asked to study the impact of a name change announcement on the subsequent return generated by the firm's stock. In a sample of 400 companies that have made such announcements, you discover that over the 28-day period after a name change announcement, the average company experiences a 17 percent increase in price, with a standard deviation of 8 percent.

a. What is a 90 percent confidence interval for the mean stock price change for companies announcing a name change?

b. The range from 16 percent to 18 percent would constitute what (percentage) confidence interval for the mean change?

c. Do the data suggest that there is at least a 75 percent chance that a company's stock price will go up after a name change announcement?

8. Five years ago, an automobile manufacturer started offering an extended warranty to buyers of its sport-utility vehicle. The extended warranty covered defects occurring after the initial three-year warranty expired. Of the 10,000 people who bought the sport-utility vehicle in the first year of the program, 15 percent purchased the extended warranty.

In the Warranty Department, you have recently received data on a random sample of 200 of the cars sold in the first year that the extended warranty was available. For this sample, the average extended-warranty expenditure per car for the one-year period after the initial warranty elapsed was $350 with a standard deviation of $100.

a. What is a 95 percent confidence interval for the mean one-year extended-warranty expenditure per automobile?

b. At its introduction, the extended warranty was priced at $225 per year per automobile. Compute a 95 percent confidence interval for the one-year profitability of the extended warranty.

c. How large a sample would the Warranty Department require if it wanted its 95 percent confidence interval for the mean warranty expenditure to be no more than ±$5?

9. The Luxor Computer Company plans to introduce a pyramid-shaped desktop computer. The company is interested in the proportion of prospective customers who find the unusual shape a positive selling point. In a random sample of 350 potential customers, 203 of the respondents indicated that the shape was a positive selling point.

a. What is an estimate of the proportion of prospective customers who find the unusual shape a positive selling point?

b. What is a 90 percent confidence interval for the proportion of prospective customers who find the unusual shape a positive selling point?

c. How many prospective customers would have to be queried for Luxor to be 90 percent certain that its estimated proportion was within five percent of the true value?

10. The number of staff personnel needed to handle patients at a medical center is determined by the mean time that patients must wait before being attended to by a physician. For a random sample of 100 previously recorded emergencies, the sample mean waiting time was 72 minutes, with a standard deviation of 28 minutes.

a. What is a 50 percent confidence interval for the actual mean waiting time?

b. What is a 99 percent confidence interval for the actual mean waiting time?

11. Oxbridge University is contemplating a policy under which they would pay employees to not bring their vehicles to campus. Instead of paying an annual fee for on-campus parking, employees would receive a rebate from the university, provided that they found alternative means of getting back and forth to work. Since this idea is unusual, the university wants to estimate the proportion of its employees who would sign up. When the option was offered to a random sample of 40 employees, 5 signed up.

a. What is the estimated proportion that will sign up? What is the estimated standard deviation of the proportion that will sign up?

b. What is a 95 percent confidence interval for the proportion that will sign up?

c. How large a sample size is required to obtain a 95 percent confidence interval of ±0.05?

12. An engineer working on the auto assembly line is preparing to estimate the mean time required to install a dashboard. Assuming a required standard deviation of 10 seconds in the estimated mean, determine the sample size under the following conditions:

a. The desired confidence level of being in error by no more than one second (in either direction) is 0.99.

b. The desired confidence level is 0.95 for a tolerable error of one second.

c. A confidence level of 0.99 is desired with a tolerable error of two seconds. How does the sample size you obtain compare with your answer to (a)?

d. Repeat (a), assuming that $\sigma = 20$ seconds. By how much does the sample size decrease?

8 Regression Analysis

8.1 INTRODUCTION

Spreadsheet models consist of numerical inputs (data and perhaps decision variables) and calculated variables that are related by equations. These equations, or relationships among variables, are drawn from a variety of sources. Some are essentially definitions, such as *Profit = Revenue − Cost*, or *Net Cash Flow = Cash Income + Depreciation − Capital Expenditures*. Other relationships are essentially logical, such as this IF statement for units sold: `IF(Demand>Units available, Units available, Demand)`. Another class of relationships attempts to describe the behavior of individuals or other entities. The relationship between advertising and sales in the Advertising Budget example of Chapters 5 and 6 (*Unit sales = 35 × Seasonal factor × SQRT*(3000 + *Advertising*)) is such a behavioral relationship, because it describes how advertising influences the decisions of consumers.

Two aspects of a behavioral relationship are important: its structural form and its parameters. In the relationship for unit sales above, the parameters are the numbers 35 and 3,000, whereas the structural form is nonlinear. The ultimate outcome of a spreadsheet model can depend, of course, on both the values of the parameters and the functional form of the relationship. This is why in Chapter 6 we advocated performing sensitivity analysis on both the parameters and the structure of the key relationships in a model.

In Chapter 2 we pointed out that we can incorporate parameters into a model without first collecting data, provided we later carry out a sensitivity analysis. In a similar fashion, we can incorporate a particular relationship into a model by specifying its structural form and parameters without collecting data, if we later test the sensitivity of our results to our assumptions.

In some circumstances, however, data can be valuable in helping to determine the parameters in a relationship or its structural form. The process of using data to formulate relationships is known as **regression analysis**. In this approach, we identify one variable as the **response variable**, which means that it can be predicted from the values of other variables. In other words, the response variable can be explained—at least in part and in a quantitative fashion—by the other variables. Those other variables are called **explanatory variables**. Regression models that involve one explanatory variable are called **simple** regressions; when two or more explanatory variables are involved, the relationships are called **multiple** regressions. Regression models are also divided into **linear** and **nonlinear** models, depending on whether the relationship between the response and explanatory variables is linear or nonlinear.

In this chapter we discuss the basic tools of regression analysis that are needed by spreadsheet analysts. We do not cover various advanced methods that might be important to those specializing in data analysis. As always, our focus is on practical methods that can be used in the context of modeling a business problem using spreadsheets.

This chapter is organized around an example in which a firm must decide how much capacity it needs to build to produce a new drug. This decision problem gives us a realistic context within which to demonstrate how regression analysis supplements the other modeling tools we have discussed. After presenting this example and an initial analysis of the capacity decision, we introduce two tools for exploratory data analysis: scatter plots and correlation. We next introduce simple linear regression and methods for testing how well a given relationship fits the available data. Then we move on to simple nonlinear regression and multiple regression. Finally, we discuss the important assumptions behind regression analysis. The chapter concludes with an optional section on Trendline and LINEST, two of Excel's many methods for executing regression analysis.

8.2   A DECISION-MAKING EXAMPLE

Forecasts of future sales are an essential ingredient in selecting the capacity of a new manufacturing facility. While capacity can be adjusted up or down during the life of a plant, it is usually less expensive to build the appropriate size at the start. In this example, we illustrate how to build a model to help determine the size for a new plant.

EXAMPLE
Bundy
Pharma-
ceuticals, Inc.

Bundy Pharmaceuticals, Inc. (BPI) is planning to shift production of its popular arthritis drug from overseas contract suppliers to domestic manufacturing. The question BPI faces is how big a plant to build. Sales of the drug have been growing over the past decade, but future sales cannot be known for certain. Too small a plant will leave some demand unsatisfied and revenues lost, but too large a plant will lead to inefficiencies and excess costs.

The current price of the drug is $10 per unit. Since sales have increased from around 500,000 units to more than one million units over the past 10 years, BPI is currently considering plant capacities in the range from 1.2 million to 2.5 million units annually. Within this range, it costs a minimum of $5 million to build a plant, with an incremental cost of approximately $10 per unit of annual capacity. For example, a 1.5 million-unit plant costs $20 million.

Once a plant has been built, its capacity determines both its variable and fixed costs of operation. The fixed costs are estimated to be $1.50 for each unit of capacity. Assuming a capacity of at least one million units, the maximum variable costs are $6 per unit. Each incremental 100,000 units of capacity above one million reduces variable costs by $0.10. For example, variable costs are $5.50 for a 1.5 million-unit plant. Corporate policy specifies that new plant decisions be made on the basis of a 10-year NPV using a discount rate of 10 percent. ∎

8.2.1   Base-case Analysis

Our first cut at creating a model for this situation should be based on simple but reasonable assumptions. The purpose of this prototype is primarily to translate the given information into a usable model structure with limited effort and rework. As shown in Figure 8.1[*], the model includes seven parameters that are given in the problem description. The model also has one decision variable (plant capacity), which is arbitrarily set to 1.5 million at this stage. One area that needs special consideration is the forecast of demand over the next 10 years. Historical data on sales over the past 10 years are given in the accompanying table. (*Note*: Since offshore production capacity has been used, there has not been a year in which demand exceeded sales.)

Year	Unit Sales
1	487,000
2	560,000
3	601,000
4	689,000
5	788,000
6	854,000
7	902,000
8	957,000
9	991,000
10	1,010,000

[*]To download spreadsheets for this chapter, go to the Student Companion Site at www.wiley.com/college/powell.

FIGURE 8.1 Base-case Spreadsheet for BPI

	A	B	C	D	E	F	G	H	I	J
1	Bundy Pharmaceuticals Inc.									
2	SGP/KRB									
3	1/1/2006									
4										
5		Parameters	Interest rate		10%					
6			Unit revenue		$10.00					
7			Plant construction cost							
8				fixed	$5,000,000					
9				variable	$10.00					
10			Fixed operating cost		$1.50					
11			Variable operating cost							
12				maximum	$6.00					
13				decline rate	$0.10					
14			Demand							
15				Initial level	1,010,000					
16				Annual growth	50,000					
17										
18		Decisions		Capacity	1,500,000					
19										
20		Results		NPV	$561,374					
21										
22		Model	Plant Cost	$20,000,000						
23										
24			Year	Demand	Sales	Vcost	Fcost	Cash F		
25			0	1010000				($20,00		
26			1	1060000	1060000	5.50	2250000	$2,520,000		
27			2	1110000	1110000	5.50	2250000	$2,745,		
28			3	1160000	1160000	5.50	2250000	$2,970,		
29			4	1210000	1210000	5.50	2250000	$3,195,		
30			5	1260000	1260000	5.50	2250000	$3,420,		
31			6	1310000	1310000	5.50	2250000	$3,645,		
32			7	1360000	1360000	5.50	2250000	$3,870,000		
33			8	1410000	1410000	5.50	2250000	$4,095,		
34			9	1460000	1460000	5.50	2250000	$4,320,		
35			10	1510000	1500000	5.50	2250000	$4,500,		
36							NPV	$561,374		
37										

Construction costs occur throughout year 0. They are recognized at the end of the year and discounted back to the start of the

Ongoing revenues and costs are recognized at the end of each year.

All costs are discounted back to the start of year 0.

8.1

It is too early in the analysis process to undertake an elaborate and time-consuming statistical analysis of these data. At this early stage we have no idea how critical the demand forecast is to the decision at hand. For this first prototype, we will look for a way to incorporate the essential features of the given data with minimal effort.

A quick glance at the demand history shows that sales grew from about 500,000 ten years ago to about one million last year. A simple but plausible forecast of future demand would be to assume that this rate of increase (about 50,000 units per year) will continue for the next 10 years. We need two parameters to represent demand according to these assumptions: an initial value (1.01 million) and the annual growth rate (50,000). Accordingly, demand next year is 1.06 million, growing to 1.51 million 10 years out. We will continue to assume a capacity of 1.5 million, since the task of finding the *best* capacity level is yet to come. Under these assumptions, demand first exceeds 1.5 million (causing unsatisfied demand) only in the tenth year. The NPV for this case is $0.561 million, as shown in Figure 8.1.

8.2.2 Sensitivity Analysis

Given that the base-case model accurately represents our understanding of the problem, we next wish to explore the implications for the capacity decision. Since we have only a single decision variable, we can use the Data Sensitivity tool to find the optimal capacity. The results are shown in Figure 8.2. It appears that the best we can do is an NPV of $1.811 million with a 1.25 million-unit plant. Notice that with a capacity of 1.25 million, demand begins to exceed capacity in year 5. The optimal capacity level balances the costs of building additional capacity with the benefits of increased sales and lower variable costs. This result is, of course, only a first estimate—an initial, rough idea of where the best capacity level may lie, given a simple model and a number of assumptions, each of which should be tested. (A more detailed search for the optimum capacity shows that a slight improvement can be made by choosing capacity of 1.26 million, but at this stage in the analysis, that is more precision than necessary.)

One way to test our model is to determine the sensitivity of the NPV to each of the input parameters. This can be accomplished using a tornado chart, as shown in Figure 8.3. In this chart, each of the parameters was varied by 10 percent from its base-case value. Keeping in mind the caveats we mentioned in Chapter 6 about

FIGURE 8.2 Optimal Capacity Determination for BPI

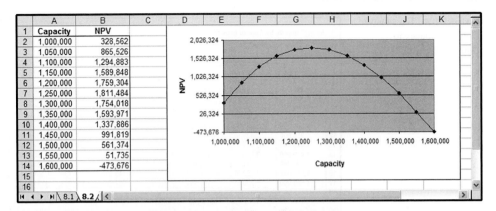

tornado charts, we find that this chart shows that two parameters, unit revenue and maximum variable operating cost, have the largest impacts on NPV. The initial demand level has some impact on the NPV, but the growth rate in demand has a relatively small impact, assuming that a 10 percent deviation is an accurate representation of the true uncertainty. This is at least partly because with a capacity of 1.25 million, sales reach capacity in year 4, so later growth in demand has no impact on the NPV.

Another useful insight can be derived from sensitivity analysis. For example, let's examine the annual growth rate of 50,000 units. How sensitive is the optimal capacity to this assumption? We can repeat the sensitivity test of capacity for a variety of growth parameters. This gives rise to a two-way sensitivity table (see Figure 8.4)— resembling the first sensitivity table but with a different column for each different growth rate. We've used a bold font in the table to highlight the maximum NPV in each column, showing the location of the optimal capacity for each growth rate. The results show that optimal capacity is relatively *insensitive* to the growth parameter. When we vary the growth parameter from 10,000 to 90,000 units per year, an increase of 900 percent, the optimal capacity increases from 1.05 million to 1.5 million, only about 50 percent. Now, it is unlikely that future growth is as uncertain as we have depicted it here. If, in fact, future growth lies somewhere between 40,000 and 60,000 units per year, and we build a plant based on an assumed rate of 50,000 units, our resulting NPV will fall short of the optimum by less than 5 percent.

FIGURE 8.3 Tornado Chart for BPI

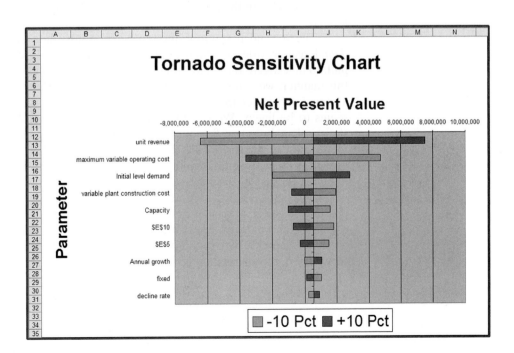

FIGURE 8.4 Sensitivity of Optimal Capacity to Demand Growth

	A	B	C	D	E	F	G	H	I	J
1	NPV: Capacity by Annual growth									
2										
3	Capacity					Annual growth				
4		10,000	20,000	30,000	40,000	50,000	60,000	70,000	80,000	90,000
5	1,000,000	328,562	328,562	328,562	328,562	328,562	328,562	328,562	328,562	328,562
6	1,050,000	676,594	798,584	832,055	865,526	865,526	865,526	865,526	865,526	865,526
7	1,100,000	437,074	929,742	1,134,702	1,230,195	1,294,883	1,328,767	1,362,651	1,396,536	1,430,420
8	1,150,000	-126,759	782,213	1,203,273	1,436,501	1,589,848	1,686,505	1,783,161	1,817,459	1,851,756
9	1,200,000	-704,963	388,960	1,092,607	1,497,187	1,759,304	1,943,185	2,069,693	2,167,514	2,265,335
10	1,250,000	-1,283,166	-161,324	821,985	1,423,897	1,811,484	2,103,111	2,289,181	2,475,251	2,574,237
11	1,300,000	-1,861,370	-726,330	393,639	1,207,210	1,754,018	2,146,165	2,441,222	2,656,181	2,844,440
12	1,350,000	-2,439,573	-1,291,335	-143,097	880,120	1,593,971	2,104,522	2,501,229	2,799,717	3,044,185
13	1,400,000	-3,017,777	-1,856,341	-694,904	451,110	1,337,886	1,981,568	2,475,409	2,876,675	3,178,595
14	1,450,000	-3,595,981	-2,421,346	-1,246,712	-72,077	991,819	1,780,584	2,390,062	2,866,679	3,272,505
15	1,500,000	-4,174,184	-2,986,352	-1,798,519	-610,686	561,374	1,504,737	2,245,112	2,819,452	3,278,332
16	1,550,000	-4,752,388	-3,551,357	-2,350,326	-1,149,295	51,735	1,157,081	2,002,165	2,689,017	3,269,739
17	1,600,000	-5,330,591	-4,116,362	-2,902,133	-1,687,905	-473,676	724,431	1,706,492	2,502,337	3,153,818
18										
19	Max NPV	$676,594	$929,742	$1,203,273	$1,497,187	$1,811,484	$2,146,165	$2,501,229	$2,876,675	$3,278,332
20	Best Capacity	1,050,000	1,100,000	1,150,000	1,200,000	1,250,000	1,300,000	1,350,000	1,400,000	1,500,000
21										
22			Pct of Optimal							
23			for Capacity = 1.25M		95.1%		98.1%			
24										

H ◄ ► H \ 8.1 / 8.2 / 8.3 \ 8.4 / |◄ |

8.2.3 Base-case Summary

Our base-case results suggest that if demand growth is around 50,000 units per year over the next 10 years, we should build about 1.25 million units of capacity. Sensitivity analysis shows that if we are confident that actual demand growth will be between, say, 40,000 and 60,000 units annually, then 1.25 million is close to the optimal level. This may well be enough precision for making a good decision. After all, many things about the future are uncertain, in addition to demand. Recommending an optimal plant capacity of 1.234567 million units would suggest an implausible level of precision in the analysis. Later, we return to this example and apply statistical methods to explore their impact.

8.3   EXPLORING DATA: SCATTER PLOTS AND CORRELATION

In our initial approach to the BPI case, we created a simple linear growth model for forecasting demand. Starting in year 1 this relationship can be written as

$$Demand = 101,000 + 50,000 \times Time$$

Now we will begin the process of exploring the historical data on sales to refine this model.

The first and most important step in exploratory data analysis is simply to *plot the data*. Excel provides us with the option of building an X–Y chart, also called a **scatter plot**, to investigate the relationship between two variables. When we look at data in this manner, we can get an indication as to whether there is a positive or negative association between the variables, how strong that association is, and whether or not it seems to be linear. We can then back up our visual impressions with some basic statistical analyses to refine our understanding of the dependency. Figure 8.5 shows a scatter plot of the historical sales data against time. This plot confirms the steady growth in sales over time, and it suggests that a linear model may be reasonable, although there is also a suggestion that growth has been slowing in recent years.

The first statistical step in analyzing this data is to measure the strength of a possible linear relationship between *Sales* and *Time*. Suppose we have a sample consisting of n pairs of observations for the variables x and y. Using the definitions given in Chapter 7, we can compute the average and the standard deviation for x and for y. Then, the **correlation** is defined as

$$r = \frac{1}{(n-1)} \sum_{i=1}^{n} \left(\frac{(x_i - \bar{x})}{s_x} \right) \left(\frac{(y_i - \bar{y})}{s_y} \right)$$

FIGURE 8.5   Scatter Plot for BPI Sales History

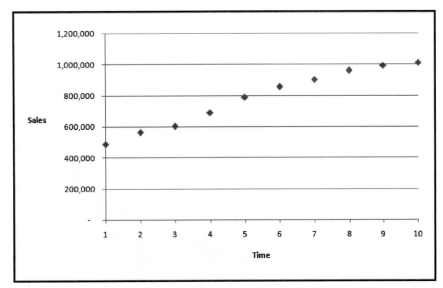

Here, we use $\bar{x}$ to represent the average of the variable x and similarly for $\bar{y}$. We also use s_x to represent the standard deviation of the variable x and similarly for s_y. The quantity r measures the strength of a linear association between the two variables x and y. In other words, it is a measure of the degree to which the relationship between x and y follows a straight line.

The r-statistic has a number of convenient features. The value of r will always lie in the range between -1 and 1. A value of $r > 0$ indicates a positive association between the two variables. In other words, when one variable is above its mean, the other tends to be above its mean as well. A value of $r < 0$ indicates a negative relationship; that is, when one variable is above its mean, the other tends to be below its mean. When r is close to 1 (or -1), the association is a strong one, but when r is close to 0, the association is weak. Also, because the calculation of r is based on z-values, it is independent of the units of measurement. In other words, we may scale the variables x and y before we make the calculation, but we still get the same value for r.

If we find that r is close to zero, the data do not show a strong linear association between the two variables. We may then look for a different kind of data set, or we may retreat from the assumption that a linear relationship exists between the two variables. If we find that r is large (although there is no formal cutoff for "large"), we know that a strong linear relationship exists between the variables, and we can proceed to investigate what straight line best describes that relationship.

As an example, suppose we take the 10-year history of annual sales at BPI. Even a casual look at the figures will suggest a linear relationship, but the scatter plot (see Figure 8.5) underscores the possibility. The calculation of the correlation r can be obtained from the Excel function CORREL(A8:A17,B8:B17), which yields a value of $r = 0.988$. This high value for the correlation suggests that demand has risen over time in a near-linear fashion. We may ultimately decide that a nonlinear relationship makes more economic sense, but the scatter plot and the calculation of r provide strong evidence that a simple linear trend model is justifiable, at least over the range of the given observations.

For a different example we turn to the Executives database, first introduced in Figure 7.3 of Chapter 7. We are curious about the relationship between executive salaries (column D) and company sales (column N). We calculate the correlation as $r = 0.473$. This positive value tells us that salaries tend to be high in firms whose sales are high (and vice versa). However, when we look at a scatter plot of the data (Figure 8.6), we may be able to detect a bit of a positive relationship, but there is a great deal of scatter. In other words, although the relation is a positive one, we do not

FIGURE 8.6 Scatter Plot for Company Sales and Executive Salaries

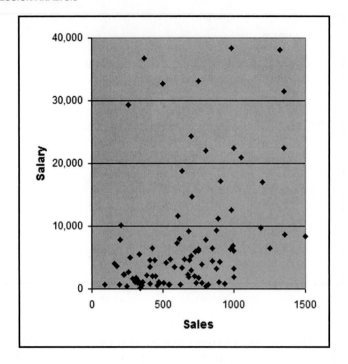

have a strong indication of a linear relationship between sales and salary. (Note that Figure 8.6 omits a small number of points representing very high salaries.)

8.4 SIMPLE LINEAR REGRESSION

The simple linear regression equation takes the form

$$y = a + bx + e \tag{8.1}$$

where y is the response variable, x is the explanatory variable, and the constants a and b represent the intercept and slope, respectively, of the regression line. The term e represents an "error" term. In other words, we may think of the relationship between x and y as if it follows the straight line formed by the function $y = a + bx$, subject to some unexplained factors captured in the error term. The unexplained factors may simply represent the limitations of our knowledge about the true relationship. Alternatively, we can think of the response variable as following a probability model, with y as its mean value, for any given value of x. The error term then represents the random deviation of the response variable from its mean value, y. We will write the error term explicitly when introducing a new type of model, but we'll omit it when discussing examples.

Regression is a means to find the line that most closely matches the observed relationship between x and y. Although the concept of "most closely" could be implemented in alternative ways, the most common approach is to minimize the sum of squared differences between the observed values and the model values. (Approaches to the problem of finding the closest match fall into the general category of optimization methods that we cover in more detail in Chapters 10–13.)

Why is minimizing the sum of squared differences such a popular approach? At first, we might think that it would be a good idea to minimize just the sum of differences between the observed values and the model values. However, it is possible to show that the sum of differences is always zero when y is set equal to the mean y-value. Since this value obviously ignores the relationship between y and x, it would not be satisfactory; we therefore need some other measure of how closely a line fits the data. The sum of squared differences is almost as simple as the sum of differences, and it has the virtue of "penalizing" large differences more than small differences, so it is a natural candidate. (The sum of squared differences has some technical virtues as well, but they involve statistical concepts that go beyond our coverage here.)

Specifically, let's suppose that our sample contains n observations of x–y pairs. Let x_i represent the ith observation of the explanatory variable, and let y_i represent the corresponding observation of the response variable. The model predicts that when the explanatory variable takes on the value x_i, then the response variable should be $y = a + bx_i$. The difference between the observed value and the model's prediction is called the **residual**, which can be written as

$$e_i = y_i - y = y_i - (a + bx_i) \tag{8.2}$$

and the sum of squared differences (between observation and model) becomes

$$SS = \sum_{i=1}^{n} e_i^2 = \sum_{i=1}^{n} (y_i - a - bx_i)^2$$

The regression problem can be reduced to choosing a and b so that we minimize SS. Regression theory gives us the following formulas that solve the simple regression problem:

$$b = \frac{n \sum_{i=1}^{n} x_i y_i - \sum_{i=1}^{n} x_i \sum_{i=1}^{n} y_i}{n \sum_{i=1}^{n} x_i^2 - \left(\sum_{i=1}^{n} x_i \right)^2} \quad \text{and} \quad a = \bar{y} - b\bar{x} \tag{8.3}$$

It is not necessary to solve these equations, however, as Excel can perform these calculations once we have recorded the observed data in a spreadsheet.

As an example, we return to the Executives database and examine the relation between executive salaries and company sales. Our regression equation takes the form

$$Salary = a + b \times Sales + e$$

where Salary is in thousands and Sales in million. For our sample of 100 executives, the formulas in 8.3 yield the estimates $a = 583$ and $b = 0.00897$. These results suggest that an increase of \$1 million in sales is associated with an increase of about \$8,970 in salary.

8.5 GOODNESS-OF-FIT

Having found the values of the constants a and b that give the best fit of the model to the observed data, we might still wonder, how *good* a fit is the best fit? Given that we are working with a linear regression model, the three graphs in Figure 8.7 suggest the spectrum of outcomes. In Figure 8.7a, the regression is perfect: every observation falls right on the regression line, and the residual values are all zero. Another way to interpret this outcome is that *all* of the variation in y-values is completely accounted for (or "explained") by their dependence on x-values (and therefore on the variation in x-values). In Figure 8.7b, the regression is imperfect, so the residuals are nonzero but small. Nevertheless, *much* of the variation in y-values can be explained by variation in x. That is, changes in x account for most of the variation in y, although there is also some "unexplained" variation. Finally, in Figure 8.7c, there is little or no dependency between y and x. In this case, the variation in the residuals is roughly the same as the variation in the y-values; *none* of the variation in y-values can be explained by variation in x.

FIGURE 8.7 Three Types
of Regression Results

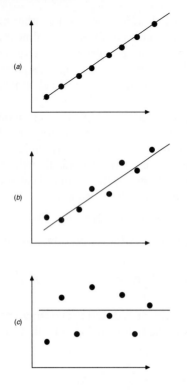

In order to quantify the outcomes and to provide a measure of how well the regression equation fits the data, we introduce the **coefficient of determination**, known as R^2, to measure the closeness of fit. Values of R^2 must lie between zero and one, and the closer R^2 is to one, the better the fit. (Its square root is the correlation, r.) A useful interpretation is that R^2 is relatively large when the model explains much of the variation in observed y-values. When R^2 is equal to one, the regression equation is perfect—it explains all of the observed variation. (This would be the case for Figure 8.7a.) When R^2 is zero, the regression equation explains none of the observed variation. (This would be approximately the case for Figure 8.7c.) Thus, R^2 measures how much of the variation in y-values is explained by the relation in the model.

In our example involving executive salaries and company sales, $R^2 = 0.223$. In other words, about 22 percent of the variation in salaries can be explained by variation in company sales. The rest of the variation is due either to "noise" or to systematic factors—other than sales—that we have not included in the regression equation.

Excel's Data Analysis tool contains a Regression option that automates the calculations we have just discussed. To use the regression tool, we select Data▶Analysis▶Data Analysis▶Regression. The Regression window, shown in Figure 8.8, asks for a range for the y-values and for the x-values. If we use the original Executives database, we can specify the y-range as D1:D101 and the x-range as N1:N101, checking the `Labels` box to reflect the fact that these ranges include field names. For this illustration, we need not check other boxes, although the `Line Fit Plots` option provides a convenient graphical look at the results. The figure illustrates the output option of using a new worksheet (named Regression) as a home for the regression report. When we click OK, Excel produces the regression tables shown in Figure 8.9, which have been slightly modified for display purposes.

Much of the information in the regression tables is quite detailed and beyond the scope of our coverage. We focus on four measures of how well the regression model is supported by the data: R^2, the F-statistic, the p-statistics, and confidence intervals. The first two of these measures apply to the regression model as a whole; the last two apply to individual regression coefficients.

FIGURE 8.8 The Regression Window in the Data Analysis Tool

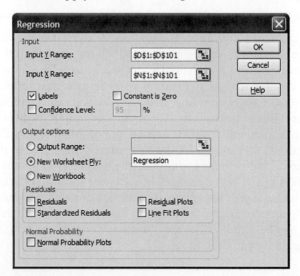

FIGURE 8.9 Regression Results for the Executives Example

	A	B	C	D	E	F	G	H	I
1	SUMMARY OUTPUT								
2									
3	*Regression Statistics*								
4	Multiple R	0.4727							
5	R Square	0.2234							
6	Adjusted R Square	0.2155							
7	Standard Error	304.7							
8	Observations	100							
9									
10	ANOVA								
11		*df*	*SS*	*MS*	*F*	*Significance F*			
12	Regression	1	2616776.788	2616777	28.1941	6.85223E-07			
13	Residual	98	9095657.386	92812.8					
14	Total	99	11712434.17						
15									
16		Coefficients	Standard Error	t Stat	P-value	Lower 95%	Upper 95%	Lower 95.0%	Upper 95.0%
17	Intercept	582.9412	35.4450	16.4464	6.1E-30	512.6018	653.2806	512.6018	653.2806
18	SALES	0.00897	0.0017	5.3098	6.9E-07	0.0056	0.0123	0.0056	0.0123
19									

Database / Glossary / Summary / Sheet1 / Correlation \ **Regression** /

As we have seen, the R^2 value (cell B5) provides an overall, quantitative measure of how close the regression model fits the data. The higher the R^2, the more the regression model explains, or accounts for, the variation in the response variable. There is, however, no magic level for R^2 that distinguishes a good model from a bad model. All we can really say is that if we have two competing models, the one with the higher R^2 fits the data more closely. But there are situations in which our business judgment would suggest that we prefer a model with a lower R^2 than a competing model.

The **F-statistic** (cell E12) and its significance (cell E13) provide a different measure of the overall quality of the regression. The significance level answers this question: How likely is it that we would get the R^2 we observe (or higher) if, in fact, all the true regression coefficients were zero? In other words, if our model really had no explanatory power at all, how likely is it that, sampling at random, we would encounter the explained variation we observed? If sufficient thought has gone into a model before turning to regression, so that the analyst has cogent reasons for believing the form of the model is realistic and the initial parameter values are plausible, it is very unlikely that the F-statistic will suggest that the R^2 we observe could have come about when all the true coefficients are zero. In effect, this result would imply that the data do not support *any* aspect of the model. If the F-statistic suggests that it is *unlikely* that the observed R^2 could occur when all the true regression coefficients are zero, this should not be taken as a positive sign that the model is somehow proven, since we had strong reasons before performing the regression to believe that the overall form of the model was realistic. If, however, the F-statistic suggests that it is *likely* that the R^2 we observe could occur when all the true coefficients are zero, the most sensible conclusion is that the data are not appropriate for refining the parameter estimates in our model, and we should look for more appropriate data or rely on our judgment for our parameter estimates.

We turn our attention now from evaluating the regression model as a whole to evaluating each regression coefficient individually, using p-statistics and confidence intervals. The **p-statistic** (or **p-value**) is somewhat akin to the significance level of the F-statistic. It answers this question: How likely is it that we would get an estimate of the regression coefficient at least this large (either positive or negative) if, in fact, the true value of the regression coefficient were zero? In other words, if there really was no influence of this particular explanatory variable on the response variable, how likely is it that we would encounter the estimated coefficient we observed? Again, this is not usually a particularly strong test of the model. Imagine, for example, that we are attempting to determine the impact of a growing patient population on the sales of a drug. We have hypothesized, based on expert experience in the industry, that an additional 100 patients will increase annual sales by 800 to 1,200 doses. We would expect, then, that the regression coefficient would be around 10 but could be as low as 8 or as high as 12. After collecting data and running a regression (perhaps getting an estimated coefficient of 9.5), we would probably not be surprised to find that it is very unlikely that the estimated coefficient would have arisen by chance when the true coefficient was zero. After all, we know that an increase in the patient population has *some* positive effect on sales. What we are really interested in is whether the coefficient is 8 or 12 or somewhere in between, and we hope that the regression procedure will shed light on this question. The most useful way to determine the range of uncertainty in a regression coefficient is to form a confidence interval. (A check box is provided in the Regression window for confidence intervals for the regression coefficients. Excel automatically provides a report on the 95 percent confidence intervals, so the user needs to check this box only when a different confidence interval is desired.) A confidence interval for the coefficient in our example will tell us whether the actual parameter is likely to lie between 9.0 and 10.0, for example, or between 8.0 and 11.0. This information, along with the point estimate of the coefficient itself and our judgment, will help us to select a final parameter value for this coefficient in our model.

Returning to the regression results in Figure 8.9, we first observe that R^2, displayed in cell B5, is 0.223. In cell F12, under the heading *Significance F*, we find the probability of observing this R^2 or higher when all the true regression coefficients are zero. The reported value is 6.852×10^{-7} (or 0.0000006852), which means that this probability is negligible.

In rows 17 and 18, we find results for each of the regression coefficients, the constant or intercept, and Sales. In cells B17 and B18, we find point estimates for the values of the coefficients: $a = 583$ for the constant term and $b = 0.00897$ for the coefficient of Sales. The *p*-values in cells E17 and E18 are both essentially zero, suggesting that these estimated coefficients would be unlikely to occur randomly if the true coefficients were zero. In cells F17 and G17, we are given the 95 percent confidence interval on the intercept: 512.6 to 653.3. Finally, in cells F18 and G18, we have the 95 percent confidence interval for the coefficient on Sales: 0.0056 to 0.0123. Thus, while our point estimate for the coefficient on Sales is about 0.009, these data suggest that it could range between 0.006 and 0.012, approximately.

To provide another example, we turn to the Applicants database first introduced in Figure 7.2 of Chapter 7 and the analysis of GMAT levels in different admission rounds. The regression model we wish to analyze in this case takes the form

$$GMAT\ score = a + b \times Round + e$$

For the Regression tool, we specify the *y*-range as B5:B9 and the *x*-range as A5:A9 (see Figure 8.10). The regression table reveals the following results:

- The value of R^2 is about 0.745, which suggests that the model fits the data rather well.

FIGURE 8.10 Regression Results for the Applicants Example

	A	B	C	D	E	F	G	H	I
13	SUMMARY OUTPUT								
14									
15	*Regression Statistics*								
16	Multiple R	0.8631							
17	R Square	0.7449							
18	Adjusted R Squar	0.6598							
19	Standard Error	29.5452							
20	Observations	5							
21									
22	ANOVA								
23		*df*	*SS*	*MS*	*F*	*Significance F*			
24	Regression	1	7646.3	7646.3	8.7595	0.0596			
25	Residual	3	2618.8	872.9					
26	Total	4	10265.1						
27									
28		*Coefficients*	*Standard Error*	*t Stat*	*P-value*	*Lower 95%*	*Upper 95%*	*Lower 95.0%*	*Upper 95.0%*
29	Intercept	708.0815	30.9873	22.8507	0.0002	609.466	806.697	609.4661666	806.6969278
30	X Variable 1	-27.6520	9.3430	-2.9596	0.0596	-57.386	2.082	-57.38566179	2.08165021
31									

Database / Glossary / Nonprofit / Oldest / GMAT \ Regression /

- The probability under *Significance F* is about 6 percent, which suggests that it is unlikely that this R^2 value could have arisen when all the true coefficients were zero.

- The estimated coefficients are $a = 708$ and $b = -27.7$, indicating that the average GMAT scores drop by almost 28 points each round in the admission process. The *p*-value for the intercept is very small, which suggests that this estimate would be unlikely if the true value of the coefficient were zero. However, the *p*-value for Round is 6 percent, which suggests that we cannot be so sure that this estimate could not have arisen by chance when the true coefficient was zero. The 95 percent confidence interval for Round is extremely wide, from -57 to $+2$. This suggests that our point estimate, from which we concluded that GMAT scores drop by almost 28 points each round, is rather imprecisely estimated. (Notice that the confidence interval for this coefficient does extend past zero, which is consistent with the low but nonzero *p*-value.)

EXAMPLE
Regression Statistics

Four measures are used to judge the statistical qualities of a regression:

R^2: Measures the percent of variation in the response variable accounted for by the regression model.

F-statistic (Significance F): Measures the probability of observing the given R^2 (or higher) when all the true regression coefficients are zero.

p-value: Measures the probability of observing the given estimate of the regression coefficient (or a larger value, positive or negative) when the true coefficient is zero.

Confidence interval: Gives a range within which the true regression coefficient lies with given probability. ∎

8.6 SIMPLE REGRESSION IN THE BPI EXAMPLE

In our base-case model for Bundy Pharmaceuticals, we used a very simple idea to project demand. We calculated very roughly the average annual growth in demand over the past 10 years, and we used that figure to project forward from the previous year. Thus, our initial conclusions were based on demand growing from about 1.01 million to 1.51 million units over the life of the plant. This initial model was only loosely derived from past experience. But since we have historical data on past sales, it is natural to ask whether we could use regression methods to create demand models that exploit the available historical data more fully. Whether these models will materially change the *conclusions* of the base case is an open question. We test three such models here, using time, lagged demand, and the number of patients with arthritis as explanatory variables.

First, we look at time as the explanatory variable. Perhaps the simplest interpretation of the available data is that demand increases over time at a constant rate. In fact, this is the reasoning behind our base-case model, although, for the purposes of that model, we made a quick calculation of the growth rate without using statistical methods. Later, we used a scatter plot, along with the calculation of correlation, to support the original reasoning. Here, we assume that there is a linear model describing the relation between demand and time (with time indexed from 1 to 10). The Data Analysis tool, applied to the 10 years of historical data, produces the following regression equation:

$$Demand = 443,600 + 61,873 \times Time$$

The fit of this regression is very good: the R^2 is high (0.98); the probability corresponding to the *F*-value (*Significance F*) is essentially zero; and the *p*-values for both the slope and intercept are essentially zero as well. The 95 percent confidence interval for the slope coefficient is 53,964 to 69,782. Recall that in our base model, we assumed sales growth of 50,000 each year, so the regression results suggest a point estimate closer to 60,000, although our original estimate is not far outside the confidence interval for this parameter.

When we introduce annual growth of 61,873 into the base-case spreadsheet, demand grows to 1.63 million units 10 years out, compared to the base-case value of 1.51 million units. After creating a sensitivity table for NPV as a function of capacity, we find that the best capacity choice for this model is 1.3 million units, with an estimated NPV of $2.201 million. This contrasts to our base-case conclusion that capacity of 1.25 million would give an optimal NPV of $1.811 million.

It is worth asking how wrong we would be if this current model were actually to represent reality, and we were to choose instead a capacity of 1.25 million units, as suggested by our base-case analysis. The NPV at 1.25 million units is about $2.138 million. The difference between this value and the optimum of $2.201 million is about 3 percent—not a particularly large error, especially given the errors that are likely to be caused by inaccuracies in other aspects of the model.

It is also instructive to test the sensitivity of these conclusions to the regression parameters, the slope parameter in particular. Suppose we vary the slope parameter from 50,000 to 70,000, which is roughly the range of the 95 percent confidence interval from the regression. Repeated visits to a sensitivity table show that the optimal capacity varies from 1.25 million to 1.35 million units over this range. As in the base case, we conclude that optimal capacity is only moderately sensitive to the annual growth in demand.

A second regression approach takes lagged demand as the explanatory variable. While it is plausible that demand grows as a function of time alone, it is more likely that demand is influenced directly by economic and business forces. One way to incorporate these influences is to use last year's demand to forecast this year's demand, on the assumption that this year's activity will be influenced by much the same underlying factors as last year's.

The Data Analysis tool produces the following regression model:

$$Demand = 124,247 + 0.913 \times LastYearDemand$$

This regression also fits quite well, with high R^2 (0.99); the probability corresponding to the F-value (*Significance F*) is essentially zero, and the p-values for both the slope and intercept are essentially zero as well. The 95 percent confidence interval for the slope coefficient is 0.81 to 1.01. This model, however, suggests that demand will grow only to 1.24 million in year 10, far lower than in our base-case model. Why is this? The answer lies in the estimated regression equation, which suggests that demand in any given year is a constant plus 91 percent of the previous year's demand. According to this equation, demand would actually *decline* over time were it not for the influence of the constant term. Not surprisingly, under these assumptions, the optimal value of capacity is lower, around 1.15 million, and the best NPV we can expect is only $1.219 million.

A better model for demand based on lagged values would force the regression constant to be zero. (This is a check-box option offered in the Regression window shown, for example, in Figure 8.8.) This model would take the form $Demand = b \times LastYearDemand$, so we would expect the parameter b to exceed 1.0. The Data Analysis tool produces the following regression model:

$$Demand = 1.069 \times LastYearDemand$$

This regression fits well, with an R^2 of 0.96 and the other indicators in line. The slope coefficient indicates that annual growth will occur at a rate just under 7 percent. (Its 95 percent confidence interval is from 1.03 to 1.10, suggesting that annual growth could range from 3 to 10 percent.) Under this model, demand reaches 1.97 million units by year 10, and the optimal plant capacity is 1.40 million units (with an NPV of $2.708 million), higher than the base case, but more in line with the results using the first regression model, with time as the explanatory variable.

How sensitive is our decision to the slope coefficient? Suppose we vary the annual growth rate from 1 to 15 percent. (Recall that the estimated value is 6.9

percent.) Optimal capacity varies from 1.05 million to more than 3 million units in this range. How should we interpret these results? The answer to this question depends on how much we know about the growth rate in demand over the next 10 years. If we actually believe that any growth rate between 1 and 15 percent is equally likely, we can say only that the optimal capacity choice is indeterminate over a wide range. However, suppose we believe that growth will lie in a range around 7 percent—perhaps between 3 and 10 percent, as suggested by the confidence interval. Then, we can conclude that the optimal plant capacity lies between 1.14 million and 1.80 million units.

A third regression approach takes the number of arthritis patients as the explanatory variable. The two previous models fit the given data well, from a purely statistical point of view. However, neither relates demand directly to any of the underlying economic forces. Such a model, while it may involve more effort to build, may also provide insights unachievable with the previous models.

Sales of an antiarthritis drug obviously have a direct connection to the number of people suffering from this condition. Drawing on some work done by an industry association, BPI has gathered the following data covering the past 10 years on the number of patients diagnosed with arthritis.

Year	Demand	Patients
1	487,000	9,123,000
2	560,000	10,189,000
3	601,000	11,570,000
4	689,000	12,584,000
5	788,000	13,956,000
6	854,000	15,191,000
7	902,000	17,321,000
8	957,000	19,247,000
9	991,000	21,096,000
10	1,010,000	23,095,000

Two plausible models suggest themselves: either demand is proportional to the number of patients (and the regression line goes through the origin), or it is linear in the number of patients. The first approach does lead to a plausible model (*Demand* $= 0.050 \times$ *Patients*), with R^2 of 0.84 and the other statistical measures in line. However, this model may overestimate the growth in demand if some doctors experiment with a new drug and prescribe it frequently to the first patients they see, but prescribe it less often to subsequent patients. The alternative approach, using a nonzero intercept, produces the following regression equation:

$$Demand = 190,543 + 0.0387 \times Patients$$

This regression has a higher R^2 (0.93) than the previous model. It suggests that if the number of patients were to rise by 100,000, demand would rise by 3,870. However, the 95 percent confidence interval on the critical slope parameter is 0.030 to 0.047, so the actual increase in demand could be as low as 3,000 or as high as 4,700. In a detailed analysis, we would want to test the sensitivity of our results to values in this range.

Before we can use this regression model to forecast demand, we need to develop a forecast for the explanatory variable, the number of arthritis patients. If we assume the number of patients will grow at a constant 5 percent over the 10-year horizon, demand will grow to 1.65 million units by year 10. The optimal capacity for this case is 1.35 million, with an estimated NPV of $2.696 million. Again, this conclusion is in line with earlier results from regressions based on time and based on lagged sales. However, this conclusion depends both on our forecast of the number of arthritis patients *and* on our estimated relationship between patients and demand. Therefore, errors in forecasting the growth in arthritis patients will lead to errors in selecting the optimal plant capacity.

To test the sensitivity of the optimal capacity to the assumed growth in the number of patients, we determined the optimal capacity for growth rates between 0 and 10 percent by incorporating the patient-based regression equation into our model and then building a sensitivity table to compare different capacity choices. If there is no future growth in the patient population, the optimal capacity is 1.10 million. With 5 percent growth, we should build a plant for 1.35 million; at 10 percent, the optimal capacity is 1.80 million. Any uncertainty we have about the growth of the patient population adds to the uncertainty in determining the optimal plant capacity. This is a major drawback of regression models based on explanatory variables that themselves require forecasting.

8.7 SIMPLE NONLINEAR REGRESSION

In many cases, a straight-line relationship will not be the most plausible description of a dependency between two variables. Consider the dependency of sales volume on advertising, or any relationship involving diminishing returns. When we compare linear and nonlinear equations, the nonlinear version may well be better.

How should we attack the nonlinear case in regression? Since the formulas for the linear case are so convenient, the approach most widely used is to transform a nonlinear model back into a linear one. For example, suppose we are trying to estimate the parameters (*a* and *b*) of a power function

$$y = ax^b \tag{8.4}$$

Following the approach introduced for simple linear regression, we could calculate predicted values from this equation and compare them to the observed values, minimizing the sum of squared differences between the observations and the predictions. There are no simple formulas available for this case, analogous to those in (8.3), Moreover, it is difficult to locate software that automates the calculations, as Excel does for linear regression. (We can, however, create our own custom analysis for this purpose, using optimization techniques, and we discuss this application in Chapter 10.)

Alternatively, we can transform the equation in (8.4) by taking the logarithm of both sides:

$$\log y = \log a + b \times \log x$$

Note that this transformation creates a *linear* equation: log *a* is the constant term, and the constant *b* now plays the role of a slope, not an exponent. With this transformation, we can use all of the results for simple linear regression, including the Data Analysis tool in Excel. However, this also means that we have to think in terms of a graph that plots log *y* versus log *x*, rather than *y* versus *x*. Because most of us find it difficult to think in "logarithm space," this version of the model is probably not as intuitive or transparent as the original. So we give up some intuition for the convenience of using the transformed model.

We should not expect to get identical answers from the two approaches. To illustrate this point, we analyze the following example.

EXAMPLE
*Van Winkle's
Pharmacy*

Van Winkle's Pharmacy, a chain of drugstores, owns pharmacies in different types of locations, such as shopping malls, grocery stores, and independent storefronts. Stores in different types of locations are open for different hours, and the company can therefore study a natural experiment to see how revenue varies with store hours. For a sample of 10 stores, the following data show the number of hours the store is open each week and the average revenue.

Store	Hours	Revenue
1	40	5,958
2	44	6,662
3	48	6,004
4	48	6,011
5	60	7,250
6	70	8,632
7	72	6,964
8	190	11,097
9	100	9,107
10	168	11,498

∎

If we work with the data directly, with the form of (8.4), we need a specialized analysis to find the best fit. It is possible to show (using methods that we introduce in Chapter 10) that the best fit is given by the equation

$$Revenue = 1,022 \times Hours^{0.482}$$

The choice of $a = 1,022$ and $b = 0.482$ leads to a sum of squared differences equal to approximately 7.55 million.

By contrast, if we work with the transformed equation, we can use Excel's Regression tool to analyze the relation between the logarithm of Revenue and the logarithm of Hours. The best fit turns out to be

$$\log(Revenue) = 2.954 + 0.510 \times \log(Hours)$$

When this equation is transformed back into the original dimensions, it becomes

$$Revenue = 899.2 \times Hours^{0.510}$$

Obviously, the two equations are not very different; however, the sum of squared differences for the transformed equation is equal to about 7.68 million, or nearly 2 percent higher than the best fit. This example illustrates the trade-off in a choice of a modeling strategy. If we use the direct equation (8.4), we need to develop a specialized analysis, but we can find the best fit. On the other hand, if we use the transformed equation, we can take advantage of Excel's built-in regression analysis, but we will likely not find the best fit.

The power function in (8.4) is just one example of the model structures that could be useful in describing the dependence of one variable on another. As we discussed in Chapter 2, it is helpful to be familiar with a few families of functions. In the regression context, these functions would be the curves we might sketch to fit data points on a scatter plot. In Chapter 10, we present a general method for fitting nonlinear curves to data.

8.8 MULTIPLE LINEAR REGRESSION

A simple regression equation with one explanatory variable may not always be sufficient for our purposes. The use of a single explanatory variable may lead to acceptable results in statistical terms, but to be useful, the relationship may need additional variables. In these cases, an appropriate relationship contains multiple explanatory variables. When there are m such variables, the linear regression model takes the form

$$y = a_0 + a_1x_1 + a_2x_2 + \ldots + a_mx_m + e \tag{8.5}$$

Here, we're using subscripts differently than in the discussion of simple regression. In (8.5), the subscripts are used to index the different explanatory variables, from

1 to m. However, the main regression concepts resemble those for the case of simple regression. As before, we work with n observations, where each observation consists of one value for the response variable and one value for each of the m explanatory variables. We compare the observations with the prediction of the equation and find the sum of squared differences. Then, we find the values of the coefficients, a_0 through a_m, that minimize this sum. These coefficients provide the best fit.

Excel's Regression tool provides an extensive analysis of the regression equation. Its first table lists a number of statistics, including three measures of fit. As in the case of simple regression, we can use R^2 as a basic measure of fit. In the case of multiple regression, R^2 is called the **coefficient of multiple determination**, and its square root, R, is called the **multiple R**, or the **multiple correlation coefficient**. Excel reports both values. The table also reports an **adjusted R^2**. The reason for introducing another measure is that adding explanatory variables to the regression equation will never decrease the value of R^2 and will usually increase it, even if there is no reason why the added variable should help predict the response variable. A suitable adjustment accounts for the effect of the number of variables in the equation and will cause the adjusted R^2 to decrease unless there is a compensating reduction in the differences between observed and predicted values. One informal guideline for how many explanatory variables to include in a regression equation is to find the largest value of the adjusted R^2. However, we strongly recommend including variables that can be justified on practical or theoretical grounds, even if the adjusted R^2 is not at its largest possible value.

The regression report also lists a value corresponding to the F-statistic (labeled *Significance F*), which has the same interpretation as in a simple regression: it measures the probability of getting the observed R^2 or higher if, in fact, all the true regression coefficients were zero. This is a measure of the overall fit of the regression model to the data, but it is not a particularly stringent test. We would expect this probability to be low in any well-considered model for which relevant data were being used.

The estimated coefficients of the regression equation, which we denoted as a_0 through a_m, can be found under the *Coefficients* heading in the Excel regression output. Corresponding to each coefficient, the table provides a *p*-value, which measures the probability that we would get an estimate at least this large if the true regression coefficient were zero. While the *p*-value does provide a quick check on each coefficient, the respective confidence intervals generally provide more useful information.

As a brief example, we return to the Executives database. This time we explore a multiple regression model for the relation between executive salaries and various measures of firm performance. In particular, for explanatory variables, we select Sales, Profits, Assets, and ROA, because one or more of these financial measures would seem to be logical explanatory variables. Thus, our regression equation takes the following form:

$$Salary = a_0 + a_1 \times Sales + a_2 \times Profit + a_3 \times Assets + a_4 \times ROA$$

To invoke Excel's tool for multiple regression, we must have the explanatory variables in contiguous cells on the spreadsheet, so that we can specify a single range for the *x*-variables. In this case, that range is N1:Q101, with labels included. The output table is shown in Figure 8.11. We observe the following:

- The multiple regression model achieves an R^2 of 0.275. If we are comparing the multivariable model to the simple regression model we examined earlier, a relevant comparison involves the Adjusted R^2, which has gone up slightly, from 0.215 to 0.244.

- The F-value of 3.277×10^{-6} shows that it would be extremely unlikely to observe this value of the R^2 if all the true regression coefficients were zero.

- Although the increased value of R^2 is achieved with four explanatory variables, two of them (*Assets* and *ROA*) have high *p*-values (0.63 and 0.20, respectively),

FIGURE 8.11 Multiple Regression Results for Executive Salaries

	A	B	C	D	E	F	G	H	I
1	SUMMARY OUTPUT								
2									
3	*Regression Statistics*								
4	Multiple R	0.5244							
5	R Square	0.2750							
6	Adjusted R Square	0.2444							
7	Standard Error	299.0							
8	Observations	100							
9									
10	ANOVA								
11		*df*	*SS*	*MS*	*F*	*Significance F*			
12	Regression	4	3220345.342	805086.3	9.0064	3.27673E-06			
13	Residual	95	8492088.832	89390.4					
14	Total	99	11712434.17						
15									
16		*Coefficients*	*Standard Error*	*t Stat*	*P-value*	*Lower 95%*	*Upper 95%*	*Lower 95.0%*	*Upper 95.0%*
17	Intercept	541.3234	44.3163	12.2150	3.46E-21	453.3445	629.3023	453.3445	629.3023
18	SALES	0.0172	0.0037	4.6128	1.24E-05	0.0098	0.0246	0.0098	0.0246
19	PROFIT	-0.0513	0.0260	-1.9714	0.0516	-0.1030	0.0004	-0.1030	0.0004
20	ASSETS	-0.0002	0.0005	-0.4788	0.6332	-0.0012	0.0007	-0.0012	0.0007
21	ROA	6.9400	5.4625	1.2705	0.2070	-3.9043	17.7844	-3.9043	17.7844
22									

Glossary / Summary / Sheet1 / Correlation / Regression \ Multiple /

which suggests that these estimates would not be unlikely even when the true coefficients are zero. As we would expect, the confidence intervals for these coefficients range on either side of zero. As for the coefficient on *Sales*, the point estimate is 0.0172, with a 95 percent confidence interval from 0.0098 to 0.0246. The coefficient on *Profit* has a point estimate of −0.0513, with a 95 percent confidence interval from −0.1030 to 0.0004. Notice that this confidence interval extends over zero, and the *p*-value of 5.16 percent suggests that there is a nonnegligible chance of observing the estimate we have when the true coefficient is zero.

Our attempts to develop a model for executive salaries have not gone very far at this point. Although the level of company sales appears to be a key explanatory factor in our analysis, we must also recognize that we are limited by the data. In particular, if we had a larger data set, with data from successive years, we might be able to fashion a more convincing model by relating salaries to *changes* in profits or returns. Here again, judgment about the nature of salaries in practice might be more beneficial than a series of regression runs in helping us formulate a good predictive model.

8.9 MULTIPLE REGRESSION IN THE BPI EXAMPLE

Could we improve the capacity decision by adding explanatory factors to the demand model—in other words, by performing a multiple regression? We have already discussed data on the number of patients with arthritis; additional data are available in Figure 8.12 on the average price of the drug and on the level of sales effort (measured in terms of the size of the sales force dedicated to this product). Let's see if we can improve our decision with this information.

First, we should think through the implications of a multiple regression model in this context. The regression equation would take the form

$$Demand = a_0 + a_1 \times Patients + a_2 \times Price + a_3 \times Effort$$

We expect that two factors, *Patients* and *Effort*, would have positive effects on Demand, so a_1 and a_3 should be positive numbers. Similarly, we expect *Price* to have a negative effect, so a_2 would be negative. However, since most patients don't pay for drugs directly, or don't pay the full price, it is possible that this effect is weak.

This model is based on the following strong assumptions:

- *Demand* would be a_0 even if *Patients*, *Price*, and *Effort* were all zero.

- If any one of the explanatory variables—for example, *Price*—were to increase by x, *Demand* would increase by $a_2 \times x$, regardless of the level of *Price*. Thus, an

FIGURE 8.12 Multiple Regression Results for BPI Demand

	A	B	C	D	E	F	G
1	Year	Demand	Patients	Price	Effort		
2	1	487000	9123000	10.11	100		
3	2	560000	10189000	9.43	110		
4	3	601000	11570000	8.76	115		
5	4	689000	12584000	7.51	120		
6	5	788000	13965000	7.25	119		
7	6	854000	15191000	6.93	115		
8	7	902000	17321000	6.79	123		
9	8	957000	19247000	6.33	134		
10	9	991000	21096000	6.06	145		
11	10	1010000	23095000	5.92	142		
12							
13	SUMMARY OUTPUT						
14							
15	*Regression Statistics*						
16	**Multiple R**	0.994373061					
17	R Square	0.988777784					
18	**Adjusted R Square**	0.983166675					
19	Standard Error	24601.59061					
20	Observations	10					
21							
22	ANOVA						
23		*df*	*SS*	*MS*	*F*	*Significance F*	
24	Regression	3	3.19961E+11	1.067E+11	176.21791	3.07857E-06	
25	Residual	6	3631429562	605238260			
26	Total	9	3.23593E+11				
27							
28		*Coefficients*	*Standard Error*	*t Stat*	*P-value*	*Lower 95%*	*Upper 95%*
29	Intercept	1397473.03	237341.4827	5.8880269	0.001065	816718.9217	1978227.1448
30	Patients	0.025820	0.006541285	3.9471715	0.007562	0.009814	0.041826
31	Price	-79350.92	14770.29026	-5.372333	0.001708	-115492.5467	-43209.2973
32	Effort	-3383.08	1806.158	-1.873078	0.110207	-7802.5882	1036.4371
33							

8.1 / 8.2 / 8.3 / 8.4 / 8.5 \ **8.12** /

increase in *Price* from \$10 to \$11 will have the same effect as an increase from \$100 to \$101.

- The effects of two or more explanatory variables are independent. Thus, an increase of \$1 in *Price* has the same impact on *Demand* whether *Effort* is high or low.

In a first attempt, we include all three explanatory variables. Our results (see Figure 8.12) show an adjusted R^2 of 0.98, which is higher than what we achieved with the simple regression (0.93) using patients only. (*Significance F* is once again essentially zero.) The regression equation takes the following form:

$$Demand = 1{,}397{,}473 + 0.0258 \times Patients - 79{,}351 \times Price - 3{,}383 \times Effort$$

However, a high *p*-value (11 percent) suggests that the estimated coefficient on *Effort* could arise even when the true coefficient is zero. (The 95 percent confidence interval is −7,803 to 1,036.) Worse than that, the estimated coefficient on *Effort* is *negative*. Unless our sales force is utterly inept, this is not a very reasonable result. If we include it in the model, it will lead us to conclude that less sales effort is better than more, when more appropriate conclusions might be that the data on effort are somehow biased or that we should fix a broken sales process.

With these results in hand, we estimate another equation in which we use only *Patients* and *Price* as explanatory variables. This equation takes the following form:

$$Demand = 1{,}100{,}233 + 0.0169 \times Patients - 76{,}745 \times Price$$

The adjusted R^2 is 0.99, and now all three regression coefficients have low *p*-values. Moreover, the coefficients on *Patients* and *Price* have the sign we would expect. However, substantial uncertainty remains as to the true value of the coefficients, as indicated by their confidence intervals. For example, the coefficient on *Price*, which may be crucial to determining future pricing policy, is estimated at −76,745 but could lie between −117,269 and −36,220. In other words, increasing price by \$1 could lower demand by anywhere from 36 to 117 thousand units.

If we accept this equation as the best regression model possible using these data, what implications does it have for the capacity decision? First, notice that to use this equation, we have to make projections of the explanatory variables, *Patients* and *Price*, just as we did before when we used only *Patients* as the explanatory variable. To keep this manageable, we assume that *Patients* will grow at 10 percent and that *Price* will not grow at all over the next 10 years. Under these assumptions, the optimal capacity is about 1.28 million units, with an associated NPV of $1.963 million.

But does this multiple regression really make our decision better? Even if our regression model is highly accurate, how accurate are our forecasts of *Patients* and *Price*? If those forecasts are inaccurate, and actual demand differs from our forecasts, then our decision on capacity may be off as well. We can test this by varying our growth rate assumptions for *Patients* and *Price* and then testing the sensitivity of optimal capacity. For example, if the growth in *Patients* is 0 percent, capacity should be 1.04 million; if the growth is 20 percent, capacity should be 1.81 million. Setting the growth rate for *Patients* back to 10 percent, we find that if Price grows by 10 percent, capacity should be set at 1.00 million units; if Price declines at 10 percent, capacity should be 1.46 million. Clearly, forecasting the growth rates in Patients and Price is particularly critical to making a good decision in this case.

These results suggest that inaccuracy in our forecasts of explanatory variables could have a major impact on our decision. Thus, we should not be too confident in the value of this model to improve our decision making unless we think we can make a fairly accurate forecast of the growth in *Patients* and *Price*. The lesson is this: always remember that regression models require forecasts of the explanatory variables. If these forecasts themselves cannot be made with precision, the regression equation may not provide a better decision than a simpler approach that does not require forecasting.

8.10   REGRESSION ASSUMPTIONS

We have introduced the regression equation as a means of estimating relationships between two or more parameters in our model. We have not attempted to develop the full coverage of regression as a statistical topic; rather, we have drawn on statistical results where they suit our purposes in modeling. Nevertheless, we should point out that the validity of statistical inferences from regression analysis rests on several important assumptions. These are as follows:

- Errors in the regression model follow a normal distribution.
- Errors in the regression model are mutually independent.
- Errors in the regression model have the same variance.
- Linearity is assumed to hold (for simple and multiple linear regression).

The first of these assumptions relates to our basic probabilistic model. The response variable is viewed as having a mean value on the regression line, and the observation is viewed as being equal to the mean value plus an error term. The error terms are assumed to follow a normal distribution. This might be a plausible assumption whenever differences between observed and model values can be thought of as the combined effect of several unobservable explanatory factors, such as would be the case for the relationship between sales and advertising. One way to use the data to help confirm this assumption is to examine the distribution of the residual values by displaying them in a histogram and checking that they appear to follow a normal distribution.

The second assumption states that there are no systematic dependencies among different observations. This would be the case, for example, if we hypothesized a linear relationship when there was actually a cycle in operation. In this situation, some observations would fall above the regression equation, and others below it, in a discernible, systematic pattern. Such dependencies can also be detected by looking for systematic rather than random patterns in the residuals.

The third assumption states that the normal distribution for errors does not become more narrow, or more spread out, as we proceed through the data. Qualitatively, this means that the size of the errors should be roughly the same early in the sample as late in the sample. Again, we would look for evidence to the contrary by scanning the residuals to see whether small and large values are distributed randomly throughout the sample. We could also compare the distribution of residuals from early observations with the distribution from late observations.

The regression tool in the Analysis Toolpak provides several methods for displaying residuals. The most useful are the Residual Plot and the Line Fit Plot. The Residual Plot is a graph of the residuals against the values of the explanatory variable. Any nonrandom patterns in this plot indicate a violation of the regression assumptions. The Line Fit Plot shows the fitted values of the regression line plotted against the actual observations. This plot can also be used for detecting violations of the assumptions.

Finally, the fourth assumption may be based on our knowledge of the underlying economics in a model, or may derive from a well-intended attempt at a reasonable first cut. If linearity is a poor assumption, the evidence is likely to show up in the pattern of residuals. For example, if the plot of residuals shows values that are first negative, then positive for a while, and finally negative again, there is good reason to believe that a nonlinear relationship exists in the data.

8.11* USING THE EXCEL TOOLS TRENDLINE AND LINEST

Excel provides several alternative methods for performing regression analysis. The Regression option in the Analysis Toolpak, which we have discussed in this chapter, is the most flexible and complete. In this section we will discuss two other useful methods. Trendline is a charting option that allows the user to fit one of six families of curves to a set of data and to add the resulting regression line to the plot. LINEST is an array function that can be used to compute regression statistics and use them directly as parameters in a model.

8.11.1 Trendline

As an example, we open the worksheet that contains the chart of BPI sales history (Figure 8.5). When we click on the chart, Excel augments the ribbon with three Chart Tools tabs (Design, Layout, and Format). We select Layout▶Analysis▶Trendline and from the list, we then select More Trendline Options, displaying the Format Trendline window shown in Figure 8.13.

Trendline offers the option to fit any one of the following six families of curves:

Exponential	$y = ae^{bx}$
Linear	$y = a + bx$
Logarithmic	$y = a + b \times ln(x)$
Polynomial	$y = a + bx + cx^2 + dx^3 + \ldots$ (the user selects the Order of the polynomial, which is the largest exponent of x)
Power	$y = ax^b$
Moving average	$y = $ Average of previous n y-values (the user selects the Period for the moving average, which is n, the number of previous values used to calculate the result)

Select the linear option and Excel will plot the best-fitting linear regression line on the chart. In addition, select both Display Equation on chart and Display

FIGURE 8.13 Format
Trendline Window

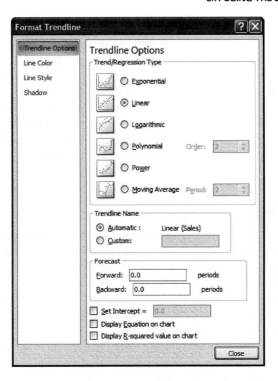

R-squared value on chart. With these options selected, the chart should resemble Figure 8.14. Note that the equation of the linear regression $(y = 443,600 + 61,873x)$ is identical to the regression line we derived earlier using the Regression procedure in the Analysis Toolpak. The R^2 values are also identical. Trendline minimizes the sum of squared residuals when fitting a line to data.

One of the useful features of Trendline is that it can be used to fit nonlinear curves directly, without linearizing them, as we did earlier with the power function $y = ax^b$. We observed earlier that while demand has grown steadily over the past 10 years, there is a hint in the chart that the growth may be tapering off. A power function with a fractional exponent would be a reasonable choice for capturing diminishing returns. As Figure 8.15 shows, a power function fits this data quite well ($R^2 = 0.97$). In fact, the power curve fits just about as well as the straight line, and it may be the better choice if we have good reasons to believe that growth in the future will slow down.

This example demonstrates how easy it is to experiment with fitting different curves to data using Trendline. This leads some users to attempt to find a curve that fits the data exactly, or at least to find the curve that gives the highest possible R^2 value. This is an extremely dangerous approach. We have

FIGURE 8.14 Linear
Trendline for BPI Data

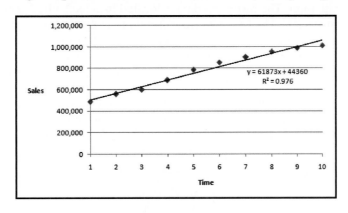

FIGURE 8.15 Power
Trendline for BPI Data

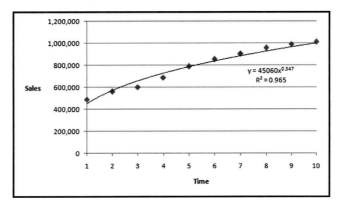

stressed repeatedly the importance of bringing judgment to any data analysis. When using Trendline, the user's judgment should guide the choice of which family of curves to use, not a mechanical procedure based on maximizing R^2. As we showed in the Bundy example, we might well choose a power curve over a straight line, even though the R^2 is slightly lower, because the shape of the power curve is closer to what we expect to see in the future. Furthermore, achieving a high R^2 is almost always possible with a polynomial of high order, but it can lead to nonsensical results. The best-fitting 6th order polynomial fits the data in the Bundy example with an R^2 of 0.993. However, it leads to a forecast of *negative* demand in the 12th year!

8.11.2 LINEST

LINEST is an Excel function that calculates regression parameters and measures of goodness-of-fit for simple or multiple regressions. It is one of a set of functions including SLOPE, INTERCEPT, and TREND, which can be used as alternatives to the Data Analysis add-in. LINEST is an **array function**, which means that it physically occupies more than one cell in the spreadsheet. Like all Excel functions, it is linked to the underlying data, so if the data change the regression parameters calculated by LINEST change automatically. This is not true of results calculated using the Regression tool: if the underlying data change, the user must be careful to rerun the Regression procedure. (It is true of Trendline: the results of Trendline will adjust if the underlying data changes.)

LINEST can be useful for situations in which we want to use a regression parameter as an input to a model, but the underlying data on which the parameter is calculated is anticipated to change frequently. A typical example involves a regularly updated sales forecast, in which we base our forecast for the next four quarters on data over the last 20 quarters. Each quarter we enter the latest data, run a regression analysis to determine the parameters of the best-fitting line, and use that to forecast for the next four quarters.

The model shown in Figure 8.16 demonstrates how LINEST can be used in this situation. The historical data is located in cells A3:B22. The most recent quarter is quarter 20. The LINEST array formula {LINEST(B3:B22,A3:A22,,TRUE)} appears in cells D2:E6. In this case, we have used LINEST to estimate the slope and intercept for a simple regression of Sales on time. The slope parameter appears in cell D2, and the intercept parameter in cell E2. These parameters are then used to forecast sales for the next four quarters, 21–24, in cells E10:E13.

To use the LINEST function, the user must first anticipate how many cells its results will occupy. LINEST will require one column for each regression parameter (thus, two for a simple regression, three for a multiple regression with two explanatory variables, and so on) and five rows. In entering the LINEST function in this

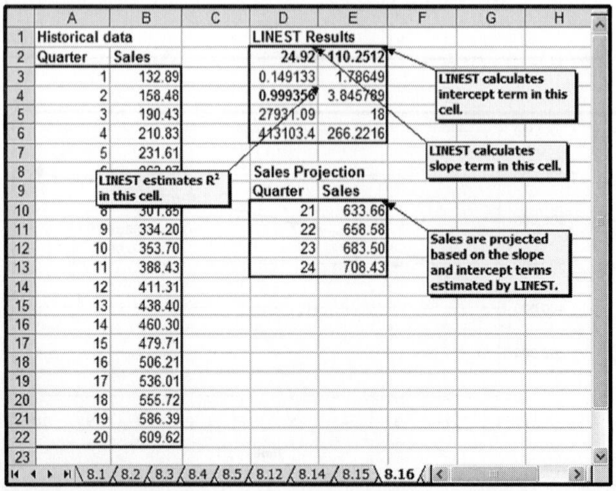

FIGURE 8.16 Forecasting Model Using LINEST

FIGURE 8.17 Function Wizard for LINEST

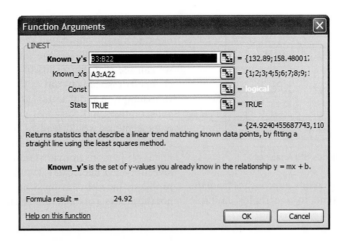

model, we first highlighted cells D2:E6. Then we entered the function arguments as needed; finally, we entered the function by using Control + Shift + Enter. This procedure is necessary to enter any array function. Array functions are always set off by curly braces when they appear in the formula window.

The function wizard for LINEST is shown in Figure 8.17. The first two inputs are the ranges for the y- and x-values. The third input allows the user to set the regression constant to zero. The fourth input allows the user to control the number of regression statistics that are displayed. For a complete description of the regression statistics calculated by LINEST and how they are displayed, go to Excel Help.

As this example shows, LINEST can be used to embed the regression procedure into the spreadsheet in such a way that the user does not have to consider the results each time a new regression is run. This is appropriate when there is good reason to think that the regression model will be plausible for any of the data inputs on which it will be based. It would not be appropriate during early testing of the model when the analyst is trying to determine the appropriate form of the regression model. LINEST does calculate the R^2 value for the regression (in cell D4 in our example), so it is possible to check the overall fit of the regression each time new data is entered.

8.12 SUMMARY

Our premises in this chapter are that modeling is the central task for the analyst and that data collection and statistical analysis are not an end in themselves but support the modeling task where appropriate. This implies that both parameters and relationships can be created for a prototype model without extensive reliance on data. However, when sensitivity testing indicates that certain parameters or relationships must be determined precisely, we often collect data and perform statistical analysis to refine the parameters and relations in our models.

Regression analysis is a means for using data to help formulate relationships among variables. It can be used to help determine the appropriate functional form of a relationship, whether linear or nonlinear. It can also help determine appropriate values for individual parameters in a relationship. In any case, it must be used in conjunction with the judgment of the modeler, who can temper the results of the regression analysis with a broad understanding of the limitations of the data and the context of the problem.

All regression methods are based on the idea of fitting a family of curves to data by choosing parameters that minimize the sum of squared residuals. The simplest regression model is a linear relationship with one explanatory variable. Regression provides not only estimates for the two parameters in this relationship, but also a variety of measures of the goodness-of-fit, such as R^2. Regression can also be applied in cases where there are multiple explanatory variables and nonlinear relationships.

Excel provides several methods for conducting regression analyses. The most complete method is the Regression option within the Analysis Toolpak add-in. Other useful methods include Trendline, which can be used to fit any one of six families of curves to plotted data, and LINEST, which can be used to calculate regression estimates dynamically.

Throughout this chapter we have used the Bundy Pharmaceuticals example to illustrate how regression can be used in a broader modeling context. Our initial approach to modeling this problem was to build a very rough first model without extensive data analysis. This prototype was sufficient to generate an initial estimate of the optimal capacity. We then refined our model for forecasting

	A	B	C
1	Review of BPI analyses		
2			
3	Case	Optimal Capacity	Optimal NPV
4	Base Case	1.25	$1.811
5	Time regression	1.30	$2.201
6	Lagged demand	1.15	$1.303
7	Proportional regression	1.40	$2.708
8	Patients regression	1.35	$2.816
9	Patients & Price	1.15	$1.566
10			

| ◄ ◄ ► ► | \ 8.16 \ 8.17 \ 8.18 \ | ◄ | | ► |

FIGURE 8.18 Summary of the Various BPI Analyses

demand, using five different regression approaches from the simplest regression against time to a complex multiple regression approach. We found that different forecasts of demand modify our original conclusion in only minor ways. Figure 8.18 summarizes the various cases we examined, and we can see that the results of our first prototype were not changed drastically by any of the statistical embellishments. Its assumption about annual growth in demand was perhaps conservative, and the most convincing statistically based enhancements would lead us to a capacity choice of 1.30 million. On the other hand, an argument could be made that, linear projections notwithstanding, demand is beginning to level off, and a choice of 1.25 million is well justified. In most problems faced by business analysts, it is *model structure*, not the analysis of data, that has the largest effect on results.

SUGGESTED READINGS

The popularity of spreadsheets, both in education and in industry, has influenced the writing of textbooks in several areas, including statistics. The following list contains textbooks on basic statistics, mostly with a classical treatment of the subject, except that they rely on a spreadsheet perspective.

Albright, S. C., W. L. Winston, and C. Zappe. 2006. *Data Analysis and Decision Making with Microsoft Excel*. 3d ed. Mason, OH: Thomson South-Western.

Evans, J. R. 2007. *Statistics, Data Analysis, and Decision Modeling*. 3d ed. Upper Saddle River, NJ: Prentice-Hall.

Levine, D. M., D. Stephan, T. C. Krehbiel, and M. L. Berenson. 2004. *Statistics for Managers Using Microsoft Excel*. 4th ed. Upper Saddle River, NJ: Prentice-Hall.

Pelosi, M. K., and M. Sandifer. 2002. *Doing Statistics for Business with Excel*. 2d ed. New York: John Wiley & Sons.

EXERCISES

1. A food products company believes that storing frozen foods at low temperatures for several weeks might cause a noticeable weight loss in the product. Some data were collected to test this belief, as summarized in the table below:

Weeks stored	26	32	35	27	25	31	30	36
Weight loss (%)	1.05	1.35	1.32	1.12	1.01	1.24	1.28	1.41

a. Explore the possibility of a linear relation between percentage weight loss and weeks in storage. Does there seem to be a strong linear relationship, based on a scatter plot and the correlation?

b. Build a linear model to represent the relation between storage time and weight loss. What weight loss would the model predict for this product if it were stored at low temperatures for 28 weeks? For 52 weeks?

c. As an alternative way of building the model, suppose we measure excess storage time as weeks beyond 24 along with weight loss in percentage above 1 percent. (In other words, subtract 24 from the data on weeks stored and 1.01 from the data on weight loss.) Find the coefficients of the linear model corresponding to this alternative specification of the variables. How do they compare to the coefficients in (b)? Explain your results.

2. A toy company has been marketing souvenir toys in conjunction with various professional sports teams in a number of cities. Over the past few years, this experience has provided some data on the effect of advertising on sales revenues because the advertising expenditures have tended to be different in each case. Although the lengths of advertising campaigns vary, the vast majority of the sales occur within the first three months, which is the time period covered in the data. A summary is shown in the table.

Advertising ($M)	18	12	5	4	24	26	15	12	16	10	15	12
Revenues ($M)	105	72	40	44	135	122	88	77	105	67	98	54

a. Explore the possibility of a linear relation between advertising expenditures and three-month sales revenue. Does there seem to be a strong linear relationship, based on a scatter plot and the correlation?

b. Build a linear model to represent the relation between advertising and revenue. What revenues would the model predict for expenditures of $2 million and $30 million?

c. As an alternative to the linear model in (b), build a nonlinear model using the power function $y = ax^b$. What revenues would the model predict for expenditures of $2 million and $30 million? What are the advantages and disadvantages of a nonlinear model for this relationship?

3. A marketing manager for a computer manufacturer was interested in whether consumers could evaluate the price of laptops and desktops with different features. An experiment was devised in which a set of consumers were randomly shown one computer from an inventory and were asked to guess its price. Four computers were used in the study, with list prices of $1,800, $2,500, $3,000, and $4,500. The following table summarizes the findings. Each column represents a different computer, with its price in the first row. The rest of the column contains the various guesses by randomly selected customers. (Each guess came from a different customer.)

	C1	C2	C3	C4
Actual price	1,800	2,500	3,000	4,500
Guesses	1,400	2,500	3,600	3,600
	2,300	2,600	3,300	5,500
	2,200	2,400	3,600	4,900
	3,000	2,700	3,600	5,600
	1,000	2,500	3,700	4,600
	1,500	2,600		4,300
	1,400	1,800		6,100
		2,400		

a. Explore the possibility of a linear relation between a customer's guesses and actual prices. Does there seem to be a strong linear relationship, based on a scatter plot and the correlation?

b. Build a linear model to represent a customer's price guess for a given computer price. What guess would the model predict for a computer that has a list price of $3,600?

c. What is the probability that the intercept term in the model of (a) is actually zero? Build a linear model with an intercept of zero to represent a customer's price guess for a given computer price. What guess would the model predict for a computer that has a list price of $3,600?

d. What advantages or disadvantages does the model in (b) have?

4. The Centers for Disease Control has collected the following data on cigarette advertising and brand preferences among adolescents and adults.

	Advertising	Brand preference	
Brand	**($ million)**	**Adolescent (%)**	**Adult (%)**
Marlboro	75	60.0	23.5
Camel	43	13.3	6.7
Newport	35	12.7	4.8
Kool	21	1.2	3.9
Winston	17	1.2	3.9
Benson & Hedges	4	1.0	3.0
Salem	3	0.3	2.5

a. Explore the possibility of a linear relation between advertising and brand preference for adults and for ado-

lescents separately. Do there seem to be strong linear relationships, based on a scatter plot and the correlation?

b. Build linear models to represent the relation between advertising and brand preference for these two groups. What preferences would the models predict for advertising of $60 million?

c. Build nonlinear models to represent the relation between advertising and brand preference for these two groups, using the power function $y = ax^b$. What preferences would the models predict for advertising of $60 million? What are the advantages and disadvantages of a nonlinear model for this relationship?

5. The Energy Conservation Committee at National Electronics Company is trying to understand energy use at their plant. As a first step, the committee wants to build a model that will predict monthly energy use as a function of production volumes (*Production*), daily outside temperature (*Temperature*), and number of workdays (*Days*). The following table summarizes the data they have been able to collect for the previous year.

Month	Energy use	Temperature	Days	Production
1	450	42	24	121
2	442	56	21	116
3	499	62	24	132
4	484	68	25	109
5	479	78	25	115
6	507	85	26	119
7	515	89	25	118
8	501	81	24	116
9	513	73	24	132
10	480	67	25	127
11	492	58	24	122
12	466	50	23	117

a. Build a linear model to predict energy use based on all three potential explanatory variables.

b. What level of energy use would the model in (a) predict for a month in which there was an average temperature of 44, monthly production of 120, and 25 days of work at the plant?

c. What percentage of the variability in energy use is accounted for by the model in (a)?

d. According to the model in (a), what are the marginal impacts on energy use of a one-unit increase in temperature and a one-unit increase in production?

e. Evaluate each of the four regression parameters in (a) to determine whether any are likely to be zero. Eliminate those parameters with a high probability of being zero from the model and estimate a new model. Compare the advantages and disadvantages of this model to the one in (a).

6. The National Transportation Safety Board collects data by state (including the District of Columbia) on traffic fatalities. Part of this data is shown in the following table, along with potentially related factors including population, number of licensed drivers, number of registered vehicles, and total number of vehicle miles driven. (The complete data are available in the file *Traffic.xls*.) You have been asked to develop a model to help explain the factors that underlie traffic fatalities.

State	Traffic fatalities	Population (thousands)	Licensed drivers (thousands)	Registered vehicles (thousands)	Vehicle miles traveled (millions)
AL	1,083	4,219	3,043	3,422	48,956
AK	85	606	443	508	4,150
AZ	903	4,075	2,654	2,980	38,774
AR	610	2,453	1,770	1,560	24,948
CA	4,226	31,431	20,359	23,518	271,943
CO	585	3,656	2,620	3,144	33,705
CT	310	3,275	2,205	2,638	27,138
DE	112	706	512	568	7,025
DC	69	570	366	270	3,448
FL	2,687	13,953	10,885	10,132	121,989

a. Build a linear model to predict traffic fatalities based on all four potential explanatory variables as they are measured in the table. Evaluate the model in terms of overall goodness-of-fit. Evaluate the results for each regression parameter: Are the signs appropriate? Are the values different from zero?

b. Can you improve the model in (a) by *removing* one or more of the explanatory variables from the regression? If so, compare the advantages and disadvantages of the resulting regression from the one in (a).

c. Can you improve the models in (a) or (b) by *transforming* one or more of the explanatory variables from the regression? If so, compare the advantages and disadvantages of the resulting regression from the ones in (a) and (b).

7. A commission on state parks is interested in identifying the factors that determine park revenues. Data is available at the state level on total revenues, acreage, number of day visitors, number of overnight visitors, and operating expenses. A portion of this data is displayed here; the entire data set is available in the file *Parks.xls*.

State	Acreage	Day visitors	Overnight visitors	Operating expenses	Total revenue
Alabama	50	4,740	1,175	28,279	25,724
Alaska	3,250	3,567	703	5,294	1,957
Arizona	46	1,721	580	11,392	4,114
Arkansas	51	6,931	683	23,364	12,805
California	1,345	64,765	6,187	175,189	63,689
Colorado	347	11,973	727	15,771	10,708
Connecticut	176	7,672	357	8,875	3,571
Delaware	17	2,795	207	8,829	5,013
Florida	454	11,302	1,189	44,738	21,606
Georgia	67	13,272	673	54,596	16,917

a. Build a linear model to predict total revenues based on the four potential explanatory variables as they are measured in the table. Evaluate the model in terms of overall goodness-of-fit. Evaluate the results for each regression parameter: Are the signs appropriate? Are the values different from zero?

b. Can you improve the model in (a) by *removing* or *transforming* one or more of the explanatory variables from the regression? If so, compare the advantages and disadvantages of the resulting regression from the one in (a).

8. Cost-of-living indices are often used to measure the desirability of living in a particular geographical area. The data in the following table gives a composite index and six component indices for several urban areas in the United States. (The complete data on 321 areas is available in the file *COL.xls*.)

a. Build a linear model to predict the composite index based on the component indices. Evaluate the model in terms of overall goodness-of-fit. Evaluate the results for each regression parameter: Are the signs appropriate? Are the values different from zero?

b. Can you improve the model in (a) by *removing* or *transforming* one or more of the explanatory variables from the regression? If so, compare the advantages and disadvantages of the resulting regression to the one in (a).

Urban area	Composite index	Grocery items	Housing	Utilities	Transportation	Health care	Miscellaneous goods and services
Birmingham, AL	98.4	97.7	94.8	102.6	95.5	98.3	101.5
Cullman County, AL	95.0	98.9	88.1	98.7	97.4	87.1	98.9
Decatur-Hartselle, AL	94.7	95.8	87.4	89.8	102.2	96.3	99.3
Gasden, AL	93.2	101.5	79.1	101.8	87.0	87.4	101.7
Huntsville, AL	95.6	94.1	85.1	88.6	101.9	99.3	104.6
Marshall County, AL	91.2	101.5	84.6	97.6	87.3	83.1	92.9
Mobile, AL	96.0	100.5	82.0	105.2	102.6	91.1	102.6
Montgomery, AL	100.8	98.5	94.9	102.0	99.3	94.1	108.3
Anchorage, AK	123.0	120.1	132.3	88.0	112.0	170.1	119.3
Fairbanks, AK	128.7	118.4	134.0	166.7	119.6	168.1	115.3
Juneau, AK	140.0	122.6	164.2	157.2	117.2	165.5	125.2

9 Short-Term Forecasting

9.1 INTRODUCTION

The physicist Nils Bohr once quipped: "Prediction is very difficult, especially about the future." While prediction, or forecasting, is always difficult, some kinds are more difficult than others. Long-term forecasting is the most difficult because information is limited, competing trends exist, and many variables can influence future outcomes. An example would be forecasting the development of new technologies. A decade ago, could we have developed good forecasts for the sales of cholesterol-reducing drugs? Or the demand for downloadable music? Or the uses for geographic information systems? Forecasting those phenomena at that early stage would certainly have been challenging.

Short-term forecasting is another matter. Predicting the volume of activity in an established market is relatively manageable when we have access to good records based on recent observations. For example, what if we want to predict how much gas we'll use in our car next month? Or the interest rate on 6-month CDs next week at our local bank? Or the number of callers requesting maintenance service on their kitchen appliances tomorrow? When quantities such as these play the role of input parameters in our models, the task becomes one of making intelligent extrapolations from the history of observations. Practical techniques are available for this kind of short-term forecasting.

Regression analysis can sometimes be useful in short-term forecasting. As we saw in Chapter 8, regression represents a general modeling approach to predicting the value of one variable based on knowledge of other variables. In particular, if we know the values of the explanatory variables, we may be in a good position to predict the value of the response variable. However, when we want to forecast the routine behavior of parameters in the short run, regression may be of limited usefulness. Although it does afford us an opportunity to "explain" one variable's behavior in terms of several other variables, it still leaves us with the task of finding or predicting those values. In short, regression replaces the problem of forecasting the response variable with the problem of forecasting the explanatory variables. The alternative we will explore in this chapter is to base the forecast of a variable on its own history, thereby avoiding the need to specify a causal relationship and to predict the values of explanatory variables.

Our focus in this chapter is on time series methods for forecasting. For our purposes, a **time series** is a set of observations taken at regular intervals over time. The use of time series methods presumes that the future will be enough like the past that we can obtain reasonably accurate forecasts by using only past values to predict future values.

Finally, a note on terminology. Some people use the term **forecasting** to imply the use of a routine computational method, preferring to reserve the term **prediction** to suggest the use of subjective judgment in addition to calculations. In that sense, we are dealing here with forecasting techniques.

9.2 FORECASTING WITH TIME SERIES MODELS

The basic problem in short-term forecasting is to estimate the value of an important parameter, such as next week's demand for a product. Two features of short-term

FIGURE 9.1 Three Components of Time Series Behavior

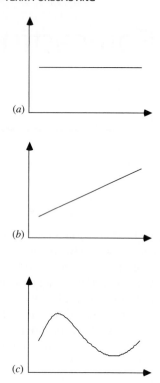

forecasting are important. First, we make use of historical data for the phenomenon we wish to forecast. In other words, we have some recent data on hand, and we assume that the near-term future will resemble the past. That assumption makes it sensible to project historical observations into the future. Second, we seek a routine calculation that may be applied to a large number of cases and that may be automated, without relying on any qualitative information about the underlying phenomena. Short-term forecasts are often used in situations that involve forecasting many different variables at frequent intervals. Some inventory systems, for example, track thousands of items. To forecast demand for each item every day requires efficient methods that do not require manual intervention.

At the outset, we hypothesize a model for systematic behavior in the time series of interest. The major components of such a model are usually the following:

- A base level
- A trend
- Cyclic fluctuations

Figure 9.1 shows these three basic categories in graphical form. Thus, we start by adopting one of these models, or a combination of them, as a representation of the process we're forecasting. Later, we will see how we might choose one of the models based on how well the forecasts match our observations.

By adopting one of the models in Figure 9.1, we assume that future observations will be samples drawn from a probability distribution whose mean value follows the model. The simplest case is the model for a constant mean (Figure 9.1a), without trend or cyclic effects. In that case, our model becomes:

$$x_t = a + e_t \tag{9.1}$$

where x_t represents the observed value for time period t and a represents the mean value. Later on, when we introduce other factors, we'll refer to a as the **base value**. The term e represents randomness. In other words, the actual observations can be thought of as a systematic but unknown mean value (a), modified by a random or "noise" term (e). The random term captures all of the uncertainty, and our purpose is to forecast the nonrandom term—the mean value—as precisely as possible. In order to produce that forecast, we can draw on the existing observations, x_t, x_{t-1}, x_{t-2}, and so on.

9.2.1 The Moving Average Model

If we were perfectly confident that our assumption about the model in (9.1) would remain unchanged forever, then we could use our entire history of observations to construct a forecast. The more of our past data we used, the more precise our forecast would tend to be. However, we may suspect that there has been, or will be, some systematic change in the mean of the process (that is, a change in a). If such a change occurred without our realizing it, then some of the data used in the construction of the forecast could be outdated when we drew on the entire history. To guard against this possibility, we can limit ourselves to only the most recent observations in order to construct a forecast. In particular, the n-period **moving average** builds a forecast by averaging the observations in the most recent n periods:

$$A_t = (x_t + x_{t-1} + \ldots + x_{t-n+1})/n \tag{9.2}$$

where x_t represents the observation made in period t and A_t denotes the moving average calculated after making the observation in period t. If we let F_{t+1} represent the forecast for period $(t + 1)$, then our forecasting procedure sets $F_{t+1} = A_t$. Of course, for the model in (9.1) there is no difference between the mean demand in period t and the mean demand in period $(t + 1)$, so we could also think of A_t as a forecast for the mean value of demand at period t as well as at period $(t + 1)$. However, when there is a trend or a seasonality factor, it is important to be clear about the target period for the forecast. We adopt the following convention for the steps in forecasting:

1. Make the observation in period t.
2. Carry out the necessary calculations.
3. Use the calculations to forecast period $(t + 1)$.

The formula in (9.2) simply takes the average of the n most recent observations. One period from now, there will be a new observation to include in the average, while the oldest observation will be dropped. Thus, in the event that a systematic change occurs in the underlying process, the oldest data point, which reflects how the process looked prior to the change, will be purged from the forecast calculation.

EXAMPLE
Curtis
Distributors (1)

Curtis Distributors is a distributor of office products. Among the many items it handles is a particular folding table that is in constant demand. The actual demands in each of the previous 10 weeks have been tracked by Curtis's information system, as reproduced in the following table.

Week	1	2	3	4	5	6	7	8	9	10
Sales	73	106	76	89	106	113	96	66	104	73

Now the distributor's task is to develop a forecast for week 11 (and beyond) from this history. ∎

For the purposes of illustration, we use a 4-week moving average. In the worksheet of Figure 9.2*, we find the observations in column B and the moving average in column C. The forecast calculations appear in column D, using the moving average at period t as the forecast for period $(t + 1)$. The first forecast we can calculate occurs after the fourth observation, so we see entries in the Forecast column starting in week 5. Cell C8 contains the formula AVERAGE(B5:B8), and this formula has been copied to the cells below it. The last calculation in column C contains the moving average after the observation in week 10, a value of 85.50, which becomes our forecast for week 11. (Given our model of constant mean demand, this value is also our forecast, at this stage, for week 12 and beyond.)

In our example, it is interesting to note that the largest forecast (101) occurs after an observation (96) that is lower than the previous two observations. However,

FIGURE 9.2 Worksheet for Calculating Moving Averages

	A	B	C	D	E	F	G
1	Moving Average Example						
2							
3	Period		4-week Moving Average				
4	t	Observed	A(t)	Forecast	Error	Deviation	Percent
5	1	73					
6	2	106					
7	3	76					
8	4	89	86.00				
9	5	106	94.25	86.00	20.00	20.00	19%
10	6	113	96.00	94.25	18.75	18.75	17%
11	7	96	101.00	96.00	0.00	0.00	0%
12	8	66	95.25	101.00	-35.00	35.00	53%
13	9	104	94.75	95.25	8.75	8.75	8%
14	10	76	85.50	94.75	-18.75	18.75	25%
15	11			85.50			
16							

*To download spreadsheets for this chapter, go to the Student Companion Site at www.wiley.com/college/powell.

we can understand why that might be the case here: the 4-week moving average has just dropped the observation of 76 from week 3 and added the observation of 96 from week 7. As a result, the moving average is larger than before. With two observations above 100 from weeks 5 and 6 also included in the moving average, we can see why the forecast might peak at this stage. The low observation of 66 in week 8 causes the moving average to drop, for similar reasons.

How many periods' worth of observations should we include in the moving average? There is no definitive answer to this question, but there is a trade-off to consider. Suppose the mean of the underlying process remains stable. If we include very few data points, then the moving average exhibits more variability than if we include a larger number of data points. In that sense, we get more *stability* from including more points. Suppose, however, there is an unanticipated change in the mean of the underlying process. If we include very few data points, our moving average will tend to track the changed process more closely than if we include a larger number of data points. In that case, we get more *responsiveness* from including fewer points.

A stylized example, containing no randomness, helps to demonstrate the responsiveness feature. Suppose the mean of a process is stable at 100 and then jumps to 180 in period 10, where it remains. In Figure 9.3, we see that the 4-week moving average detects the change and raises the forecast in column D to 120 for period 11. After week 13, the 4-week moving average has fully recovered, and the forecast stays at 180 thereafter.

For comparison, a 6-week moving average is calculated for the same observations and shown in column I, with forecasts in column J. Here, we see that the change is detected in period 10, but the response is more gradual. Full recovery occurs only after week 15. As the example suggests, the longer moving average responds more slowly to a step change in the mean. If there were randomness in the observations, in addition to the systematic change in the mean, the results might be harder to discern, but the essence of the comparison would be similar. To the extent that we value responsiveness in our forecasts, we prefer a shorter moving average to a longer one.

The other side of the trade-off, as mentioned above, involves stability. We return to the data from the Curtis Distributors example in Figure 9.2 and compute a 6-week moving average for comparisons with the original 4-week moving average. In Figure 9.4, we can see that the 4-week moving average fluctuates more than the 6-week moving average. In the five weeks in which both methods generate forecasts, the 4-week moving average forecasts range from a low of 85.50 to a high of 101.00.

FIGURE 9.3 Moving Average Calculations in a Stylized Example

	A	B	C	D	E	F	G	H	I	J	K	L	M
1	Moving Average Example												
2													
3	Period		4-week Moving Average						6-week Moving Average				
4	t	Observed	A(t)	Forecast	Error	Deviation	Percent		A(t)	Forecast	Difference	Deviation	Percent
5	1	100											
6	2	100											
7	3	100											
8	4	100	100.00										
9	5	100	100.00	100.00	0.00	0.00	0%						
10	6	100	100.00	100.00	0.00	0.00	0%		100.00				
11	7	100	100.00	100.00	0.00	0.00	0%		100.00	100.00	0.00	0.00	0%
12	8	100	100.00	100.00	0.00	0.00	0%		100.00	100.00	0.00	0.00	0%
13	9	100	100.00	100.00	0.00	0.00	0%		100.00	100.00	0.00	0.00	0%
14	10	180	120.00	100.00	80.00	80.00	44%		113.33	100.00	80.00	80.00	44%
15	11	180	140.00	120.00	60.00	60.00	33%		126.67	113.33	66.67	66.67	37%
16	12	180	160.00	140.00	40.00	40.00	22%		140.00	126.67	53.33	53.33	30%
17	13	180	180.00	160.00	20.00	20.00	11%		153.33	140.00	40.00	40.00	22%
18	14	180	180.00	180.00	0.00	0.00	0%		166.67	153.33	26.67	26.67	15%
19	15	180	180.00	180.00	0.00	0.00	0%		180.00	166.67	13.33	13.33	7%
20	16	180	180.00	180.00	0.00	0.00	0%		180.00	180.00	0.00	0.00	0%
21	17	180	180.00	180.00	0.00	0.00	0%		180.00	180.00	0.00	0.00	0%
22	18	180	180.00	180.00	0.00	0.00	0%		180.00	180.00	0.00	0.00	0%
23	19	180	180.00	180.00	0.00	0.00	0%		180.00	180.00	0.00	0.00	0%
24	20	180	180.00	180.00	0.00	0.00	0%		180.00	180.00	0.00	0.00	0%
25													
26					MSE	MAD	MAPE				MSE	MAD	MAPE
27		For periods 10-15			2000.00	33.33	18.5%				2696.30	46.67	25.9%
28													

9.2 9.3

FIGURE 9.4 Comparison of 4-week and 6-week Moving Averages

	A	B	C	D	E	F	G	H	I	J	K	L	M
1	Moving Average Example												
2													
3	Period		4-week Moving Average						6-week Moving Average				
4	t	Observed	A(t)	Forecast	Error	Deviation	Percent		A(t)	Forecast	Difference	Deviation	Percent
5	1	73											
6	2	106											
7	3	76											
8	4	89	86.00										
9	5	106	94.25	86.00	20.00	20.00	19%						
10	6	113	96.00	94.25	18.75	18.75	17%		93.83				
11	7	96	101.00	96.00	0.00	0.00	0%		97.67	93.83	2.17	2.17	2%
12	8	66	95.25	101.00	-35.00	35.00	53%		91.00	97.67	-31.67	31.67	48%
13	9	104	94.75	95.25	8.75	8.75	8%		95.67	91.00	13.00	13.00	13%
14	10	76	85.50	94.75	-18.75	18.75	25%		93.50	95.67	-19.67	19.67	26%
15				85.50						93.50			
16													

H ◄ ► H \ 9.2 ⟨ 9.3 ⟩ 9.4 / | ◄

The range for the 6-week moving average is 91.00 to 97.67, a much tighter interval. To the extent that we value a small range in our forecast, we prefer a longer moving average to a shorter one.

To resolve the trade-off, we have to consider what is likely to happen in the process that generates the observations. If we are confident in the model of a stable mean—that is, a constant value of a—then we should value stability in the forecast and prefer a longer moving average. To the extent that we believe that the value of a is subject to change, we should value responsiveness and prefer a shorter moving average.

9.2.2 Measures of Forecast Accuracy

How good are the forecasts produced by a moving average calculation? There is no universal measure of performance for forecast accuracy, but several measures are used frequently. We suggest three measures:

- MSE: the Mean Squared Error between forecast and actual
- MAD: the Mean Absolute Deviation between forecast and actual
- MAPE: the Mean Absolute Percent Error between forecast and actual

The MSE is a traditional squared-error calculation that echoes results in statistics; the MAD looks only at absolute error sizes, without squaring them; and the MAPE looks at relative error sizes. The relevant formulas are as follows (where F_t represents the forecast and x_t the actual observation), assuming that forecasts have been calculated for periods u through v. The number of periods is therefore $(u - v + 1)$.

$$\text{MSE} = \frac{1}{(u - v + 1)} \sum_{t=u}^{v} (F_t - x_t)^2$$

$$\text{MAD} = \frac{1}{(u - v + 1)} \sum_{t=u}^{v} |F_t - x_t|$$

$$\text{MAPE} = \frac{1}{(u - v + 1)} \sum_{t=u}^{v} \left| \frac{F_t - x_t}{x_t} \right|$$

The MAD and MAPE calculations are similar: one is absolute, the other is relative. We usually reserve the MAPE for comparisons in which the magnitudes of two cases are different. For example, we might be evaluating forecasts for two of a distributor's products, a standard product that sells about 100 per period and a custom product that sells about 10 per period. The forecast deviations for the standard product are likely to be much larger than the deviations for the custom product, so a comparison seeking a small value of the MAD would intrinsically favor the custom product. A fairer comparison might be the MAPE because it adjusts for the differences in scale.

In Figure 9.3, we have included the calculations of these three measures, covering periods 10–15, where there are forecast errors. Here, we can see that all

FIGURE 9.5 Extended
Comparison of 4-week and
6-week Moving Averages

	A	B	C	D	E	F	G	H	I	J	K	L	M
1	Moving Average Example												
2													
3	Period		4-week Moving Average						6-week Moving Average				
4	t	Observed	A(t)	Forecast	Error	Deviation	Percent		A(t)	Forecast	Difference	Deviation	Percent
5	1	73											
6	2	106											
7	3	76											
8	4	89	86.00										
9	5	106	94.25	86.00	20.00	20.00	19%						
10	6	113	96.00	94.25	18.75	18.75	17%		93.83				
11	7	96	101.00	96.00	0.00	0.00	0%		97.67	93.83	2.17	2.17	2%
12	8	66	95.25	101.00	-35.00	35.00	53%		91.00	97.67	-31.67	31.67	48%
13	9	104	94.75	95.25	8.75	8.75	8%		95.67	91.00	13.00	13.00	13%
14	10	76	85.50	94.75	-18.75	18.75	25%		93.50	95.67	-19.67	19.67	26%
15	11	97	85.75	85.50	11.50	11.50	12%		92.00	93.50	3.50	3.50	4%
16	12	112	97.25	85.75	26.25	26.25	23%		91.83	92.00	20.00	20.00	18%
17	13	117	100.50	97.25	19.75	19.75	17%		95.33	91.83	25.17	25.17	22%
18	14	84	102.50	100.50	-16.50	16.50	20%		98.33	95.33	-11.33	11.33	13%
19	15	79	98.00	102.50	-23.50	23.50	30%		94.17	98.33	-19.33	19.33	24%
20	16	62	85.50	98.00	-36.00	36.00	58%		91.83	94.17	-32.17	32.17	52%
21	17	60	71.25	85.50	-25.50	25.50	43%		85.67	91.83	-31.83	31.83	53%
22	18	92	73.25	71.25	20.75	20.75	23%		82.33	85.67	6.33	6.33	7%
23	19	68	87.57	73.25	-5.25	5.25	8%		88.81	82.33	-14.33	14.33	21%
24	20	87	85.71	87.57	-0.57	0.57	1%		88.69	88.81	-1.81	1.81	2%
25													
26					MSE	MAD	MAPE				MSE	MAD	MAPE
27		For periods 11-20			444.06	18.56	23.3%				384.47	16.58	21.6%
28													

\9.2 \ 9.3 \ 9.4 \ 9.5 \

three measures are lower for the 4-week moving average than for the 6-week alternative. Thus, the more responsive 4-week moving average is preferred here.

In Figure 9.5, we have extended the Curtis Distributors example through 20 periods in order to allow for a longer comparison interval. Here, the three error measures, calculated for periods 11–20, happen to be smaller for the 6-week moving average. Such a result is typical when the mean is stable and we observe the process for a relatively long interval.

EXCEL TIP
Moving
Average
Calculations

Moving averages are simple enough to calculate on a spreadsheet, and we don't necessarily need specialized software or commands to do the work. However, Excel's Data Analysis tool does contain an option for calculating moving averages (Data▶Analysis▶Data Analysis▶Moving Average). Excel assumes that the data appear in a single column, and the tool provides an option of recognizing a title for this column, if it is included in the data range. Other options include a graphical display of the actual and forecast data and a calculation of the standard error after each forecast. (This is equivalent to the square root of the MSE; however, Excel pairs the forecast F_{t+1} and the observation x_t. In the calculations of Figure 9.2, we adopted a more intuitive convention in which the forecast F_{t+1} is compared with the next observation, x_{t+1}).   ■

9.3   THE EXPONENTIAL SMOOTHING MODEL

All time series forecasts involve weighted averages of historical observations. In the case of a four-period moving average, the weights are 0.25 on each of the last four observations and zero on all of the previous observations. But if the philosophy is to weight recent observations more than older ones, then why not allow the weights to decline gradually as we go back in time? This is the approach taken in **exponential smoothing**.

For the stable demand model (9.1), exponential smoothing involves taking a weighted average of the latest observation x_t and our previous forecast S_t:

$$S_t = \alpha x_t + (1 - \alpha)S_{t-1} \qquad (9.3)$$

The parameter α is a number between zero and one, called the **smoothing constant**. We refer to S_t as the **smoothed value** of the observations, and we can think of it as our "best guess" as to the value of the mean. Our forecasting procedure sets the forecast $F_{t+1} = S_t$.

Similarly, one period previously, we would have made the calculation

$$S_{t-1} = \alpha x_{t-1} + (1 - \alpha)S_{t-2}$$

Substituting this equation into (9.3) yields

$$S_t = \alpha x_t + \alpha(1-\alpha)x_{t-1} + (1-\alpha)^2 S_{t-2}$$

Continuing to substitute in this way, we can eventually express (9.3) as follows:

$$S_t = \alpha x_t + \alpha(1-\alpha)x_{t-1} + \alpha(1-\alpha)^2 x_{t-2} + \alpha(1-\alpha)^3 x_{t-3} + \cdots \qquad (9.4)$$

Because $\alpha < 1$, the term $\alpha(1-\alpha)^t$ declines as t increases. Thus, we can see that the forecast is a weighting of all the observations, applying the largest weight to the most recent observation, the second largest weight to the second most recent observation, and so on. The exponential smoothing formula is not as drastic as the moving average formula because it doesn't discard old data after n periods. Instead, the exponential smoothing calculation simply gives less weight to observations as they become older. Indeed, the exponential decay exhibited by the weights in (9.4) is the basis for the name of the forecasting technique.

As written in (9.3), the new forecast is a weighted average of the most recent observation and the last smoothed value. Another way to express the same relationship is the following:

$$S_t = S_{t-1} + \alpha(x_t - S_{t-1}) \qquad (9.5)$$

In other words, our new smoothed value (S_t) is equal to our old one (S_{t-1}), modified by an amount proportional to the difference, or error, between our latest observation and our previous best guess. Thus, we are willing to adjust our best guess in the direction of that difference, and in some sense, the value of α describes the strength of that adjustment. A larger value of α gives more weight to the adjustment. However, there is likely to be some randomness in the difference between the last observation x_t and our last forecast (which is equivalent to S_{t-1}), so we do not want to make the value of α too large.

The forecasting process described by (9.4) strikes something of a balance between stability (by including all observations) and responsiveness (by weighting recent observations most heavily). However, this balance can be influenced by the choice of the smoothing constant. When α is large (close to 1), the forecasts are responsive but tend to be volatile; when α is small (close to 0), the forecasts tend to be stable but relatively unresponsive. Most analysts opt for a conservative choice—that is, a relatively small value of α. This means using a stable forecast and accepting the risk that the true mean may change. When evidence mounts that a systematic change has occurred in the mean, it would then make sense to manually override the calculated value of S_{t-1}, essentially reinitializing the calculations.

We can get an additional perspective by examining the coefficients in the expression (9.4). Figure 9.6 shows the weight applied to observation x_{t-k} (the observation that is k periods old) for two values of the smoothing constant, $\alpha = 0.2$ and $\alpha = 0.6$. The use of the larger value, $\alpha = 0.6$, leads to 99 percent of the weight being placed on the most recent five observations, whereas the use of the smaller value, $\alpha = 0.2$, leads to only 67 percent of the weight being placed on the same observations. The graph also shows that the weights for $\alpha = 0.2$ are almost identical from period to period, while for $\alpha = 0.6$, the weights decline rapidly for earlier periods.

To illustrate the calculations for exponential smoothing, we return to the Curtis Distributors example. In Figure 9.7, we show the calculation of the smoothed value in column C. The parameter $\alpha = 0.2$ appears in cell C3. The initial smoothed value S_1 is taken to be equal to the first observation in cell C6. The Excel implementation of the exponential smoothing formula in (9.3) appears in cell C7 as: $C3*B7+(1-$C3*C6. Then this formula is copied to the cells below. The smoothed value becomes the forecast for the following period in column D.

In cells E28:G28, we calculate the three error measures covering periods 5–20 for the exponential smoothing approach. Comparable measures for the 4-week moving average method are calculated in cells K28:M28. We see that the accuracies

FIGURE 9.6 Comparison
of Weights Placed on
k-Year-Old Data

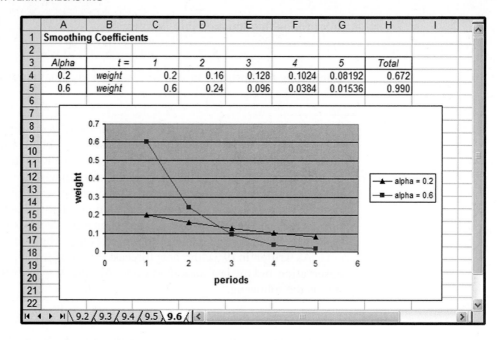

of the two procedures are roughly comparable. The MSE favors exponential smoothing, whereas the two absolute deviation methods favor the moving average. Although there is no theoretical reason to prefer exponential smoothing, some research suggests that, across a wide spectrum of applications, exponential smoothing tends to produce more accurate forecasts than moving averages. One of the questions we have not explored in this comparison is whether the error measures could be improved for a different choice of the smoothing constant. (We may already suspect, based on a different calculation in Figure 9.5, that an alternative moving average may achieve better error measures).

Figure 9.8 displays the smoothed and averaged data against the actual observations. The graph provides a good reminder that the two forecasting methods serve to estimate the mean of the underlying process. In this example, the process also has quite a bit of randomness, reflected by the fact that the time series for the observations fluctuates more drastically than either of the forecasts.

FIGURE 9.7 Worksheet
for Exponential Smoothing
Calculations

	A	B	C	D	E	F	G	H	I	J	K	L	M
1	Exponential Smoothing Example												
2													
3		Alpha	0.2										
4	Period								4-week Moving Average				
5	t	Observed	S(t)	Forecast	Error	Deviation	Percent		A(t)	Forecast	Difference	Deviation	Percent
6	1	73	73.00										
7	2	106	79.60	73.00	Initial value S(1) = x(1)					A(t) = [X(t)+X(t-1)+X(t-2)+X(t-3)] / 4			
8	3	76	78.88	79.60									
9	4	89	80.90	78.88					86.00				
10	5	106	85.92	80.90	25.10	25.10	24%		94.25	86.00	20.00	20.00	19%
11	6	113	91.34	85.92	S(t) = αx(t) + (1-α)S(t-1)		24%		96.00	94.25	18.75	18.75	17%
12	7	96	92.27	91.34	4.66	4.66	5%		101.00	96.00	0.00	0.00	0%
13	8	66	87.02	92.27	-26.27	26.27	40%		95.25	101.00	-35.00	35.00	53%
14	9	104	90.41	87.02	16.98	16.98	16%		94.75	95.25	8.75	8.75	8%
15	10	73	86.93	90.41	-17.41	17.41	24%		84.75	94.75	-21.75	21.75	30%
16	11	77	84.94	86.93	-9.93	9.93	13%		80.00	84.75	-7.75	7.75	10%
17	12	119	91.76	84.94	34.06	34.06	29%		93.25	80.00	39.00	39.00	33%
18	13	84	90.20	91.76	-7.76	7.76	9%		88.25	93.25	-9.25	9.25	11%
19	14	71	86.36	90.20	-19.20	19.20	27%		87.75	88.25	-17.25	17.25	24%
20	15	88	86.69	86.36	1.64	1.64	2%		90.50	87.75	0.25	0.25	0%
21	16	97	88.75	86.69	10.31	10.31	11%		85.00	90.50	6.50	6.50	7%
22	17	69	84.80	88.75	-19.75	19.75	29%		81.25	85.00	-16.00	16.00	23%
23	18	117	91.24	84.80	32.20	32.20	28%		92.75	81.25	35.75	35.75	31%
24	19	80	88.99	91.24	-11.24	11.24	14%		90.75	92.75	-12.75	12.75	16%
25	20	73	85.79	88.99	-15.99	15.99	22%		84.75	90.75	-17.75	17.75	24%
26													
27					MSE	MAD	MAPE				MSE	MAD	MAPE
28		For periods 5-20			391.99	17.47	19.7%				409.02	16.66	19.1%
29													

FIGURE 9.8 Comparison of Smoothed and Averaged Forecasts

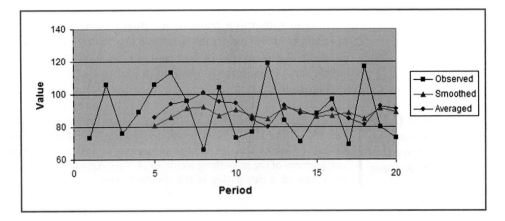

It's helpful to look at a stylized example (with no randomness) to appreciate how exponential smoothing works. For example, imagine that we were tracking a process for which the observations were stable at 100, with no variability. In other words, the observation in each period is exactly 100. How does exponential smoothing perform?

In Figure 9.9, we show the calculations for the case of $\alpha = 0.2$ and an initial value of $S_1 = 0$. The observations appear in column B, the calculation of S_t in column C, and the forecast in column D. As the table shows, the forecast underestimates the observation from the outset, but the gap gradually narrows. After approximately 20 periods, the forecasts are virtually on target. Thus, the responsiveness feature of exponential smoothing can eventually overcome an inaccurate initialization of the smoothed value.

In addition, we would expect that the forecast would be better if the initial value of S_1 were larger. The sensitivity table in Figure 9.9 shows how the value of the forecast after period 10 varies with α and with S_1. Note that when $S_1 = 100$, the forecasts are on target for any choice of α (and this turns out to be the case in every period). In a sense, this is exactly how we would hope a forecasting procedure would operate: if we start with a good guess for the mean, then the procedure stays on target; if we start with a poor guess, then the procedure at least converges to the figure we desire, and it converges faster for larger values of the smoothing constant.

FIGURE 9.9 Exponential Smoothing Calculations in a Stylized Example

	A	B	C	D	E	F	G	H	I	J	K
1	Exponential Smoothing Example										
2											
3		Alpha	0.2								
4	Period										
5	t	Observed	S(t)	Forecast					S(1)		
6	1	100	0.00				83.22	0	50	100	150
7	2	100	20.00	0.00			0.2	83.22	91.61	100.00	108.39
8	3	100	36.00	20.00		alpha	0.4	98.32	99.16	100.00	100.84
9	4	100	48.80	36.00			0.6	99.93	99.97	100.00	100.03
10	5	100	59.04	48.80			0.8	100.00	100.00	100.00	100.00
11	6	100	67.23	59.04							
12	7	100	73.79	67.23							
13	8	100	79.03	73.79							
14	9	100	83.22	79.03							
15	10	100	86.58	83.22							
16	11	100	89.26	86.58							
17	12	100	91.41	89.26							
18	13	100	93.13	91.41							
19	14	100	94.50	93.13							
20	15	100	95.60	94.50							
21	16	100	96.48	95.60							
22	17	100	97.19	96.48							
23	18	100	97.75	97.19							
24	19	100	98.20	97.75							
25	20	100	98.56	98.20							
26											

9.9

Ready | | | | | | | | | | NUM

One remaining concern we might have about the exponential smoothing formula is how it performs when we are wrong about the underlying model—that is, when the mean is not constant. In the next two sections, we examine how to adapt the exponential smoothing model to the trend and cyclical effects pictured in Figure 9.1.

EXCEL TIP
Implementing
Exponential
Smoothing

Excel's Data Analysis tool contains an option for calculating forecasts using exponential smoothing. The Exponential Smoothing module resembles the Moving Average module, but instead of asking for the number of periods, it asks for the **damping factor**, which is the complement of the smoothing factor, or $(1 - \alpha)$. Again, there is an option for chart output and an option for a calculation of the standard error. ■

9.4   EXPONENTIAL SMOOTHING WITH A TREND

In the previous discussion, we assumed in equation (9.1) that the underlying model is stable. But what if that isn't the case: how will the procedure perform? To shed some light on this problem, consider another stylized case, without any variability. Suppose that we have been operating with a stable mean of 100 for some time but that an upward trend occurs and then persists. The observations in Figure 9.10 illustrate this case. The observations remain at 100 until period 4 and then increase by 10 each period. The value of $S_1 = 100$, as would be the case if there were a past history of stable behavior not shown in the figure.

Once the trend begins, the value of S_t increases, but the forecast always lags behind the corresponding observation. Given the form of (9.5), this pattern is not surprising, because we are always updating our best guess by a fraction of the forecast error. In fact, as the example shows, the forecast error $(F_t - x_t)$ eventually stabilizes at a gap of approximately 50. (In general, for other values of the smoothing constant, the size of the gap would be a factor of $1/\alpha$ multiplied by the trend, if we waited long enough). When randomness is present and we assume the model for a stable mean when in reality a trend exists, our forecasts will tend to underestimate the actual mean. Therefore, it will be necessary to modify the basic model if we want to generate accurate forecasts in the presence of a trend.

FIGURE 9.10 Exponential Smoothing Calculations with a Trend in the Data

	A	B	C	D	E	F	G	H	I	J
1	Basic Model with Trend in Data				Trend	10				
2										
3		Alpha	0.2							
4	Period				Initial value					
5	t	Observed	S(t)	Forecast	Error					
6	1	100	100.00							
7	2	100	100.00	$S(t) = \alpha x(t) + (1-\alpha)S(t-1)$			Sensitivity of Error to α at t=25			
8	3	100	100.00	100.00	0.00			49.63		1/α
9	4	110	102.00	100.00	10.00		0.1	90.15		100.00
10	5	120	105.60	102.00	18.00		0.2	49.63		50.00
11	6	130	110.48	105.60	24.40		0.3	33.32		33.33
12	7	140	116.38	110.48	29.52		0.4	25.00		25.00
13	8	150	123.11	116.38	33.62		0.5	20.00		20.00
14	9	160	130.49	123.11	36.89		0.6	16.67		16.67
15	10	170	138.39	130.49	39.51		0.7	14.29		14.29
16	11	180	146.71	138.39	41.61		0.8	12.50		12.50
17	12	190	155.37	146.71	43.29		0.9	11.11		11.11
18	13	200	164.29	155.37	44.63					
19	14	210	173.44	164.29	45.71					
20	15	220	182.75	173.44	46.56					
21	16	230	192.20	182.75	47.25					
22	17	240	201.76	192.20	47.80					
23	18	250	211.41	201.76	48.24					
24	19	260	221.13	211.41	48.59					
25	20	270	230.90	221.13	48.87					
26	21	280	240.72	230.90	49.10					
27	22	290	250.58	240.72	49.28					
28	23	300	260.46	250.58	49.42					
29	24	310	270.37	260.46	49.54					
30	25	320	280.30	270.37	49.63					
31										

14 4 ▶ ▶I \ 9.6 \ 9.7 \ 9.8 \ 9.9 \ 9.10 \ | <

Our introduction to moving average and exponential smoothing methods for forecasting was based on a model with a stable mean, $x_t = a + e$. Now we consider a model with a linear trend:

$$x_t = a + bt + e_t \tag{9.6}$$

where a is called the **base value**, b is the **trend**, and t is the time period. The observation is assumed to be drawn from a probability distribution with a mean value of $a + bt$. In other words, the mean value follows a straight line with a slope of b, and there is variability as well. We can think of the parameter a as the initial value, or the base value for the mean.

When a trend is present, there are two tasks—to forecast the mean and to forecast the trend. Loosely speaking, we ask, where is the process now and how fast is it changing? A pair of smoothing formulas does the work:

$$S_t = \alpha x_t + (1 - \alpha)S_{t-1} \tag{9.7}$$

$$T_t = \alpha(S_t - S_{t-1}) + (1 - \alpha)T_{t-1} \tag{9.8}$$

As before, S_t is the **smoothed value** after the observation has been made in period t, and T_t is the **estimated trend.** Equation (9.8) is similar to the basic smoothing calculation, but because we cannot observe the trend directly, we use the difference in the two most recent smoothed values as a proxy. Then we weight that value along with our previous best guess for the trend.

With these two values in hand, we construct a forecast for the next period. First, we must answer the question, where is the process now? Knowing that S_t contains a systematic lag, as mentioned earlier, we must compensate for the lag. Then we can use the estimated trend to forecast where the process will be one period from now. The forecast is thus:

$$F_{t+1} = S_t + (1/\alpha)T_t \tag{9.9}$$

In our stylized trend example, we can see the effect of using (9.9) in Figure 9.11. The calculations in (9.7) and (9.8) appear in columns C and D. The forecast is calculated in column E, and the error in column F. As the error values show, the adjustment in (9.9) does not produce accurate forecasts in the periods immediately after the trend begins, but the forecasts do approach the desired values eventually. By period 25, the forecast is quite accurate; moreover, the error virtually disappears by this stage for α values above 0.3. The lesson here is that the forecasting model may need several periods' worth of data to "warm up," after which it can produce fairly accurate forecasts.

Note that the same smoothing constant is used in both (9.7) and (9.8). As an alternative, we might prefer to use a different smoothing constant for the smoothed value than for the estimated trend because we may view the trade-off between

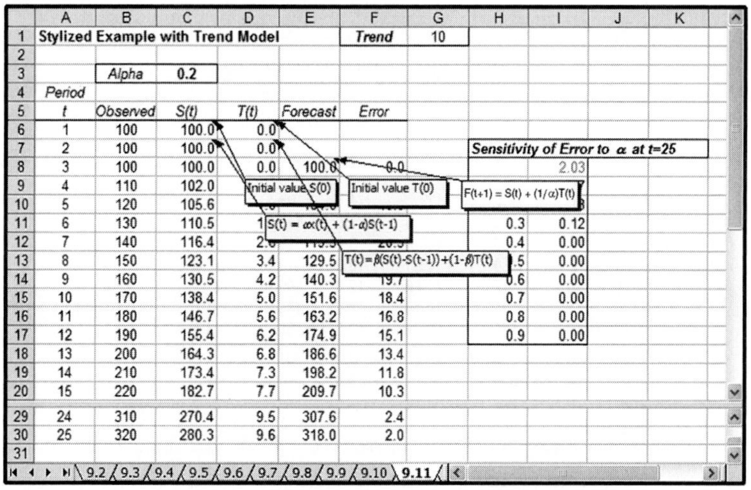

	A	B	C	D	E	F	G	H	I	J	K
1	Stylized Example with Trend Model					Trend	10				
2											
3		Alpha	0.2								
4	Period										
5	t	Observed	S(t)	T(t)	Forecast	Error					
6	1	100	100.0	0.0							
7	2	100	100.0	0.0				Sensitivity of Error to α at t=25			
8	3	100	100.0	0.0	100.0	0.0			2.03		
9	4	110	102.0	[illegible]	[illegible]	[illegible]		[illegible]	[illegible]		
10	5	120	105.6	[illegible]	[illegible]	[illegible]		[illegible]	[illegible]		
11	6	130	110.5	1[illegible]	[illegible]	[illegible]		0.3	0.12		
12	7	140	116.4	2.[illegible]	[illegible]	[illegible]		0.4	0.00		
13	8	150	123.1	3.4	129.5	[illegible]		[illegible].5	0.00		
14	9	160	130.5	4.2	140.3	19.7		0.6	0.00		
15	10	170	138.4	5.0	151.6	18.4		0.7	0.00		
16	11	180	146.7	5.6	163.2	16.8		0.8	0.00		
17	12	190	155.4	6.2	174.9	15.1		0.9	0.00		
18	13	200	164.3	6.8	186.6	13.4					
19	14	210	173.4	7.3	198.2	11.8					
20	15	220	182.7	7.7	209.7	10.3					
29	24	310	270.4	9.5	307.6	2.4					
30	25	320	280.3	9.6	318.0	2.0					
31											

FIGURE 9.11 Trend Model Calculations with a Trend in the Data

responsiveness and stability differently for those two factors. In fact, it is common practice to prefer stability in the smoothed value and responsiveness in the estimated trend. This more flexible procedure, known as **Holt's method**, uses two smoothing constants, as shown in the following formulas.

$$S_t = \alpha x_t + (1 - \alpha)(S_{t-1} + T_{t-1}) \tag{9.10}$$

$$T_t = \beta(S_t + S_{t-1}) + (1 - \beta)T_{t-1} \tag{9.11}$$

Note that the form of (9.10) differs from that of (9.7) and therefore leads to a different smoothed value. The trend formula in (9.11) has the same form as (9.8), but because the S_t values are different, we should expect the T_t values to be different. These calculations allow the forecast for period $(t + 1)$ to be constructed from the following formula.

$$F_{t+1} = S_t + T_t \tag{9.12}$$

Note that (9.10) produces a new smoothed value by computing a weighted average of the observation in period t and the forecast for period t. The estimated trend again uses a proxy for the observed trend, along with the last estimated trend, to produce a new estimated trend. In Holt's method, especially where we initialize the trend forecast at zero, it makes sense to use a relatively large smoothing factor β in the trend equation (9.11), whereas a smaller factor α is still reasonable for the main equation (9.10).

Figure 9.12 shows how Holt's method works in the stylized trend example from Figure 9.11. In the calculations shown, we set $\alpha = 0.2$ as before, but we take $\beta = 0.5$ for greater responsiveness in the trend estimate. Again, we see that there is a warm-up period, and eventually the forecast becomes quite accurate.

EXAMPLE
Curtis Distributors (2)

The following table displays historical data on the orders placed for a relatively new product stocked by Curtis Distributors. Obviously, there are fluctuations in week-to-week figures, but there is clearly an upward trend in the observations. The task is to develop a forecast for week 21 (and beyond).

Week	1	2	3	4	5	6	7	8	9	10
Sales	66	69	75	72	92	83	94	105	90	112

Week	11	12	13	14	15	16	17	18	19	20
Sales	99	107	120	114	138	124	146	143	131	151

■

FIGURE 9.12 Holt's Method with a Trend in the Data

	A	B	C	D	E	F	G	H	I	J	K	L	M
1	**Stylized Example for Holt's Method**												
2													
3		Alpha	0.2	Beta	0.5					*Sensitivity of Error at t=25*			
4	*Period*										*Beta*		
5	*t*	*Observed*	*S(t)*	*T(t)*	*Forecast*	*Error*			1.9	*0.2*	*0.4*	*0.6*	*0.8*
6	1	100	100.0	0.0					*0.2*	-3.9	-0.6	2.8	0.9
7	2	100	100.0	0.0				*Alpha*	*0.4*	-0.2	0.1	-0.1	0.0
8	3	100	100.0	0.0	100.0	0.0			*0.6*	0.1	0.0	0.0	0.0
9	4	110	102.0	1.0	100.0	10.0			*0.8*	0.1	0.0	0.0	0.0
10	5	120	106.4	2.7	103.0	17.0							
11	6	130	113.3	4.8	109.1	20.9							
12	7	140	122.5	7.0	118.1	21.9							
13	8	150	133.6	9.0	129.4	20.6							
14	9	160	146.1	10.8	142.6	17.4							
15	10	170	159.5	12.1	156.9	13.1							
16	11	180	173.3	12.9	171.6	8.4							
17	12	190	187.0	13.3	186.2	3.8							
28	23	300	299.9	8.9	299.8	0.2							
29	24	310	309.0	9.0	308.8	1.2							
30	25	320	318.4	9.2	318.1	1.9							
31													

9.9 9.12

Ready NUM

FIGURE 9.13 Trend Model for the Curtis Distributors Example

	A	B	C	D	E	F	G	H	I
1	Example with Trend Model					Trend	10		
2									
3		Alpha	0.2						
4	Period								
5	t	Observed	S(t)	T(t)	Forecast	Error			
6	1	66	66.0	0.0					
7	2	69	66.6	0.1					
8	3	75	68.3	0.4	67.2	7.8			
9	4	72	69.0						
10	5	92	73.6						
11	6	83	75.5	1					
12	7	94	79.2	1					
13	8	105	84.4	2.5	88.6				
14	9	90	85.5	2.3	97.0	-7.0			
15	10	112	90.8	2.9	96.8	15.2			
16	11	99	92.4	2.6	105.1	-6.1			
17	12	107	95.3	2.7	105.5	1.5			
18	13	120	100.3	3.1	108.7	11.3			
19	14	114	103.0	3.1	115.9	-1.9			
20	15	138	110.0	3.8	118.3	19.7			
21	16	124	112.8	3.6	129.2	-5.2			
22	17	146	119.5	4.2	131.0	15.0			
23	18	143	124.2	4.3	140.6	2.4			
24	19	131	125.5	3.7	145.8	-14.8			
25	20	151	130.6	4.0	144.2	6.8			
26									

Callouts: Initial value S(0); Initial value T(0); $F(t+1) = S(t) + (1/\alpha)T(t)$; $S(t) = \alpha x(t) + (1-\alpha)S(t-1)$; $T(t) = \beta(S(t)-S(t-1)) + (1-\beta)T(t)$

Figure 9.13 shows the calculations in our first exponential smoothing procedure, using $\alpha = 0.2$. Figure 9.14 shows the calculations for Holt's method, using $\alpha = 0.2$ and $\beta = 0.5$. Holt's model achieves a slightly lower value of MSE, which may reflect the fact that it uses two smoothing constants. When Holt's method is used, the forecast for period 21 is obtained from (9.12):

$$F_{21} = S_{20} + T_{20} = 149.1 + 4.0 = 153.1$$

By using the most recent estimated trend, we can calculate forecasts for later periods:

$$F_{22} = F_{20} + 2T_{20} = 157.1$$

$$F_{23} = F_{20} + 3T_{20} = 161.1$$

In this way, we can extrapolate to any number of future periods, under the assumption that the base value and the trend in the model in (9.6) remain unchanged.

FIGURE 9.14 Holt's Method for the Curtis Distributors Example

	A	B	C	D	E	F	G	H	I
1	Example for Holt's Method								
2									
3		Alpha	0.2	Beta	0.5				
4	Period								
5	t	Observed	S(t)	T(t)	Forecast	Error			
6	1	66	66.0	0.0					
7	2	69	66.6	0.3					
8	3	75	68.5	1.1					
9	4	72	70.1	1.3	69.6	2.4			
10	5	92	75.6	3					
11	6	83	79.8	3.8	79.0	4.0			
12	7	94	85.7	4.8	83.6				
13	8	105	93.4	6.3	90.5				
14	9	90	97.8	5.3	99.7	-9.7			
15	10	112	104.9	6.2	103.1	8.9			
16	11	99	108.7	5.0	111.1	-12.1			
17	12	107	112.3	4.3	113.7	-6.7			
18	13	120	117.3	4.7	116.7	3.3			
19	14	114	120.4	3.9	122.0	-8.0			
20	15	138	127.0	5.2	124.3	13.7			
21	16	124	130.6	4.4	132.3	-8.3			
22	17	146	137.2	5.5	135.0	11.0			
23	18	143	142.8	5.5	142.7	0.3			
24	19	131	144.9	3.8	148.3	-17.3			
25	20	151	149.1	4.0	148.7	2.3			
26									

Callouts: Initial value of S(t); Initial value of T(t); $S(t) = \alpha x(t) + (1-\alpha)(S(t-1)+T(t-1))$; $F(t+1) = S(t) + T(t)$; $T(t) = \beta(S(t)-S(t-1)) + (1-\beta)T(t-1)$

9.5 EXPONENTIAL SMOOTHING WITH TREND AND CYCLICAL FACTORS

We can take the exponential smoothing model further and include a *cyclical* factor, as anticipated by Figure 9.1. This type of factor is usually called a "seasonal" factor, but a literal interpretation of that term may seem restrictive. A seasonal factor suggests a cycle containing four periods, one for each season in the year. However, we can also conceive of a cycle containing 12 periods, one for each month in the year. We can even conceive of a cycle containing 52 periods, one for each week in the year. Therefore, we rely on the term *cyclical* as a reminder that the number of periods in a cycle need not be four.

For a cyclical effect, there are two types of models: an additive model and a multiplicative model. The form of the additive model is as follows.

$$x_t = a + d_t + e_t \tag{9.13}$$

When a trend is included, the more general form of the additive model becomes

$$x_t = a + bt + d_t + e_t \tag{9.14}$$

Adapting the terminology introduced earlier, we call a the **base value**, b the **trend**, d_t the **cyclical factor**, and t the time period. The observation is assumed to be drawn from a probability distribution with a mean value of $a + bt + d_t$, with $b = 0$ if there is no trend. In these two models, the cyclical factor adds to (or subtracts from) the mean value an amount that depends on the position of time t in the cycle. Thus, if the cycle is quarterly, with four periods in the cycle, the effect would be represented by one of the four values d_1, d_2, d_3, d_4, depending on where in the cycle period t falls. Usually, we require that the four values of d_t sum to zero.

For the model in (9.13), we need two smoothing formulas. The first produces the smoothed value using observations from which the seasonal effect has been removed. The second produces the estimated cyclical factor. For flexibility, we use different smoothing constants in the two formulas.

$$S_t = \alpha(x_t - C_{t-p}) + (1 - \alpha)S_{t-1} \tag{9.15}$$

$$C_t = \gamma(x_t - S_t) + (1 - \gamma)C_{t-p} \tag{9.16}$$

where p represents the number of periods in a cycle. Incorporating the trend, with the more general model in (9.14), we need three smoothing formulas. The first produces the smoothed value, the second produces the trend estimate, and the third produces the estimated cyclical factor. Three smoothing constants are employed (α for the smoothed value, β for the trend, and γ for the cyclical factor).

$$S_t = \alpha(x_t - C_{t-p}) + (1 - \alpha)(S_{t-1} + T_{t-1}) \tag{9.17}$$

$$T_t = \beta(S_t - S_{t-1}) + (1 - \beta)T_{t-1} \tag{9.18}$$

$$C_t = \gamma(x_t - S_t) + (1 - \gamma)C_{t-p} \tag{9.19}$$

For the additive model, the forecast takes the following form.

$$F_{t+1} = (S_t + T_t) + C_{t+1-p} \tag{9.20}$$

where S_t is the smoothed value, T_t is the estimated trend, and C_{t+1-p} is the estimated cyclical factor for period $(t + 1)$, which would have been estimated most recently at period $(t + 1 - p)$.

For a multiplicative factor, the form of the model is as follows.

$$x_t = ad_t + e_t \tag{9.21}$$

When a trend is included, the more general form of the multiplicative model becomes the following.

$$x_t = (a + bt)d_t + e_t \tag{9.22}$$

Following the structure of the additive models, we can anticipate that we again need three smoothing formulas for the model in (9.22), as follows.

$$S_t = \alpha(x_t/C_{t-p}) + (1 - \alpha)(S_{t-1} + T_{t-1}) \tag{9.23}$$

$$T_t = \beta(S_t - S_{t-1}) + (1 - \beta)T_{t-1} \tag{9.24}$$

$$C_t = \gamma(x_t/S_t) + (1 - \gamma)C_{t-p} \tag{9.25}$$

For the multiplicative model, the forecast takes the following form.

$$F_{t+1} = (S_t + T_t)C_{t+1-p} \tag{9.26}$$

where, again, S_t is the smoothed value, T_t is the estimated trend, and C_{t+1-p} is the estimated cyclical factor for period $(t + 1)$, which would have most recently been estimated at period $(t + 1-p)$. This form of the forecasting procedure is often called the **Holt-Winters method**.

We have presented four variations of the cyclical model, depending on which type of cyclical factor is assumed and whether a trend is assumed. We emphasize the Holt-Winters method (multiplicative with trend) in our examples, because that seems to be the most widely used in practice.

First, we demonstrate the cyclical model with another stylized example. The observations in Figure 9.15 exhibit both cyclic fluctuation (over four periods) and a trend but no randomness. We start with a history of four quarterly observations of demand. Based on the first cycle of observations, the components of the forecast are initialized as follows:

$$S_t = (x_1 + x_2 + x_3 + x_4)/4, \quad \text{for } t = 1 \text{ to } 4$$

$$T_t = 0, \quad \text{for } t = 1 \text{ to } 4$$

$$C_t = 4x_t/(x_1 + x_2 + x_3 + x_4), \quad \text{for } t = 1 \text{ to } 4$$

Thus, the smoothed values S_t are initialized in the first four periods as the average observation in the first four periods. The trend T_t is initialized at zero. Finally, for each of the first four periods, the cyclical factor is initialized as the ratio of the observation in period t to the average of the first four observations. Then, starting with the second cycle (period 5), formulas (9.23)–(9.25) are used to compute new values of S_t, T_t, and C_t each time a new observation is made.

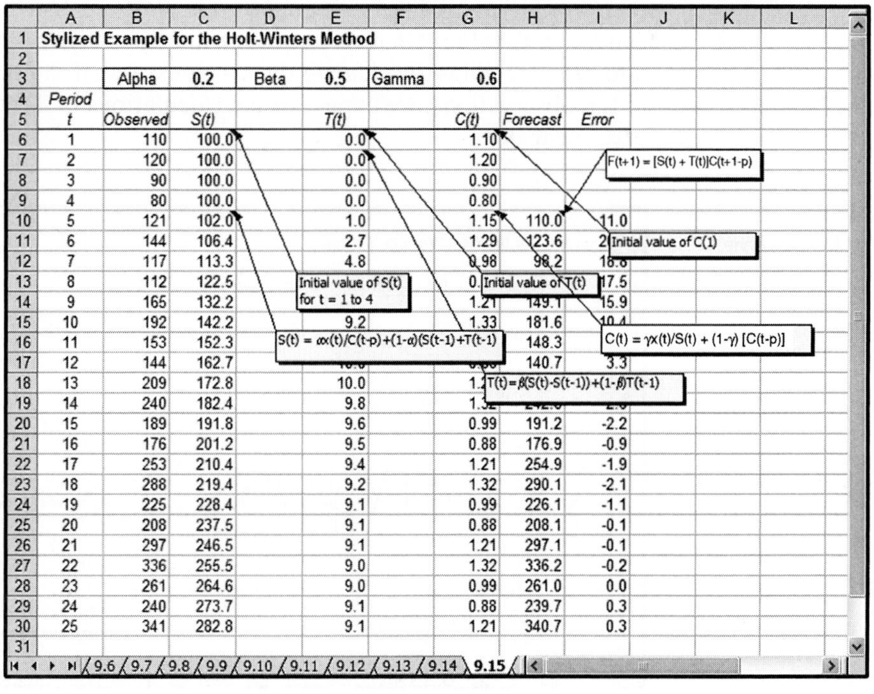

FIGURE 9.15 Stylized Model with Trend and Cyclic Fluctuations

Stylized Example for the Holt-Winters Method

t	Observed	S(t)	T(t)	C(t)	Forecast	Error
	Alpha 0.2	Beta 0.5	Gamma 0.6			
1	110	100.0	0.0	1.10		
2	120	100.0	0.0	1.20		
3	90	100.0	0.0	0.90		
4	80	100.0	0.0	0.80		
5	121	102.0	1.0	1.15	110.0	11.0
6	144	106.4	2.7	1.29	123.6	
7	117	113.3	4.8	0.98	98.2	
8	112	122.5		0.		17.5
9	165	132.2		1.21	149.1	15.9
10	192	142.2	9.2	1.33	181.6	10.4
11	153	152.3			148.3	
12	144	162.7			140.7	3.3
13	209	172.8	10.0	1.1		
14	240	182.4	9.8	1.3		
15	189	191.8	9.6	0.99	191.2	-2.2
16	176	201.2	9.5	0.88	176.9	-0.9
17	253	210.4	9.4	1.21	254.9	-1.9
18	288	219.4	9.2	1.32	290.1	-2.1
19	225	228.4	9.1	0.99	226.1	-1.1
20	208	237.5	9.1	0.88	208.1	-0.1
21	297	246.5	9.1	1.21	297.1	-0.1
22	336	255.5	9.0	1.32	336.2	-0.2
23	261	264.6	9.0	0.99	261.0	0.0
24	240	273.7	9.1	0.88	239.7	0.3
25	341	282.8	9.1	1.21	340.7	0.3

In Figure 9.15, we take the three smoothing constants to be $\alpha = 0.2, \beta = 0.5$, and $\gamma = 0.6$. We use a relatively large value of β because the initial trend estimate is zero, and we can expect that the forecasting procedure will have to respond to the data to produce a good trend estimate. We use a relatively large value of γ because we have an opportunity to update our estimates of the individual cyclical factors only once for every four observations. Nevertheless, as the error values in column I demonstrate, the forecasts become fairly accurate after period 12.

EXAMPLE ***Town of Lincoln***

The town of Lincoln tracks its water use on a quarterly basis so that it can anticipate capacity needs in its town water system and in its water treatment plant. The following table shows a three-year history of water use (in thousands of gallons), and the town wants to forecast water use in each of the upcoming four quarters.

	Quarter											
	1	2	3	4	5	6	7	8	9	10	11	12
Sales	8,216	9,196	3,768	4,032	7,481	7,889	3,996	3,764	6,664	7,011	4,356	3,565

■

Figure 9.16 contains the calculations for exponential smoothing using the Holt-Winters model for this time series. To initialize the calculations, we use the same convention as in Figure 9.15. Then, for the observations starting in period 5, we invoke (9.23)–(9.25). We can clearly detect a higher-than-average seasonal factor in each of the first two periods of the cycle, with lower values in the last two periods. We also detect a slight negative trend. Our forecasts for the next four quarters are as follows.

$$F_{13} = (S_{12} + T_{12})C_9 = (5{,}683.6 - 29.5)(1.19) = 6{,}682.3$$

$$F_{14} = (S_{12}+T_{12})C_{10} = (5{,}683.6 - 29.5)(1.31) = 7{,}337.6$$

$$F_{15} = (S_{12} + T_{12})C_{11} = (5{,}683.6 - 29.5)(0.71) = 4{,}016.8$$

$$F_{16} = (S_{12} + T_{12})C_{12} = (5{,}683.6 - 29.5)(0.63) = 3{,}555.1$$

In the spreadsheet, this set of formulas provides a general and powerful way to create forecasts with exponential smoothing. In particular, if there is no trend, then we can set all T-values equal to zero. If there is no cyclical behavior, then we can set all C-values equal to one in the multiplicative model. Alternatively, we can allow the formulas to calculate these values, and, if there is not too much volatility in the observations, we expect to see calculations of T_t near zero and calculations of C_t near one.

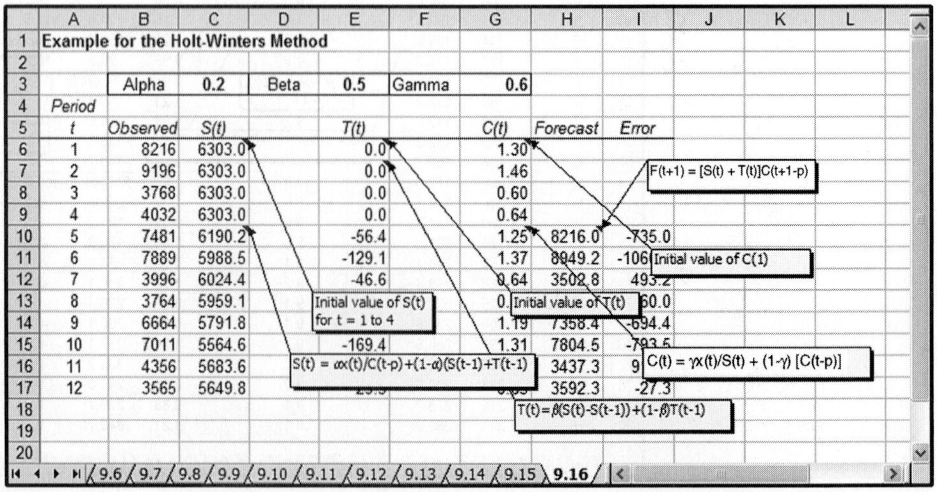

	A	B	C	D	E	F	G	H	I
1	**Example for the Holt-Winters Method**								
2									
3		Alpha	**0.2**	Beta	**0.5**	Gamma	**0.6**		
4	*Period*								
5	*t*	*Observed*	*S(t)*		*T(t)*		*C(t)*	*Forecast*	*Error*
6	1	8216	6303.0		0.0		1.30		
7	2	9196	6303.0		0.0		1.46		
8	3	3768	6303.0		0.0		0.60		
9	4	4032	6303.0		0.0		0.64		
10	5	7481	6190.2		-56.4		1.25	8216.0	-735.0
11	6	7889	5988.5		-129.1		1.37	8949.2	-106
12	7	3996	6024.4		-46.6		0.64	3502.8	493.2
13	8	3764	5959.1		[illegible]		0.	[illegible]	60.0
14	9	6664	5791.8		[illegible]		1.19	7358.4	-694.4
15	10	7011	5564.6		-169.4		1.31	7804.5	-793.5
16	11	4356	5683.6		[illegible]		[illegible]	3437.3	9
17	12	3565	5649.8		[illegible]		[illegible]	3592.3	-27.3
18									
19									
20									

FIGURE 9.16 The Holt-Winters Method for the Town of Lincoln Example

9.6* USING CB PREDICTOR

CB Predictor is a software application for constructing short-term forecasts on a spreadsheet. It is included in the Crystal Ball software package. (Crystal Ball 7 Academic is provided with this book. In order to follow the coverage in this section, install Crystal Ball before proceeding. Crystal Ball installs a Ribbon with four groups of commands: Define, Run, Analyze, and Help. CB Predictor can be invoked by choosing Crystall Ball▶Run▶Tools▶CB Predictor). In this section, we show how to use CB Predictor to create a variety of short-term forecasting models.

CB Predictor is an alternative to constructing spreadsheet formulas for the specific purposes of short-term forecasting. As we've mentioned, implementing time series forecasting methods on a spreadsheet is relatively straightforward. Compared to using specialized software like CB Predictor, building custom spreadsheets allows us a great deal of flexibility. We can design the spreadsheets to suit our purposes, and the calculations are transparent. There is also no new software to master; our knowledge of Excel will suffice. However, we always face the need to debug our own spreadsheets and the risk that some logical errors might persist. CB Predictor has been debugged and has a user-friendly interface, although it takes some time to learn how to run the software. CB Predictor also provides a number of analyses and reports automatically, whereas we might view the time required to add such reports to our own spreadsheet models counterproductive. Thus, for certain kinds of applications, it may make sense to rely on CB Predictor rather than our own custom spreadsheet models.

CB Predictor offers eight alternative forecasting procedures, organized into the following categories:

- Nonseasonal data with no trend
  - Single Moving Average
  - Single Exponential Smoothing
- Nonseasonal data with a trend
  - Double Moving Average
  - Double Exponential Smoothing
- Seasonal data with no trend
  - Seasonal Additive
  - Seasonal Multiplicative
- Seasonal data with a trend
  - Holt-Winters' Additive
  - Holt-Winters' Multiplicative

Single moving average corresponds to the method we presented in Section 9.2.1, and single exponential smoothing to the method of Section 9.3. Double exponential smoothing (Holt's method) was covered in Section 9.4; whereas Holt-Winters' Multiplicative method was covered in Section 9.5. Details on how to use the remaining methods in CB Predictor can be found in the User Manual. We illustrate how to use CB Predictor to develop single moving average and single exponential smoothing forecasts.

9.6.1 Single Moving Average

We introduce the use of CB Predictor with moving averages. Recalling the example in Figure 9.2, we find that our spreadsheet holds the 10 observations, as shown in Figure 9.17. We select Run▶CB Predictor..., which brings up the CB Predictor window shown in Figure 9.18. This window contains four tabs which we visit in succession, following the numbered steps described in the window.

At Step 1, we specify the location of the data set in the window provided, or we click on the Select... button and use the cursor to highlight the input range, A4:B14. At Step 2, we check the box for Data in columns and the box for First column has

FIGURE 9.17   Data for the
Curtis Distributors
Example

	A	B	C	D
1	**Moving Average Example**			
2				
3		**4-week Moving Average**		
4	Period	Observed		
5	1	73		
6	2	106		
7	3	76		
8	4	89		
9	5	106		
10	6	113		
11	7	96		
12	8	66		
13	9	104		
14	10	73		
15				

dates. (We would have left the latter box unchecked had we specified the input range as A5:B14.) Step 3 is optional.

On the Data Attributes tab (see Figure 9.19), we specify `Data is in periods with no seasonality` at Step 4, and we skip Step 5. Then, on the Method Gallery, we are presented with the eight choices shown in Figure 9.20. For our purposes, we check the box for Single Moving Average and leave the other boxes unchecked, as shown in the figure. Next, we double-click on the window containing the check box for `Single Moving Aver-age`, bringing up the Single Moving Average window shown in Figure 9.21. This window allows us to specify the number of periods in the moving average by selecting the `User defined button` and entering 4 for `Periods`. If we were to select the `Automatic` button, CB Predictor would decide for us how many periods to use. (In the case of simple moving averages, the default is three periods). Once we override the default and return to the gallery, we can see that Single Moving Average appears with a double asterisk in the Method Gallery, to indicate that its parameter has been specified by the user.

This brings us to the Results tab (Figure 9.22). At Step 7, we specify the number of forecasts. In the case of a simple moving average, it is sufficient to specify one forecast. If we ask for more, they will all be identical to the first, because we specified no seasonality. For now, we select none in Step 8, although we could generate confidence intervals if we wished. At Step 9, we first select a cell to hold the forecast (say, A15) and then check the boxes for the four different results (`Report`, `Charts`, `Results table`, and `Methods table`). Each check generates a separate worksheet describing some aspect of the results. Finally, we click on Run to perform the analysis.

Of the new worksheets generated by CB Predictor, the most important is probably the sheet labeled Report. (If we run CB Predictor a second time in the same workbook, the report worksheet will be labeled Report2, and so on). The Report sheet tells us that the forecast for period 11 is 84.75 (in cell D28). This forecast is also added to our original worksheet, in row 15, as we had requested. In row 55 of the report, we can also see the values of the square root of the MSE (labeled RMSE), MAD, and MAPE, should we wish to make some comparisons later with other methods.

The Chart sheet produces a graph comparing the observations with the moving average forecasts. The Results Table sheet shows the period-by-period calculations

FIGURE 9.18   CB Predictor
Window: Input Data Tab

CB Predictor

Input Data | Data Attributes | Method Gallery | Results

Step 1.   Enter a cell range on your spreadsheet that contains one or more data series:

Range: $A$4:$B$14   Select...

Step 2.   Show how your data is arranged:

☐ First row has headers

○ Data in rows

● Data in columns

☑ First column has dates

Step 3.   Optional -- view a graph of your data along with summary statistics: View Data...

<< Back   Next >>   Preview...   Run   Cancel   Help

FIGURE 9.19   CB Predictor Window: Data Attributes Tab

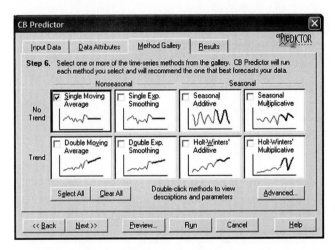

FIGURE 9.20   CB Predictor Window: Method Gallery Tab

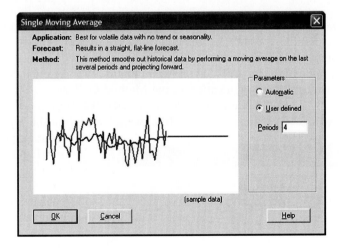

FIGURE 9.21   Single Moving Average Window in CB Predictor

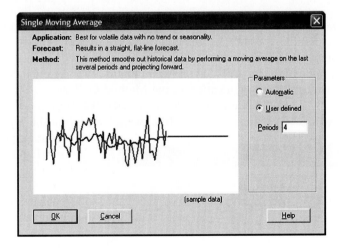

of the moving average, provided in the form of a pivot table. Finally, the Methods Table sheet provides another pivot table, this one summarizing the error criteria, two specialized statistics, and the parameter of the method chosen.

9.6.2 Single Exponential Smoothing

We next illustrate how to add a single exponential smoothing forecast to the moving average forecast we have already created. We run CB Predictor, and when we come to the Method Gallery tab, we check the box for Single Exponential Smoothing as

FIGURE 9.22 CB Predictor: Results Tab

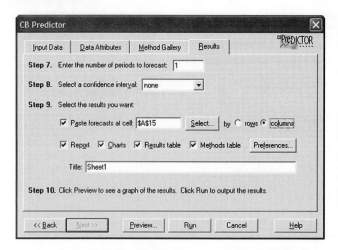

FIGURE 9.23 Single Exponential Smoothing Window in CB Predictor

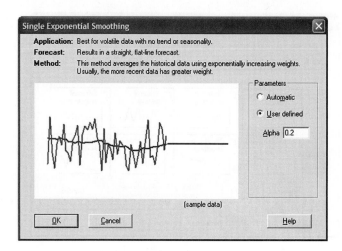

well as the one for Single Moving Average. Then, we double-click on the window containing the check box and proceed to the window for Single Exponential Smoothing. Here, we can select the button for a User defined parameter and enter a value of 0.2 for alpha, as shown in Figure 9.23. Again, a double asterisk appears in the corresponding location in the Method Gallery.

From the Method Gallery, we click the Advanced button, and examine the Advanced Options window. Here, we select MAD in the top portion and Standard Forecasting in the bottom portion, as shown in Figure 9.24. Then we return to the Results tab and click on Preferences.... At this level, we are offered five tabs (Paste, and one for each output report). On each of these last four tabs, we select Current Workbook and Replace Sheet. These selections ensure that CB Predictor will replace the four output worksheets instead of creating four new ones. On the Report tab, a minimal set of check boxes are the following: Summary, Forecast values, Methods (All methods), Errors, and Parms, as shown in Figure 9.25.

Returning to the Results tab, we click on Run to obtain the analysis. In the Report worksheet generated by CB

FIGURE 9.24 Advanced Options Window in CB Predictor

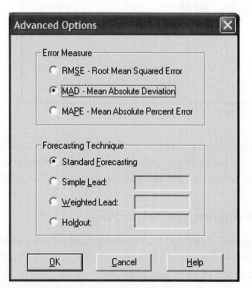

FIGURE 9.25 Preferences Window in CB Predictor

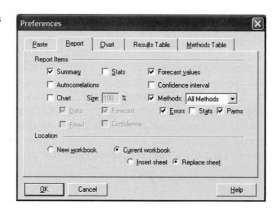

Predictor, we again see the forecast of 84.75, just as we did when we ran the four-period moving average. A further look at the report helps explain why. Figure 9.26 reproduces selected portions of the Report worksheet. In the Method Errors section (rows 23–24 of the figure), the table shows a comparison of the two forecasting methods, with the moving average procedure achieving the smaller value of MAD. Because we chose MAD as the criterion for selection (recall Figure 9.24), this means that the moving average method was ranked as the "Best" of the two methods, and therefore, the forecast for period 11 was taken from the moving average procedure.

FIGURE 9.26 A Portion of the Report from CB Predictor

	A	B	C	D	E	F	G	H	
1	**Summary:**								
2		Number of series: 1							
3		Periods to forecast: 1							
4		Seasonality: none							
5		Error Measure: MAD							
6									
7	**Series: Observed**						Range: B5:B14		
8									
9		Method: Single Moving Average							
10		Parameters: (user defined)							
11			Periods: 4						
12		Error: 17.375							
13									
14		Forecast:							
15									
16			Date	Forecast					
17			11	84.75					
18									
19									
20		Method Errors:							
21									
22			Method			RMSE	MAD	MAPE	
23		Best:	Single Moving Average			20.519	17.375	21.12%	
24		2nd:	Single Exponential Smoothing			20.739	18.247	19.97%	
25									
26									
27		Method Parameters:							
28									
29			Method			Parameter	Value		
30		Best:	Single Moving Average			Periods*	4		
31		2nd:	Single Exponential Smoothing			Alpha*	0.2		
32						*=user defined			
33									

|◄ ◄ ► ►|\ 9.17 ⟋ 9.18 ⟋ 9.19 ⟋ 9.20 ⟋ 9.21 ⟋ 9.22 ⟋ 9.23 ⟋ 9.24 ⟋ 9.25 \ **9.26** ⟋ |< >|

9.7 SUMMARY

Moving averages and exponential smoothing are widely used for routine short-term forecasting. They rely on historical observations of a particular process, and they project the pattern of observations into the future. By making projections from past data, these methods assume that the future will resemble the past. However, the exponential smoothing procedure is sophisticated enough to permit representations of a linear trend and a cyclical factor in its calculations. Thus, if we are sure that historical data exhibits a trend or follows a systematic cycle, we can build those structures into the exponential smoothing calculations.

Exponential smoothing procedures are adaptive. If the underlying process changes, and the size of a trend or the size of a seasonal factor changes, then the calculations will respond to this change and eventually produce accurate forecasts. Even if we fail to notice that a trend exists and rely on the basic exponential smoothing model, it will respond somewhat to the actual pattern in the observations, although its forecasts will exhibit a systematic lag.

Implementing an exponential smoothing procedure requires that initial values be specified and a smoothing factor be chosen. In most cases, when forecasts will be calculated for an extended period, the results eventually become insensitive to the initial values. Therefore, it is often reasonable to use coarse estimates or default values (zero) for initial values. At the same time, the smoothing factor should be chosen to trade off stability and responsiveness in an appropriate manner.

Although specialized software for moving average and exponential smoothing procedures is available, routine forecasting is easy to adapt to the spreadsheet, as a means of tracking and predicting future values of key

parameters. Although Excel contains a Data Analysis tool for calculating moving average forecasts and exponentially smoothed forecasts, the tool does not accommodate the most powerful version of exponential smoothing, which includes trend and cyclical components. Fortunately, the formulas for these calculations are straightforward and lend themselves easily to spreadsheet use. Even without an add-in to perform the work, analysts can adapt exponential smoothing techniques to spreadsheets without extensive preparation.

SUGGESTED READINGS

A comprehensive source on forecasting methods is the textbook by Makridakis, Wheelwright, and Hyndman.

Makridakis, S., S. C. Wheelwright, and R. J., Hyndman. 1998. *Forecasting: Methods and Applications.* New York: John Wiley & Sons.

The following paper reviews progress in research over the first quarter century of time series forecasting developments.

Armstrong, J. S. 1984. "Forecasting by Extrapolation: Conclusions from Twenty-Five Years of Research." *Interfaces* 14, 52–66.

EXERCISES

1. For the moving average example in Figure 9.2, compute the three error measures based on the forecasts for periods 5–10

a. What is the value of MSE?

b. What is the value of MAD?

c. What is the value of MAPE?

2. Consider the stylized example of Figure 9.3, in which there is a jump in the mean value. Using the same worksheet as a template, enter the exponential smoothing calculations for these periods. Assume that $S_1 = 100$.

a. Take $\alpha = 0.2$. Calculate the forecasts generated by exponential smoothing, and compute the values of MSE, MAD, and MAPE for periods 10–15.

b. Repeat the calculations in part (a) but with $\alpha = 0.6$.

c. If we suspect that there might be a jump in the underlying process, which of the two values of α examined in parts (a) and (b) would be preferred?

3. Brad's Burritos provides a simple set of lunch offerings in college town. The shop has recently decided to implement a forecasting system and is testing the use of exponential smoothing methods. The owner is willing to assume that by now, the number of customers who come to the shop at lunchtime (noon to 2 P.M.) does not exhibit trends or cyclic effects on weekdays. Data collection has gone on for two weeks (10 weekdays), counting the number of lunchtime customers. The observations are shown in the table.

Day	M	T	W	T	F	M	T	W	T	F
Customers	108	130	96	144	136	113	120	119	120	106

a. Compute a forecast for the number of lunchtime customers on the next weekday by using a 3-day moving average. What is the forecast? What is the MAD for the last five observations?

b. Compute a forecast for the number of lunchtime customers on the next weekday by using exponential smoothing with $\alpha = 0.3$. What is the forecast? What is the MAD for the last five observations?

4. Garish Motors sells new and used automobiles. Sales of new cars over the past 50 weeks are given in the following table (week 50 is the most recent).

Week	Sales	Week	Sales
1	36	26	48
2	42	27	40
3	50	28	55
4	59	29	49
5	72	30	58
6	54	31	52
7	49	32	57
8	37	33	51
9	59	34	54
10	41	35	53
11	53	36	47
12	42	37	44
13	52	38	47
14	55	39	37
15	45	40	51
16	69	41	58
17	64	42	58
18	44	43	39
19	64	44	42

20	59	45	33
21	55	46	50
22	30	47	68
23	60	48	53
24	53	49	44
25	47	50	43

a. Compute a forecast for sales next week by using a 4-week moving average. What is the forecast? What is the MSE for the last five observations?

b. Can you reduce the MSE for the last five observations by changing the moving average window (try 5- to 10-week windows).

c. Compute a forecast for sales next week by using exponential smoothing with $\alpha = 0.25$. What is the forecast? What is the MSE for the last five observations?

d. Can you improve the MSE for the last five observations by changing the smoothing constant α?

5. Data covering the most recent 30 days are given in the following table for the price per gallon of regular gasoline at a local station.

Day	Price	Day	Price
1	2.53	16	2.46
2	2.35	17	2.60
3	1.91	18	2.10
4	2.20	19	2.01
5	1.77	20	2.14
6	3.26	21	2.03
7	1.63	22	2.68
8	2.73	23	2.59
9	2.41	24	2.99
10	2.72	25	2.94
11	2.87	26	1.77
12	1.49	27	2.62
13	2.92	28	3.19
14	3.53	29	3.01
15	2.74	30	2.10

a. Compute a forecast for the next day's price by using a 3-day moving average. What is the forecast? What is the MSE for the last five observations?

b. Can you reduce the MSE for the last five observations by changing the moving average window (try 4- to 10-day windows)?

c. Compute a forecast for the next day's price by using exponential smoothing with $\alpha = 0.25$. What is the forecast? What is the MSE for the last five observations?

d. Can you improve the MSE for the last five observations by changing the smoothing constant α?

6. Contributions to the disaster relief fund for a national charity average around $1 million a month and do not exhibit trend or seasonal effects. Data on the most recent 12 months is given in the following table.

Month	Contributions
1	1,074,844
2	780,433
3	1,082,218
4	1,009,653
5	1,066,739
6	1,297,010
7	978,685
8	1,108,218
9	1,019,778
10	999,380
11	1,041,070
12	821,189

a. Compute a forecast for next month's contributions by using a 4-month moving average. What is the forecast? What is the MSE for the last five observations?

b. Can you reduce the MSE for the last five observations by changing the moving average window (try 5- to 7-week windows)?

c. Compute a forecast for next month's contributions by using exponential smoothing with $\alpha = 0.25$. What is the forecast? What is the MSE for the last five observations?

d. Can you reduce the MSE for the last five observations by changing the smoothing constant α?

7. Consider the example of Figure 9.7, in which the smoothing constant was taken to be $\alpha = 0.2$. Repeat the calculations for smoothing constants between 0.1 and 0.9, in steps of 0.1.

a. Identify the α–value that achieves the smallest value of MSE.

b. Identify the α–value that achieves the smallest value of MAD.

8. Consider the example of the new product at Curtis Distributors, which was analyzed in Figure 9.13, in which the smoothing constant was taken to be $\alpha = 0.2$. Repeat the calculations for smoothing constants between 0.1 and 0.9, in steps of 0.1.

a. Identify the α–value that achieves the smallest value of MSE.

b. Identify the α–value that achieves the smallest value of MAD.

9. Consider the example of the new product at Curtis Distributors, which was analyzed using Holt's method in Figure 9.14. Repeat the forecasts using one smaller value of α than the value of 0.2 used in the figure, and also one larger value. Then do the same, using one smaller value of β than the value of 0.5 used in the figure, and also one larger value. (This means nine pairs of values in all, one of which is illustrated in the figure).

a. Which pair (α, β) achieves the smallest value of MSE?

b. Which pair (α, β) achieves the smallest value of MAD?

10. Consider the stylized example in Figure 9.15. Repeat the forecasts using the additive model with trend, using the same smoothing constants.

a. What is the value of MSE corresponding to the multiplicative model in Figure 9.15?

b. What is the value of MSE corresponding to the additive model with the same smoothing constants?

11. Consider the example of the new product at Curtis Distributors, which was analyzed using a multiplicative model in Figure 9.16. Repeat the forecasts using the additive model, with the same smoothing constants.

a. What is the value of MSE corresponding to the multiplicative model in Figure 9.16?

b. What is the value of MSE corresponding to the additive model with the same smoothing constants?

12. The operations manager at a manufacturing facility is about to begin an energy-efficiency initiative. As this program begins, it will be helpful to have benchmark data on energy use, in order to determine whether the initiative is having an effect. The facilities department has provided data on the monthly energy use (in kilowatt hours) over the past three years, as shown in the following table:

Year 1	Usage	Year 2	Usage	Year 3	Usage
Jan	31,040	Jan	24,540	Jan	32,410
Feb	28,720	Feb	26,560	Feb	21,380
Mar	20,540	Mar	22,060	Mar	20,370
Apr	22,260	Apr	16,220	Apr	18,300
May	11,550	May	12,920	May	10,020
Jun	13,100	Jun	9,740	Jun	11,420
Jul	14,790	Jul	10,160	Jul	10,020
Aug	12,360	Aug	12,740	Aug	11,800
Sep	12,890	Sep	9,240	Sep	13,120
Oct	9,790	Oct	11,220	Oct	10,410
Nov	14,840	Nov	13,780	Nov	13,510
Dec	14,610	Dec	19,040	Dec	17,340

a. Use the Holt-Winters method to estimate the monthly usage for the coming 12 months. Use smoothing parameters of $\alpha = 0.3$, $\beta = 0.4$, and $\gamma = 0.5$.

b. For the forecasting problem in (a), which value of α achieves the minimum value of MSE, holding the other smoothing parameters constant?

13. The town of Hillside has a surface reservoir that supplies water to the homes in the town's central residential district. A committee of residents is concerned about the system's capacity and wants to project future use. The town's water department has promised to develop its best forecast of water use in the next two years. The department has collected quarterly data on water use (in millions of gallons) over the past decade, as shown in the following table:

Year	Q1	Q2	Q3	Q4
1	55	34	39	65
2	59	54	46	46
3	41	38	33	65
4	37	36	35	51
5	34	21	23	60
6	39	27	23	47
7	42	25	21	55
8	23	22	25	40
9	28	26	21	53
10	30	25	21	54

a. Use the Holt-Winters method to estimate the quarterly water use for the coming eight quarters. Use smoothing parameters of $\alpha = 0.3$, $\beta = 0.4$, and $\gamma = 0.5$

b. For the forecasting problem in (a), which value of α achieves the minimum value of MSE, holding the other smoothing parameters constant?

14. Big Box, the local discount retailer, is negotiating a major expansion with the Planning Board. It has been asked as part of this process to develop a sales forecast for the next several years. Quarterly sales data for the past 10 years are given in the following table:

Year	Q1	Q2	Q3	Q4
1	94.28	83.80	115.23	125.71
2	97.89	87.02	119.65	130.52
3	104.45	92.84	127.66	139.26
4	111.11	98.77	135.81	148.15
5	115.56	102.72	141.24	154.08
6	121.47	107.97	148.47	161.96
7	127.90	113.69	156.33	170.54
8	134.20	119.29	164.02	178.93
9	141.00	125.33	172.33	188.00
10	148.94	132.39	182.04	198.59

a. Develop an appropriate forecast using a moving average approach.

b. Develop an appropriate forecast using a simple exponential smoothing approach.

c. Develop an appropriate forecast using an exponential smoothing with a trend (Holt's method).

d. Develop an appropriate forecast using an exponential smoothing with trend and cyclicality (the Holt-Winters method).

e. Which of the four forecasts developed above would you recommend using?

15. Coastal Fuel Oil is a distributor of fuel oil products in the Northeast. It contracts with shippers for deliveries of home heating oil and distributes product in its own trucks.

Since its storage capacity is limited, and purchasing storage for fuel oil it cannot store itself is expensive, accurate demand forecasts are valuable. Monthly data covering the past 10 years are given in the following table:

a. Develop an appropriate forecast using a moving average approach.

b. Develop an appropriate forecast using a simple exponential smoothing approach.

c. Develop an appropriate forecast using exponential smoothing with trend (Holt's method).

d. Develop an appropriate forecast using exponential smoothing with trend and cyclicality (Holt-Winters method).

e. Which of the four forecasts developed above would you recommend using?

Year	Jan	Feb	Mar	Apr	May	Jun	Jul	Aug	Sep	Oct	Nov	Dec
1	194.92	222.77	250.62	278.46	306.31	334.15	222.77	250.62	278.46	306.31	334.15	362.00
2	203.71	232.81	261.92	291.02	320.12	349.22	232.81	261.92	291.02	320.12	349.22	378.32
3	209.84	239.81	269.79	299.77	329.74	359.72	239.81	269.79	299.77	329.74	359.72	389.70
4	213.67	244.19	274.71	305.24	335.76	366.28	244.19	274.71	305.24	335.76	366.28	396.81
5	219.20	250.52	281.83	313.15	344.46	375.77	250.52	281.83	313.15	344.46	375.77	407.09
6	230.43	263.34	296.26	329.18	362.10	395.02	263.34	296.26	329.18	362.10	395.02	427.93
7	237.36	271.27	305.17	339.08	372.99	406.90	271.27	305.17	339.08	372.99	406.90	440.81
8	241.77	276.31	310.85	345.39	379.93	414.47	276.31	310.85	345.39	379.93	414.47	449.01
9	252.63	288.72	324.81	360.90	396.99	433.08	288.72	324.81	360.90	396.99	433.08	469.17
10	260.01	297.16	334.30	371.45	408.59	445.73	297.16	334.30	371.45	408.59	445.73	482.88

10 Nonlinear Optimization

10.1 INTRODUCTION

Optimization is the process of finding the best set of decisions for a particular measure of performance. For example, in the Advertising Budget example of Chapter 5, we measure performance in terms of annual profit, and optimization allows us to set advertising expenditures in the four quarters so that we achieve the *maximum* annual profit.

In Chapter 6, we introduced a framework for spreadsheet analysis in which optimization represents one of the higher order levels of analysis, generally coming after a base case has been established, some what-if questions have been explored, and perhaps some back-solving calculations have been made. In this chapter, we'll assume that the steps in that framework have already been carried out. However, the entire framework does not necessarily apply to every spreadsheet model. There are spreadsheets that do not lend themselves to optimization. In some models, for example, the purpose is to explore past relationships or to forecast future outcomes. But managers and analysts generally use models in order to *improve* future operations. We refer to the levers they use to bring about improved performance as **decision variables**. If there are decision variables in a model, it is natural to ask, what are the *best* values of those variables? The measure of performance that defines our notion of "best" is called the **objective function**, or simply the **objective**. Once we have specified the objective in a model, it is also natural to ask what is the best value of that objective? This chapter explores in some detail how to answer these questions by building and analyzing optimization models.

Optimization refers both to the goal of finding the best values of the decision variables and to a set of procedures that accomplish that goal. These procedures are known as **algorithms** and are usually implemented by software. In the case of Excel, the optimization software is known as **Solver**. A version of Solver (referred to as the Standard Solver) is built into every copy of Excel. In this book, we use **Premium Solver for Education**, which is a more advanced version than the Standard Solver in Excel. Premium Solver for Education is available to users of this book and should be installed before proceeding with this chapter. It is this version that we refer to as Solver.

These days, the word "solver" is often a generic reference to optimization software, whether or not it is implemented in a spreadsheet. However, optimization tools have been available on computers for several decades, predating the widespread use of spreadsheets and even personal computers. Before spreadsheets, optimization was available through stand-alone software but was often accessible only by technical experts. Managers and business analysts had to rely on those experts to build and interpret optimization models. Building such models typically meant constructing algebraic statements to define the problem mathematically. Now, however, the spreadsheet permits end users to develop their own models without having to rely on algebra. Moreover, the same end users can then call on Solver themselves to find optimal solutions for the models they build.

Finding the optimal values of decision variables in a spreadsheet model can sometimes present a challenge. Although Solver is a very powerful and highly sophisticated piece of software, it is still possible to formulate otherwise acceptable spreadsheet models for which Solver cannot find the optimal solution. To use Solver effectively, end users should understand how to formulate spreadsheet models that exploit the power of Solver while avoiding its pitfalls. This chapter and the three that follow are designed to provide that understanding.

One way to avoid some of the pitfalls is to follow the principles of spreadsheet design covered in Chapter 5. For instance, it remains desirable to modularize the spreadsheet, to isolate parameters, and to separate decision variables from calculations and intermediate calculations from final results. In the chapters on optimization, we also advocate some additional guidelines for optimization models. These guidelines help us to debug our own models, and when we're finished debugging and testing, the guidelines help us communicate our results to others. Solver actually permits users considerable flexibility in designing models, but if we were to use all of that flexibility, we might confuse the people we want to communicate with, as well as ourselves. For that reason, it is good practice to impose some discipline on the building of optimization models.

Optimization problems are categorized according to the algorithm used to solve them. In the optimization chapters, we discuss the three main categories: nonlinear, linear, and integer optimization problems. In each case, we provide several examples, give advice on how to formulate models appropriately, show how to find solutions, and illustrate how to interpret the results.

In this chapter, we concentrate on the nonlinear solver, which is the default option when we invoke Solver. We begin by demonstrating the optimization approach in the Advertising Budget example. We next provide general principles for building models for Solver. Then, we elaborate on the use of the nonlinear solver and provide additional examples.

10.2   AN OPTIMIZATION EXAMPLE

Recall that in the Advertising Budget example of Chapters 5 and 6, the goal is to plan the spending of advertising dollars over the coming year. Planning is done on a quarterly basis, so we must choose advertising expenditures for each of the four quarters. Whatever plan we devise, we will evaluate it in terms of annual profits. Also, we have an annual advertising budget of $40,000 that we should not exceed. Figure 10.1[*] reproduces the spreadsheet model that we initially developed in Chapter 5.

10.2.1   Optimizing Q1

We first consider a limited optimization question: What is the best choice of advertising expenditures in the first quarter (Q1)? For the moment, we ignore the existence of the budget, and we assume that the expenditures in the three other quarters remain at $10,000. We could approach this problem by using the Data Sensitivity tool. In Figure 10.2, we show a table of Q1 expenditures and the corresponding annual profits, along with a graph of the relationship. The graph reveals that expenditures beyond the base-case level of $10,000 can increase annual profits; but eventually, such expenditures become counterproductive, and annual profits drop. The graph and the table both show that the maximum profit level is achieved for expenditures of about $17,000. With two or three systematic refinements of this table, we could easily determine the optimal expenditures to a higher level of precision. However, we would not be able to extend the sensitivity table to more than two variables, which is our goal given that we have four decision variables.

To illustrate the optimization approach to this problem, we invoke Solver by selecting Add-ins▶Menu Commands▶Premium Solver (assuming the software has already been installed.) The Solver Parameters window (shown in Figure 10.3) contains four key inputs to describe the model:

---

[*]To download spreadsheets for this chapter, go to the Student Companion Site at www.wiley.com/college/powell.

FIGURE 10.1 Base-Case Model for the Advertising Budget Example

	A	B	C	D	E	F	G	H	I	J
1	Advertising Budget Model									
2	SGP/KRB									
3	1/1/2006									
4										
5	PARAMETERS									
6				Q1	Q2	Q3	Q4			Notes
7		Price	$40.00							Current price
8		Cost	$25.00							Accounting
9		Seasonal		0.9	1.1	0.8	1.2			Data analysis
10		OHD rate	0.15							Accounting
11		Sales Parameters								
12			35							Consultants
13			3000							
14		Sales Expense		8000	8000	9000	9000			Consultants
15		Ad Budget	$40,000							Current budget
16										
17	DECISIONS							Total		
18		Ad Expenditures		$10,000	$10,000	$10,000	$10,000	$40,000		sum
19										
20	OUTPUTS									
21		Profit	$69,662		Base case	$69,662				
22										
23	CALCULATIONS									
24		Quarter		Q1	Q2	Q3	Q4	Total		
25		Seasonal		0.9	1.1	0.8	1.2			
26										
27		Units Sold		3592	4390	3192	4789	15962		given formula
28		Revenue		143662	175587	127700	191549	638498		price*units
29		Cost of Goods		89789	109742	79812	119718	399061		cost*units
30		Gross Margin		53873	65845	47887	71831	239437		subtraction
31										
32		Sales Expense		8000	8000	9000	9000	34000		given
33		Advertising		10000	10000	10000	10000	40000		decisions
34		Overhead		21549	26338	19155	28732	95775		rate*revenue
35		Total Fixed Cost		39549	44338	38155	47732	169775		sum
36										
37		Profit		14324	21507	9732	24099	69662		GM -TFC
38		Profit Margin		9.97%	12.25%	7.62%	12.58%	10.91%		pct of revenue
39										

- A **target cell** (sometimes called the **set cell**)
- A choice to **maximize** or **minimize**
- A set of **changing cells**
- A set of **constraints**

The Solver window requires that the target cell be maximized by altering the changing cells, subject to constraints. In our problem, there are no constraints; we are simply interested in maximizing profit (our target cell) by altering Q1 expenditures (our single changing cell). In the Solver Parameters window, we enter the references to the target cell (C21) and the changing cell (D18). Then, we select the Standard GRG Nonlinear algorithm from the pull-down menu, as shown in Figure 10.4.

When we click on the Solve button, Solver searches for the optimal expenditure level and places it in the changing cell. If no technical problems are encountered, Solver displays a window stating, Solver found a solution. All constraints and optimality conditions are satisfied, as shown in

FIGURE 10.2 Data Sensitivity Results for Varying Q1 Expenditures

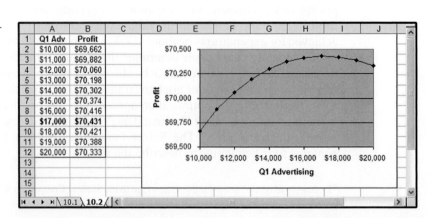

	A	B
1	Q1 Adv	Profit
2	$10,000	$69,662
3	$11,000	$69,882
4	$12,000	$70,060
5	$13,000	$70,198
6	$14,000	$70,302
7	$15,000	$70,374
8	$16,000	$70,416
9	**$17,000**	**$70,431**
10	$18,000	$70,421
11	$19,000	$70,388
12	$20,000	$70,333

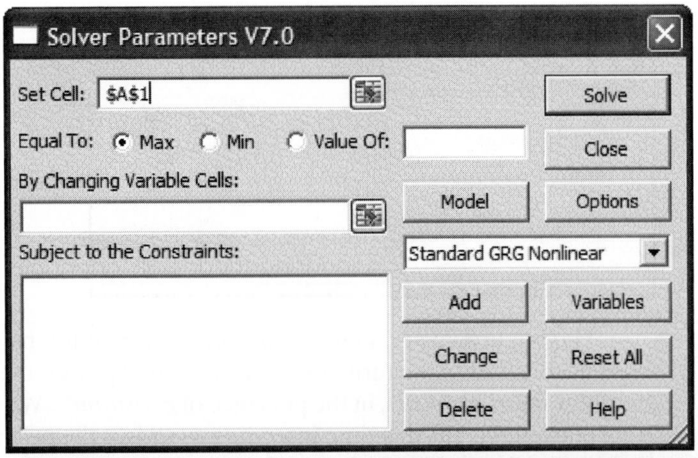

FIGURE 10.3 Solver Parameters Window for the Premium Solver for Education

FIGURE 10.4 Selecting the Nonlinear Solver

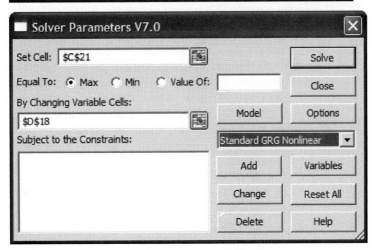

Figure 10.5. We refer to this as the *optimality message*, and we can simply choose OK in the corresponding window. In this case, the optimal expenditure in Q1 is $17,093, and the corresponding revenue is $70,431. This is essentially the same result we found using the Data Sensitivity tool in Figure 10.2, but with somewhat more precision.

10.2.2 Optimization Over All Four Quarters

If we optimized the advertising expenditures in each of the other quarters individually, as we did with Q1, we would find a different optimal level of expenditures for each quarter. The following table summarizes the results of those four one-at-a-time optimization runs.

	Quarter			
	1	**2**	**3**	**4**
Expenditures	17,093	27,016	12,876	32,721
Profits	70,431	73,171	69,806	75,284

We get the same results if we optimize all four quarters simultaneously, by entering the range of their cell addresses (D18:G18) as changing cells. Unfortunately, this result is infeasible because it calls for total expenditures of more than $40,000 ($89,706, in fact). Although this solution is infeasible, it is useful to explore our model in this way. For one thing, this solution immediately suggests that we may want to lobby for a larger budget. It also reveals interesting structure in the solution in that the expenditure profile reflects the seasonal factors, with the highest and lowest values coming in the last two quarters.

FIGURE 10.5 Solver's Optimality Message

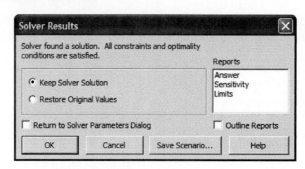

Having provided a glimpse of Solver's capability by optimizing our decisions without constraints, we turn next to Solver's real power, the optimization of decision variables *simultaneously*, in the presence of *constraints*. We return to the Advertising Budget example but this time intending to satisfy the original $40,000 budget. How should we allocate this budget across the four quarters?

10.2.3 Incorporating the Budget Constraint

To investigate this question, we return to the base-case model and invoke Solver. The Solver Parameters window offers the three key inputs: a target cell, a set of changing cells, and a set of constraints. Again, the Solver window requires that we set the target cell equal to a maximum by altering designated changing cells subject to specified constraints. We proceed with the following steps.

- Verify that the target cell is specified as C21.
- For the Changing Cells, enter D18:G18.
- Click on the Add button, which brings up the Add Constraint window.
- Enter the constraint H18 ≤ C15, as shown in Figure 10.6.
- Click OK, and return to the Solver Parameters window.
- Select the Standard GRG Nonlinear algorithm from the pull-down menu.

In filling out the Add Constraint window, we follow one of our design guidelines for Solver models by referencing a *formula* in the left-hand window and referencing a *number* in the right-hand window when specifying constraints. In this case, cell H18 contains a formula, and cell C15 contains a number. By relying on cell references rather than entering numbers directly, we ensure that the key parameters are visible on the worksheet itself, rather than in the less accessible windows of the Solver interface.

At this point, the model has been specified well enough to solve, but it is always a good habit to examine the options before proceeding. Clicking on the Options button in the Solver Parameters window displays the options menu shown in Figure 10.7. The main options correspond to check boxes on the General tab. In this example, the decision variables must be nonnegative, so we check the `Assume Non-Negative` box. We leave the box to `Bypass Solver Reports` unchecked, although we usually skip the reports. The option to `Show Iteration Results` might occasionally be used to help in debugging, but it is normally unchecked. We leave the option to `Use Automatic Scaling` unchecked as well, although there are some exceptions, as we discuss later.

Although the optimization of a model such as the Advertising Budget model can be done quickly and smoothly, we don't advocate running Solver without forethought. We recommend pausing before running Solver, in order to think about what the outcomes might be. In the case at hand,

FIGURE 10.6 Entering Constraint Information in the Add Constraint Window

FIGURE 10.7   The Solver
Options Window

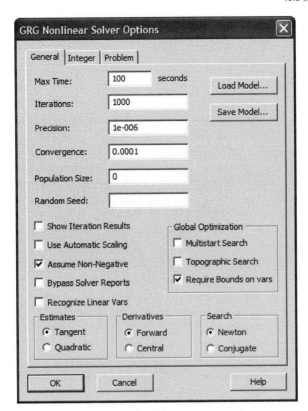

- Should we expect the budget to be allocated equally across the quarters?
- If so, why should this occur?
- If not, should we expect one of the allocations to be zero?

These kinds of questions are informal hypotheses that can be very valuable to an analyst. They provide an opportunity for us to test our intuition with respect to the model. Only two things can happen, and they are both good. Either our intuition will be confirmed, in which case our confidence in the model will increase; or else our intuition will be contradicted, in which case we can learn something unexpected about the situation that might improve our understanding.

In this example, we have already explored the differences among the quarters, so we should expect the allocations to be unequal across quarters, reflecting differences in the seasonal factors. Our limited examination of the relationship between Q1 expenditures and profit (Figure 10.2) revealed decreasing marginal returns, suggesting that nonzero expenditures could be productive in any quarter.

By entering the addresses of the target cell and the changing cells and by specifying a constraint, we have prepared the model for optimization. When we click the `Solve` button, Solver searches for the optimal expenditures and displays the results in the worksheet. The Solver Results window allows us to either keep the optimal solution and write over the original contents, or restore the values that were in the worksheet before Solver ran. In this case, we keep the solution and note that the optimal profit is $71,447, as shown in Figure 10.8. As we can see in the figure, the optimal allocation contains different expenditures in each quarter, and in every quarter the expenditure exceeds $5,000. The highest expenditures occur in Q4 and Q2, as we might have predicted, given their high seasonal factors. Finally, we note that the entire $40,000 advertising budget is used.

10.3   BUILDING MODELS FOR SOLVER

As we mentioned earlier, most of our general guidelines about effective spreadsheet design apply to the specific case of building models for use with Solver. In addition,

FIGURE 10.8 The Optimal Allocation in the Advertising Budget Model

	A	B	C	D	E	F	G	H	I	J
1	Advertising Budget Model									
2	SGP/KRB									
3	1/1/2006									
4										
5	PARAMETERS									
6				Q1	Q2	Q3	Q4			Notes
7		Price	$40.00							Current price
8		Cost	$25.00							Accounting
9		Seasonal		0.9	1.1	0.8	1.2			Data analysis
10		OHD rate	0.15							Accounting
11		Sales Parameters								
12			35							Consultants
13			3000							
14		Sales Expense		8000	8000	9000	9000			Consultants
15		Ad Budget	$40,000							Current budget
16										
17	DECISIONS							Total		
18		Ad Expenditures		$7,273	$12,347	$5,117	$15,263	$40,000		sum
19										
20	OUTPUTS									
21		Profit	$71,447		Base case	$69,662				
22										
23	CALCULATIONS									
24		Quarter		Q1	Q2	Q3	Q4	Total		
25		Seasonal		0.9	1.1	0.8	1.2			
26										
27		Units Sold		3193	4769	2523	5676	16161		given formula
28		Revenue		127709	190777	100905	227038	646430		price*units
29		Cost of Goods		79818	119236	63066	141899	404019		cost*units
30		Gross Margin		47891	71542	37840	85139	242411		subtraction
31										
32		Sales Expense		8000	8000	9000	9000	34000		given
33		Advertising		7273	12347	5117	15263	40000		decisions
34		Overhead		19156	28617	15136	34056	96965		rate*revenue
35		Total Fixed Cost		34430	48963	29253	58319	170965		sum
36										
37		Profit		13461	22578	8587	26820	71447		GM -TFC
38		Profit Margin		10.54%	11.83%	8.51%	11.81%	11.05%		pct of revenue
39										

Solver requires specific information about our optimization problem, so we must be able to identify a target cell, a set of changing cells, and the constraints (if any). The process of identifying these elements is called **formulating** an optimization problem.

10.3.1 Formulation

Every optimization model is made up of **decision variables**, an **objective function**, and a set of **constraints**. Before setting up a worksheet for optimization, it is a good idea to identify these elements, at least in words if not in symbols. To get started, we can ask three key questions.

- What must be decided?
- What measure should we use to compare alternative sets of decisions?
- What restrictions limit our choice?

To guide us toward decision variables, we ask ourselves, "What must be decided?" Decision variables must be under the control of the decision maker. (Quantitative inputs that are *not* under the decision maker's control are treated as parameters.) From the start, we should be explicit about the units in which we measure each decision variable. Common examples of decision variables would include quantities to buy, quantities to deploy, quantities to produce, and quantities to deliver (or combinations of the above list). Whatever the decision variables are, once we know their numerical values, we should have a resolution of the problem. In Solver models, the changing cells contain the values of decision variables.

In the Advertising Budget model of Figure 10.1, the decision variables are the advertising expenditures in each of the four quarters. Once we know their values, we have a resolution of the budget allocation problem. The specific values appear in the range D18:G18.

To guide us toward an objective function, we ask ourselves, "What measure should we use to compare alternative sets of decisions?" Imagine that two consultants have come to us with their recommendations on what action to take (i.e., what decision variables to use), and we must choose which action we prefer. For this purpose, we need a yardstick—a single performance measure that tells us which action is better. That quantity is affected by the choice of decision variables, and it will normally be obvious whether we wish to maximize or minimize. Maximization criteria usually focus on such measures as profit, revenue, return, or efficiency. Minimization criteria usually focus on cost, time, distance, size, or investment. In Solver models, the target cell contains a reference to the objective function.

In many optimization models, the formula for the objective function directly references decision-variable cells. In complicated cases, there may be intermediate calculations, and the logical relation between objective function and decision variables may be indirect. In such cases, we might want to use the Trace Dependents command (Formulas▶Formula Auditing) to confirm that each decision variable is linked to the objective function. Similarly, we can use the Trace Precedents option to confirm that the objective function is ultimately linked to each decision variable.

To guide us toward constraints, we ask ourselves, "What restrictions limit our choice of decision variables?" Seldom are we free to choose any set of decisions we like; instead, we may have to respect certain limitations that are intrinsic to the decision problem. For example, we may look for capacities that provide upper limits on certain activities or commitments that place thresholds on other activities. Sometimes, we may specify equations to ensure consistency among a set of variables.

A constraint consists of a comparison between one measured quantity and a parameter of the problem. The measured quantity depends on the decision variables, and the role of the constraint is to make sure that the decision variables, alone or in combination, meet the requirements of the problem. By convention, each constraint involves a relationship between a measured quantity on the left-hand side (or LHS) and a parameter of the problem on the right-hand side (or RHS). We refer to the parameter as the **constraint constant**, the **RHS constant**, or simply the RHS. Constraints appear in three varieties in optimization models:

$$\text{LHS} \leq \text{RHS} \quad \text{(less-than constraint)}$$

$$\text{LHS} \geq \text{RHS} \quad \text{(greater-than constraint)}$$

$$\text{LHS} = \text{RHS} \quad \text{(equality constraint)}$$

We use less-than constraints to represent capacities or ceilings or in places where we find it necessary to say "at most" or "no more than" a certain quantity. For example, we might require that the labor hours scheduled must be no more than the labor hours available. In that case, the number of hours scheduled would make up the LHS, and the number of hours available would be the RHS of a less-than constraint.

We use greater-than constraints to represent commitments or thresholds or in places where we find it necessary to say "at least" or "no less than" a certain quantity. For example, we might require that components purchased must be at least as large as the obligation in the purchasing contract. In that case, components purchased would make up the LHS, and the contractual commitment would be the RHS of a greater-than constraint.

Finally, we use equality constraints to represent material balance or simply to define related variables consistently. For example, we might include a material-balance constraint that end-of-month inventory must equal start-of-month inventory plus production minus demand. In symbols, this relationship translates into the following algebraic expression:

Ending Inventory = Starting Inventory + Production − Demand

In such a case, the demand level usually plays the role of a given parameter, and the other quantities are usually related to decision variables. To be consistent with the convention of placing parameters on the right-hand side, we can rewrite the expression as

$$Starting\ Inventory + Production - Ending\ Inventory = Demand$$

Like the objective function, the LHS is a formula that references the decision variables directly, or else we can use the Trace Precedents command to trace the linkage back to the decision variables through one or more intermediate quantities. We reference the LHS formula on the left-hand side of the Add Constraint window, while we reference the RHS constant on the right-hand side of the window.

In the Advertising Budget model, there is only one constraint: The total advertising expenditure over the year must be at most $40,000. The left-hand side of this less-than constraint amounts to the sum of the quarterly expenditures and appears in cell H18. With the Trace Precedents command, we can quickly see how this quantity is linked directly to the decision variables.

10.3.2 Layout

We prefer a disciplined approach to building optimization models, and we advocate conformance to a relatively standardized model template. Standardization helps us in several ways. First, it enhances our ability to communicate with others. A standardized structure provides a common language for describing optimization problems and reinforces our understanding about how these models are shaped. This is especially true when spreadsheet models are being shown to someone knowledgeable about optimization. Second, it improves our ability to diagnose errors while we are building the model. A standardized structure has certain recognizable features that make it easier to spot modeling errors or simple typographical errors than in an unstructured approach. Third, it permits us to "scale up" the model more easily. That is, we may later want to expand a model by adding variables or constraints, allowing us to move from a prototype to a practical size, or from a "toy" version to an "industrial strength" version.

Here are the main elements of our structured approach:

- Organize the worksheet into modules. We suggest separate portions of the worksheet for decision variables, objective function, and constraints; but sometimes other forms of organization are more appropriate. For data-intensive models, it is also a good idea to devote a separate module to the input data.

- Place all decision variables in a single row (or column) of the worksheet if possible. (It is sometimes advantageous to use a rectangular range for decision variables.)

- Use color highlighting or borders for the decision variable cells.

- Place the objective function in a single cell, also highlighted.

- Arrange constraints to facilitate visual comparison of left-hand and right-hand sides. For the most part, "left" and "right" can be respected in the layout, although other formats occasionally make more sense. Sometimes, it is also helpful to calculate the difference between the left- and right-hand sides for each constraint, or at least to indicate whether the constraint has been met exactly.

On occasion, there are reasonable exceptions to these guidelines. However, the standard features provide a useful starting point for the several reasons we have enumerated.

SOLVER TIP
Ranges for Decision Variables

In the Solver Parameters window, we could reference the changing cells one at a time, separating the references by commas. We prefer, however, to arrange the worksheet so that all the decision variables are in adjacent cells, since this allows us to make a single reference to their range. Because most optimization problems have several decision variables, it saves time if we place all of them in adjacent cells. This design also makes the Solver Parameters window easier to interpret if someone else is trying to follow our work, or if we are reviewing it after not having seen it for a long time. ∎

10.3.3 Interpreting Results

Just as there are three modules in our worksheet, there are three kinds of information to examine in the optimization results. First, there are the optimal values of the decision variables. They tell us the best course of action. Second, there is the optimal value of the objective function, which tells us the best level of performance we can achieve. Third, there are the constraint outcomes. In particular, a constraint in which the left-hand side equals the right-hand side is called a tight, or **binding**, constraint. Prior to solving the model, *every* constraint is a potential limitation on the set of decisions, but optimization generally leads to an outcome where only *some* of the constraints are actually binding. These are the true economic limitations in the model: they are the constraints that actually prevent us from achieving even better levels of performance.

We can think of the solution to an optimization problem as providing what we might call **tactical** information and **strategic** information. By tactical information, we mean that the optimal solution prescribes the best possible set of decisions under the conditions given. Thus, if the model represents an actual situation, its optimal decisions represent a plan to be implemented. By strategic information, we mean that the optimal solution tells us what factors could lead us to even better levels of performance. If we are not faced with the need to implement a course of action immediately, we can think about altering one of the problem's parameters in a way that could improve the situation. Thus, if the model represents a situation with given parametric conditions, we can examine the possibility of changing the "givens" in order to raise the level of performance.

10.4   MODEL CLASSIFICATION AND THE NONLINEAR SOLVER

Optimization models come in only a few basic types or categories. It is important to recognize the category into which a model falls, because the algorithm used to optimize the model should match its type. The fundamental distinction among models arises from linearity.

Every relationship in a model is either **linear** or **nonlinear**. In a linear relationship, each variable is multiplied by a constant, such as the straight line

$$y = ax + b$$

where x and y represent variables, or the plane

$$z = ax + by$$

where x, y, and z represent variables.

Any relationship that is *not* of this form is nonlinear; for example, the power function

$$y = ax^b$$

when $b \neq 1$, or the product function

$$z = axy$$

where x, y, and z represent variables.

Optimization problems are classified as linear if the objective function and all the constraints are linear functions of the decision variables. If any one of these components is not linear, the problem is classified as a nonlinear optimization problem. We also refer to linear optimization as **linear programming** and to nonlinear optimization as **nonlinear programming**. As the default choice, the Solver Parameters window always shows the selection of the nonlinear solver (Standard GRG Nonlinear) when we first enter information describing our model. The nonlinear solver can be used for both linear or nonlinear problems, although it is not always the best algorithm to use for linear problems. The main alternative is the linear solver

(Standard LP Simplex), which is specialized for linear cases. We examine linear models in the next chapter.

The algorithm used by Solver for nonlinear optimization is called the **GRG algorithm** (short for Generalized Reduced Gradient), which is often likened to hill climbing in the fog. Because of the fog, we can't tell where the peak is located relative to our starting point, so we can use only the conditions close around us to choose a search direction. One practical approach, or heuristic, would be to follow the steepest path we can see. After we proceed a short distance in that direction, we look again for the steepest path available from our new location and proceed in that direction. Again, after a short distance, we reach the limit of what we were able to see in the fog, and we reassess which direction is the steepest, modifying our path as we go. Eventually, we come to a point from which no path leads up. As far as we can tell, this must be the peak, so we stop.

The GRG algorithm uses a very similar procedure to locate a maximum for an objective function. It starts at the point represented by the values of the decision variables in the changing cells, tests different directions in which it could modify those variables, and selects the direction that goes up most steeply—that is, in which the objective function increases the fastest. After moving in that direction, the procedure tests different directions from its new location and again selects the steepest path. Eventually, the procedure comes to a point where no step in any direction goes up. At that point, the procedure stops. (In a minimization problem, we could think of the procedure as descending into a crater, looking for the lowest point.)

The GRG algorithm has some additional intelligence built into its procedure. For example, it is capable of adjusting the size of its steps—taking large steps while steep paths are available, but then taking smaller steps as the path levels out. The algorithm can also cope with constraints. However, hill climbing in the fog has one serious limitation. When we stop the search, fog obscures our long-range view, so we can't see whether another location some distance away is higher than where we stopped. In other words, the fog may prevent us from seeing a higher peak than the one we found. In an analogous fashion, the GRG algorithm may stop at a solution that we call a **local optimum**. This point is better than any other point close by, but there could well be an even better solution some distance away, unseen by the search procedure. Although we wish to find the highest peak, or **global optimum**, the GRG procedure will not guarantee that we always find it with one run, except in special circumstances.

A graphical interpretation should underscore this point. Figure 10.9 shows a graph of a hypothetical performance measure, where the single decision variable is plotted along the horizontal axis. The actual formula for performance is the following.

$$f(x) = 100 + 300x - 60x^2 - 17.5x^3 + 5.32x^4 - 0.33x^5$$

The maximum value of the function is about 700, attained when $x = 8.36$. However, if we begin our hill-climbing procedure at points below $x = 4.85$, Solver will stop at the point $x = 1.95$, where the function reaches a local optimum of about 395.

FIGURE 10.9 Graph of a Hypothetical Performance Measure

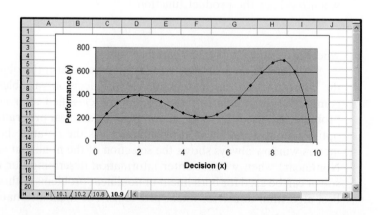

On the other hand, if we start above $x = 4.85$, our hill-climbing procedure will take us to the global optimum, as desired.

As our graph shows, the final solution produced by the GRG algorithm may depend on where it started. This would be true in problems where there are several local optima distinct from the global optimum. In such cases, there can never be a guarantee that a single run of Solver has found the optimal solution, so it makes sense to rerun Solver several times, trying a different starting point each time. The **starting point** is the set of values of the decision variables in the worksheet when Solver begins its search. If Solver finds the same solution from many different starting points, that should increase our confidence that we have found the global optimum. On the other hand, there is no recipe for how many starting points to try or where they should be located.

In many practical cases, the objective function has only one local optimum, which is also a global optimum. A figure corresponding to Figure 10.9 for this type of function would exhibit only one peak. Such functions are sometimes said to be shaped like an "inverted bowl." (In minimization problems, the analogy would be a "bowl-shaped" function.) For these kinds of functions, the GRG algorithm in Solver is perfectly **reliable** when the model contains either no constraints or a set of linear constraints. We use the term reliable to mean that the algorithm finds the global optimum.

10.5 NONLINEAR PROGRAMMING EXAMPLES

Because nonlinear functions include a wide variety of possible relationships, many different kinds of problems lend themselves to solution with the nonlinear solver. The Advertising Budget example was such a problem, in which the nonlinearity arose in the function relating sales and advertising. Thus, we found ourselves confronting a nonlinear objective function and (in the case of the advertising budget) a linear constraint. In this section, we illustrate the formulation and solution of nonlinear programs related to some other common problem structures. Each involves the maximization or minimization of a nonlinear objective function.

10.5.1 Facility Location

A common logistics problem is to locate a facility that serves many customer sites, The customer sites already exist, so their locations are known. The service facility is to be centrally located according to some measure of "central." Most often, the location problem arises in two dimensions, as in the case of the Kilroy Paper Company.

EXAMPLE
Kilroy Paper Company

The Kilroy Paper Company distributes specialty papers to big-box stores in 10 major U.S. metropolitan areas and plans to consolidate its warehouses into one national distribution center (DC). To identify a suitable location, Kilroy's distribution manager first maps the 10 stores on a two-dimensional grid, so that coordinates (x_k, y_k) can be associated with each site. These values are shown in the following table.

Site (k)	x_k	y_k
1	5	41
2	20	10
3	44	48
4	60	58
5	100	4
6	138	80
7	150	40
8	170	18
9	182	2
10	190	56

For any distribution center location (x, y), it is possible to calculate the distance from the DC to each of the stores and to sum the distances. This total can be thought of as a proxy for the total annual cost incurred by Kilroy's trucks, since they will make regular trips to the individual stores. Minimizing the sum of distances therefore represents an objective that is consistent with minimizing annual distribution cost. Kilroy wishes to determine the location that achieves the minimum sum of distances. ∎

To begin the analysis, we ask, "What must be decided?" The answer is clearly the site for the distribution center, which is given by a pair of coordinates (x, y). In the worksheet of Figure 10.10, we place initial guesses for the coordinates (x, y) in cells C4 and D4.

To develop an objective function, we ask, "What measure of performance can we use?" As the problem statement indicates, the measure of interest is the sum of the distances between the distribution center and the various stores. This measure takes some effort to construct. The straight-line distance in two dimensions (also known as the **Euclidean distance**) between the distribution center and the kth store is given by

$$Distance = \text{SQRT}[(x\text{-}distance)^2 + (y\text{-}distance)^2]$$

or

$$D_k(x, y) = \text{SQRT}[(x - x_k)^2 + (y - y_k)^2]$$

For each store k, this distance is calculated in column G of Figure 10.10. The sum of these distances is the measure of performance:

$$f(x, y) = \sum_{k=1}^{10} D_k(x, y)$$

This sum is calculated in cell D6 of the worksheet.

The optimization problem is to find the decision variables (x, y) that minimize the objective function $f(x, y)$. The problem has no explicit constraints. In Figure 10.10, the decision variables appear in cells C4 and D4, and the objective function appears in cell D6.

In the Solver Parameters window, we enter the following information.

Target cell	D6 (minimize)
Changing cells	C4:D4
Constraints	None

When we click on the Solve button, Solver searches for a solution. The optimal solution, as displayed in Figure 10.11, is the location (114.1, 35.2), for which the

FIGURE 10.10 Model for the Kilroy Paper Company Example

	A	B	C	D	E	F	G
1	Locating a Distribution Center						
2							
3	Decisions		x	y			
4		Location	10.0	10.0			
5							
6	Result		Sum	1059.1			
7							
8	Data				Calculations		
9		Site (k)	x(k)	y(k)	x-dist	y-dist	Distance
10		1	5	41	-5.000	31.000	31.401
11		2	20	10	10.000	0.000	10.000
12		3	44	48	34.000	38.000	50.990
13		4	60	58	50.000	48.000	69.311
14		5	100	4	90.000	-6.000	90.200
15		6	138	80	128.000	70.000	145.890
16		7	150	40	140.000	30.000	143.178
17		8	170	18	160.000	8.000	160.200
18		9	182	2	172.000	-8.000	172.186
19		10	190	56	180.000	46.000	185.785
20							

10.10

FIGURE 10.11 Optimal Solution for the Kilroy Paper Company Example

	A	B	C	D	E	F	G
1	Locating a Distribution Center						
2							
3	Decisions		x	y			
4		Location	114.1	35.2			
5							
6	Result		Sum	670.6			
7							
8	Data				Calculations		
9		Site (k)	x(k)	y(k)	x-dist	y-dist	Distance
10		1	5	41	-109.071	5.828	109.226
11		2	20	10	-94.071	-25.172	97.380
12		3	44	48	-70.071	12.828	71.235
13		4	60	58	-54.071	22.828	58.692
14		5	100	4	-14.071	-31.172	34.201
15		6	138	80	23.929	44.828	50.815
16		7	150	40	35.929	4.828	36.252
17		8	170	18	55.929	-17.172	58.506
18		9	182	2	67.929	-33.172	75.596
19		10	190	56	75.929	20.828	78.734
20							

objective function reaches a minimum of approximately 670.6. This location is the central site for Kilroy's distribution center.

SOLVER TIP
Target Cell Options in Solver

Solver provides us with the opportunity to maximize a target cell, or to minimize a target cell, simply by choosing a button in the Solver Parameters window. A third option allows us to specify a target value and find for our variables a set of values that achieves the target value. This target capability is similar to that of the Goal Seek tool, except that Solver can handle many variables at once. However, it is the maximization and minimization modes for which Solver is primarily used. ■

10.5.2 Revenue Maximization

A common business problem involves maximizing revenue in the presence of a demand curve. A **demand curve** is simply a function that relates demand volume to price. But because revenue is the product of price and volume, and volume depends on price, revenue is generally a nonlinear function of price. In some cases, volume also depends on another product's price. We illustrate with the following example.

EXAMPLE
Coastal Telephone Company

Coastal Telephone Company (CTC) is a regional supplier of long-distance telephone services. CTC is trying to determine the optimal pricing structure for its daytime and evening long-distance calling rates. The daytime price applies from 8:00 A.M. to 6:00 P.M., and the evening price applies the rest of the time. With the help of a consultant, the company has estimated the average demand for phone lines (per minute) as follows:

Daytime Lines Demanded $= 600 - 5000 \times Day\ Price + 300 \times Evening\ Price$
Evening Lines Demanded $= 400 + 600 \times Day\ Price - 2500 \times Evening\ Price$

CTC wants to find prices that maximize its revenue. ■

To determine the decision variables in this problem, we ask, "What must be decided?" Here, the answer is obviously the pair of prices, which we write as DP for the daytime price and EP for the evening price.

To determine the objective function, we ask, "What measure should we use?" As stated, CTC is interested in maximizing its total revenue. Total revenue consists of a daytime component and an evening component. The daytime component per minute is $DD \times DP$, where DD represents daytime demand. Similarly, the evening component per minute is $ED \times EP$, where ED represents evening demand. Noting that there are 600 minutes in the daytime period and 840 minutes in the evening period, we can write our objective function as follows:

$$Revenue = 600DD \times DP + 840ED \times EP$$

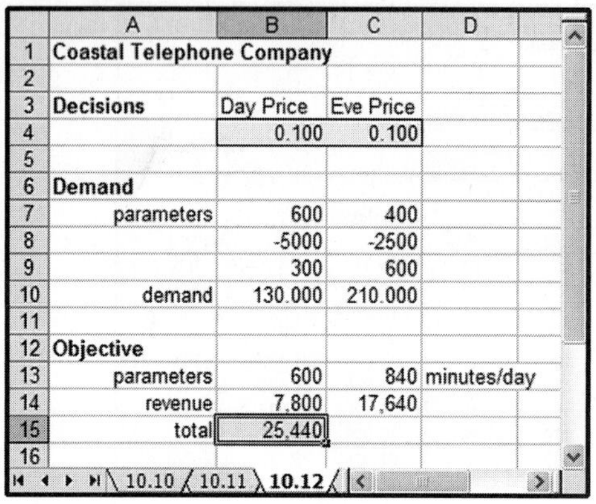

FIGURE 10.12 Model for
the Coastal Telephone
Company Example

	A	B	C	D
1	Coastal Telephone Company			
2				
3	Decisions	Day Price	Eve Price	
4		0.100	0.100	
5				
6	Demand			
7	parameters	600	400	
8		-5000	-2500	
9		300	600	
10	demand	130.000	210.000	
11				
12	Objective			
13	parameters	600	840	minutes/day
14	revenue	7,800	17,640	
15	total	25,440		
16				

`10.10 / 10.11 \ 10.12 /`

Note that since DD is a function of both DP and EP, the objective function is nonlinear because it involves products of decision variables (i.e., $DP \times DP$ and $DP \times EP$). Moreover, DD is not, strictly speaking, a decision variable. Rather, we can view it as a *derived* variable, or an intermediate variable, in the sense that its value is determined once we know the values of the decision variables.

A formal statement of the optimization problem is as follows, including the demand curve constraints:

$$\text{Maximize } Revenue = 600DD \times DP + 840ED \times EP$$

Subject to

$$DD = 600 - 5000DP + 300EP$$

$$ED = 400 + 600DP - 2500EP$$

In the worksheet shown in Figure 10.12, we devote column B to daytime variables and column C to evening variables. Model construction takes the following steps.

- We place the daytime and evening prices in row 4. Since we do not know the optimal prices when we are building the worksheet, we can place initial guesses (such as $0.10) in these cells.

- The demand parameters appear in the next module, with demands calculated in row 10. The revenues are calculated in row 14 from the demands in row 10.

- These last two figures are summed to obtain total revenue in cell B15.

To find a solution to the problem, we invoke Solver and specify:

Target cell	B15 (maximize)
Changing cells	B4:C4
Constraints	None

When we click on the `Solve` button, Solver searches for an optimal solution. The optimal prices turn out to be roughly $DP = 0.070$ and $EP = 0.091$, with maximum revenue of $28,044 per day. (When the objective is a quadratic function, as it is here, and no constraints apply, the GRG algorithm reliably finds the global optimum. This could be confirmed by running Solver from a variety of initial starting values for the decision variables.)

SOLVER TIP
*Settings for
the Solver
Options*

Before we run Solver, we should click on the `Options` button and examine the Solver Options window. Four check boxes are available:

Show Iteration Results. Leave this box unchecked. Checking this box stops the nonlinear solver at each step of its search, displaying the latest solution found. But there is no reason to intervene in the search procedure except very rarely, when a model needs debugging.

Use Automatic Scaling. Leave this box unchecked. Occasionally, this box may be checked if there is some suspicion that the model contains numbers of rather different magnitudes. However, this option is something of a last resort if there seem to be numerical difficulties in finding an optimal solution.

Assume Non-Negative. Check this box whenever the variables make sense only if they are nonnegative (which is in the vast majority of applications). Alternatively, it is possible to enter explicit constraints that force decision variables to be positive or zero, but the check box is an easier mechanism and avoids clutter in the Solver Parameters window.

Bypass Solver Reports. Leave this box unchecked. Even if we're sure we want to avoid the Solver reports, there is no advantage in checking the box. The only exception might be when Solver is called in a subroutine of a VBA macro, but this is an advanced use. ■

10.5.3 Curve Fitting

As another example of optimization without constraints, we describe a general approach to regression, or, more accurately, the process of fitting a function to observed data points. In particular, we return to the Van Winkle's Pharmacy example we encountered in Chapter 8, where we want to predict pharmacy revenue as a function of the number of hours the store is open in a week. The given data consist of 10 observations of store hours and revenue. These are shown in cells B5:C14 in the worksheet of Figure 10.13.

The scatter plot in Figure 10.13 suggests a nonlinear relationship, so we will work with a simple nonlinear function. Recalling our list of functions in Figure 2.12, we first hypothesize that the relationship takes the form of the power curve with diminishing returns

$$Revenue = a \times Hours^b$$

What must be decided? As we know from our coverage of regression in Chapter 8, the decision variables are the parameters a and b. What measure should we use? The traditional objective function is the sum of squared differences between the model and the data. What constraints apply? None: the choices for a and b are not restricted at all.

In the worksheet of Figure 10.14, we reserve cells D1 and D2 for the parameters a and b, respectively, and we enter the formula for Revenue into cells D5:D14. As tentative values, we set $a = 1,000$ and $b = 0.5$, knowing those arbitrary choices can likely be improved. We now have the observed values and the model values for *Revenue* next to each other in columns C and D. In column E, we calculate the difference between model and observation and in column F, the square of each difference. The sum of these squared differences appears in cell F2 and represents the objective function. We invoke Solver and specify:

Target cell   F2 (minimize)
Changing cells   D1:D2
Constraints   None

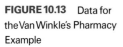

FIGURE 10.13 Data for the Van Winkle's Pharmacy Example

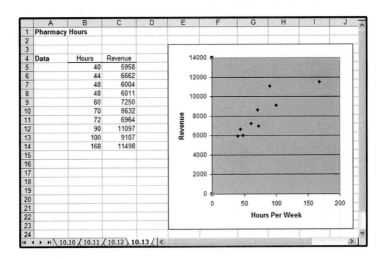

FIGURE 10.14 Model for Curve Fitting in the Van Winkle's Pharmacy Example

	A	B	C	D	E	F	G
1	Pharmacy Hours		a·	1000		Sum of Squared Differences	
2			b	0.5		9,993,184	
3							
4	Data	Hours	Revenue	Model	Difference	Sq. Diff.	
5		40	5958	6325	-367	134363	
6		44	6662	6633	29	827	
7		48	6004	6928	-924	854152	
8		48	6011	6928	-917	841262	
9		60	7250	7746	-496	245983	
10		70	8632	8367	265	70437	
11		72	6964	8485	-1521	2314297	
12		90	11097	9487	1610	2592638	
13		100	9107	10000	-893	797449	
14		168	11498	12961	-1463	2141778	
15							

⟨ 10.10 / 10.11 / 10.12 / 10.13 \ 10.14 / ⟩

No constraints need be specified, not even nonnegativity of the decision variables (although we expect the optimal value of *b* to be greater than zero because revenue should increase with hours). When we click on the Solve button, Solver searches for the optimal values of the model parameters. In this case, the values turn out to be $a = 1,022$ and $b = 0.482$, with a minimum sum of squares approximately equal to 7.55 million, as shown in Figure 10.15. (When the objective is in the form of a sum of squared differences, the GRG algorithm reliably finds the global optimum. This could be confirmed by running Solver from a variety of initial starting values for the decision variables.) As we pointed out in Chapter 8, standard regression software does not achieve a sum of squares as small as this value.

The model that we have built is quite flexible because of its modular structure. For example, we could easily modify the worksheet to fit an alternative model of diminishing returns in the form

$$Revenue = a + b \times log(Hours)$$

This modification requires that we enter the model function into cell D5 and then copy it throughout the column below. Thus, column D serves as a module corresponding to the *form* of the model we wish to fit. (In Chapter 8, we summarized the results of using a variation of the logarithmic model.)

A second module corresponds to the measure of fit. Although minimizing the sum of squared differences would be the typical objective function for regression analysis, other measures of fit are sometimes appropriate. For example, we could minimize the sum of *absolute* differences. Under this criterion, large deviations between the function and the data have less influence on the results than they would under the least squares criterion. For this criterion, we calculate the absolute difference between model and observation in column F, as shown in Figure 10.16. The function in cell F2 does not have to change. When we run Solver, we do not have to modify the information in the Solver Parameters window, because the necessary modifications have all been made on the worksheet. The target cell and changing cells remain the same. Thus, column F is a module corresponding to the *criterion* for the

FIGURE 10.15 Optimal Solution for the Van Winkle's Pharmacy Example

	A	B	C	D	E	F	G
1	Pharmacy Hours		a	1022.0345		Sum of Squared Differences	
2			b	0.4817852		7,554,649	
3							
4	Data	Hours	Revenue	Model	Difference	Sq. Diff.	
5		40	5958	6044	-86	7372	
6		44	6662	6328	334	111650	
7		48	6004	6599	-595	353747	
8		48	6011	6599	-588	345470	
9		60	7250	7348	-98	9549	
10		70	8632	7914	718	515249	
11		72	6964	8022	-1058	1120079	
12		90	11097	8933	2164	4683482	
13		100	9107	9398	-291	84689	
14		168	11498	12067	-569	323363	
15							

⟨ 10.10 / 10.11 / 10.12 / 10.13 / 10.14 \ 10.15 / ⟩

FIGURE 10.16 Second Revenue Model for the Van Winkle's Pharmacy Example

	A	B	C	D	E	F	G	H
1	Pharmacy Hours		a	1022.0345		Sum of Absolute Differences		
2			b	0.4817852		6500		
3								
4	Data	Hours	Revenue	Model	Difference	Abs. Diff.		
5		40	5958	6044	-86	86		
6		44	6662	6328	334	334		
7		48	6004	6599	-595	595		
8		48	6011	6599	-588	588		
9		60	7250	7348	-98	98		
10		70	8632	7914	718	718		
11		72	6964	8022	-1058	1058		
12		90	11097	8933	2164	2164		
13		100	9107	9398	-291	291		
14		168	11498	12067	-569	569		
15								

⏮ ◀ ▶ ⏭ \ 10.10 / 10.11 / 10.12 / 10.13 / 10.14 / 10.15 \ **10.16** /

model we wish to fit. Together, the modules for form and criterion give us a handy tool for fitting a model to data, a tool that provides flexibility unavailable in the standard regression package.

Starting with the *a* and *b* values of Figure 10.16, Solver produces a solution with an objective function of 5,719, as shown in Figure 10.17. However, in the Solver Results window, we read the message, Solver has converged to the current solution. All constraints are satisfied. This message indicates that Solver may not have reached even a local optimum. In fact, Solver's stopping criterion is related to the Convergence parameter on the Options menu, for which the default is usually 0.0001. This means that Solver will stop when the last few solutions in its hill-climbing procedure have been unable to improve the objective function by more than 0.01 percent. In response to this stopping message, we should simply rerun Solver, starting from the latest solution. In this instance, Solver achieves an improved value of the objective function of 5,717, and the message in the Solver Results window now reads, Solver found a solution. All constraints and optimality conditions are satisfied. This is the message we're looking for, as it indicates that a local optimum has been found.

Starting Values		Final Values		
a	**b**	**a**	**b**	**Objective**
1,022	0.482	1,108	0.457	5,717
500	0.5	1,142	0.451	5,712
500	0	1,136	0.452	5,713
1,000	1	1,003	0.479	5,911
1,000	0	1,129	0.453	5,714
2,000	2	1,663	0.369	7,323

FIGURE 10.17 Optimal Solution for the Second Revenue Model

	A	B	C	D	E	F	G	H
1	Pharmacy Hours		a	1107.9075		Sum of Absolute Differences		
2			b	0.4566191		5719		
3								
4	Data	Hours	Revenue	Model	Difference	Abs. Diff.		
5		40	5958	5971	-13	13		
6		44	6662	6236	426	426		
7		48	6004	6489	-485	485		
8		48	6011	6489	-478	478		
9		60	7250	7185	65	65		
10		70	8632	7709	923	923		
11		72	6964	7809	-845	845		
12		90	11097	8647	2450	2450		
13		100	9107	9073	34	34		
14		168	11498	11498	0	0		
15								

⏮ ◀ ▶ ⏭ \ 10.10 / 10.11 / 10.12 / 10.13 / 10.14 / 10.15 / 10.16 \ **10.17** /

Unlike the minimization of the sum of squares, this nonlinear program has several local optima. If we had started the search at a different pair of values for a and b, Solver could have produced a different solution. The table on the previous page summarizes some alternative results.

This example illustrates one of the potential problems with the nonlinear solver: Its solution may depend on the starting point. As a result, we normally want to try out a variety of starting points, to give us the best chance to find the global optimum.

SOLVER TIP	
Solutions from the GRG Algorithm	The GRG algorithm may stop with the message, Solver has converged to the current solution. All constraints are satisfied. We refer to this result as the *convergence message*. The convergence message indicates that the algorithm should be rerun from the stopping point. This message may then reappear, in which case Solver should be rerun once more. Eventually, the algorithm should conclude with the message, Solver found a solution. All constraints and optimality conditions are satisfied. We refer to this result as the *optimality message*. This message signifies that Solver has found a local optimum. (If the first message persists, it may be helpful either to check the box for Automatic Scaling or to increase the Convergence parameter by a factor of 10, for example, from 0.0001 to 0.001.) To help determine whether the local optimum is also a global optimum, Solver should be restarted at a different set of decision variables and rerun. If several widely differing starting solutions lead to the same local optimum, that is some evidence that the local optimum is likely to be a global optimum, but in general there is no way to know for sure.

Although there are conditions under which we can guarantee that the GRG algorithm is reliable—that is, it finds a global optimum—the theoretical details are beyond the scope of our treatment. It is always a good idea to try starting with different sets of decision variables, to see whether Solver will always converge to the same local optimum. If we encounter two different local optima in this process, we know that we had better test a variety of starting points if we hope to find the global optimum. ∎

10.5.4 Economic Order Quantity

A basic inventory problem requires balancing ordering costs and carrying costs to minimize total costs. We are given a product's annual demand, D, and we need to determine the quantity to order, Q.

Suppose that a fixed ordering cost of K is incurred with each order, independent of the order size. If the quantity ordered is Q, then the *number* of orders placed per year is D/Q. It then follows that the ordering cost per year is

$$Ordering\ cost = (Cost\ per\ order) \times (Orders\ per\ year) = KD/Q$$

By placing orders so that replenishment occurs just as stock is depleted, we ensure that the inventory level fluctuates between a low of zero and a high of Q. The average inventory is therefore $Q/2$. Suppose also that items held in inventory incur an annual carrying cost of h. (This cost is often expressed as a percentage of the product's unit cost, in the form $h = ic$, where i denotes the carrying cost percentage and c denotes an item's cost.) Then the annual inventory carrying costs are

$$Inventory\ cost = (Carrying\ charge) \times (Average\ Inventory) = hQ/2$$

Then, the average total cost (ATC) is the sum of these two components:

$$ATC = Ordering\ cost + Inventory\ cost = KD/Q + hQ/2 \qquad (10.1)$$

The formula for ATC represents the annual total of ordering and holding costs, provided that demand D and holding cost h are annual figures. If those are weekly figures, then ATC represents the *weekly* total of ordering and holding costs. The formula thus adapts to the time scale of the input parameters.

Notice that the economic order quantity model is a single-item model. If we have two items in an inventory system, we can analyze them separately, as two independent problems, to find optimal order quantities and optimal costs for the system. However, in most multiproduct inventory systems, interactions among the items occur. For example, the items may compete for a limited resource, as we see in the case of the Woodstock Appliance Company.

EXAMPLE
Woodstock Appliance Company

The Woodstock Appliance Company carries four products. The annual demands for these products range from 300/year for a high-end vacuum cleaner to 30,000/year for a table fan. The order cost, holding cost, and purchase cost, as well as how much space each product occupies, are known for each of the four products. The numerical information is summarized in the following table.

Product	1	2	3	4
Demand/yr.	5,000	10,000	30,000	300
Order cost	400	700	100	250
Holding cost	10%	10%	10%	10%
Purchase cost	500	250	80	1,000
Space/unit	12	25	5	20

Woodstock stores inventory in its warehouse, which contains 12,000 square feet that can be dedicated to any combination of the four products. The problem is to find the order quantities that minimize cost while respecting the limit on storage space. ■

What must be decided? We want to determine the four order quantities, and these serve as decision variables in our model. How do we measure performance? We evaluate a set of order quantities by calculating the total annual cost across all four products. For product j, the total annual cost is given by a function ATC_j, which follows equation (10.1). The sum of the four functions ATC_j serves as the objective function. What constraints apply? The only important constraint is the ceiling on storage space. In words, we require that the storage space consumed must be less than or equal to the space available. In addition, we might want to add the constraints $Q_j \geq 1$, just to be explicit that order quantities of less than 1 are not feasible. An algebraic formulation of our problem becomes:

$$\text{Minimize } ATC = ATC_1 + ATC_2 + ATC_3 + ATC_4$$

Subject to

$$12Q_1 + 25Q_2 + 5Q_3 + 20Q_4 \leq 12,000$$

$$Q_1 \geq 1$$

$$Q_2 \geq 1$$

$$Q_3 \geq 1$$

$$Q_4 \geq 1$$

In Figure 10.18, the individual product costs are calculated in cells B17:E17. Cell B18 then sums the four individual product costs in order to determine the cost for the product line. The space required for each product is calculated in cells B21:E21, and the total space used is calculated in cell F21.

We invoke Solver and specify:

Target cell	B18 (minimize)
Changing cells	B10:E10
Constraints	F12 ≤ H21
	B10:E10 ≥ 1

When we click on the Solve button, we obtain a solution with a minimum annual cost of $43,916. Once again, we test this solution by choosing different initial

FIGURE 10.18 Optimal Solution for the Woodstock Applicance Company Example

	A	B	C	D	E	F	G	H
1	Economic Order Quantity							
2								
3	Parameters	Product 1	Product 2	Product 3	Product 4			
4	Demand	5000	10000	30000	300			
5	Fixed cost	400	700	100	250			
6	Holding cost	10%	10%	10%	10%			
7	Purchase cost	500	250	80	1000			
8	Space	12	25	5	20			
9	Decisions							
10	Order quantity	272	643	784	37			
11								
12	Objective							
13	Orders/yr.	18.4	15.6	38.3	8.0			
14	Ordering cost/yr.	7,366	10,886	3,829	2,004			
15	Avg. Inventory	135.8	321.5	391.8	18.7			
16	Carrying cost/yr.	6,788	8,038	3,134	1,871			
17	Total product cost	14,154	18,924	6,963	3,875			
18	Total cost	43,916						
19								
20	Constraint							
21	Avg. Space required	1,629	8,038	1,959	374	12,000	<=	12,000
22								

⏮ ◀ ▶ ⏭ \ 10.18 / ◀

values of the decision variables as starting points. The results indicate that the solution is likely to be a global optimum.

SOLVER TIP
Avoid Dis-continuous Functions

A number of functions familiar to experienced Excel programmers should be avoided when using the nonlinear solver. These include logical functions (such as IF or AND), mathematical functions (such as ROUND or CEILING), lookup and reference functions (such as CHOOSE or VLOOKUP), and statistical functions (such as RANK or COUNT). In general, any function that *changes discontinuously* is to be avoided. For example, the IF function

$$\text{IF}(X < 0, 0, 1)$$

jumps abruptly from 0 to 1 when the variable X reaches 0.

The problem these functions create for the hill-climbing algorithm in Solver is that they can turn a smooth hill into one with abrupt cliffs. Since the hill-climbing procedure cannot "see" beyond its immediate surroundings, when it comes to a cliff, it simply stops. Thus, the Solver may stop prematurely when used on models that include these functions.

For an example, consider the Advertising Budget model. Suppose we ensure that the figures for Units Sold (row 27 of the worksheet in Figure 10.1) are integers by using the ROUND function in making those calculations. When we implement Solver starting from the base case, it stops almost immediately at an objective of $69,668. By using the round-off function, for what is essentially a cosmetic purpose, we have introduced a discontinuous function that undermines the nonlinear solver.

Premium Solver for Education contains an algorithm called the Evolutionary Solver, which is better suited to nonlinear optimization problems that have discontinuities, as would be the case if the model were to use the IF, CHOOSE, or ROUND functions. However, the principles behind this algorithm are beyond the scope of our coverage. ∎

10.6 SENSITIVITY ANALYSIS FOR NONLINEAR PROGRAMS

Sensitivity analysis involves testing our initial assumptions to see what impact they have on our conclusions. In previous chapters we have recommended performing sensitivity analysis on all of the numerical inputs to a model, whether they are parameters or decision variables. Sensitivity analysis of one or two decision variables (perhaps using the Data Sensitivity tool) can lead us to the optimal values of those variables, but this approach cannot be used for more than two variables. An optimization procedure such as Solver performs this kind of search in a sophisticated manner and can handle large numbers of decision variables and constraints. Thus, we can think of optimization as an ambitious form of what-if analysis with respect to decision variables.

FIGURE 10.19 First Input Window for the Solver Sensitivity Tool

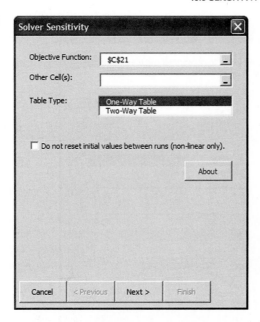

When we are dealing with an optimization model, there are two types of sensitivity analysis that are often confused. Consider, for example, the Advertising Budget model from Section 10.2.3, which led to a maximum profit of $71,447. We first ask how the results change when the price drops by 10 percent, to $36. A simple what-if analysis gives us the answer: The new profit is $16,500. This, of course, assumes that the advertising allocation does not change. In other words, if we fix the budget allocation and then vary the price, the result is a profit of $16,500. But what would happen if we could optimize the budget allocation *after* the price dropped to $36? Would the optimal profit still be $16,500? A run of Solver at the lower price answers this question. In fact, the optimal profit at a price of $36 is $17,376, not $16,500. So in general, there is a difference between the sensitivity of a model to a parameter *without* re-optimization and the sensitivity *with* re-optimization.

Because these two types of sensitivity are different, it is important to recognize which one is appropriate for a given situation. In the Advertising Budget example, we might find ourselves in the situation where we do not know next year's price at the present time, but we will know it before we have to implement our advertising plan. In this case, we would like to vary the price and determine both the optimal advertising plan and the optimal profit for each possible price. For this purpose, we need to run Solver for each value of the price that we wish to study. Fortunately, there is an analogous tool to Data Sensitivity, called **Solver Sensitivity**, which automates this procedure. It is also a module in the Sensitivity Toolkit add-in. Before using Solver Sensitivity, we must run Solver on the active worksheet. Then, after optimizing the base-case model, we can select Solver Sensitivity (Add-ins▶ Menu Commands▶Sensitivity Toolkit).

We illustrate the use of Solver Sensitivity by revisiting the Advertising Budget example of Figure 10.8. In our first sensitivity analysis, we vary the unit price, which is $40.00 in the base case. The first step is to optimize the base-case model. Then, when we select Solver Sensitivity, the input window in Figure 10.19 appears. Solver Sensitivity automatically identifies the objective function as cell C21. For Other Cell(s), we specify the decision variables (in this case, the range D18:G18), although, in general, we could track any set of cells on the worksheet. Finally, we select One-Way table and click on Next. On the next input screen (see Figure 10.20), we select C7, which contains the price, as Cell to Vary. Using the Begin, End, Increment mode of data entry, we enter a First Value (or minimum) of 30.00, a Last Value (or maximum) of 40.00, and an Increment of 0.50. (Dollar signs should be omitted.) Figure 10.20 shows the Solver Sensitivity input window after this information has been entered, just before clicking Finish.

The Solver Sensitivity add-in runs Solver 21 times, once for each value of price from $30.00 to $40.00. It then produces a new worksheet, containing the information shown in Figure 10.21 after some reformatting. Column A contains the values we specified for Price: $30.00 to $40.00 in steps of $0.50. In column B, we find the corresponding optimal profit values, each produced by a Solver run. In column C, Solver Sensitivity calculates the rate of change in the optimal values, from one price to the next. Finally, the last four columns (D–G) show the values of the OtherCells we designated, with column headings showing the cell addresses for each of those outputs.

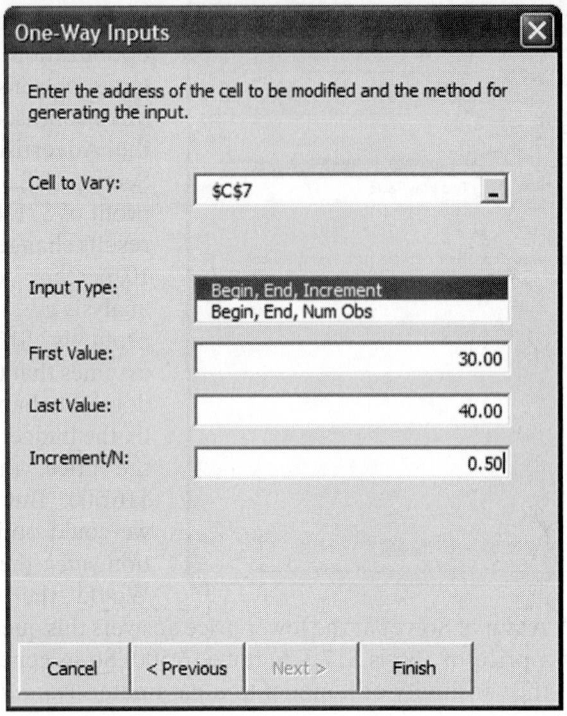

FIGURE 10.20 Second
Input Window for the
Solver Sensitivity Tool

In the figure, we can see in one place how the optimal solution (that is, the objective function value and the optimal values of the decision variables) varies with the unit price. At relatively low prices (at or below $32.00), the margins are so small that it is best not to spend anything on advertising. As the unit price increases, it first becomes desirable to spend advertising money in Q4; then in Q2 as well; then in Q1 as well; and, at $34.50, it becomes desirable to spend advertising money in all four quarters. When the price rises to $37.00, the advertising budget is completely spent, and the allocation of the $40,000 budget remains the same as price rises even further. Thus, we can see that the base-case result (that the budget should be completely spent) is dependent, in part, on the fact that the unit price is sufficiently high. That is not an insight we could reach without doing this kind of sensitivity analysis.

A sensitivity analysis can also show the effects on the optimal solution of altering the budget. This is a common type of sensitivity analysis in which we explore the consequences of altering a constraint that is binding in the base case.

FIGURE 10.21 Output
Table Produced by the Solver
Sensitivity Tool

	A	B	C	D	E	F	G
1	Price	Objective	Change	$D$18	$E$18	$F$18	$G$18
2	$30.00	-$30,166		$0	$0	$0	$0
3	$30.50	-$26,907	$6,517.89	$0	$0	$0	$0
4	$31.00	-$23,648	$6,517.89	$0	$0	$0	$0
5	$31.50	-$20,389	$6,517.89	$0	$0	$0	$0
6	$32.00	-$17,130	$6,517.89	$0	$0	$0	$0
7	$32.50	-$13,871	$6,518.16	$0	$0	$0	$39
8	$33.00	-$10,511	$6,720.85	$0	$447	$0	$1,101
9	$33.50	-$6,875	$7,271.23	$0	$1,475	$0	$2,325
10	$34.00	-$2,902	$7,946.11	$773	$2,636	$0	$3,708
11	$34.50	$1,487	$8,778.44	$1,640	$3,932	$666	$5,249
12	$35.00	$6,330	$9,685.58	$2,597	$5,361	$1,422	$6,950
13	$35.50	$11,626	$10,592.76	$3,643	$6,924	$2,249	$8,810
14	$36.00	$17,376	$11,499.96	$4,779	$8,621	$3,147	$10,830
15	$36.50	$23,580	$12,407.14	$6,005	$10,452	$4,115	$13,009
16	$37.00	$30,237	$13,313.80	$7,273	$12,346	$5,117	$15,263
17	$37.50	$37,105	$13,736.64	$7,273	$12,346	$5,117	$15,263
18	$38.00	$43,974	$13,736.64	$7,273	$12,346	$5,117	$15,263
19	$38.50	$50,842	$13,736.64	$7,273	$12,346	$5,117	$15,263
20	$39.00	$57,710	$13,736.65	$7,273	$12,346	$5,117	$15,263
21	$39.50	$64,578	$13,736.65	$7,273	$12,346	$5,117	$15,263
22	$40.00	$71,447	$13,736.65	$7,273	$12,346	$5,117	$15,263
23							

10.21

FIGURE 10.22 Sensitivity of the Advertising Budget Model Results to Changes in Price

	A	B	C	D	E	F	G	H	I	J	K
1	Budget	Objective	Change	$D$18	$E$18	$F$18	$G$18	Q1	Q2	Q3	Q4
2	$30,000	$66,715.5		$5,298	$9,395	$3,556	$11,751	17.7%	31.3%	11.9%	39.2%
3	$35,000	$69,277.5	0.512	$6,285	$10,871	$4,337	$13,507	18.0%	31.1%	12.4%	38.6%
4	$40,000	$71,446.8	0.434	$7,273	$12,346	$5,117	$15,263	18.2%	30.9%	12.8%	38.2%
5	$45,000	$73,279.0	0.366	$8,261	$13,822	$5,898	$17,020	18.4%	30.7%	13.1%	37.8%
6	$50,000	$74,817.5	0.308	$9,249	$15,298	$6,678	$18,776	18.5%	30.6%	13.4%	37.6%
7	$55,000	$76,097.3	0.256	$10,237	$16,773	$7,459	$20,532	18.6%	30.5%	13.6%	37.3%
8	$60,000	$77,146.8	0.210	$11,224	$18,249	$8,239	$22,288	18.7%	30.4%	13.7%	37.1%
9	$65,000	$77,989.6	0.169	$12,212	$19,724	$9,020	$24,044	18.8%	30.3%	13.9%	37.0%
10	$70,000	$78,645.7	0.131	$13,200	$21,200	$9,800	$25,800	18.9%	30.3%	14.0%	36.9%
11	$75,000	$79,131.8	0.097	$14,188	$22,676	$10,580	$27,556	18.9%	30.2%	14.1%	36.7%
12	$80,000	$79,462.3	0.066	$15,176	$24,151	$11,361	$29,312	19.0%	30.2%	14.2%	36.6%
13	$85,000	$79,649.9	0.038	$16,163	$25,627	$12,141	$31,068	19.0%	30.1%	14.3%	36.6%
14	$90,000	$79,705.6	0.011	$17,093	$27,016	$12,876	$32,721	19.0%	30.0%	14.3%	36.4%
15	$95,000	$79,705.6	0.000	$17,093	$27,016	$12,876	$32,721	18.0%	28.4%	13.6%	34.4%
16	$100,000	$79,705.6	0.000	$17,093	$27,016	$12,876	$32,721	17.1%	27.0%	12.9%	32.7%
17											

Ⅰ◀ ◀ ▶ ▶Ⅰ ╱ 10.21 ╲ **10.22** ╱ Ⅰ ◀

Figure 10.22, created with Solver Sensitivity, shows how optimal profit changes when we increase the budget from $30,000 to $100,000 in steps of $5,000. These inputs are shown in column A, with the corresponding optimal profit given in column B. In column C, we see a calculation of the rate at which profit changes, per unit change in the budget. For example, the first nonblank entry indicates that, between $30,000 and $35,000, each additional $1.00 of advertising budget adds 51.2 cents to profit.

A graphical perspective on these results is shown in Figure 10.23. The top chart plots the optimal profit as a function of the budget. In this graph, we can see that optimal profits expand as the budget increases. However, the graph reveals **diminishing marginal returns**, reflecting the fact that the profit function gets flatter as the budget increases. Eventually, profit actually levels out, because the advertising budget is more than we can effectively use. The bottom chart plots the rate of change in profit as a function of the budget. Here, we observe diminishing returns in the form of a declining rate of change. The rate of change in profit reaches zero when the budget exceeds a useful level, around $90,000.

FIGURE 10.23 Graphical Display of the Sensitivity Results

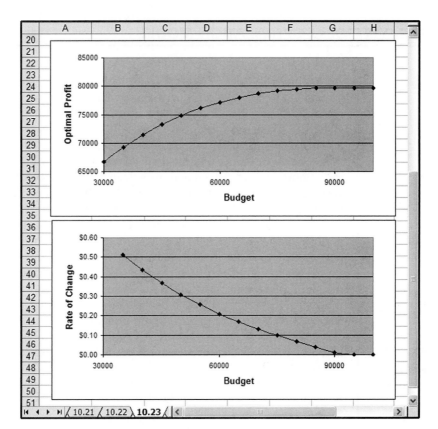

We have added four columns in Figure 10.22 (columns H:K) that translate the quarterly expenditures into percentages of the overall budget. As we can see, the percentage split changes very slightly over this range. For a budget of $30,000, the optimal expenditure in Q4 is about 39 percent of the year's budget, and for a budget of $90,000, this figure drops to about 36 percent.

Perhaps the most important feature of these results is a qualitative one. *When we relax a binding constraint, the objective function cannot get worse.* In fact, it usually gets better, as illustrated in Figure 10.22. This is an intuitive but important result, and we will encounter it in both linear and nonlinear optimization models.

SOLVER TIP
Data Sensitivity or Solver Sensitivity?

It is easy to be confused as to when to use the Data Sensitivity tool and when to use the Solver Sensitivity tool. Both tools explore the results of varying an input parameter, but they answer different types of questions.

Solver Sensitivity answers questions about how the *optimal solution* changes with a change in a parameter. In this case, Solver Sensitivity varies an input parameter *and* reruns Solver to determine the optimal values of the decision variables for that parameter. The output can trace the implications for a result cell (or several result cells). However, it is not appropriate to use Solver Sensitivity unless the decision maker actually has the opportunity to optimize decisions in response to a parameter change.

The Data Sensitivity tool answers questions about how specific outputs change with a change in one or two parameters. In this case, Data Sensitivity varies an input parameter and traces the implications through the model to a result cell (or several result cells). If there are decision variables in the model, they remain fixed when the input parameter changes, and they are not re-optimized.

The Data Sensitivity tool can also be used to answer questions about how specific outputs change with a change in one or two *decision variables*. This usage amounts to a simple search for optimal decision variables. It is a form of what-if analysis that explores the change in outputs when an input is varied, where the input just happens to be a decision variable. For this purpose, Solver itself would be a more powerful tool. However, Data Sensitivity may be appropriate if we are interested in the nonoptimal values of the decision variables as well as the optimal values.   ∎

10.7*   THE PORTFOLIO OPTIMIZATION MODEL

A **portfolio** is a collection of assets. In a stock portfolio, the investor chooses the stocks, and the dollar value of each, to hold in the portfolio at the start of an investment period. Over this period, the values of the stocks may change. At the end of the period, performance can be measured by the total value of the portfolio. For a given size (or dollar value) of the portfolio, the key decision is how to allocate the portfolio among its constituent stocks.

The performance of individual stocks can be measured in two ways: return and risk. **Return** is the percentage growth in the value of the stock, and **risk** is the variability associated with the returns on the stock. The information on which stock performance is evaluated is a series of historical returns, typically compiled on a monthly basis. This history provides an empirical distribution of a stock's return performance. For stock k in the portfolio, this return distribution can be summarized by a mean (r_k) and a standard deviation (s_k).

The performance of a portfolio of stocks is also measured in terms of return and risk. When we create a portfolio of stocks, our goals are usually to maximize the mean return and to minimize the risk. Both goals cannot be met simultaneously, but we can use optimization to explore the trade-offs involved.

EXAMPLE
Advising Ms. Womack

Suppose we are providing investment advice to Ms. Womack, who has some savings to invest and very clear ideas about her preferred stocks. She has identified stocks in five different industries that she believes would constitute a good portfolio. The performance of the five stocks over the last two years is summarized by the means and standard deviations of monthly stock prices, as shown in the following table.

Stock	Mean	St. Dev.
National Computer	0.0209	0.0981
National Chemical	0.0121	0.0603
National Power	0.0069	0.0364
National Auto	0.0226	0.0830
National Electronics	0.0134	0.0499

Ms. Womack is stumped only by the question of how to allocate her investment among these five stocks. National Computer Company and National Auto Company stocks have achieved the best average returns in the two-year period, but they also have relatively high volatility, as measured by their standard deviations. National Power Company is the least volatile, but it also has the lowest average return. Ms. Womack wishes to navigate between these different extremes. Our task is to organize the quantitative information so that we can help her make the allocation decision. ∎

Figure 10.24 shows a worksheet containing the monthly returns for Ms. Womack's five stocks over the last two years. The data can be found in columns I through N. The mean returns are calculated using the AVERAGE function in cells B4:F4, and the standard deviations are calculated using the STDEV function in cells B5:F5.

The next task is to combine the individual stock behaviors into a summary for the portfolio as a whole—that is, the portfolio mean and variance. For the portfolio mean, we use a weighted average of individual stock returns. Thus, if we allocate a proportion p_k of our portfolio to stock k, then the return on the five-stock portfolio is the following weighted average:

$$R = p_1 r_1 + p_2 r_2 + p_3 r_3 + p_4 r_4 + p_5 r_5$$

This calculation lends itself to the SUMPRODUCT formula and appears in the worksheet in cell C26. The proportions themselves, highlighted as decision variables, appear in cells B15:F15, with their sum in cell G15.

For the portfolio variance, we use a standard statistical formula for the variance of a sum. For this purpose, we must know the covariance σ_{kj} between every pair of stocks (k, j). The covariance values are calculated from the historical data with Excel's COVAR function. These figures appear in the worksheet in cells B8:F12.

EXCEL TIP
The COVAR Function

The COVAR function in Excel calculates the covariance between two equal-sized sets of numbers representing observations of two variables. The covariance measures the extent to which one variable tends to rise or fall with increases and decreases in the other variable. If the two variables rise and fall in unison, their covariance is large and positive. If the two variables move in opposite directions, then their covariance is negative. If the two variables move independently, then their covariance is close to zero. The basic form of the function is the following:

COVAR(Array1,Array2)
- *Array1* references the observations of the first variable.
- *Array2* references the observations of the second variable. ∎

In cell C11 of Figure 10.24, the function COVAR($M5:$M28,$K5:$K28) finds the covariance between the returns of National Auto Company and those of National Chemical Company. In this case, the function generates the value −0.0006. The fact that it is a small number in absolute value indicates that the two sets of returns are nearly independent; the fact that it is negative indicates that there is a slight tendency for National Auto's returns to go up when National Chemical's returns go down, and vice versa.

The formula for the portfolio variance V often appears in statistics books in different but equivalent forms. Nevertheless, it is straightforward to make the

FIGURE 10.24 The Portfolio Optimization Model

	A	B	C	D	E	F	G	H
1	**Portfolio Model**							
2								
3	**Data Summary**	*Computer*	*Chemical*	*Power*	*Auto*	*Electronic*		
4	*Avg. Return*	0.0209	0.0121	0.0069	0.0226	0.0134		
5	*St. Deviation*	0.0981	0.0603	0.0364	0.0830	0.0499		
6								
7	***Covariances***						*Proportions*	
8	*Computer*	0.0092	-0.0006	0.0003	0.0026	0.0012	0.132	
9	*Chemical*	-0.0006	0.0035	0.0000	-0.0006	0.0003	0.304	
10	*Power*	0.0003	0.0000	0.0013	0.0006	-0.0001	0.158	
11	*Auto*	0.0026	-0.0006	0.0006	0.0066	0.0017	0.225	
12	*Electronic*	0.0012	0.0003	-0.0001	0.0017	0.0024	0.181	
13								
14	***Proportions***							
15		0.132	0.304	0.158	0.225	0.181	1.000	
16								
17	***Calculations***							
18		0.000161	-0.000025	0.000006	0.000077	0.000028		
19		-0.000025	0.000322	-0.000002	-0.000038	0.000016		
20		0.000006	-0.000002	0.000032	0.000020	-0.000004		
21		0.000077	-0.000038	0.000020	0.000333	0.000070		
22		0.000028	0.000016	-0.000004	0.000070	0.000078		
23								
24	*Portfolio Variance*	Risk	0.00122		Risk ceiling	0.0015		
25								
26	*Weighted Average*	Return	0.0150		Return floor	0.015		
27								
28								
29								

	I	J	K	L	M	N
1						
2	**Data**					
3						
4	Month	*Computer*	*Chemical*	*Power*	*Auto*	*Electronic*
5	1	0.22816	-0.07205	0.01730	0.22266	0.08202
6	2	0.09134	0.02588	0.05646	0.01278	-0.03499
7	3	-0.01288	-0.04771	0.02280	0.00379	0.01662
8	4	-0.17196	0.06342	0.00000	0.04101	-0.07496
9	5	0.16557	0.03670	0.00510	0.07576	-0.00810
10	6	-0.00789	0.01372	0.02244	0.06817	0.05446
11	7	-0.04909	0.05960	0.06583	-0.07143	-0.08607
12	8	0.22967	-0.02083	0.00812	-0.02564	0.01712
13	9	0.10117	0.00681	0.02360	0.12632	-0.00510
14	10	-0.10530	-0.05128	0.00865	0.16406	0.08376
15	11	-0.02767	0.04730	-0.02926	-0.05593	0.04890
16	12	0.00813	-0.01247	0.00893	0.01327	0.08498
17	13	0.05323	0.11894	-0.00885	0.15493	0.09790
18	14	0.05364	0.00197	-0.06917	-0.07317	-0.00382
19	15	-0.01818	-0.04479	-0.06473	-0.08640	-0.01546
20	16	-0.09556	0.04366	0.01384	-0.07952	0.03534
21	17	0.02459	0.08765	0.00259	0.03665	0.02402
22	18	-0.06400	-0.03260	-0.01379	-0.03535	-0.02736
23	19	0.01393	0.05736	0.06993	0.01316	0.04604
24	20	0.10971	0.08680	0.02588	-0.00260	0.05501
25	21	-0.06464	0.05025	0.00645	-0.05990	-0.00350
26	22	0.01114	-0.06070	0.01603	0.08357	-0.03981
27	23	0.01610	-0.12925	0.04076	-0.00257	-0.03415
28	24	0.01188	0.06094	-0.06442	0.01856	0.00763
29						

10.21 / 10.22 / 10.23 \ **10.24** /

calculation in Excel. The value of the product $p_k \sigma_{kj} p_j$ is computed as the (k, j)th element of the array in cells B18:F22. (For this purpose, it is convenient to replicate the proportions from row 15 in cells G8:G12.) Then the elements of this array are summed in cell C24 to form V. Thus, the risk measure V appears in cell C24, and the return measure R appears in C26.

The portfolio optimization problem is to choose the investment proportions so that we minimize risk subject to a floor (lower bound) on the return. That is, we want to minimize V subject to a minimum value of R, with the p-values as the decision variables. A value for the lower bound appears in cell F26. In the Solver Parameters window, we enter the following information.

Target cell	C24 (minimize)
Changing cells	B15 : F15
Constraints	C26 $\geq$ F26
	G15 $=$ 1

For a return floor of 1.5 percent, Solver returns the solution shown in Figure 10.24. All five stocks appear in the optimal portfolio, with allocations ranging from 30 percent of the portfolio in National Chemical to 13 percent of the portfolio in National Computer.

For this model, the worksheet layout is a little different from the others we have examined, due mainly to the close relationship between the historical data and the elements of the analysis. Note that the worksheet, as constructed, could easily be adapted to the optimization of any five-stock portfolio. For this purpose, we need only the set of returns data, which we can copy into the data section of the worksheet. For a data collection period of longer than 24 periods, the formulas for average, standard deviation, and covariance would have to be adjusted. The Calculations section separates the decision variables from the objective function, but the logic of the computations flows from Proportions to Calculations to Risk and Return.

Beyond a single optimization of the portfolio model, investors are usually interested in the trade-off between risk and return. If we minimize risk subject to a floor on the return, we can repeat the optimization for several values of the floor. This process traces out points along the so-called **efficient frontier**, which plots the best risk achievable for any desired level of return. A complementary approach is available if we maximize return subject to a ceiling on risk. Results from the Solver Sensitivity tool for these two approaches, along with summary plots, are shown in Figure 10.25. Both plots describe the same risk–return trade-off; they just happen to take slightly different forms. By exploring Ms. Womack's preferences as they play out in these graphs, we can make a more persuasive recommendation on how her investment funds should be allocated.

FIGURE 10.25 Graphs of the Efficient Frontier in the Portfolio Example

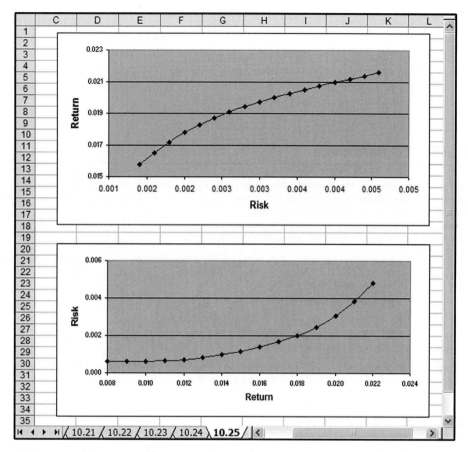

10.8 SUMMARY

We introduced optimization in Chapter 6 as one phase in a general analytic procedure for spreadsheet models. Optimization answers the question, "What's the best we can do?" or to put it more formally, "What values of the decision variables lead to the best possible value of the objective?" In a sense, optimization is simply a sophisticated tool for performing what-if analysis.

In Excel, optimization is carried out using Solver. Solver is actually a collection of optimization procedures, and in this chapter, we illustrated the use of the nonlinear solver, which is Solver's default choice.

To develop facility with Solver, it helps to practice formulating, solving, and interpreting optimization problems. Formulation and layout for optimization require some additional considerations that tend not to arise in simpler kinds of modeling, and we mentioned a number of principles that bear repeating. These are guidelines for the model builder and, in our experience, the craft skills exhibited by experts:

• Follow a standard form whenever possible.

• Enter cell references in the Solver windows; keep numerical values in cells.

• Try out some feasible (and infeasible) possibilities as a way of debugging the model and exploring the problem.

• Test intuition and suggest hypotheses before running Solver.

Along with our examples, these guidelines provide help in learning how to implement optimization analyses in spreadsheet models.

Sometimes, difficulties arise in using the nonlinear solver to find optimal solutions. The most frequent difficulties and the appropriate responses are as follows.

• The search doesn't seem to move away from the initial solution. This symptom usually indicates that the model contains some discontinuity, most likely caused by the use of one of Excel's special functions (IF, MAX, ROUND, LOOKUP, etc.). To avoid the problem, make sure that the model contains only functions that are polynomials or functions that involve the LOG or EXP functions.

• The search seems to stop at an inferior solution. This symptom occurs when the problem contains local optima. To help circumvent this difficulty, rerun the search from a number of different starting points. Doing so will either provide evidence of local optima or build confidence that a global optimum has been found.

• An infeasible solution occurs. This symptom occurs when the initial set of decision variables is infeasible, and the nonlinear solver cannot locate a feasible solution, let alone an optimal one. To avoid this problem, make sure the initial values of the decision variables are feasible in the constraints. (Very rarely, the nonlinear solver starts with a feasible solution and then goes infeasible. Should this happen, rerun with a very different starting solution.)

• Solver claims that no feasible solution exists, even when the initial values of the decision variables are feasible. This symptom suggests a scaling problem. Try rerunning after checking the Automatic Scaling check box. Occasionally,

the difficulty can be resolved by resetting the Convergence parameter on the Solver Options menu to a value 10 times larger than the default value.

Thus, a little troubleshooting effort can overcome unexpected behavior by the nonlinear solver.

SUGGESTED READINGS

Some advanced perspectives on optimization techniques, along with some guidance in constructing optimization models, can be found in several books. A partial list is given here.

A book that fleshes out the coverage in our optimization chapters, retaining an emphasis on spreadsheet modeling, is the following:

Baker, K. R. 2006. *Optimization Modeling with Spreadsheets*. Belmont, CA: Duxbury Press.

A thorough discussion of applications can be found in the following book:

Williams, H. P. 1999. *Model Building in Mathematical Programming*, 3d ed. Chichester: John Wiley & Sons.

If we want to explore alternatives to Excel as the software platform, we are drawn to algebraic modeling languages. Two

popular and accessible approaches are represented by AMPL and LINDO, described in the following books:

Fourer, R., D. F. Gay, and B. W. Kernighan. 2003. *AMPL: A Modeling Language for Mathematical Programming*. Belmont, CA: Duxbury Press.

Schrage, L. 1997. *Optimization Modeling with LINDO*, 5th ed. Belmont, CA: Duxbury Press.

For a more theoretical treatment of optimization, the following books provide up-to-date treatments:

Rardin, R. L. 1998. *Optimization in Operations Research*. Upper Saddle River, NJ: Prentice-Hall.

Winston, W. L., and M. Venkataramanan. 2003. *Introduction to Mathematical Programming*. 4th ed. Belmont, CA: Duxbury Press.

EXERCISES

1. *Location Problem (revisited)*. Return to the Kilroy Paper Company example introduced in this chapter. Upon further consideration, the logistics manager points out that the trucks do not make an equal number of trips to the various stores. Thus, a better proxy for total distribution costs would be obtained by weighting the distance from distribution center to store k by the annual number of trips to store k (represented as n_k). The expanded set of input data is as follows.

Site (k)	Coordinates		Trips
	x_k	y_k	n_k
1	5	41	12
2	20	10	20
3	44	48	15
4	60	58	27
5	100	4	8
6	138	80	16
7	150	40	10
8	170	18	18
9	182	2	25
10	190	56	14

a. Find the optimal location for Kilroy's distribution center in this expanded version of the problem.

b. What is the optimal value of the objective function?

2. *Location Problem with Two Sites*. Oliveira Office Supply has a large retail system consisting of 12 stores spread around the country, often in direct competition with Kilroy.

However, managers at Oliveira have decided to use two national distribution centers. When Oliveira's stores are mapped on the same grid as Kilroy's, the store locations occur at the coordinates listed in the following table. As in the previous exercise, there is also data to indicate how many trips are made annually to each store.

Site (k)	Coordinates		Trips
	x_k	y_k	n_k
1	2	96	21
2	5	41	12
3	20	10	20
4	44	48	15
5	60	58	27
6	100	4	8
7	122	94	21
8	138	80	16
9	150	40	10
10	170	18	18
11	182	2	25
12	190	56	14

a. Find the optimal location for Oliveira's two distribution centers in this expanded version of the problem.

b. What is the optimal value of the objective function?

3. *Cost Modeling*. General Widget Corporation has collected data on the daily output and daily production cost of widgets produced at its factory. (Data for the study are shown in the following table.) The company believes that daily output (DO) and daily production cost (PC) ought to be linearly related. Thus, for some numbers a and b:

$$PC = a + b \times DO$$

	Output	Production Cost
Day 1	5,045	2,542
Day 2	6,127	2,812
Day 3	6,360	2,776
Day 4	6,645	3,164
Day 5	7,220	4,102
Day 6	9,537	4,734
Day 7	9,895	4,238
Day 8	10,175	4,524
Day 9	10,334	4,869
Day 10	10,855	4,421

a. Build a least squares model to estimate the parameters a and b in the linear relationship. In other words, minimize the sum of squared differences between the model's predicted values and the observations. What are the best values of the parameters a and b for this criterion? What is the minimum value of the objective function? (Verify your results by using Excel's Regression tool.)

b. Suppose instead that a better criterion is thought to be minimizing the sum of absolute deviations between the model's predicted values and the observations. What are the best values of the parameters a and b for this criterion? What is the minimum value of the objective function?

c. Suppose instead that a better model than the linear model is thought to be the power function

$$PC = a(DO)^b$$

Using the sum of absolute deviations (as in the previous part), what values of a and b provide the best fit? What is the minimum value of the objective function?

4. *Curve Fitting with Constraints.* A bank's economist has been interested in developing a production function for the bank. The model recognizes three explanatory variables, which are measures of resources available to the bank. These are Labor Hours, Operating Expenses, and Capital Expenses. The response variable, which measures output activity, is a weighted average of the transactions processed by all departments in the course of a month. The economist's model takes the form:

$$Q = a_0 x_1^{a_1} x_2^{a_2} x_3^{a_3}$$

Because the fitted curve is a production function, it represents the ideal output level that could be achieved for any choice of inputs. Thus, the notion is to fit the model to actual data as well as possible, subject to the requirement that the predicted value be at least as large

as the observed value for each combination of inputs in the data set.

Branch	Labor Hours	Operating Expenses	Capital Expenses	Output
1	34,515	6,543	591	289,130
2	49,960	11,830	550	506,808
3	20,652	3,464	427	143,653
4	49,024	7,603	478	385,421
5	36,923	8,723	830	253,525
6	28,967	4,606	474	219,992
7	28,452	7,425	182	193,284
8	45,911	8,013	790	257,253
9	26,890	14,662	447	173,266
10	47,376	7,576	764	326,752
11	57,913	12,035	875	478,533
12	43,477	7,255	1,109	337,643
13	49,786	10,909	405	244,127
14	30,045	4,264	479	139,447
15	56,579	8,895	840	380,206
16	43,824	12,690	801	178,769
17	33,823	4,143	381	216,168

a. What are the best-fitting values of a_0, a_1, a_2, and a_3?

b. Using the model determined in part (a), what ideal output is predicted for Branch 2? for Branch 4?

5. *Profit Maximization with Demand Curves.* Campbell Motors is an auto dealership that specializes in the sale of station wagons and light trucks. Because of its reputation for quality and service, Campbell has a strong position in the regional market, but demand remains somewhat sensitive to price. While evaluating the new models, Campbell's marketing consultant has come up with the following demand curves:

$$Truck\ Demand = 500 - 18\,(Truck\ Price)$$
$$Wagon\ Demand = 400 - 11\,(Wagon\ Price)$$

The dealership's unit costs are \$20,000 for trucks and \$25,000 for wagons. Each truck requires three hours of prep labor, and each wagon requires two hours of prep labor. The current staff can supply 250 hours of labor.

a. Determine prices at which Campbell Motors can maximize the profit it generates from combined sales of trucks and wagons.

b. What is the marginal value of the current staff's labor hours?

6. *Allocation.* A regional beer distributor has \$100,000 to spend on advertising in four markets, where each market responds differently to advertising. Based on observations of the market's response to several advertising initiatives, the distributor has estimated the sales response by fitting a power curve $R = ax^b$, where R represents sales revenue and x represents advertising dollars, both measured in thousands. The estimated curves are described in the following table:

Market	Sales Revenue
Domestic	$100x^{0.4}$
Premium	$80x^{0.5}$
Light	$120x^{0.3}$
Microbrew	$60x^{0.6}$

a. Determine how the advertising dollars should be allocated to the four markets so that the sales revenue for the distributor is maximized.

b. If the distributor had $1,000 additional funds in the advertising budget, by how much could total revenue be increased?

c. If the distributor had $2,000 additional funds in the advertising budget beyond the base case in part (a), by how much could total revenue be increased?

d. Construct a graph showing the optimal total revenue as a function of the advertising budget, for budget sizes in the range $50,000 to $150,000.

7. *Selecting an Advertising Budget.* A well-known charity is interested in conducting a television campaign to solicit contributions. The campaign will be conducted in two metropolitan areas. Past experience indicates that, in each city, the total contributions are a function of the amount of money expended for TV advertisements. Specifically, the charity has estimated response functions that indicate the percentage of the population making a donation as a function of the dollars spent on TV advertising. The form of this function is $y = 1 - \text{EXP}(-\alpha x)$, where x represents the advertising expenditure (in thousands of dollars), y represents the percentage donating, and α is a parameter that differs from city to city. The charity has earmarked a fund of $400,000 for advertising between the two cities and wants to determine the best allocation of these funds.

	City 1	City 2
Response parameter (α)	0.006	0.004
Population	750,000	600,000
Average donation per donor	$2.00	$1.50

a. Suppose the charity decides to maximize total donations, given its budget limit on advertising. How should advertising funds be spent, and what amount will be raised in donations as a result?

b. Is the budget binding in the solution of (a)? If so, how much additional budget would the charity like to obtain? If not, how much of the budget should actually be spent?

c. Suppose the charity maximizes total donations net of the cost of advertising. (This would make sense if surplus advertising funds can be put toward the charity's other services.) From the perspective of this objective, how should advertising funds be spent, and what amount will be raised in donations as a result?

8. *Joint Ordering.* A firm uses the policy of ordering two particular items at a time because they come from the same supplier. The characteristics of these items are shown in the following table.

Item	Demand	Fixed Cost	Unit Cost	Holding Cost
1	800/year	$3	$10	30%
2	40/year	$3	$ 2	30%

a. Find the optimal cycle length for the joint orders. What are the optimal order quantities for the two items? What is the average annual cost for the two items combined?

b. Suppose the two items are managed independently, and each uses its own optimal order quantity. What is the average annual cost for the two items combined?

c. Suppose that there is a savings in the fixed cost due to joint ordering. Instead of $6, the ordering cost is only $3, because some activities cover both items. Which strategy (joint or independent) is preferable?

9. *Ordering fuels.* Three liquid fuels are stored in tanks for use in a blending process. Each fuel is characterized by a demand rate, a fixed replenishment cost, and a unit cost. Inventory carrying costs are assessed at the rate of 12 percent per year.

In order to save money on insurance rates, the operating policy is to limit the average value of stock on hand to no more than $7,500.

Fuel	Demand	Fixed Cost	Unit Cost
1	1,000/year	$100	$ 50
2	250/year	$ 75	$100
3	500/year	$ 50	$ 20

a. What are the optimal order quantities for the three items when they are ordered jointly, assuming that the fixed ordering costs are incurred for each item? What is the average annual cost for the three items combined?

b. Suppose the items are managed separately, but the overall limit on stock value still holds. What are the order quantities for the individual items? What is the average annual cost for the three items combined?

c. Suppose the stock limit in the base case is relaxed. If the limit is raised by $500, what is the impact on the optimal average annual cost?

10. *Learning-Based Production Planning.* Many labor-intensive production operations experience a learning curve effect. The learning curve specifies that the cost to produce a unit is a function of the unit number—that is, as production volume increases, the cost to produce each unit drops. One form of the learning curve is as follows: $C_i = a(i)^b$ where C_i is the cost of unit i, a is called the first unit cost, and b is the learning "slope" parameter. The total cost of producing a batch of size x can then be approximated by $(ax^{1+b})/(1 + b)$. Now consider a production setting where there is learning. We have the following single-product production planning data: demands for the next five periods are 100, 150, 300, 200, 400. Holding cost per unit per period is $0.30, and production cost follows a learning curve with $a = 15$ and $b = -0.2$.

a. Assume that there is no transfer of learning between time periods and that at most one batch is produced per time period. Solve the production planning problem of minimizing the sum of production and inventory costs, while satisfying demand. What are the optimal batch sizes?

b. Solve the same production planning problem ignoring the learning curve, that is, assume that every unit costs $15.

c. Assume we must have an ending inventory in period 5 of at least 50. Re-solve the problem in part (a). What are the optimal batch sizes? How much of a required ending inventory in period 5 induces a change in the optimal batch sizes?

11. *Curve Fitting.* Managers at Office Products, Inc. are planning their sales campaigns for the coming year. As one part of this effort, they are attempting to determine the relationship between the number of sales reps that are assigned to a product and the sales of that product. The subjective estimates of a group of experienced managers are summarized in the following table, which relates sales effort to sales.

Sales Reps	Sales (000)
50	433
75	478
100	545
125	745
150	987
175	1,156
200	1,235
225	1,288
250	1,345

a. Build a least squares model to fit an S-shaped curve to this data. An appropriate function has the form

$$Sales = b + (a - b)(Reps^c/(d + Reps^c))$$

What values of the four parameters a, b, c, and d minimize the sum of squared differences between the model's predicted values and the observations? (Note that good starting points for the four parameters are helpful in achieving a good fit.) In general, the parameter b represents the lowest level of the function and a its highest level.

b. Determine whether there are local optima in the optimization problem in part (a) by providing Solver different initial values for the four parameters.

12. *Assigning Sales Representatives.* Managers at Industrial Supply, Inc. are planning a sales campaign for the coming year in which they must determine how many sales representatives they will assign to seven product lines. S-shaped sales response functions of the form

$$\%Sales = b + (a - b)(\%Reps^c/(d + \%Reps^c))$$

have been fitted to subjective data provided by a group of experienced managers. (Both variables *Sales* and *Reps* have been measured relative to base levels. Thus %*Reps* represents the ratio between proposed reps and base reps, while %*Sales* represents the ratio between proposed sales and base sales.) The fitted values for the four parameters for each product are given in the following table.

Response Parameters				
	a	b	c	d
Product A	1.6574	0.4722	2.0322	1.1954
Product B	1.3792	0.1493	2.5622	0.4562
Product C	1.2798	0.3101	2.3345	0.4033
Product D	1.0971	0.4497	3.0420	0.1910
Product E	1.2527	0.5603	1.7734	0.5576
Product F	1.1152	0.5899	2.8685	0.2851
Product G	2.0276	0.1575	1.7337	1.0381

The following table gives the current number of reps assigned to each product and current sales, along with the contribution margin on each product. The cost of each rep is $63,000 per year.

	Current Reps	Current Sales	Contribution Margin
Product A	96.8	214,400	0.70
Product B	142.4	36,500	0.55
Product C	52.7	21,200	0.72
Product D	24.1	37,200	0.72
Product E	27.3	38,000	0.62
Product F	29.7	14,600	0.53
Product G	56.8	11,200	0.52

a. Build a financial model to calculate the total net profit over all seven product lines for any proposed allocation of reps. What is the optimal allocation of reps and resulting optimal profit if we use no more reps than we currently have?

b. What is the optimal allocation of reps and the resulting optimal profit if we can hire an unlimited number of reps?

11 Linear Programming

11.1 INTRODUCTION

In Chapter 10, we introduced optimization with Solver, and we focused on nonlinear programming. The nonlinear solver is the default algorithm in Premium Solver,[1] and it can be applied to a variety of optimization problems. *Linear programming* is a special case for which certain mathematical conditions must hold, but it is much more widely used in practice than nonlinear programming. Because of the mathematical structure of a linear program, it is possible to harness a more powerful algorithm (called the *simplex method*) for linear problems than for nonlinear problems, and we can accommodate larger numbers of variables and constraints. In this chapter, we cover the use of the linear solver, and we examine several examples that illustrate the wide applicability of linear programming models. In the 50 years or so that computers have been available for this kind of decision support, linear programming has proven to be a valuable tool for understanding business decisions.

As in the previous chapter, our optimization models contain a set of decision variables, an objective function, and a set of constraints. But in the case of linear models, we can impose additional design guidelines on our worksheets that lead to a more standardized approach than we were able to adopt with nonlinear models. These additional guidelines help us develop models efficiently, debug our models quickly, and communicate our results effectively.

11.1.1 Linearity

The term *linear* in linear programs refers to a feature of the objective function and the constraints. A linear function exhibits three properties:

- Additivity
- Proportionality
- Divisibility

By **additive**, we mean that the contribution from one decision gets added to (or sometimes subtracted from) the contributions of other decisions. In an additive function, we can separate the contributions that come from each decision. By **proportional**, we mean that the contribution from any given decision grows in proportion to the value of the corresponding decision variable. When a decision variable doubles, then its contribution to the objective also doubles. By **divisible,** we mean that a fractional decision variable is meaningful.

As an example, suppose that we compute profit from the function

$$Profit = (Unit\ Revenue) \times (Quantity\ Sold) - (Unit\ Cost) \times (Quantity\ Purchased)$$

where *Unit Revenue* and *Unit Cost* are parameters known to be 100 and 60, respectively, whereas *Quantity Sold* and *Quantity Purchased* are decisions, which

---

[1]**Premium Solver for Education** is an advanced version of the Standard Solver in Excel and is available to users of this book. It should be installed before proceeding with this chapter.

we'll denote by x and y, respectively. In symbols, we can simply write:

$$\text{Profit} = 100x - 60y$$

where x and y are decision variables. Note that *Profit* separates into two additive terms, which we can call total revenue and total cost. The total revenue term ($100x$) is proportional to the decision variable *Quantity Sold*. Likewise, the total cost term ($60y$) is proportional to the decision variable *Quantity Purchased*. Fractional values for the decisions could well make sense. Suppose, for example, that the product is fuel and that the unit of measurement is gallons. Then certainly a fractional value such as $x = 72.4$ is plausible. Even if we think of discrete items, such as televisions, the unit of measurement could be dozens, in which case a fractional value such as $x = 15.5$ would also be meaningful. In summary, our *Profit* function exhibits all three of the linearity properties.

We turn now to an algebraic perspective. When we have several decision variables, we may give them letter names, such as x, y, and z, or we may number them and denote them by x_1, x_2, x_3, and so on. When there are n decision variables, we can write a linear objective function as follows:

$$z = c_1 x_1 + c_2 x_2 + \cdots + c_n x_n$$

where z represents the value of the objective function, and the c's are a set of given parameters called **objective function coefficients**. Note that the x's appear in separate terms (i.e., they are additive), they appear with exponents of 1 (i.e., their contributions to the objective function are proportional), and they are not restricted to integers (i.e., they are divisible). In a worksheet, we recognize the structure of z as a calculation that could be made by the SUMPRODUCT function. Thus, for spreadsheet purposes, we can recognize a linear function if it consists of a sum of pairwise products—where one of the pairs in each product is a parameter and the other is a decision variable.

For a constraint to be linear, its left-hand side must be a linear function. In other words, the left-hand side can be represented by a SUMPRODUCT function made up of a sum of pairwise products, where one element of each product is a parameter and the other is a decision variable. In most cases, we will actually use the SUMPRODUCT formula, although, as we will see in the next chapter, we sometimes prefer the SUM formula.

EXCEL TIP
The
SUMPRODUCT
Function

The SUMPRODUCT function in Excel takes the pairwise products of two sets of numbers and sums the products. This operation is sometimes called the scalar product. For our purposes, the form of the function is the following:

SUMPRODUCT(*Array1, Array2*)

- *Array1* references the first set of numbers.
- *Array2* references the second set of numbers.

The two arrays must have identical layouts. Specifically, if *Array1* comprises a set of numbers in a single row, then *Array2* must also be a set of numbers in a single row. Both arrays must be of the same size.

Suppose, for example, that we had three items with unit prices of 2, 3, and 4 and with sales volumes of u, v, and w, respectively. Then total revenue would come to $2u + 3v + 4w$, which could be computed from the formula SUMPRODUCT($\{2,3,4\}, \{u, v, w\}$). When the volumes are $u = 30$, $v = 33$, and $w = 36$, the total revenue function takes on the value 303. ∎

11.1.2 Simplex Algorithm

The solution procedure for linear models is referred to as the **simplex algorithm**, or the linear solver. The simplex algorithm employs a strategy that shares some of the features of hill climbing, but it is able to exploit the special properties of linearity to find an optimal solution efficiently. For instance, if we can imagine a diamond that represents the set of feasible decision variables, then the simplex algorithm can be viewed as a procedure for moving along the edges of the diamond's surface until an optimal point is encountered. The simplex algorithm does not require a starting point in the worksheet; or to put it another way, it determines its own starting solution. This means that Solver ignores the initial information in the changing cells when solving a linear model. Once the solution procedure finds a **feasible solution**—one that satisfies all the constraints—it proceeds from there to an optimal solution. An **optimal solution** must satisfy all constraints, and its objective function must equal the best value that can be achieved. Moreover, the simplex method *guarantees* that it will find a global optimum (if there is one), and in that sense, the simplex method is completely reliable. We cannot say the same for the GRG algorithm except in special circumstances.

In mathematical terms, linear models are a special case of nonlinear models, and in principle, the GRG algorithm could be used as a solution procedure for the examples we present here. However, the simplex algorithm is especially suited to linear models, and it avoids numerical problems that sometimes affect the performance of the GRG algorithm. The linear solver is the preferred choice for any linear programming problem.

Linear programming models come in many sizes and shapes, but there are only a few standard types. It is helpful, therefore, to think in terms of a few basic structures when learning how to build and interpret linear programming models. In this chapter and the next, we present four different types. Most linear programming models are, in fact, combinations of these four types, but understanding the building blocks helps to clarify the key modeling concepts. In our framework, the four types are

- Allocation models
- Covering models
- Blending models
- Network models

We cover network models separately in Chapter 12.

11.2 ALLOCATION MODELS

The allocation model calls for maximizing an objective (usually profit) subject to less-than constraints on capacity. Consider the Veerman Furniture Company as an example.

EXAMPLE
Veerman Furniture Company

Veerman Furniture Company makes three kinds of office furniture: chairs, desks, and tables. Each product requires some labor in the parts fabrication department, the assembly department, and the shipping department. The furniture is sold through a regional distributor, which has estimated the maximum potential sales for each product in the coming quarter. Finally, the accounting department has provided some data showing the profit contributions on each product. The decision problem is to determine the product mix—that is, to maximize Veerman's profit for the quarter by choosing production quantities for the chairs, desks, and tables. The data shown in the accompanying table summarize the parameters of the problem:

| Department | Hours per Unit | | | Hours Available |
	Chairs	Desks	Tables	
Fabrication	4	6	2	1,850
Assembly	3	5	7	2,400
Shipping	3	2	4	1,500
Demand Potential	360	300	100	
Profit	$15	$24	$18	

∎

11.2.1 Formulation

As recommended in the previous chapter, we approach the formulation of the optimization model by asking three basic questions. To determine the decision variables, we ask, "What must be decided?" The answer is the product mix, so we define decision variables as the number of chairs, desks, and tables produced. For the purposes of notation, we use C, D, and T to represent the number of chairs, desks, and tables in the product mix, respectively.

Next we ask, "What measure can we use to compare alternative sets of decision variables?" To choose between two different product mixes, we would calculate the total profit contribution for each one and choose the higher profit. To calculate profit, we add the profit from chairs, from desks, and from tables. Thus, an algebraic expression for total profit is:

$$\text{Profit} = 15C + 24D + 18T$$

To identify the model's constraints, we ask, "What restrictions limit our choice of decision variables?" In this scenario, there are two kinds of limitations: one due to production capacity and the other due to demand potential. In words, a production capacity constraint states that the number of hours *consumed* in the fabrication department must be less than or equal to the number of hours *available*. In symbols, we write:

Fabrication hours consumed $= 4C + 6D + 2T \leq 1{,}850$ (Fabrication hours available)

Similar constraints hold for the assembly and shipping departments:

Assembly hours consumed $= 3C + 5D + 7T \leq 2{,}400$ (Assembly hours available)

Shipping hours consumed $= 3C + 2D + 4T \leq 1{,}500$ (Shipping hours available)

Another type of constraint relates to demands. We require that the number of chairs *produced* must be less than or equal to the estimated demand *potential* for chairs. In symbols, we write:

Chairs produced $= C \leq 360$ (Chair demand potential)

Similar constraints hold for desks and tables:

Desks produced $= D \leq 300$ (Desk demand potential)

Table produced $= T \leq 100$ (Table demand potential)

We now have six constraints that describe the restrictions limiting our choice of decision variables C, D, and T. The entire model, stated in algebraic terms, reads as follows:

$$\text{Maximize } z = 15C + 24D + 18T$$

subject to

$$4C + 6D + 2T \leq 1{,}850$$
$$3C + 5D + 7T \leq 2{,}400$$
$$3C + 2D + 4T \leq 1{,}500$$
$$C \qquad\qquad\ \leq\ 360$$
$$D \qquad\ \leq\ 300$$
$$T \leq\ 100$$

11.2.2 Spreadsheet Model

This algebraic statement reflects a widely used format for linear programs. Variables appear in columns, constraints appear as rows, and the objective function appears as a special row at the top of the model. We will adopt this layout as a standard for spreadsheet display.

FIGURE 11.1 Spreadsheet Model for the Veerman Furniture Company Example

	A	B	C	D	E	F	G	H
1	Allocation: Furniture Production							
2								
3	Decision Variables							
4			C	D	T			
5	Product mix	100	200	50				
6								
7	Objective Function				Total			
8	Profit	15	24	18	$7,200			
9								
10	Constraints				LHS		RHS	
11	Fabrication	4	6	2	1700	<=	1850	Not Binding
12	Assembly	3	5	7	1650	<=	2400	Not Binding
13	Shipping	3	2	4	900	<=	1500	Not Binding
14	Chair market	1	0	0	100	<=	360	Not Binding
15	Desk market	0	1	0	200	<=	300	Not Binding
16	Table market	0	0	1	50	<=	100	Not Binding
17								

A worksheet for this allocation problem appears in Figure 11.1[*]. Notice the three modules in the worksheet:

- A highlighted row for the decision variables (B5:D5)
- A highlighted single cell for the objective function value (E8)
- A set of constraint relationships (rows 11–16).

In the Constraints module, cells containing the symbol ≤ have no function in the operation of the worksheet; they are intended as a visual aid, helping to convey a sense of the information in the constraints. We place them between the left-hand-side value of the constraint (a formula) and the right-hand-side value (a parameter). To the right of each constraint parameter, we construct a cell that displays the status of the constraint. In cell H11, for example, the formula is IF(E11=G11, "Binding", "Not Binding"). The constraint is **binding** if it is satisfied as an equality; otherwise, it is nonbinding. (Although this status indicator is a desirable feature of linear programming models for most beginners, we will often omit it, so that we can focus on the information in the constraints themselves.)

Figure 11.2 shows the formulas in this model. Note here that, aside from labels, the model contains only two kinds of cells: those containing a number (either a parameter or a decision variable) and those containing a SUMPRODUCT formula.

The set of values for the decision variables in Figure 11.1 was an arbitrary one. We could try different sets of three values in order to see whether we could come up with a good product mix by trial and error. Such an attempt might also be a useful debugging step, to provide some assurance that the model is correct. For example, suppose we start by fixing the number of desks and tables at zero and varying the number of chairs. For fabrication capacity, chairs consume 4 hours each, and there are 1,850 hours available, so we could put $1{,}850/4 = 462.5$ chairs

FIGURE 11.2 Formulas in the Veerman Furniture Company Worksheet

	A	B	C	D	E	F	G	H
1	Allocation: Furniture							
2								
3	Decision Variables							
4			C	D	T			
5	Product mix	100	200	50				
6								
7	Objective Function				Total			
8	Profit	15	24	18	=SUMPRODUCT($B$5:$D$5,B8:D8)			
9								
10	Constraints				LHS		RHS	
11	Fabrication	4	6	2	=SUMPRODUCT($B$5:$D$5,B11:D11)	<=	1850	=IF(E11=G11,"Binding","Not Binding")
12	Assembly	3	5	7	=SUMPRODUCT($B$5:$D$5,B12:D12)	<=	2400	=IF(E12=G12,"Binding","Not Binding")
13	Shipping	3	2	4	=SUMPRODUCT($B$5:$D$5,B13:D13)	<=	1500	=IF(E13=G13,"Binding","Not Binding")
14	Chair market	1	0	0	=SUMPRODUCT($B$5:$D$5,B14:D14)	<=	360	=IF(E14=G14,"Binding","Not Binding")
15	Desk market	0	1	0	=SUMPRODUCT($B$5:$D$5,B15:D15)	<=	300	=IF(E15=G15,"Binding","Not Binding")
16	Table market	0	0	1	=SUMPRODUCT($B$5:$D$5,B16:D16)	<=	100	=IF(E16=G16,"Binding","Not Binding")
17								

[*]To download spreadsheets for this chapter, go to the Student Companion Site at www.wiley.com/college/powell.

into the mix (that is, into cell B5), and the result would be feasible for the first constraint. However, we can see immediately—by comparing LHS and RHS values—that this solution violates the ceiling on chair demand. So we can reduce the number of chairs to 360, which will give us a feasible product mix and a profit of $5,400. (Recall that a feasible solution must satisfy *all* constraints.) Keeping the number of chairs fixed, we can now add desks to the product mix (by entering a number into cell C5). Using trial and error (or Excel's Goal Seek tool), we can determine that it is possible to raise the number of desks to 68, achieving a profit of $7,032. However, this choice consumes all of the remaining fabrication capacity, leaving no room for tables in the product mix. Similar kinds of explorations, with other values of the decision variables, can help us confirm that the model is working properly and give us a feel for the profit that might be achievable. Although we will not discuss this step as we build other models in this chapter, we wouldn't skip it unless we were dealing with a familiar type of problem.

11.2.3 Optimization

Once we are satisfied that the model is valid, we proceed to the optimization procedure. We invoke Solver, and in the Solver Parameters window, we specify:

Target cell	E8 (maximize)
Changing cells	B5:D5
Constraints	E11:E16 ≤ G11:G16

Note that in this last step, we reference parameters that have been entered in the worksheet. We usually do *not* enter the right-hand side constants in the Add Constraint window, even though Solver permits us to do so.

We select the linear solver (Standard LP Simplex) from the pull-down menu in the Solver Parameters window (see Figure 11.3). Next, we proceed to the Options menu and check the box for Assume Non-Negative, as in Figure 11.4. Our decision variables will be meaningful in this model only if they are nonnegative.

Before running Solver, we should create some hypotheses about the solution. For example,

- Do we expect the optimal solution to call for all three products?

- Will the optimal solution consume all of the available hours?

- Should desks, which have the highest profit margin, be produced at the maximum amount the market allows?

As we mentioned earlier, this is an excellent opportunity to test our intuition by posing and trying to answer such questions.

As we see in Figure 11.5, the optimal solution calls for no chairs, 275 desks, and 100 tables. Evidently, the profit margin on chairs is not sufficiently attractive for us to want to devote scarce resources to their production. The maximum profit contribution is $8,400, and the two binding constraints are fabrication hours and the demand ceiling

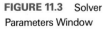

FIGURE 11.3 Solver Parameters Window

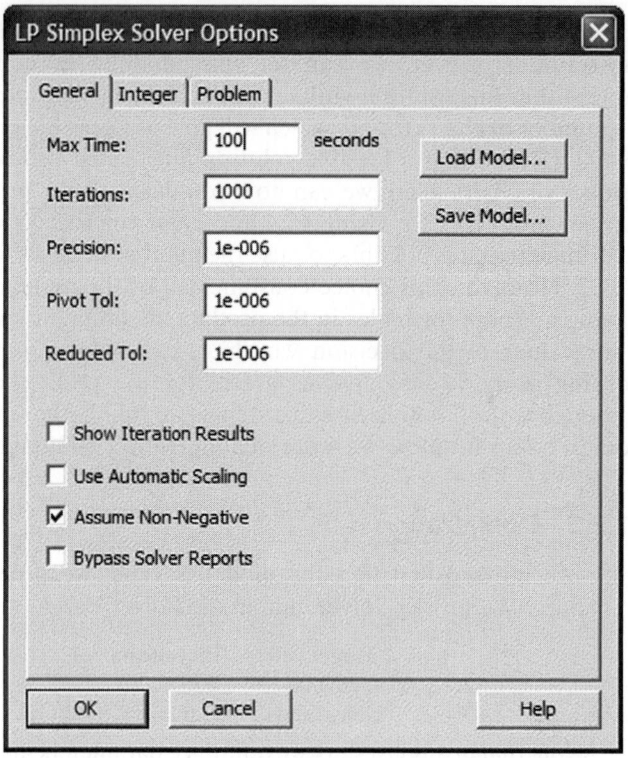

FIGURE 11.4 Solver
Options Window

FIGURE 11.5 Optimal
Solution for the Veerman
Furniture Company Model

	A	B	C	D	E	F	G	H
1	**Allocation: Furniture Production**							
2								
3	**Decision Variables**							
4			C	D	T			
5	Product mix	0	275	100				
6								
7	**Objective Function**				*Total*			
8	Profit	15	24	18	$8,400			
9								
10	**Constraints**				*LHS*		*RHS*	
11	Fabrication	4	6	2	1850	<=	1850	Binding
12	Assembly	3	5	7	2075	<=	2400	Not Binding
13	Shipping	3	2	4	950	<=	1500	Not Binding
14	Chair market	1	0	0	0	<=	360	Not Binding
15	Desk market	0	1	0	275	<=	300	Not Binding
16	Table market	0	0	1	100	<=	100	Binding
17								

for tables. (We also have unused time in assembly and shipping and unmet demand in chairs and desks.) These results—decision variables, objective function, and binding constraints—are the three key pieces of information provided in the solution.

Recall the distinction made in Chapter 10 between tactical and strategic information in the solution to an optimization problem. If we are faced with implementing a production plan for the next quarter at Veerman Furniture, we would pursue the tactical solution, producing no chairs, 275 desks, and 100 tables. (We might first want to make sure that our marketing department approves the idea of bringing a limited range of products to the market in order to maximize short-term profits. This is one of the places where the simplifications in a model must be assessed against the realities of the actual situation.) On the other hand, if there is time to adjust the resources available at Veerman Furniture, we should explore the possibility of acquiring more fabrication capacity or expanding the demand potential for tables, as these are the binding constraints. In addition, if there is time to adjust marketing policies, we might also want to look into the possibility of raising the price on chairs.

11.3 COVERING MODELS

The covering model calls for minimizing an objective (usually cost) subject to greater-than constraints on required coverage. Consider Dahlby Outfitters as an example.

EXAMPLE
Dahlby Outfitters

Dahlby Outfitters wishes to introduce a packaged trail mix as a new product. The ingredients for the trail mix are seeds, raisins, flakes, and two kinds of nuts. Each ingredient contains certain amounts of vitamins, minerals, protein, and calories. The marketing department has specified that the product be designed so that a certain minimum nutritional profile is met. The decision problem is to determine the optimal product composition—that is, to minimize the product cost by choosing the amount for each of the ingredients in the mix. The data shown in the accompanying table summarize the parameters of the problem.

| | Grams per Pound | | | | | Nutritional |
Component	Seeds	Raisins	Flakes	Pecans	Walnuts	Requirement
Vitamins	10	20	10	30	20	20
Minerals	5	7	4	9	2	10
Protein	1	4	10	2	1	15
Calories	500	450	160	300	500	600
Cost/pound	$4	$5	$3	$7	$6	

■

11.3.1 Formulation

What must be decided? Here, the answer is the amount of each ingredient to put into a package of trail mix. For the purposes of notation, we use S, R, F, P, and W to represent the number of pounds of each ingredient in a package.

What measure will we use to compare sets of decision variables? This should be the total cost of a package, and our goal is the lowest possible total cost. To calculate the total cost of a particular composition, we add the cost of each ingredient in the package:

$$Cost = 4S + 5R + 3F + 7P + 6W$$

What restrictions limit our choice of decision variables? In this scenario, the main limitation is the requirement to meet the specified nutritional profile. Each dimension of this profile gives rise to a separate constraint. An example of such a constraint would state, in words, that the number of grams of vitamins *provided* in the package must be greater than or equal to the number of grams *required* by the specified profile. In symbols, we write:

$$Vitamin\ content = 10S + 20R + 10F + 30P + 20W \geq 20 \text{ (Vitamin floor)}$$

Similar constraints must hold for the remainder of the profile:

$$Mineral\ content = 5S + 7R + 4F + 9P + 2W \geq 10 \text{ (Mineral floor)}$$
$$Protein\ content = 1S + 4R + 10F + 2P + 1W \geq 15 \text{ (Protein floor)}$$
$$Calorie\ content = 500S + 450R + 160F + 300P + 500W \geq 600 \text{ (Calorie floor)}$$

In this basic scenario, no other constraints occur, although we could imagine that there might also be limited quantities of the ingredients available, expressed as less-than constraints, or a weight requirement for the package, expressed as an equality constraint. Putting the algebraic statement together in one place, we obtain the following model.

$$\text{Minimize } z = 4S + 5R + 3F + 7P + 6W$$

subject to

$$10S + 20R + 10F + 30P + 20W \geq 20$$
$$5S + 7R + 4F + 9P + 2W \geq 10$$
$$1S + 4R + 10F + 2P + 1W \geq 15$$
$$500S + 450R + 160F + 300P + 500W \geq 600$$

FIGURE 11.6 Worksheet for the Dahlby Outfitters Model

	A	B	C	D	E	F	G	H	I	J
1	Covering: Trail Mix Composition									
2										
3	Decision Variables									
4		S	R	F	P	W				
5	Amounts	0.50	0.40	0.30	0.70	0.20				
6										
7	Objective Function						Total			
8	Cost	4	5	3	7	6	$11.00			
9										
10	Constraints						LHS		RHS	
11	Vitamins	10	20	10	30	20	41	>=	20	Not Binding
12	Minerals	5	7	4	9	2	13.2	>=	10	Not Binding
13	Protein	1	4	10	2	1	6.7	>=	15	Not Binding
14	Calories	500	450	160	300	500	788	>=	600	Not Binding
15										

11.1 / 11.2 / 11.5 \ **11.6** /

11.3.2 Spreadsheet Model

A worksheet for this model appears in Figure 11.6. Again, we see three modules:

- A highlighted row for the decision variables (B5:F5)
- A highlighted single cell for the objective function value (G8)
- A set of constraint relationships (rows 11–14).

If we were to display the formulas in this worksheet, we would again see that the model is made up of only numbers and cells containing the SUMPRODUCT formula.

11.3.3 Optimization

Once we are satisfied that the model is valid, we proceed to the optimization procedure. We invoke Solver and specify:

Target cell	G8 (minimize)
Changing cells	B5:F5
Constraints	G11:G14 ≤ I11:I14

We select the linear solver and, in the Options menu, check the box for Assume Non-Negative. After contemplating some hypotheses about the problem (for example, will the solution require all five ingredients?), we run Solver and obtain a solution. The optimal solution, shown in Figure 11.7, calls for 1.32 pounds of flakes, 0.33 pound of raisins, and 0.48 pound of seeds, with no nuts at all. Evidently, nuts are prohibitively expensive, given the nature of the required nutritional profile and the other ingredients available. The optimal mix achieves all of the nutritional requirements at a minimum cost of $7.54. The three binding constraints in this solution are the requirements for minerals, protein, and calories.

Of course, we might decide that a trail mix without nuts is not an appealing product. If we wish, we can amend the model in order to force nuts into the optimal mix. One way to do so is to specify a minimum amount of nuts. In Figure 11.8, we show an amended model that requires at least 0.15 pound of *each* ingredient. The value of

FIGURE 11.7 Optimal Solution for the Dahlby Outfitters Model

	A	B	C	D	E	F	G	H	I	J
1	Covering: Trail Mix Composition									
2										
3	Decision Variables									
4		S	R	F	P	W				
5	Amounts	0.48	0.33	1.32	0.00	0.00				
6										
7	Objective Function						Total			
8	Cost	4	5	3	7	6	$7.54			
9										
10	Constraints						LHS		RHS	
11	Vitamins	10	20	10	30	20	24.642	>=	16	Not Binding
12	Minerals	5	7	4	9	2	10	>=	10	Binding
13	Protein	1	4	10	2	1	15	>=	15	Binding
14	Calories	500	450	160	300	500	600	>=	600	Binding
15										

11.1 / 11.2 / 11.5 / 11.6 \ **11.7** /

FIGURE 11.8 Worksheet for the Amended Dahlby Outfitters Model

FIGURE 11.9 Optimal Solution for the Amended Dahlby Outfitters Model

0.15 is placed in row 6, just below the corresponding decision variable. In the Solver Parameters window, we add the constraint that the range B5:F5 must be greater than or equal to the range B6:F6. A requirement that a particular decision variable must be greater than or equal to a given value is called a **lower bound** constraint. Similarly, a requirement that a particular decision variable must be less than or equal to a given value would be called an **upper bound** constraint. It is usually convenient to locate the upper or lower bound on the worksheet in close proximity to the corresponding decision variable, as we have done in row 6.

After including the lower bound constraints, a new run of Solver produces the optimal solution shown in Figure 11.9. Note that the lower bounds create an optimal solution that contains all five of the ingredients, as expected. We might have anticipated that nuts would appear at their lower limit, because before we added the lower bound constraints, the optimization process kept nuts completely out of the mix. The cost is also higher in the amended model than in the original, at $8.33. This fact reflects an intuitive principle that complements the one we stated earlier: *When we add constraints to a model, the objective function cannot improve.* In most cases, as in this example, the objective function will get worse when we add a constraint.

11.4 BLENDING MODELS

Blending relationships are very common in linear programming applications, yet they remain difficult for beginners to identify in problem descriptions and to implement in spreadsheet models. Because of this difficulty, we begin with a special case—the representation of proportions. As an example, let's return to the product mix example of Veerman Furniture which was introduced earlier in this chapter. Recall from Figure 11.5 that the optimal product mix consisted of no chairs, 275 desks, and 100 tables. Suppose that this outcome is unacceptable because of the imbalance in volumes. For more balance, the marketing department might require that each of the products must make up at least 25 percent of the total units sold.

11.4.1 Blending Constraints

When we describe outcomes in terms of proportions, and when we place a floor (or ceiling) on one or more of those proportions, we are using blending constraints of a special type. Because the total number of units sold is $C + D + T$, a direct statement of the requirement for chairs is the following.

$$\frac{C}{C + D + T} \geq 0.25 \tag{11.1}$$

This greater-than constraint has a parameter on the right-hand side and all the decision variables on the left-hand side, as is usually the case. Although this is a valid constraint, it is not in *linear* form, because the quantities C, D, and T appear in both the numerator and denominator of the fraction. (In effect, the ratio divides decision variables by decision variables.) However, with a bit of algebra we can convert the nonlinear inequality to a linear one. First, multiply both sides of the inequality by $(C + D + T)$, yielding:

$$C \geq 0.25(C + D + T)$$

Next, collect terms involving the decision variables on the left-hand side, so that we get:

$$0.75C - 0.25D - 0.25T \geq 0 \tag{11.2}$$

This form conveys the same requirement as the original fractional constraint, and we recognize it immediately as a linear form. The coefficients on the left-hand side of (11.8) turn out to be either the complement of the floor $(1 - 0.25)$ or the floor itself (but with a minus sign). In a similar fashion, the requirement that the other products must respect the floor leads to the following two constraints.

$$-0.25C + 0.75D - 0.25T \geq 0$$
$$-0.25C - 0.25D + 0.75T \geq 0$$

Appending these three constraints to the product mix model (in rows 17–19) gives rise to the linear program described in Figure 11.10. Note that the first of the three new constraints is not satisfied by the existing solution. A Solver run produces the solution in Figure 11.11, where we can see that the new optimal mix becomes 100 chairs, 200 desks, and 100 tables. Thus, swapping chairs and tables for desks in the product mix, we can achieve the best possible level of profit, at $8,100. Also, as we might have expected, chairs comprise exactly 25 percent of the optimal output in this solution.

Whenever we encounter a constraint in the form of a lower limit or an upper limit on a proportion, we can take the following steps:

FIGURE 11.10 Product Mix Model with Added Constraints

	A	B	C	D	E	F	G
1	Allocation: Furniture Production						
2							
3	Decision Variables						
4			C	D	T		
5	Product mix	0	275	100			
6							
7	Objective Function				Total		
8	Profit	15	24	18	$8,400		
9							
10	Constraints				LHS		RHS
11	Fabrication	4	6	2	1850	<=	1850
12	Assembly	3	5	7	2075	<=	2400
13	Distribution	3	2	4	950	<=	1500
14	Chair market	1	0	0	0	<=	360
15	Desk market	0	1	0	275	<=	300
16	Table market	0	0	1	100	<=	100
17	Chair fraction	0.75	-0.25	-0.25	-93.75	>=	0
18	Desk fraction	-0.25	0.75	-0.25	181.25	>=	0
19	Table fraction	-0.25	-0.25	0.75	6.25	>=	0
20							

FIGURE 11.11 Optimal Solution to the Product Mix Model with Added Constraints

	A	B	C	D	E	F	G
1	Allocation: Furniture Production						
2							
3	Decision Variables						
4			C	D	T		
5	Product mix	100	200	100			
6							
7	Objective Function				Total		
8	Profit	15	24	18	$8,100		
9							
10	Constraints				LHS		RHS
11	Fabrication	4	6	2	1800	<=	1850
12	Assembly	3	5	7	2000	<=	2400
13	Distribution	3	2	4	1100	<=	1500
14	Chair market	1	0	0	100	<=	360
15	Desk market	0	1	0	200	<=	300
16	Table market	0	0	1	100	<=	100
17	Chair fraction	0.75	-0.25	-0.25	0	>=	0
18	Desk fraction	-0.25	0.75	-0.25	100	>=	0
19	Table fraction	-0.25	-0.25	0.75	0	>=	0
20							

⏮ ◀ ▶ ⏭ / 11.5 / 11.6 / 11.7 / 11.8 / 11.9 / 11.10 \ **11.11** / ◀ ▶

1. Write the fraction that expresses the constrained proportion.
2. Write the inequality implied by the lower bound or upper bound.
3. Multiply both sides of the inequality by the denominator and collect terms.
4. The result is a linear inequality, ready to incorporate in the model.

In Step 3, it is not actually necessary to collect terms because Solver allows us to leave a SUMPRODUCT formula on both sides of the inequality. However, we recommend collecting terms so that the variables appear on the left-hand side of the inequality and a constant appears on the right. This format is consistent with allocation and blending constraints and may make it easier to debug a model.

In general, the blending model involves mixing materials with different individual properties and describing the properties of the blend with weighted averages. We might be familiar with the phenomenon of mixing if we have spent time in a chemistry lab mixing fluids with different concentrations, but the concept extends beyond lab work. Consider the Diaz Coffee Company as an example.

EXAMPLE
The Diaz Coffee Company

The Diaz Coffee Company blends three types of coffee beans (Brazilian, Colombian, and Peruvian) into ground coffee to be sold at retail. Suppose that each kind of bean has a distinctive aroma and strength, and the company has a chief taster who can rate these features on a scale of 1 to 100. The features of the beans are tabulated as follows.

Bean	Aroma Rating	Strength Rating	Cost/lb.	Pounds Available
Brazilian	75	15	$0.50	150,000
Colombian	60	20	$0.60	120,000
Peruvian	85	18	$0.70	200,000

The company would like to create a blend that has an aroma rating of at least 78 and a strength rating of at least 16. Its supplies of the various beans are limited, however. The available quantities are specified above. All beans are delivered under a previously arranged purchase agreement. Diaz wants to make 4,000,000 pounds of the blend at the lowest possible cost. ∎

11.4.2 Formulation

Suppose, for example, that we blend Brazilian and Peruvian beans in equal quantities of 25 pounds each. Then we should expect the blend to have an aroma rating of 80, just halfway between the two pure ratings of 75 and 85. Mathematically, we take the weighted average of the two ratings:

$$\text{Aroma rating} = \frac{25(75) + 25(85)}{25 + 25} = 80$$

Now suppose that we blend the beans in amounts B, C, and P. The blend will have an aroma rating calculated by a weighted average of the three ratings, as follows:

$$\text{Aroma rating} = \frac{B(75) + C(60) + P(85)}{B + C + P}$$

To impose a constraint that requires an aroma rating of at least 78, we write:

$$\frac{B(75) + C(60) + P(85)}{B + C + P} \geq 78 \qquad (11.3)$$

This greater-than constraint has a parameter on the right-hand side of (11.2) and all the decision variables on the left-hand side, as is usually the case. Although this is a valid constraint, it is not in *linear* form, because the quantities B, C, and P appear in both the numerator and denominator of the fraction. If we were to include this form of the constraint in Solver, we would be forced to use the nonlinear solver to get a solution. However, we can convert the nonlinear inequality to a linear one by following the steps listed earlier and thus satisfy the linear solver. First, multiply both sides of the inequality by $(B + C + P)$, yielding:

$$75B + 60C + 85P \geq 78(B + C + P)$$

Next, collect terms on the left-hand side, so that we get:

$$-3B - 18C + 7P \geq 0 \qquad (11.4)$$

This form conveys the same requirement as the original fractional constraint in (11.3), and we recognize it immediately as a linear constraint. The coefficients on the left-hand side turn out to be just the *differences* between the individual aroma ratings $(75, 60, 85)$ and the requirement of 78, with the signs indicating whether the individual rating is above or below the target. In a similar fashion, a requirement that the strength of the blend must be at least 16 leads to the constraint

$$-1B + 4C + 2P \geq 0$$

Thus, blending requirements are stated initially as fractions in (11.1) and (11.3), and in that form, they lead to nonlinear constraints. We are interested in converting these to linear constraints, as in (11.2) and (11.4), because with a linear model, we can harness the power of the linear solver. As discussed earlier, this means that we can find a global optimum reliably.

Now, with an idea of how to incorporate the blending requirements, we return to our scenario.

- What must be decided? The decision variables are the quantities to purchase, which we can continue to represent as B, C, and P. However, due to the scale of the model, it is convenient to take the dimensions of these three quantities to be thousands of pounds.

- What measure will we use? Evidently, it is the total purchase cost of meeting our 4 million pound requirement.

- What restrictions must we meet? In addition to the blending constraints, we need a constraint that generates a 4 million pound blend, along with three constraints that limit the supplies of the different beans.

11.4.3 Spreadsheet Model

Figure 11.12 shows the spreadsheet for our model, which contains a greater-than constraint and three less-than constraints, in addition to the blending constraints. In addition, the model has been scaled by taking the supply and output constraints, as well as the decision variables, to be in thousands of pounds. The three decision variables have been set arbitrarily to 100,000 in the figure. In a sense, the model has two key blending constraints, and it also has what we might think of as covering and

FIGURE 11.12 Worksheet for the Diaz Coffee Company Model

	A	B	C	D	E	F	G	H
1	Blending: Coffee beans							
2								
3	Decision Variables							
4		B	C	P				
5	Inputs	100	100	100			in '000	
6								
7	Objective Function				Total			
8	Cost	0.50	0.60	0.70	$180		in '000	
9								
10	Constraints				LHS		RHS	
11	Blend aroma	-3	-18	7	-1400	>=	0	Not Binding
12	Blend strength	-1	4	2	500	>=	0	Not Binding
13	Output	1	1	1	300	>=	4000	Not Binding
14	B-supply	1	0	0	100	<=	1500	Not Binding
15	C-supply	0	1	0	100	<=	1200	Not Binding
16	P-supply	0	0	1	100	<=	2000	Not Binding
17	Actual aroma	75	60	85	73.3		78	
18	Actual strength	15	20	18	17.7		16	
19								

⏮ ◀ ▶ ⏭ \ 11.5 / 11.6 / 11.7 / 11.8 / 11.9 / 11.10 / 11.11 \ **11.12** / ◀ ▶

allocation constraints. Each of the constraints takes the same form: a SUMPRODUCT formula on the left-hand side and a parameter on the right-hand side. Note that this model contains both less-than and greater-than constraints, and it is helpful, when filling in the Solver Parameters window, to keep like constraints together.

Notice that the Output constraint requires that we produce *at least* 4 million pounds, not *exactly* 4 million pounds. Thus, as formulated here, there is some flexibility in the Output constraint. Although Diaz wishes to produce 4 million pounds, our model allows the production of a larger quantity if this will reduce costs. (Our intuition probably tells us that we should be able to minimize costs with a 400,000-pound blend, but we would accept a solution that lowered cost while producing more than this amount because we could simply throw away the excess and remain better off.) In many situations, it is a good idea to use the weaker form of a constraint, giving the model some additional flexibility and avoiding equality constraints. In other words, *we build the model with some latitude in satisfying the constraints of the decision problem, whenever possible.* The solution will either confirm our intuition (as this one does) or else teach us a lesson about the limitations of our intuition.

11.4.4 Optimization

We now invoke Solver and specify:

Target cell	E8 (maximize)
Changing cells	B5:D5
Constraints	E11:E13 ≥ G11:G13
	E14:E16 ≤ G14:G16

We select the linear solver and check the box for Assume Non-Negative. When we run Solver, we obtain the optimal blend of 1,500,000 pounds of Brazilian, 520,000 pounds of Colombian, and 1,980,000 pounds of Peruvian beans, for a total cost of $2.448 million (see Figure 11.13). Of the two blending constraints, only the first (aroma) constraint is binding; the optimal blend actually has better-than-required strength. The output constraint is also binding (consistent with our intuitive expectation), as is the limit on Brazilian supply.

In Figure 11.13, which displays the optimal solution, rows 17 and 18 on the worksheet are strictly speaking not part of our Solver model. (In other words, the model's constraints and objective function are not influenced by the calculations in these two rows.) Instead, they provide a more conventional calculation of the blended properties, and we include them simply for convenience when interpreting the results. Thus, where the first constraint of the model (row 11) is binding, the aroma calculation in row 17 shows that the weighted average exactly equals the requirement of 78. Although the second constraint (row 12) shows that the strength requirement is not binding, the comparison of the left-hand side (4,540) with the right-hand side

FIGURE 11.13   Optimal Solution for the Diaz Coffee Company Model

	A	B	C	D	E	F	G	H
1	Blending: Coffee beans							
2								
3	Decision Variables							
4		B	C	P				
5	Inputs	1500	520	1980			in '000	
6								
7	Objective Function				Total			
8	Cost	0.50	0.60	0.70	$2,448		in '000	
9								
10	Constraints				LHS		RHS	
11	Blend aroma	-3	-18	7	0	>=	0	Binding
12	Blend strength	-1	4	2	4540	>=	0	Not Binding
13	Output	1	1	1	4000	>=	4000	Binding
14	B-supply	1	0	0	1500	<=	1500	Binding
15	C-supply	0	1	0	520	<=	1200	Not Binding
16	P-supply	0	0	1	1980	<=	2000	Not Binding
17	Actual aroma	75	60	85	78.0		78	
18	Actual strength	15	20	18	17.1		16	
19								

11.5 / 11.6 / 11.7 / 11.8 / 11.9 / 11.10 / 11.11 / 11.12 / **11.13** /

(zero) may not be very useful. However, the last row of the worksheet shows that the optimal blend's strength is 17.1 (see cell E18), giving us a clearer sense of the cushion between the strength achieved and the requirement of 16.

SOLVER TIP
Rescaling the Model

Rescaling the decisions and parameters of a model—using thousands or even millions as a unit of measure—has the virtue that it saves us the work of entering lots of zeros. As a consequence, we may avoid some data-entry errors, and the spreadsheet looks a little less crowded than it would with many large numbers on it. However, there is an important practical reason for rescaling. The way that Solver carries out its arithmetic sometimes makes rescaling desirable. As a guideline, the parameters in the objective function and the constraints should not differ from each other, or from the values of the decision variables, by more than a factor of 100,000. In the Diaz Coffee example, the ratio of the largest right-hand-side constant to the smallest constraint coefficient would be 4,000,000 if there were no rescaling. Although a model as simple as this one would likely run correctly, it is safer (as well as more convenient) to do the rescaling.

One symptom of a need for rescaling would be a response from Solver stating that there is no feasible solution to a problem in which we're sure that feasible solutions can be found. In these circumstances, we should try to multiply a constraint by some constant or redefine the decision variables using a different unit of measure. Sometimes, however, scaling problems are difficult to avoid completely when we're trying to keep the model easy for another user to understand. In these cases, we can ask Solver to perform some internal rescaling of the model if we check the option box for Use Automatic Scaling. The Automatic Scaling option may be helpful; however, it is always preferable for the model builder to do the rescaling. (Unfortunately, in some instances, the Automatic Scaling option causes the linear solver to go awry when it would otherwise have functioned perfectly.)

Finally, if we need to display our model results in units that are more natural for our audience, we can create a separate presentation worksheet. On this sheet, the numbers can be "unscaled" and displayed in any desired format without affecting the optimization process. ■

11.5   SENSITIVITY ANALYSIS FOR LINEAR PROGRAMS

As we stressed in Chapter 6, sensitivity analysis is a vital part of all spreadsheet modeling. In optimization modeling, some of the most valuable insights come not from the optimal solution itself, but from a sensitivity analysis around the optimal solution. As we will see, the special structure of linear programs gives rise to certain characteristic results. We again use the Solver Sensitivity option in the Sensitivity Toolkit.

We implement the Solver Sensitivity tool with the Veerman Furniture model to illustrate some of the features of sensitivity analysis in linear programs. Recall that the model allows us to find the profit-maximizing product mix among chairs, desks, and tables. The optimal product mix (see Figure 11.5) is made up of desks and tables, with no chairs. Two constraints are binding: fabrication hours and the tables market. The optimal total profit contribution in the base case is $8,400.

11.5.1 Sensitivity to Objective Function Coefficients

Suppose that we are using the Veerman Furniture model as a planning tool and that we wish to explore a change in the price of chairs. We might not yet know what the exact price will be, pending more information about the competition, but we want to explore the impact of a price change, which translates into a change in the profit contribution of chairs. For the time being, let's assume that if we vary the price, there will be no effect on the demand potential for chairs. We invoke Solver Sensitivity with the entries shown in Figures 11.14 and 11.15.

Objective Function	E8
Other Cell(s)	B5:D5
Cell to Vary	B8
First Value	12
Last Value	24
Increment	1

The Solver Sensitivity report appears on a new worksheet (see Figure 11.16). These results show how the optimal product mix and the optimal profit both change as the profit contribution on chairs increases. For the range of profit contributions we chose ($12 to $24), we see two distinct profiles. For values up to $16, the base-case solution prevails, but above $16, the optimal mix changes, as follows:

- Chairs stay at zero until the unit profit contribution on chairs reaches $16; then chairs enter the optimal mix at a quantity of 330.
- When the unit contribution reaches $21, the number of chairs in the optimal mix increases to 360.
- Desks and tables are not affected until the unit contribution on chairs reaches $16; then the optimal number of desks drops from 275 to 55. When the unit profit on chairs reaches $21, the optimal number of desks drops again, to 40.
- Tables stay level at 100 until the unit contribution on chairs reaches $21; then the optimal number of tables drops to 85.
- The optimal total profit remains unchanged until the unit contribution on chairs reaches $16; thereafter, it increases.

From this information, we can conclude that the optimal solution is insensitive to changes in the unit profit contribution of chairs, up to $16. Beyond that point, however, the profit contribution on chairs becomes sufficiently attractive that we want to have

FIGURE 11.14 First Input Window for Solver Sensitivity

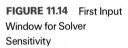

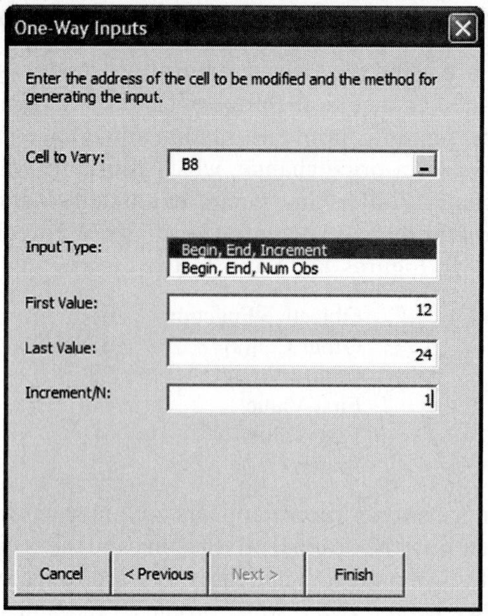

FIGURE 11.15 Second Input Window for Solver Sensitivity

FIGURE 11.16 Solver Sensitivity Report for the Change in Price

	A	B	C	D	E	F
1	Unit Profit	Objective	Change	C	D	T
2	$12	$8,400		0	275	100
3	$13	$8,400	$0	0	275	100
4	$14	$8,400	$0	0	275	100
5	$15	$8,400	$0	0	275	100
6	$16	$8,400	$0	0	275	100
7	$17	$8,730	$330	330	55	100
8	$18	$9,060	$330	330	55	100
9	$19	$9,390	$330	330	55	100
10	$20	$9,720	$330	330	55	100
11	$21	$10,050	$330	360	40	85
12	$22	$10,410	$360	360	40	85
13	$23	$10,770	$360	360	40	85
14	$24	$11,130	$360	360	40	85
15						

all three products in the mix. In effect, chairs substitute for desks (though not at a ratio of 1:1) when the profit contribution exceeds $16. Subsequently, when the profit contribution exceeds $21, chairs substitute for both desks and tables and are limited only by their demand potential. Thus, if we decide to alter the price for chairs, we can anticipate the impact on our product mix from the information in the sensitivity table.

In all linear programs, there is a distinct pattern to the changes in the optimal solution when we vary a coefficient of a decision variable in the objective function. In some interval around the base-case value, there is no change at all in the optimal decisions, but the objective function value will change if the decision variable is positive. Outside of this interval, a different set of values for the decision variables becomes optimal. As we saw in this example, the change from one set of values to the other will not be gradual. Instead, it will often be dramatic, as illustrated by the optimal number of chairs changing from 0 to 330 when the profit contribution increases from $16 to $17.

11.5.2 Sensitivity to Constraint Constants

Turning to another question, we noticed in the optimal solution to the base case that two constraints are binding: fabrication hours and the demand for tables. If fabrication time is limiting our ability to increase profits, perhaps we should acquire more of it. How much should we pay for additional time? Notice that this is a sensitivity question that involves one of the right-hand side constants rather than an objective function coefficient. To obtain an answer, we can invoke Solver Sensitivity again. In this case, our entries are shown in Figures 11.17 and 11.18.

Objective Function	E8
Other Cell(s)	B5:D5
Cell to Vary	G12
First Value	1,500
Last Value	2,400
Increment	100

The Solver Sensitivity tool adds another new worksheet, as shown in Figure 11.19. The table shows how the optimal product mix and the optimal profit both change as the number of fabrication hours increases. Its columns correspond to the same outputs as in the first table, and its rows correspond to the values we designated for the input. Thus, we see the following changes in the optimal product mix:

- Chairs stay at zero until the number of fabrication hours reaches 2,000; then chairs enter the optimal mix and continue to increase thereafter.

FIGURE 11.17 First Input Window for Solver Sensitivity

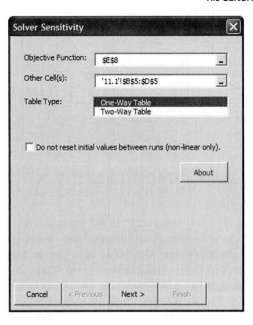

- Desks increase until the number of fabrication hours reaches 2,000; then desks stay level at 300.
- Tables stay level at 100 until the number of fabrication hours reaches 2,200; then tables drop.
- The optimal total profit increases as the number of fabrication hours increases, but not at a constant rate.

From this information, we can conclude that as we increase fabrication capacity, we should alter the product mix—first by increasing the number of desks, next by adding chairs to the mix, and then by swapping chairs for tables.

To determine how much we should be willing to pay for additional time, we examine the marginal value of additional fabrication hours. The **marginal value** is defined as the improvement in the objective function from a unit increase in the number available (i.e., an increase of 1 in the right-hand side of the fabrication constraint). We could calculate this marginal value by changing the number of fabrication hours to 1,851, re-solving the problem, and noting the improvement in the objective function. (It increases to $8,404, an improvement of $4.)

Marginal values are calculated automatically by the Solver Sensitivity tool and are displayed in the third column of the table, where we see that the marginal value of fabrication hours is $4.00 in the region of the base case. As the number of fabrication hours increases, the marginal value stays level for a while, then drops to $3.75, stays level at this value for a while, then later drops to about $2.32. This pattern is an instance of *diminishing marginal returns*: if someone were to offer us more and more of a scarce resource, its value would eventually decline. In this case, the scarce resource (or binding constraint) is fabrication capacity. Limited fabrication hours prevent us from achieving higher total profits; that is what makes fabrication hours economically scarce.

FIGURE 11.18 Second Input Window for Solver Sensitivity

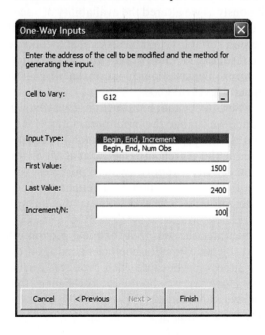

Starting with the base case, we should be willing to pay up to $4.00 for each additional fabrication hour because profit increases by this amount. This marginal value is also called the **shadow price**. In economic terms, the shadow price is the breakeven price at which it would be attractive to acquire more of a scarce resource. In other words, imagine that someone were to offer us additional fabrication hours (for example, if we could lease fabrication equipment). We can improve total profit by acquiring those additional hours, as long as their price is less than $4.00 each.

FIGURE 11.19 Solver Sensitivity Report for the Change in Fabrication Hours

	A	B	C	D	E	F
1	RHS	Objective	Change	C	D	T
2	1,500	$7,000.00		0.00	216.67	100.00
3	1,600	$7,400.00	$4.00	0.00	233.33	100.00
4	1,700	$7,800.00	$4.00	0.00	250.00	100.00
5	1,800	$8,200.00	$4.00	0.00	266.67	100.00
6	1,900	$8,600.00	$4.00	0.00	283.33	100.00
7	2,000	$9,000.00	$4.00	0.00	300.00	100.00
8	2,100	$9,375.00	$3.75	25.00	300.00	100.00
9	2,200	$9,750.00	$3.75	50.00	300.00	100.00
10	2,300	$10,077.27	$3.27	77.27	300.00	95.45
11	2,400	$10,309.09	$2.32	109.09	300.00	81.82
12						

In this example, we observe that the marginal value of the scarce resource remains constant in a neighborhood around the base-case value. In particular, the $4.00 shadow price holds for additional fabrication hours until we reach 2,000; then it drops to $3.75. In the interval from 1,850 hours to 2,000 hours, the incremental hours allow more desks to be manufactured. In fact, we can see from Figure 11.19 that each additional 100 hours leads to an increment of 16.67 desks in the product mix. This increment, in turn, accounts for an increase of $400.00 in total profit, since desks contribute $24.00 each.

Above 2,000 fabrication hours, the pattern is a little different. With additional hours available, there are more chairs in the optimal product mix, and the optimal profit grows by $375.00 for each additional 100 hours. Thus, the shadow price is $3.75, and this value persists until around 2,200 hours. Actually, the shadow price changes at 2,266.67 hours, but our table is too coarse for us to see the precise change point. (We could see it more readily if we were to repeat the analysis with a step size of 1 hour.) Above 2,266.67 fabrication hours, the total profit increases at an even smaller rate ($2.32). In this interval, we see that chairs are added to the product mix, and tables are removed from it. Chairs consume more fabrication time than do tables. Therefore, with a relatively small amount of fabrication capacity (1,850 hours), we are better off not making chairs. As fabrication capacity increases (to, say, 2,300 hours), we are willing to swap chairs for tables, in light of other capacities available, in pursuit of optimal profits.

Linear programs typically exhibit a distinct pattern in sensitivity tables when we vary the availability of a scarce resource. The marginal value of capacity remains constant over some interval of increase or decrease. (This contrasts with the marginal value in nonlinear models, such as Figure 10.23, where we saw marginal values that changed continuously as we altered the availability of a scarce resource.) Within this interval, some of the decision variables change linearly with the change in capacity, while other decision variables stay the same. If someone were to continually give us more of a scarce resource, its value would drop and eventually fall to zero. In the case of our product mix problem, we could confirm that the value of additional hours drops to zero at a capacity level of 3,000.

The Solver Sensitivity tool has the limitation that we must specify in advance the grid over which we change the input parameter. If we choose too coarse a grid, we may not identify the precise point at which the solution changes. In that case, we can always refine the search and run the analysis again. An alternative is to use Solver's own Sensitivity Report, which provides information on the local sensitivity to both objective function coefficients and right-hand sides. (The chapter appendix provides some details on the information in the Sensitivity Report.)

We have illustrated the sensitivity of linear programs to two fundamental types of parameters: an objective function coefficient and a constraint constant. These cases are particularly interesting because each produces a characteristic pattern in the optimal solution. However, we should not lose sight of the fact that with the Solver Sensitivity tool, we can analyze the sensitivity of the optimal solution to *any* parameter in the model.

SOLVER TIP
Solver Sensitivity and Shadow Prices

Solver Sensitivity is a general-purpose tool for sensitivity analysis of optimization models. It is used to determine the sensitivity of the optimal solution to *any* input parameter. It automatically calculates the change in the objective function per unit change in the input parameter, which we call the *marginal change* in the objective.

Solver Sensitivity can, of course, be used to assess the impact on the optimal solution of changes in the constraint constants, which typically represent resources. In this case, the marginal change in the objective can be interpreted as the marginal value of the resource. The marginal value of a resource is the change in the objective per unit change in the resource, which can usually be interpreted as the maximum amount we would be willing to pay to acquire additional resource.

The marginal value of a resource is given the special name **shadow price**. In linear programs, shadow prices are constant for some range of changes in the RHS. This feature is central to our interpretation of the economic patterns in the solutions to linear optimization models. In nonlinear models, by constrast, the marginal values of resources are typically not constant.   ∎

11.6   PATTERNS IN LINEAR PROGRAMMING SOLUTIONS

In linear programming models, one form of insight comes from seeing a qualitative pattern in the solution. Stated another way, the optimal solution tells a "story" about a pattern of economic priorities, and it's the recognition of those priorities that provides useful insight. When we know the pattern, we can explain the solution more convincingly than when we simply read Solver results. When we know the pattern, we can also anticipate some of the answers to "what-if" questions without having to modify the worksheet. In short, the pattern provides a level of understanding that enhances decision making. Therefore, after we optimize a linear programming model, we should always try to discern the qualitative pattern in the optimal solution.

11.6.1   Identifying Patterns

Spotting a pattern involves observations about both variables and constraints. In the optimal solution, we pay special attention to which constraints are binding and which are not, as well as to which decision variables are positive and which are zero. Grasping the pattern of binding constraints and positive decision variables often allows us to reconstruct the solution in a step-by-step fashion. To the untrained observer, we seem to be solving the problem methodically, from scratch; in fact, we are only providing a retrospective interpretation of the solution, and we need to know that solution before we can devise the interpretation. Nevertheless, we are not merely reflecting information in the computer output. Rather, we are describing a set of economic imperatives at the heart of the model. When we can see those imperatives, and communicate them, then we have gained some insight. In the examples that follow, we show how to uncover these patterns.

While it can be extremely helpful to identify the pattern in the solution to a linear program, we should not assume that the pattern holds for anything other than small changes in the parameters. We can always check whether the pattern changes by rerunning Solver with new input parameters.

To illustrate the process of identifying a pattern, recall the solution of the product mix problem in Figure 11.5. The display in Figure 11.20 highlights the positive variables and the binding constraints. When we concentrate on these variables and constraints, we see that the problem becomes one of optimizing the choice of the variables D and T, subject to two constraints:

$$6D + 2T = 1,850$$

$$T = 100$$

The second equation dictates the value of T because it is a binding constraint containing only one variable. Once we know that $T = 100$, we can substitute into

FIGURE 11.20 Optimal
Product Mix Model,
Highlighting Elements
of the Pattern

	A	B	C	D	E	F	G
1	Allocation: Furniture Production						
2							
3	Decision Variables						
4			C	D	T		
5	Product mix		0	275	100		
6							
7	Objective Function				Total		
8	Profit		15	24	18	$8,400	
9							
10	Constraints					LHS	RHS
11	Fabrication		4	6	2	1850 <=	1850
12	Assembly		3	5	7	2075 <=	2400
13	Distribution		3	2	4	950 <=	1500
14	Chair market		1	0	0	0 <=	360
15	Desk market		0	1	0	275 <=	300
16	Table market		0	0	1	100 <=	100
17							

the first constraint and deduce that $D = 275$. The solution is constructed as if we determine T first and then D. The construction of the solution goes like this:

- First, remove C from further consideration.
- Next, let the market ceiling for tables dictate the value of T.
- Finally (with T fixed), let the fabrication capacity dictate the value of D.

Note that this description describes the solution fully but does not use any numbers. In that sense, the pattern is a qualitative interpretation of the solution. However, once we supply the parameters of the constraints (here, that means 100 and 1,850), the pattern gives us a scheme for computing the optimal quantitative solution. It is almost as if Solver first spots the optimal pattern and then says, "Give me the numerical information in your problem." For any specification of the numbers (within certain limits), Solver could then compute the optimal solution by simply following the sequential steps in the pattern. In reality, of course, Solver cannot know the pattern until the solution is determined, because the solution is a critical ingredient in the pattern.

Let's return to the point that the patterns hold for any set of numbers within certain limits. What limits are we referring to? Suppose we make a change in the size of the market ceiling for tables and increment the ceiling by one, to 101. Then, the steps in the pattern lead us to a new optimal solution: $T = 101$ and $D = 274.667$. The impact on the objective function is an increment of $24(-0.333) + 18(+1) = 10$. In other words, a unit increase in the market ceiling for tables allows the optimal mix to increase profits by $10.

In effect, we have derived the shadow price for the market ceiling constraint. (We could confirm this result by rerunning Solver with a market ceiling of 101 for tables.) Thus, if we increment the ceiling by two units, the new optimal solution becomes $T = 102$ and $D = 274.333$, with an increase of $20 in the objective. How long can we continue incrementing the market ceiling for tables? To answer this question, we have to consider the impact on the constraints we have been ignoring, as well as on the decision variables. In the latter case, the optimal value of D drops 0.333 for every unit increase in the ceiling. At this rate, the ceiling could become as large as 825. But let's look at the nonbinding constraints.

- The Assembly constraint had a surplus of 325 hours in the original problem. Increasing T by one and reducing D by 0.333 consume an additional 5.333 Assembly hours. At this rate, there is room to increase the ceiling by at most $325/5.333 = 60.9375$.
- The Shipping constraint had a surplus 550 hours in the original problem. Increasing T by one and reducing D by 0.333 consume an additional 3.333

Shipping hours. At this rate, there is room to increase the ceiling by at most $550/3.333 = 165$.

- The chair ceiling is unaffected by the change.
- The desk ceiling had a surplus of 25 desks in the original solution, but because the change involves a reduction in the number of desks, the desk ceiling does not come into play.

Taking the tightest of the relevant limits, we conclude that the market ceiling for tables could be increased as much as 60.9375 without changing the pattern.

In the opposite direction, suppose we *reduce* the size of the market ceiling for tables.

- Reducing the ceiling for tables directly affects the variable T. There is room to decrease the ceiling by at most 100 tables.
- The desk ceiling had a surplus of 25 desks in the original solution. Decreasing T by one and increasing D by 0.333 consumes an additional 0.333 of the surplus in the constraint. At this rate, there is room to increase the ceiling by at most $25/0.333 = 75$ tables.

Taking the tighter of these two limits, we conclude that the market ceiling for tables could be reduced by as much as 75 without changing the pattern. Thus, the analysis of both directions leads to the conclusion that the shadow price holds for market ceilings from 25 to 160.9375. Beyond this range, the pattern changes: in particular, there is a change in the set of binding constraints or the set of nonzero variables (or both).

11.6.2 Further Examples

The following examples illustrate patterns in the optimal solution of other linear programs.

EXAMPLE
A Product
Portfolio Decision

The product portfolio problem asks which products a firm should be making. If there are contracts that obligate the firm to enter certain markets, then the question is which products to make in quantities beyond the required minimum. Consider Grocery Distributors (GD), a company that distributes 15 different vegetables to grocery stores. GD's vegetables come in standard cardboard cartons that each take up 1.25 cubic feet in the warehouse. The company replenishes its supply of frozen foods at the start of each week and rarely has any inventory remaining at week's end. An entire week's supply of frozen vegetables arrives each Monday morning at the warehouse, which can hold up to 18,000 cubic feet of product. In addition, GD's supplier extends a line of credit amounting to $30,000. That is, GD is permitted to purchase up to $30,000 worth of product each Monday.

GD can predict sales for each of the 15 products for the coming week. This forecast is expressed in terms of a minimum and a maximum level of sales. The minimum quantity is based on a contractual agreement that GD has made with a few retail grocery chains; the maximum quantity represents an estimate of the sales potential in the upcoming week. The unit cost and unit selling price for each product are known. The given data are compiled in the following table.

Product	Cost	Price	Minimum	Maximum
Whipped Potatoes (WP)	2.15	2.27	300	1,500
Creamed Corn (CC)	2.20	2.48	400	2,000
Blackeyed Peas (BP)	2.40	2.70	250	900
Artichokes (AR)	4.80	5.20	0	150
Carrots (CR)	2.60	2.92	300	1,200
Succotash (SU)	2.30	2.48	200	800
Okra (OK)	2.35	2.20	150	600
Cauliflower (CL)	2.85	3.13	100	300
Green Peas (GP)	2.25	2.48	750	3,500
Spinach (SP)	2.10	2.27	400	2,000

Lima Beans (LB)	2.80	3.13	500	3,300
Brussel Sprouts (BS)	3.00	3.18	100	500
Green Beans (GB)	2.60	2.92	500	3,200
Squash (SQ)	2.50	2.70	100	500
Broccoli (BR)	2.90	3.13	400	2,500

■

GD solves the linear programming model shown in Figure 11.21. In this model, the objective is to maximize profit for the coming week. Sales for each product are constrained by a minimum quantity and a maximum quantity. In addition, constraints come from aggregate limits on warehouse space and purchase expenditures.

We invoke Solver and specify:

Target cell	R11 (maximize)
Changing cells	C9:Q9
Constraints	C9:Q9 ≥ C6:Q6
	C9:Q9 ≤ C7:Q7
	R14:R15 ≤ T14:T15

The solution shows that all of the decision variables are positive except for artichokes, and the minimum cost is $3,395.50.

Examining the variables in the solution in more detail, we notice that all but one of the purchase quantities match either the maximum or the minimum, with lima beans as the only exception. Any product that has a nonzero minimum must appear in the solution at a positive amount, but some products are purchased at even higher levels. These can be considered high-priority products. Products purchased at their minimum levels can be considered low-priority products. In either case, however, the values corresponding to high-priority products and low-priority products are dictated by one binding constraint containing one variable.

Examining the other constraints in the solution, we see that the credit limit is binding, but the space constraint is not. In effect, the credit limit serves as a bottleneck on purchases, but we can ignore the space constraint, because other constraints dictate how much space is used. A description of the pattern could take the following form:

- Set the volume of each high-priority product equal to its maximum level.
- Set the volume of each low-priority product equal to its minimum level.
- Use the entire credit limit.

In other words, we are actually solving a simpler problem than originally given: produce the highest possible value from the 15 products under a tight credit limit. To solve this problem, we can use a common-sense rule: pursue the products in the order of highest to lowest *profit-to-cost ratio*. Meanwhile, we must meet the given minimum quantities. Therefore, we can convert the pattern into a calculation scheme for the decision variables, as follows:

- Purchase each product at its minimum sales level.
- Rank the products from highest to lowest ratio of profit to cost.

FIGURE 11.21 Optimal Solution for the GD Model

	A	B	C	D	E	F	G	H	I	J	K	L	M	N	O	P	Q	R	S	T
1	General Distributors																			
2																				
3	Data	Vegetable	WP	CC	BP	AR	CR	SU	OK	CL	GP	SP	LB	BS	GB	SQ	BR			
4		Cost	2.15	2.20	2.40	4.80	2.60	2.30	2.35	2.85	2.25	2.10	2.80	3.00	2.60	2.50	2.90			
5		Price	2.27	2.48	2.70	5.20	2.92	2.48	2.20	3.13	2.48	2.27	3.13	3.18	2.92	2.70	3.13			
6		Min	300	400	250	0	300	200	150	100	750	400	500	100	500	100	400			
7		Max	1500	2000	900	150	1200	800	600	300	3500	2000	3300	500	3200	500	2500			
8																				
9	Decisions	Cartons	300	2000	900	0	1200	200	150	100	750	400	2150	100	3200	100	400			
10																				
11	Objective	Profit $	0.12	0.28	0.30	0.40	0.32	0.18	-0.15	0.28	0.23	0.17	0.33	0.18	0.32	0.20	0.23	$3,395.50		
12																				
13																			LHS		RHS
14	Constraints	Credit	2.15	2.20	2.40	4.80	2.60	2.30	2.35	2.85	2.25	2.10	2.80	3.00	2.60	2.50	2.90	30,000.00	<=	30,000
15		Space	1.25	1.25	1.25	1.25	1.25	1.25	1.25	1.25	1.25	1.25	1.25	1.25	1.25	1.25	1.25	14,937.50	<=	18,000
16																				
17	Ratios		1.056	1.127	1.125	1.083	1.123	1.078	0.936	1.098	1.102	1.081	1.118	1.060	1.123	1.080	1.079			
18																				

11.16 / 11.19 / 11.20 \ 11.21 /

- For the highest-ranking product, raise the purchase quantity toward its maximum sales level. As we increase the purchase quantity, only two things can happen: either we reach the maximum for that product (in which case we go to the next highest priority product), or we use up the credit limit (in which case we are done).

The ranking mechanism prioritizes the products. Using these priorities, we essentially separate the products into three groups: a set of high-priority products, produced at their maximum levels; a set of low-priority products, produced at their minimum levels; and a *single* medium-priority product, produced at a level somewhere between its minimum and maximum. (This product is the one we are adding to the purchase plan when we use up the credit limit.) This procedure is complete and unambiguous, and this pattern describes the optimal solution without explicitly using any numbers. At first, the solution was just a collection of positive decision variables and binding constraints. But we were able to convert the solution into a prioritized list of allocations that establish the values of the decision variables one at a time.

Actually, Solver's solution merely distinguishes the three priority classes; it does not reveal the profit-to-cost ratio rule explicitly. That insight might come from reviewing the makeup of the priority classes, or from some intuition about how single-constraint problems are optimized. (The profit-to-cost ratios are shown for confirmation in row 17 of Figure 11.21.) But this brings up an important point. Solver does not usually reveal the economic reason why a variable should have high priority, and it is not always necessary (or even possible) for us to know why an allocation receives high priority. We simply notice a binding constraint containing just one positive variable, and that leads us toward a better understanding of the solution.

Again, we can alter the base-case model slightly and follow the consequences for the optimal purchase plan. For example, if we raise the credit limit, the only change in the solution will be the purchase of additional cartons of the medium-priority product. Thus, the marginal value of raising the credit limit by a dollar is equivalent to the incremental profit per dollar of purchase cost for the medium-priority product, or $0.118. We could confirm this result by rerunning Solver with one additional dollar of credit.

Suppose instead that we were to increase the amount of a low-priority product in the purchase plan. Then, following the optimal pattern, we would have to purchase less of the medium-priority product owing to the tight credit limit. Consider the purchase of more squash than the 100-carton minimum. Each additional carton of squash will cost $2.50, substituting for about 0.892 carton of lima beans in the credit constraint. The net effect on profit is as follows:

- Add a carton of squash (increase profit by $0.20).
- Remove 0.892 carton of lima beans (decrease profit by $0.2946).
- Therefore, net cost = $0.0946.

Thus, each carton of squash we force into the purchase plan, above the minimum sales level of 100, will reduce profits by 9.46 cents. If we were to rerun the model requiring 101 cartons of squash, we would confirm that profit declines by exactly this amount.

Comparing the analysis of GD's decision with the product mix example considered earlier, we see that the optimal pattern, when translated into a computational scheme, is complete and unambiguous in both cases. We can use the pattern to determine the shadow price on a binding constraint or to derive marginal costs of introducing nonoptimal decisions. A specific feature of GD's model is the focus on one particular bottleneck constraint. This feature helps us understand the role of a binding constraint when we interpret a pattern; however, in many problems, there is more than one binding constraint.

EXAMPLE
Production Planning

The production planning problem has several formulations. In one version, a company has contracted to meet a certain demand schedule and faces constraints on production capacity. The problem is to find a least-cost production plan. In our example, a company produces two products (A and B) using two types of machines (X and Y) over a planning period of three months. The products can be produced on either machine, and the following table describes the machine hours required to make a single unit of each product.

	Product A	Product B
Hours on Machine X	2.0	1.5
Hours on Machine Y	2.5	2.0

Machine capacities in hours on X and Y are given for each of the three months. In addition, the quantities to be delivered each month, according to the contract, are also given.

Month	X-Capacity	Y-Capacity	A-Demand	B-Demand
1	140	250	50	30
2	60	80	100	60
3	150	100	50	50

The relevant costs are labor on each machine ($30.00/hour) and inventory held ($10.00/unit/month, for either product). ■

Figure 11.22 provides a linear programming model for this problem, with the optimal solution shown. The variables in this model are of two kinds. One kind is the number of units of each product scheduled for production, broken down by machine and by month—for example, $AX1$. The other kind is the inventory of each product held from one month to the next—for example, $AI1$. The inventory variables allow us to express demand constraints using the basic accounting definition of inventory: Final inventory must be equal to starting inventory plus production minus shipments. One such equation applies to each product in each month (rows 21–26).

Our Solver parameters are as follows:

Target cell	R13 (maximize)
Changing cells	B10:Q10
Constraints	R15:R20 $\leq$ T15:T20
	R21:R26 = T21:T26

A look at the optimal solution in Figure 11.22 leads us to the following description of the pattern:

FIGURE 11.22 Optimal Solution for the Production Planning Model

	A	B	C	D	E	F	G	H	I	J	K	L	M	N	O	P	Q	R	S	T	U	V
1	**Production Planning**																					
2																						
3	**Parameters**																					
4			Hrs/unit	*A*	*B*	$/hr	*A*	*B*	$/unit	*A*	*B*											
5			*X*	2.0	1.5	*X*	30	30	*X*	60	45											
6			*Y*	2.5	2.0	*Y*	30	30	*Y*	75	60											
7	**Decisions**																					
8				*Month 1*						*Month 2*					*Month 3*							
9		*AX1*	*AY1*	*BX1*	*BY1*	*AI1*	*BI1*	*AX2*	*AY2*	*BX2*	*BY2*	*AI2*	*BI2*	*AX3*	*AY3*	*BX3*	*BY3*					
10	*Units*	32.5	85.5	50.0	0.0	68.0	20.0	0.0	32.0	40.0	0.0	0.0	0.0	37.5	12.5	50.0	0.0					
11																		**Total**				
12	**Objective**																	**Cost**				
13	*$*	60	75	45	60	10	10	60	75	45	60	10	10	60	75	45	60	$21,130				
14	**Constraints**																	*LHS*		*RHS*		
15	*X1*	2.0	0	1.5	0	0	0	0	0	0	0	0	0	0	0	0	0	140	<=	140	*X1*	
16	*Y1*	0	2.5	0	2.0	0	0	0	0	0	0	0	0	0	0	0	0	214	<=	250	*Y1*	
17	*X2*	0	0	0	0	0	0	2.0	0	1.5	0	0	0	0	0	0	0	60	<=	60	*X2*	Machine
18	*Y2*	0	0	0	0	0	0	0	2.5	0	2.0	0	0	0	0	0	0	80	<=	80	*Y2*	Capacities
19	*X3*	0	0	0	0	0	0	0	0	0	0	0	0	2.0	0	1.5	0	150	<=	150	*X3*	
20	*Y3*	0	0	0	0	0	0	0	0	0	0	0	0	0	2.5	0	2.0	31	<=	100	*Y3*	
21	*A1*	1	1	0	0	-1	0	0	0	0	0	0	0	0	0	0	0	50	=	50	*A1*	
22	*B1*	0	0	1	1	0	-1	0	0	0	0	0	0	0	0	0	0	30	=	30	*B1*	
23	*A2*	0	0	0	0	1	0	1	1	0	0	-1	0	0	0	0	0	100	=	100	*A2*	Product
24	*B2*	0	0	0	0	0	1	0	0	1	1	0	-1	0	0	0	0	60	=	60	*B2*	Shipments
25	*A3*	0	0	0	0	0	0	0	0	0	0	1	0	1	1	0	0	50	=	50	*A3*	
26	*B3*	0	0	0	0	0	0	0	0	0	0	0	1	0	0	1	1	50	=	50	*B3*	
27																						

11.16 / 11.19 / 11.20 / 11.21 / **11.22**

- All product shipment constraints are binding (because they were cast as equations in the model).
- Capacity constraints on machine X capacity are binding in each period, but machine Y capacity is binding only in month 2.
- In the optimal production plan, the following variables are positive:

  *AX*1, *AX*3
  *AY*1, *AY*3
  *BX*1, *BX*2, *BX*3

- The positive inventory variables are *AI*1 and *BI*1.

To convert this pattern into a scheme for calculating the values of the decision variables, we again start by noticing which variables are positive and which are zero. If we focus on product–month combinations, we may not see a distinct pattern, although it becomes clear that the optimal schedule calls for overproduction in the first month, creating inventory that gets consumed in the second month (*AI*2 and *BI*2 are both zero). In the third month, production matches demand exactly. When we focus on product–machine combinations, on the other hand, a detailed pattern begins to take shape. We see that product B is never produced on machine Y (*BY*1, *BY*2, and *BY*3 are all zero), whereas product A is produced on both X and Y. Since machine X capacity is binding in each month, it is evidently important to produce B on X and to avoid producing B on Y. We see that it is also preferable to produce B on X in an earlier period, and to hold it in inventory, as compared to producing B on Y in the period when demand occurs. This observation suggests that the solution can be constructed by the following procedure:

- First, assign X-capacity in each month to make the number of units of B-demand in the same period.
- If X-capacity is inadequate to meet current B-demand, then assign X-capacity in the previous month and hold the items in inventory.
- If X-capacity is more than adequate for B-demand, then assign X-capacity to make the number of units of A-demand in the current period.
- If X-capacity is fully consumed, then assign Y-capacity to make the remaining number of units of A-demand in the current period.
- If Y-capacity is inadequate to meet current A-demand, then assign Y-capacity in the previous month and hold the items in inventory.

Clearly, machine X has a cost advantage over machine Y in making both products: Its hourly cost is the same, and it takes less time to produce either product. It is this relative cost advantage that leads to the pattern in the optimal solution. Here again, we have interpreted the optimal solution without explicitly using a number, yet we have provided a complete and unambiguous description of the solution. This description can be viewed as a system of priorities that determines the variables one at a time, in sequence.

Again, we can test our characterization of the optimal pattern by deriving the shadow prices. For example, suppose that the capacity of X were increased by one hour in month 1. Given the optimal pattern, we should want to transfer some production of A at the margin from machine Y to machine X. The extra hour of X would accommodate 1/2 unit of A. This would reduce production of A by 5/4 of an hour on Y. In cost terms, the extra hour of X incurs a cost of $30.00, while 5/4 of an hour on Y will be saved, at a benefit of $37.50. The net benefit is $7.50, which is the shadow price on the capacity constraint for machine X in month 1. We could, of course, confirm this result by rerunning Solver with one more hour of capacity on X.

As another example of altering the problem slightly, suppose that we increase by one unit the quantity of product A to be delivered in month 1. The marginal cost of meeting this shipment is just the cost of producing one more unit of product A on Y.

This amount is $75.00, which turns out to be the shadow price for the corresponding constraint. Suppose instead that we increase by one unit the quantity of product A to be delivered in month 2. In this case, the marginal cost is $85.00, since the marginal unit must be produced in month 1 (at a cost of $75.00) and held in inventory one month (at a cost of $10.00), because no capacity remains in month 2 under the optimal plan.

Suppose now that we increase by one unit the quantity of product B to be delivered in month 2. According to the pattern, we prefer to make this unit on machine X, but X is fully committed to product B during month 2. Following the pattern, we want to make product B on X during month 1 and hold it in inventory; to do so, however, we will have to transfer some production of A from machine X to machine Y. To find the marginal cost of this entire adjustment, we have to follow the economic implications of each element of the marginal change:

- Make one unit of B on X (time $= 1.5$ hrs; cost $= 45.00).
- Hold one unit of B one month (cost $= 10.00).
- Remove 1.5 hrs of A production from X (cost saved $= $45.00; \frac{3}{4}$ unit).
- Add $\frac{3}{4}$ unit of A production to Y (time $= \frac{15}{8}$ hrs; cost $= 56.25).
- Therefore, net cost $= $45.00 + $10.00 - $45.00 + $56.25 = 66.25.

Once again, knowing the qualitative pattern in the optimal solution allows us to anticipate how that solution will change when the problem is modified. Moreover, we can calculate shadow prices by quantifying the implications of the pattern for changes in the constraint constants.

11.6.3 Review

The foregoing examples illustrate the process of extracting insight from the solution to a linear programming problem. By focusing just on positive variables and binding constraints, we try to rebuild the optimal solution from the given parameters, with the determination of one variable at a time, if possible. At the first step, we look for a binding constraint containing a single variable. That combination allows us to deduce the value of the variable immediately. Then, with that value known, we look for another binding constraint containing just one other variable, and we continue in this fashion. This construction can often be interpreted as a list of priorities, and those priorities reveal the economic forces at work.

Answers to two diagnostic questions help determine whether we have been successful at extracting a pattern:

- Is the pattern complete and unambiguous?
- Where do the shadow prices come from?

The answer to the first question takes us to a full solution of the problem, specifying all of the decision variables in the optimal solution uniquely. The second question invites us to alter one constraint constant in the original problem and trace the incremental changes in the variables, allowing us to derive the shadow price for the corresponding constraint. Note that this derivation is not necessary except to achieve a deeper interpretation of the results, because we can determine the value of the shadow price simply by running Solver Sensitivity.

Patterns, as we have suggested, have certain limits. If we test our specification of a pattern by deriving shadow prices, we have to recognize that a shadow price has a limited range over which it holds. (Recall from Figure 11.19 that the shadow price on fabrication time was $4.00 up to 2,000 hours and then dropped to $3.75.) Beyond this range, a different pattern prevails. As we change a right-hand side constant, there will eventually be a change in the shadow price. The same is true of the pattern: beyond the range in which the shadow price holds, the pattern may change. In the production planning example, however, we were able to describe the pattern in a fairly general way, so that it holds even when the shadow price changes.

Unfortunately, the pattern cannot always be reduced to a list of assignments in priority order. Occasionally it happens that, once we identify the positive variables and the binding constraints in the optimal solution, we might be able to say no more than that the pattern comes from solving a system of equations determined by the binding constraints and the positive variables. Nevertheless, in most cases, as the foregoing examples indicate, we can learn a great deal about the underlying economics by looking for patterns in the optimal solution.

11.7* DATA ENVELOPMENT ANALYSIS

Data Envelopment Analysis (DEA) is a linear programming application aimed at evaluating the efficiencies of similar organizational departments or *decision-making units* (DMUs, as they are called). The DMUs are characterized in terms of their inputs and outputs, but not in terms of their operating details. A DMU is considered **efficient** if it gets the most output from its inputs. In the diagram of Figure 11.23, for example, a DMU has three outputs (y_1, y_2, and y_3) and two inputs (x_1 and x_2). Its efficiency is defined as the value of its outputs divided by the value of its inputs. An inefficient DMU could potentially produce greater output value from the same inputs, or it could produce the same outputs from smaller input value. The purpose of DEA is to identify inefficient DMUs when there are multiple outputs and multiple inputs.

When inputs and outputs are treated as multidimensional, we need to use weighting factors to produce an overall efficiency measure. We compute the total value of two *inputs* x_1 and x_2 as $v_1x_1 + v_2x_2$. The input quantities are obtained from historical data, and the weights v_1 and v_2 are determined in the analysis. Similarly, we compute the total value of three *outputs* as $u_1y_1 + u_2y_2 + u_3y_3$, where the output quantities (y_1, y_2, y_3) are historical data and the weights (u_1, u_2, u_3) are determined in the analysis. The efficiency measure is then the ratio of weighted outputs to weighted inputs:

$$E = \frac{u_1y_1 + u_2y_2 + u_3y_3}{v_1x_1 + v_2x_2}$$

EXAMPLE
Burritoville
Restaurants

Juan Pimiento has been a successful entrepreneur, developing a chain of Mexican restaurants in the Southwest. A few years ago, he opened his first Burritoville store. When it became profitable and popular in its first two years, Juan built some new stores, bought similar competing stores, and eventually found himself the owner of a restaurant chain. Because some of the stores in the chain had been existing restaurants, and because he was inclined to experiment with store designs and menus, there were differences in the way the various stores operated. From his new vantage point, Juan thought that it might be a good idea to evaluate where in the chain things were going well and where they were not.

After reading up on DEA, Juan has come up with some historical data to summarize performance of his stores. The key outputs in his analysis are monthly profit and peak daily volume. The key inputs are labor hours and monthly facility cost. He has gathered the following data for the restaurants in the chain.

Store ID	Monthly Profit	Peak Volume	Labor Hours	Facility Cost
1	761	109	56	1,476
2	925	103	72	1,613
3	788	119	64	1,612
4	858	114	63	1,381
5	928	107	70	1,748
6	758	120	72	1,645
7	963	104	66	1,290
8	918	119	60	1,779
9	876	94	61	1,325
10	997	102	72	1,453

The data for monthly profit and facility cost have come directly from accounting records in the company. The average daily labor hours have been pulled together by store managers, working from daily personnel schedules. Peak volumes have been determined by having someone stand at the front door to count (and greet) customers coming into the store. With the data collection effort finished, Juan hopes that DEA can provide some insight into levels of efficiency at the various locations. ∎

Let's address the efficiency analysis for Store 1. Given the historical data, we know that the efficiency measure for Store 1 takes the following form

$$E_1 = \frac{u_1 y_1 + u_2 y_2}{v_1 x_1 + v_2 x_2} = \frac{761 u_1 + 109 u_2}{56 v_1 + 1476 v_2}$$

with the weights yet to be determined. The DEA method imposes two conditions on the analysis. First, to rescale the efficiency measure, the denominator is set equal to 1. Thus:

$$56 v_1 + 1476 v_2 = 1$$

Second, by convention, DEA requires that output value cannot exceed input value, for any of the DMUs, or:

$$761 u_1 + 109 u_2 - 56 v_1 - 1476 v_2 \leq 0 \quad \textit{for Store 1}$$
$$925 u_1 + 103 u_2 - 72 v_1 - 1613 v_2 \leq 0 \quad \textit{for Store 2}$$

and similarly for the eight remaining DMUs.

At this stage, the analysis turns to linear programming to find the weights that produce the largest efficiency value for Store 1. Because the denominator (input value) of E_1 is scaled to 1, the optimization problem for Store 1 simplifies to maximizing the output value, $761 u_1 + 109 u_2$.

Figure 11.24 shows the worksheet for the analysis, using the standard format for an allocation model. The objective function in this model corresponds to the output value of Store 1, computed by a SUMPRODUCT formula in cell G18. The equality constraint that fixes the value of inputs can be found in row 20, while the normalizing convention (requiring that output values never exceed input values) can be found in rows 21–30.

In the Solver Parameters window, we enter the following information.

Target cell	G18 (maximize)
Changing cells	C16:F16
Constraints	G20 = I20
	G21:G30 ≤ I21:I30

When we run Solver on this model, we obtain an objective function of 1.00, as shown in the figure, along with the following weights:

Output	Profit weight (u_1)	0.00027
Output	Volume weight (u_2)	0.00728
Input	Labor weight (v_1)	0.01199
Input	Facilities weight (v_2)	0.00022

With these weights, the input value is 1.0 and the output value is 1.0 for Store 1, resulting in an efficiency of 100 percent. In effect, we have imagined that the manager of Store 1 has been acting to optimize some measure of efficiency. Our model tells us that if that measure were based on weights of 0.00027, 0.00728, 0.01199, and 0.00022, then indeed, Store 1 would have the highest efficiency among the stores in the chain. In other words, there is at least one set of weights for which Store 1 performs as well as any other store in the set. In that sense, we can conclude that Store 1 is operating efficiently.

Figure 11.25 shows the analysis for Store 2. The format is the same as that for Store 1, and only two changes occur. First, the objective function now contains data for Store 2 in row 18. Second, the coefficients for the constraint on input value

FIGURE 11.23 Conceptual Description of a Decision Making Unit

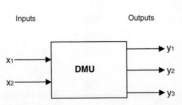

FIGURE 11.24 Analysis of Store 1 in the Burritoville DEA Model

	A	B	C	D	E	F	G	H	I
1	Restaurants								
2			*Outputs*		*Inputs*				
3	Data	*DMU*	*Profit*	*Volume*	*Hours*	*Cost*			
4		Store 1	761	109	56	1476			
5		Store 2	925	103	72	1613			
6		Store 3	788	119	64	1612			
7		Store 4	858	114	63	1381			
8		Store 5	928	107	70	1748			
9		Store 6	758	120	72	1645			
10		Store 7	963	104	66	1290			
11		Store 8	918	119	60	1779			
12		Store 9	876	94	61	1325			
13		Store 10	997	102	72	1453			
14									
15								DMU	1
16	Decisions	*Weights*	0.00027	0.00728	0.01199	0.00022			
17									
18	Objective	*Efficiency*	761	109	56	1476	1.000		
19									
20	Constraints	Input	0	0	56	1476	1.000	=	1
21		Store 1	761	109	-56	-1476	0.000	<=	0
22		Store 2	925	103	-72	-1613	-0.221	<=	0
23		Store 3	788	119	-64	-1612	-0.046	<=	0
24		Store 4	858	114	-63	-1381	0.000	<=	0
25		Store 5	928	107	-70	-1748	-0.198	<=	0
26		Store 6	758	120	-72	-1645	-0.150	<=	0
27		Store 7	963	104	-66	-1290	-0.060	<=	0
28		Store 8	918	119	-60	-1779	0.000	<=	0
29		Store 9	876	94	-61	-1325	-0.104	<=	0
30		Store 10	997	102	-72	-1453	-0.173	<=	0
31									

| ◄ ◄ ► ► \ 11.24 / ◄ | | |

contain data for Store 2 in row 20. Otherwise, the parameters of the linear program remain unchanged from the analysis of Store 1. When we run Solver on this model, we obtain an objective function of 0.869, as shown in the figure, along with the following weights:

Output	Profit weight (u_1)	0.00094
Output	Volume weight (u_2)	0.0
Input	Labor weight (v_1)	0.01241
Input	Facilities weight (v_2)	0.00007

With these weights, the input value is 1.0, and the output value is 0.869, resulting in an efficiency of 86.9 percent. Note that cells G27 and G28 are zero. This means that the normalizing constraint is binding for Stores 7 and 8. In other words, Stores 7 and 8 have efficiencies of 100 percent, even at the most favorable weights for Store 2. In effect, we have imagined that the manager of Store 2 has been acting to optimize

FIGURE 11.25 Analysis of Store 2 in the Burritoville DEA Model

	A	B	C	D	E	F	G	H	I
1	Restaurants								
2			*Outputs*		*Inputs*				
3	Data	*DMU*	*Profit*	*Volume*	*Hours*	*Cost*			
4		Store 1	761	109	56	1476			
5		Store 2	925	103	72	1613			
6		Store 3	788	119	64	1612			
7		Store 4	858	114	63	1381			
8		Store 5	928	107	70	1748			
9		Store 6	758	120	72	1645			
10		Store 7	963	104	66	1290			
11		Store 8	918	119	60	1779			
12		Store 9	876	94	61	1325			
13		Store 10	997	102	72	1453			
14									
15								DMU	2
16	Decisions	*Weights*	0.00094	0.00000	0.01241	0.00007			
17									
18	Objective	*Efficiency*	925	103	0	0	0.869		
19									
20	Constraints	Input	0	0	72	1613	1.000	=	1
21		Store 1	761	109	-56	-1476	-0.078	<=	0
22		Store 2	925	103	-72	-1613	-0.131	<=	0
23		Store 3	788	119	-64	-1612	-0.161	<=	0
24		Store 4	858	114	-63	-1381	-0.067	<=	0
25		Store 5	928	107	-70	-1748	-0.113	<=	0
26		Store 6	758	120	-72	-1645	-0.290	<=	0
27		Store 7	963	104	-66	-1290	0.000	<=	0
28		Store 8	918	119	-60	-1779	0.000	<=	0
29		Store 9	876	94	-61	-1325	-0.022	<=	0
30		Store 10	997	102	-72	-1453	-0.053	<=	0
31									

| ◄ ◄ ► ► \ 11.24 \ 11.25 / ◄ | | |

some measure of efficiency. Our model tells us that if that measure were based on weights of 0.00094, 0.0, 0.01241, and 0.00007, then Store 2 would achieve the highest efficiency it could reach, 0.869. But even then, two other stores in the chain would achieve higher efficiency values. In that sense, we can conclude that Store 2 is operating inefficiently. When we analyze other stores in the chain, we can discover which ones are operating efficiently.

We could construct similar worksheets for the analysis of other stores following the same format. However, much of the content on those worksheets would be identical, so we can design a more streamlined approach to the analysis. Figure 11.25 contains a version of the model that actually handles the analysis for all 10 stores. The array in rows 4–13, as before, contains the problem data. Cell I15 contains the store number for the DMU being analyzed. Based on this choice, two adjustments must be made in the linear programming model. First, the outputs for the store being analyzed must be selected for use in the objective function, in cells C18:D18. Second, the inputs for the store being analyzed must be selected for use in the equality constraint, in cells E20:F20. These selections are highlighted in bold in Figure 11.25. The INDEX function uses the store number in cell I15 to copy the objective function coefficients from the data array into cells C18:D18. It also copies the input values from the data array into cells E20:F20. The four cells in bold format thus change when we enter a different selection in cell I15.

EXCEL TIP
The INDEX Function

The INDEX function in Excel finds a value in a rectangular array according to the row number and column number of its location. The basic form of the function, as we use it for DEA models, is the following:

INDEX(*Array, Row, Column*)

- *Array* references a rectangular array.
- *Row* specifies a row number in the array.
- *Column* specifies a column number in the array. If *Array* has just one column, then this argument can be omitted.

In the example of Figure 11.25, suppose *Array* = C4:C13 and *Row* = I15. When cell I15 contains the number 4, the function INDEX(C4:C13, $I$15) finds the element in the fourth row of the array in cells C4:C13. In this case, the function returns the Profit output value for Store 4, or 858. This calculation would be suitable for cell C18, and the formula could be copied to cell D18, producing the entry INDEX(D4:D13, $I$15) and the corresponding value of 114. ∎

The analysis of the stores in the chain requires that we solve the model in Figure 11.25 several times, once for each DMU. In our example, we vary the contents of cell I15 from 1 to 10. For each value, we save the essential results in some other place before switching to a new DMU. In particular, we want to save the weights and the value of the objective function. Figure 11.26 shows a worksheet containing a summary of the 10 optimizations for the 10-store example (one from each choice of cell G16). This summary can be generated automatically with one run of the Solver Sensitivity tool.

As we can see in Figure 11.26, there are four efficient stores in our example: Stores 1, 4, 7, and 8. The other stores are inefficient, at levels ranging from 87 to 97 percent.

FIGURE 11.26 Sensitivity Report for the Allocation Example

	A	B	C	D	E	F	G
1	DMU	Efficiency	Profit	Volume	Hours	Cost	
2	1	1.000	0.00027	0.00728	0.01199	0.00022	
3	2	0.869	0.00094	0.00000	0.01241	0.00007	
4	3	0.973	0.00000	0.00818	0.00927	0.00025	
5	4	1.000	0.00012	0.00786	0.00000	0.00072	
6	5	0.885	0.00095	0.00000	0.01261	0.00007	
7	6	0.907	0.00000	0.00756	0.00856	0.00023	
8	7	1.000	0.00104	0.00000	0.00000	0.00078	
9	8	1.000	0.00109	0.00000	0.01440	0.00008	
10	9	0.974	0.00111	0.00000	0.01470	0.00008	
11	10	0.946	0.00095	0.00000	0.01254	0.00007	
12							

◄ ◄ ► ►I \ 11.26 / ◄ | ► |

This means that the inefficient stores could probably learn something by examining the way that the efficient stores are run. For this reason, DEA is often used to organize benchmarking visits within the divisions or branches of a large organization.

11.8 SUMMARY

Linear programming represents the most widely used optimization technique in practice. In this chapter, we have taken note of the special features of a linear program: a linear objective function and linear constraints. Linearity in the optimization model allows us to apply the simplex method as a solution procedure, which in turn guarantees finding a global optimum whenever an optimum of any kind exists. Therefore, when we have a choice, we are better off with a linear formulation of a problem than with a nonlinear formulation.

To develop facility with the linear solver, it helps to practice formulating, solving, and interpreting linear programming problems. The spreadsheet layout can be somewhat standardized, and a number of additional guidelines become helpful.

- Follow a standard form whenever possible, relying on the SUMPRODUCT function.

- Enter cell references in the Solver windows; keep numerical values in cells.

- Use a linear model in preference to a nonlinear model.

- If the model contains simple bounds, place them near the decision variable cells.

- Show constraint relationships ($\leq, =, \geq$) on the worksheet.

- Group like constraints together (i.e., similar in logical direction.)

- Align data with decisions when appropriate.

- Use the weak form of a constraint and give the model maximum flexibility.

- For blending models, add redundant but more intuitive calculations of blending constraints, outside of the Solver model.

- Explore some feasible (and infeasible) possibilities as a way of debugging the model.

- Test intuition and suggest hypotheses before running Solver.

- Identify the patterns of economic priorities that appear in the solution.

Along with the technical information that we have covered, these guidelines help accelerate the process of building and applying linear programming models successfully.

One last caveat: While optimization is a powerful technique, we should not assume that a solution that is optimal for a model is also optimal for the real world. Because every model is a simplification, any optimal solution from a model must be interpreted before it can be applied in the real world. Often, the realities of the application will force changes in the optimal solution determined by the model. One powerful method for making this translation is to look for the pattern, or the economic priorities, in the optimal solution. These economic priorities are often more valuable to decision makers than the precise solution to a particular instance of the model.

SUGGESTED READINGS

Some advanced perspectives on optimization techniques, along with some guidance in constructing optimization models, can be found in the following books:

Baker, K. R. 2006. *Optimization Modeling with Spreadsheets.* Belmont, CA: Duxbury Press.

Fourer, R., D. F. Gay, and B. W. Kernighan. 2003. *AMPL: A Modeling Language for Mathematical Programming.* Belmont, CA: Duxbury Press.

Rardin, R. L. 1998. *Optimization in Operations Research.* Upper Saddle River, N J: Prentice–Hall.

Schrage, L. 1997. *Optimization Modeling with LINDO.* 5th ed. Belmont, CA: Duxbury Press.

Williams, H. P. 1999. *Model Building in Mathematical Programming.* 3d ed. Chichester: John Wiley & Sons.

EXERCISES

1. *Production Planning.* The Bogard Corporation produces three types of bookcases, which it sells to large office supply companies. The production of each bookcase requires two machine operations, trimming and shaping, followed by assembly, which includes inspection and packaging. All three types require 0.4 hour of assembly time, but the machining operations have different processing times, as shown here, in hours per unit:

	Standard	Narrow	Wide
Trimmer	0.2	0.4	0.6
Shaper	0.6	0.2	0.5

Each machine is available 150 hours per month, and the current size of the assembly department provides capacity of 600 hours. Each bookcase produced yields a unit profit contribution as follows:

	Standard	Narrow	Wide
Profit	$8	$6	$10

a. What are the optimal production quantities for the company?

b. What is the pattern in the optimal allocation?

2. *Fertilizing the Lawn.* The facilities manager at Oxbridge University is planning to apply fertilizer to the grass in the quadrangle area in the spring. The grass needs nitrogen, phosphorus, and potash in at least the amounts given in the following table.

Mineral	Minimum Weight (lb)
Nitrogen	12
Phosphorus	14
Potash	18

Three kinds of commercial fertilizer are available, with mineral content and prices per 1,000 pounds as given in the following table. There is virtually unlimited supply of each kind of fertilizer.

Fertilizer	Nitrogen Content (lb)	Phosphorus Content (lb)	Potash Content (lb)	Price ($)
A	20	10	5	10
B	10	5	15	8
C	15	10	5	7

How much of each fertilizer should be purchased to satisfy the requirements at minimum cost?

3. *Coordinating Production and Marketing.* The Andrews Apple Products Company purchases apples from local growers and makes applesauce and apple juice. It costs $0.80 to produce a jar of applesauce and $0.60 to produce a bottle of apple juice. The company has a policy that at least 20 percent but not more than 60 percent of its output must be applesauce.

The company wants to meet but not exceed the demand for each product. The marketing manager estimates that the demand for applesauce is a maximum of 5,000 jars, plus an additional 3 jars for each $1 spent on advertising for applesauce. The maximum demand for apple juice is estimated to be 4,000 bottles, plus an additional 5 bottles for every $1 spent on advertising for apple juice. The company has $16,000 to spend on producing and advertising its two products. Applesauce sells for $1.75 per jar; apple juice sells for $1.75 per bottle. The company wants to know how many units of each product to produce, and how much advertising to spend on each product, in order to maximize profit.

a. What are the optimal quantities of applesauce and apple juice for Andrews to produce? (Rounding off is acceptable.)

b. What is the optimal amount to spend on advertising? What is the optimal profit?

c. Describe the qualitative pattern in the solution.

4. *Managing a Portfolio.* A local bank wants to build a bond portfolio from a set of five bonds with $1 million available for investment. The expected annual return, the worst-case annual return on each bond, and the "duration" of each bond are given in the following table. (The duration of a bond is a measure of the bond's sensitivity to interest rates.)

	Expected Return	Worst Case Return	Duration
Bond 1	12.5%	8.0%	8
Bond 2	11.5%	7.5%	7
Bond 3	10.5%	6.8%	6
Bond 4	9.5%	7.0%	5
Bond 5	8.5%	7.4%	3

- The average worst-case return for the portfolio must be at least 7.2 percent.
- The average duration of the portfolio must be at most 6.
- Because of diversification requirements, at most 40 percent of the total amount invested can be invested in a single bond.

a. What is the maximum return on the $1 million investment? How should the investment be distributed among the bonds to achieve this return? (Assume that bonds can be purchased in fractional amounts.)

b. What is the qualitative pattern in the optimal solution?

c. What is the marginal rate of return on the investment amount? That is, what would be the percentage return on an additional dollar invested? (Give the percentage to four significant figures.)

5. *Planning Automobile Production.* The Auto Company of America (ACA) produces four types of cars: subcompact, compact, intermediate, and luxury. ACA also produces trucks and vans. Vendor capacities limit total production capacity to at most 1.2 million vehicles per year. Subcompacts and compacts are built together in a facility with a total annual capacity of 620,000 cars. Intermediate and luxury cars are produced in another facility with capacity of 400,000; and the truck/van facility has a capacity of 275,000. ACA's marketing strategy requires that subcompacts and compacts must constitute at least half of the product mix for the four car types. The Corporate Average Fuel Economy (CAFE) standards in the Energy Policy and Conservation Act require an average fleet fuel economy of at least 27 mpg.

Profit margins, market potential, and fuel efficiencies are summarized as follows:

Type	Profit Margin ($/vehicle)	Market Potential (sales in '000)	Fuel Economy (mpg)
Subcompact	150	600	40
Compact	225	400	34

Intermediate	250	300	15
Luxury	500	225	12
Truck	400	325	20
Van	200	100	25

a. What is the optimal profit for ACA?

b. What is the pattern in the optimal allocation?

c. How much would optimal annual profits drop if the fuel economy requirement were raised to 28 mpg?

6. *Making Beer.* The Schutzberg Brewery has received an order for 1500 gallons of 3 percent beer (that is, 3 percent alcoholic content). This is a custom order because Schutzberg does not produce a 3 percent product. They do brew the following products.

Product	Percent Alcohol	Cost per Gallon
Free	0.25	0.55
Light	2.50	0.65
Amber	4.50	0.80
Dark	6.00	0.75

There are 500 gallons of each of these products on hand. Rather than brewing a 3 percent beer from scratch, the brewmaster has decided to mix existing stocks, perhaps with some water (0 percent alcoholic content), to satisfy this small order in the shortest possible time, hoping that the taste will be adequate. In case the taste is bad and he has to throw the mixture out, he would like to minimize the cost of the mix.

a. What are the components of the least-cost blend that will result in a 3 percent beer?

b. What is the total cost for the 1,500 gallons of product?

c. Use the pattern in (b) to trace the effects of increasing the order by 10 percent. How will the optimal mix change? How will the optimal cost change?

7. *Make or Buy.* A sudden increase in the demand for smoke detectors has left Acme Alarms with insufficient capacity to meet demand. The company has seen monthly demand from its retailers for its electronic and battery-operated detectors rise to 20,000 and 10,000, respectively. Acme's production process involves three departments: fabrication, assembly, and shipping. The relevant quantitative data on production and prices are summarized as follows.

Department	Monthly Hours Available	Hours/Unit (Electronic)	Hours/Unit (Battery)
Fabrication	2,000	0.15	0.10
Assembly	4,200	0.20	0.20
Shipping	2,500	0.10	0.15
Variable cost/unit		$18.80	$16.00
Retail price		$29.50	$28.00

The company also has the option to obtain additional units from a subcontractor, who has offered to supply up to 20,000 units per month in any combination of electric and battery-operated models, at a charge of $21.50 per unit. For this price, the subcontractor will test and ship its models directly to the retailers without using Acme's production process.

a. What are the maximum profit and the corresponding make/buy levels? (Fractional decisions are acceptable.)

b. Describe the qualitative pattern in the solution.

c. Use the pattern in (b) to trace the effects of increasing the fabrication capacity by 10 percent. How will the optimal make/buy mix change? How will the optimal profit change?

d. For how much of a change in fabrication capacity will the pattern persist?

8. *Leasing Warehouse Space.* Cox Cable Company needs to lease warehouse storage space for five months at the start of the year. Cox knows how much space will be required in each month, and the company can purchase a variety of lease contracts to meet these needs. For example, Cox can purchase one-month leases in each month from January to May. The company can also purchase two-month leases in January through April, three-month leases in January through March, four-month leases in January and February, or a five-month lease in January. In total, the company could use 15 possible leases. Cox must decide which leases to purchase and how many square feet to purchase on each lease.

Since the space requirements differ month to month, it may be economical to lease only the amount needed each month on a month-by-month basis. On the other hand, the monthly cost for leasing space for additional months is much less than for the first month, so it may be desirable to lease the maximum amount needed for the entire five months. Another option is the intermediate approach of changing the total amount of space leased (by adding a new lease and/or having an old lease expire) at least once, but not every month. Two or more leases for different terms can begin at the same time.

The space requirements (in square feet) are shown in the following table.

	Month				
	Jan	Feb	Mar	Apr	May
Required space	15,000	10,000	20,000	5,000	25,000

Leasing costs (in dollars per thousand square feet) are given in the next table.

	Length of Lease				
	1	2	3	4	5
Cost ($/TSF)	$280	450	600	730	820

The task is to find a leasing schedule that provides the necessary amounts of space at the minimum cost.

a. Determine the optimal leasing schedule. What is the optimal total cost and the corresponding schedule?

b. Describe the qualitative pattern in the solution.

c. Use the pattern in (b) to trace the effects of increasing the space required for January. How will the leasing schedule change? How will the total cost change?

d. For how much of a change in January's requirement will the pattern persist?

9. *Oil Blending.* An oil company produces three brands of oils: Regular, Multigrade, and Supreme. Each brand of oil is composed of one or more of four crude stocks, each having a different viscosity index. The relevant data concerning the crude stocks are:

Crude Stock	Viscosity Index	Cost ($/barrel)	Supply per day (barrels)
1	20	7.10	1,000
2	40	8.50	1,100
3	30	7.70	1,200
4	55	9.00	1,100

Each brand of oil must meet a minimum standard for viscosity index, and each brand thus sells at a different price. The relevant data concerning the three brands of oil are:

Brand	Minimum Viscosity Index	Selling Price ($/barrel)	Daily Demand (barrels)
Regular	25	8.50	2,000
Multigrade	35	9.00	1,500
Supreme	50	10.00	750

a. The daily demands represent potential sales. In other words, the model should contain demand ceilings (upper limits). What is the optimal profit under these assumptions?

b. The daily demands are to be met precisely. In other words, the model should contain demand constraints in the form of equalities. What is the optimal profit under these assumptions?

c. The daily demands represent minimum sales commitments, but all output can be sold. In other words, the model should permit production to exceed daily demand. What is the optimal profit under these assumptions?

10. *Coffee Blending and Sales.* Hill-O-Beans Coffee Company blends four component beans into three final blends of coffee: one is sold to luxury hotels, another to restaurants, and the third to supermarkets for store-label brands. The company has four reliable bean supplies: Robusta, Javan Arabica, Liberica, and Brazilian Arabica. The following: table summarizes the very precise recipes for the final coffee blends, the cost and availability information for the four components, and the wholesale price per pound of the final blends. The percentages indicate the fraction of each component to be used in each blend.

Component	Hotel	Restaurant	Market	Cost per Pound	Max Weekly Availability (lbs)
Robusta	20%	35%	10%	$0.60	40,000
Javan Arabica	40%	15%	35%	$0.80	25,000
Liberica	15%	20%	40%	$0.55	20,000
Brazilian Arabica	25%	30%	15%	$0.70	45,000
Wholesale Price Per Pound	$1.25	$1.50	$1.40		

The processor's plant can handle no more than 100,000 pounds per week, but there is virtually unlimited demand for the final blends. However, the marketing department requires minimum production levels of 10,000, 25,000, and 30,000 pounds, respectively, for the hotel, restaurant, and market blends.

a. In order to maximize weekly profit, how many pounds of each component should be purchased?

b. What is the economic value of an additional pound's worth of plant capacity?

c. How much (per pound) should Hill-O-Beans be willing to pay for additional pounds of Liberica in order to raise total profit?

d. Construct a graph to show how the optimal profit varies with the minimum weekly production level of the hotel blend.

e. Construct a graph to show how the optimal profit varies with the unit cost of Robusta beans.

11. *Coordinating advertising and production.* The Hawley Lighting Company manufactures four families of household lighting at its factory. The product families are table lamps, floor lamps, ceiling fixtures, and pendant lamps. The following table shows the average material costs for each of the products.

Product	Table	Floor	Ceiling	Pendant
Material cost	$66	85	50	80

Each product is made in one of two production processes by purchasing components, assembling and testing the product, and finally packaging it for shipping. Table lamps and floor lamps go through the assembly and finishing process in Department 1, while ceiling fixtures and pendant lamps go through the process in Department 2. Variable production costs and capacities (measured in units of product) are shown in the following table. The capacities are measured in units of product. Note that there are regular and overtime possibilities for each department.

| Process | Regular Time | | Overtime | |
	Unit Cost	Capacity	Unit Cost	Capacity
Department 1	$16	100,000	18	25,000
Department 2	12	90,000	15	24,000

Average selling prices for the four products are known, and estimates have been made of the market demand for each product at these prices. These figures are shown in the following table.

	Table	Floor	Ceiling	Pendant
Selling price	$120	150	100	160
Potential sales (000)	60	20	100	35
Advertising effect	12%	10%	8%	15%

Sales levels can also be affected by advertising expenditures. Starting with the demand levels in the table, an increase of up to $10,000 in advertising raises the demand by the percentage shown in the last row. An expenditure of less than $10,000 in advertising will lead to a proportional effect on demand. For example, an increase in advertising of $5,000 for table lamps would raise demand by 6 percent, or 3,600 units. However, there is a budget limit of $18,000 on the total amount to be spent on advertising among all four products.

a. What is an optimal output plan for the company?

b. For each department, what is the marginal value of additional overtime capacity?

c. What is the marginal value of additional advertising dollars?

d. What is the marginal value of additional sales for each product?

12. *Scheduling staff.* You are the director of the Computer Center for Gaillard College and responsible for scheduling the staffing of the center, which is open from 8 A.M. until midnight. You have monitored the usage of the center at various times of the day and determined that the following number of computer consultants are required:

Time of Day	Minimum Number of Consultants Required to Be on Duty
8 A.M. – noon	4
Noon – 4 P.M.	8
4 P.M. – 8 P.M.	10
8 P.M. – midnight	6

Two types of computer consultants can be hired: full-time and part-time. The full-time consultants work for eight consecutive hours in any of the following shifts: morning (8 A.M. – 4 P.M.), afternoon (noon – 8 P.M.), and evening (4 P.M. – midnight). Full-time consultants are paid $14 per hour.

Part-time consultants can be hired to work any of the four shifts listed in the table. Part-time consultants are paid $12 per hour. An additional requirement is that during every time period, at least one full-time consultant must be on duty for every part-time consultant on duty.

a. Determine a minimum-cost staffing plan for the center. How many full-time and part-time consultants will be needed? What is the minimum cost?

b. After thinking about this problem for a while, you have decided to recognize meal breaks explicitly in the schedul-

ing of full-time consultants. In particular, full-time consultants are entitled to a one-hour lunch break during their eight-hour shift. In addition, employment rules specify that the lunch break can start after three hours of work or after four hours of work, but those are the only alternatives. Part-time consultants do not receive a meal break. Under these conditions, what staffing schedule minimizes costs? What is the minimum cost?

13. *Project Scheduling.* A construction contractor is responsible for a project with seven key tasks. Some of the tasks can begin at any time, but others have predecessor tasks that must be completed previously. The individual tasks can be carried out at standard times, or they can be expedited ("crashed"). The cost of executing the task increases by a certain cost per day if its time is shortened. The following table shows the information describing the tasks of the project, their standard and minimum times (in days), their standard costs, the crashing cost per day shortened, and the predecessor(s).

Task Number	Minimum Time	Standard Time	Standard Cost	Cost/Day to Shorten	Predecessor Tasks
1	6	12	$ 1,600	$100	None
2	8	16	2,400	75	None
3	16	24	2,900	120	2
4	14	20	1,900	100	1, 2
5	4	16	3,800	140	3
6	12	16	2,900	165	3
7	2	12	1,300	60	4

The project has a deadline of 40 days, which the contractor is committed to meet.

a. If no crashing is done, how long will the project take, and what will be its cost?

b. Which activities should be crashed to achieve the least-cost schedule that meets a 40-day deadline? What is the difference between its cost and the cost in part (a)?

14. *Cargo Loading.* You are in charge of loading cargo ships for International Cargo Company (ICC) at a major East Coast port. You have been asked to prepare a loading plan for an ICC freighter bound for Africa. An agricultural commodities dealer would like to transport the following products aboard this ship:

Commodity	Tons Available	Volume per Ton (cu ft)	Profit per Ton ($)
1	4,000	40	70
2	3,000	25	50
3	2,000	60	60
4	1,000	50	80

You can elect to load any or all of the available commodities. However, the ship has three cargo holds with the following capacity restrictions:

Cargo Hold	Weight Capacity (tons)	Volume Capacity (cu ft)
Forward	3,000	100,000
Center	5,000	150,000
Rear	2,000	120,000

More than one type of commodity can be placed in the same cargo hold. However, because of balance considerations, the weight in the forward cargo hold must be within 10 percent of the weight in the rear cargo hold, and the center cargo hold must be between 40 and 60 percent of the total weight on board.

a. Determine a profit-maximizing loading plan for the commodities. What is the maximum profit and the loading plan that achieves it?

b. Suppose each one of the cargo holds could be expanded. Which holds and which forms of expansion (weight or volume) would allow ICC to increase its profits on this trip, and what is the marginal value of each form of expansion?

15. *Evaluating Performance.* Fidelity Savings & Loans (FS&L) operates a number of banking facilities throughout its region of the country. The officers of FS&L would like to analyze the efficiency of the various branch offices using DEA. The following data set has been selected to represent appropriate input and output measures of each banking facility. (Labor hours and Operating costs are considered inputs; Customer Satisfaction, New Loans and Return on Assets (ROA) are considered outputs.)

Branch	Labor Hrs.	Op. Costs	ROA	New Loans	Customer Satisfaction
1	3.73	6.34	5.32	770	92
2	3.49	4.43	3.39	780	94
3	5.98	6.31	4.95	790	93
4	6.49	7.28	6.01	730	82
5	7.09	8.69	6.40	910	98
6	3.46	3.23	2.89	860	90
7	7.36	9.07	6.94	880	89
8	6.38	7.42	7.18	970	99
9	4.74	6.75	5.98	770	94
10	5.04	6.35	4.97	930	91

a. Which branches are efficient?

b. Which branches are inefficient? For each inefficient branch, which other branches would be good benchmarking targets?

APPENDIX 11.1 THE SENSITIVITY REPORT

The Solver Sensitivity tool duplicates for optimization models the functionality of the Data Sensitivity tool for basic spreadsheet models. That parallelism makes Solver Sensitivity the vehicle of choice for most of the sensitivity analyses we might want to perform with optimization models. However, it is sometimes useful to draw on Excel's own sensitivity tool. The Sensitivity Report is one of three reports offered after a Solver run, once the optimal solution has been found. The other two reports are completely superfluous if a model has been constructed effectively, but the Sensitivity Report sometimes provides additional insight or efficiency.

To provide access to the Sensitivity Report, we must uncheck the box for Bypass Solver Reports in the Solver Options menu. After the optimal solution has been produced, we highlight Sensitivity in the Reports list in the Solver Results window. The Sensitivity Report for linear programs has two sections. The top section (titled Adjustable Cells) deals with the objective function and, in particular, with the coefficients in the objective function corresponding to each of the decision variables. The bottom section (titled Constraints) deals with the values of the constants on the right-hand sides. Figure 11A1 shows the Sensitivity Report for the Veerman Furniture (allocation) example.

In the top section, the report provides the values of the decision variables in the optimal solution (under Final Value) and the values of the coefficients in the objective function (under Objective Coefficient). The Allowable Increase and Allowable Decrease show how much we could change any one of the objective function coefficients without altering the optimal product mix—that is, without altering any of the decision variables. For example, the objective function coefficient for desks is $24.00 in the base case. This figure could rise to $54.00 or drop to $22.50 without having an impact on the optimal product mix. (Of course, the optimal profit would change because the number of desks remains fixed.) A similar range is provided for the other two variables, with 1E+30 symbolizing infinity in the report's output. Finally, there is a column labeled Reduced Cost. Entries in this column are zero for variables that are not at their bound (in this case, the bounds are zero). For chairs, the reduced cost of −1 reflects the fact that the objective function coefficient of $15 would have to improve by more than $1 before there would be an incentive to use chairs in the optimal mix. However, this same information is available in the Allowable Increase column for chairs. In most cases, the Reduced Cost information in the report is redundant.

In the bottom section, the report provides the values of the constraint left-hand sides (under Final Value) and the right-hand-side constraint constants (under Constraint R.H. Side), along with the shadow price for each constraint. The Allowable Increase and Allowable Decrease show how much we could change any one of the constraint constants without altering any of the shadow prices. For

FIGURE 11A1 Sensitivity Report for the Allocation Example

Microsoft Excel 11.0 Sensitivity Report							
Worksheet: [Sheets11.1W.xls]11.5							
Adjustable Cells							
Cell	Name	Final Value	Reduced Cost	Objective Coefficient	Allowable Increase	Allowable Decrease	
$B$5	Product mix C	0	-1	15	1	1E+30	
$C$5	Product mix D	275	0	24	30	1.5	
$D$5	Product mix T	100	0	18	1E+30	10	
Constraints							
Cell	Name	Final Value	Shadow Price	Constraint R.H. Side	Allowable Increase	Allowable Decrease	
$E$11	Fabrication LHS	1850	4	1850	150	1650	
$E$12	Assembly LHS	2075	0	2400	1E+30	325	
$E$13	Shipping LHS	950	0	1500	1E+30	550	
$E$14	Chair market LHS	0	0	360	1E+30	360	
$E$15	Desk market LHS	275	0	300	1E+30	25	
$E$16	Table market LHS	100	10	100	60.9375	75	

FIGURE 11A2 Sensitivity Report for the Covering Example

Microsoft Excel 11.0 Sensitivity Report
Worksheet: [Sheets11.1W.xls]11.9

Adjustable Cells

Cell	Name	Final Value	Reduced Cost	Objective Coefficient	Allowable Increase	Allowable Decrease
$B$5	Amounts S	0.39	0.00	4	1.064766839	3.7
$C$5	Amounts R	0.15	0.85	5	1E+30	0.849173554
$D$5	Amounts F	1.36	0.00	3	2.651612903	1.72
$E$5	Amounts P	0.15	4.35	7	1E+30	4.351239669
$F$5	Amounts W	0.15	2.00	6	1E+30	2

Constraints

Cell	Name	Final Value	Shadow Price	Constraint R.H. Side	Allowable Increase	Allowable Decrease
$G$11	Vitamins LHS	27.97004132	0	16	11.97004132	1E+30
$G$12	Minerals LHS	10.07913223	0	10	0.079132231	1E+30
$G$13	Protein LHS	15	0.17768595	15	7.29375	0.319166667
$G$14	Calories LHS	600	0.007644628	600	5836.5	8.326086957

example, the number of Fabrication hours (1,850 in the base case) could change from 200 to 2,000 without affecting the shadow price of $4.00.

The ranging analysis for right-hand side constraint constants is omitted for constraints that involve a simple lower bound or upper bound. That is, if the form of the constraint is Variable ≤ Ceiling or else Variable ≥ Floor, then the sensitivity analysis will not appear. But, if the same information is incorporated into the model using the standard SUMPRODUCT constraint form, as in the case of the product mix model, then the Sensitivity Report will treat the constraint in its usual fashion and include it in the Constraints table. As an example, consider the modified version of the Dahlby Outfitters (covering) example, with a floor of 0.15 for each of the decision variables. Although there are four original constraints and five additional constraints limiting the decision variables to values no less than 0.15, the Sensitivity Report shows information for only the four original constraints (see Figure 11A2).

Compared to the Solver Sensitivity output, the Sensitivity Report is more precise but less flexible. The Sensitivity Report is more precise than Solver Sensitivity with respect to the question of where the decision variables change or where a shadow price changes. For our allocation example, recall that we could not tell precisely when the shadow price drops from $3.75 to $2.32. Only by searching on a smaller grid could we detect where the change takes place, and even that would require some careful interpolation in the table to obtain the exact value. By contrast, if we were to solve a base-case model in which there were 2,200 Fabrication hours, and if we asked for the Sensitivity Report, we would be able to see from the Allowable Increase on Fabrication hours that the shadow price holds up to 2,666.67 hours.

The Sensitivity Report is less flexible than Solver Sensitivity output with respect to the user's ability to tailor the analysis. The Sensitivity Report cannot "see" beyond the Allowable Increase or the Allowable Decrease. However, a coarse grid search using Solver Sensitivity can show how values in the model change beyond these ranges. In addition, Solver Sensitivity can track the effect of varying a parameter on any cells in the spreadsheet. The Sensitivity Report, by contrast, does not tell us explicitly how the objective function changes when we vary one of the objective function coefficients, nor does it tell us how the decision variables change when we vary one of the constraint constants. Solver Sensitivity can even track the effect of varying a parameter that is not, strictly speaking, within the model itself. For example, suppose there were several constraint constants that represented capacities and that these capacities could all be increased by a common percentage. Solver Sensitivity could be set up to track the decision variables and the objective function as functions of this percentage.

In addition, Solver Sensitivity can perform two-way analyses, in the same spirit as the two-way analysis in the Data Table tool. When we also consider the user's ability to tailor the analysis, something that is lacking in the Sensitivity Report, we conclude that the Solver Sensitivity is usally the preferred way of doing sensitivity analysis, in spite of the loss in precision.

12 Network Models

12.1 INTRODUCTION

As mentioned in the previous chapter, there are four main types of linear programming structures, three of which we covered in that chapter. The fourth type is the **network model**, which is the subject of this chapter. We find it useful to subdivide network models into three subcategories, but common to all network models is our use of a diagram to help formulate and solve linear programming problems.

The network model describes patterns of flow in a connected system, where the flow might involve material, people, or funds. The system elements may be locations, such as cities, warehouses, or assembly lines; or they may be points in time rather than points in space. When we construct diagrams to represent such systems, the elements are represented by **nodes**, or circles, in the diagram. The paths of flow are represented by **arcs**, or arrows. Figure 12.1 shows a very simple diagram, in which the network elements are a factory (node 1) and two warehouses (nodes 2 and 3). The arc from node 1 to node 2 carries the flow (truckloads of goods, perhaps) from the factory to the first warehouse; similarly, the arc from node 1 to node 3 carries the flow from the factory to the second warehouse.

As we shall see, drawing a network diagram helps us formulate an appropriate linear programming model, and if we encounter difficulties in getting our model to work, the diagram can also be a helpful device for troubleshooting.

12.2 THE TRANSPORTATION MODEL

A very common supply chain involves the shipment of goods from suppliers at one set of locations to customers at another. The supplier may own several factories that fabricate component parts, while the customers are assembly plants that build and test products. Alternatively, the supplier may be a wholesaler who stocks food in several warehouses, while the customer is part of a chain of grocery stores that reorder separately on a regular basis. A supply-chain structure of this sort lends itself to representation as a **transportation model**. The classic transportation model is characterized by a set of supply sources (each with known capacities), a set of demand locations (each with known requirements), and the unit costs of transportation between supply–demand pairs. A case in point is Bonner Electronics.

FIGURE 12.1 A Simple Network Diagram

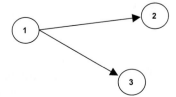

EXAMPLE
Bonner
Electronics

Bonner Electronics is planning next week's shipments from its three manufacturing plants to its four distribution warehouses and is seeking a minimum-cost shipping schedule. Each plant has a potential capacity, expressed in cartons of product, and each warehouse has a week's requirement that must be met. There are 12 possible shipment routes, and for each route, the unit shipping cost is known. The following table below provides the given information for this example.

Plant	Warehouse				
	Atlanta	Boston	Chicago	Denver	Capacity
Minneapolis	$0.60	$0.56	$0.22	$0.40	9,000
Pittsburgh	0.36	0.30	0.28	0.58	12,000
Tucson	0.65	0.68	0.55	0.42	13,000
Requirement	7,500	8,500	9,500	8,000	

■

12.2.1 Flow Diagram

A flow diagram, showing the possible routes, is depicted in Figure 12.2. In the diagram, the node letters on the left designate manufacturing plants, which supply the product. The node letters on the right stand for warehouses, where the demands occur. In this case, all supply–demand pairs represent feasible routes for the shipment plan.

Each route of flow incurs a cost: the unit cost of flow from any plant to any warehouse is given in the table containing the parameters of the problem. The flows along each of the 12 possible routes constitute the decision variables in the model. Although the diagram does not contain labels for the arcs, it would be natural to use the notation *MA* for the quantity shipped on the route from Minneapolis to Atlanta, *MB* for the quantity shipped on the route from Minneapolis to Boston, and so on. In the network diagram, each arc represents a decision.

12.2.2 Formulation

The transportation model has two kinds of constraints: less-than capacity constraints and greater-than demand constraints, assuming total demand does not exceed capacity. For the Minneapolis plant, we can express the capacity constraint as follows:

$$MA + MB + MC + MD \leq 9,000$$

In words, the total amount shipped out of Minneapolis must be less than or equal to the Minneapolis capacity. For Pittsburgh and Tucson, we have similar constraints:

FIGURE 12.2 Diagram for Bonner Electronics

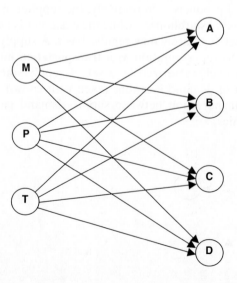

$$PA + PB + PC + PD \leq 12,000$$
$$TA + TB + TC + TD \leq 13,000$$

Note that the left-hand side of these constraints simply adds the outbound shipment quantities from a given location. For that reason, we don't really need to use the SUMPRODUCT formula in a spreadsheet representation; we can get by with the simpler SUM formula.

For the Atlanta warehouse, the demand constraint reads:

$$MA + PA + TA \geq 7,500$$

In words, the amount received at Atlanta must be greater than or equal to the Atlanta requirement. Similarly, for the other three warehouses, the demand constraints become

$$MB + PB + TB \geq 8,500$$
$$MC + PC + TC \geq 9,500$$
$$MD + PD + TD \geq 8,000$$

Again, the left-hand sides of these constraints can easily be expressed using the SUM formula. Putting both kinds of constraints together, and building an objective function from the same set of variables, we can create the following algebraic statement of the model.

$$\text{Maximize } z = 0.60\,MA + 0.56MB + 0.22MC + 0.40MD + 0.36PA + 0.30PB$$
$$+ 0.28PC + 0.58PD + 0.65TA + 0.68TB + 0.55TC + 0.42TD$$

subject to

$$
\begin{aligned}
MA + MB + MC + MD &\leq 9,000 \\
PA + PB + PC + PD &\leq 12,000 \\
TA + TB + TC + TD &\leq 13,000 \\
MA + PA + TA &\geq 7,500 \\
MB + PB + TB &\geq 8,500 \\
MC + PC + TC &\geq 9,500 \\
MD + PD + TD &\geq 8,000
\end{aligned}
$$

12.2.3 Spreadsheet Model

Figure 12.3[*] displays a worksheet for this problem. Notice the distinctive From/To structure in the table describing the problem's data. This structure lends itself readily to a row-and-column format, which is the essence of spreadsheet layout. Here, we adopt the convention that flow moves conceptually *from* the rows of the worksheet *to* the columns—for example, from Minneapolis to Atlanta. Because of this From/To structure, it is helpful to depart from the standard linear programming layout of the previous chapter and adopt a special format for this type of model. In particular, we can construct a model in rows and columns to mirror the table of parameters that describes the problem. In the Parameters module of the worksheet, we see all of the unit costs displayed in an array. In the Decisions module, the decision variables (shaded for highlighting) appear in an array of the same size. At the right of each decision row is the "Sent" quantity, which is simply the sum of the flows along the row. These figures align with the capacities given in the Parameters module. Below each decision column is the "Received" quantity, which is the sum down the column. These figures align with the demands given

FIGURE 12.3 Worksheet for the Bonner Electronics Model

	A	B	C	D	E	F	G
1	Transportation Model						
2							
3	Parameters						
4		From/To	Atl	Bos	Chi	Den	Capacity
5		Minn	0.60	0.56	0.22	0.40	9000
6		Pitt	0.36	0.30	0.28	0.58	12000
7		Tucs	0.65	0.68	0.55	0.42	13000
8		Required	7500	8500	9500	8000	
9							
10	Decisions						
11			Atl	Bos	Chi	Den	Sent
12		Minn	0	4000	5000	0	9000
13		Pitt	7500	4500	0	0	12000
14		Tucs	0	0	4500	8000	12500
15		Received	7500	8500	9500	8000	
16							
17	Objective						
18		Total Cost	$13,225				
19							

|◄ ◄ ► ►|\ 12.1 ⟨ 12.2 ⟩ 12.3 ⟨|◄

*To download spreadsheets for this chapter, go to the Student Companion Site at www.wiley.com/college/powell.

in the Parameters module. The objective function, which is expressed as a SUMPRODUCT in cell C18, is the total transportation cost for the system. A useful exercise for someone encountering the transportation model for the first time is to clear the decision-variable cells C12:F14 and search by trial and error for a low-cost shipment plan.

EXCEL TIP
The
SUMPRODUCT
Function

The SUMPRODUCT function in Excel takes the pairwise products of two sets of numbers and sums the products. The form of the function is the following:

SUMPRODUCT(*Array 1*, *Array 2*)

- *Array 1* references the first set of numbers.
- *Array 2* references the second set of numbers.

In the standard layout for linear programs, introduced in Chapter 11, the two arrays were each laid out as one row and several columns. However, in general, the arrays can be *m* rows by *n* columns, as long as both arrays are of the same size. It is this more general structure that we employ in the transportation model and other, similar models. ∎

12.2.4 Optimization

Now, with this formulation in mind, we can invoke Solver and specify:

Target cell	C18 (minimize)
Changing cells	C12:F14
Constraints	C15:F15 ≥ C8:F8 (*Received ≥ Required*)
	G12:G14 ≤ G5:G7 (*Sent ≤ Capacity*)

We select the linear solver and check the box for Assume Non-Negative. We obtain the solution shown in Figure 12.4, which achieves the minimum cost of $12,025. All requirement constraints in this solution are binding, even though we permitted the model to send more than the requirement to each warehouse. This result makes intuitive sense, because shipping more than is required to any warehouse would merely incur excess cost. Once we understand why there is no incentive to exceed demand, we can anticipate some excess capacity in the solution. This follows from the fact that total capacity comes to 34,000 cartons, while total demand is only 33,500. In particular, capacity constraints are binding at Pittsburgh and Minneapolis, but an excess capacity of 500 cartons remains at Tucson.

Now let's return to the diagram for our problem and check the figures. This time, we simplify the diagram by ignoring the variables that turned out to be zero, and we include just the nonzero shipments. Figure 12.5 shows the revised version of the network diagram.

At each node, arcs enter and arcs leave. We want to check that the configurations make sense at each location. For example, at node M, there is one outbound flow of 9000 cartons, which exactly meets capacity. At node P, there are two outbound

FIGURE 12.4 Optimal Solution to the Bonner Electronics Model

	A	B	C	D	E	F	G
1	Transportation Model						
2							
3	Parameters						
4		*From/To*	Atl	Bos	Chi	Den	Capacity
5		Minn	0.60	0.56	0.22	0.40	9000
6		Pitt	0.36	0.30	0.28	0.58	12000
7		Tucs	0.65	0.68	0.55	0.42	13000
8		*Required*	7500	8500	9500	8000	
9							
10	Decisions						
11			Atl	Bos	Chi	Den	Sent
12		Minn	0	0	9000	0	9000
13		Pitt	3500	8500	0	0	12000
14		Tucs	4000	0	500	8000	12500
15		Received	7500	8500	9500	8000	
16							
17	Objective						
18		Total Cost	$12,025				
19							

12.1 / 12.2 / 12.3 \ 12.4 /

FIGURE 12.5   Revised Flow Diagram for Bonner Electronics

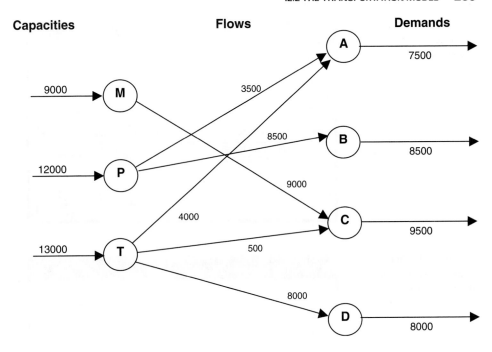

flows totaling 12,000, also meeting capacity. And at note T, there are three outbound flows totaling 12,500, which is less than capacity. A similar check shows that the inbound flows meet the various demand requirements.

12.2.5 Modifications to the Model

The model layout in Figure 12.4 has another virtue: it is easily expandable. Consider, for example, how to adapt the model to the situation in which Bonner Electronics adds a warehouse facility to its system. In Excel, select column E and then select Home▶Cells ▶Insert Sheet Columns. Figure 12.6 shows the result: both arrays (unit costs and decision variables) are expanded. The following steps are required to update the worksheet:

- Enter the location of the new warehouse in cells E4 and E11.
- Enter the inbound costs to the new warehouse in cells E5:E7.
- Enter the demand at the new warehouse in cell E8.
- Copy the formula in cell D15 to E15.

After taking these steps, a look at the Solver Parameters windows tells us that the model is ready to solve, as shown in Figure 12.7. In other words, the formulas in

FIGURE 12.6   Expanded Version of the Spreadsheet Model

	A	B	C	D	E	F	G	H
1	Transportation Model							
2								
3	Parameters							
4		*From/To*	Atl	Bos		Chi	Den	*Capacity*
5		Minn	0.60	0.56		0.22	0.40	9000
6		Pitt	0.36	0.30		0.28	0.58	12000
7		Tucs	0.65	0.68		0.55	0.42	13000
8		*Required*	7500	8500		9500	8000	
9								
10	Decisions							
11			Atl	Bos		Chi	Den	*Sent*
12		Minn	0	0		9000	0	9000
13		Pitt	3500	8500		0	0	12000
14		Tucs	4000	0		500	8000	12500
15		*Received*	7500	8500		9500	8000	
16								
17	Objective							
18		Total Cost	$12,025					
19								

◄ ► ►◄\ 12.1 ⟨ 12.2 ⟨ 12.3 ⟨ 12.4 ⟨ 12.5 ⟩ **12.6** ⟨ ‹

FIGURE 12.7 Solver Parameters Window for the Expanded Version of the Model

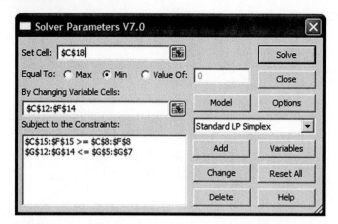

FIGURE 12.8 Bonner Electronics Model with Range Names Added

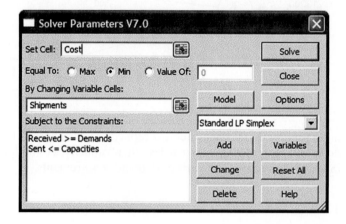

cells H12:H14 have automatically adapted to the expansion, and so has the objective function formula in cell C18.

One last feature of the transportation model is worth noting: It lends itself readily to the use of range names in Excel. Working with the model of Figure 12.4, we can add range names in the following locations:

- Cell C18 named "Cost"
- Cells C12:F14 named "Shipments"
- Cells G5:G7 named "Capacity"
- Cells G12:G14 named "Sent"
- Cells C8:F8 named "Demands"
- Cells C15:F15 named "Received"

With these names assigned, the Solver Parameters window takes the form shown in Figure 12.8. This format communicates the model to the user in a different way. The Solver Parameters window is somewhat self-documenting in this form. The range names would be useful when the model is fully debugged and offered to users who are not comfortable with the cell details that usually appear.

12.2.6 Sensitivity Analysis

The concepts of sensitivity analysis that were introduced in the previous chapter apply here as well. This means that the Solver Sensitivity tool may be used with network linear programming models with no new considerations. It also means that we can interpret patterns in the optimal solution in terms of economic priorities. We look at shadow prices in our network example to illustrate the concepts involved. (Recall from Chapter 11 that a shadow price is the breakeven price at which it would be attractive to acquire more of a scarce resource.)

FIGURE 12.9 Solver Sensitivity Output for the Bonner Electronics Model

	A	B	C	D	E	F	G	H	I	J	K	L	M	N	O
1	BosDemand	Total Cost	Change	MA	MB	MC	MD	PA	PB	PC	PD	TA	TB	TC	TD
2	8200	$11,848		0	0	9000	0	3800	8200	0	0	3700	0	500	8000
3	8300	$11,907	0.59	0	0	9000	0	3700	8300	0	0	3800	0	500	8000
4	8400	$11,966	0.59	0	0	9000	0	3600	8400	0	0	3900	0	500	8000
5	8500	$12,025	0.59	0	0	9000	0	3500	8500	0	0	4000	0	500	8000
6	8600	$12,084	0.59	0	0	9000	0	3400	8600	0	0	4100	0	500	8000
7	8700	$12,143	0.59	0	0	9000	0	3300	8700	0	0	4200	0	500	8000
8	8800	$12,202	0.59	0	0	9000	0	3200	8800	0	0	4300	0	500	8000
9															

12.9

In the transportation model, we have supply and demand constraints, and the solution to the model provides shadow prices on each. The shadow price on a demand constraint tells us how much it costs to ship the marginal unit to the corresponding location, and sometimes, this figure is not obvious without some careful thought.

Consider the demand at the Boston warehouse in the Bonner Electronics example. In the base case, shown in Figures 12.4 and 12.5, Boston demand is 8,500 cartons. All this quantity is supplied from Pittsburgh, incurring a shipping cost of $0.30 per carton. Suppose we vary the demand parameter from 8,200 to 8,800 in steps of 100 and examine the optimal solution. Figure 12.9 shows the resulting output from the Solver Sensitivity tool. As expected, the optimal total cost increases when Boston demand increases, but from the Change column of the report, we note that the marginal cost of meeting this demand is $0.59.

How do we reconcile the direct cost of $0.30 on the Pittsburgh–Boston route with the marginal cost of $0.59? One way to see the connection involves identifying the qualitative pattern in the problem's solution. In the previous chapter, we introduced the process of discovering a pattern in the optimal solution to a linear programming model. The main idea was to focus on positive variables and binding constraints, and then to identify a priority list that specifies the sequence in which the variables may be calculated. In network models, the steps can be facilitated by using network diagrams.

In this example, there are three supplies and four demands, giving rise to 12 possible shipment routes. Note, however, that the solution contains only six nonzero shipments: *MC*, *PA*, *PB*, *TA*, *TC*, and *TD*. The other routes can be ignored when constructing the pattern. This observation allows us to work with the simplified network diagram of Figure 12.5.

As we previously observed, all of the demand constraints are binding. The solution also tells us that two of the supply capacities are binding—in particular, the capacities at Minneapolis and Pittsburgh. The decision variables associated with Tucson are not determined by the capacity at Tucson; instead, as we shall see, they are determined by other constraints in the model.

In the optimal solution, some demands are met entirely from a unique source. For example, demand at Boston is all met from Pittsburgh, and demand at Denver is all met from Tucson. In some sense, these are high-priority allocations, and we can think of them as if they were made *first*. There is also a symmetric feature: supply from Minneapolis all goes to Chicago. Dedicating capacity to a unique demand also marks a high-priority allocation. Each of these variables appears alone (with no other positive variables) in a binding constraint.

Once we assign the high-priority allocations, we can ignore the supply at Minneapolis and the demands at Boston and Denver, and we can turn to the problem that remains. Thus, we proceed to a second-priority level, where we are left with a reduced problem containing two sources and two destinations, as shown in Figure 12.10. Here *PA* and *TC* are the high-priority allocations in the reduced problem. Setting *PA* = 3,500 consumes the remaining capacity at Pittsburgh; setting *TC* = 500 covers the remaining demand at Chicago.

Having made the second-priority assignments, we can ignore the supply at Pittsburgh and the demand at Chicago. We are left with a net demand at Atlanta and unallocated supply at Tucson, as shown in Figure 12.11. Thus, the last step, at the third-priority level, is to meet the remaining demand with a shipment along route *TA*. This allocation leaves an excess supply of 500 cartons at the Tucson factory,

FIGURE 12.10 Diagram for the Reduced Problem

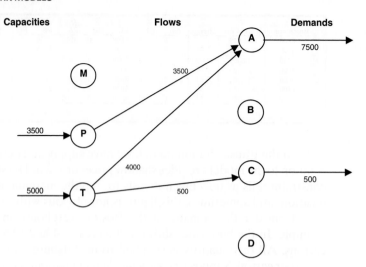

demonstrating that the utilization of the Tucson supply has been dictated by the supply and demand constraints elsewhere in the problem.

Here is a brief statement of the process, as it applies in general to the solution of a transportation model.

- Identify a high-priority demand—one that is covered by a unique source—and allocate the entire demand to this route. Remove this demand from consideration.

- Identify a high-priority capacity—one that supplies a single destination—and allocate the entire supply to this route. Remove this supply from consideration.

- Repeat the previous two steps using remaining demands and remaining supplies each time, until all shipments are accounted for.

Using this set of steps in the example problem,

1. Ship as much as possible on routes *PB*, *TD*, and *MC*.

2. Proceed to the reduced problem at the second-priority level and ship as much as possible on routes *PA* and *TC*.

3. Proceed to the reduced problem at the third-priority level and ship as much as possible on route *TA*.

At each allocation, "as much as possible" is dictated by the minimum of remaining capacity and remaining demand. Looking back, we can see that this three-stage description characterizes the optimal solution without explicitly using a number. By describing the optimal solution without using the parameters in the problem, we have portrayed a qualitative pattern in the solution and translated it

FIGURE 12.11 Diagram for the Last Stage of the Reduced Problem

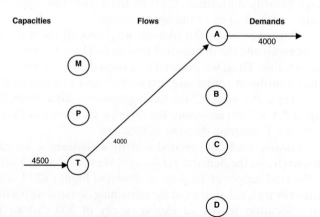

FIGURE 12.12 Changes in the Diagram for the Altered Problem

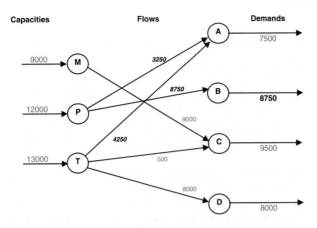

into a list of economic priorities. This retrospective description of the solution is complete and unambiguous. Anyone who constructs a solution using these steps will reach the same result.

This pattern holds not just for the specific problem that we solved, but also for similar problems that have some of the parameters slightly altered. For example, suppose that demand at Boston were raised to 8,750. We could verify that the same pattern applies. The revised details of implementing the same pattern are shown in Figure 12.12, where we can see that three of the decision variables have been altered in response to the increased demand at Boston. Furthermore, if we track the cost implications of these changes, we can calculate that the increase in total transportation cost is $0.30(250) - 0.36(250) + 0.65(250) = 0.59(250) = \$147.50$.

Thus, our calculations reveal that the incremental cost of shipment to Boston is $0.59. Although the direct cost is only $0.30, the limited capacity at Pittsburgh forces us to compensate for the additional shipment to Boston by making adjustments elsewhere (while maintaining the optimal pattern). These adjustments lead us to a marginal cost of $0.59.

More generally, we can alter the original problem in several ways at once. Suppose demands at Atlanta, Boston, and Chicago are *each* raised by 100 simultaneously. What will the optimal plan look like? In qualitative terms, we already know. The qualitative pattern of economic priorities allows us to write down the optimal solution to the revised problem without rerunning Solver, but rather by using the pattern's three-stage priority list and adjusting the shipment quantities for the modifications in demands.

Tracing the cost implications, as shown in the diagram of Figure 12.13, we find that the 100-unit increases in the three demands will combine to increase the optimal total cost by $179. On a per-unit basis, this is an increase of $1.79, which corresponds to the sum of the shadow prices on the first three demand constraints.

FIGURE 12.13 Changes in the Diagram When Three Demands Change

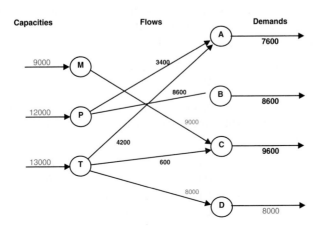

12.3 THE ASSIGNMENT MODEL

An important special case of the transportation problem occurs when all capacities and all requirements are equal to one. In addition, total supply equals total demand. This special case is known as the **assignment problem**. The classic assignment model is characterized by a set of people, a set of tasks, and a score for each possible assignment of a person to a task. The problem is to find the best assignment of people to tasks. This model can be applied to the medley relay in swimming.

EXAMPLE
The Buchanan Swim Club

Coach Kemppel is the coach of the Buchanan Swim Club's co-ed team. Her team competes against other swim clubs, and a perennial question for the coach is how to organize the medley relay team. The medley relay requires each of four swimmers to swim a different stroke: butterfly, breaststroke, backstroke, and freestyle. The relay is the final event in the competitions, and the outcome of the swim meet often depends on the performance of the relay team.

During practice, Coach Kemppel has asked each of her top four swimmers to try each of the four strokes, and she has tracked their times (in seconds), as shown in the following table.

	Stroke			
	BF	BR	BK	FR
Todd	38	75	44	27
Betsy	34	76	43	25
Lee	41	71	41	26
Carly	33	80	45	30

With this information, Coach Kemppel is ready to assign swimmers to strokes in the relay race, but she can see that a lot of combinations are possible. ∎

12.3.1 Formulation

We can think of an **assignment** as a selection of four numbers from the table of swim times, one from each row and one from each column. (Because the number of swimmers is the same as the number of strokes, we can think of either assigning strokes to swimmers or assigning swimmers to strokes.) The total time associated with such an assignment is the sum of the numbers selected. This is merely another way of saying that the problem is a special transportation problem in which the row "capacities" are each 1 and the column "demands" are also 1. As such, we could easily construct a flow diagram to represent the decision problem in much the same way as we did with the transportation model of Figure 12.2.

For an algebraic statement of our model, we define our decision variables as the possible swimmer-stroke combinations, $T1, T2, \ldots, C4$, where the letter refers to the swimmer's name and the number refers to the stroke (1 for Butterfly, etc.). Our objective function (denoted z) is the total time for an assignment, which can be expressed as the sum of sixteen products. Each term in this sum is an assignment cost multiplied by a decision variable.

$$\text{Total Time} = z = 38T1 + 75T2 + 44T3 + 27T4 + 34B1 + 76B2 + 43B3 + 25B2$$
$$+ 41L1 + 71L2 + 41L3 + 26L4 + 33C1 + 80C2 + 45C3 + 30C4$$

There are eight constraints—four for the swimmers and four for the strokes. The row constraints, which require that each swimmer be assigned to at most one stroke, are as follows:

$$
\begin{aligned}
T1 + T2 + T3 + T4 &\leq 1 \\
B1 + B2 + B3 + B4 &\leq 1 \\
L1 + L2 + L3 + L4 &\leq 1 \\
C1 + C2 + C3 + C4 &\leq 1
\end{aligned}
$$

Meanwhile, the column constraints, which require that each stroke be assigned at least one swimmer, are as follows:

$$
\begin{array}{ccccccccc}
T1 & + & B1 & + & L1 & + & C1 & \geq & 1 \\
T2 & + & B2 & + & L2 & + & C2 & \geq & 1 \\
T3 & + & B3 & + & L3 & + & C3 & \geq & 1 \\
T4 & + & B4 & + & L4 & + & C4 & \geq & 1
\end{array}
$$

All of these constraints could be written as equalities without affecting the problem's solution, but sometimes using the inequalities can avoid confusion.

The assignment problem is to minimize z subject to the eight constraints on the variables. We might wonder whether additional conditions should be imposed to help us avoid fractional values for the decision variables. For example, if we assigned every variable the value 0.25, we would have a feasible solution to the model, but not one that we could implement in practice. However, we don't need to worry about this problem because the optimal values of the decision variables turn out to be integers in any assignment problem. We elaborate on this point later in this chapter.

12.3.2 Spreadsheet Model

Figure 12.14 shows a spreadsheet model for the assignment problem. It resembles the spreadsheet for the transportation model introduced in Figure 12.3. The upper portion contains a 4×4 array of assignment costs. The decisions are shown in the lower 4×4 array and highlighted. To the right of each row is the row sum, and below each column is the column sum. As in the transportation model of Figure 12.3, these cells use the SUM formula. Finally, in cell C17, we highlight the value of the objective function, or total cost, which is computed as the SUMPRODUCT of the cost array and the decision array.

Conceptually, there are capacities of 1 for each plant and requirements of 1 for each product, in analogy to the transportation model. Rather than include these parameters on the spreadsheet itself, they are entered as right-hand-side constants in the constraints. Normally, it is not good practice to enter right-hand side constants in the Solver Parameters window, because we prefer to show parameters of the model on the spreadsheet itself, where we might want to explore some what-if questions. However, we make an exception here because the right-hand sides will not change: values of 1 represent the essence of the assignment problem. In the Solver Parameters window, we enter the following information.

Target cell	C17 (maximize)
Changing cells	C11:F14
Constraints	C15:F15 $\geq$ 1
	G11:G14 $\leq$ 1

FIGURE 12.14

Spreadsheet Model for the Assignment Problem

	A	B	C	D	E	F	G
1	Assignment Model						
2							
3	Data		Butterfly	Breast	Back	Free	
4		Todd	38	75	44	27	
5		Betsy	34	76	43	25	
6		Lee	41	71	41	26	
7		Carly	33	80	45	30	
8							
9							
10	Decisions		Butterfly	Breast	Back	Free	Row sum
11		Todd	0	0	1	0	1
12		Betsy	0	0	0	1	1
13		Lee	0	1	0	0	1
14		Carly	1	0	0	0	1
15		Column sum	1	1	1	1	
16							
17	Objective	Total Time	173				
18							

12.14

The less-than constraints assure that at most one swimmer is assigned to each stroke, and the greater-than constraints assure that each stroke has at least one swimmer assigned to it. (As mentioned earlier, we could also express all of the constraints as equations.)

12.3.3 Optimization

Figure 12.14 displays the optimal solution, which achieves a minimum total time of 173 seconds. This optimum is achieved by assigning Todd to the backstroke, Betsy to the freestyle, Lee to the breaststroke, and Carly to the butterfly. By solving this linear programming problem, Coach Kemppel can make optional use of her team's talent, thus giving them the best chance of winning their medley relay race.

12.3.4 Sensitivity Analysis

As suggested earlier, it is rare that we would want to perform sensitivity analysis with respect to either the supply parameters or the demand parameters in an assignment model. For that reason, we can enter the right-hand constant (1) in the Solver Parameters window. However, we may well be interested in sensitivity analysis with respect to the cost parameters. In the medley-relay example, this translates to sensitivity analysis with respect to the swimming times.

Few swimmers can consistently swim the same distance in precisely the same length of time. We might ask, what if one of the swimmers took longer than expected: Would we have been better off with an alternative assignment? We focus this example on Todd's time in the backstroke. The following table shows how the optimal solution varies as his time increases from 44 to 46 seconds.

T3 Time	Optimal Relay Time	Todd's Assignment
44	173	Backstroke
45	174	Backstroke
46	174	Breaststroke

In the base case, Todd's time is 44 seconds, and he is optimally assigned to the backstroke even though two other swimmers are faster at that stroke. If his time is 45 seconds, the team's relay time increases from 173 seconds to 174 as a result, but there is no incentive to reallocate. If his time is 46 seconds, however, a reallocation would allow the team to reach a 174-second time. In that reallocation, Todd would be assigned to the breast stroke.

The situation is slightly different for Carly's time in the butterfly, as shown in the following table.

C1 Time	Optimal Relay Time	Carly's Assignment
33	173	Butterfly
34	174	Butterfly
35	175	Butterfly
36	176	Butterfly
37	177	Butterfly
38	177	Breast stroke

In the base case, her time is 33 seconds, fastest on the team. If her time is 34 seconds, the team's relay time increases to 174. If her time is 35 seconds, slower than Betsy's time in the butterfly, it remains optimal to assign Carly to the butterfly, and the team's relay time increases again, to 175. Not until her time rises to 38 seconds is there an incentive to reallocate. At 38 seconds and above, Carly would be assigned to the backstroke, and the relay time would be 177.

12.4   THE TRANSSHIPMENT MODEL

In the previous section, we saw that the assignment problem is a simplified version of the transportation problem, with unit supplies and demands. By contrast, the **transshipment problem** is a more complex version of the transportation problem, characterized by two stages of flow instead of just one. In the Bonner Electronics diagram of Figure 12.2, there are two levels in the system (plants and warehouses), and all of the flow takes place in one stage, from plants to warehouses. In more complex logistics systems, there are three major levels—plants, distribution centers (DCs), and warehouses—and in such systems, the flow often takes place in two stages.

EXAMPLE
Western
Paper
Company

The Western Paper Company manufactures paper at two factories (F1 and F2) on the West Coast. Their products are shipped by rail to a pair of depots (D1 and D2), one in the Midwest and one in the South. At the depots, the products are repackaged and sent by truck to three regional warehouses (W1, W2, and W3) around the country, in response to replenishment orders.

Each of the factories has a known monthly production capacity, and the three regional warehouses have placed their demands for next month. The following tables summarize the data that have been collected for this planning problem.

(From) Factory	(To) DC		Capacity
	D1	D2	
F1	$1.28	1.36	2500
F2	1.33	1.38	2500
F3	1.68	1.55	2500

(From) DC	(To) Warehouse				
	W1	W2	W3	W4	W5
D1	$0.60	0.42	0.32	0.44	0.68
D2	0.57	0.30	0.40	0.38	0.72
Requirement	1200	1300	1400	1500	1600

Knowing the costs of transporting goods from factories to DCs and from DCs to warehouses, Western Paper is interested in scheduling its material flow at the minimum possible cost.   ∎

12.4.1   Formulation

A good first step in modeling is to build a diagram of the Western Paper system, as shown in Figure 12.15. The left-hand side of the diagram shows the potential flows from factories to DCs, and the right-hand side shows the potential flows from DCs to warehouses. The DCs are called **transshipment points** because material arrives at those locations and is then subject to further shipment. At the heart of the transshipment structure is the need to coordinate the two transportation stages at the transshipment points. This coordination is governed by the **conservation law** of flows in networks: The total quantity flowing out of a node must equal the total quantity flowing in.

In order to describe the conservation law algebraically, we introduce some notation for the decision variables. We use x to represent a first-stage flow, from

FIGURE 12.15 Diagram for
Western Paper

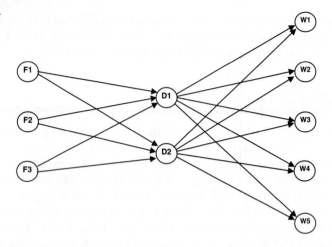

factory to DC, and y to represent a second-stage flow, from DC to warehouse. Thus, let x_{21} represent the quantity shipped from F2 to D1, and let y_{23} represent the quantity shipped from D2 to W3. With this notation, we can write the conservation relationship for D1 as follows:

$$(\text{Flow Out}) = (\text{Flow in})$$

or

$$(\text{Flow Out}) - (\text{Flow In}) = 0$$

or

$$(y_{11} + y_{12} + y_{13} + y_{14} + y_{15}) - (x_{11} + x_{21} + x_{31}) = 0$$

Similarly, for D2, we have:

$$(y_{21} + y_{22} + y_{23} + y_{24} + y_{25}) - (x_{12} + x_{22} + x_{32}) = 0$$

We can see that the conservation law takes the form of an equality constraint for particular nodes in the network. This equality constraint is sometimes called a **balance equation** because it assures perfect balance between inputs and outputs.

We can now develop an algebraic statement of the transshipment model by combining the types of supply and demand constraints we saw in the transportation model with the balance equations introduced here for transshipment nodes. Our model takes the following form.

$$\text{Minimize } z = 1.28x_{11} + 1.36x_{12} + 1.33x_{21} + 1.38x_{22} + 1.68x_{31} + 1.55x_{32}$$
$$+ 0.60y_{11} + 0.42y_{12} + 0.32y_{13} + 0.44y_{14} + 0.68y_{15}$$
$$+ 0.57y_{21} + 0.30y_{22} + 0.40y_{23} + 0.38y_{24} + 0.72y_{25}$$

subject to

$$
\begin{array}{ll}
x_{11} + x_{12} & \le 2,500 \\
x_{21} + x_{22} & \le 2,500 \\
x_{31} + x_{32} & \le 2,500 \\
y_{11} + y_{21} & \ge 1,200 \\
y_{12} + y_{22} & \ge 1,300 \\
y_{13} + y_{23} & \ge 1,400 \\
y_{14} + y_{24} & \ge 1,500 \\
y_{15} + y_{25} & \ge 1,600 \\
-x_{11} - x_{21} - x_{31} + y_{11} + y_{12} + y_{13} + y_{14} + y_{15} & = 0 \\
-x_{12} + x_{22} - x_{32} + y_{21} + y_{22} + y_{23} + y_{24} + y_{25} & = 0
\end{array}
$$

Note that in our formulation, the balance equations give rise to a set of equality constraints in the model. These constraints could also be expressed in the form of inequalities—that is, the total flow into a DC node must be greater than or equal to the flow out of that node. That version would be consistent with our modeling principle of posing constraints in their most flexible form. However, because of the cost structure, we also know that there is no incentive to ship material to a DC if it is not subsequently brought to a warehouse. Furthermore, by using equality constraints here, we associate a different constraint type (less-than constraint, greater-than constraint, equality constraint) with each of the three different roles (factories, warehouses, and DCs), so that the algebraic structure of the model mirrors the physical structure of the system.

12.4.2 Spreadsheet Model

With a network diagram and an algebraic model in hand, we turn now to the question of spreadsheet layout. The diagram for the Western Paper example depicts two side-by-side transportation problems, and we can lay out a worksheet similarly, showing two stages horizontally on a worksheet, each resembling Figure 12.2 for the transportation model.

In Figure 12.16, we show a worksheet for the Western Paper example, where the left-hand portion corresponds to the first (3×2) stage, and the right-hand portion corresponds to the second (2×5) stage. Cell E15 contains a SUMPRODUCT formula that accounts for the total transportation cost in the first stage. Cell M15 serves the purpose for the second stage. The total cost for the entire system, equal to the sum of the first and second stage costs, is calculated in cell E17.

12.4.3 Optimization

In the Solver Parameters window, we enter the following information.

Target cell	E17 (minimize)
Changing cells	C10:D12, H10:L11
Constraints	C13:D13 = M10:M11
	E10:E12 ≤ E5:E7
	H12:L12 ≥ H7:L7

The formulation contains three less-than constraints (one per factory), five greater-than constraints (one per warehouse), and two equality constraints (one per DC). The optimal solution in this example is shown in Figure 12.16 with a total cost of $12,881. Thus, Western Paper can recognize both stages of its supply chain when it optimizes its distribution costs in one comprehensive model.

Once more, it is a good idea to label the diagram with the values from the optimal solution in order to ensure that the solution makes sense. Figure 12.17 shows the optimal flows for the Western Paper example. Again, we drop the arcs with no flow so that we can focus on the feasibility of the decisions. At node D1, we can see that the total inflow is 4,200, and the total outflow is 4,200. At node D2, the total inflow

FIGURE 12.16 Worksheet for the Western Paper Model

	A	B	C	D	E	F	G	H	I	J	K	L	M
1	Transshipment Model												
2													
3	Parameters			*Stage 1*						*Stage 2*			
4			D1	D2	Capacity			W1	W2	W3	W4	W5	
5		F1	1.28	1.36	2500		D1	0.60	0.42	0.32	0.44	0.68	
6		F2	1.33	1.38	2500		D2	0.57	0.30	0.40	0.38	0.72	
7		F3	1.68	1.55	2500		Required	1200	1300	1400	1500	1600	
8													
9	Decisions		D1	D2	Sent			W1	W2	W3	W4	W5	Flow out
10		F1	2500	0	2500		D1	1200	0	1400	0	1600	4200
11		F2	1700	800	2500		D2	0	1300	0	1500	0	2800
12		F3	0	2000	2000		Received	1200	1300	1400	1500	1600	
13		Flow in	4200	2800									
14													
15	Objective		Stage 1 Cost		9665							Stage 2 Cost	3216
16													
17			Total Cost		$12,881								
18													
19													

12.14 / 12.15 / **12.16** /

FIGURE 12.17   Optimal
Solution for Western
Paper

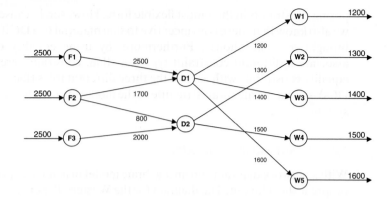

is 2,800, matching the total outflow of 2,800. Thus, we can use the diagram to produce a quick visual check that the decision variables in the optimal solution are consistent with the balance equations for the transshipment points. Then, as in the transportation diagram (Figure 12.5), we can check at the factory nodes and at the warehouse nodes to ensure that total outflow is consistent with total inflow. The network diagram serves as a convenient visual check, and, of course, as a visual aid for communicating the results of the analysis.

12.4.4   Sensitivity Analysis

Examining the optimal solution in Figure 12.16, and focusing on the shipments from the two DCs to the five warehouses, we may be surprised to see that demand at the first warehouse is met from DC1, even though shipments from DC2 would be cheaper per unit. In particular, the optimal solution uses a route that costs $0.60 per unit as part of the solution, in preference to a route that costs $0.57. We might wonder how much cheaper the cost on the latter route would have to be in order to provide an incentive to switch.

To answer this question, we can use the Solver Sensitivity tool to test the sensitivity of the optimal solution to the cost parameter in cell H6. We find that at a unit cost below $0.55, the optimal solution uses the route from D2 to W1.

12.5   A STANDARD FORM FOR NETWORK MODELS

The transportation, assignment, and transshipment problems constitute a special class of network models in linear programming. They all lend themselves easily to the use of a flow diagram, and they all contain a From/To flow structure that suggests a corresponding array layout in a worksheet. When we specify the changing cells in the Solver Parameters window, we do not enter a *row* of adjacent cells, as in the standard format. Instead, we enter an *array*, or, in the case of the transshipment model, a pair of arrays. (This feature could obviously be generalized to cases in which we have three or more stages in the model.) With the array format at the heart of the model, the constraints involve restrictions on totals across a row or down a column, allowing us to use the SUM formula, rather than the SUMPRODUCT formula that we saw throughout Chapter 11.

One interesting feature of this class of models is that an optimal solution always consists of an integer-valued set of decision variables as long as the right-hand-side parameters are integers. Recall that the linearity assumption in linear programming allows for divisibility in the values of decision variables. As a result, we may find that some or all of the decision variables in an optimal solution are fractional, and this sometimes makes the result difficult to implement or interpret. However, no such problem arises with these three network models; they will always produce integer-valued solutions as long as the constraint parameters are themselves integers.

Finally, the three network models feature less-than constraints for capacities and greater-than constraints for requirements, along with balance equations in the case of the transshipment model. In the case of the assignment model, we could actually use equality constraints from the outset. However, as we shall discover next, it is possible to formulate any of these problems as linear programs built exclusively on balance equations. Although this approach may not seem as intuitive, it does link the flow diagram and the spreadsheet model more closely, as suggested at the beginning of the chapter, and it allows us to see a more general structure that encompasses other network models as well.

Some network structures do not lend themselves as easily as the transportation model to an array layout for decision variables. For these networks, it is desirable to use the standard linear programming format, with decision variables in a single row and a SUMPRODUCT function in each of the constraints. The distinguishing features of this approach are a flow diagram and the use of material-balance equations.

In a classical network model, each node in the network corresponds to a material-balance equation—the requirement that total outflow must equal total inflow. Figure 12.5 shows the solution to a model in which the total flow into the network (supply capacity) is 34,000 but the total flow out of the network (demand requirements) is only 33,500. To convert this situation to a classical network, we add a "virtual" warehouse to the model—a fifth warehouse (labeled E) with a demand of 500. With this demand quantity, total supply matches total demand.

Next, to make sure that the solution to the original problem is not corrupted, we take the unit transportation costs associated with the virtual warehouse to be zero. Therefore, no additional cost is incurred for material shipped to the location E. The revised diagram is shown in Figure 12.18.

Once we have a network diagram for a problem, we can translate it into a linear program by following these simple steps:

- Define a variable for each arc.
- Include supplies as input flows and demands as output flows.
- Construct the balance equation for each node.

In this version of the model, *every* constraint is a balance equation. Thus, the constraints take the following form.

$$(\text{Flow Out}) - (\text{Flow In}) = 0$$

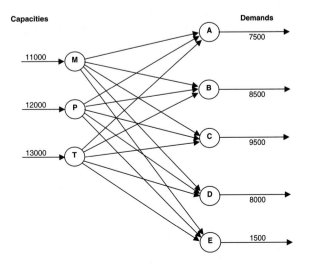

FIGURE 12.18 Revised Diagram with a Virtual Destination

$$MA + MB + MC + MD + ME - 9000 = 0$$
$$PA + PB + PC + PD + PE - 12,000 = 0$$
$$TA + TB + TC + TD + TE - 13,000 = 0$$
$$7,500 - MA - PA - TA = 0$$
$$8,500 - MB - PB - TB = 0$$
$$9,500 - MC - PC - TC = 0$$
$$8,000 - MD - PD - TD = 0$$
$$500 - ME - PE - TE = 0$$

One step remains, and that is to rearrange the equations so that the constraint constants appear on the right-hand side. In this step, we still have a choice, and we adopt a sign convention for right-hand-side constants that can provide improved clarity. Under this convention, we write a balance equation with a positive right-hand side when there is flow *into* the network and with a negative right-hand side when there is flow *out of* the network. Thus, the constraint equations take the following form for the purposes of building a spreadsheet model.

$$MA + MB + MC + MD + ME = 9,000$$
$$PA + PB + PC + PD + PE = 12,000$$
$$TA + TB + TC + TD + TE = 13,000$$
$$-MA - PA - TA = -7,500$$
$$-MB - PB - TB = -8,500$$
$$-MC - PC - TC = -9,500$$
$$-MD - PD - TD = -8,000$$
$$-ME - PE - TE = -2,500$$

The worksheet of Figure 12.19 follows the standard form for linear programs. The 15 variable names are listed in row 4, with their values in the highlighted cells of the next row. The objective function is in the form of a SUMPRODUCT, as is usually the case in standard form. Finally, the constraints are all balance equations, one for each node.

The standard form in Figure 12.19 has features that link it closely to the diagram in Figure 12.18.

- Each variable corresponds to an arc in the diagram (and vice versa).

- Each constraint corresponds to a node in the diagram (and vice versa).

- The right-hand-side constants of the model show up in the network as supplies and demands, with the convention that supply values are positive and demand values negative.

- The coefficients of a given variable in the constraint equations include only two nonzero values, +1 and −1, which occur in constraints corresponding to the tail and head of the corresponding arc, respectively.

The standard form of Figure 12.19 may not be as intuitive as the simpler model in Figure 12.3. Nevertheless, the standard form bears a close relation to the network diagram of Figure 12.18, which provides us with a debugging tool for the spreadsheet model. That is, we can use the diagram as a checklist to make sure that all variables

FIGURE 12.19 Worksheet for the Revised Model

	A	B	C	D	E	F	G	H	I	J	K	L	M	N	O	P	Q	R	S	T
1	Tuition Problem																			
2																				
3	Decisions																			
4		Routes	MA	MB	MC	MD	ME	PA	PB	PC	PD	PE	TA	TB	TC	TD	TE			
5			0	0	9000	0	0	3500	8500	0	0	0	4000	0	500	8000	500			
6	Objective																	Total cost		
7		Costs	0.60	0.56	0.22	0.40	0.00	0.36	0.30	0.28	0.58	0.00	0.65	0.68	0.55	0.42	0.00	$12,025		
8																				
9	Constraints																	LHS		RHS
10		M supply	1	1	1	1	1											9000	=	9000
11		P supply						1	1	1	1	1						12000	=	12000
12		T supply											1	1	1	1	1	13000	=	13000
13		A demand	-1					-1					-1					-7500	=	-7500
14		B demand		-1					-1					-1				-8500	=	-8500
15		C demand			-1					-1					-1			-9500	=	-9500
16		D demand				-1					-1					-1		-8000	=	-8000
17		E demand					-1					-1					-1	-500	=	-500
18																				

12.18 \ **12.19**

and all constraints are contained in the model. We can also ensure that the supply and demand parameters are properly reflected, and we can even confirm that the $(+1)$ and (-1) coefficients are located correctly.

Using the standard form enables us to draw on the network diagram as a debugging aid. This benefit may not seem to be large enough to warrant using the standard form when the classical layout of Figure 12.3 is so intuitive. But the concept becomes helpful in models that are more complicated than the transportation model. We present an example in the next section.

12.6 NETWORK MODELS WITH YIELDS

In network diagrams for the transportation, assignment, and transshipment models, arcs carry flow from one node to another. One feature of those models is that the quantity sent out from a source node is precisely the quantity that arrives at the destination node. However, we can extend network models to cases in which this type of conservation requirement need not apply. If the flows of interest are subject to positive or negative yields, we can incorporate that feature as well. Waste in a manufacturing process is an example of a negative yield and interest on a bank balance is an example of a positive yield. Two examples should illustrate the role of yields.

12.6.1 Yields as Reductions in Flow

One common type of yield phenomenon involves technologies that produce waste. When wood is cut, shaped, and sanded in a manufacturing process, the amount of usable wood that exits the process is less than the amount that entered. When metal enters a process that involves grinding, drilling, and polishing, the same is true of the amount of metal at the end of the process compared to the amount at the start. This type of reduction in the amount of a flow is called **process yield**.

EXAMPLE
Planning
Recycling
Operations

The Ligon Paper Company specializes in paper recycling. The company owns several facilities that obtain paper from commercial or municipal sources, and they produce paper for a variety of markets where customers are looking for recycled content.

Ligon Paper collects three types of input, which they classify as White Paper, Mixed Paper, and Newsprint. Applying various processes, they produce three products: high-quality Office Paper, lower-quality Catalog Paper, and napkin-grade Tan Stock.

One of the processes at Ligon Paper takes White Paper and converts it to Office Paper. For each ton of White Paper input, the process generates 0.85 ton of Office Paper. Alternatively, a ton of White Paper can be converted to Catalog Paper; here the yield is 0.90 ton. Third, White Paper can be converted to Tan Stock, with a yield of 95 percent. For the other types of input, different yields apply, and it is not possible to convert Newsprint to Office Paper. The following table gives a complete set of yield factors, stated as percentages.

	Office	Catalog	Tan Stock
White Paper	85%	90%	95%
Mixed Paper	60%	70%	80%
Newsprint	—	65%	60%

In the coming planning period, Ligon's contracts with suppliers have generated 300 tons of White Paper, 600 tons of Mixed Paper, and 400 tons of Newsprint. In existing markets, Ligon could sell 150 tons of Office Paper at the market price of \$25/ton, 750 tons of Catalog Paper at \$20/ton, and 550 tons of Tan Stock at \$18/ton. The problem is to determine how much of each product to produce. ∎

Except for the effect of yields, the planning problem at Ligon Paper can be represented as a transportation problem. We show the network diagram in

FIGURE 12.20 Diagram for Ligon Paper

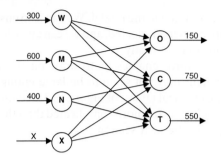

Figure 12.20. If there were no yield factors, this diagram would translate into a 3×3 transportation model, and the standard transportation layout would be convenient. However, yield factors make it a little more difficult to use the array-based layout, so we adopt the network layout. In the Ligon Paper example, there is excess supply capacity, so our model contains four supply nodes and three demand nodes. The fourth node is a virtual, or fictitious, node that accounts for meeting excess demand. However, because of the yield factors, we cannot calculate the excess demand in advance. Even if we consume the entire supply of 1,300 tons, we can't tell how many tons of product that generates because the amount depends on the specific allocation. Thus, in our diagram, we treat the virtual capacity for meeting excess demand as a variable (X).

Again, there is an intimate relation between the network diagram and the spreadsheet model, which is shown in Figure 12.21. Each arc in the network corresponds to a variable, each node in the network corresponds to a constraint, and all constraints are written as balance equations. The variables are measured in tons of supply; these are the quantities that are *started* into the various processes. To compute the quantities in tons of *output*, we have to apply yield factors. The objective function computes the revenue from the schedule of outputs, as supply costs are fixed for the purposes of this decision. In the Solver Parameters window, we enter the following information:

Target cell	P10 (maximize)
Changing cells	C5:N5
Constraints	P12:P18 = R12:R18

Figure 12.21 displays the optimal solution to the model, which dictates that White Paper should be processed into Office Paper and Catalog Paper; Mixed Paper should be processed into Tan Stock; and Newsprint should be processed into Catalog Paper. This production plan results in total revenue of $19,814. Thus, the yield-based model provides Ligon Paper with a revenue-maximizing allocation of its capacity.

12.6.2 Yields as Expansions in Flow

In production processes, yields are typically less than one: outputs are smaller than inputs because some waste is generated along the way. However, in other kinds of processes, yields can be greater than one. An example of this feature arises in funds-flow models. The following example is a case in point.

EXAMPLE
Planning for Tuition Expenses

Parents Patti and Russ want to provide for their daughter's college expenses with some of the $100,000 they have recently inherited. They hope to set aside part of the money and establish an account that would cover the needs of their daughter's college education, which begins four years from now, with a one-time investment. Their estimate is that first-year college expenses will come to $24,000 and will increase $2,000 per year during each of the remaining three years of college. The following investment instruments are available:

Investment	Available	Matures	Return at maturity
A	every year	in 1 year	5%
B	in years 1, 3, 5, 7	in 2 years	11%
C	in years 1, 4	in 3 years	16%
D	in year 1	in 7 years	44%

Faced with this prospect, Patti and Russ wish to set aside the *minimum* amount of money initially that will guarantee that the college expenses will be met. In other words, they seek an investment plan that will cover college financial needs with the smallest possible initial investment. ∎

Investment and funds-flow problems of this sort lend themselves to network modeling. In this type of problem, nodes represent points in time at which funds flows occur. We can imagine tracking a bank account, with funds flowing in and out, depending on our decisions. In this problem, there needs to be a node for Now (the start of year 1) and for the start of years 2 through 8. (Note that the end of year 3 and the start of year 4 are, in effect, the same point in time.) To construct a typical node, we list the potential inflows and outflows that can occur:

Inflows

Initial investment

Appreciation of investment A from one year ago

Appreciation of investment B from two years ago

Appreciation of investment C from three years ago

Appreciation of investment D from seven years ago

Outflows

Expense payment for the coming year

Investment A for the coming year

Investment B for the coming two years

Investment C for the coming three years

Investment D for the coming seven years

Not all of these inflows and outflows apply at every point in time, but if we sketch the eight nodes and the flows that do apply, we come up with a diagram such as the one shown as Figure 12.22. In this diagram, $A1$ represents the amount allocated to investment A at the start of year 1, $A2$ represents the amount allocated to investment A at the start of year 2, and so on. The initial fund in the account is shown as V, and the expense payments are shown as $E5$ through $E8$.

FIGURE 12.21 Worksheet for the Ligon Paper Model

	A	B	C	D	E	F	G	H	I	J	K	L	M	N	O	P	Q	R
1	Recycling Planning																	
2																		
3	Decisions																	
4		Routes	WO	WC	WT	MO	MC	MT	NC	NT	XO	XC	XT	X				
5			176	124	0	0	0	600	400	0	0	379	70	449				
6																		
7		Yields	0.85	0.90	0.95	0.60	0.70	0.80	0.65	0.60	1	1	1					
8	Objective																	
9		Gross Revenue	25	20	18	25	20	18	20	18	0	0	0	0		Total Revenue		
10		Net Revenue	21.25	18.00	17.10	15.00	14.00	14.40	13.00	10.80	0	0	0	0		$19,814		
11	Constraints															LHS		RHS
12		W supply	1	1	1											300	=	300
13		M supply				1	1	1								600	=	600
14		N supply							1	1						400	=	400
15		X supply									1	1	1	-1		0	=	0
16		O demand	-0.85			-0.60						-1				-150	=	-150
17		C demand		-0.90			-0.70		-0.65				-1			-750	=	-750
18		T demand			-0.95			-0.80		-0.60				-1		-550	=	-550
19																		

12.18 / 12.19 / 12.20 \ 12.21

FIGURE 12.22 Diagram for the Investment Problem

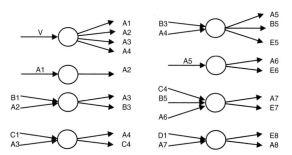

FIGURE 12.23 Alternative
Diagram for the Investment
Problem

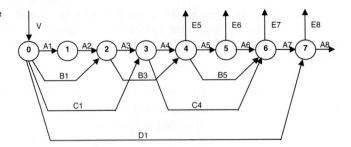

The diagram shows the end-of-year nodes as independent elements, which is all we really need; however, Figure 12.23 shows a tidier diagram in which the nodes are connected in a single network.

Note that there is no variable $B7$ in the model. A two-year investment starting in year 7 would extend beyond the eight-year horizon, so this option is omitted. However, the variable $A8$ does appear in the model. We can think of $A8$ as representing the final value in the account. Perhaps it is intuitive that, if we are trying to minimize the initial investment, there is no reason to have money left in the account in the end. Still, to verify this intuition, we include $A8$ in the model, anticipating that we will find $A8 = 0$ in the optimal solution.

The next step is to convert the diagram into a linear programming model. For this purpose, the flows on the arcs become decision variables, and each node gives rise to a balance equation, as follows.

Start of year 1	$A1 + B1 + C1 + D1 - V$	$= 0$
Start of year 2	$A2 - 1.05A1$	$= 0$
Start of year 3	$A3 + B3 - 1.05A2 - 1.11B1$	$= 0$
Start of year 4	$A4 + C4 - 1.05A3 - 1.16C1$	$= 0$
Start of year 5	$A5 + B5 - 1.05A4 - 1.11B3$	$= -24{,}000$
Start of year 6	$A6 - 1.05A5$	$= -26{,}000$
Start of year 7	$A7 - 1.05A6 - 1.11\,B5 - 1.16\,C4$	$= -28{,}000$
Start of year 8	$A8 - 1.05A7 - 1.44D1$	$= -30{,}000$

The resulting model is shown on the worksheet of Figure 12.24. Notice the systematic pattern formed by the coefficients in the columns of the constraint equations. Each column has two nonzero coefficients: a positive coefficient (of 1), in the row corresponding to the time the investment is made, and a negative coefficient (reflecting the appreciation rate), in the row corresponding to the time the investment matures. The only exceptions are V and $A8$, which represent flows into and out of the network. In other funds-flow models, the column coefficients portray the investment-and-return profile for each of the variables, on a per-unit basis. The right-hand side constants, following our sign convention, show the profile of planned flows into and out of the system over the various time periods.

The objective function in this example is simply the initial size of the investment account, which is the variable V. Thus, we can depart slightly from the standard format and designate the objective function in cell C7 simply by referencing cell B5.

FIGURE 12.24 Worksheet
for the Investment Model

	A	B	C	D	E	F	G	H	I	J	K	L	M	N	O	P	Q	R	S
1	Tuition Problem																		
2																			
3	Decisions																		
4		V	A1	A2	A3	A4	A5	A6	A7	A8	B1	B3	B5	C1	C4	D1			
5		80.883	0.00	0.00	0.00	0.00	24.76	0.00	0.00	0.00	60.05	66.66	25.23	0.00	0.00	20.83			
6	Objective																		
7		$80.883																	
8																			
9	Constraints																		
10	Year																		
11	0	-1	1	0	0	0	0	0	0	0	1	0	0	1	0	1	0	=	0
12	1	0	-1.05	1	0	0	0	0	0	0	0	0	0	0	0	0	0	=	0
13	2	0	0	-1.05	1	0	0	0	0	0	-1.11	1	0	0	0	0	0	=	0
14	3	0	0	0	-1.05	1	0	0	0	0	0	0	0	-1.16	1	0	2.69E-15	=	0
15	4	0	0	0	0	-1.05	1	0	0	0	0	-1.11	1	0	0	0	-24	=	-24
16	5	0	0	0	0	0	-1.05	1	0	0	0	0	0	0	0	0	-26	=	-26
17	6	0	0	0	0	0	0	-1.05	1	0	0	0	-1.11	0	-1.16	0	-28	=	-28
18	7	0	0	0	0	0	0	0	-1.05	1	0	0	0	0	0	-1.44	-30	=	-30
19																			

K ◀ ▶ H \ 12.18 / 12.19 / 12.20 / 12.21 / 12.22 / 12.23 \ **12.24** / | ◀

Once again, there is a close relationship between the network diagram and the spreadsheet model. This relationship allows the diagram to be used as a debugging aid for checking the spreadsheet. After we have checked the spreadsheet for consistency with the diagram, we can proceed with the analysis.

We invoke Solver and specify:

Target cell	B7 (minimize)
Changing cells	B5:P5
Constraints	Q11:Q18 = S11:S18

When we minimize V, Solver provides the optimal solution shown in Figure 12.24, calling for an initial investment of about \$80,883.

Note that the optimal value of the objective function in our spreadsheet model appears as 80.883, because we have rescaled our model in thousands of dollars. The rescaling was accomplished by entering the tuition expenses in thousands of dollars on the right-hand side of the last four constraints. In a model such as this one, rescaling is obviously convenient. It allows us to avoid entering a lot of zeros when we type in the model, and it makes the model easier to debug.

SOLVER TIP
Rescaling the Model

Rescaling the parameters of a model—so that they appear in thousands (or even millions)—has the virtue that it saves us the work of entering lots of zeros. As a consequence, we may avoid some data-entry errors, and the spreadsheet looks a little less crowded than it would with many large numbers on it. However, there is an important practical reason for rescaling as well. The way that Solver carries out its arithmetic sometimes makes rescaling desirable. As a guideline, the parameters in the objective function and the constraints should not differ from each other, or from the values of the decision variables, by more than a factor of 10,000. A model that tracks cash flows in the millions while also computing percentage returns as decimal fractions violates this rule.

Sometimes, rescaling problems are difficult to avoid when we're trying to keep the model easy to understand. In these cases, we can ask Solver to perform some internal rescaling of the model if we check the option box for Use Automatic Scaling. As helpful as the Automatic Scaling option is, however, it is always preferable for the model builder to do the rescaling.

Finally, if we need to display our model results in units that are more natural for our audience, we can create a separate presentation worksheet. On that sheet, the numbers can be displayed in any desired format without affecting the optimization process. ∎

12.6.3 Patterns in General Network Models

To reinforce the concept of identifying patterns in optimal solutions, we explore the tuition-planning model in more detail. The optimal solution is shown on the worksheet in Figure 12.24 and on the network diagram in Figure 12.25. In the diagram, we have removed nonzero variables as the first step in identifying a pattern. (Recall that in searching for a pattern, we normally ignore nonbinding constraints, but in network models, all constraints are balance equations and therefore binding.)

The diagram in Figure 12.25 makes the pattern easy to see. First, with respect to the variables, investment A is seldom used, and investment C is never used. In addition, there is no money left over at the end of the scenario ($A8 = 0$), as we might have anticipated. Most of the investment is allocated toward instruments B and D. The initial investment B1 is reinvested at year 3 and must appreciate sufficiently to

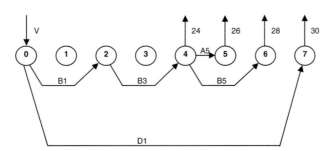

FIGURE 12.25 Diagram for the Optimal Decisions in the Investment Model

cover the first year of tuition, the investment in $A5$, and the reinvestment in $B5$. Thereafter, $A5$ covers the second year of tuition, $B5$ covers the third, and the initial investment in $D1$ covers the fourth. This is the qualitative pattern in the solution.

When we make a priority list of variables, we must account for the logical sequence in which these variables can be calculated. For this purpose, we start from the end of the problem and work backward. The individual calculation steps are as follows.

1. The expense outflow at node 7 dictates the size of the investment in $D1$. (Specifically, the investment returns 44 percent, so to cover a flow of $30,000, the amount invested must be $30,000/1.44 = 20,833$.

2. The expense at node 6 dictates the size of $B5$ as $28,000/1.11 = 25,225$.

3. The expense at node 5 dictates the size of $A5$ as $26,000/1.05 = 24,762$.

4. The expense at node 4 must be considered in conjunction with the investment outflows for $A5$ and $B5$, which have been determined in steps 2 and 3. Combining the three outflows and dividing by 1.11, we obtain 66,655.

5. The outflow at node 2 dictates the size of $B1$ as $66,655/1.11 = 60,050$.

6. Since the outflows at node 1 ($B1$ and $D1$) are now determined, we simply sum them to compute the required initial investment of 80,883.

The shadow prices in funds-flow networks are useful as well. Consider the second-year expense of $26,000. If it were to increase by $1, what would be the impact on the objective function? We can answer this question by repeating the calculation steps and including the change.

1. No change in $D1$.

2. No change in $B5$.

3. Increase $A5$ by $1/1.05 = 0.952$.

4. Increase $B3$ by $0.952/1.11 = 0.858$.

5. Increase $B1$ as $0.858/1.11 = 0.773$.

6. The initial investment must increase by the increment in $B1 = 0.773$.

The conclusion is that a dollar's increase in the expense at year 5 can be covered by an increase in the initial investment of $0.773. This amounts to a rate of return of 29.3 percent over the five-year period, or an average annual return of about 5.28 percent. In financial terms, we can reconstruct this rate as a combination of a 5 percent return (in year 5 from investment A) and a 5.36 percent annual return (in years 1–4, from investment B). Thus, the shadow price effectively tells us the cost of funds for meeting expenses in any particular year.

12.7* NETWORK MODELS FOR PROCESS TECHNOLOGIES

In the networks we have examined thus far, nodes conform to a conservation law requiring that total outflow equals total inflow. This is the case even in networks where flows are subject to yields. In all of our examples, the material flowing out of a node (money, materials, people, etc.) has been identical to the material flowing into the node. In this section, we consider a generalization in which some nodes represent production operations that actually transform the substance between inflow and outflow. This type of network is particularly suitable for the analysis of production plans in process industries, such as paper, steel, or chemicals. We illustrate the generality with an example from oil refining.

EXAMPLE
Production at
Delta Oil

The refining process at Delta Oil Company separates crude oil into components that eventually yield gasoline, heating oil, jet fuel, lubricating oil, and other petroleum products. In particular, gasoline is produced from crude oil by either a distillation process alone or by a distillation process followed by a catalytic-cracking process. The outputs of these processes are subsequently blended to obtain different grades of gasoline.

The distillation tower at Delta's refinery uses five barrels of crude oil to produce three barrels of distillate and two barrels of other "low-end" by-products. Some distillate is blended into gasoline products; the rest becomes feedstock for the catalytic cracker.

The catalytic-cracking process produces high-quality catalytic gasoline (or catalytic, for short) from the feedstock. Delta's catalytic cracker requires 2.5 barrels of distillate to produce 1.6 barrels of catalytic and 1 barrel of "high-end" by-products. (The cracking process creates output volume that exceeds input volume.)

Finally, distillate from the distillation tower is blended with catalytic to make regular gasoline and premium gasoline. The blend of distillate and catalytic must be at least 50 percent catalytic to meet the quality requirements of regular and at least 75 percent catalytic to meet the quality requirements of premium. ∎

12.7.1 Formulation

At the Delta Oil Refinery, as in most facilities of this type, it is not hard to find a diagram of the production process. Such a diagram may not have been devised for the purposes of building network models, but it is usually not too different from one that would suit our modeling purposes. Our network model is shown in Figure 12.26. The process has been simplified by aggregating distinct products into such categories as high-end and low-end, but the main process steps are represented.

In the figure, we label each of the arcs in the network, recognizing that these labels will also serve as the names of decision variables in the linear programming model. For convenience, we use some abbreviations, such as *CR*, which represents the amount of catalytic that is combined into regular gasoline. Next, we create node T to represent the tower and node C to represent the cracker. We also add nodes 1, 2, and 3 to represent allocations of flow. At node 1, the distillate must be split into a portion that is directly blended into gasoline and a portion that is used as a feedstock for the cracker. At node 2, the distillate allocated to blending must be split between regular and premium grades of gasoline, and similarly at node 3 for the catalytic produced by the cracker. Finally, nodes 4 and 5 represent the output of the two blending decisions, one for regular and one for premium.

For each node in the diagram, we write a balance equation. Conceptually, however, there is a twist here. Because the nodes represent production processes, the input material may differ from the output material, and there may be multiple input materials and multiple output materials. We then must write a balance equation for each output material. For example, the equations for the tower node (T) take the following form:

$$\text{Flow Out} - \text{Flow In} = 0$$

or

$$Dist - 0.60\,Crude = 0$$
$$Low - 0.40\,Crude = 0$$

Thus, there are two balance equations, one each for distillate and low-end by-products. Each equation contains one input term, for crude. The coefficients of 0.60 and 0.40 correspond to a fractional split of five barrels into flows of three barrels and two barrels, respectively, for the split between distillate (*Dist*) and low-end by-products (*Low*).

FIGURE 12.26   Diagram for Delta Oil

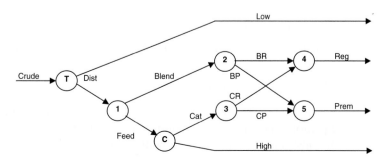

A similar pair of equations applies to the cracker node (C):

$$\text{Flow Out} - \text{Flow In} = 0$$

or

$$Cat - 0.64\,Feed = 0$$
$$High - 0.40\,Feed = 0$$

The numbered nodes are similar to transshipment nodes in our distribution models, because the inputs and outputs are the same material. At node 1, distillate must be split into either feedstock (*Feed*) or gasoline blending input (*Blend*). The balance equation becomes:

$$Feed + Blend - Dist = 0$$

Nodes 2 and 3 have a similar structure.

$$BP + BR - Blend = 0$$
$$CP + CR - Cat = 0$$

Nodes 4 and 5 are also of this type:

$$Prem - BP - CP = 0$$
$$Reg - BR - CR = 0$$

The system of balance equations and the network flow diagram are different representations of the same model. We can use one form to debug the other by checking for consistency and eliminating structural errors.

In addition to the network flows in this problem, other types of information are needed, including:

- Production capacities for each production process
- Sales potentials for final products
- Blending specifications for gasoline

The first two of these can be stated in appropriate dimensions, such as barrels per day, while the third describes limits on the ratio in which gasoline inputs may be mixed. To illustrate the entire model, suppose the following parametric assumptions apply.

- Tower and cracker capacities: 50,000 and 20,000 barrels/day
- Sales potential for regular and premium gasoline: 16,000 barrels/day each
- Sales potential for by-products: unlimited
- Blending floor for catalytic in regular gasoline: at least 50 percent catalytic
- Blending floor for catalytic in premium gasoline: at least 75 percent catalytic

To complete the model, we need the economic factors that make up the objective function. Suppose the following parametric assumptions apply.

- Cost of crude oil: $28 per barrel
- Cost of operating the tower: $5 per barrel of crude
- Cost of operating the cracker: $6 per barrel of feedstock
- Revenue for high-end and low-end by products: $44 and $36 per barrel, respectively
- Revenue for regular and premium gasoline: $50 and $55 per barrel, respectively

12.7.2 Spreadsheet Model

Figure 12.27 shows a spreadsheet model for the entire problem. We see the balance equations in the first portion of the Constraints module, in rows 12–20. The next pair of constraints, in rows 21–22, contains the blending quality requirements for the grades of gasoline. Finally, the four constraints in rows 23–26 contain the ceilings on production capacities and sales volumes. These could alternatively be incorporated as upper bounds on the variables *Crude*, *Prem*, *Reg*, and *Prem*.

The objective function is made up of revenue from the sales of outputs, the cost of operations, and the cost of input materials. For clarity, we devote a row of the spreadsheet to each of these components of the objective function, recognizing that several of these cells do not apply. In fact, intermediate products such as distillate are not directly associated with either costs or revenues. The value of the objective function, calculated as a SUMPRODUCT, appears in cell O9.

12.7.3 Optimization

In the Solver Parameters window, we enter the following information.

Target cell	O9 (maximize)
Changing cells	B4:N4
Constraints	O12:O20 = Q12:Q20
	O21:O22 ≥ Q21:Q22
	O23:O26 ≤ Q23:Q26

Figure 12.27 displays the optimal solution to the Delta Oil Company model. In brief, the solution achieves a profit contribution of $466,400. It calls for purchases of 49,300 barrels of crude oil. This quantity leaves the tower with a small amount of excess capacity, but cracker capacity is fully utilized by the optimal allocation of distillate. Sales of regular gasoline are limited by market potential, but this is not the case for premium. Both gasoline products are blended at their minimum quality requirements, suggesting that catalytic is a scarce resource. A brief look at the decision variables reveals that there is flow on every arc in the network diagram.

Viewed as strategic information, the optimal solution provides useful insights into the determinants of profitability at Delta Oil. Of the two main pieces of process equipment, the cracker is currently the more constraining; however, the tower is not far behind. Capacity may have to be raised in both places for Delta to significantly increase its profits. On the output side, profits are also constrained by demand for regular gasoline. If the marketing department could find additional customers for regular gasoline, this could also lead to increased profits. In short, the strategic implications of the Delta Oil model are typical of product mix models; however, the construction of the model itself is driven by the principles of network modeling.

FIGURE 12.27 Worksheet for the Delta Oil Model

	A	B	C	D	E	F	G	H	I	J	K	L	M	N	O	P	Q
1	Refinery Planning Problem																
2																	
3	Decisions	Crude	Dist	Low	Blend	Feed	Cat	High	BR	BP	CR	CP	Reg	Prem			
4	Kbbl.	49.3	29.6	19.7	9.6	20.0	12.8	8.0	8.00	1.60	8.00	4.80	16.0	6.4			
5	Objective																
6	price			36				44					50	55			
7	cost	5				6											
8	cost	28															
9	net	-33	0	36	0	-6	0	44	0	0	0	0	50	55	466.400		
10	Constraints															LHS		RHS
11																	
12	Tower	-0.60	1	0	0	0	0	0	0	0	0	0	0	0	0.0	=	0
13	Tower	0	0	1	0	0	0	0	0	0	0	0	0	0	0.0	=	0
14	Distillate split	0	-1	0	1	1	0	0	0	0	0	0	0	0	0.0	=	0
15	Cracker	0	0	0	0	-0.64	1	0	0	0	0	0	0	0	0.0	=	0
16	Cracker	0	0	0	0	-0.40	0	1	0	0	0	0	0	0	0.0	=	0
17	Blend split	0	0	0	-1	0	0	0	1	1	0	0	0	0	0.0	=	0
18	Catalytic split	0	0	0	0	0	-1	0	0	0	1	1	0	0	0.0	=	0
19	Reg composition	0	0	0	0	0	0	0	-1	0	-1	0	1	0	0.0	=	0
20	Prem composition	0	0	0	0	0	0	0	0	-1	0	-1	0	1	0.0	=	0
21	Reg quality	0	0	0	0	0	0	0	-0.50	0	0.50	0	0	0	0.0	>=	0
22	Prem quality	0	0	0	0	0	0	0	0	-0.75	0	0.25	0	0	0.0	>=	0
23	Tower capacity	1	0	0	0	0	0	0	0	0	0	0	0	0	49.3	<=	50
24	Cracker capacity	0	0	0	0	1	0	0	0	0	0	0	0	0	20.0	<=	20
25	Reg sales	0	0	0	0	0	0	0	0	0	0	0	1	0	16.0	<=	16
26	Prem sales	0	0	0	0	0	0	0	0	0	0	0	0	1	6.4	<=	16
27																	

I ◀ ▶ ▶I \ 12.18 / 12.19 / 12.20 / 12.21 / 12.22 / 12.23 / 12.24 / 12.25 / 12.26 \ 12.27 / |◀ ▶|

12.8 SUMMARY

Network models, like the allocation, covering, and blending models of the previous chapter, represent a distinct class of linear programs. Network models have special advantages because network diagrams can be used in the modeling process.

- The diagram helps delineate the scope of the model (that is, what to include and what to exclude).
- The diagram defines decision variables by creating arcs.
- The diagram specifies material balance constraints by creating nodes.
- The diagram is relatively easy to understand because it is a visual model.
- The diagram serves as a debugging tool because its elements match up with the elements of an algebraic model or a spreadsheet model.
- The diagram serves as a communication tool because it conveniently displays system structure, model solution, and even sensitivity analysis.

Transportation, assignment, and transshipment models exhibit a characteristic From/To structure that lends itself readily to spreadsheet display. Rather than laying out decisions along a single row, as in the standard form, this structure allows the model to be built with an array layout for decisions and key objective-function parameters. One additional feature of these models is that they produce integer-valued decisions in the optimal solution.

The balance equations that were first encountered in transshipment nodes are the key constraint format for network models, extending to models in which yield factors apply and even to process models where the inflow and outflow may not be of the same material. The constraints in some network linear programs consist exclusively of balance equations, whereas constraints in more complicated models may include allocation, covering, and blending constraints appended to a central network representation.

Finally, the concepts of sensitivity analysis that were introduced in the previous chapter apply as well to network models. In particular, when it comes to interpreting optimal solutions, the network diagram is a convenient device for constructing patterns. The diagram often provides visual hints that lead to a systematic description of the economic priorities in the solution of a network linear program.

EXERCISES

1. *Transporting Coal.* The Calcio Coal Company produces coal at three mines and ships it to four power plants (P1–P4). The cost per ton of producing coal and the production capacity (in tons) for each mine are known. The number of tons of coal demanded by each customer is also known. The cost (in dollars) of shipping a ton of coal from a mine to each plant is available as well. The following table provides the data.

	P1	P2	P3	P4	Capacity	Cost
Mine 1	9	15	8	10	125	50
Mine 2	7	15	14	12	100	57
Mine 3	5	5	11	12	150	55
Mine 4	3	6	8	11	120	61
Demands	110	115	135	130		

a. Calcio wishes to minimize the cost of transporting coal from its mines to its plants. What is the minimum cost?

b. What is the transportation schedule that achieves the minimum cost in (a)?

2. *Planning Procurement.* An automobile manufacturer wants to award contracts for the supply of five different engine components. Some of the components are used in most models, while other components are specialized to one or two models—therefore, the volumes differ. Five contractors have submitted bids on the components, and the following table summarizes the prices bid per unit. Where no entry appears, the contractor did not bid.

	Component				
	C1	C2	C3	C4	C5
Supplier 1	25	—	55	42	40
Supplier 2	28	78	—	44	41
Supplier 3	30	80	58	40	—
Supplier 4	—	82	57	43	—
Supplier 5	32	88	60	—	42
Demand	40,000	10,000	25,000	10,000	30,000

The manufacturer wants to determine how many units of each component should be awarded to each contractor in order to minimize total cost for the purchases. (For these purposes, fractional solutions in the model are acceptable.)

a. What is the minimum total cost for the manufacturer, if no other conditions are imposed?

b. In fact, Supplier 2 is capacity constrained and cannot provide more than 25,000 units in total. In addition, the manufacturer does not want more than $2 million allocated to any one of the suppliers. Recognizing these limitations, what is the minimum total cost for the manufacturer?

c. Describe the qualitative pattern (computational scheme) in the solution for (b).

3. *Shipping Carpets.* A manufacturer of nylon carpets produces rolls of carpeting at four factories and ships them to distributors in five locations The following table shows the capacities at the factories and the demands at the distributors for the next quarter, all given in thousands of rolls. Also shown are the unit transportation costs between each factory and each distributor, stated in cost per roll.

To Distributor:	D1	D2	D3	D4	D5	Capacity
From F1	11	16	18	22	15	40
From F2	12	24	20	21	18	50
From F3	18	17	15	15	20	50
From F4	17	22	14	24	21	60
Demand	30	24	42	36	48	

a. What is the optimal distribution plan for the quarter?

b. What is the cost of the distribution plan in part (a)?

c. Suppose instead that demand at D4 increases and demand at D3 decreases, each by 1,000 rolls. What is the new optimal cost, assuming that the schedule can be revised? (Answer this question using the pattern in the optimal solution, not by rerunning the model.)

4. *Distributing Locks.* The Lannon Lock Company manufactures commercial security locks at plants in Atlanta, Louisville, Detroit, and Phoenix. The unit cost of production at each plant is $35.50, $37.50, $37.25, and $36.25, respectively; the annual capacities are 18,000, 15,000, 25,000, and 20,000, respectively. The locks are sold through wholesale distributors in seven locations around the country. The unit shipping cost for each plant–distributor combination is shown in the following table, along with the demand forecast from each distributor for the coming year:

	Tacoma	San Diego	Dallas	Denver	St. Louis	Tampa	Balti- more
Atlanta	2.50	2.75	1.75	2.00	2.10	1.80	1.65
Louisville	1.85	1.90	1.50	1.60	1.00	1.90	1.85
Detroit	2.30	2.25	1.85	1.25	1.50	2.25	2.00
Phoenix	1.90	0.90	1.60	1.75	2.00	2.50	2.65
Demand	5,500	11,500	10,500	9,600	15,400	12,500	6,600

a. Determine the least costly way of producing and shipping locks from plants to distributors.

b. Suppose that the unit cost at each plant were $10 higher than the original figure. What change in the optimal distribution plan would result? What general conclusions can you draw for transportation models with nonidentical plant related costs?

5. *Scheduling Umpires.* Chris Pearson is running a tennis tournament and is in the process of scheduling the umpires for each match in today's rounds. There are five matches to be played today, and six umpires are available.

Every match needs exactly one umpire, and no umpire can be assigned to more than one match. The following table shows the number of times (in the past) that each umpire has been scheduled for a match involving one of the competing players in each of the matches. Chris wants to assign umpires to matches in a way that avoids placing umpires with players they have seen many times.

	Previous Pairings				
Umpire	Singles Semifinal 1	Singles Semifinal 2	Doubles Semifinal 1	Doubles Semfinal 1	Junior Final
1	2	1	2	2	2
2	3	0	1	4	1
3	2	2	2	2	0
4	3	2	0	2	3
5	3	3	4	1	0
6	0	1	1	5	1

a. Chris has decided to minimize the sum of the number of times the umpires have previously been paired with the players. What is the optimal assignment of umpires to matches?

b. Suppose Chris were to apply a weighting factor to the assignments, treating the assignments in the three singles matches as if they counted double the other assignments. Does this change the optimal assignments?

6. *Assigning Engineers.* A small engineering firm has four senior designers available to work on the firm's four current projects over the next two weeks. The firm's manager has developed the following table of quality scores, which show each designer's design quality on each type of project, on a scale of 100. Also shown is an estimate of the time required for each project.

	Project			
Designer	1	2	3	4
1	90	80	25	50
2	60	70	50	65
3	70	40	80	85
4	65	55	60	75
Time	70	50	85	35

a. Assume that one designer is assigned to each project. What assignment of designers to projects maximizes the sum of the quality scores assigned?

b. Suppose that each designer has 80 hours available over the next two weeks. Assuming that more than one designer can work on a project, what assignment schedule maximizes the sum of quality scores assigned?

7. *Shipping fruit.* Wollmer Distribution Company collects fruit from several small farms in the region, consolidates its collections, and then ships the fruit to a regional wholesale fruit market by truck. Having made their collections, the company has in stock 57 tons of grapes, 62 tons of peaches, and 81 tons of bananas.

Wollmer owns four trucks that can transport fruit to market. Each truck has its own capacity, and Wollmer has discovered that yield losses occur at different rates depending on which fruit is carried in which truck. The truck suspension system and the efficiency of the refrigeration system seem to account for most of the losses. The following table shows the loss as a percentage.

	Grapes	Peaches	Bananas	Capacity (T)
Truck 1	12%	10%	4%	40
Truck 2	12%	14%	5%	50
Truck 3	16%	13%	6%	55
Truck 4	18%	17%	8%	75

The current market prices for the three fruits are as follows.

Fruit	Price/Ton
Grapes	$500
Peaches	1,000
Bananas	1,750

a. As a logical way of loading the trucks, Wollmer's dispatcher follows a standard rule: take the largest yield from the table of yields and assign as many tons as possible; then go on to the next largest yield available, and so on. For this rule, what is the resulting revenue, and how many tons are brought to market?

b. What shipping plan will bring in the most revenue for Wollmer? What is the optimal total revenue?

c. In the optimal solution, how many tons of fruit are delivered to market? What is the maximum possible number of tons brought to market?

8. *Buying and Selling a Commodity.* A small firm buys and sells wheat. It owns a warehouse with a capacity of 10,000 bushels, and as of late August, there will be 2,000 bushels in the warehouse. Wheat is delivered to the warehouse during the first week of the month, and it is sold and shipped around the middle of the month. All transactions are on a cash basis because the season is short, and the firm expects to have $20,000 in its accounts at the end of August. This amount is available for making September purchases.

The latest predictions of market prices are shown in the following table.

	Sep 15	Oct 15	Nov 15
Buy	$5.45	$5.75	$6.00
Sell	$6.05	$6.25	$6.30

a. What buy-and-sell schedule will produce the maximum profit for the firm?

b. What is the optimal profit in part (a)?

c. How does the optimal plan change as a function of the firm's account balance? (Consider amounts both above and below the current $20,000.)

9. *Planning Investments.* Your uncle has $90,000 that he wishes to invest now in order to use the accumulation for purchasing a retirement annuity in five years. After consulting with his financial adviser, he has been offered four types of fixed income investments, labeled as investments A, B, C, and D.

Investments A and B are available at the beginning of each of the next five years (call them years 1 to 5). Each dollar invested in A at the beginning of a year returns $1.20 (a profit of $0.20) two years later, in time for immediate reinvestment. Each dollar invested in B at the beginning of a year returns $1.36 three years later.

Investments C and D will each be available at one time in the future. Each dollar invested in C at the beginning of year 2 returns $1.66 at the end of year 5. Each dollar invested in D at the beginning of year 5 returns $1.12 at the end of year 5.

Your uncle is obligated to make a balloon payment on an existing loan, in the amount of $24,000, at the end of year 3. He wants to cover that payment out of these funds as well.

a. Devise an investment plan for your uncle that maximizes the amount of money that can be accumulated at the end of five years. How much money will be available for the annuity in five years?

b. Describe the pattern in the optimal plan.

10. *Financial Planning.* Your sister has just won $300,000 (tax-free) in the state lottery. She's decided to quit her job and devote herself to writing novels for the next 10 years, using her lottery winnings to support herself. She figures that she will need $30,000 of income at the start of the coming year, $31,000 at the start of next year, $32,000 for the third year, and so on. In order to meet these expenses, she plans to invest her lottery winnings all at once, in bonds. If she finds that she has extra cash in any year (including the first), she plans to place it in her savings account, which pays 3 percent annual interest, but she does not want to purchase any additional bonds in the future.

At the start of the coming year, bonds with 1-, 3-, 5-, and 10-year maturities will become available on the market. If a bond matures in k years, it pays $100 at the end of each of k years, as well as $1000 at the end of the kth year. Currently, 1-year bonds sell for $1,075, 3-year bonds for $1,100, 5-year bonds for $1,200, and 10-year bonds for $1,300.

Your sister wants to make sure that the income from her investments will provide for her living expenses year by year. She has asked you to advise her on how many bonds to purchase and has offered to give you any funds left over at the end of the 10-year period.

a. Assume that you wish to maximize the amount of money available to you at the end of 10 years. How many of each type of bond should your sister purchase? (Assume that these bonds can be purchased in fractional amounts, as part of an investment pool.)

b. How much money will be available to you at the end of 10 years?

c. Suppose you investigate other savings banks and find that interest rates higher than 3 percent are available. What is the minimum interest rate that would alter which of the four types of bonds your sister should buy?

11. *Planning Inventories.* The National Tire Company (NTC) manufactures only one type of tire and wants to plan its production and inventory levels for the next five months. Company policy is to schedule all of its overtime production during one month. The following table provides the relevant data for each month, where the inventory-level requirements refer to the level at the end of each month.

Month	Unit Demand	Production Cost	Maximum Production Level	Minimum Production Level	Maximum Inventory Level	Minimum Inventory Level
1	12,000	$11.00	18,000	6,000	10,000	2,000
2	18,000	$11.00	18,000	6,000	10,000	2,000
3	24,000	$11.50	30,000	6,000	15,000	2,000
4	20,000	$11.00	18,000	6,000	10,000	2,000
5	22,000	$11.00	18,000	6,000	10,000	2,000

Other relevant information is as follows:

- NTC estimates that it costs $1 to hold one tire in inventory from one month to the next.
- NTC currently has an inventory level of 4,000 tires.
- NTC wants to meet its demand with no backorders; that is, all demand must be met no later than the month in which it occurs.

a. Construct a network diagram to represent the NTC scenario. Using the diagram, build a spreadsheet model for the production and inventory plan.

b. What is the minimum total cost, including production and inventory costs, for the five-month period (ignoring the cost of the initial inventory)? What production levels minimize total cost?

12. *Scheduling a Refinery.* Coastal Refining Company operates a refinery with a distillation capacity of 12,000 barrels per day. As a new member of Coastal's management team, you have been given the task of developing a production schedule for the refinery, that is, determining how much of which products to produce and how.

In simplified form, the refinery process starts with distillation, which feeds crude oil into a *pipestill*, as it is commonly called. Here the crude is heated, and as the temperature rises, different products are given off in vapor form. These products can be collected separately and sold as produced, or blended and sold, or else processed further in a *catalytic cracker*. In the cracker, less profitable products such as heating oil can be converted to more profitable products such as naphtha. Finally, the various products of the pipestill and the cracker are blended and sold on the marketplace.

To streamline the analysis, the lighter distillation products have been grouped under the single category of *naphtha*. Similarly, the lighter streams from the catalytic cracker have been grouped under the single category of *catalytic naphtha*. Based on the present operation, a satisfactory gasoline blend can be obtained by combining the straight-run naphtha (directly from the pipestill) and catalytic naphtha in the ratio of at most 5 parts straight run to 4 parts catalytic.

Two crude oil sources are available to the refinery, in quantities up to 10,000 barrels per day for each source of crude. The yields from distillation and the delivered cost of the inputs are as follows:

	Crude 1	Crude 2
Naphtha	0.20	0.15
Diesel Fuel	0.25	0.20
Gasoil	0.40	0.30
Heating Oil	0.10	0.20
Pitch	0.05	0.10
Cost/barrel	$34	$32

The yields for each of the crude oil sources add to less than one because there is always some residue from the process, averaging 10 percent.

Heating oil can be used as feedstock to the catalytic cracker, or alternatively, it can be treated and sold in the form produced by the pipestill. Gasoil can also be fed to the cracker, or, with some blending, it can be sold as equipment fuel. The blending process requires that at least 1 part diesel fuel must be mixed with 4 parts gasoil.

In the catalytic cracking process, the feedstock is recycled through the cracker until fully converted. For example, each barrel of gasoil originally fed into the catalytic cracker uses an average of 4 barrels of capacity when fully cycled. The products of this process will be catalytic naphtha, catalytic heating oil, and pitch. When heating oil is used as feedstock, the possibilities are a bit more complicated. In normal mode, each barrel of heating oil originally fed into the catalytic cracker uses an average of 2.5 barrels of capacity when fully cycled; but there is also a "high-severity" mode of operation, which uses an average of 2.0 barrels of capacity. The capacity of the catalytic cracker is 15,000 barrels of throughput per day, and its yields are as follows:

	Heating Oil Normal	Heating Oil Hi-severity	Gasoil
Catalytic naphtha	30%	35%	50%
Catalytic heating oil	70%	80%	50%
Pitch	10%	5%	15%

The sums exceed 100 percent; because the cracking process reduces the density of the output.

Current prices (in dollars per barrel) for the major final products are as follows: gasoline $42, diesel fuel $38, catalytic heating oil $36, straight-run heating oil $35, equipment fuel $32, and pitch $25. The marketing department has indicated that the company could probably not sell more than 4,000 barrels per day each of diesel fuel and catalytic heating oil, but it could sell as much of the other products as the refinery is able to produce.

A recent internal study has reported that the direct processing cost per barrel of crude oil going into the pipestills is $1.20 and that the direct cost for the catalytic cracker is $1.50 per barrel of input, with a 15 percent premium for the high-severity mode of operation.

a. What is the optimal schedule for Coastal Refining?

b. What is the optimal total cost?

c. What are the shadow prices for pipestill capacity and cracker capacity? Over what ranges do these figures hold? What do they tell us about the value of capacity expansion?

13 Integer Programming

13.1 INTRODUCTION

One of the basic assumptions in linear programming models relates to divisibility of the decision variables: Fractional values of decision variables make sense either literally (12.6 tons of steel can be produced) or as a modeling approximation (1,776.2 trucks is the same as 1,776). The optimal solution of a linear program may therefore contain fractional decision variables, and this is appropriate—or at least tolerable—in most applications. In some cases, however, it may be necessary to ensure that some or all of the decision variables take on integer values. Accommodating the requirement that variables must be integers is the subject of **integer programming**. In this chapter, we examine the formulation and solution of integer programs.

Before we discuss how to handle the integer requirement with Solver, we review what we have already covered that relates to the subject of fractional values for decision variables. There are, for example, some problem types where the occurrence of fractional decision variables can be avoided entirely. In transportation, assignment, and transshipment models, which were covered in the previous chapter, integer solutions are always produced (provided the supply and demand parameters are integers) without an explicit requirement. As those examples might suggest, there are categories of linear programs that can guarantee integer solutions, but a comprehensive treatment of those special cases is beyond the scope of our coverage.

In some cases, we might be interested mainly in the strategic information that comes with a linear program's solution. That is, we may want to identify the qualitative pattern in the optimal solution, or we may want to find the shadow prices as a guide for strategic initiatives. Neither of these goals is inhibited by a solution that contains fractions. In fact, imposing integer requirements can make it harder to identify certain strategic information. But on some occasions, only an integer solution will do.

Consider the product mix for chairs, desks, and tables discussed in the Veerman Furniture model of Chapter 11. As it turned out, the optimal solution contains no chairs, 275 desks, and 100 tables, so that all the decision variables happen to be integers. Suppose instead that only 1,800 fabrication hours are available, rather than the 1,850 of the base case. As we can see in Figure 13.1[*], the optimal product mix includes 266.67 desks. Is the fractional number of desks meaningful?

On the surface, it may seem to make no sense to talk about two-thirds of a desk in the product mix. Certainly, if we were interested in the tactical implications of the solution, it would not make sense for us to prescribe the production of two-thirds of a desk to help meet demand. However, there are two interpretations of the fraction that do make sense. For one, we may be willing to round off or truncate fractional values. That is, we might interpret the optimal solution as 266 desks and 100 tables. Although this truncated solution does not use every last hour of capacity, the unused time is about a tenth of a percent of fabrication capacity. The impact on the objective function is equally small. The underlying uncertainty in our knowledge of all the parameters in the model is likely to be much larger than a tenth of 1 percent. Thus, *any* solution to the model is somewhat approximate. Therefore, rounding is often a perfectly acceptable way of dealing with fractional decision variables.

[*]To download spreadsheets for this chapter, go to the Student Companion Site at www.wiley.com/college/powell.

FIGURE 13.1 Optimal Solution to the Example

	A	B	C	D	E	F	G
1	Allocation: Furniture Production						
2							
3	Decision Variables						
4			C	D	T		
5	Product mix		0	266.667	100		
6							
7	Objective Function				Total		
8	Profit	15	24	18	$8,200		
9							
10							
11	Constraints				LHS		RHS
12	Fabrication	4	6	2	1800	<=	1800
13	Assembly	3	5	7	2033.333	<=	2400
14	Shipping	3	2	4	933.3333	<=	1500
15	Chair market	1	0	0	0	<=	360
16	Desk market	0	1	0	266.6667	<=	300
17	Table market	0	0	1	100	<=	100
18							

13.1

A second interpretation is also possible. We might want to think of the solution as resulting from a planning model that specifies conditions in a typical week. In that context, when we encounter a figure such as 266.67 in the optimal mix, we could interpret it as prescribing 267 desks for the first two weeks and then 266 desks in the third. That is, we might interpret the solution as the long-run average of a repeated activity, where, again, fractions could easily make sense. Thus, rounded-off values and planning averages provide us with two reasons why we might tolerate fractional answers to linear programming problems when they seem impractical in literal terms.

13.2 INTEGER VARIABLES AND THE INTEGER SOLVER

Rounded solutions and planning averages aside, there are still situations where only integers will suffice (for example, when projects must be funded in full or not at all, or when producing a small quantity of large items such as airplanes). In those cases, we must be able to specify that the decision variables be integers.

Solver allows us to directly designate decision variables as integer valued. Adding an integer requirement to a model that is otherwise a nonlinear programming problem or a linear programming problem will give rise to an **integer nonlinear programming problem**, or to an **integer linear programming problem**. In the case of integer linear programs, Solver employs an algorithm that checks all possible assignments of integer values to variables, although some of the assignments may not have to be examined explicitly. This procedure may require the solution of a large number of linear programs, but because Solver can do this quickly and reliably with the simplex algorithm, it will eventually locate a global optimum. In the case of integer nonlinear programs, however, certain difficulties can arise, although Solver will always attempt to find a solution. Because it builds on the GRG algorithm, which cannot distinguish local optima from global optima, Solver is somewhat handicapped in its solution procedure for those problems. Because integer versions of nonlinear programs are particularly challenging, we concentrate here on integer linear programs.

The use of Solver for integer programming models, once they are formulated, is relatively straightforward. The requirement that a variable must be an integer is treated in Solver much like an additional constraint. Along with the constraint choices of ≤, ≥, and =, the Solver constraint window also permits the choice of **int** and **bin**. The *int* constraint forces a variable to be *int*eger valued, and the *bin* constraint forces a variable to be either zero or one (*bin*ary valued). As an example, we return to the fractional version of Veerman Furniture from Figure 13.1. In the Solver Parameters window we click on the Add button. Then, we can designate all three variables as integers in the Add Constraint window, as shown in Figure 13.2.

After the model has been built and particular variables have been designated as integer or binary, the next step is to select the Integer tab in the Options window. The key option is the Tolerance parameter, for which the default value is normally set at 5 percent. At this setting, Solver is guaranteed only to find a solution that is no worse

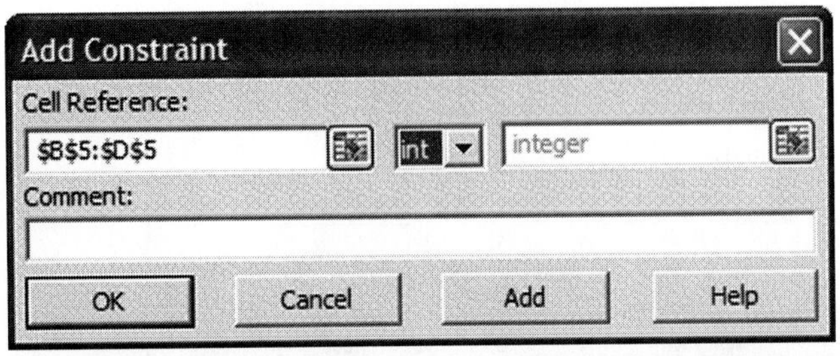

FIGURE 13.2 Designating
Variables as Integers

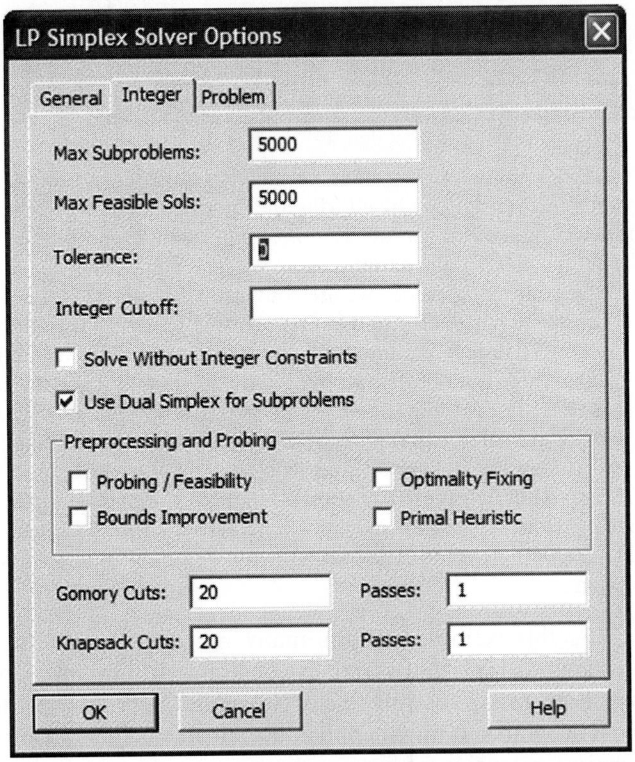

Add Constraint   ☒

Cell Reference:

$B$5:$D$5   ▦   int ▾   integer   ▦

Comment:

[   ]

| OK | Cancel | Add | Help |

FIGURE 13.3 Setting the
Tolerance Parameter

LP Simplex Solver Options   ☒

General | **Integer** | Problem |

Max Subproblems: 5000

Max Feasible Sols: 5000

Tolerance: 0

Integer Cutoff: [   ]

☐ Solve Without Integer Constraints

☑ Use Dual Simplex for Subproblems

┌ Preprocessing and Probing ──────────────────────────┐
│ ☐ Probing / Feasibility   ☐ Optimality Fixing   │
│ ☐ Bounds Improvement   ☐ Primal Heuristic   │
└──┘

Gomory Cuts: 20   Passes: 1

Knapsack Cuts: 20   Passes: 1

| OK | Cancel | Help |

than 5 percent away from the optimal solution. Clearly, we want to find the very best solution, and this calls for setting the Tolerance parameter equal to 0 percent. However, the tighter Tolerance level may require the solution procedure to take much more time, especially in larger models. Therefore, we sometimes keep the level at 5 percent while we are debugging the model, and we leave it at that level if we find ourselves working on a large problem. If we find that Solver can locate a solution at the 5 percent Tolerance level in a reasonable amount of time, we can experiment by lowering the Tolerance toward the 0 percent level. In our example, which is not a large problem, we set the Tolerance to 0 percent as shown in Figure 13.3. We return to the Solver Parameters window and invoke Solver with the following problem specification:

Target cell	E8 (maximize)
Changing cells	B5:D5
Constraints	B5:D5 = integer
	E12:E17 ≤ G12:G17

We obtain the solution shown in Figure 13.4. There are two features of the solution we should anticipate. First, because designating a variable as an integer imposes a constraint that did not originally apply, the objective function cannot get better and will likely get worse. Second, no fractions should occur in the decision variables. This is precisely what we find in the optimal solution: The objective function drops from \$8,200 to \$8,199, and the optimal mix consists of 1 chair, 266 desks, and 100 tables. This solution is close to the fractional solution, although it is neither a rounded-down solution nor a rounded-off solution. (Of course, Veerman Furniture is unlikely to adopt a plan that calls for just one chair, even if it is optimal for the model.)

FIGURE 13.4 Optimal
Solution to the Integer
Version of the Example

	A	B	C	D	E	F	G
1	Allocation: Furniture Production						
2							
3	Decision Variables						
4			C	D	T		
5	Product mix		1	266	100		
6							
7	Objective Function					Total	
8		Profit	15	24	18	$8,199	
9							
10							
11	Constraints					LHS	RHS
12		Fabrication	4	6	2	1800 <=	1800
13		Assembly	3	5	7	2033 <=	2400
14		Shipping	3	2	4	935 <=	1500
15		Chair market	1	0	0	1 <=	360
16		Desk market	0	1	0	266 <=	300
17		Table market	0	0	1	100 <=	100
18							

H ◂ ▸ H \ 13.1 \ 13.4 /

SOLVER TIP
Integer
Options

Having designated at least one variable to be integer valued, we should always examine Solver's integer options by clicking the Options button in the Solver Parameters window and selecting the Integer tab. The most important integer option is the Tolerance parameter. The default value of the parameter is 5 percent, and we may leave this value undisturbed while we debug our model. Once we are convinced that our model is running correctly, we can set the Tolerance parameter to 0 percent so that an optimal solution is guaranteed.

The Tolerance parameter is always nonzero when we build a model in a fresh worksheet, and there is no explicit warning from Solver that this is the case. Because it is not hard to forget that the Tolerance parameter needs attention, it may be a good idea to set the Tolerance parameter to 0 percent at an early stage of building the model.

Among the integer options available are Max Subproblems and Max Feasible Solns. Although these parameters can limit the extent of the calculations performed in a large problem, it is usually more convenient to use Max Time in the first of the Solver options tabs. The default value of 100 seconds can be raised to allow a longer search for an optimal solution. ∎

As this example suggests, many integer programming models are simply linear programs with certain variables constrained to be integers. To solve these models using Solver requires only one or two additional steps beyond those required to solve linear programs. It might appear, therefore, that integer programming is just a minor technical extension of linear programming. However, binary variables allow us to model a number of frequently occurring situations that cannot be modeled using standard linear programming techniques. In the remainder of the chapter, we discuss examples of that class of models.

13.3 BINARY VARIABLES AND BINARY CHOICE MODELS

A binary variable, which takes on the values zero or one, can be used to represent a "go/no-go" decision. We can think in terms of discrete projects, where the decision to accept the project is represented by the value 1, and the decision to reject the project is represented by the value 0. In this section, we examine two problem types that involve **binary choice**.

13.3.1 The Capital Budgeting Problem

Companies, committees, and even households often find themselves facing a problem of allocating a capital budget. As the problem arises in many firms, there is a specified budget for the year, to be invested in multiyear projects. Several proposed projects are also under consideration. Often, a high-level committee is responsible for reviewing the proposals and for deciding which projects to undertake. In modeling terms, the committee's job is to determine how to maximize the value of the projects selected, subject to the limitation on expenditures represented by the capital budget.

In the classic version of the **capital budgeting problem**, each project is described by two values: the expenditure required and the value of the project.

As a project is typically a multiyear activity, its value is represented by the net present value (NPV) of its cash flows over the project life. The expenditure, combined with the expenditures of other projects selected, cannot be more than the budget available.

EXAMPLE
The Marr Corporation

Division A of the Marr Corporation has been allocated $160 million for capital projects this year. Managers in Division A have examined various possibilities and have proposed five projects for Marr's capital budgeting committee to consider. The projects cover a variety of activities, as listed below.

P1 Implement a new information system.
P2 License a new technology from another firm.
P3 Build a state-of-the-art recycling facility.
P4 Move the receiving department to new facilities on site.
P5 Install an automated machining center in production.

There is just one project of each type. Each project has an estimated NPV, and each requires a capital expenditure, which must come out of the budget for capital projects. The following table summarizes the possibilities, with all figures in millions of dollars.

	Project				
	P1	P2	P3	P4	P5
NPV	10	17	6	8	14
Expenditure	48	96	80	32	64

The committee would like to maximize the total NPV from projects selected, subject to the budget limit of $160 million. ■

We can formulate this problem as an allocation model with one constraint. To construct an algebraic model, we let

$$y_j = 1 \text{ if project } j \text{ is accepted, and } 0 \text{ otherwise}$$

The decision variables y_j represent binary choice. When $y_j = 1$, project j is selected to be part of the set of projects undertaken; when $y_j = 0$, project j is rejected. Only these two binary values have meaning as decisions. An algebraic statement of the model is the following.

$$\text{Maximize } z = 10y_1 + 17y_2 + 6y_3 + 8y_4 + 14y_5$$

subject to

$$48y_1 + 96y_2 + 80y_3 + 32y_4 + 64y_5 \leq 160$$

The corresponding worksheet is shown in Figure 13.5. (A feasible but suboptimal set of choices is displayed in the model.) Let's first solve this model as a linear programming problem without binary constraints. In the Solver Parameters window, we enter the following information.

Target cell	H7 (maximize)
Changing cells	C5:G5
Constraints	H9 ≤ J9

If we optimize this model, the optimal NPV is $40 million, but the solution (see Figure 13.6) would be to select project P4 *five times*. This is because P4 has the lowest

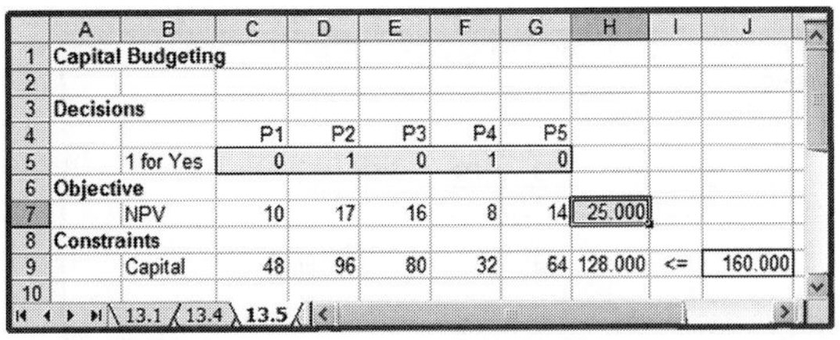

	A	B	C	D	E	F	G	H	I	J
1	Capital Budgeting									
2										
3	Decisions									
4			P1	P2	P3	P4	P5			
5		1 for Yes	0	1	0	1	0			
6	Objective									
7		NPV	10	17	16	8	14	25.000		
8	Constraints									
9		Capital	48	96	80	32	64	128.000	<=	160.000
10										

FIGURE 13.5 Worksheet for the Capital Budgeting Model

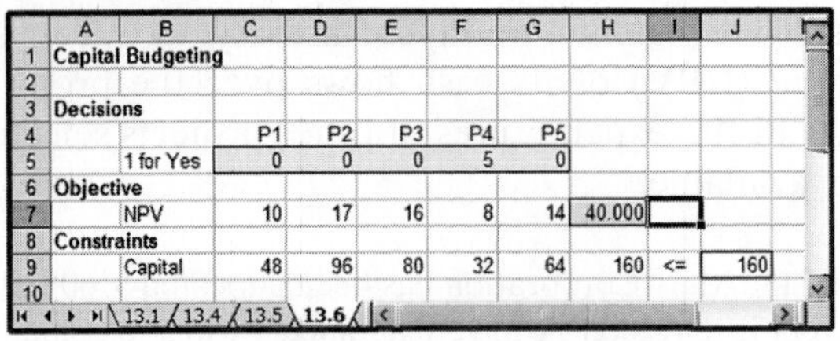

	A	B	C	D	E	F	G	H	I	J
1	Capital Budgeting									
2										
3	Decisions									
4			P1	P2	P3	P4	P5			
5		1 for Yes	0	0	0	5	0			
6	Objective									
7		NPV	10	17	16	8	14	40.000		
8	Constraints									
9		Capital	48	96	80	32	64	160	<=	160
10										

FIGURE 13.6 Solution to the Linear Version of the Capital Budgeting Model

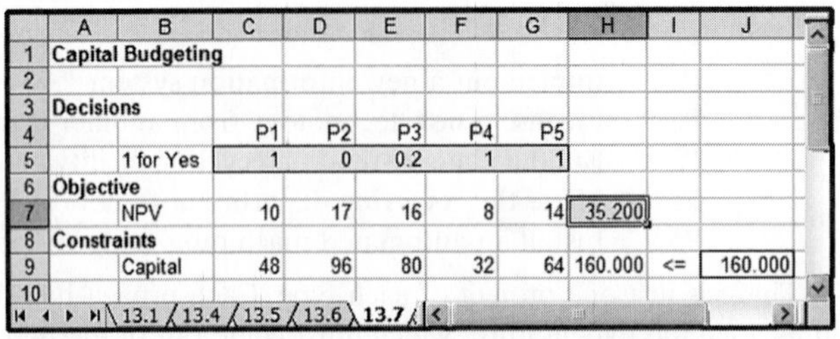

	A	B	C	D	E	F	G	H	I	J
1	Capital Budgeting									
2										
3	Decisions									
4			P1	P2	P3	P4	P5			
5		1 for Yes	1	0	0.2	1	1			
6	Objective									
7		NPV	10	17	16	8	14	35.200		
8	Constraints									
9		Capital	48	96	80	32	64	160.000	<=	160.000
10										

FIGURE 13.7 Solution to the Constrained Linear Version of the Capital Budgeting Model

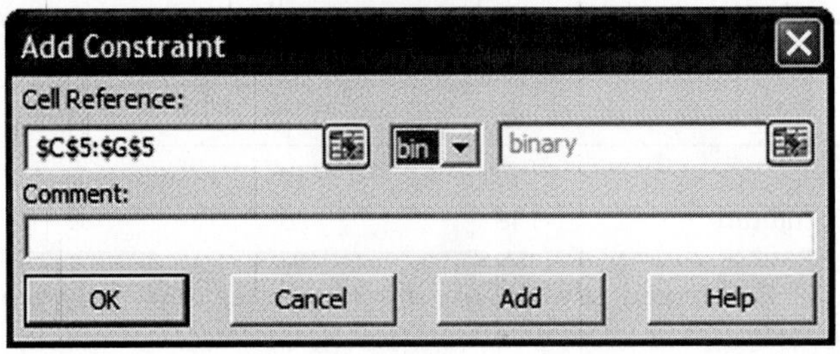

FIGURE 13.8 Designating Variables as Binary Integers

cost per dollar of NPV. However, these are one-of-a-kind projects; none can be implemented more than once.

If we were to optimize the model as a linear program with each of the variables constrained to be no more than 1, the NPV would be $35.2 million (see Figure 13.7), and the optimal mix of projects would be P1, P4, P5, and 20 percent of P3. However, no fractional projects are possible. We must treat the projects as indivisible: The decision on each one is to either accept it or reject it entirely. Therefore, we must use binary variables, as all-or-nothing variables, for this purpose.

When we add the constraint that each variable is binary, as shown in Figure 13.8, we obtain the maximum NPV of $34 million by accepting projects P1, P3, and P4 (and consuming the entire $160 million budget). The worksheet containing the optimal solution is shown in Figure 13.9. In this example, we were able to set the Tolerance parameter equal to 0 from the start. Unless otherwise noted, that is the presumption in all of the integer programming models we cover.

13.3.2 The Set Covering Problem

In Chapter 11, we encountered the covering model as one of the basic structures in linear programming. The **set covering problem** is a variation of the covering model in which the variables are all binary. In addition, the parameters in the constraints are all zeroes and ones.

In the classic version of the set covering problem, each project is described by a subset of locations that it "covers." The problem is to cover all locations with a minimal number of projects.

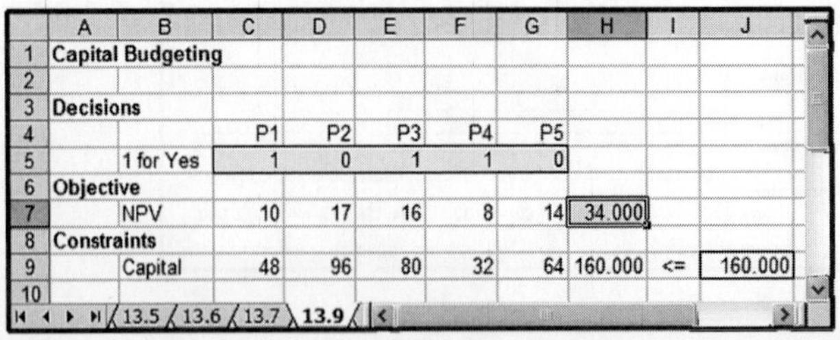

	A	B	C	D	E	F	G	H	I	J
1	Capital Budgeting									
2										
3	Decisions									
4			P1	P2	P3	P4	P5			
5		1 for Yes	1	0	1	1	0			
6	Objective									
7		NPV	10	17	16	8	14	34.000		
8	Constraints									
9		Capital	48	96	80	32	64	160.000	<=	160.000
10										

FIGURE 13.9 Optimal Solution to the Capital Budgeting Model

EXAMPLE
Emergency Coverage in Metropolis

The city of Metropolis is in the process of designing a new public emergency system, and its design calls for locating emergency vehicles around the city. The city is divided into nine districts, and seven potential sites have been identified as possible locations for emergency vehicles. Equipment located at each potential site can reach some (but not all) of the districts within the three-minute time requirement specified by the city. In the following table, an entry of 1 means that the district can be serviced from the corresponding site within the time requirement.

Site	S1	S2	S3	S4	S5	S6	S7
District D1	0	1	0	1	0	0	1
District D2	1	0	0	0	0	1	1
District D3	0	1	0	0	0	1	1
District D4	0	1	1	0	1	1	0
District D5	1	0	1	0	1	0	0
District D6	1	0	0	1	0	1	0
District D7	1	0	0	0	0	0	1
District D8	0	0	1	1	1	0	0
District D9	1	0	0	0	1	0	0

The city wants to provide coverage to all nine districts within the specified time, using the minimum number of sites. ■

The name *set covering* comes from the fact that each site can be associated with a set of districts that it covers. For example, site S1 is associated with the set {0 1 0 0 1 1 1 0 1} that appears as the first column of the table. If we select S1 to be a site for emergency equipment, then we will have covered districts D2, D5, D6, D7, and D9. For a solution to be feasible, we would have to choose the remaining sites so that they cover D1, D3, D4, and D8.

To formulate a model, we let $y_j = 1$ if site j is selected and 0 otherwise. Then our optimization problem may be stated as follows.

Minimize $z = y_1 + y_2 + y_3 + y_4 + y_5 + y_6 + y_7$

subject to:

$$
\begin{array}{llllll}
& y_2 & +y_4 & & +y_7 & \geq 1 \\
y_1 & & & +y_6 & +y_7 & \geq 1 \\
& y_2 & & +y_6 & +y_7 & \geq 1 \\
& y_2 & +y_3 & +y_5 & +y_6 & \geq 1 \\
y_1 & & +y_3 & +y_5 & & \geq 1 \\
y_1 & & +y_4 & +y_6 & & \geq 1 \\
y_1 & & & & +y_7 & \geq 1 \\
& y_3 & +y_4 & +y_5 & & \geq 1 \\
y_1 & & & +y_5 & & \geq 1
\end{array}
$$

In this algebraic form, we can see that all coefficients in the objective function are 1, all constraint coefficients are 1, and all right-hand-side constants are 1. Thus, the model is a specialized covering model but with the added provision that all variables are binary.

A spreadsheet model for the set covering example is shown in Figure 13.10, although the solution shown is not feasible. If we optimize this model as a linear program, we find that the decision variables turn out fractional, so it is essential to add the binary constraints on the variables. In the Solver Parameters window, we enter the following information.

Target cell	J6 (minimize)
Changing cells	C4:I4
Constraints	C4:I4 = binary
	J9:J17 ≥ L9:L17

The optimal solution, shown in Figure 13.11, requires three sites to cover all districts.

FIGURE 13.10 Worksheet for the Set Covering Model

	A	B	C	D	E	F	G	H	I	J	K	L
1	Set Covering											
2												
3	Decisions	Site	S1	S2	S3	S4	S5	S6	S7			
4		1=Yes	0	1	1	1	0	1	0			
5												
6	Objective	Sites	1	1	1	1	1	1	1	4		
7												
8	Constraints									cover?		
9		D1	0	1	0	1	0	0	1	2	>=	1
10		D2	1	0	0	0	0	1	1	1	>=	1
11		D3	0	1	0	0	0	1	1	2	>=	1
12		D4	0	1	1	0	1	1	0	3	>=	1
13		D5	1	0	1	0	1	0	0	1	>=	1
14		D6	1	0	0	1	0	1	0	2	>=	1
15		D7	1	0	0	0	0	0	1	0	>=	1
16		D8	0	0	1	1	1	0	0	2	>=	1
17		D9	1	0	0	0	1	0	0	0	>=	1
18												

H ◀ ▶ H / 13.5 / 13.6 / 13.7 / 13.9 \ 13.10 / | ◀

FIGURE 13.11 Optimal Solution for the Set Covering Model

	A	B	C	D	E	F	G	H	I	J	K	L
1	Set Covering											
2												
3	Decisions	Site	S1	S2	S3	S4	S5	S6	S7			
4		1=Yes	1	0	0	1	0	1	0			
5												
6	Objective	Sites	1	1	1	1	1	1	1	3		
7												
8	Constraints									cover?		
9		D1	0	1	0	1	0	0	1	1	>=	1
10		D2	1	0	0	0	0	1	1	2	>=	1
11		D3	0	1	0	0	0	1	1	1	>=	1
12		D4	0	1	1	0	1	1	0	1	>=	1
13		D5	1	0	1	0	1	0	0	1	>=	1
14		D6	1	0	0	1	0	1	0	3	>=	1
15		D7	1	0	0	0	0	0	1	1	>=	1
16		D8	0	0	1	1	1	0	0	1	>=	1
17		D9	1	0	0	0	1	0	0	1	>=	1
18												

H ◀ ▶ H / 13.5 / 13.6 / 13.7 / 13.9 / 13.10 \ 13.11 / | ◀

In the capital budgeting and set covering examples, we encountered models that resemble linear programming formulations except that the decisions involve binary choice. The use of binary variables was critical because linear programming formulations would not be able to find optimal solutions. In the next section, we study how binary variables can help us accommodate additional information in an otherwise linear model.

13.4 BINARY VARIABLES AND LOGICAL RELATIONSHIPS

We sometimes encounter additional conditions affecting the selection of projects in problems like capital budgeting. These include relationships among projects, fixed costs, and quantity discounts.

13.4.1 Relationships among Projects

Projects can be related in any number of ways. We cover five types of relationships here:

- At least m projects must be selected.
- At most n projects must be selected.
- Exactly k projects must be selected.
- Some projects are mutually exclusive.
- Some projects have contingency relationships.

To illustrate, we return to the solution of our capital budgeting example, shown in Figure 13.9, where the solution is to adopt projects P1, P2, and P4. Suppose now that projects P2 and P5 are international projects, while the others are domestic. Suppose also that the committee wishes to select *at least one* of its projects from the international arena. We can then add a covering constraint to the base case:

$$y_2 + y_5 \geq 1$$

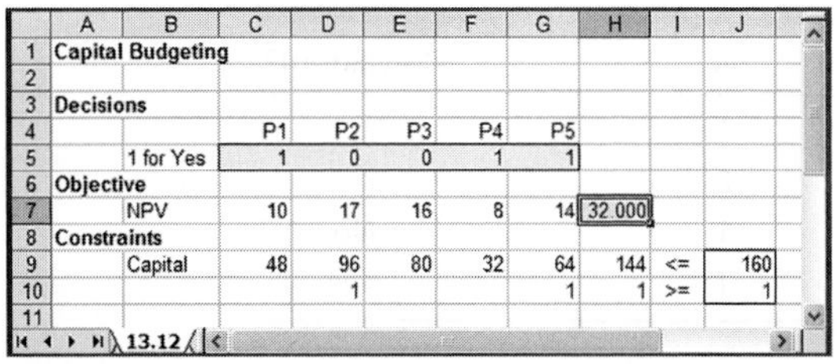

FIGURE 13.12 Capital Budgeting Model with Minimum Level Constraint

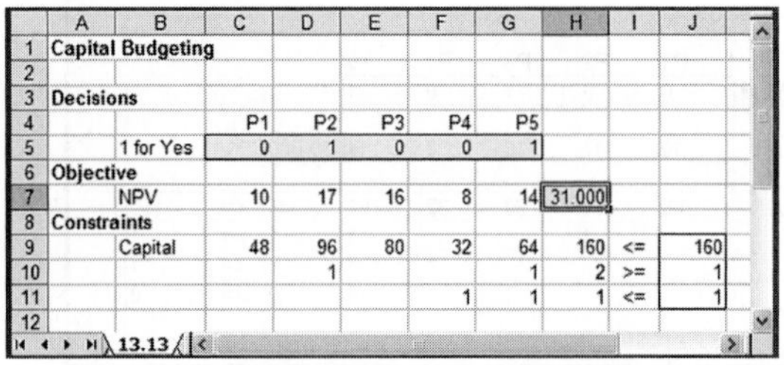

FIGURE 13.13 Capital Budgeting Model with Mutually Exclusive Constraint

Because the variables are all binary, this constraint ensures that the combination

$$y_2 = y_5 = 0$$

is not allowed. Therefore, P2, or P5, or both, will be selected, thus satisfying the requirement of one international selection. We can append this covering constraint to the model in row 10 of the worksheet. Of course, the addition of a constraint may make the objective function worse, and in this case, the optimal NPV drops to $32 million. Figure 13.12 shows that we can achieve this value by accepting projects P1, P4, and P5 (and incurring expenditures of only $144 million).

This additional constraint illustrates the fact that we can use binary variables to represent structural or policy relationships of the form

- Select *at least m* of the possible projects.
- Select *at most n* of the possible projects.

Alternatively, management at Marr Corporation may believe that it lacks sufficient personnel to oversee three projects, so it might impose the constraint that exactly two of the projects be chosen. Then we could write

$$y_1 + y_2 + y_3 + y_4 + y_5 = 2$$

This constraint limits the selection to exactly two projects.

Other relationships that we normally think of as "logical" relationships can also be expressed with binary variables. Suppose that projects P4 and P5 are **mutually exclusive** (for example, they could require some of the same staff resources). Then we could write:

$$y_4 + y_5 \leq 1$$

This constraint prohibits the combination

$$y_4 = y_5 = 1$$

The mutual exclusivity requirement is just a special case of the *at most n* relationship, but with $n = 1$. Figure 13.13 shows the worksheet for the expanded model, with the mutual exclusivity constraint entered in row 11. As the figure indicates, the new constraint alters the optimal solution, and the best choice is to adopt projects P2 and P5. This solution achieves an optimal NPV of only $31 million, while consuming the entire capital budget.

In addition, we sometimes encounter **contingency** relationships. Suppose that project P5 requires that P3 be selected. In other words, P5 is contingent on P3. To analyze logical requirements of this sort, consider all of the selection combinations for the binary variables. The following table shows that three of the four combinations are consistent with the contingency condition:

y_3	y_5	Consistent?
0	0	Yes
1	0	Yes
0	1	No
1	1	Yes

FIGURE 13.14 Capital Budgeting Model with Contingency Constraint

	A	B	C	D	E	F	G	H	I	J
1	Capital Budgeting									
2										
3	Decisions									
4			P1	P2	P3	P4	P5			
5		1 for Yes	0	0	1	0	1			
6	Objective									
7		NPV	10	17	16	8	14	30.000		
8	Constraints									
9		Capital	48	96	80	32	64	144	<=	160
10				1			1	1	>=	1
11						1	1	1	<=	1
12					1		-1	0	>=	0
13										

We can accommodate the three consistent combinations and exclude the one inconsistent combination by adding the following constraint:

$$y_3 - y_5 \geq 0$$

Figure 13.14 shows the result of entering the contingency constraint into row 12 of the worksheet. This time the objective function drops to $30 million, and projects P3 and P5 are selected, consuming $144 million of the budget.

The contingency constraint is an example of how we can include requirements that seem qualitative, or at least nonlinear, in a linear model by employing binary variables. Binary variables provide us with a convenient indicator of a project's status. With binary variables, we can represent qualitative or logical information about the set of projects in the model.

13.4.2 Linking Constraints and Fixed Costs

One of the assumptions in linear models is strict proportionality: The cost contributed by an activity is proportional to its activity level. However, we commonly encounter situations in which activity costs are composed of fixed costs and variable costs, with only the variable costs being proportional to activity level. With an integer programming model, we can also integrate the fixed component of cost.

Imagine that we have already built a linear programming model, but one variable (x) has a fixed cost that we want to represent in the objective function. To incorporate this fixed cost into the model, we separate the fixed and variable components of cost. In algebraic terms, we write cost as

$$Cost = Fy + cx$$

where F represents the fixed cost and c represents the linear variable cost. The variables x and y are decision variables where x is a normal (continuous) variable and y is a binary variable. (See Figure 13.15.) Constraints in the linear program involve only the variable portion—that is, they involve only the variable x, not the variable y. In this situation, we also want to make sure that the variables x and y work together consistently. In particular, we want to have $y = 1$ (so that we incur the fixed cost) when $x > 0$, and we want to have $y = 0$ (so that we avoid the fixed cost) when $x = 0$. To achieve consistent linking of the two variables, we add the following generic **linking constraint** to the model:

$$x \leq My$$

where the number M represents an upper bound on the variable x. In other words, M is at least as large as any value we can feasibly choose for x.

FIGURE 13.15 Graph of a Cost Function with a Fixed-Cost Component

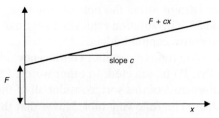

Why does the linking constraint work? As seen by Solver, this is just another feasibility condition to be satisfied. When $y = 0$ (and therefore no fixed cost is incurred), the right-hand side becomes zero, and Solver interprets the constraint as $x \leq 0$. Since we also require $x \geq 0$, these two constraints together force x to be zero. Thus, when $y = 0$, it will be consistent to avoid the fixed cost. On the other hand, when $y = 1$, the right-hand side will be so large that Solver does not need to restrict x at all, permitting its value to be positive while we incur the fixed cost. Thus, when $y = 1$, it will be consistent to incur the fixed cost. Of course, because we are optimizing, Solver will never produce a solution with the combination of $y = 1$ and $x = 0$, because it would always be preferable to set $y = 0$.

The following example illustrates the use of linking constraints for modeling fixed costs.

EXAMPLE
Mayhugh Manufacturing Company

Mayhugh Manufacturing, a medium-size job shop, has been producing and selling three product families. Each product family requires production hours in each of three departments. In addition, each product family requires its own sales force, which must be supported no matter how large or small the sales volume happens to be. The parameters describing the situation are summarized in the following table.

	Product Family		
	F1	F2	F3
Profit per unit	$1.20	$1.80	$2.20
	Hours Required Per Thousand Units			Hours Available
Department A	3	4	8	2,000
Department B	3	5	6	2,000
Department C	2	3	9	2,000
Sales cost ($000)	60	200	100	

■

At the heart of this situation lies a product mix problem. The linear programming representation of the product mix problem (with no fixed costs) is shown in Figure 13.16. By defining the x-values in thousands, we scale the model so that the objective function is in thousands of dollars. The optimal product mix calls for producing all three families, with F1 at 400,000, F2 at 100,000 and F3 at 50,000. This product mix creates $770,000 in variable profits. If we subtract the total fixed costs of $360,000, we are left with a net profit of $410,000, as calculated in cell F19 of the worksheet.

The linear programming solution might represent the situation for a firm that has introduced and supported various new products over the years and that now finds itself carrying out activities in three product markets. The linear programming framework suggests how to allocate capacity, provided that all three product families are active. However, there is no basis for determining whether any one of the families should be dropped, because fixed-cost considerations are not within the scope of the linear programming analysis.

To formulate the full problem as an integer programming model, we make two changes. First, we write the objective function with separate terms for variable profit and fixed cost:

FIGURE 13.16 Worksheet for a Product Mix Version of the Mayhugh Example

$$Net\ Profit = 1.20x_1 - 60y_1 + 1.80x_2$$

$$-200y_2 + 2.20x_3 - 100y_3$$

where x_j represents the volume for family j, in thousands. Here, y_j is a binary variable that must take either the value 1 when x_j is positive (and the fixed cost is incurred) or the value 0 when x_j is zero (and the fixed cost is avoided). Next, we add three linking constraints to assure consistency between the x–y pairs:

$$x_1 - My_1 \leq 0$$
$$x_2 - My_2 \leq 0$$
$$x_3 - My_3 \leq 0$$

Now we need to identify a large number to play the role of M. Essentially, we need a number large enough so that it will not limit the choice of these variables in any of the other (demand and supply) constraints. For example, a value of 400 (thousand) would work, since that represents the largest demand ceiling, and none of the volumes could ever be larger.

Thus, when $y_2 = 1$, the linking constraint for product family F2 becomes $x_2 \leq 400$; and when $y_2 = 0$, the constraint becomes $x_2 \leq 0$. Similar interpretations apply to families F1 and F3. These are valid linking constraints, but we can streamline the model slightly. Instead of retaining separate constraints to represent the demand ceilings and the linking constraints, we can let the linking constraint do "double duty" if we choose a different value of M for each family and set it equal to the demand ceiling. For example, the value of M selected for the F2 constraint could be 300 instead of 400. Then, when $y_2 = 1$, the constraint on product family F2 becomes $x_2 \leq 300$, which also serves as a demand-ceiling constraint. When $y_2 = 0$, the constraint becomes $x_2 \leq 0$, and the choice of M does not matter. The streamlined model becomes:

Maximize $1.20x_1 - 60y_1 + 1.80x_2 - 200y_2 + 2.20x_3 - 100y_3$

subject to

$$
\begin{array}{rrrrrrl}
3x_1 & + & 4x_2 & + & 8x_3 & & \leq 2,000 \\
3x_1 & + & 5x_2 & + & 6x_3 & & \leq 2,000 \\
2x_1 & + & 3x_2 & + & 9x_3 & & \leq 2,000 \\
x_1 & & & & & -400y_1 & \leq \quad 0 \\
& & x_2 & & & -300y_2 & \leq \quad 0 \\
& & & & x_3 & -50y_3 & \leq \quad 0
\end{array}
$$

Our spreadsheet model, shown in Figure 13.17, uses just three columns (one for each product family), where the corresponding pairs of x and y variables appear in the same column. In this spreadsheet, the left-hand side of the linking constraint for each x–y pair appears in the corresponding column. For example, the formula in cell C16 is C5 - C15*C6, and this value is constrained to be negative or zero. We invoke Solver and specify:

Target cell	F9 (maximize)
Changing cells	C5:E6
Constraints	C16:E16 $\leq$ 0
	C6:E6 = binary
	F11:F13 $\leq$ H11:H13

FIGURE 13.17 Optimal Solution for the Mayhugh Example

	A	B	C	D	E	F	G	H
1	Product Mix with Fixed Costs							
2								
3	Decisions							
4			F1	F2	F3			
5			400	160	0	K-units		
6			1	1	0	binary		
7	Objective							
8		Variable profit	1.20	1.80	2.20			
9		Fixed cost	60	200	100	508	K$	
10	Constraints							
11		X	3	4	8	1840	<=	2000
12		Y	3	5	6	2000	<=	2000
13		Z	2	3	9	1280	<=	2000
14								
15		demand	400	300	50	K-units		
16		linking	0	-140	0			
17								

The optimal solution achieves a net profit of $508,000. In order to attain this level of profits, the company must produce family F1 up to its ceiling, produce family F2 at the level of 160,000, and eliminate production of product family F3. In other words, the integer programming model detects that family F3 does not cover its fixed cost, and the company would be better off not producing and selling that family at all.

SOLVER TIP

Logical Functions and Integer Programming

In setting up integer programming models, an experienced Excel programmer might be tempted to use the logical functions in Excel (IF, AND, OR, etc.) to express certain relationships among decision variables. A direct means of linking a continuous variable *x* to its fixed costs would be to substitute the formula IF($x>0,1,0$) in the cell containing the binary variable. For example, in the model of Figure 13.17, we would use the following formula in cell C6.

$$IF(C5 > 0, 1, 0)$$

We could then copy this formula into cells D6 and E6. The resulting model has no binary variables and only the three decision variables in C5:E5. It also contains no linking constraints (see Figure 13.18). To run the model we specify:

Target cell	F9 (maximize)
Changing cells	C5:E5
Constraints	C5:E5 $\leq$ C15:E15
	F11:F13 $\leq$ H11:H13

Although this approach is logically sound, when we run Solver, we obtain the error message reproduced in Figure 13.19, informing us that the model is not linear. We cannot run the linear solver because the IF function is nonlinear. Unfortunately, the linear solver does not always detect the nonlinearity caused by the use of logical functions, so it is important to remember *never* to use an IF function in a model built for the linear solver.

What if we use the nonlinear solver instead? The answer is that our results depend on our initial solution. An initial solution of all zeroes cannot be improved by the nonlinear solver; an initial solution of all 50s leads to a solution worth $410,000. Neither, as we already know, is optimal. The presence of the IF function tends to make the nonlinear solver stop its search at a local optimum. For these reasons, we want to avoid using the IF function and the other logical functions in optimization models. ■

FIGURE 13.18 Using Logical Functions to Represent Fixed Costs

FIGURE 13.19 The Nonlinearity Message from Solver

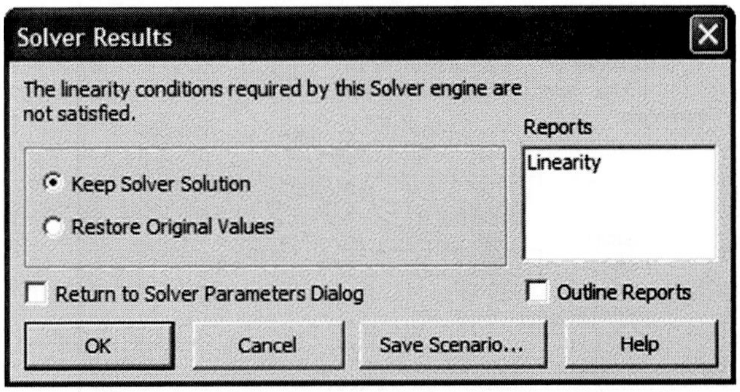

13.4.3 Threshold Levels and Quantity Discounts

Sometimes we encounter situations where, in order to do business, we are required to participate at a specified minimum level. For example, in purchasing, we might be able to qualify for a discounted price if we buy in quantity. As another example, in manufacturing, a setup is sufficiently disruptive that the line would be set up to assemble a batch of motors only if we're making at least a dozen of them, not merely one or two. These examples illustrate a **threshold-level requirement**: a decision variable is either at least as large as a specified minimum, or else it is zero.

The existence of a threshold level does not directly affect the objective function of a model, and it can be represented in the constraints with the help of binary variables. Suppose we have a variable x that is subject to a threshold requirement. Let m denote the minimum feasible value of x if it is nonzero. Then we can capture this structure in an integer programming model by including the following *pair* of constraints:

$$x - my \geq 0$$
$$x - My \leq 0$$

where, as before, M is a large number that is greater than or equal to any value x could feasibly take. To see how these two requirements work, consider the two possibilities for the binary variable. When $y = 1$, the constraints reduce to $m \leq x \leq M$, so that x is forced to be at or above the threshold level. When $y = 0$, the constraints reduce to $x = 0$. Thus, the pair x and y will behave consistently.

For example, in the Mayhugh example, we might want to require that product family F2 have a production level of at least 250 units. Since the model already includes the linking constraint $x_2 - 300y_2 \leq 0$, we need only to add the threshold constraint $x_2 - 250y_2 \geq 0$, and the search for an F2 level will be restricted to production values between 250 and 300, or zero. Figure 13.20 shows the amended model, with the linking constraint entered in cell D19. Because we are adding a constraint that eliminates our former optimal product mix, we can expect that the optimal profit must drop. To run the model we specify:

Target cell	F9 (maximize)
Changing Cells	C5:E6
Constraints	C16:E16 $\leq$ 0
	C6:E6 = binary
	D10 $\geq$ 0
	F11:F13 $\leq$ H11:H13

Figure 13.20 displays the optimal solution, where the threshold constraint is binding, and we achieve a maximum profit of $490,000.

FIGURE 13.20 Mayhugh Example with a Constraint on the Minimum Volume in Family 2

	A	B	C	D	E	F	G	H
1	Product Mix with Fixed Costs							
2								
3	Decisions							
4			F1	F2	F3			
5			250	250	0	K-units		
6			1	1	0	binary		
7	Objective							
8		Variable profit	1.20	1.80	2.20			
9		Fixed cost	60	200	100	490	K$	
10	Constraints							
11		X	3	4	8	1750	<=	2000
12		Y	3	5	6	2000	<=	2000
13		Z	2	3	9	1250	<=	2000
14								
15		demand	400	300	50	K-units		
16		linking	-150	-50	0			
17								
18		minimum		250				
19				0				
20								

14 ◀ ▶ ▶◀\ 13.15 / 13.16 / 13.17 / 13.18 \ **13.20** / ◀

13.5* THE FACILITY LOCATION MODEL

The transportation model, discussed in Chapter 12, is typically used to find optimal shipping schedules in supply chains and logistics systems. The applications of the model can be viewed as tactical problems, in the sense that the time interval of interest is usually short, say a week or a month. Over that time period, the supply capacities and locations are unlikely to change at all, and the demands can be predicted with reasonable precision. Given such information, the model represents shipment patterns as decisions and finds their optimal configuration.

Over a longer time frame, a strategic version of the problem arises. In this setting, the decisions relate to the selection of supply locations as well as the shipment schedule. These decisions are strategic in the sense that, once determined, they influence the system for a relatively long time interval. The basic model for choosing supply locations is called the **facility location model.**

EXAMPLE
Levinson
Foods
Company

Levinson Foods is in the process of expanding its distribution system. After some planned acquisitions, the company will have 10 distribution centers, with monthly volumes (in cartons) as listed below. Six of these sites will be able to support warehouses, in terms of the infrastructure available, and are designated by (W).

Center	Volume	Center	Volume
Albuquerque (W)	3,200	Oklahoma City	3,500
Boise	2,500	Phoenix (W)	5,000
Dallas (W)	6,800	Salt Lake City	1,800
Denver (W)	4,000	San Antonio (W)	7,400
Houston (W)	9,600	Wichita	2,700

Because the properties have been acquired under different circumstances, they would have different characteristics if Levinson Foods were to open warehouses at the sites. Their potential capacities (in cartons) and monthly operating costs are summarized in the following table.

Warehouse	Capacity	Cost
Albuquerque	16,000	$140,000
Dallas	20,000	150,000
Denver	10,000	100,000
Houston	10,000	110,000
Phoenix	12,000	125,000
San Antonio	10,000	120,000

Information has been compiled showing the cost per carton of shipping between any pair of locations in the system. Levinson could open warehouses at any of the designated locations, but its criterion is to minimize total cost, including fixed operating costs and variable shipment costs. ■

13.5.1 The Capacitated Problem

Conceptually, we can think of this problem as having two stages. In the first stage, decisions must be made about how many warehouses to open and where they should be. Then, once we know where the warehouses are, we can construct a transportation model to optimize the actual shipments. The costs at stake are also of two types: fixed costs associated with keeping a warehouse open and variable transportation costs associated with shipments from the open warehouses.

Imagine that we have built the 6×10 transportation model for this problem, using the following variables:

$$x_{ij} = \text{quantity shipped from warehouse } i \text{ to center } j$$

Now we want to add considerations for the warehouses. Let

$$y_i = 1 \text{ if warehouse } i \text{ is open, and } 0 \text{ otherwise}$$

We associate these binary variables with the fixed costs, and so we add the following cost expression to the transportation model.

$$\text{Total Fixed Cost} = 140y_1 + 150y_2 + 100y_3 + 110y_4 + 125y_5 + 120y_6$$

In addition, we want to link the binary variables to the corresponding continuous variables, so we add linking constraints of the form:

$$x_{ij} - My_i \leq 0$$

for every combination of i and j. As usual, the linking constraints ensure consistency between the shipment quantities x_{ij} and the binary variables that signify whether a warehouse is open.

The resulting model is shown in Figure 13.21, using a format that is meant to look similar to the transportation model of Chapter 12:

- Capacities are entered in cells M4:M9 (with their total in M10).
- Demands are entered in cells C10:L10.
- Unit costs are entered in cells C4:L9.
- Shipment decisions are entered in C14:L19, with row and column totals labeled *Sent* and *Received*.

In addition to the transportation model that lies at the heart of this formulation, the worksheet contains fixed costs in cells B4:B9 and binary variables in B14:B19. With these additions, the objective function (cell B11) can be expressed as the sum of two SUMPRODUCT calculations:

Total Fixed Cost	=	SUMPRODUCT(B14:B19, B4:B9)
Total Variable Cost	=	SUMPRODUCT(C14:L19, C4:L9)
Objective function	=	Total Fixed Cost + Total Variable Cost

When we turn to constraints, we start with the supply and demand constraints of the transportation model (*Sent* ≤ *Capacity* and *Received* ≥ *Demand*); then we must add the linking constraints. These are set up in the array C23:L27. Each entry is of the form $x_{ij} - My_i$. For simplicity, we use the total capacity

FIGURE 13.21 Optimal Solution to the Levinson Foods Model

	A	B	C	D	E	F	G	H	I	J	K	L	M
1	Warehouse Location												
2													
3		*Fixed Cost*	Alb	Boise	Dall	Denv	Hous	Okla	Phoe	Salt	SanA	Wich	*Capacity*
4	Albuquerque	140,000	0.00	47.00	32.00	22.00	42.50	27.00	23.00	30.00	36.50	29.50	16,000
5	Dallas	150,000	32.00	79.50	0.00	39.00	12.50	10.50	50.00	63.00	13.50	17.00	20,000
6	Denver	100,000	21.00	42.00	39.00	0.00	51.50	31.50	40.50	24.00	47.50	26.00	10,000
7	Houston	110,000	42.50	91.00	12.50	51.50	0.00	23.00	58.00	72.00	10.00	31.00	10,000
8	Phoenix	125,000	23.00	49.00	50.00	40.50	58.00	49.00	0.00	32.50	50.00	52.00	12,000
9	San Antonio	120,000	36.50	83.50	13.50	47.50	10.00	24.00	50.00	66.50	0.00	32.00	12,000
10	*Volume*		3200	2500	6800	4000	9600	3500	5000	1800	7400	2700	80,000
11		884,550											
12													
13		*Open?*					*Shipments*						*Sent*
14	Albuquerque	0	0	0	0	0	0	0	0	0	0	0	0
15	Dallas	1	0	0	6800	0	0	3500	0	0	7000	2700	20,000
16	Denver	1	1700	2500	0	4000	0	0	0	1800	0	0	10,000
17	Houston	1	0	0	0	0	9600	0	0	0	400	0	10,000
18	Phoenix	1	1500	0	0	0	0	0	5000	0	0	0	6,500
19	San Antonio	0	0	0	0	0	0	0	0	0	0	0	0
20		*Received*	3200	2500	6800	4000	9600	3500	5000	1800	7400	2700	46,500
21													
22		*Linking*	0	0	0	0	0	0	0	0	0	0	
23			-80,000	-80,000	-73,200	-80,000	-80,000	-76,500	-80,000	-80,000	-73,000	-77,300	
24			-78,300	-77,500	-80,000	-76,000	-80,000	-80,000	-80,000	-78,200	-80,000	-80,000	
25			-80,000	-80,000	-80,000	-80,000	-70,400	-80,000	-80,000	-80,000	-79,600	-80,000	
26			-78,500	-80,000	-80,000	-80,000	-80,000	-80,000	-75,000	-80,000	-80,000	-80,000	
27			0	0	0	0	0	0	0	0	0	0	
28													

13.21

(80,000) as the value for M, although smaller values would also work. In the Solver window, we specify:

Target cell	B11 (minimize)
Changing Cells	B14:L19
Constraints	B14:B19 = binary
	C20:L20 = C10:L10
	C22:L27 ≤ 0
	M14:M19 ≤ M4:M9

One modification has been made in the usual statement of constraints. The demand constraints, normally posed as inequalities, are entered here as equations. This modification is made here because the problem contains some unit costs of zero, so there is no disincentive for shipping more than the demand requirement from some warehouse to a center at its own location. (If a small handling cost were added to all of the unit costs, this would not be an issue.) When we run the model, Solver produces the optimal solution shown in Figure 13.21, which achieves a minimum total cost of $884,550. Four of the six warehouse possibilities are selected, incurring $485,000 in fixed costs and the remainder in variable distribution costs.

An alternative formulation exists that is sometimes more convenient to use. In this alternative model, we substitute for the linking constraints. Instead of one linking constraint for each distribution variable, we use one linking constraint for each warehouse. For example, for the first warehouse:

$$x_{11} + x_{12} + x_{13} + \cdots + x_{1,10} - My_1 \leq 0$$

and similarly for the other five warehouses. This type of constraint ensures consistency between the binary variable y_i and the set of shipment variables emanating from warehouse i. If any shipment is positive, y_i must be 1; if y_i is zero, then no shipments from the corresponding warehouse are possible. Instead of 60 linking constraints, we need only six. These appear in Figure 13.22, in cells N14:N19. We can streamline the model a bit further by choosing M values in each of these constraints so that they do "double duty." Thus, the formula in cell N14 reads M14 – M4*B14. The reference to M4 means that the capacity of the first warehouse plays the role of M, so that when $y_1 = 1$, the linking constraint functions as a capacity constraint. This approach allows us to simplify the information in the Solver window, which reads as follows.

Target cell	B11 (minimize)
Changing Cells	B14:L19
Constraints	B14:B19 = binary
	C20:L20 = C10:L10
	N14:N19 ≤ 0

A run of this model reproduces the optimal solution, as shown in the figure.

FIGURE 13.22 Streamlined Worksheet for the Levinson Foods Model

	A	B	C	D	E	F	G	H	I	J	K	L	M	N
1	Warehouse Location													
2														
3		Fixed Cost	Alb	Boise	Dall	Denv	Hous	Okla	Phoe	Salt	SanA	Wich	Capacity	
4	Albuquerque	140,000	0.00	47.00	32.00	22.00	42.50	27.00	23.00	30.00	36.50	29.50	16,000	
5	Dallas	150,000	32.00	79.50	0.00	39.00	12.50	10.50	50.00	63.00	13.50	17.00	20,000	
6	Denver	100,000	21.00	42.00	39.00	0.00	51.50	31.50	40.50	24.00	47.50	26.00	10,000	
7	Houston	110,000	42.50	91.00	12.50	51.50	0.00	23.00	58.00	72.00	10.00	31.00	10,000	
8	Phoenix	125,000	23.00	49.00	50.00	40.50	58.00	49.00	0.00	32.50	50.00	52.00	12,000	
9	San Antonio	120,000	36.50	83.50	13.50	47.50	10.00	24.00	50.00	66.50	0.00	32.00	12,000	
10	Volume		3200	2500	6800	4000	9600	3500	5000	1800	7400	2700	80,000	
11		884,550												
12														
13		Open?					Shipments						Sent	Linking
14	Albuquerque	0	0	0	0	0	0	0	0	0	0	0	0	0
15	Dallas	1	0	0	6800	0	0	3500	0	0	7000	2700	20,000	0
16	Denver	1	1700	2500	0	4000	0	0	0	1800	0	0	10,000	0
17	Houston	1	0	0	0	0	9600	0	0	0	400	0	10,000	0
18	Phoenix	1	1500	0	0	0	0	0	5000	0	0	0	6,500	-5,500
19	San Antonio	0	0	0	0	0	0	0	0	0	0	0	0	0
20	Received	3200	2500	6800	4000	9600	3500	5000	1800	7400	2700	46,500		
21														

13.21 13.22

FIGURE 13.23 Worksheet for the Uncapacitated Version of the Location Model

	A	B	C	D	E	F	G	H	I	J	K	L	M	N
1	Warehouse Location													
2														
3		*Fixed Cost*	Alb	Boise	Dall	Denv	Hous	Okla	Phoe	Salt	SanA	Wich	*Capacity*	
4	Albuquerque	140,000	0.00	47.00	32.00	22.00	42.50	27.00	23.00	30.00	36.50	29.50	46,500	
5	Dallas	150,000	32.00	79.50	0.00	39.00	12.50	10.50	50.00	63.00	13.50	17.00	46,500	
6	Denver	100,000	21.00	42.00	39.00	0.00	51.50	31.50	40.50	24.00	47.50	26.00	46,500	
7	Houston	110,000	42.50	91.00	12.50	51.50	0.00	23.00	58.00	72.00	10.00	31.00	46,500	
8	Phoenix	125,000	23.00	49.00	50.00	40.50	58.00	49.00	0.00	32.50	50.00	52.00	46,500	
9	San Antonio	120,000	36.50	83.50	13.50	47.50	10.00	24.00	50.00	66.50	0.00	32.00	46,500	
10	*Volume*		3200	2500	6800	4000	9600	3500	5000	1800	7400	2700	279,000	
11		857,050												
12														
13		*Open?*					*Shipments*						*Sent*	*Linking*
14	Albuquerque	0	0	0	0	0	0	0	0	0	0	0	0	0
15	Dallas	1	0	0	6800	0	0	3500	0	0	0	2700	13,000	-33,500
16	Denver	1	3200	2500	0	4000	0	0	0	1800	0	0	11,500	-35,000
17	Houston	1	0	0	0	0	9600	0	0	0	7400	0	17,000	-29,500
18	Phoenix	1	0	0	0	0	0	0	5000	0	0	0	5,000	-41,500
19	San Antonio	0	0	0	0	0	0	0	0	0	0	0	0	0
20		*Received*	3200	2500	6800	4000	9600	3500	5000	1800	7400	2700	46,500	
21														

⏮ ◀ ▶ ⏭ 13.21 / 13.22 / **13.23** / ◀

13.5.2 The Uncapacitated Problem

Once we see how to solve the facility location problem with capacities given, it is not difficult to adapt the model to the uncapacitated case. Obviously, we could choose a virtual capacity for each warehouse that is as large as total demand, so that capacity would never interfere with the optimization. We show this approach in Figure 13.23, where we modify the previous worksheet by taking all capacities to be 46,500, which is the total demand in the problem. As the figure shows, removing the capacity constraints allows us to reach a lower cost, but the improvement is only about 3 percent.

An alternative formulation of the uncapacitated facility location model is sometimes useful. It is based on a simple insight about the nature of an optimal shipment pattern in the uncapacitated case. Notice that, in the optimal solution of Figure 13.23, each center is supplied by a unique warehouse. In particular, supply comes from the cheapest of the open warehouses. That form must always hold in an optimal solution, and this fact permits us to use a slightly different representation of the model.

In the uncapacitated model, we know that if warehouse i provides supply to center j, then the corresponding cost must be the demand at center j multiplied by the unit cost on the route from i to j. In Figure 13.24, we compute these costs in advance, in cells C14:L19. Then we can use decision variables of zero or one to indicate whether a given warehouse-center combination is selected as part of the

FIGURE 13.24 Alternative Version of the Uncapacitated Location Model

	A	B	C	D	E	F	G	H	I	J	K	L	M	N
1	Warehouse Location													
2														
3			Alb	Boise	Dall	Denv	Hous	Okla	Phoe	Salt	SanA	Wich	*Centers*	
4	Albuquerque		0.00	47.00	32.00	22.00	42.50	27.00	23.00	30.00	36.50	29.50	10	
5	Dallas		32.00	79.50	0.00	39.00	12.50	10.50	50.00	63.00	13.50	17.00		
6	Denver		21.00	42.00	39.00	0.00	51.50	31.50	40.50	24.00	47.50	26.00		
7	Houston		42.50	91.00	12.50	51.50	0.00	23.00	58.00	72.00	10.00	31.00		
8	Phoenix		23.00	49.00	50.00	40.50	58.00	49.00	0.00	32.50	50.00	52.00		
9	San Antonio		36.50	83.50	13.50	47.50	10.00	24.00	50.00	66.50	0.00	32.00		
10	*Volume*		3200	2500	6800	4000	9600	3500	5000	1800	7400	2700		
11		857,050												
12														
13		*Fixed Cost*	Alb	Boise	Dall	Denv	Hous	Okla	Phoe	Salt	SanA	Wich		
14	Albuquerque	140,000	0	117,500	217,600	88,000	408,000	94,500	115,000	54,000	270,100	79,650		
15	Dallas	150,000	102,400	198,750	0	156,000	120,000	36,750	250,000	113,400	99,900	45,900		
16	Denver	100,000	67,200	105,000	265,200	0	494,400	110,250	202,500	43,200	351,500	70,200		
17	Houston	110,000	136,000	227,500	85,000	206,000	0	80,500	290,000	129,600	74,000	83,700		
18	Phoenix	125,000	73,600	122,500	340,000	162,000	556,800	171,500	0	58,500	370,000	140,400		
19	San Antonio	120,000	116,800	208,750	91,800	190,000	96,000	84,000	250,000	119,700	0	86,400		
20														
21		*Open?*					*Shipments*						*Sent*	*Linking*
22	Albuquerque	0	0	0	0	0	0	0	0	0	0	0	0	0
23	Dallas	1	0	0	1	0	0	1	0	0	0	1	3	-7
24	Denver	1	1	1	0	1	0	0	0	1	0	0	4	-6
25	Houston	1	0	0	0	0	1	0	0	0	1	0	2	-8
26	Phoenix	1	0	0	0	0	0	0	1	0	0	0	1	-9
27	San Antonio	0	0	0	0	0	0	0	0	0	0	0	0	0
28		*Received*	1	1	1	1	1	1	1	1	1	1		

⏮ ◀ ▶ ⏭ 13.21 / 13.22 / 13.23 \ **13.24** / ◀

solution. The "indicator" variables appear in the array C22:L27. A solution is feasible whenever the sum of the indicator variables in every column is equal to 1.

For convenience, we place the fixed costs in rows 14–19, so that the objective function can be expressed with the formula SUMPRODUCT (B14 : L19, B22 : L27). Next, we revise the linking constraints by using $M = 10$, which is the number of centers. Thus, in cell N22, the formula reads M22 – $M$4* B22, where the number of centers has been entered in cell M4.

Thus, we specify the problem as follows in the Solver window:

Target cell	B11 (minimize)
Changing cells	B22:L27
Constraints	B22:B27 = binary
	C28:L28 = 1
	N22:N27 $\leq$ 0

As Figure 13.24 confirms, this formulation produces the optimal solution as well. The advantage of this form of the model relates to the indicator variables. They are allowed to be fractional, but they behave like binary variables—that is, they are never fractional in the optimal solution. This means that logical conditions (contingency, mutual exclusivity, etc.) can be added to the model, using indicator variables in the role of binary variables.

13.5.3 The Assortment Model

The facility location model, with or without capacity constraints, clearly has direct application to the design of supply chains and the choice of locations from a discrete set of alternatives. But the model can actually be used in other types of problems because it captures the essential trade-off between fixed costs and variable costs. An example from the field of Marketing is the **assortment problem,** which asks which items in a product line should be carried, when customers are willing to substitute.

EXAMPLE
Togawa Steel
Company

Togawa Steel Company (TSC) manufactures structural beams of a standard length. The strength of a beam depends on its weight, and industry standards specify eight beam weights ranging from 50 pounds to 750 pounds. If a customer requests a given strength, then TSC may meet the demand by substituting a beam of greater strength. In this case, TSC incurs the material cost of providing the heavier beam. For every substitution, the incremental material cost is the difference in weight between the beam demanded and the beam supplied, multiplied by the variable cost of $2 per pound. If TSC decides to manufacture a particular weight, then it incurs a setup cost of $120,000.

The beam weights and their demand requirements for the coming month are tabulated as follows.

	Category							
	1	2	3	4	5	6	7	8
Weight	50	100	150	200	250	400	500	750
Demand	1,000	2,000	400	800	1,000	500	200	100

TSC intends to meet all demand and wants to determine an optimal assortment of beam weights to manufacture. ∎

Although the scenario at Togawa Steel appears to have little in common with locating warehouses, there is a key structural similarity: TSC faces the problem of trading off the fixed setup costs associated with greater variety in its product line with the variable substitution costs of meeting demand with heavier beams than necessary. In fact, this trade-off is structurally identical to trading off the fixed costs of operating warehouses with the variable costs of distributing from those warehouses.

FIGURE 13.25 Optimal Solution to the Togawa Steel Model

	A	B	C	D	E	F	G	H	I	J	K	L	M
1	Assortment Problem												
2													
3	Data	Weight		750	500	400	250	200	150	100	50	Total	
4		Demand		100	200	500	1000	800	400	2000	1000	6000	
5													
6		Weight	Line				Weight Demanded						Material
7		Produced	Cost	750	500	400	250	200	150	100	50		Cost
8		750	120	0	0.500	0.700	1.000	1.100	1.200	1.300	1.400		2
9		500	120	99	0	0.200	0.500	0.600	0.700	0.800	0.900		
10		400	120	99	99	0	0.300	0.400	0.500	0.600	0.700		
11		250	120	99	99	99	0	0.100	0.200	0.300	0.400		
12		200	120	99	99	99	99	0	0.100	0.200	0.300		
13		150	120	99	99	99	99	99	0	0.100	0.200		
14		100	120	99	99	99	99	99	99	0	0.100		
15		50	120	99	99	99	99	99	99	99	0		
16													
17	Objective		Total Cost		840								
18													
19	Decisions		Produce									Sum	Linking
20		750	1	5800	200	0	0	0	0	0	0	6000	0
21		500	0	0	0	0	0	0	0	0	0	0	0
22		400	1	0	0	6000	0	0	0	0	0	6000	0
23		250	1	0	0	0	6000	0	0	0	0	6000	0
24		200	1	0	0	0	0	5600	400	0	0	6000	0
25		150	0	0	0	0	0	0	0	0	0	0	0
26		100	1	0	0	0	0	0	0	5000	1000	6000	0
27		50	0	0	0	0	0	0	0	0	0	0	0
28				5800	200	6000	6000	5600	400	5000	1000		
29													

13.25

Each beam weight that Togawa Steel produces incurs a fixed setup cost. Demands for beam weights that TSC does not produce represent substitution costs. We can imagine an array that contains the unit cost of substituting beam weight i for beam weight j. Figure 13.25 shows this array in cells D8:K15, where the cost entries are in thousands. For example, cell J10 contains the cost of substituting 400-pound beams for 100-pound beams. The cost per beam is $2(400 - 100) = \$600$, which appears in the worksheet as 0.600 due to rescaling.

Notice that the diagonal elements are zero because no substitution is involved. Entries below the diagonal would correspond to the substitution of lighter beams than the size demanded, which is infeasible. Rather than exclude those decisions, we have built the model as if they are permitted, but the model imposes a very large cost on these alternatives to make sure that they are never used in the solution. Here, we use the number 99, partly because it is quite a bit larger than the other unit costs in the model (and therefore discourages the use of the corresponding decision variables) and partly because it is a distinct number that signals an arbitrarily large value whose purpose is to inhibit certain decisions.

With the cost array in place, our decision variables appear in the array C20:K27, with the first column filled with binary decision variables signifying which setup costs TSC incurs. The rest of the array represents production quantities, although we should not expect to see a solution with nonzero entries below the diagonal. The objective function is calculated in the same way as in the location models, here with the formula SUMPRODUCT(C8:K15,C20,K27). The Solver Parameters window resembles the form in location models:

Target cell	E17 (minimize)
Changing Cells	C20:K27
Constraints	C20:C27 = binary
	D28:K28 ≥ D4:K4
	M20:M27 ≤ 0

Figure 13.25 displays the optimal solution, showing that Togawa Steel should produce weights of 750, 400, 250, 200, and 100. Demand for 500-pound beams should be met by supplying 750-pound beams, demand for 150-pound beams should be met by supplying 200-pound beams, and demand for 50-pound beams should be met by supplying 100-pound beams. This production plan costs \$840,000, which is the minimum cost achievable in the problem.

13.6 SUMMARY

Integer programming problems are optimization problems in which at least one of the variables is required to be an integer. The Solver Parameters window does not explicitly offer a special solution algorithm for integer programs. Instead, whenever the problem formulation specifies an integer (int) variable or a binary (bin) variable among the changing cells, Solver uses a specialized solution procedure that produces integer values as required.

Solver permits integer or binary variables to be used with the linear solver or the nonlinear solver. However, use of the nonlinear solver with integer constraints is problematic. Because the nonlinear solver is vulnerable to local optima, its effectiveness with integer variables is open to question. There are no guarantees that Solver's solution to a nonlinear integer program will be at all reliable. On the other hand, Solver's solution to linear integer programs is reliable: A global optimal solution always occurs as long as the Tolerance parameter has been set to zero.

In this chapter, we examined several examples of linear integer programming problems. The new formulation lessons occurred in conjunction with the use of binary variables. Binary variables can represent all-or-nothing decisions that allow only accept/reject alternatives. Binary variables can also be instrumental in capturing complicated logic in linear form so that we can harness the linear solver to find solutions. Binary variables make it possible to accommodate problem information on

- Contingency conditions between projects
- Mutual exclusivity among projects
- Linking constraints for consistency
- Threshold constraints for minimum activity levels

With the capability of formulating these kinds of relationships in optimization problems, our modeling abilities expand well beyond the basic capabilities of the linear and nonlinear solvers.

SUGGESTED READINGS

Some advanced perspectives on integer programming techniques can be found in the following books:

Garfinkel, R., and G. Nemhauser. 1999. *Integer and Combinatorial Optimization*. New York: John Wiley & Sons.

Schrage, L. E. 1997. *Optimization Modeling with LINDO.*, 5th ed. Pacific Grove, CA: Duxbury Press.

Williams, H. P. 1999. *Model Building in Mathematical Programming*, 3d ed. Chichester: John Wiley & Sons.

EXERCISES

1. *Selecting Projects.* The Texas Electronics Company (TEC) is contemplating a research and development program encompassing eight major projects. The company is constrained from embarking on all projects by the number of available scientists (40) and the budget available for projects ($300,000). Following are the resource requirements and the estimated profit for each project.

Project	Expense ($000)	Scientists Required	Profit ($000)
1	60	7	36
2	110	9	82
3	53	8	29
4	47	4	16
5	92	7	56
6	85	6	61
7	73	8	48
8	65	5	41

a. What is the maximum profit, and which projects should be selected?

b. Suppose that management decides that projects 2 and 5 are mutually exclusive. That is, TEC should not undertake both. As a result, what are the revised project portfolio and the revised maximum profit?

c. Suppose that management also decides to undertake at least two of the projects involving consumer products. (These happen to be projects 5–8.) As a result, what are the revised project portfolio and the revised maximum profit?

2. *Buying Equipment.* Oriental Airlines is considering a capital expansion in which it will purchase new aircraft for its Pacific runs. Oriental is looking at the purchase of Boeing B797s, Airbus A450s, and Lockheed L120s. The budget for new purchases is $750 million. Boeing B797s cost $42 million, Airbus A450s cost $30 million, and Lockheed L120s cost $27.5 million. On the average, these planes are expected to generate annual profits of $3.5 million, $2.8 million, and $3.0 million, respectively. In an effort to achieve some uniformity with respect to spare parts and maintenance procedures, airline executives have specified that they will not buy fewer than 10 airplanes of any type. Their objective is to maximize total annual profit.

Oriental has allocated up to $10 million for additional personnel to support the operation of the new aircraft. Each B797 requires $200,000 in new hires; each A450 requires $180,000; and each L120 requires $190,000.

Currently, the available maintenance facilities allow 800 days of maintenance per year for new purchases. Each B797 requires 45 days of annual maintenance; each A450 requires 38 days; and each L120 requires 42 days. It is possible, however, to increase the available annual maintenance to 1,250 days. To accomplish this, the maintenance facilities would have to be expanded at a capital cost of $16 million, which would come out of the budget for new purchases. In addition, the expansion would augment operating costs by $18 million annually, an expense that would reduce annual profits.

a. What is the optimal purchasing plan, and what is the corresponding annual profit for Oriental?

b. Suppose the maintenance expansion were to augment operating cost $24 million instead of $18 million. Then, what would be the optimal purchasing plan?

c. Suppose that, in addition to the augmented operating cost of $24 million, the uniformity policy required a minimum of only 8 airplanes of the same type rather than 10 as

That is, the solution must contain integer decisions. What are the optimal make/buy levels?

c. Is the solution in part (b) a rounded-off version of the fractional solution in part (a)?

4. *Investment Planning.* Perry Enterprises is considering a number of investment possibilities. Specifically, each investment under consideration will draw on the capital account during each of its first three years, but in the long run, each is predicted to achieve a positive net present value (NPV). Listed below are the investment alternatives, their NPV's, and their capital requirements, and all figures are in thousands of dollars. In addition, the amount of capital available to the investments in each of the next three years is predicted to be $9.5 million, 7.5 million, and $8.8 million, respectively.

	Project					
	One-Phase Expansion	Two-Phase Expansion	Test Market	Advertising Campaign	Basic Research	Purchase Equipment
NPV	4,200	6,800	9,600	4,400	8,700	3,500
Year 1 Capital	3,000	2,500	6,000	2,000	5,000	1,000
Year 2 Capital	1,000	3,500	4,000	1,500	1,000	500
Year 3 Capital	4,000	3,500	5,000	1,800	4,000	900

at present. What would be the optimal purchasing plan under these assumptions?

3. *Make or Buy.* A sudden increase in the demand for smoke detectors has left Acme Alarms with insufficient capacity to meet demand. The company has seen monthly demand from its retailers for its electronic and battery-operated detectors rise to 20,000 and 10,000, respectively. Acme's production process involves three departments: fabrication, assembly, and shipping. The relevant quantitative data on production and prices are summarized as follows:

Department	Monthly Hours Available	Hours/Unit (Electronic)	Hours/Unit (Battery)
Fabrication	2,000	0.15	0.10
Assembly	4,200	0.20	0.20
Shipping	2,500	0.10	0.15
Variable cost/unit		$18.80	$16.00
Retail price		$29.50	$28.00

The company also has the option to obtain additional units from a subcontractor, who has offered to supply up to 20,000 units per month in any combination of electric and battery-operated models, at a charge of $21.50 per unit. For this price, the subcontractor will test and ship its models directly to the retailers without using Acme's production process.

a. What are the maximum profit and the corresponding make/buy levels? (Fractional decisions are acceptable.)

b. Suppose that Acme requires that the solution provided by the model be implementable without any rounding off.

a. Assuming that any combination of the investments is permitted, which ones should Perry make to maximize NPV?

b. What is the optimal NPV in the combination chosen in part (a)?

c. Suppose that the expansion investments are mutually exclusive and only one of them can be made. How does this alter the solution in part (a)?

d. Suppose that the test market cannot be carried out unless the advertising campaign is also adopted. How does this contingency alter the solution in (a)?

5. *Cutting Stock.* Poly Products sells packaging tape to industrial customers. All tape is sold in 100-foot rolls that are cut in various widths from a master roll, which is 15 inches wide. The product line consists of the following widths: 2″, 3″, 5″, 7″, and 11″. These can be cut in different combinations. For example, one combination might consist of three cuts of 5″ each. Another combination might consist of two 2″ cuts and an 11″ cut. Both of these configurations use the entire 15-inch roll without any waste, but other configurations are also possible. For example, another combination might consist of two 7″ cuts. This combination creates 1 inch of waste for every roll cut this way.

Each week, Poly Products collects demands from its customers and distributors and must figure out how to configure the cuts in the master rolls. To do so, the production manager lists all possible combinations of cuts and tries to fit them together so that waste is minimized while demand is met. (In particular, demand must be met exactly, because Poly Products does not keep inventories of its tape.) This week's demands are shown in the following table.

Size	2″	3″	5″	7″	11″
Demand	60	50	40	30	20

a. How many configurations can be cut from a 15-inch master roll so that there is less than 2 inches of waste (i.e., the smallest quantity that can be sold) left on the roll?

b. What is the minimum amount of waste that can be created if all demand is met exactly?

6. *Optimizing Product Mix.* California Products Company has the capability of producing and selling three products. Each product has an annual demand potential (at current pricing and promotion levels), a variable contribution, and an annual fixed cost. The fixed cost can be avoided if the product is not produced at all. This information is summarized as follows.

Product	Demand	Contribution	Fixed Cost
I	290,000	$1.20	$60,000
J	200,000	1.80	200,000
K	50,000	2.30	55,000

Each product requires work on three machines. The standard productivities and capacities are as follows.

	Hours per 1,000 Units			
Machine	Product I	Product J	Product K	Hours Available
A	3.205	3.846	7.692	1,900
B	2.747	4.808	6.410	1,900
C	1.923	3.205	9.615	1,900

a. Determine which products should be produced, and how much of each should be produced, in order to maximize profit contribution from these operations.

b. Suppose the demand potential for product K were doubled. What would be the maximum profit contribution?

7. *Purchasing with Price Breaks.* Universal Technologies, Inc. has identified two qualified vendors with the capability to supply certain of its electronic components. For the coming year, Universal has estimated its volume requirements for these components and has obtained price break schedules from each vendor. (These are summarized as "all-units" price discounts in the table below.) Universal's engineers have also estimated each vendor's maximum capacity for producing these components, on the basis of available information about equipment in use and labor policies in effect. Finally, because of its limited history with vendor A, Universal has adopted a policy that permits no more than 60 percent of its total unit purchases on these components to come from vendor A.

a. What is the minimum total cost for Universal's purchases?

b. In the optimal solution to part (a), which purchases are made at discounted prices?

8. *Purchasing with an Incremental Quantity Discount.* In the previous problem, suppose that vendor A provides a new price discount schedule for component 3. This one is an "incremental" discount, as opposed to an "all-units" discount, as follows:

Unit price $= $60 on all units up to 1,000
Unit price $= $56 on the next 1,000 units
Unit price $= $51 on the next 500 units

a. What is the minimum total cost for Universal's purchases?

b. In the optimal solution to part (a), which purchases are made at discounted prices?

9. *Establishing a Product Line.* National Metals Company (NMC) manufactures titanium shafts. Its equipment is capable of producing shafts in 10 lengths, reflecting settings on its machinery. These lengths are essentially 32 cm to 50 cm in steps of 2 cm. Setting up the machinery to produce one of these lengths (which is done once a week) costs $250. As a result, NMC has decided to make only a selected number of lengths. When a customer requests a given length, NMC may supply it from stock, if it happens to match one of the lengths in the production schedule. Otherwise, NMC trims a longer length to meet the order. The variable cost for producing the shafts is $20 per cm, and NMC receives revenue of $40 per cm. Trim waste can be sold to a recycler for $15 per cm.

Product	Requirement	Vendor A		Vendor B	
		Unit Price	Volume Required	Unit Price	Volume Required
1	500	$225	0–250	$224	0–300
		$220	250–500	$214	300–500
2	1,000	$124	0–600	$120	0–1,000
		$115	600–1,000	(no discount)	
3	2,500	$60	0–1,000	$54	0–1,500
		$56*	1,000–2,000	$52	1,500–2,500
		$51	2,000–2,500		
Total Capacity (Units)		2,800		2,400	

*For example, if 1,400 units are purchased from vendor A, they cost $56 each, for a total of $78,400.

The demand requirements for the coming week are tabulated as follows; all demand must be satisfied.

Length	32	34	36	38	40	42	44	46	48	50
Demand	12	4	7	8	16	7	12	5	8	3

a. What is an optimal assortment of lengths for NMC to manufacture?

b. What is the optimal profit in the coming week?

10. *Plant Location.* The Spencer Shoe Company manufacturers a line of inexpensive shoes in one plant in Pontiac and distributes to five main distribution centers (Milwaukee, Dayton, Cincinnati, Buffalo, and Atlanta) from which the shoes are shipped to retail shoe stores. Distribution costs include freight, handling, and warehousing costs. To meet increased demand, the company has decided to build at least one new plant with a capacity of 40,000 pairs per week. Surveys have narrowed the choice to three locations: Cincinnati, Dayton, and Atlanta. As expected, production costs would be low in the Atlanta plant, but distribution costs are relatively high compared to those of the other two locations. Other data are as follows:

Distribution Costs per Pair

To Distribution Centers	From				Demand (pairs/wk)
	Pontiac	Cincinnati	Dayton	Atlanta	
Milwaukee	$0.42	$0.46	$0.44	$0.48	10,000
Dayton	0.36	0.37	0.30	0.45	15,000
Cincinnati	0.41	0.30	0.37	0.43	16,000
Buffalo	0.39	0.42	0.38	0.46	19,000
Atlanta	0.50	0.43	0.45	0.27	12,000
Capacity (pairs/wk.)	27,000	40,000	40,000	40,000	
Production cost/pair	$2.70	$2.64	$2.69	$2.62	
Fixed cost /wk.	$7,000	$4,000	$6,000	$7,000	

a. Assume that the Pontiac plant has no resale value and must remain open. What are the plant locations that will minimize total costs, including production, distribution, and fixed costs? What is the optimal total cost?

b. Assume that the Pontiac plant could be closed at zero net cost. What are the optimal locations? What is the optimal total cost?

11. *Project Team Assignment.* A project-based course assigns students to project teams at the start of the term. For this purpose, each student is asked to examine the set of projects available and to identify three of the alternatives as preferred assignments. A preference of 3 indicates the most preferred project. When these preferences are collected, the instructor assigns the students to project teams, aiming for an optimal assignment of students to teams. The criterion for the assignment is to maximize the total of the preferences assigned.

This year, there are 10 available projects and 16 students enrolled. There is a maximum team size between 2 and 4 on each project, according to the nature of the work to be done. It is not permissible for a student to work alone on a project (that is, in a team of size 1). The following table shows the student preferences and the limits for the team sizes.

a. What is the best value of the criterion—that is, the maximum sum of assigned preferences?

b. In the solution of part (a), how many students are assigned to their first choice? What is the maximum number of students who could be assigned to their first choice, if that were the only criterion?

12. *Designing a Supply Chain.* The Van Horne Company manufactures air conditioners that are sold to five large retail customers around the country. Van Horne is evaluating its manufacturing and logistics strategy to ensure that it is operating as efficiently as possible. The company can produce air conditioners at six plants and stock these units in any of four different warehouses. The cost of manufacturing and shipping a unit between each plant and warehouse is summarized in the following table along with the fixed operating cost and monthly capacity for operating each plant

	WH 1	WH 2	WH 3	WH 4	Fixed Cost	Plant Capacity
Plant 1	$700	$1,000	$900	$1,200	$55,000	300
Plant 2	800	500	600	700	$40,000	200
Plant 3	850	600	700	500	$45,000	300
Plant 4	600	800	500	600	$50,000	250
Plant 5	500	600	450	700	$42,000	350
Plant 6	700	600	750	500	$40,000	400

	S1	S2	S3	S4	S5	S6	S7	S8	S9	S10	S11	S12	S13	S14	S15	S16	limit
P1	0	3	0	3	0	3	0	3	0	0	0	0	0	0	2	0	3
P2	0	0	3	0	0	0	3	2	0	3	0	0	0	2	0	0	3
P3	2	2	0	0	0	2	0	0	0	0	0	2	2	0	0	0	3
P4	0	0	0	1	2	0	2	0	3	0	0	0	0	0	3	0	4
P5	0	1	0	0	0	1	0	0	0	2	0	1	3	3	0	0	4
P6	1	0	0	0	0	0	1	0	0	0	0	0	0	0	1	2	3
P7	0	0	2	0	3	0	0	0	2	0	3	3	0	0	0	3	3
P8	3	0	0	0	0	0	0	1	0	1	1	0	1	0	0	0	2
P9	0	0	1	2	0	0	0	0	0	0	2	0	0	0	0	0	2
P10	0	0	0	0	1	0	0	0	1	0	0	0	0	1	0	1	2

Similarly, the per-unit cost of shipping units from each warehouse to each customer is given in the following table, along with the monthly fixed cost of operating each warehouse.

	Cust1	Cust2	Cust3	Cust4	Cust5	Fixed Cost
WH 1	$40	$80	$60	$90	$50	$40,000
WH 2	60	50	75	40	35	50,000
WH 3	55	40	65	60	80	35,000
WH 4	80	30	80	50	60	60,000

The monthly demand from each customer is summarized as follows.

	Cust1	Cust2	Cust3	Cust4	Cust5
Demand	200	300	200	150	250

a. Considering all of the costs and demands tabulated above, what is the minimum monthly operating cost for Van Horne's supply chain?

b. Which plants and warehouses should Van Horne operate to meet demand in the most cost-effective manner?

14 Decision Analysis

14.1 INTRODUCTION

In previous chapters, we have generally assumed that all the information we need for our models is known with certainty. When we recognized uncertainty at all, we addressed it using sensitivity analysis (as in Chapter 6). In the chapters on optimization, we tended to ignore uncertainty because Solver requires us to assume that the parameters in our models are fixed. But many business problems contain uncertain elements that are impossible to suppress without losing the essence of the situation. In this chapter, we introduce some basic methods for analyzing decisions affected by uncertainty.

In the typical spreadsheet model, there are two kinds of inputs: decisions and parameters. Decisions are subject to the control of the decision maker, whereas parameters are beyond the control of the decision maker. Whether based on judgment or derived from empirical data, parameters are usually treated as fixed—known in advance with certainty. Now, we broaden our viewpoint to include **uncertain inputs**—that is, parameter values that are subject to uncertainty. Uncertain parameters become known only after a decision is made.

When a parameter is uncertain, we treat it as if it could take on two or more values, depending on influences beyond our control. These influences are called **states of nature**, or more simply, **states**. In many instances, we can list the possible states, and for each one, the corresponding value of the parameter. Finally, we can assign probabilities to each of the states so that the parameter outcomes form a probability distribution.

EXAMPLE
Wertz Game and Toy Company

Wertz Game and Toy (WGT) Company has developed an electronic toy for preschoolers that promises to be fun to play with while it provides a sophisticated learning experience. WGT believes that its design is innovative enough that it can capture sales in this year's toy market before competitors can copy the major features and bring competing products to market. Nevertheless, WGT also has some doubts about how appealing its design will be. Because the toy is more sophisticated than the mechanical toys historically sold to this age group, the market could be very enthusiastic or it could be indifferent.

As WGT's marketing manager, we have some choices about how to bring this new toy to market. A conservative approach would be to introduce a single version of the toy and see how it fares. This option would keep the costs down in case the market response is unenthusiastic. A bold approach would be to bring out two versions of the toy—basic and advanced—along with a line of accessories based on the original toy. This option would be quite profitable if the market response were positive but unprofitable if the response were indifferent. Finally, there is a compromise option, which involves bringing out the two versions but none of the accessories.

Reviewing introductions of other products, our staff believes that it's possible to classify market responses to a new product into three categories: Good, Fair, and Poor. Taking these one at a time, they have estimated the costs and revenues associated with each option, for each possible category of market response. Their economic analysis is summarized in the following table of profit figures (given in thousands).

		Market Response		
		Good	Fair	Poor
	Single Version	100	60	−10
Decisions	Two Versions	200	50	−40
	Full Line	300	40	−100

■

The entries in the table represent estimated profits for the next year for every combination of action and state. We ignore profits beyond next year because this product will likely have a very short lifetime. Although detailed analyses were required to produce each of these profit estimates, all we need here is the profit estimate itself.

At WGT we face a situation in which uncertainty plays an important role, and we must choose a decision by selecting from among the three actions available. Which action is best? We consider several ways of addressing this question.

14.2 PAYOFF TABLES AND DECISION CRITERIA

The table of profits in the WGT example is sometimes called a **payoff table**. The rows correspond to alternative actions and the columns to possible states. For each action–state combination, the entry in the table is a measure of the economic result. Typically, the payoffs are measured in monetary terms, but they need not be profit figures. They could be costs or revenues in other applications, so we use the more general term *payoff*.

The question we face in the WGT example would be much easier to answer if each action had only one payoff value associated with it. Then we could simply identify the best payoff (e.g., the largest profit) and select the corresponding action. But as we can see in the table, each action has not one but *three* payoff values associated with it. In a sense, the complication in this type of problem is that more information is available than we are used to processing when it comes to selecting a course of action. We'd like to condense the information in the table and produce one value for each action, thus simplifying the choice.

14.2.1 Benchmark Criteria

There are some simple ways to condense the information in each row of the table into one summary value for each action. For example, suppose we focus on the largest profit potential for each action and compute the maximum payoff in each row as a summary value. This approach corresponds to taking an optimistic view of the possible outcomes: we look only at the best case and ignore the others. In the WGT example, the most profitable outcome happens to occur with the Good market response for each of the decisions, yielding the following choices:

	States			Max
	Good	**Fair**	**Poor**	**Payoff**
Single Version	100	60	−10	**100**
Two Versions	200	50	−40	**200**
Full Line	300	40	−100	**300**

Now that we've condensed the information into one value for each action, we can make a straightforward choice. We are led to the Full Line as the best decision. This approach is called the **maximax payoff criterion** because it seeks the largest of the maximum payoffs among the actions.

An obvious alternative is to be pessimistic. We could instead take as the summary value the smallest payoff in each row. These happen to occur with the Poor market response, yielding the following choices:

| | States | | | Min Payoff |
	Good	Fair	Poor	
Single Version	100	60	−10	**−10**
Two Versions	200	50	−40	**−40**
Full Line	300	40	−100	**−100**

Again, we have a single value for each action, but here the Single Version is the best decision. This approach is called the **maximin payoff criterion** because it seeks the largest of the minimum payoffs among the actions. As the example illustrates, optimistic and pessimistic perspectives can lead to different choices. The broader point is that the choice of a criterion is critical: depending on what we choose as a criterion, a different action may turn out to be the best decision.

Although optimistic and pessimistic possibilities would appear to represent the two extremes of choice, there is actually another way to implement conservative thinking. Instead of using the nominal profit values, let's interpret them in relative terms. Suppose, for example, that the Good market state occurs. If we had chosen the Single Version action, then the profit of $100,000 does not convey our feeling about the choice. Sure, a profit of $100,000 is nice, but we would still be aware that, had we chosen the Full Line, we could have been better off by $200,000. In other words, it's the fact that we *could* have done better that influences how we feel about the result. To formalize this approach we define a measure called the **regret**. For any state and any specific action, the regret is the monetary difference between the best possible payoff for that state and the payoff for the specific action.

In the case of WGT, for the Good state, the Single Version generates regret of $200,000 (= 300,000 − 100,000); Two Versions generates a regret of $100,000 (= 300,000 − 200,000); and the Full Line generates a regret of zero (= 300,000 − 300,000). The following table shows the complete set of regrets, in the same format as our original decision table.

| | Market Response | | |
	Good	Fair	Poor
Single Version	200	0	0
Two Versions	100	10	30
Full Line	0	20	90

To condense the information into a summary value for each action, we again assume that the worst (state) will happen, and we ignore the other outcomes. Thus, we compute the maximum regret in each row, giving rise to the following summary values:

| | States | | | Max Regret |
	Good	Fair	Poor	
Single Version	200	0	0	**200**
Two Versions	100	10	30	**100**
Full Line	0	20	90	**90**

Having condensed the information down to one value for each action, the choice is straightforward. Keep in mind that when we use a regret measure, we want to achieve as *small* a value as possible, so we would choose the Full Line as the best decision. This approach is called the **minimax regret criterion** because it seeks the smallest of the maximum regrets among the actions. As the example shows, the minimax regret criterion and the maximin payoff criterion can lead to different decisions, although they both represent pessimistic approaches.

14.2.2 Incorporating Probabilities

The three criteria introduced in the previous section are benchmarks in the following sense. Each one ignores some of the given information as a means of condensing the data down to one value for each action. By focusing on just one extremely optimistic or one extremely pessimistic outcome, we could be ignoring information that could be quite relevant. To develop a more persuasive method for making a decision, we would like to incorporate all the information given.

The three criteria from the previous section also ignore information that we may have about the relative likelihoods of the possible states of nature. If we know something about the probabilities of the various states, our decision will generally improve if we take that information into account.

At WGT, for example, we might come up with the following assessment of the probabilities for different market responses:

	States		
	Good	Fair	Poor
Probability	0.2	0.5	0.3

Here, we think of the events Good, Fair, and Poor as three mutually exclusive and exhaustive outcomes. We can immediately translate this information into probability distributions for the payoffs corresponding to each of the potential actions. For the Single Version, we have the following distribution of profit:

Profit($000)	100	60	−10
Probability	0.2	0.5	0.3

Previously, we had three possible (profit) outcomes for each state; now, we have three outcomes along with three probabilities. That's six pieces of information, but our task is still to condense this information into one number for each action so that we can make a straightforward choice.

Given that we have a probability distribution, a standard way to summarize it numerically is to compute its **mean** or **expected value**. The expected value is the weighted average outcome, where the weights are the probabilities of each state. For the Single Version, the calculation of expected profit takes the following form:

$$EP(\text{Single Version}) = (0.2)(100,000) + (0.5)(60,000) + (0.3)(-10,000) = 47,000$$

We use the notation EP to represent an expected payoff—in this case, the expected profit. Note that the expected payoff calculation ignores *no* information: All outcomes and probabilities are incorporated into the result. Using the expected payoff as a summary measure, we can reduce our comparison to the following:

	States			EP
	Good	Fair	Poor	
Probability	0.2	0.5	0.3	
Single Version	100	60	−10	**47**
Two Versions	200	50	−40	**53**
Full Line	300	40	−100	**50**

Thus, with the **expected payoff criterion**, the best choice is Two Versions, which has an expected payoff of $53,000.

To justify the use of expected payoff as a criterion, we might imagine hypothetically that we face a large number of independent opportunities to repeat this same decision (or at least a decision very much like it). Each time, one of the states will occur, and in the long run, the Good state, the Fair state, or the Poor state will occur with frequencies that match their probabilities. Then the action that achieves the maximum profit in the long run would be Two Versions. It would generate a long-run average of $53,000 per opportunity, which would be larger than the long-run average of either of the other two options. In general, the long-run profit would be maximized by the action that achieves the largest expected value at each opportunity.

The analysis of payoff tables captures the main principles of decision making with uncertain outcomes. Furthermore, the necessary calculations could easily be made in a spreadsheet, but we have avoided showing spreadsheet models for these calculations because the table format can sometimes become unwieldy. Decision trees offer a more flexible modeling format, especially when a set of decisions must be made in series. Decision trees are the topic of the next section. Subsequent sections introduce TreePlan, software for drawing and analyzing trees in spreadsheets.

14.3 USING TREES TO MODEL DECISIONS

A **probability tree** depicts one or more random factors. For example, if we believe that demand for our product is uncertain, we might model that uncertainty using the probability tree in Figure 14.1. In this simple tree, we assume that demand may take on one of the three alternative values: High, Medium, or Low. The node from which the branches emanate is called a **chance node**, and each branch represents one of the possible states that could occur. Each state, therefore, is a possible resolution of the uncertainty represented by the chance node. Eventually, we'll specify probabilities for each of the states and create a probability distribution to describe uncertainty at the chance node.

In other circumstances, we might want to show greater detail than just three qualitative states for demand, so we might use a tree with more branches, perhaps quantifying the states as $10 million, $20 million, $30 million, $40 million, and $50 million, as shown in Figure 14.2. Again, the tree is meant to show that demand is uncertain and that just one of the alternative states will actually occur. When we specify the probabilities for each of these five states, we create a probability distribution for the dollar value of demand.

Probability trees can accommodate more than one source of uncertainty. In addition to the demand uncertainty in Figure 14.1, suppose we face uncertainty in both the number of competing products and the competitive effectiveness of our advertising. We can draw a tree with three chance nodes. The first chance node represents demand states, characterized as High, Medium, or Low. For each demand state, one of several possible numbers of competitors will occur. Likewise, for each combination of demand and number of competitors, one of several levels of advertising effectiveness will occur. We can depict this situation either in a telegraphic form (Figure 14.3), in which only one chance node of each type is displayed, or in exhaustive form (Figure 14.4), where all possible combinations are displayed. In either case, the tree conveys the idea that there are 45 possible states, corresponding to the following calculation:

$$\text{States} = (\text{demand levels}) \times (\text{number of competitors})$$
$$\times (\text{levels of advertising effectiveness})$$
$$\text{States} = 3 \times 5 \times 3 = 45$$

FIGURE 14.1 Simple Probability Tree

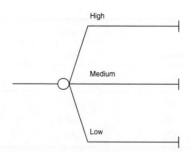

FIGURE 14.2 Probability Tree with Five States

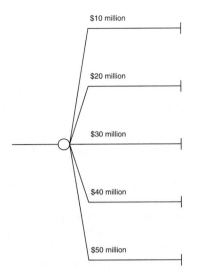

$10 million

$20 million

$30 million

$40 million

$50 million

Once we realize this fact, we could equivalently represent the outcomes with one chance node and 45 states. To perform the steps in analyzing the tree, we would need to examine the details for each of these states. For that purpose, the telegraphic form is not sufficiently detailed, and we would instead need to represent the entire set of 45 alternatives, as in Figure 14.4.

Although probability trees are helpful for displaying chance events and their outcomes, they can quickly become complex when there are several sources of uncertainty, as our 45-state example suggests. At an early stage in building a tree, however, it is not necessary to be precise in specifying the number of alternatives at a chance node. It is more important to recognize which outcomes are uncertain and how to represent them logically.

14.3.1 Decision Trees

Decision-tree models offer a visual tool that can represent the key elements in a model for decision making under uncertainty and help organize those elements by distinguishing between decisions (controllable variables) and random events (uncontrollable variables). In a **decision tree**, we describe the choices and uncertainties facing a single decision-making agent. This usually means a single decision maker, but it could also mean a decision-making group or a company. In our example, we may think of ourselves in the role of the marketing manager, who is also the decision-making agent. Alternatively, we may prefer to think of WGT as the agent because the benefits and costs belong to the firm.

FIGURE 14.3 Three Chance Nodes in Telegraphic Form

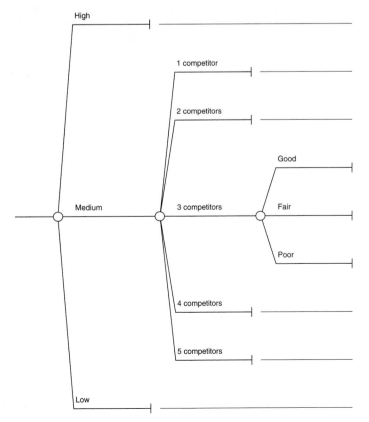

High

1 competitor

2 competitors

Good

Medium   3 competitors   Fair

Poor

4 competitors

5 competitors

Low

FIGURE 14.4 Three
Chance Nodes in Exhaustive
Form

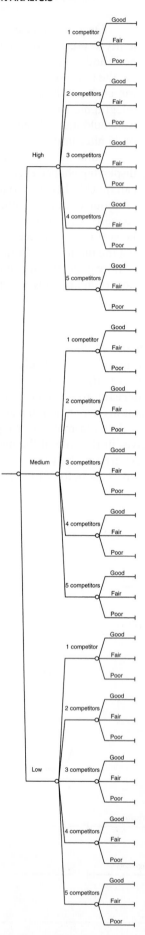

In a decision tree, we represent decisions as square nodes (boxes), and for each decision, the alternative choices are represented as branches emanating from the decision node. These are potential actions that are available to the decision maker. In addition, for each uncertain event, the possible alternative states are represented as branches emanating from a chance node, labeled with their respective probabilities. For the WGT example, the tree contains three possible actions, and each action is associated with a random event with three possible states, as shown in Figure 14.5. The layout, showing the actions on the left and the uncertain events to their right, mirrors the time sequence in which the elements occur: WGT *first* chooses an action, and *then* the uncertain event takes place. Finally, depending on the action chosen and the uncertain event that follows, a specific monetary payoff occurs, shown on the diagram to the right of the corresponding branch.

Whereas we *build* the tree left to right, to reflect the temporal sequence in which a decision is followed by a chance event, we *evaluate* the tree in the reverse direction. At each chance node, we can calculate the expected payoff represented by the probability distribution at the node. This value becomes associated with the corresponding action branch of the decision node. (In Figure 14.6, the three expected values are 47, 53, and 50.) Then, at the decision node, we calculate the largest expected payoff to determine the best action, and we enter the maximum *EP* (53). These calculations confirm that Two Versions is the best decision and that the expected profit for that decision is $53,000. This process of making the calculations is usually referred to as **rolling back** the tree.

After we identify the optimal decision, it is usually a good idea to examine the probability distribution that describes payoffs in the optimal case. For the WGT example, this task is straightforward because the outcomes for the Two Versions decision have been treated explicitly. The distribution is the following.

Profit($000)	200	50	−40
Probability	0.2	0.5	0.3

The distribution associated with a particular action is called its **risk profile**. The risk profile shows all the possible economic outcomes and provides the probability of each: it is a probability distribution for the principal output of the model. This form reinforces the notion that, when some of the input parameters are described in probabilistic terms, we should examine the outputs in probabilistic terms. In the WGT example, uncertainty about market response means that we need probability models to describe the profits for alternative decisions. After we determine the optimal decision, we can use a probability model to describe the profit outcome. In particular, examining the distribution in the table

FIGURE 14.5 Decision
Tree for Wertz Game
and Toy

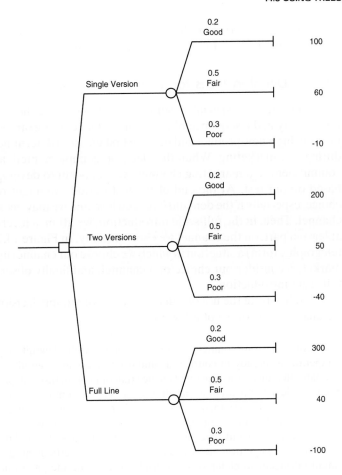

FIGURE 14.6 Analysis of
the Tree for Wertz Game
and Toy

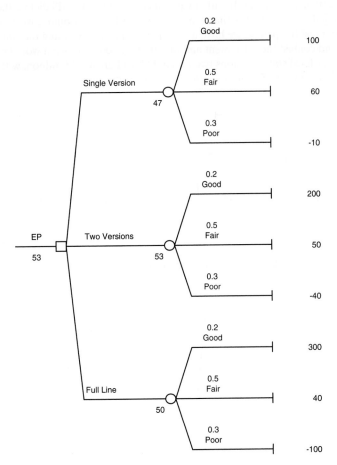

above, we can confirm that the expected payoff is $53,000, and we can see that there is a 30 percent chance of negative profits with this decision.

14.3.2 Decision Trees for a Series of Decisions

Decision trees are especially useful in situations where there are multiple sources of uncertainty and a sequence of decisions to make. For example, suppose that we are introducing a new product and that the first decision determines which channel to use during test-marketing. When this decision is implemented, and we make an initial commitment to a marketing channel, we can begin to develop estimates of demand based on our test. At the end of the test period, we might reconsider our channel choice, especially if the demand has been low, and we may decide to switch to another channel. Then, in the full-scale introduction, we attain a level of profit that depends, at least in part, on the channel we chose initially. In Figure 14.7, we have depicted (in telegraphic form) a situation in which we choose our channel initially, observe the test market, reconsider our choice of a channel, and finally observe the demand during full-scale introduction.

To illustrate the use of a decision tree containing decisions in a serial structure, we analyze the course of a lawsuit.

EXAMPLE
A Patent Infringement Suit

One of our corporate competitors is threatening us with a lawsuit for patent infringement. The competitor is already in court in a similar lawsuit against another firm, and our legal staff estimates that there is a 50 percent chance that our competitor will prevail. One option open to us is to settle out of court now; the alternative is to wait until the current case is resolved before taking action. If our competitor loses the other suit, it will not pursue an action against us. On the other hand, if the competitor wins, it is likely to sue us. Our legal staff estimates that likelihood at 80 percent. They further estimate that the suit would be brought for $10 million.

If the competitor sues us, we can negotiate a settlement, go to trial and contest the patent-infringement claim, or go to trial and concede the patent infringement but fight the settlement amount. In either case, of course, the trial will dictate the monetary outcome. Our legal staff estimates that a negotiated settlement would cost us roughly $8 million. If we contest the patent, we have a 30 percent chance of winning the suit. If we concede the patent and contest the settlement amount, then the only question would be the size of that amount. Our legal staff envisions two possibilities: High, at $15 million, with a 60 percent probability, and Low, at $5 million, with a 40 percent probability. ∎

FIGURE 14.7 Decision Tree with Sequential Decisions

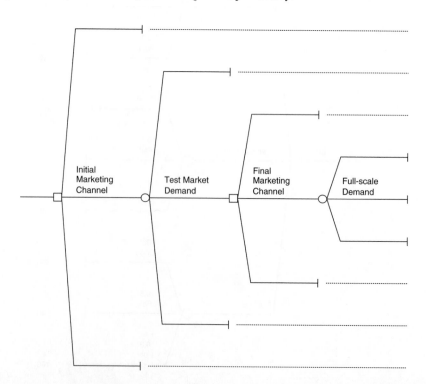

Initial Marketing Channel

Test Market Demand

Final Marketing Channel

Full-scale Demand

Figure 14.8 shows a decision tree for this case, with a display of payoffs and probabilities. The first decision is whether to settle now or wait for the outcome of the competitor's current suit. At this stage, we know very little about what the settlement amount could be, so we have simply labeled it X. If we wait and if the current suit fails, then we will not be sued, and there will be no monetary consequences. However, if the competitor prevails, we show a chance node with an 80 percent probability that our competitor will sue us. If there is no suit, there are again no monetary consequences. If our opponent sues, we have the three choices shown as branches on the tree. First, we could choose to settle. We represent that branch with the estimated cost of $8 million. Next, the outcome of each trial branch is shown as random. If we contest the patent, then the outcome is represented with win/lose outcomes and a 30 percent chance of winning the suit. If we concede the patent and contest the settlement amount, then we represent the outcomes with two settlement amounts and probabilities indicated by our legal staff.

This example illustrates a case in which two sets of decisions must be made and shows how the decisions available to us later on depend on choices made earlier, as well as on chance events. The result is an asymmetric tree, with chance events interspersed among decision opportunities. One important feature of legal proceedings is that both parties have a series of options, and at least as a first cut, we can represent the outcomes of the other party's choices (such as whether to sue) as random events, just like the outcomes of trials.

The objective of a quantitative analysis in this case is not simply to determine the optimal decision but also to choose an appropriate value for settling the suit now. For this purpose, we can assign an arbitrary but large amount as the settlement figure so that we can evaluate the expected outcome if we choose to wait. In Figure 14.8, we have denoted this amount as X, and we have included the necessary probabilities and outcome values elsewhere. Note that the outcomes are all costs, so our objective is to minimize expected cost.

We roll back the tree from right to left, calculating expected values at chance nodes and minimizing costs at decision nodes, as shown in Figure 14.9. In the figure, we have arbitrarily set the settlement amount at $4 million. If the opponent wins the current suit and sues us, we have three choices (at node A):

- Settle
- Go to Trial/Contest Patent
- Go to Trial/Concede Patent and Contest Settlement

The expected values for the last two options are $7 million and $11 million, respectively. Because settling at this stage would cost us $8 million, the lowest-cost choice is to contest the patent.

FIGURE 14.8 Decision Tree for the Patent Infringement Example

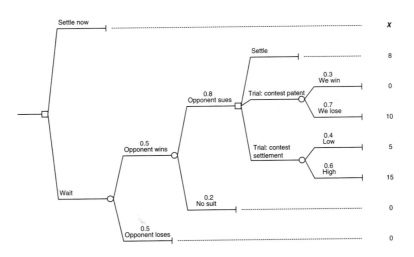

FIGURE 14.9 Analysis of the Patent Infringement Example

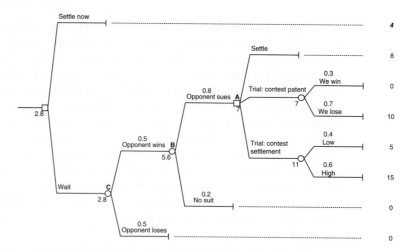

At node B, we will either be sued and lose $7 million in expected value, or we will not be sued and lose nothing. Given that the probability of a suit is 0.8, the expected value at node B is $5.6 million ($= 0.8 \times 7 + 0.2 \times 0$). At node C, we have a 50 percent chance of losing an expected value of $5.6 million and a 50 percent chance of losing nothing. The expected value here is $2.8 million ($= 0.5 \times 5.6 + 0.5 \times 0$).

The result of making these calculations is that we have identified an optimal *decision strategy*; that is:

- If the current suit loses, then we need not do anything.
- If the current suit wins and if our competitor does not sue us, then we need not do anything.
- If the current suit wins and if our competitor sues us, then we should contest the patent.

We refer to this set of contingencies as a strategy because we cannot be certain which states will occur; however, we have determined our best course of action for each possible state.

Now we can see that if we could settle the suit today for $2.8 million, we would be no better or worse off than if we were to wait, at least in terms of expected costs. But the risks of these two choices are quite different. No uncertainties attach to settling now. If we wait, however, we have a 72 percent chance of losing nothing and a 28 percent chance of losing $10 million. We lose nothing in three cases:

- If the opponent loses the current suit (probability 0.5)
- If the opponent wins and does not sue (probability $0.1 = 0.5 \times 0.2$)
- If the opponent wins and sues and we win (probability $0.12 = 0.5 \times 0.8 \times 0.3$)

The probabilities of these outcomes sum to 0.72, but the complement, 0.28, represents the probability of a substantial loss. The following simple table represents the risk profile under the optimal strategy.

Cost($Million)	0	10
Probability	0.72	0.28

Given the 28 percent chance of an outcome we'd like to avoid, we might even decide that it's preferable to offer somewhat more than $2.8 million to settle immediately.

Suppose we consider offering $4 million now to avoid a suit entirely. We can then compare two risk profiles. One risk profile is the two-outcome table shown above, with potential losses of \$0 and \$10 million. The other risk profile is a one-outcome table corresponding to the settlement amount. The decision boils down to whether we prefer the payment of \$4 million to ensure that we will avoid the possible cost of \$10 million. It is our preference for one of these risk profiles that will be expressed as a decision. Thus, the decision tree provides some useful quantitative guidance for a possible settlement decision that might otherwise seem entirely subjective.

As this example demonstrates, when there are other players or agents in the scenario, their actions can be depicted as chance nodes, although this may be an oversimplification. If we were to sue a competitor for patent infringement, it is unlikely that they would toss a coin to decide whether to settle or go to court against us. More likely, they would act as we would in that situation—that is, they would study the situation and make a decision aimed at reaching the best outcome for *them*. The analysis of the interrelated decisions of two (or more) actors is quite difficult, and we will not discuss it at length except to mention that representing a competitor's actions as random probably overstates the value we can extract from the situation.

14.3.3 Principles for Building and Analyzing Decision Trees

Decision trees can be built using a fairly standard procedure. Judgment is required, however, in determining which decisions and uncertainties are critical to the situation and therefore must be captured in the tree, as well as in selecting the specific choices and states to recognize. Beginners tend to draw overly complex trees. The more experienced analyst starts with a small number of nodes and a small number of outcomes and expands only when the results suggest that more detail is required. Here is a general procedure for constructing trees:

1. Determine the essential decisions and uncertainties.
2. Place the decisions and uncertainties in the appropriate temporal sequence.
3. Start the tree with a decision node representing the first decision.
4. Select a representative (but not necessarily exhaustive) number of possible choices for the decision node.
5. For each choice, draw a chance node representing the first uncertain event that follows the initial decision.
6. Select a representative (but not necessarily exhaustive) number of possible states for the chance node.
7. Continue to expand the tree with additional decision nodes and chance nodes until the overall outcome can be evaluated.

Decision trees can be used to develop a purely qualitative understanding of a situation, although they are usually used for quantitative analysis as well. This quantitative analysis can identify which decisions are best and can construct the probability distribution of results. To carry out this analysis, we need two types of information: the probability for each possible state and the overall value of arriving at the end of the tree along a particular path. Here is the rollback procedure for analyzing trees:

1. Start from the last set of nodes—those leading to the ends of the paths.
2. For each chance node, calculate the expected payoff as a probability-weighted average of the values corresponding to its branches.
3. Replace each chance node by its expected value.
4. For each decision node, find the best expected value (maximum benefit or minimum cost) among the choices corresponding to its branches.
5. Replace each decision node by the best value, and note which choice is best.

6. Continue evaluating chance nodes and decision nodes, backward in sequence, until the optimal outcome at the first node is determined.

7. Construct its risk profile.

In the rollback procedure, any chance node, or any decision node, can be evaluated once the nodes connected to its emanating branches have been evaluated. In that way, the calculations move from the end of the tree toward the beginning, ultimately identifying the optimal choice at the initial decision node.

14.3.4 The Cost of Uncertainty

In the decision trees we have considered so far, a decision node precedes a chance node. Indeed, the crux of the problem is that an action must be chosen *before* learning how an uncertain event will unfold. The situation would be much more manageable if we could learn about the uncertain event first and *then* choose an action. Reversing the sequence in this way may not be feasible in practice, but it can provide us with some useful insight.

In the WGT example, suppose we could wait to decide on an action until after learning how the market will respond. It's as if we had a crystal ball and could see into the future. Peering into the crystal ball, we could learn one of three things:

- The market will be Good.
- The market will be Fair.
- The market will be Poor.

Each of these conditions places us in a specific column of the original payoff table. If the Good market prevails, then our best choice is the Full Line. The corresponding profit is $300,000. If the Fair market prevails, then our best choice is the Single Version (profit: $60,000). And if the Poor market prevails, then our best choice is again the Single Version (net loss: $10,000).

Of course, we can't know beforehand which state we'll see in the crystal ball, but we already know the probabilities of the three outcomes. These probabilities correspond to the original probability estimates. When we initially quantified the elements of the problem, we took the probability of the Good market response to be 0.2, and therefore, the probability that we will see the Good market response when we peer into the crystal ball is also 0.2. Similarly, the probability that we will see the Fair market response is 0.5, and the probability that we will see the Poor market response is 0.3. Thus, we have three profit outcomes and a probability for each. The probability distribution of profit outcomes then takes the following form.

Profits($000)	300	60	−10
Probability	0.2	0.5	0.3

The mean of this distribution is $87,000. This value represents the *EP* when we can determine the state first and then choose the most appropriate action. We call this quantity the Expected Payoff with Perfect Information (*EPPI*). In the original decision problem, when the choice had to be made in advance of knowing the state, the expected profit was only $53,000. The difference between these two expected values, equal to $34,000, measures the economic benefit of being able to reverse the order of decision and state. In short, this is the cost of uncertainty: having to make a decision before the uncertainty is resolved leaves us worse off by $34,000 (on average) compared to what we could gain if uncertainty could be resolved before making the decision.

The $34,000 quantity we computed for the WGT example is called the **expected value of perfect information**, abbreviated *EVPI*. Here, the term *perfect* refers to the resolution of uncertainty. When we have to make a decision before

FIGURE 14.10   Decision
Tree for the EVPI
Calculation

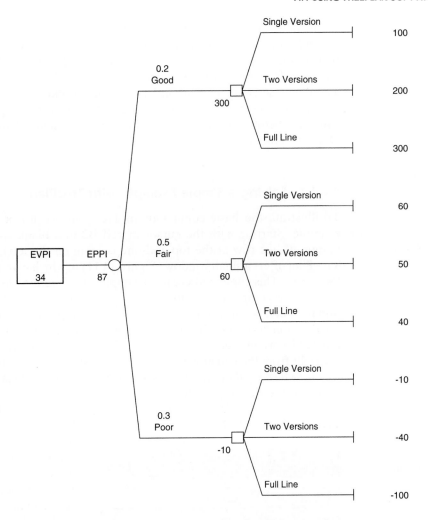

uncertainty is resolved, we are operating with imperfect information (uncertain knowledge) about the state of nature. When we can make a decision after uncertainty is resolved, we can respond to perfect information about the state of nature. Our probability assessments of event outcomes remain unchanged, and we are still dealing with expected values.

To review, the two expected values in the comparison are:

The expected profit from following the optimal policy (in the original problem)

The expected profit from choosing an action with perfect information

In this comparison, the expected payoff with perfect information must always be at least as large as the expected payoff from following the optimal policy in the original problem, and it will usually be larger. The *EVPI* measures the difference, or the gain due to perfect information.

The calculation of *EVPI* can also be represented with a tree structure, where we reverse the sequence of decision and chance event in the tree diagram, just as we did in the calculations. Figure 14.10 shows how the diagram would be redrawn for the WGT example and how the *EVPI* is calculated.

14.4   USING TREEPLAN SOFTWARE

As our examples demonstrate, the calculations required to roll back a decision tree are not sophisticated—they require multiplications and additions, and they require finding the maximum or minimum of several numbers. The calculations themselves can be done quite readily in a spreadsheet. However, it is often difficult to create a layout for the calculations that is tailored to the features of a particular example. For that reason, it makes sense to take advantage of software that has been designed expressly for representing decision trees in Excel. Here, we illustrate the use of TreePlan, a software application for constructing and analyzing decision trees, which is available to users of this book. In order to follow the coverage in this section, install TreePlan before proceeding. TreePlan can be invoked by selecting Add-ins▶ Decision Tree...

14.4.1 Solving a Simple Example with TreePlan

To illustrate the basic commands in TreePlan, we use it to analyze the WGT example. Starting with the cursor in cell B2 in a blank spreadsheet (to leave a margin of one row at the top and one column on the left), we invoke TreePlan. TreePlan offers a small window (Figure 14.11) in which we can select the button for New Tree. This command creates a simple tree diagram, displayed on the spreadsheet in a rectangle whose upper left-hand corner is cell B2, where the cursor had initially been, as shown in Figure 14.12[*]. The important feature of this diagram is the decision node (in cell C6) and the two branches emanating from it, generically labeled Decision 1 and Decision 2. TreePlan builds its analysis moving down and to the right from the cell at which the new tree starts. Therefore, if input data for the tree is to be stored on the same worksheet, it should be located entirely to the left or above the starting cell for the tree.

If we were analyzing a model containing two actions, this would be an initial structure for our decision node, but in the WGT example, we have three actions. In order to expand the diagram, we return to the Tools menu, and, with the cursor on cell C6, we select Add-ins▶Decision Tree. This time we encounter TreePlan's Decision window (Figure 14.13), which gives us an option to add a branch to the decision node. (An early lesson here is that TreePlan tailors the choice of options to where we place the cursor. Had we placed the cursor in a different cell, we would likely have encountered a window other than the Decision window.)

After we add a branch, we obtain the diagram shown in Figure 14.14, with three actions, labeled Decision 1, Decision 2, and Decision 3. (Although we could edit these three names, we usually advise waiting until more of the tree is completed before editing the labels.) Next, we place chance nodes in the tree, starting with the cursor on cell G4. This time, TreePlan opens the Terminal window (Figure 14.15), which offers the option to Change to event node. On the right-hand side of this window, we have some options for

FIGURE 14.11 Initial Window in TreePlan

FIGURE 14.12 Initial Tree Diagram Produced by TreePlan

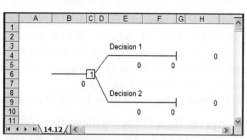

FIGURE 14.13 Decision Window in TreePlan

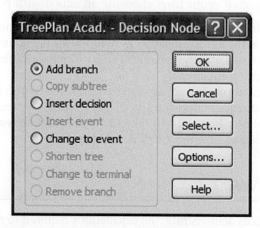

[*]To download spreadsheets for this chapter, go to the Student Companion Site at *www.wiley.com/college/powell.*

FIGURE 14.14 Expanded Initial Tree Diagram

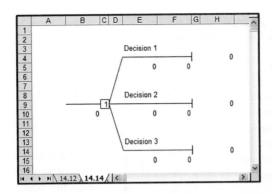

FIGURE 14.15 Terminal Window in TreePlan

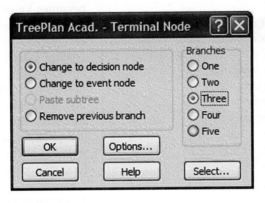

the number of branches in the event node, and we select Three. When we press OK, the desired chance node appears (see Figure 14.16) with three states, labeled Event 4, Event 5, and Event 6. In addition, three probabilities appear (in cells I2, I7, and I12). As a default, TreePlan uses equal probabilities for the number of branches specified, so in this case, each probability is equal to 1/3. At this stage, we can change the event names to Good, Fair, and Poor and the probabilities to 0.2, 0.5, and 0.3, respectively. Next we will copy this information to another chance node.

With the cursor on the chance node (cell G9), we invoke TreePlan again, and this time we see the Event window (Figure 14.17), which provides an opportunity for us to select the option Copy subtree. (Copying subtrees is not always a step in building the model, but the WGT example happens to have a chance node that appears in the tree three times.) Next, we place the cursor on cell G19, which is the location of the second chance node, and we invoke TreePlan once more. This time, in the Terminal window (Figure 14.18), we can choose to Paste subtree, and the entire structure of the first chance node is duplicated, including the probabilities, as shown in Figure 14.19. In order to paste once more, we first have to copy a subtree (with our cursor on either cell G4 or cell G24). Then we can paste the subtree to cell G34. At this stage, the full tree structure is developed, as we can see in Figure 14.20, and we can now edit the generic decision names by entering Single Version, Two Versions, and Full Line.

The next step is to enter the various payoffs, and there are two approaches we can take. To follow the format of TreePlan faithfully, we enter payoffs in

FIGURE 14.16 First Chance Node Produced by TreePlan

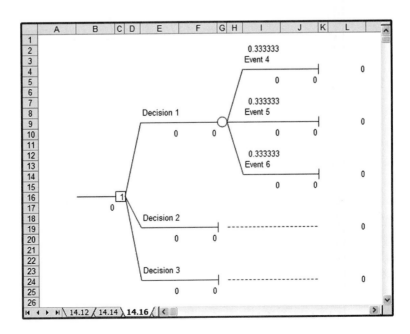

FIGURE 14.17   Event Window in TreePlan

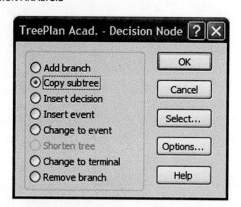

column I. The payoff immediately appears as well at the end of the branch, in column L, where we would have placed the payoff if we had been drawing the tree by hand. TreePlan allows us to associate payoffs with decisions as well as with events. In the WGT example, we might imagine that the decision to implement the Single Version action incurs a set of costs that become relevant as soon as the action is selected. Later, when the market state becomes known, various revenues are obtained. In the tree, the costs would be entered in column E and the revenues in column I, with the net revenue calculated in column L. However, our original description of the WGT problem did not break out the costs and revenues this way; instead, each combination of action and state was associated with a specific net revenue. It is this net amount that we now enter in column I, allowing it to be carried into column L, as shown in Figure 14.21.

FIGURE 14.18   Terminal Window in TreePlan with Paste Option

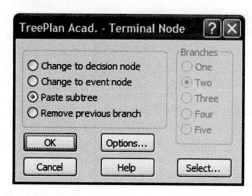

Once we enter the payoffs for all action–state combinations, TreePlan performs the rollback calculations automatically. Column J duplicates the value in column L. Then column F calculates an expected payoff, based on the probabilities in column I and the payoffs in column J. At the decision node, the best available expected payoff is reproduced in column B. The decision node in column C contains the number of the action (2) that produced the maximum payoff. Figure 14.21 shows all of these results.

FIGURE 14.19   Expanded Diagram with Second Chance Node Copied

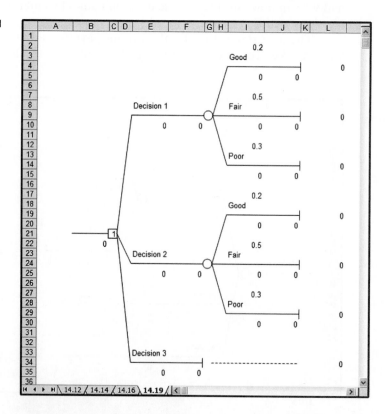

FIGURE 14.20 Full Diagram for the Wertz Game and Toy Example

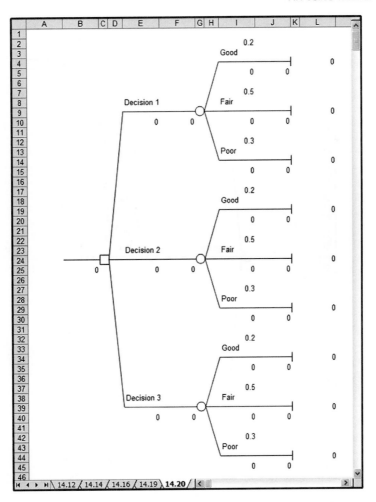

In a straightforward decision-tree analysis, such as we encounter in the case of the WGT example, we can use an alternative way of entering the payoffs. Because each action–state pair corresponds to a payoff, we can enter the payoff figures in column L, without placing the same information in the body of the tree structure. This procedure actually overwrites formulas in column L, but the rollback still executes correctly, as we can see in Figure 14.22. Although this procedure preempts some of TreePlan's features, it corresponds more closely to the way we would lay out a decision tree by hand. In particular, the input parameters representing payoffs can all be found along the right-hand side of the model.

14.4.2 Sensitivity Analysis with TreePlan

It is important to remember that a decision-tree analysis, such as we see in Figure 14.21, retains the properties of a spreadsheet. That is, the worksheet produced by TreePlan contains inputs, formulas, and outputs, just as we would find in any well-designed model. Thus, we can perform sensitivity analyses in the usual ways.

As an example, we explore the sensitivity of the optimal solution to the profit of $200,000 that represents the payoff for the Two Versions action when the Good market state occurs. This parameter is located in cell L19 of the worksheet. To trace the effects of other profit figures for this action–state combination, we use the Data Sensitivity tool, pasting its output to the right of the decision tree, as shown in Figure 14.23. In column N, we vary the profit from zero to $300,000 in steps of $25,000. In column O, we trace the optimal expected profit, copied from cell B24, and in column P, we trace the optimal decision, copied from cell C24. As the table shows, the Full Line is the optimal decision (and $50,000 is the *EP*) when the profit figure we're varying ranges from zero up to $175,000; but at $200,000 and above, the optimal

FIGURE 14.21 Tree Diagram with Costs Entered

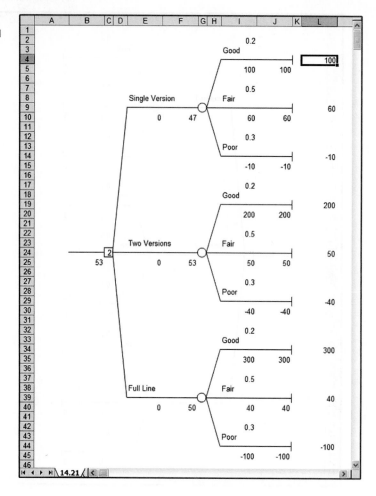

decision switches to Two Versions, and the *EP* rises with the parameter being varied. This analysis is carried out with a standard spreadsheet tool, once the model has been set up with TreePlan.

14.4.3 Minimizing Expected Costs with TreePlan

We introduced TreePlan by showing how it could be used to analyze a decision-tree problem in which the criterion is expected profit. We could just as easily apply TreePlan to a problem involving the criterion of expected cost by treating all costs as negative profits and finding the maximum expected profit. However, TreePlan can accommodate costs in a more direct fashion. If we click the Options button from the Terminal, Decision, or Event windows, we encounter the Options window shown in Figure 14.24. In the lower half of this window, we see an opportunity to choose either to Maximize (profits)/(costs), which is the default choice, or to Minimize cost, which would be an appropriate choice when we deal in costs.

To illustrate the Minimization option, we show a TreePlan model for the Patent-Infringement example that was studied earlier in this chapter. In that scenario, all payoffs were in the form of costs, and our objective was to minimize expected total cost. Figure 14.25 shows the TreePlan model, with the Minimization option selected.

14.5* MAXIMIZING EXPECTED UTILITY WITH TREEPLAN

Early in this chapter, we introduced three benchmark criteria for decision making with uncertain outcomes. In particular, the maximin payoff criterion and the minimax regret criterion represented two conservative ways of choosing an action. One

FIGURE 14.22 Tree Diagram with Costs Entered at the Ends of Branches

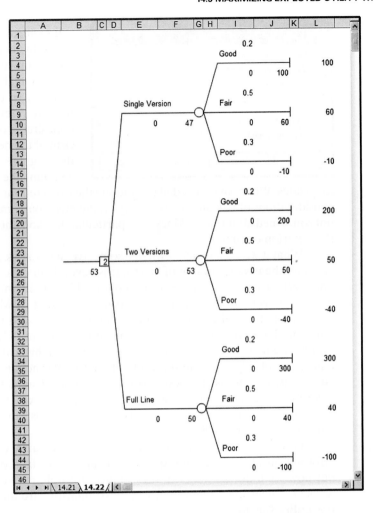

FIGURE 14.23 Sensitivity Analysis for the Example Model

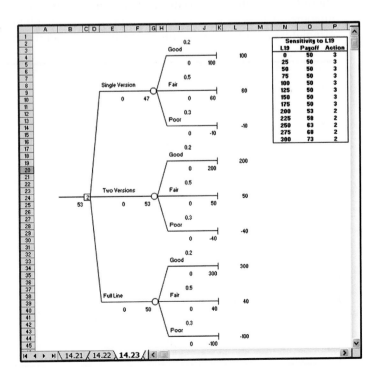

FIGURE 14.24 Options
Window in TreePlan

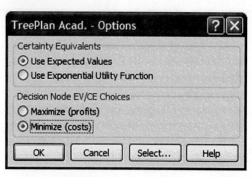

rationale for this type of conservatism is that by focusing on worst-case outcomes, the analysis tries to capture a decision maker's concern for the risk inherent in uncertain situations. By *risk*, we refer to the possibility of an undesirable outcome. Our main criticism of the benchmark criteria is that they ignore relevant information, including the probabilities of the various states. When we proceeded to examine the expected value criterion, we set aside considerations of risk and focused only on the mean outcome. If a decision maker is not concerned about the riskiness of a particular decision, then the expected payoff is the criterion of choice.

What if we wish to acknowledge some aversion to risk in our decision making? A comprehensive treatment of this topic is beyond our coverage, but we can suggest one mechanism that happens to be supported by TreePlan. Suppose that we could measure payoffs in some risk-adjusted manner—that is, with a measurement that combines notions of economic value in dollars along with the risk of an undesired outcome. To contrast this measurement with the measure of pure dollars unadjusted for risk, we'll take the name *utils* for this scale. With this scale available, the decision maker can ideally compute the value of a particular action in utils, and choose the largest such value as the best action. The value of an action, measured in utils, incorporates both outcomes and probabilities, just as expected value does, but it also acknowledges risk. We say that a decision maker who is behaving in this way seeks to maximize **expected utility**.

Our task in evaluating a decision tree remains that of condensing the information about the consequences of an action into one summary measure, but now we'll do the math in utility units, not dollars. Although there are many ways of converting dollars to utils, one straightforward method uses an **exponential utility function**:

$$U = a - b\exp(-D/R) \tag{14.1}$$

where D is the value of the outcome in dollars; U is the utility value, or the value of an outcome in utils; and $a,b,$ and R represent parameters of the utility function. Parameters a and b are essentially scaling parameters; R influences the shape of

FIGURE 14.25 TreePlan
Model for the Patent
Infringement Example

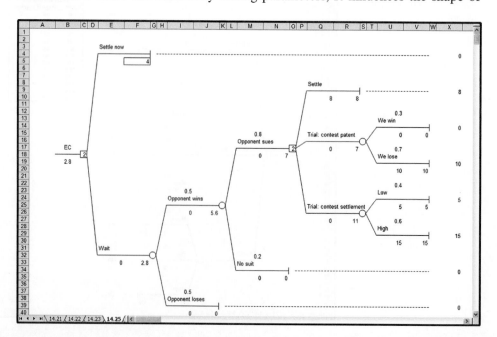

the curve and is known as the **risk tolerance**. To carry out the analysis, we use this function to convert each monetary outcome from dollars to utils, and then we determine the action that achieves the maximum expected utility. Although Tree-Plan allows the flexibility of setting three different parameters, we usually advise setting $a = b = 1$. This choice ensures that the function in (14.1) passes through the origin, so that our remaining task is finding a value of R that captures the decision maker's preferences. Typically, this is accomplished by estimating some points on the curve and finding the best fit for the parameter R.

To appreciate how the utility transformation works, consider a graph of the utility function in (14.1), shown in Figure 14.26 for the case of $R = 500$. The monetary value of an outcome is represented on the horizontal axis, and the utility value is represented on the vertical axis. We can see immediately that the graph is concave. In other words, there are diminishing marginal returns to money, when we work in utility units. An informal translation would be that another dollar is worth less to a wealthy person than to a poor person, when measured in utils. On the left-hand side of the graph, the shape indicates that large losses are more than proportionately painful compared to small losses, also when measured in utils. Working in utils, then, a decision maker tends to prefer an action that leads to outcomes near the middle of the graph to an action that leads to outcomes at the extremes, if the probabilities are roughly the same. In the WGT example, we might find that a risk-averse decision maker prefers to avoid an action that could yield profits that vary from $300,000 to as low as −$100,000. With appropriate parameters in (14.1), an exponential utility function can capture this kind of decision-making criterion.

In TreePlan, it is necessary to specify the three parameters in the exponential utility function. These three values should be entered either to the left or above the tree diagram and assigned cell names A, B, and RT, respectively. (Naming cells is covered in Chapter 4.) Then, we can return to the Options window in TreePlan (Figure 14.24) and in the upper portion, select the option `Use Exponential Utility Function`. In Figure 14.27, we show the impact on the WGT analysis, using a value of $R = 250$, which is entered in cell A9. After the option to use a utility function has been selected, TreePlan enters additional calculations in columns B, F, and J. Immediately below the monetary payoffs, which existed in the original TreePlan model (Figure 14.21), we now see the same figures converted to utils. Thus, for example, the profit of $100,000 is transformed as follows:

$$U = a - b\exp(-D/R) = 1 - \exp(-100/250) = 0.330$$

This value is calculated in cell J6, and similar calculations appear elsewhere in the column. Then, when expected values are calculated at the chance nodes in column F, these are probability-weighted *utility* values. For the Single Version action, the calculation of expected utility appears in cell F11 as follows.

$$EU = 0.2(0.330) + 0.5(0.213) + 0.3(-0.041) = 0.160$$

FIGURE 14.26 Graph of Utility Function for the Example

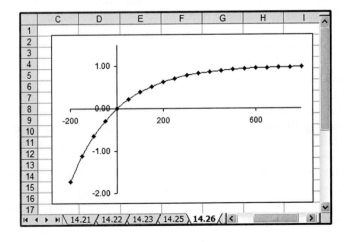

FIGURE 14.27 Modification of the Example Model for Exponential Utilities

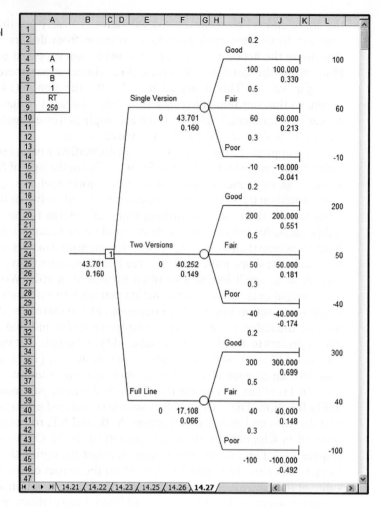

Just above this formula, in cell F10, the expected utility is converted back to a dollar value, using the inverse of the formula in (14.1). The dollar value that results ($43,701 in this case) is called the **certainty equivalent**. This figure gives the dollar value that the risk-averse decision maker would accept without any uncertainty as being equivalent to the set of utility outcomes and their respective probabilities.

Finally, the optimal decision is selected based on the dollar values corresponding to each action. (The same action would be selected if the choice were based on the maximum expected utility.) In the example shown, the optimal action for expected utility is the Single Version, with a certainty equivalent of $43,701. As this set of calculations indicates, a decision maker with an aversion to risk (as expressed by the risk tolerance value of 250) prefers a different action than the decision maker who focuses on expected payoff.

A useful sensitivity analysis aims at the risk tolerance parameter. Because we would normally have to estimate that value from the statements or actions of a unique decision maker, the accuracy in an assumed value of R is always open to question. In Figure 14.28 we show the results of running the Data Sensitivity tool, varying the value of R from 100 to 500, and tracking the expected utility for each action. As the accompanying graph shows, the decision to adopt the Single Version is relatively robust: it remains the best choice for R-values up to about 400, or almost twice the assumed value. At higher R-values, although the Two Versions action becomes optimal, its advantage over the Single Version action is slight, reinforcing our support for the Single Version as the optimal decision for a risk-averse decision maker.

FIGURE 14.28 Sensitivity to Risk Tolerance Parameter

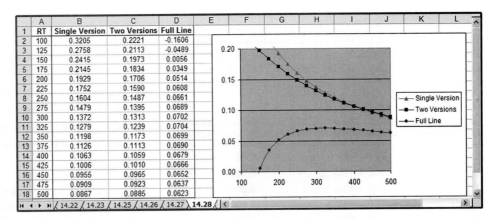

	A	B	C	D
1	RT	Single Version	Two Versions	Full Line
2	100	0.3205	0.2221	-0.1606
3	125	0.2758	0.2113	-0.0489
4	150	0.2415	0.1973	0.0056
5	175	0.2145	0.1834	0.0349
6	200	0.1929	0.1706	0.0514
7	225	0.1752	0.1590	0.0608
8	250	0.1604	0.1487	0.0661
9	275	0.1479	0.1395	0.0689
10	300	0.1372	0.1313	0.0702
11	325	0.1279	0.1239	0.0704
12	350	0.1198	0.1173	0.0699
13	375	0.1126	0.1113	0.0690
14	400	0.1063	0.1059	0.0679
15	425	0.1006	0.1010	0.0666
16	450	0.0955	0.0965	0.0652
17	475	0.0909	0.0923	0.0637
18	500	0.0867	0.0885	0.0623

14.6 SUMMARY

A decision tree is a specialized model for recognizing the role of uncertainties in a decision-making situation. Trees help us distinguish between decisions and random events, and more importantly, they help us sort out the sequence in which they occur. Probability trees provide us with an opportunity to consider the possible states in a random environment when there are several sources of uncertainty, and they become components of decision trees.

The key elements of decision trees are decisions and chance events. A decision is the selection of a particular action from a given list of possibilities. A chance event gives rise to a set of possible states, and each action-state pair results in an economic payoff. In the simplest cases, these relationships can be displayed in a payoff table, but in complex situations, a decision tree tends to be a more flexible way to represent the relationships and consequences of decisions made under uncertainty.

The choice of a criterion is a critical step in solving a decision problem when uncertainty is involved. We saw that there are benchmark criteria for optimistic and pessimistic decision making, but these are somewhat extreme criteria. They ignore some available information, including probabilities, in order to simplify the task of choosing a decision. A more suitable approach is to use probability assessments and then to take the criterion to be maximizing the expected payoff, which in the business context translates into maximizing expected profit or minimizing expected cost.

Using the rollback procedure, we can identify those decisions that optimize the expected value of our criterion. Furthermore, we can produce information in the form of a probability distribution to help assess the risk associated with any decision in the tree. TreePlan is a straightforward spreadsheet add-in that assists in the structuring of decision trees and in the calculations required for a quantitative analysis.

SUGGESTED REFERENCES

Some related material can be found in the following books:

Clemen, R. T., and T. Reilly. 2005. *Making Hard Decisions: Introduction to Decision Analysis.* 2d ed. Pacific Grove, CA: Duxbury.

Golub, A. L.. 1997. *Decision Analysis: An Integrated Approach.* New York: John Wiley & Sons.

Kammen, D. M., and D. M. Hassenzahl. 2001. *Should We Risk It?: Exploring Environmental, Health, and Technological Problem Solving.* Princeton, NJ: Princeton University Press.

EXERCISES

1. Construct a spreadsheet that makes the calculations required to analyze the decision in the WGT example. Include in the spreadsheet the calculation of the expected profit for each action and the calculation of the expected regret for each action. As a check, confirm that these two expected values match the values mentioned in the chapter.

a. Does the expected regret equal the *EVPI* for this example? Why is this true in general?

b. The probability of a Fair market response is 0.5 under the initial set of assumptions. Suppose this value were to change

by an amount p (where $0 \le p \le 0.5$). For what values of p does the Two Versions choice represent the optimal decision?

2. Gamma Construction Company has been asked to bid on the construction of 20 lighted tennis courts for State University. Each court will cost $20,000 in construction costs, and, in addition, there will be a fixed expense of $10,000 to cover the preparation and submittal of the bid. Gamma is considering five different bid levels. Each level involves a different profit margin, calculated as a percentage above total construction cost (TCC). Fixed expenses are excluded from this calculation, but they are relevant for profitability. Based on previous experience, Gamma's management is able to estimate the probability that it will win the bid at each level being considered. The bids and the probabilities are summarized in the table below.

Bid Number	Amount of Bid	Probability of Winning
1	TCC + 5%	0.80
2	TCC + 10%	0.70
3	TCC + 15%	0.50
4	TCC + 20%	0.30
5	TCC + 25%	0.20

Gamma's objective is to select the bid that maximizes its expected profit.

a. What is the optimal bid for Gamma to make?

b. What is the expected profit associated with the optimal bid in part (a)?

c. What is the risk profile for the optimal bid in part (a)?

d. Consider the probability of winning the optimal bid. If this parameter were allowed to vary, while all other parameters were kept unchanged, what values could it take without altering the optimal selection?

3. JR Davidson recently started a practice in Landscape Design and is considering the purchase of an automated drafting system. JR can purchase a system with three possible drafting capacities. The payoff for having any of these systems depends on the demands for drafting services over the next few years. The cost for each system is shown in the following table along with JR's assessment of the probability that demand will match the capacity of each one.

	Total Cost	Probability
Small system	$10,000	0.4
Medium system	$14,000	0.3
Large system	$20,000	0.3

Working at capacity, each system would generate net cash flow at a yearly rate of 50 percent of its total cost. If a system is chosen that is smaller than demand, it would work at capacity; if a system is chosen that is larger than demand, revenue from the system would be limited by demand. For convenience, JR has initially decided to count cash flow for three years, without discounting. For example, if JR chooses the Medium system and demand is Small, then the profit is calculated as follows:

$$\text{Profit} = 3(0.5 \times 10,000) - 14,000 = 1,000$$

a. What is the best decision under the maximax criterion?

b. What is the best decision under the maximin criterion?

c. What is the best decision under the minimax regret criterion?

d. What is the best decision under the expected payoff criterion?

e. Reviewing the analysis, JR decides that the assumption of a three-year horizon is too restrictive. Instead, it makes more sense to treat the horizon as uncertain, with the following probability distribution:

> Two years of cash flow has 0.4 probability
> Three years of cash flow has 0.4 probability
> Four years of cash flow has 0.2 probability

Now, what is the best decision under the expected payoff criterion?

4. You are contemplating an investment project that has two phases. As currently planned, the first phase of the project requires an investment of $100,000 today. One year from now, the project will deliver either $120,000 or $80,000, with equal probabilities. When these Phase I payouts occur, you will be able to invest an additional $100,000 in Phase II. One year later, Phase II will pay out either 20 percent more than Phase I actually delivered, or else 20 percent less, again with equal probabilities.

You may commit to both phases at the start, or you may commit to Phase I (and postpone a decision on Phase II), or you may invest in neither. If you commit to both phases at the start, there is really no reason to delay. Suppose that you can choose, in that case, to implement both phases virtually simultaneously, so that both investments are made today, and all payouts occur one year from now. (Note, however, that the size of the Phase II payout still depends on the size of the Phase I payout. Conceptually, you can think of the Phase II payouts as occurring immediately after the Phase I payouts.)

a. Using an expected payoff criterion, and discounting at 10 percent, which of the alternatives (First, Both, or Neither) is the optimal decision?

b. What is the breakeven discount rate at which Neither is a better decision than First?

c. Suppose you have access to an additional, similar investment that resembles the original but is more volatile: for the same initial investment, it delivers a Phase I return of ±40 percent (that is, either $140,000 or $60,000) with equal probabilities. Similarly, it delivers a Phase II return of ±40 percent of the Phase I payouts, again with equal probabilities. Show that this new investment is preferable to the original, with a discount rate of 10 percent.

d. Evidently, the higher volatility of the investment (±40 percent as opposed to ±20 percent) makes the potential cash flows attractive. With the discount rate at 10 percent, what levels of volatility would lead to an expected value above zero?

5. Copy Makers Inc. (CMI) has just received a credit request from a new customer who wants to purchase a copying machine. As input to its decision of whether to grant credit, CMI has made the following estimates and assumptions:

• If CMI denies the customer credit, there is a 20 percent chance that the customer will buy the copying machine with cash anyway.

• If CMI grants credit, there is a 70 percent chance that the customer will be a good credit risk.

• If CMI grants credit and the customer is a good credit risk, CMI will collect 100 percent of the purchase price.

• If CMI grants credit and the customer is a bad credit risk, CMI has two options. Under the first option, CMI would continue to send the customer a bill and hope it is eventually paid. Under this option, CMI will collect 100 percent, 50 percent, or 0 percent of the amount owed, with probabilities 0.1, 0.2, and 0.7, respectively. Under the second option, CMI would vigorously pursue the collection of the amount owed. To do so would cost CMI 25 percent of the amount owed, regardless of the amount eventually collected. Under this second option, CMI will again collect 100 percent, 50 percent, or 0 percent of the amount owed, with probabilities of 0.3, 0.5, and 0.2, respectively.

• The copy machine sells for $8,000 and costs CMI $5,000. Nonvigorous enforcement has no cost, while vigorous enforcement costs $2,000.

a. What is the complete, optimal decision strategy for CMI?

b. What is the optimal expected value?

6. TCS Corporation has recently decided to manufacture a product in its own facilities rather than outsource to Asian manufacturers. Its new plant will last about 10 years. TCS is considering two options: build a large plant now that will have sufficient capacity to handle demand into the foreseeable future, or build a small plant that can be expanded two years later, after demand is better known. TCS will not expand the small plant unless demand in the first two years exceeds a threshold level.

TCS assumes that the level of demand in subsequent years will be the same as in the first two years (e.g., if demand is high in the first two years, it will continue to be high in the next eight years).
What additional data are needed to determine the optimal decision?

7. A small manufacturer uses an industrial boiler in its production process. A new boiler can be purchased for $10,000. As the boiler gets older, its maintenance expenses increase while its resale value declines. Since the boiler will be exposed to heavy use, the probability of a breakdown increases every year.

Assume that when a boiler breaks down, it can be used through the end of the year, after which it must be replaced with a new one. Also, assume that a broken-down boiler has no resale value.

Some basic data are given in the following table:

Year of operation	Expenses	Resale Value	Breakdown Probability
1	1,500	7,000	0.1
2	2,000	5,000	0.2
3	3,000	4,000	0.4
4	4,500	2,000	0.5
5	6,000	500	0.8

a. At what year of operation should the boiler be replaced?

b. What is the expected cost per year for the boiler under the optimal replacement strategy?

8. Delta Electric Service is an electrical-utility company serving parts of several states. It is considering replacing some of its equipment at generating substations and is trying to decide whether it should replace an older, existing PCB transformer. (PCB is a toxic chemical known formally as polychlorinated biphenyl.) Although the PCB generator meets all current regulations, if an incident such as a fire were to occur, and PCB contamination caused harm either to neighboring businesses or farms or to the environment, the company would be liable for damages. Recent court cases have shown that simply meeting regulations does not relieve a utility of liability if an incident causes harm to others. In addition, courts have been awarding very large damages to individuals and businesses harmed by incidents involving hazardous material.

If Delta replaces the PCB transformer, no PCB incidents will occur, and the only cost will be the cost of the new transformer, estimated to be $85,000. Alternatively, if the company elects to keep the existing PCB transformer in operation, then, according to their consultants, there is a 50/50 chance that there will be a high likelihood of an incident or a low likelihood of an incident. For the case of a high likelihood of an incident, there is also a 0.004 probability that a fire will occur sometime during the remaining life of the transformer, and a 0.996 probability that no fire will occur. If a fire occurs, there is a 20 percent chance that it will be severe and the utility will incur a very high cost, whereas there is an 80 percent chance that it will be minor and the utility will incur a low cost. The high- and low-cost amounts, including both cleanup and damages, are estimated to be $100 million and $10 million, respectively, based on results from other incidents in the industry. For the case of a low likelihood of an incident, there is a 0.001 probability of a fire during the remaining life of the transformer and a 0.999 probability of no fire. If a fire does occur, then the same probabilities exist for the severe and minor outcomes as in the previous case. In both cases, there will be no cost if no fire occurs.

a. Should Delta replace its old transformers?

b. What is the expected cost per transformer, under the optimal replacement strategy?

9. In the early 1980s, New England Electric System (NEES) was deciding how much to bid for the salvage rights to a grounded ship, the SS *Kuniang*. If the bid were successful, the ship could be repaired and outfitted to haul coal for the company's power-generation stations. But the value of doing so depended on the outcome of a U.S. Coast Guard judgment about the salvage value of the ship. The Coast Guard's judgment involved an obscure law regarding domestic shipping in coastal waters. If the judgment were to indicate a low salvage value (an outcome with an estimated 30 percent chance of occurring), and if NEES submitted the winning bid, then NEES would be able to use the ship for its shipping needs without additional costs. If the judgment were high, the cost to NEES would run $4 million higher than if the judgment were low. The Coast Guard's judgment would not be known until after the winning bid was chosen, so there was considerable risk associated with submitting a bid. If the bid were to fail, NEES could purchase either a new ship or a tug/barge combination, both of which were relatively expensive alternatives.

Analysts at NEES estimated that purchasing a new ship for these purposes would lead to profits of $3.2 million (calculated as a net present value over 20 years of shipping). Purchasing a tug/barge combination would lead to profits of only $1.6 million. By comparison, if NEES could acquire the *Kuniang* at the low salvage value, it could achieve profits of $15.5 million, exclusive of its bid.

One of the major issues was that the higher the bid, the more likely NEES would be to win. NEES judged that a bid of $2 million would definitely not win, whereas a bid of $12 million definitely would win. As a first cut, we can represent three bids:

- A bid of $2 million would certainly not win.
- A bid of $8 million would have a 60 percent chance of winning.
- A bid of $12 million would certainly win.

The goal for NEES was to maximize its profits from supplying coal to its plants.[1]

a. What is the best of the three bids for NEES? What is the optimal expected profit?

b. Consider the estimate of a $4 million difference between the cost with a low salvage value and the cost with a high salvage value. For what range of estimates does the optimal bid in part (a) remain unchanged?

c. Enrich the bidding submodel as follows. For a bid of x (in millions of dollars), the probability of winning is $W(x)$, where $W(x)$ is a linear function between $x = 2$ and $x = 12$. What is the best value of x?

10. In early 1984, Pennzoil and Getty Oil agreed to the terms of a merger. Before any formal documents could be signed, however, Texaco offered Getty Oil a substantially better price, so Gordon Getty, who controlled most of the Getty stock, reneged on the Pennzoil deal and sold to Texaco. Naturally, Pennzoil felt it had been dealt with unfairly and filed a lawsuit against Texaco, alleging that Texaco had interfered illegally in the Pennzoil-Getty negotiations. Pennzoil won the case; in late 1985, it was awarded $11.1 billion, the largest judgment ever in the United States. A Texas appeals court reduced the judgment by $2 billion, but interest and penalties drove the total back up to $10.3 billion. James Kinnear, Texaco's chief executive officer, had said that Texaco would file for bankruptcy if Pennzoil obtained court permission to secure the judgment by filing liens against Texaco's assets. Furthermore, Kinnear had promised to fight the case all the way to the U.S. Supreme Court if necessary, arguing in part that Pennzoil had not followed the Security and Exchange Commission's regulations in its negotiations with Getty. In April 1987, just before Pennzoil began to file the liens, Texaco offered to pay Pennzoil $2 billion to settle the entire case.

Hugh Liedtke, chairman of Pennzoil, faced the choice of whether to accept the Texaco offer. His advisors were telling him that a settlement of between $3 and $5 billion would be fair, so one of his options was to make a counteroffer of $5 billion.

If Liedtke were to counteroffer, assume Texaco would be twice as likely to refuse as accept the $5 billion counteroffer. If Texaco refused, the case would go to court, where the judge would award Pennzoil $10.3 billion, or reduce the award to $5 billion, or award Pennzoil nothing. The probability that the judge would award Pennzoil nothing is about 50 percent, while the other outcomes were thought to be equally likely (25 percent probability).[2]

a. What is the best decision for Liedtke, and what is his expected payoff?

b. What is the expected payoff if Pennzoil counteroffers and Texaco refuses? Why is the expected payoff to the counteroffer higher than this?

c. Consider the probability that the judge would award Pennzoil nothing. How high would this probability have to go before the best decision would be to accept the $2 billion offer? (Assume that the probabilities of the other two outcomes are always equal.)

11. (Continuation of the previous problem) Liedtke's advisors suggest that Texaco has more options in the face of Pennzoil's $5 billion counteroffer than simply to refuse or accept. In particular, they might counteroffer, probably with an amount near $4 billion.

Modify your analysis to take this new possibility into account. Assume that Pennzoil will either accept or refuse Texaco's counteroffer of $4 billion. If it refuses, the case will go to court and the same outcomes and probabilities will apply as in the previous exercise. The probabilities that Texaco accepts, refuses, or counteroffers can be assumed to be 1/3.

a. Now what is the best decision for Liedtke, and what payoff can he expect to receive from it? Why does the expected value change in this case?

b. How sensitive is the overall expected value of this decision to the probability that Texaco counteroffers $4 billion? (Assume that the probabilities of Texaco accepting or refusing are equal.) Construct a graph to relate the expected value of the decision to this probability.

c. How would your results change if you added a possible counteroffer of $3 billion?

12. The Taiwanese government recently announced that it would begin construction of a high-speed rail system linking the northernmost city of Taipei to the southernmost city, Tai-Nan. This high-speed train will alleviate the significant traffic problems that the country is experiencing. This is a highly lucrative construction project with many international companies involved in the bidding. However, it is clear that companies that have local negotiators possess a clear advantage in the bidding process.

A construction company from Thailand has asked you to work for it in the hope that your connections will successfully help to secure a portion of the high-speed rail

[1] D. E. Bell, "Bidding for the S.S. Kuniang," *Interfaces* 14 (1984): 17–23.

[2] R. T. Clemen, and T. Reilly. 2005, *Making Hard Decisions: Introduction to Decision Analysis* 2d ed. Pacific Grove, CA: Duxbury, 65–66.

contract. You have given serious thought to the proposal and are now sitting in a meeting with the CEO. As the meeting progresses, the CEO brings up the subject of compensation. You listen intently and are surprised when he discusses the terms.

The CEO proposes the following terms: you can take $20,000 per month for a period of two years regardless of whether or not you secure the high-speed rail contract, or you can "gamble" any portion of your salary you wish. He agrees that if you successfully acquire the contract for the company, he will double the portion of the salary that you decided to gamble. But if you do not secure the contract, then you do not receive any bonus and will be paid only the amount you did not gamble. This deal applies to the entire amount that would have been "gambled" for the two-year contract no matter when the contract is obtained.

In addition, if you happen to secure a second, unrelated contract while you are there, the CEO agrees to re-double your entire "gambled" amount for the two-year period (in effect giving you four times the gambled amount). This deal applies no matter when the second contract is obtained as long as it happens within the two-year period.

The high-speed rail system is going to be built, and it will be divided between several companies. Based on your previous work and investigation into the contract, you feel that there is a 60 percent chance that you can get the contract. However, since you have done little preparation for any other projects, the likelihood of a second contract is probably only 20 percent.

You are debating whether to quit your current job, which pays $122,500 a year, to take on this opportunity. Furthermore, if you decide to take this offer, you will have to face the question of how much to "gamble" if any.

a. If you were not able to gamble any money, what should you do based on an expected-payoff analysis?

b. Suppose that you can gamble part of your salary, what amount would you gamble to be neutral to either decision?

c. Now suppose that you gamble $50,000 and have a risk aversion that can be captured in the exponential utility function $U(x) = 1 - \exp(-x/R)$. Your risk tolerance is $100,000. What is your decision based on utility, and what are the utilities of each decision to four significant digits?

d. Suppose the decision with the highest utility was to stay with your current job, how much would the Thai company have to offer as the base salary, to the nearest $100, to get you to change your mind? (Use a gamble amount of $50,000 and $R = \$100,000$.)

15 Monte Carlo Simulation

15.1 INTRODUCTION

Change and uncertainty are ubiquitous features of the business world. The effective business analyst and model builder, whose work always involves planning for an uncertain future, must therefore have tools for dealing with these aspects of business life. In earlier chapters, we generally assumed that the parameters and relationships in our models were known with certainty. We did not entirely ignore uncertainty, but we dealt with it as a secondary feature of the situation, perhaps using what-if analysis or scenario analysis to explore how our model results would change if our assumptions changed. In Chapter 14, we began to look at decision problems in which uncertainty is a central, unavoidable feature of the problem, so that if we ignore it, our analysis is sure to be flawed. In this chapter, we discuss **Monte Carlo simulation**, an important and flexible tool for modeling situations in which uncertainty is a key factor.

In order to perform Monte Carlo simulation on spreadsheet models, we use the Excel add-in **Crystal Ball**. (Crystal Ball 7 Academic is provided with this book. If you have not already done so, install Crystal Ball at this time. Crystal Ball installs a ribbon with four groups of commands: Define, Run, Analyze, and Help.) We assume in this chapter that the reader is familiar with the basic concepts of probability, because these are essential to analyzing situations involving uncertainty. The relevant concepts are reviewed in the Appendix at the end of the text (Basic Probability Concepts), which covers probability distributions (discrete and continuous), cumulative distribution functions, expected values, tail probabilities, variability, and sampling theory.

In a nutshell, simulation can describe not only what the *outcomes* of a given decision could be, but also the *probabilities* with which these outcomes will occur. In fact, the result of a simulation is the entire **probability distribution** of outcomes. In a sense, simulation is an advanced form of sensitivity analysis in which we attach a probability to each possible outcome.

We are often concerned with the **average** outcome, which is one way of summarizing the distribution of all possible outcomes and perhaps the most prominent measure of performance when outcomes are uncertain. In addition, we often wish to determine the probability of a particular set of outcomes. Such "tail probabilities" are often suitable measures of the risk associated with a decision.

Decision trees provide a simple means for analyzing decisions with uncertainty and risk. In Chapter 14 we discussed how to construct decision trees and how to determine the expected outcome and the probability distribution of outcomes given a choice of actions. Simulation provides a more general approach to similar problems. Simulation is the tool of choice when there are a large number of uncertainties, especially when these are represented by continuous distributions. Simulation is also a practical method when the underlying model is complex, as we illustrate later. However, it is important to realize that, just as with decision trees, the result of a simulation is a probability distribution for each outcome. Analyzing these distributions and extracting managerial insights are important parts of the art of simulation.

We begin this chapter with a simple demonstration of Monte Carlo simulation, using the Advertising Budget example we have analyzed in earlier chapters.

We follow this with another example, Butson Stores, in which we illustrate the steps in a complete simulation analysis. We then analyze two common business applications in detail: valuing a corporation and pricing options. In the remainder of the chapter, we systematically treat each of the steps in a simulation study. We also provide two chapter appendices that describe details of using Crystal Ball: Appendix 15.1 covers Crystal Ball settings for running simulations, while Appendix 15.2 describes specialized features of Crystal Ball.

15.2   A SIMPLE ILLUSTRATION

In this section we provide a first look at simulation analysis, using the Advertising Budget example. The goal is to develop an intuitive understanding of the inputs and outputs of a simulation analysis; we leave the details of how to use Crystal Ball to a later section.

When we introduced the Advertising Budget example in Chapter 5, we took it for granted that the price would be $40 and the cost $25. In Chapter 10, we determined that by allocating the advertising budget in the best possible way, we could attain a profit of $71,447. Of course, this result assumes that these and other input parameters are accurate forecasts of next year's values. Now we consider the more realistic case in which next year's price and cost are both subject to considerable uncertainty. Assume that the most likely value of the price is $45, but it could turn out to be as low as $30 or as high as $50. Similarly, the most likely value for cost is $20, but it could be as low as $10 or as high as $35. Given this uncertainty in the price and cost, we naturally want to know the implications for annual profit. Simulation will answer this question for us by developing the probability distribution for profit, that is, a picture of all the possible outcomes for profit along with their probabilities of occurring.

Because we already have a working model and have determined which of the input parameters are uncertain (price and cost), our first step is to choose a means for representing uncertainty in the input parameters. One way to incorporate the assumption that price can range from $30 to $50 with a most likely value of $45 is to use a triangular probability distribution, as in Figure 15.1. This distribution reflects the assumption that not all values between $30 and $50 are equally likely, but that in fact, high values are somewhat more likely than low values. We can also use a triangular distribution to represent the uncertainty in cost as in Figure 15.2, which shows a distribution in which low values are somewhat more likely than high ones.

Having chosen probability distributions for the two uncertain input parameters, it is a relatively simple process to determine the probability distribution for profit. Essentially, we draw random samples from the distributions of the inputs (using the

FIGURE 15.1 Probability Distribution for Price

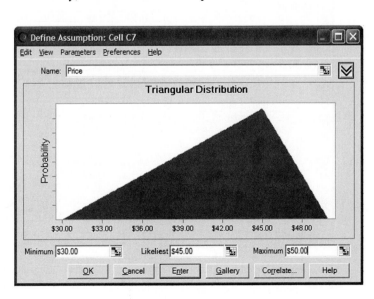

FIGURE 15.2 Probability
Distribution for Cost

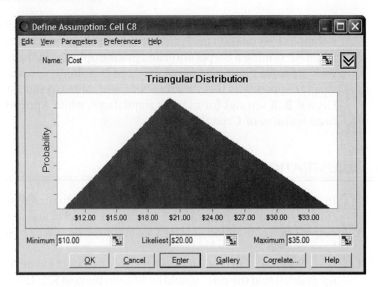

probability distributions we have chosen), and for each sample pair, we calculate the
resulting value for profit. Figure 15.3[*] shows the Advertising Budget model for one
such outcome: Profit is $38.25, cost is $23.12, and the resulting profit is $77,790. Of
course, a single random value for profit is not by itself very meaningful. The only way
to develop a realistic picture of the range of possible outcomes and their likelihoods is
to repeat this process many times. Crystal Ball makes this easy. The results for 1,000
repetitions are summarized in Figure 15.4.

This picture is a **histogram** of 1,000 repetitions of the sampling process
described above. We can interpret it as the probability distribution for profit. From

FIGURE 15.3 Advertising
Budget Model with One
Random Outcome

	A	B	C	D	E	F	G	H	I	J
1	**Advertising Budget Model**									
2	SGP/KRB			Random outcome for						
3	1/1/2006			price from a						
4				triangular						
5	PARAMETERS			distribution.						
6				Q1	Q2	Q3	Q4			Notes
7		Price	$38.25							Current price
8		Cost	$23.12							Accounting
9		Seasonal		0.9	1.1	0.8	1.2			Data analysis
10		OHD rate	0.15	Random outcome for						Accounting
11		Sales Parameters		cost from a triangular						
12			35	distribution.						Consultants
13			3000							
14		Sales Expense		8000	8000	9000	9000			Consultants
15		Ad Budget	$40,000							Current budget
16										
17	DECISIONS							Total		
18		Ad Expenditures		$7,273	$12,346	$5,117	$15,263	$40,000		sum
19										
20	OUTPUTS									
21		Profit	$77,790		Base case	$69,662				
22										
23	CALCULATIONS			Random outcome for						
24		Quarter	Q1	profit, based on			Q4	Total		
25		Seasonal	0.9	random price and cost.			1.2			
26										
27		Units Sold	3193	4769	2523	5676	16161			given formula
28		Revenue	122122	182429	96492	217106	618149			price*units
29		COGS	73816	110268	58324	131228	373637			cost*units
30		Gross Margin	48306	72161	38168	85877	244512			subtraction
31										
32		Sales Expense	8000	8000	9000	9000	34000			given
33		Advertising	7273	12346	5117	15263	40000			decisions
34		Overhead	18318	27364	14474	32566	92722			rate*revenue
35		Total Fixed Cost	33591	47711	28591	56829	166722			sum
36										
37		Profit	14715	24450	9577	29048	77790			GM -TFC
38		Profit Margin	12.05%	13.40%	9.93%	13.38%	12.58%			pct of revenue
39										

[*]To download spreadsheets for this chapter, go to the Student Companion Site at www.wiley.com/college/
powell.

FIGURE 15.4 Distribution of Profit Showing Mean Value

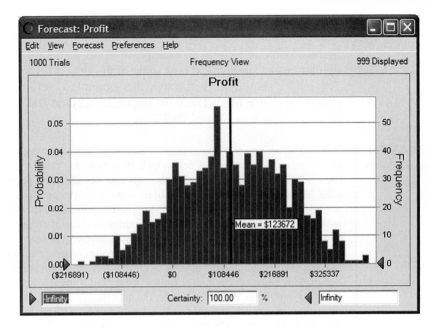

the histogram, we can see that profit ranges from less than −$100,000 to more than $300,000. The mean, or **expected value**, is $123,672 (the simple average of all 1,000 outcomes, since each is equally likely). Finally, we can determine the likelihood of making a positive profit by calculating the percentage of positive outcomes among the 1,000 repetitions. Figure 15.5 shows the results: in 84.4 percent of the cases, the profit exceeds zero.

This example illustrates all the essential features of a simulation.

1. Start with a base-case model and determine which of the input parameters to represent as uncertain.

2. Develop probability distributions for those inputs.

3. Take random samples from those inputs and calculate the resulting output, repeating the process until a clear picture of the output distribution emerges.

4. Create a histogram of the outcomes and interpret it.

Simulation provides two essential pieces of information: mean values (also called expected values) and tail probabilities (in this case, the probability of a positive profit).

FIGURE 15.5 Distribution of Profit Showing Tail Probability

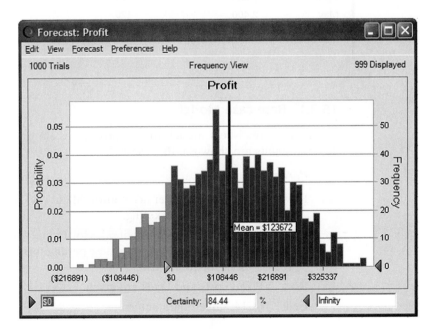

15.3 THE SIMULATION PROCESS

In this section we present an example in detail, explaining how the main concepts of simulation are applied and how some of the basic features of Crystal Ball are used. The reader should work through this example carefully, reproducing the major results we derive here. The most important Crystal Ball skills are summarized for future reference as Crystal Ball Tips.

EXAMPLE
Butson Stores

Butson Stores faces a problem in maintaining sufficient cash balances for operations over the first six months of the year. Each month, they must pay certain fixed costs and taxes (see the following table), as well as materials costs that run about 80 percent of the current month's sales. Monthly cash receipts consist of revenues from the previous month's sales, as well as 0.5 percent interest on short-term cash balances. The company enters the six-month period with a cash balance of $250,000 and wishes to maintain at least that balance each month in order to cover cash needs. December sales of $1.54 million have just been recorded. If Butson finishes a month with less than $250,000 in cash, the company can take out a one-month loan at 1 percent interest. The principal and interest are repaid in the following month. Butson's marketing department has made estimates for the mean and standard deviation of sales in each of the next six months (see the table). Given the uncertainty in sales, Butson would like to know how large their maximum monthly loan is likely to be and how likely they are to exceed their current credit limit of $750,000. Finally, the company would like to know how much they will have to pay in interest costs for loans.

Month	Fixed Costs and Taxes
January	250
February	250
March	400
April	250
May	250
June	250

Month	Mean Sales	Standard Deviation of Sales
January	1,800	80
February	1,500	80
March	1,900	100
April	2,600	125
May	2,400	120
June	1,900	90

■

15.3.1 Base-case Model

Our initial spreadsheet model for this problem is shown in Figure 15.6, where all dollar amounts are shown in thousands.

Parameters

Row 6: Sales for December are known. Mean sales for January through June are forecasts from Marketing.

Row 7: The standard deviations of sales for January through June are forecasts from Marketing. We do not use these parameters in the base-case model but record them for future use.

Row 8: Fixed costs and taxes are given.

Cells C9-C14: Given parameters.

FIGURE 15.6 Base-case
Model for Butson Stores

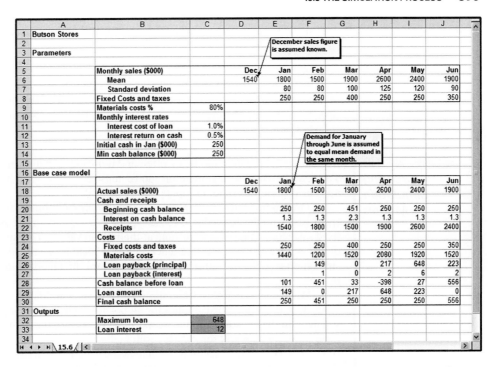

	A	B	C	D	E	F	G	H	I	J
1	Butson Stores									
2						December sales figure				
3	Parameters					is assumed known.				
4										
5		Monthly sales ($000)			Dec	Jan	Feb	Mar	Apr	May	Jun
6		Mean			1540	1800	1500	1900	2600	2400	1900
7		Standard deviation				80	80	100	125	120	90
8		Fixed Costs and taxes				250	250	400	250	250	350
9		Materials costs %	80%							
10		Monthly interest rates								
11		Interest cost of loan	1.0%							
12		Interest return on cash	0.5%				Demand for January			
13		Initial cash in Jan ($000)	250				through June is assumed			
14		Min cash balance ($000)	250				to equal mean demand in			
15							the same month.			
16	Base case model									
17					Dec	Jan	Feb	Mar	Apr	May	Jun
18		Actual sales ($000)			1540	1800	1500	1900	2600	2400	1900
19		Cash and receipts								
20		Beginning cash balance				250	250	451	250	250	250
21		Interest on cash balance				1.3	1.3	2.3	1.3	1.3	1.3
22		Receipts				1540	1800	1500	1900	2600	2400
23		Costs								
24		Fixed costs and taxes				250	250	400	250	250	350
25		Materials costs				1440	1200	1520	2080	1920	1520
26		Loan payback (principal)					149	0	217	648	223
27		Loan payback (interest)					1	0	2	6	2
28		Cash balance before loan				101	451	33	-398	27	556
29		Loan amount				149	0	217	648	223	0
30		Final cash balance				250	451	250	250	250	556
31	Outputs									
32		Maximum loan	648								
33		Loan interest	12								
34										

15.6

Model

Row 18: In the base-case model, we assume that sales each month is the same as *mean* sales (row 6).

Row 20: The beginning cash balance in January is given. The beginning cash balance in February through June is the final cash balance from the previous month (row 30).

Row 21: The interest on cash is the interest return on cash times the beginning cash balance (row 20).

Row 22: Cash receipts are actual sales from the previous month (row 18).

Row 24: Fixed costs and taxes are given data (row 8).

Row 25: Materials cost is the materials cost percentage times actual sales (row 18).

Row 26: The loan principal payback is the loan amount from the previous month (row 29).

Row 27: The interest on the loan is the loan amount from the previous month (row 29) times the interest cost of loan.

Row 28: The cash balance before the loan is the sum of the beginning cash balance, interest on cash balance, and receipts less the sum of fixed costs and taxes, materials cost, loan principal, and loan interest.

Row 29: To calculate the size of the loan, we compare the cash balance before the loan to the minimum cash balance (cell C14). If the cash balance before the loan is less than the minimum, the loan equals the difference. If the cash balance exceeds the minimum, the loan amount is zero. This logic is implemented by the function MAX($C$14-E28,0).

Row 30: The final cash balance is the sum of the cash balance before the loan and the loan amount.

Outputs

Cell C32: We calculate the largest loan taken out over the six-month horizon by calculating the maximum loan in row 29.

Cell C33: We calculate the total interest paid on loans by summing the loan interest in row 27.

Our base-case model, in which we assume no uncertainty in sales, shows that the maximum loan will be taken out in April and, at $648, will not exceed the credit limit of $750. The total interest paid on loans will be $12. (Remember: All figures are in thousands.)

MODELING TIP
Creating
Simulation
Models

Beginners to simulation modeling often find it difficult to build an initial spreadsheet model. This may be because a simulation model must correctly evaluate a large or even infinite number of different random inputs.

One useful trick is to *fix the random inputs* at some arbitrary value and build a spreadsheet model to evaluate those inputs. We did this in the Butson example when we fixed sales for January through June at their mean values. This step allowed us to build and debug a spreadsheet with no uncertainty, which is a simpler task than debugging a simulation model. Only after we had debugged this first model did we introduce uncertainty in sales.

A warning is in order: Care must be taken when building a model around a set of fixed inputs that the model logic applies for all possible values those inputs can take on when we simulate. In the Butson example, we calculate the size of the loan in row 29 recognizing that randomness in sales will sometimes result in the cash balance falling below the minimum and sometimes not. Both cases must be handled correctly by the spreadsheet so that when we simulate 1,000 different sets of monthly demands the results are always correct. ∎

15.3.2 Sensitivity Analysis

Throughout this book we have stressed the importance of sensitivity analysis in understanding a model and its implications. This principle holds as well for simulation models: The base-case model should be thoroughly explored, using Data Sensitivity, the Tornado Chart tool, or other methods, before undertaking a simulation analysis.

Most of the sensitivity analysis methods we have presented involve varying a single parameter at a time and therefore do not reveal the behavior of the model when many parameters vary. This is precisely what simulation does, which is why we can think of it as a sophisticated approach to sensitivity analysis.

In the Butson model we have two outputs: the maximum loan taken out over the six-month period and the total interest paid on loans. The tornado chart in Figure 15.7 shows how the various input parameters affect the maximum loan. Two parameters dominate here: sales in April and sales in December. The maximum loan in the base case is taken out in April, so any change in sales in that month will affect the size of the loan directly through the materials cost. Similarly, sales in December will influence receipts in January and therefore the size of the loan taken out in that month. All other parameters have a much smaller relative impact on the maximum loan taken out. Figure 15.8 shows the tornado chart for total interest paid. Here one parameter stands out as having the biggest impact: sales in December. Because the materials cost in December has already been paid (in December) and does not figure into our model, any increase in sales in December goes directly into receipts and thus into cash on hand, reducing any loan dollar-for-dollar. In any other month, the impact of an increase in sales is reduced by the amount due for materials cost.

Whereas sensitivity analysis is a necessary first step and can often reveal unexpected relationships in the model, a simulation analysis is required to analyze the combined effects of changes in many inputs. We now turn to this phase of the analysis.

15.3.3 Selecting Probability Distributions—Creating
Assumption Cells

The key uncertainty facing Butson is the level of sales in the months from January through June. Variations in sales will drive variations in receipts, which

FIGURE 15.7 Tornado
Chart for Maximum Loan

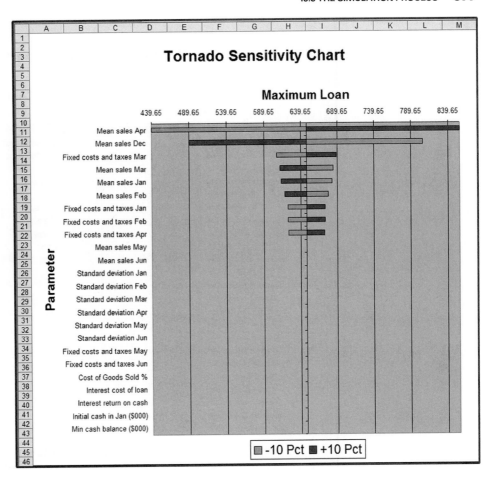

could ultimately affect the maximum loan taken out and the total interest paid. Our sensitivity analysis has shown us that the maximum loan is particularly sensitive to the level of sales in April, because the largest loan is taken out in that month.

The marketing department has provided estimates of the variability to be expected in sales each month, in terms of the mean and the standard deviation. We will assume that a normal probability distribution is appropriate here, since the normal can be defined in terms of its mean and standard deviation.

Our first task is to convert our base-case model into a simulation model by replacing our fixed (deterministic) sales assumptions in row 18 with probability distributions. In Crystal Ball, cells containing probability distributions are called **Assumption cells**. We first copy the base-case model to a new worksheet. We begin with cell E18, sales for January.

1. Select Crystal Ball▶Define▶Define Assumption from the Crystal Ball ribbon. Display the Distribution Gallery, which is an input window containing all the probability distributions that are available in Crystal Ball.

2. Scroll until the Normal distribution appears, select it, and press OK.

3. Click on the Cell Reference icon to the right of Mean and select E6 (or type in = E6), the mean of the distribution as specified by marketing. Click OK.

4. Repeat this process for the standard deviation (Std. Dev.) in cell E7.

5. The *values* in these cells will appear in the parameter boxes; you can check that the *cell references* are correct by selecting the Cell Reference icon next to each parameter or by choosing Parameters▶Show Cell References. (When we use the Distribution Gallery to enter distributions, we enter cell references using an equal sign before the cell address—for example, =E6 for Mean and =E7 for Std Dev. By using relative references here, we will then be able to enter other

FIGURE 15.8 Tornado
Chart for Total Interest Paid

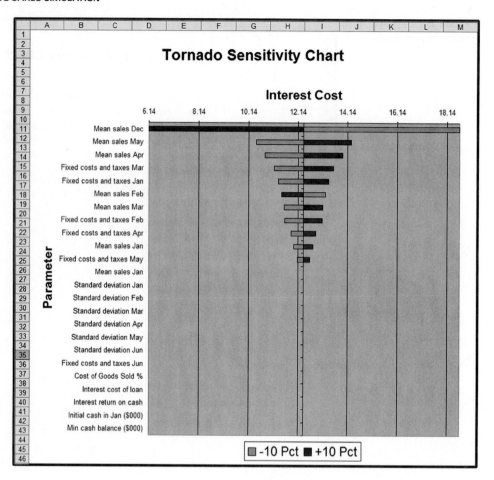

means and variances by copying the formula along the row, accessing the appropriate monthly means and standard deviations from rows 6 and 7 of the worksheet.)

6. Click on OK to enter the distribution in cell E18.

Having entered the distribution for cell E18, we then use Crystal Ball to copy this distribution to the remaining months, February through June, in cells F18:J18.

1. Highlight cell E18 and choose Crystal Ball▶Define▶Copy.

2. Highlight the range F18:J18 and choose Crystal Ball▶Define▶Paste.

The target cells change color to show they have all become Assumption cells. We can then use Crystal Ball▶Define▶Select▶ Select All Assumptions to confirm that each of these cells has the correct normal distribution. (Crystal Ball will highlight with a red border all the Assumption cells on the sheet.) Note that because we have used relative cell references in defining cell E18, the distributions for cells F18:J18 all reference the appropriate mean and standard deviation for the given month.

When copying probability distributions in Crystal Ball, we must remember to use the *Crystal Ball* commands Define▶Copy and Define▶Paste. Using the *Excel* Copy-and-Paste commands instead would copy only the *value* in the cell, not the probability distribution. Crystal Ball can be configured (through Define▶Cell Preferences) to shade each Assumption cell with a given color and to add a comment that specifies the probability distribution. This configuration is illustrated in Figure 15.9.

To check that this process has worked successfully, select Run▶Step from the Crystal Ball ribbon. We should see new random values entered into the Assumption

FIGURE 15.9 Simulation Model for Butson Stores

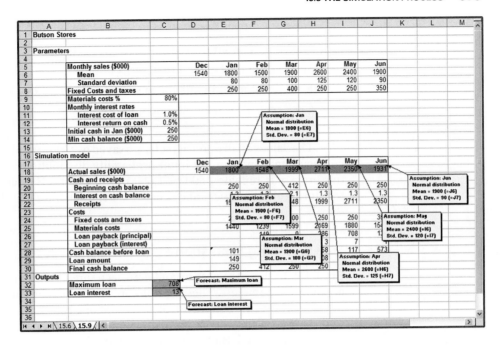

cells in E18:J18 each time we select this command. The output cells C32 and C33 also change appropriately each time a new set of random inputs is created.

CRYSTAL BALL TIP
Copy-and-Paste Errors

One of the most common errors made using Crystal Ball involves copying probability distributions from the Distribution Gallery using Excel commands rather than Crystal Ball commands. Because Crystal Ball is an add-in to Excel, Excel does not recognize every Crystal Ball feature. In particular, probability distributions entered using the Distribution Gallery (which Crystal Ball calls Assumption cells) are not visible to Excel. Excel sees only a *number* in an Assumption cell, whereas Crystal Ball sees a *distribution*. As a result, if we used Excel to copy and paste that cell to another range, we would copy only the number in the Assumption cell, not the distribution. Then, when we simulated the model, the original Assumption cell would change randomly as required, but the copied cells would not change.

To copy a probability distribution entered using the Distribution Gallery, we must use the Crystal Ball commands Define▶Copy and Define▶Paste. These commands can also be used to copy Forecast or Decision cells. ∎

15.3.4 Selecting Outputs—Creating *Forecast* Cells

The second step in setting up a simulation model is to define the model outputs so that Crystal Ball can save these values during a simulation run. In Crystal Ball, all output cells are called *Forecast cells*. In the Butson model, we have two outputs, the maximum loan and the loan interest, so we define two Forecast cells.

1. Highlight the maximum loan value in cell C32.
2. Select Define▶Define Forecast from the Crystal Ball ribbon.
3. In the Name field in the Define Forecast window, Crystal Ball enters a name for the cell if there is a label nearby. We may overwrite this entry with any other name. Similarly, we may define units for the cell, although this is optional.
4. Click on OK to save the Forecast cell.

Crystal Ball can be configured (through Define▶Cell Preferences) to shade each Forecast cell with a given color and to add a comment that specifies the name and units of the cell. This is illustrated in Figure 15.9.

Next, we repeat this process to define loan interest as a second Forecast cell.

1. Highlight loan interest in cell C33.
2. Select Define▶Define Forecast from the Crystal Ball ribbon.
3. Enter a name and units for this Forecast cell in the Define Forecast window.
4. Click on OK to save the Forecast cell.

The values of all Forecast cells are saved by Crystal Ball every time it calculates new random values for the input probability distributions. In a typical simulation, this process is repeated 500 or 1,000 times. Crystal Ball creates a temporary file for storing these outputs and creates histograms for each of them, as we will see shortly.

15.3.5   Setting Simulation Parameters

Crystal Ball allows the user to configure each simulation run by choosing values for a number of parameters. These options are located under Run▶Run Preferences on the Crystal Ball ribbon. Most of these options can safely be left at their default settings. We will set just one parameter here: the number of **trials** to run. The number of trials in Crystal Ball is the number of times model outputs (Forecasts) are calculated for different random values of the inputs.

1. Select Run▶Run Preferences from the Crystal Ball ribbon. Select the Trials tab.
2. Enter the value 1000 in the `Number of trials to run` field (see Figure 15.10).
3. Click on OK.

15.3.6   Analyzing Simulation Outputs

To run the simulation for Butson Stores, follow these steps.

1. If Run▶Reset is highlighted, select it. (This option allows Crystal Ball to erase previous simulation results.)
2. Select Run▶Start from the Crystal Ball ribbon.
3. Three windows open while Crystal Ball carries out the simulation run. One is a Control Panel that keeps track of the number of trials. The other two are Forecast windows that display histograms of the Forecast cells for the maximum loan and interest paid.

Our results are given in the form of a histogram of the 1,000 trials for each of the Forecast cells. Figure 15.11 shows the histogram for the maximum loan. We can see that the mean or average value is $644.5, but the maximum loan could be as low as $364 or as high as $963. More significantly, we can see that there is a 15 percent chance that the maximum loan amount will exceed the credit limit of $750. (To determine this tail probability, move the black triangle at the lower left of the histogram until the value $750 appears in the window on the lower left of the Forecast window. The desired probability then appears in the Certainty window.) The distribution of loan interest is shown in Figure 15.12. The mean value is $12.4, but the range is from $8 to about $17.

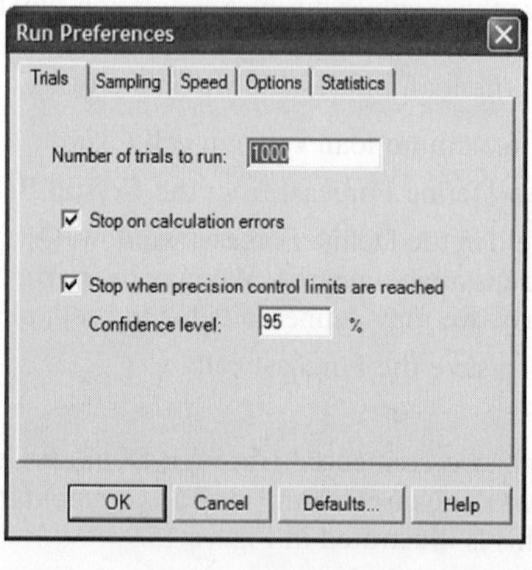

What have we learned by simulating values of sales for the six months from

FIGURE 15.10 The Run Preferences Window in Crystal Ball

FIGURE 15.11 Distribution of the Maximum Loan

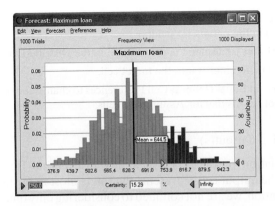

FIGURE 15.12 Distribution of Loan Interest

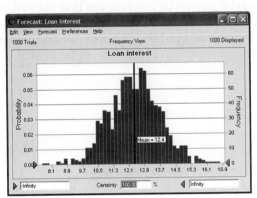

January to June for Butson Stores? Our base-case model, which was based on mean sales forecasts, showed that the maximum loan would be $648 and that we would pay $12 in loan interest. (Again, all values are in thousands.) Once we take the uncertainty in sales into account we can see the ways in which these results are accurate and the ways they are misleading. In this particular model, we find that the *mean values* of the outputs do not change significantly when we take uncertainty into account. However, we can see that the range of possible values for each of the outputs is very wide. Most importantly, there is a significant chance that we will exceed our credit limit. There is no more practical way than simulation to estimate this critical value.

We now recapitulate the simulation process, and provide recipes in capsule form for the most commonly repeated processes in Crystal Ball.

1. Selecting Uncertain Parameters

The first step in any simulation (after building an appropriate spreadsheet and performing sensitivity analysis) is to select parameters to treat as uncertain. Each of these parameters requires its own probability distribution. Because it takes time and effort to find an appropriate distribution, some economy is called for in selecting uncertain parameters. As we saw in Chapter 6, large changes in some parameters may generate only modest changes in the outcomes. These parameters probably do not warrant treatment as uncertain. Therefore, we recommend performing an initial sensitivity analysis to select those parameters that have the most influence on the results. A tornado chart is a natural tool in this selection process. Among the most influential inputs, some may be decision variables: these should *never* be considered uncertain, because they are under our control. Only the most influential and uncertain parameters should be replaced with probability distributions. In a later section, we describe in more detail how to select uncertain parameters.

2. Selecting Probability Distributions

Once we have decided that a particular input parameter should be treated as uncertain, we must develop a probability distribution for it. In most cases, this step involves a mixture of data analysis and judgment. A small set of probability distributions is commonly used in business analysis. We describe these in a later section and indicate when each is appropriate.

CRYSTAL BALL TIP
Entering Assumption Cells

1. Highlight the target cell.

2. Select Crystal Ball ▶ Define ▶ Define Assumption.

3. Click on All in the Distribution Gallery window to display all 21 available families of distributions.

4. Click on a distribution to highlight it.

5. Click OK to select it.

6. Enter the required parameters either by entering numbers or cell addresses (starting with "=") in the parameter field(s).

7. Click on Enter to display the distribution in the Distribution Gallery window.

8. Click on OK to enter it into the target cell.

9. Select Crystal Ball▶Define▶Cell Preferences to change the background color and other features of the display for Assumption cells. ■

3. Selecting Output(s)

Every simulation produces a probability distribution for one or more outputs. Generally, the output cell represents the single most important aspect of the model. But in simulation, we are not confined to considering only one output variable. In fact, one of the powerful aspects of simulation is that any cell in the spreadsheet can be considered an output cell. We might, for example, be interested not only in the profit we generate, but also in the NPV, the ratio of cost to revenues, and so on. Any variable we can represent in a single cell can be treated as an output.

CRYSTAL BALL TIP
Entering
Forecast Cells

1. Highlight the target cell.
2. Select Crystal Ball▶Define▶Define Forecast.
3. Enter a name for the Forecast in the Name field.
4. Enter units in the Units field (optional).
5. Click on OK to enter it into the target cell.
6. Select Crystal Ball▶Define▶Cell Preferences to change the background color and other features of the display for Forecast cells. ■

4. Running a Simulation

Executing a simulation consists of sampling from the input distributions and storing the results of the outputs. Crystal Ball provides a number of options for tailoring the simulation run to the situation. The key choice is how many samples to draw—or, in Crystal Ball language, selecting the number of trials. Whether we are interested in the mean profit or the probability of a loss, the more samples we take, the more precise our estimates become. We elaborate later on how to select an appropriate level of precision and how to choose other Crystal Ball settings.

CRYSTAL BALL TIP
Setting the
Number of
Trials

1. Select Crystal Ball▶Run▶Run Preferences.
2. Click on the Trials tab.
3. Enter the number of trials in the Number of trials to run field.
4. Click on OK to return. ■

5. Analyzing Outputs

The result of running a simulation is a histogram, which we interpret as a probability distribution, for each of the output cells. How we analyze this distribution depends on the problem. Often, we are concerned simply with the expected value, or mean outcome, which in Crystal Ball is listed as part of the statistical summary in the Forecast window and which can be displayed on the histogram. Many other useful aspects of the distribution, such as the minimum and maximum outcomes, are summarized under View▶Statistics. Probabilities for any event of interest can be found in various ways, which we discuss subsequently.

CRYSTAL BALL TIP
Analyzing Crystal
Ball Outputs

1. Select Crystal Ball▶Analyze▶View Charts▶Forecast Charts.
2. Click on the Forecasts of interest and select Open.
3. In the Forecast window, there are five options under View for displaying the data:

    a. Frequency

    b. Cumulative Frequency

    c. Reverse Cumulative Frequency

    d. Statistics

    e. Percentiles

4. To display the mean value on the Forecast chart, select Preferences▶Chart in the Forecast window. Select the `Chart Type` tab and select `Mean` under Marker lines.

5. To display all values of the Forecast cell, select Preferences▶Chart in the Forecast window. Select the Axis tab and select the `Fixed type` scale (from −Infinity to +Infinity). ■

15.4 CORPORATE VALUATION USING SIMULATION

In this section, we illustrate how simulation can be applied to the valuation of a company. Although valuation is often carried out with deterministic models, it is a very suitable application for Monte Carlo simulation, especially in the case of valuing a startup company.

NETSCAPE
Communications[1]

The initial public offering (IPO) of Netscape Communications Corporation on August 9, 1995, is thought to have signaled the beginning of the Internet boom. The underwriters of the IPO planned to offer five million shares at $28 per share, thereby raising $140 million. Up to that point, about $27 million had been invested in Netscape, and the company had yet to show a profit. At $28 per share, Netscape's market value would be more than $1 billion, despite a book value of just $16 million.

The IPO underwriters calculated the value of the firm by adding the present value of the free cash flows through 2005 to the present value of the firm after 2005. This latter value, known as the **terminal value**, was calculated under the assumption that the free cash flows after 2005 would grow forever at a constant rate.

The underwriters' valuation was based on an annual revenue growth rate of 65 percent. Also, the terminal value growth rate was set at 4 percent, and the tax rate was assumed to be 34 percent. Some of the other assumptions included:

Cost of sales	10.4% of revenues
R&D	34.6% of revenues
Depreciation	5.5% of revenues
Other operating expenses	80% of revenues in 1996, decreasing to 20% by 2002 and level thereafter
Capital expenses	45% of revenues in 1996, decreasing to 10% by 2000 and level thereafter
Beta	1.50
Riskless rate	6.71%
Market risk premium	7.50%

With these assumptions, a discounted cash-flow model for Netscape gave a valuation of $28 per share, supporting the underwriters' plans. ■

15.4.1 Base-case Model

Our deterministic model for this problem is shown in Figure 15.13, where all dollar amounts are shown in thousands. As usual, we have isolated the parameters in one location and grouped the calculations separately. The model includes actual values for 1995 in column B and builds the forecasts for the years 1996–2005 using recursive formulas along with growth rates and ratios given in the Assumptions section.

The free cash flows shown in row 33 are negative until 1999, but turn positive in 2000 and grow dramatically thereafter. The terminal value of the firm, which is an estimate of its value after 2005, is calculated in cell B34. Here, we take the 2005 free cash flows and project them forward one year using the

---

[1]This example is based on work of Professor Anant Sundarum.

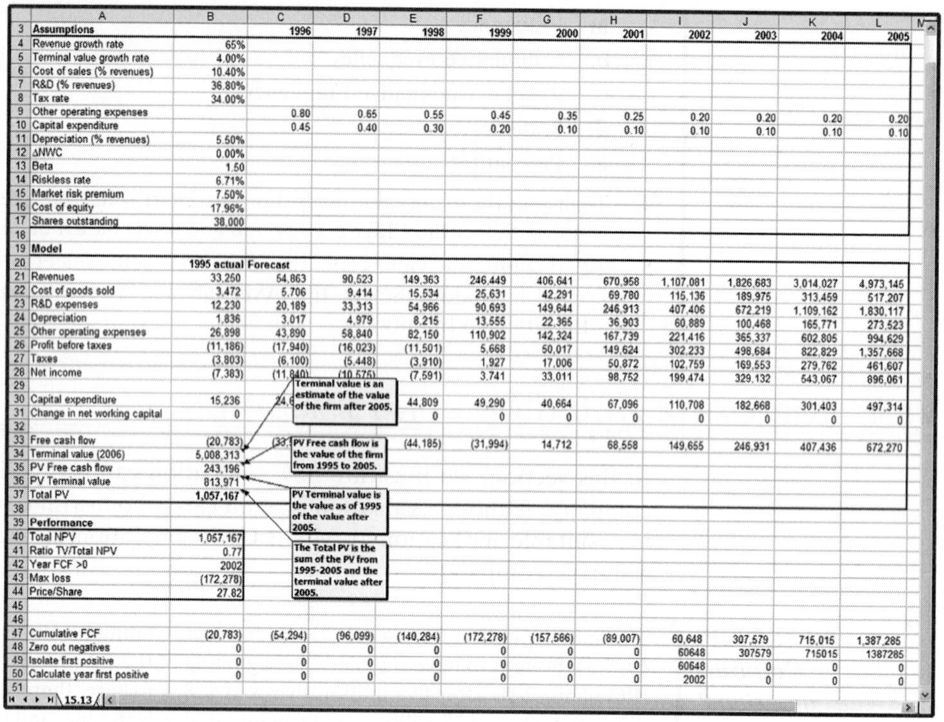

FIGURE 15.13   Deterministic Spreadsheet for Netscape

	A	B	C	D	E	F	G	H	I	J	K	L
			1996	1997	1998	1999	2000	2001	2002	2003	2004	2005
3	Assumptions											
4	Revenue growth rate	65%										
5	Terminal value growth rate	4.00%										
6	Cost of sales (% revenues)	10.40%										
7	R&D (% revenues)	36.80%										
8	Tax rate	34.00%										
9	Other operating expenses		0.80	0.65	0.55	0.45	0.35	0.25	0.20	0.20	0.20	0.20
10	Capital expenditure		0.45	0.40	0.30	0.20	0.10	0.10	0.10	0.10	0.10	0.10
11	Depreciation (% revenues)	5.50%										
12	ΔNWC	0.00%										
13	Beta	1.50										
14	Riskless rate	6.71%										
15	Market risk premium	7.50%										
16	Cost of equity	17.96%										
17	Shares outstanding	38,000										
18												
19	Model											
20		1995 actual	Forecast									
21	Revenues	33,250	54,863	90,523	149,363	246,449	406,641	670,958	1,107,081	1,826,683	3,014,027	4,973,145
22	Cost of goods sold	3,472	5,706	9,414	15,534	25,631	42,291	69,780	115,136	189,975	313,459	517,207
23	R&D expenses	12,230	20,189	33,313	54,966	90,693	149,644	246,913	407,406	672,219	1,109,162	1,830,117
24	Depreciation	1,836	3,017	4,979	8,215	13,555	22,365	36,903	60,889	100,468	165,771	273,523
25	Other operating expenses	26,898	43,890	58,840	82,150	110,902	142,324	167,739	221,416	365,337	602,805	994,629
26	Profit before taxes	(11,186)	(17,940)	(16,023)	(11,501)	5,668	50,017	149,624	302,233	498,684	822,829	1,357,668
27	Taxes	(3,803)	(6,100)	(5,448)	(3,910)	1,927	17,006	50,872	102,759	169,553	279,762	461,607
28	Net income	(7,383)	(11,840)	(10,575)	(7,591)	3,741	33,011	98,752	199,474	329,132	543,067	896,061
29												
30	Capital expenditure	15,236	24,6		44,809	49,290	40,664	67,096	110,708	182,668	301,403	497,314
31	Change in net working capital	0			0	0	0	0	0	0	0	0
32												
33	Free cash flow	(20,783)	(33,		(44,185)	(31,994)	14,712	68,558	149,655	246,931	407,436	672,270
34	Terminal value (2006)	5,008,313										
35	PV Free cash flow	243,196										
36	PV Terminal value	813,971										
37	Total PV	1,057,167										
38												
39	Performance											
40	Total NPV	1,057,167										
41	Ratio TV/Total NPV	0.77										
42	Year FCF >0	2002										
43	Max loss	(172,278)										
44	Price/Share	27.82										
45												
46												
47	Cumulative FCF	(20,783)	(54,294)	(96,099)	(140,284)	(172,278)	(157,566)	(89,007)	60,648	307,579	715,015	1,387,285
48	Zero out negatives	0	0	0	0	0	0	0	60648	307579	715015	1387285
49	Isolate first positive	0	0	0	0	0	0	0	60648	0	0	0
50	Calculate year first positive	0	0	0	0	0	0	0	2002	0	0	0

Callout notes within figure:
- Terminal value is an estimate of the value of the firm after 2005.
- PV Free cash flow is the value of the firm from 1995 to 2005.
- PV Terminal value is the value as of 1995 of the value after 2005.
- The Total PV is the sum of the PV from 1995–2005 and the terminal value after 2005.

terminal-value growth rate; then we divide by the difference between the cost of equity and the terminal-value growth rate. This calculation gives the present value in 2006 of an endless stream of cash flows growing at the terminal-value growth rate.

One interesting feature of this model is that we can measure four or five different aspects of the value of Netscape (see cells B40:B44). The single most important measure of the firm's value is the total net present value (cell B40), which adds the present value of free cash flows during 1995–2005 to the present value of the terminal value. Another interesting measure is the ratio of the terminal value to the total present value (cell B41), which reflects how much of the overall value comes after 2005. A third measure is the year in which cash flows first turn positive (cell B42), which is 2002 in the base case. Another measure that relates to financing is the cumulative loss (cell B43), or the cumulative negative free cash flow during the initial years before the cash flow turns positive. Because this is the amount that must be financed, it can indicate whether the current IPO will raise sufficient funds. Finally, we calculate the price per share (cell B44) by apportioning the total net present value of the firm to the 38,000 shares that will be outstanding after the IPO. A detailed description of the model follows.

Assumptions

Cells B4:B15: Given data.

Row 9: Other operating expenses decline from 80 percent in 1996 to 20 percent by 2002 and remain level thereafter.

Row 10: Capital expenditures decline from 45 percent in 1996 to 10 percent by 2000 and remain level thereafter.

Cell B16: Under the assumptions of the Capital Asset Pricing Model, the cost of equity for Netscape is equal to the riskless rate (cell B14), plus the product of its beta (cell B13) and market risk premium (cell B15).

Cell B17: Given data.

Model

Row 21: Data for 1995 is actual. Revenues grow at the given growth rate (cell B4) from 1996 through 2005.

Row 22: Cost of goods sold for 1996 through 2005 is revenue (row 21) times the cost of good sold percentage (cell B6).

Row 23: R&D expense for 1996 through 2005 is revenue (row 21) times the R&D percentage (cell B7).

Row 24: Depreciation for 1996 through 2005 is revenue (row 21) times the depreciation percentage (cell B11).

Row 25: Other operating expenses for 1996 through 2005 is revenue (row 21) times other operating expense percentage (row 9).

Row 26: Profit before taxes is revenues (row 21) less cost of goods sold (row 22) less R&D expenses (row 23) less depreciation (row 24) less other operating expenses (row 25).

Row 27: Taxes are profit before taxes (row 26) times the tax rate (cell B8).

Row 28: Net income is profit before taxes (row 26) less taxes (row 27).

Row 30: Capital expenditures are revenues (row 21) times the capital expenditure percentage (row 10).

Row 31: The change in net working capital is assumed to be zero throughout.

Row 33: Free cash flow is net income (row 28) plus depreciation (row 24) less capital expenditures (row 30) less change in net working capital (row 31).

Cell B34: The terminal value is calculated by taking the free cash flow in 2005 (cell L33) and multiplying it by one plus the terminal-value growth rate (cell B5). This is an estimate of the free cash flow in 2006. We then assume this value grows at the terminal-value growth rate forever. The present value of these cash flows in 2006 is calculated by discounting at the cost of equity (cell B16).

Cell B35: The present value of the free cash flows from 1995 to 2005 is the sum of the value in 1995 (cell B33) plus the net present value from 1996 to 2005 (cells C33:L33).

Cell B36: The present value of the terminal value in 2006 is the terminal value (cell B34) discounted 11 years at the cost of equity (cell B16).

Cell B37: The total present value of Netscape is the sum of the present value of free cash flows to 2005 (cell B35) and the present value of the terminal value (cell B36).

Performance

Cell B40: Total NPV is taken directly from the model (cell B37).

Cell B41: The ratio of the terminal value to the total NPV is the ratio of the terminal value (cell B36) to the total NPV (cell B37).

Cell B42: The year the free cash flow first turns positive is calculated using the intermediate calculations in rows 47 to 50. In row 47, we calculate the cumulative free cash flow by adding successive terms in row 33. In row 48, we use an IF statement to replace any negative cumulative free cash flows with zero. In row 49, we isolate the first positive free cash flow by using an AND statement to identify the cell in which free cash flow turns from negative to positive, and an IF statement to replace all other cells with zero. In row 50, we use an IF statement to determine the *year* in which the free cash flow first becomes positive. Finally, in cell B42, we add all the values across row 50, only one of which contains the year the free cash flow turns positive, all others being zero.

Cell B43: The cumulative loss is the minimum value of the cumulative free cash flows in row 47.

Cell B44: The price per share is the total present value (cell B37) divided by the number of shares outstanding (cell B17).

Our deterministic model gives us some interesting insights. The total present value of Netscape comes to more than $1 billion under this set of assumptions, apparently justifying the IPO share price. Netscape's cumulative free cash flows are expected to turn positive by 2002, but the maximum loss is more than $170 million, indicating that the proceeds from the IPO may not be sufficient to cover the investment Netscape needs to fuel its growth. Finally, the terminal value of more than $800 million makes up more than three-quarters of the total value of $1 billion. This suggests that the valuation is heavily dependent on assumptions that affect the terminal value.

15.4.2 Sensitivity Analysis

Before we turn to the uncertainty analysis, we should undertake some sensitivity testing with the deterministic model. Since we know that the terminal value makes up about 77 percent of the total present value, it is natural to ask how sensitive the terminal value is to its driving variables: the terminal-value growth rate and the market risk premium. The two-way Data Sensitivity table shown in Figure 15.14 illustrates how small changes in either the terminal-value growth rate or the market risk premium have significant effects on the terminal value of Netscape and hence on the total valuation. With the market risk premium at 7.5 percent, the terminal value ranges from about $600 million to $1.5 billion for terminal-value growth rates between 0 and 10 percent. Similarly, when we vary the market risk premium from 5 percent to 10 percent with the terminal-value growth rate at 4 percent, the terminal value ranges from $1.6 billion to $450 million.

Since we have a large number of input parameters in this model, it is also useful to create a tornado chart to evaluate which parameters most affect the valuation. The tornado chart in Figure 15.15 is based on the assumption that each parameter in the range from B4 to B15 varies up and down by the same percentage (10 percent) of its base-case value. The results suggest that the valuation is most dependent on four parameters: revenue growth rate, R&D as a percentage of revenues, beta, and the market risk premium. Since the value of beta can be estimated with reasonable accuracy from the performance of comparable companies, our uncertainty analysis focuses on the other three parameters.

15.4.3 Selecting Probability Distributions

Having built a deterministic model and having carried out various sensitivity analyses, we are now ready to undertake a risk analysis using simulation. We have identified three parameters that have a particularly strong impact on the valuation: the revenue growth rate, the R&D percentage, and the market risk premium. Based on what was known at the time about the uncertainties governing each of these parameters, we adopt the following probability distributions:

FIGURE 15.14   Two-way Data Sensitivity for Netscape

	A	B	C	D	E	F	G	H	I	J	K	L	M
1	Sensitivity of Terminal Value (TV)												
2													
3								Terminal value growth rate					
4		813971.2	0%	1%	2%	3%	4%	5%	6%	7%	8%	9%	10%
5		5.0%	1,096,993	1,191,836	1,302,215	1,432,286	1,587,836	1,777,165	2,012,615	2,313,378	2,711,005	3,261,271	4,072,946
6		5.5%	969,611	1,049,458	1,141,627	1,249,209	1,376,423	1,529,182	1,716,039	1,949,844	2,250,835	2,652,830	3,216,920
7		6.0%	859,582	927,198	1,004,677	1,094,348	1,199,334	1,323,925	1,474,179	1,658,935	1,891,616	2,193,652	2,601,479
8		6.5%	764,133	821,695	887,219	962,479	1,049,818	1,152,401	1,274,598	1,422,629	1,605,655	1,837,751	2,141,702
9	Market	7.0%	681,007	730,248	785,965	849,523	922,705	1,007,072	1,106,037	1,228,260	1,374,347	1,556,021	1,788,091
10	Risk	7.5%	608,352	650,664	698,278	752,258	813,971	Base Case: 7.5% and 4%	68	1,066,680	1,184,747	1,329,167	1,509,874
11	Premium	8.0%	544,640	581,147	622,024	668,104	720,450		62	931,129	1,027,584	1,143,906	1,286,938
12		8.5%	488,600	520,218	555,459	594,981	639,617	690,426	748,784	816,510	896,056	990,811	1,105,599
13		9.0%	439,168	466,650	497,150	531,194	569,439	612,713	662,077	718,916	785,064	863,014	956,233
14		9.5%	395,451	419,416	445,909	475,351	508,266	545,306	587,298	635,305	690,721	755,404	831,890
15		10.0%	356,693	377,656	400,745	426,303	454,747	486,595	522,498	563,282	610,016	664,103	727,429
16													

FIGURE 15.15 Tornado Chart for Netscape

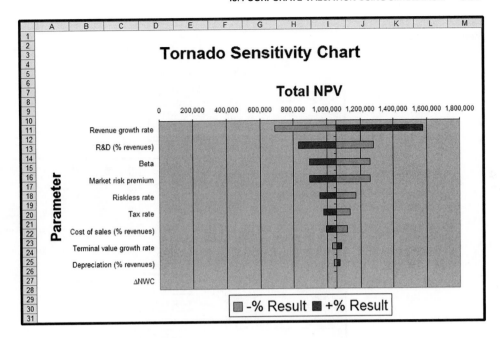

Revenue growth rate: Normal, with a mean of 65 percent and a standard deviation of 5 percent

R&D as a percentage of revenues: Triangular, with a minimum of 32 percent, most likely value of 37 percent, and a maximum of 42 percent

Market risk premium: Uniform, with a minimum of 5 percent and a maximum of 10 percent

The questions before us now are:

- How does the uncertainty in these parameters affect the valuation of Netscape?
- Was the IPO valuation justified in light of these uncertainties?

15.4.4 Simulation Analysis

Our second model for this problem, shown in Figure 15.16, includes the appropriate probability distributions for the revenue growth rate, R&D as a percentage of revenues, and the market risk premium. In the spreadsheet, these three cells are defined as Assumptions and appear with color shading. All five of the result cells discussed above are defined as Forecast cells, and they also appear with color shading. We can use the Step feature in Crystal Ball (Crystal Ball▶Run▶Step) to get a rough idea of the range of valuations that results from these uncertain inputs. We then run 1,000 trials to generate histograms for each of the five outcome measures we have described (see Figures 15.17–15.21). Analysis of these histograms sheds light on the nature of the uncertainties facing the Netscape IPO.

Figure 15.17 shows that, while the mean valuation remains around $1 billion, the present value can be as low as $236 million or as high as $3.7 billion. There is a 10 percent chance that the value will be less than about half a billion, a far cry from the deterministic valuation of $1 billion. Thus, simulation analysis allows us to quantify the extreme uncertainty in the overall value for this IPO.

Figure 15.18 shows that the terminal value is 70 to 90 percent of the total valuation. As in the deterministic case, the great majority of the total value of this firm appears to come after 10 years' time.

Figure 15.19 shows that the cumulative loss averages $173 million but can be as large as $217 million. More significantly, if the current IPO raises $140 million, there is less than a 1 percent chance that this amount will be sufficient to fund the entire future development of the company.

FIGURE 15.16 Simulation Model for Netscape

Netscape Valuation Model - Simulation Version

Assumptions

			1998	1999	2000	2001	2002	2003	2004	2005
Revenue growth rate	65%									
Terminal value growth rate	4.00%									
Cost of sales (% revenues)	10.40%									
R&D (% revenues)	36.80%									
Tax rate	34.00%									
Other operating expenses	0		0.55	0.45	0.35	0.25	0.20	0.20	0.20	0.20
Capital expenditure	0		0.30	0.20	0.10	0.10	0.10	0.10	0.10	0.10
Depreciation (% revenues)	5.50%									
ΔNWC	0.00%									
Beta	1.50									
Riskless rate	6.71%									
Market risk premium	7.60%									
Cost of equity	17.96%									
Shares outstanding	38,000									

Assumption: Revenue growth rate — Normal distribution — Mean = 65% — Std. Dev. = 5%

Assumption: R&D (% revenues) — Triangular distribution — Minimum = 32.00% — Likeliest = 37.00% — Maximum = 42.00%

Assumption: Market risk premium — Uniform distribution — Minimum = 5.00% — Maximum = 10.00%

Model

	1995 actual	Forecast									
Revenues	33,250	54,863	90,523	149,363	246,449	406,641	670,958	1,107,081	1,826,683	3,014,027	4,973,145
Cost of goods sold	3,472	5,706	9,414	15,534	25,631	42,291	69,780	115,136	189,975	313,459	517,207
R&D expenses	12,230	20,189	33,313	54,966	90,693	149,644	246,913	407,406	672,219	1,109,162	1,830,117
Depreciation	1,836	3,017	4,979	8,215	13,555	22,365	36,903	60,889	100,468	165,771	273,523
Other operating expenses	26,898	43,890	58,840	82,150	110,902	142,324	167,739	221,416	365,337	602,805	994,629
Profit before taxes	(11,186)	(17,940)	(16,023)	(11,501)	5,668	50,017	149,624	302,233	498,684	822,829	1,357,668
Taxes	(3,803)	(6,100)	(5,448)	(3,910)	1,927	17,006	50,872	102,759	169,553	279,762	461,607
Net income	(7,383)	(11,840)	(10,575)	(7,591)	3,741	33,011	98,752	199,474	329,132	543,067	896,061
Capital expenditure	15,236	24,688	36,209	44,809	49,290	40,664	67,096	110,708	182,668	301,403	497,314
Change in net working capital	0	0	0	0	0	0	0	0	0	0	0
Free cash flow	(20,783)	(33,511)	(41,805)	(44,185)	(31,994)	14,712	68,558	149,655	246,931	407,436	672,270
Terminal value (2006)	5,008,313										
PV Free cash flow	243,196										
PV Terminal value	813,971										
Total PV	1,057,167										

Performance

Total NPV	1,057,167	*Forecast: Total NPV*
Ratio TV/Total NPV	0.77	*Forecast: Ratio TV/Total NPV*
Year FCF >0	2002	*Forecast: Year FCF >0*
Max loss	(172,278)	*Forecast: Max loss*
Price/Share	27.82	*Forecast: Price/Share*

Cumulative FCF	(20,783)	(54,294)	(96,099)	(140,284)	(172,278)	(157,566)	(89,007)	60,648	307,579	715,015	1,387,285
Zero out negatives	0	0	0	0	0	0	0	60648	307579	715015	1387285
Isolate first positive	0	0	0	0	0	0	0	60648	0	0	0
Calculate year first positive	0	0	0	0	0	0	0	2002	0	0	0

Figure 15.20 shows that cumulative free cash flows turn positive in either 2002 or 2003. There is relatively little variation in the turning point.

Figure 15.21 shows that the stock price ranges from a low of about $6 to a high of $97, with a mean value of about $31. Although the stock price is closely related to the total value of the firm, this outcome measure may be more valuable to a

FIGURE 15.17 Distribution of Total NPV for Netscape

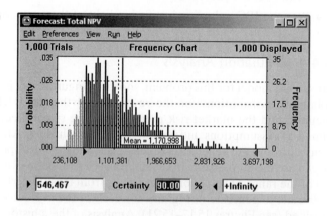

FIGURE 15.18 Distribution of Ratio of Terminal Value to Total NPV for Netscape

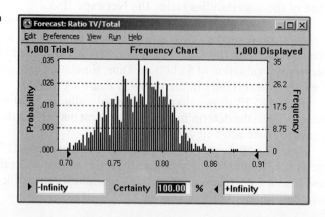

FIGURE 15.19 Distribution of Cumulative Loss for Netscape

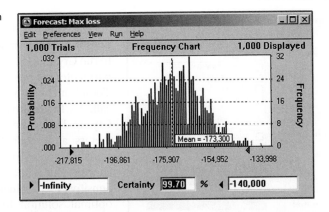

FIGURE 15.20 Distribution of Year That Cash Flows Turn Positive for Netscape

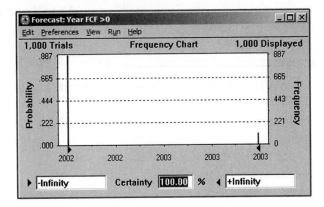

FIGURE 15.21 Distribution of Stock Price for Netscape

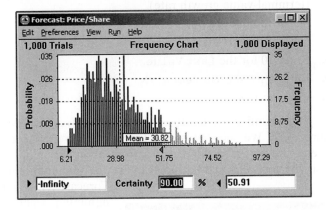

potential investor. This result shows that stock purchased at $28 today may actually be worth as little as $6; nevertheless, it has a 10 percent chance of being worth more than $50.

15.4.5 Simulation Sensitivity

The foregoing simulation analysis has allowed us to quantify the uncertainty in the future value of Netscape along a number of different dimensions. It suggests that we should be somewhat skeptical that the company's future value really supports a share price of $28. Questions remain, however. We might ask, for example, how our simulation estimates would vary if one of the underlying parameters were to change. We pointed out earlier that the terminal-value growth rate strongly influences the terminal value of the firm, which in this case accounts for most of the overall value. Thus, it is natural to ask how sensitive the expected NPV is to the terminal-value growth rate.

FIGURE 15.22 First Input Window for CB Sensitivity

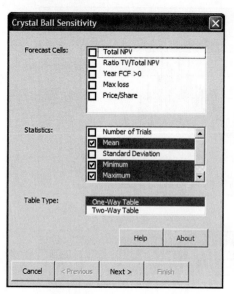

To answer this and similar sensitivity questions with a simulation model, we need to run Crystal Ball once for each value of the parameter we wish to test. Our Sensitivity Toolkit includes an option for this purpose called **CB Sensitivity**. CB Sensitivity runs Crystal Ball over a range of input parameters and records the mean (or other statistics) for as many Forecast cells as we choose. This is analogous to running Solver Sensitivity to evaluate the sensitivity of the optimal solution to an underlying parameter.

As an illustration, we run CB Sensitivity on the Netscape model, varying the terminal-value growth rate from 1 to 10 percent in increments of 1 percent.

1. Open CB Sensitivity by choosing Add-ins▶Menu Commands▶Sensitivity Toolkit▶CB Sensitivity.
2. In the first input window (see Figure 15.22), check Total NPV under Forecast cells.
3. Check Mean, Minimum and Maximum under Statistics.
4. Select One-way Table.
5. Click on Next.
6. In the second input window (see Figure 15.23) enter B5 as the Cell to Vary (terminal-value growth rate).
7. Select Input Type Begin, End, Increment.
8. Enter 1 for the First Value.
9. Enter 10 for the Last Value.
10. Enter 1 for the Increment/N.
11. Click on Finish.

The resulting values for the mean NPV are shown in graphical form in Figure 15.24. We see that as the terminal-value growth rate varies from 1 to 10 percent, the expected NPV varies from about $1 billion to $2 billion. The CB Sensitivity tool also allows us to capture the minimum and maximum values of a Forecast cell. Figure 15.24 shows that the minimum value varies little over this range, from about $0.2 billion to $0.3 billion. However, the maximum value increases from $3 billion to more than $7 billion, indicating that the likelihood of extremely high valuations increases rapidly with the terminal-value growth rate.

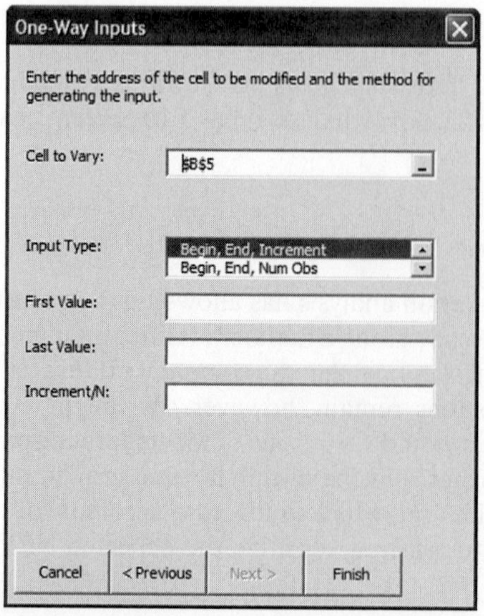

FIGURE 15.23 Second Input Window for CB Sensitivity

The Netscape valuation illustrates an approach to valuing a company that is used throughout the finance industry. One weakness of this approach is that a single growth rate is used for revenues over a period as long as 10 years, with no detailed modeling to explain the sources for this growth. Another weakness is that the terminal value often dominates the overall value of the firm, and, as we

FIGURE 15.24 NPV as a Function of Terminal Value Growth Rate

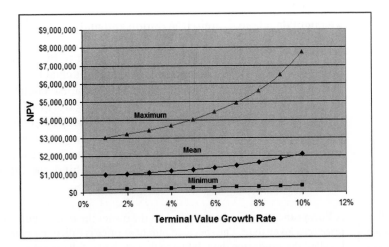

have seen, the terminal value is highly sensitive to the assumptions on which it is based. Without simulation, no insights into the effects of uncertainty would be possible, and the evaluation could easily be optimistic. Simulation reveals the range of uncertainty in the valuation itself as well as in other important aspects of the firm's future, such as the adequacy of funding.

CRYSTAL BALL TIP
Running CB Sensitivity

1. Create and run a simulation model with at least one Forecast cell.

2. Open CB Sensitivity by choosing Add-ins ▶ Menu Commands ▶ Sensitivity Toolkit ▶ CB Sensitivity.

3. In the first input window, select from among the Forecast cells listed (all Forecast cells in the selected sheet will be listed automatically).

4. Select the statistics to record from these options:

   a. Number of Trials

   b. Mean

   c. Standard Deviation

   d. Minimum

   e. Maximum

   f. Mean Standard Error

5. Select One-Way table or Two-Way table. In a one-way table, a single parameter is varied; in a two-way table, two parameters are varied independently.

6. Click on Next.

7. In the second input window, input the Cell to Vary; this is the cell that will take on a range of successive values.

8. Select Input Type:

   a. Begin, End, Increment

   b. Begin, End, Num Obs

   In the first option, the simulation is repeated for values of the parameter from the First Value to the Last Value in steps given by the Increment. In the second option, the range from First Option to Last Option is divided by the number of observations (Num Obs), and the simulation is repeated for that number of evenly spaced alternatives.

9. Input the First value, Last Value, and Increment/N.

10. Click on Finish. ■

15.5 OPTION PRICING USING SIMULATION

An **option** is the right to buy or sell an asset, without the corresponding obligation. For example, we might negotiate an option to purchase a sports franchise at any time in the coming year for a set price. If the team does well and its value increases, we might decide to exercise the option and make the purchase, but if the team does poorly, we are not obligated to buy.

Financial options, which include the right to buy or sell stocks, have become central to modern finance and investment. Financial options have value primarily because they allow the holder to hedge against changes in the value of the underlying financial asset. Billions of dollars' worth of options are traded each year. Every buyer or seller of an option has a stake in determining a fair price for the option. The theory behind option pricing is based on rather advanced mathematics, but the principles involved can be readily understood. In this example, we develop the basic concepts behind pricing options, and we use simulation to make those concepts concrete.

EXAMPLE
Pricing a European Call Option

A **European call option** on a stock gives the owner the right to purchase the stock at a specified price on a given date. The specified purchase price is called the **strike price**, and the given date is called the **expiration date**. Imagine that we had a call option with a strike price of $100 and an expiration date six months away. If the stock price on the expiration date turns out to be $105, we could make a profit of $5 by exercising the option to purchase the stock for $100 and then selling it for $105. If the stock price on the expiration date turns out to be $90, we would lose $10 if we exercised the option to buy at $100, so we would not exercise the option. This example shows that the higher the actual price is *above* the strike price, the higher the profit. But no matter how far the actual price is *below* the strike price, the owner loses nothing except the cost of acquiring the option.

A particular stock is currently selling at $35. A call option is available on this stock with an expiration date six months from today and a strike price of $40. What would be a fair market price for this option?   ∎

15.5.1 The Logic of Options

As the example shows, the value of an option depends on the actual price of the underlying stock at the expiration date. Future stock prices, of course, are not easily predicted, so it is natural to develop a probability distribution for the stock price at the expiration date. We first illustrate the concepts behind option pricing by using a simple but unrealistic distribution. Then, we develop a more realistic model for the evolution of stock prices over time, and we use it to determine option prices.

For the moment, assume there is a 50 percent chance that the stock price at expiration will be $45 and a 50 percent chance the stock price will be $35. If the price is $45, we can exercise the option and gain a profit of $5. If it is $35, we will not exercise, and we will lose nothing. The value of the option at the expiration date is called its **intrinsic value**. The intrinsic value is $5 when the price is $45; it is $0 when the price is $35.

Since we are considering buying the option today, we have to adjust for the time difference between now and the expiration date. The present value of the possible $5.00 gain is $4.83, assuming a 7 percent annual discount rate $(= 5/(1 + 0.07/2))$. The present value of the $0.00 gain if the price falls is obviously $0.00. The *expected value* of the option would be $2.41 (= 0.5 \times 4.83 + 0.5 \times 0)$. Financial theory and practice both confirm that this expected value is an appropriate market price for the option.

15.5.2 Modeling Stock Prices

Now let's return to the question of what is a realistic probability distribution for stock prices. Studies of the actual behavior of stock prices over time indicate that stocks are subject to small random changes every day, with a small upward trend. In other words, while daily prices vary, stocks show an average gain in price over longer periods. The evidence also suggests that stock prices at any date in the

FIGURE 15.25 Lognormal
Distribution

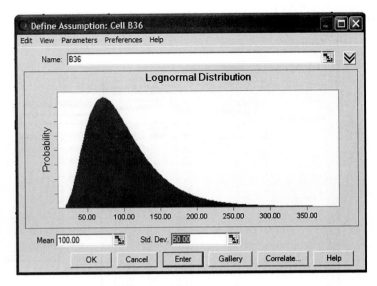

future tend to follow an asymmetric distribution, with a maximum value farther above the mean than the minimum is below it. Figure 15.25 shows a lognormal distribution, a family of distributions that is generally accepted as fitting actual stock prices quite well.

A realistic model that reproduces these aspects of actual stock prices takes the form

$$P_t = P_0 e^N \tag{15.1}$$

where P_t is the price at some future time t, P_0 is the price today, and the exponential term e^N gives the appropriate growth factor. The parameter N, which is a sample from a normal distribution, represents the return on the stock.

Stock returns are measured as the logarithm of the ratio of prices—that is, $\ln(P_t/P_0)$. Historical data on the stock's performance are used to calculate the mean μ and the standard deviation σ of the distribution of returns. Because of continuous compounding, the mean for the distribution of N is $\mu - \sigma^2/2$, while the standard deviation remains σ. Thus, the final model takes the form

$$P_t = P_0 e^{N(\mu - \sigma^2/2, \sigma)} \tag{15.2}$$

We need to convert the annual values for the parameters μ and σ to daily equivalents, in order to build a model that shows how stock prices move over shorter time periods. Since there are about 250 trading days in a year, one day represents 0.004 year. To find the daily mean, we multiply the annual price growth rate by 0.004, and we multiply the annual standard deviation by the square root of 0.004 to get a daily standard deviation. For a stock with an average annual price growth of 12 percent and an annual standard deviation of 30 percent, the equivalent daily parameters are 0.048 percent (= 0.12 × 0.004) for the mean and 1.897 percent (= 0.30 × 0.004^0.5) for the standard deviation, respectively.

Our model for projecting stock prices is shown in Figure 15.26. The key to simulating daily stock prices is generating random samples from a normal distribution with the given daily mean return and daily standard deviation. For this purpose, we use the Excel formula, EXP(CB.NORMAL($C$11,$C$12)).

The Crystal Ball function in this formula, CB.NORMAL(mean, standard deviation), takes a sample from the appropriate normal distribution. This value becomes the argument for the Excel function EXP(). Crystal Ball functions for probability distributions are a useful alternative to the Distribution Gallery for specifying Assumption cells. The list of available functions in Crystal Ball can be displayed using Formulas▶Function Library▶Insert Function and looking under the heading Crystal Ball 7.

FIGURE 15.26 Stock Price Model

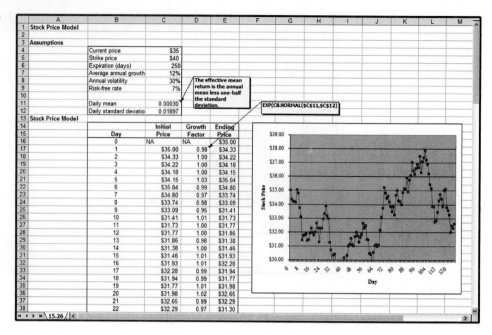

One advantage of using the Crystal Ball functions (such as CB.NORMAL) for probability distributions is that they can be copied more easily than distributions that are entered using the Distribution Gallery. Specifically, because all the formulas in cells D17:D141 involve Excel and Crystal Ball functions, we can complete the model for 125 days (six months) simply by using the Copy and Paste commands in Excel. We do not need to use the Copy Data and Paste Data commands in Crystal Ball, because the probability distributions are entered as functions, not Assumption cells. This is generally a more efficient procedure when the model involves a large number of probability distributions. A detailed description of the model follows.

Assumptions

Cells C4:C9: Given data.

Cell C11: The daily mean growth is the annual mean (cell C7) less one-half the standard deviation squared (cell C8) divided by the number of trading days in a year (cell C6).

Cell C12: The daily standard deviation of the stock price is the annual standard deviation (cell C8) divided by the square root of the number of trading days (cell C6).

Stock Price Model

Cells B16:B141: We model the evolution of the stock price from its initial value on Day 0 for 125 days, since the option to be priced is a six-month option.

Cells C17:C141: The initial price each day is the ending price from the previous day (column E).

Cells D17:D141: To determine the growth in the stock price each day, we first take a random sample from a normal distribution with the daily mean return (cell C11) and the daily standard deviation (cell C12), using the Crystal Ball function CB.NORMAL($C$11, $C$12). Then we take the exponential function (EXP()) of this quantity as specified in the model for stock price growth.

Cells E16:E141: The ending price on Day 0 is given. The ending price each subsequent day is the initial price (column C) times the growth factor for that day (column D).

FIGURE 15.27 Five Paths for Stock Prices

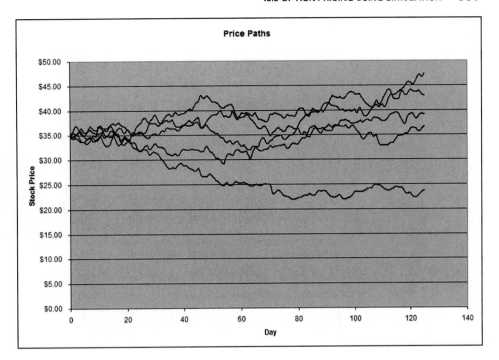

One projected price path over the six-month period is shown graphically in Figure 15.26. By using Crystal Ball▶Run▶Step and observing the graph, we can get a visual sense of the price paths this model generates. Figure 15.27 shows five of these price paths. The upward tendency in prices is evident in this graph, as well as the large degree of variability in the price.

We can determine the distribution of prices at the end of the 125-day period by designating the final price (cell E141) as a Forecast cell. Figure 15.28 shows the distribution of prices in a simulation of 1,000 trials. The mean price is $37.28, which is consistent with the 12 percent annual growth we have assumed $(\ln(37.28/35) = 6.3\%)$. The distribution also has the asymmetric shape that actual stock prices show, with a minimum value of about $20.00, or roughly half the mean, and a maximum above $80.00, more than twice the mean.

FIGURE 15.28 Distribution of Stock Prices after Six Months

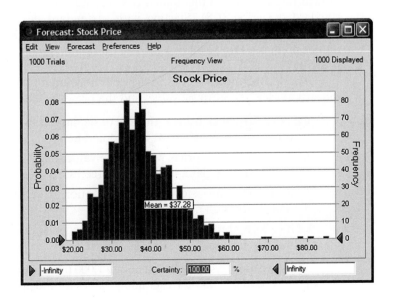

FIGURE 15.29 Option
Pricing Model

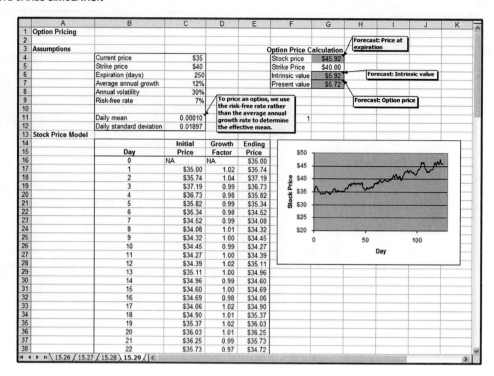

15.5.3 Pricing an Option

Now that we have a realistic model for the evolution of stock prices over time, we can return to the question of pricing the option. In the spreadsheet of Figure 15.29, we calculate the present value of the option for every randomly generated stock price. The price of an option can be calculated as the *expected value* of the *present value* of the *intrinsic value* of the option, which is its value at the terminal date. In this spreadsheet, we calculate the present value of the intrinsic value for one set of random outcomes of the daily growth factors. When we run a simulation, we create 1,000 such values and average them to calculate the expected value.

The model in Figure 15.29 is a modified version of the stock price model in Figure 15.26. First, to calculate an option price that is consistent with the risk-neutral valuation principle of finance theory, we must assume that the mean growth rate is equal to the annual risk-free rate (C9) minus one-half the squared standard deviation (C8). Starting with a standard deviation of 30 percent, we therefore obtain a mean growth rate (C7) of $2.5\% = 0.07 + (0.3)^2/2$. (For details on this point see D. L. McLeish, *Monte Carlo Simulation and Finance*, Wiley 2005, p. 109.)

The second modification creates cells in column G for the ending stock price, the strike price, the intrinsic value, and the present value:

   Cell G4: The stock price at the end of six months, when the option comes due, is calculated in cell E141 and copied here.

   Cell G5: The strike price, which is the value for which the stock can be sold at the expiration date, is given data (cell C5).

   Cell G6: The intrinsic value of the option is calculated using the formula MAX(0,G4 - G5).

   Cell G7: The present value is the intrinsic value discounted to the present at the risk-free rate.

When we use Crystal Ball to generate 1,000 trials, we obtain 1,000 values for the stock price as well as 1,000 corresponding values for the present value of the intrinsic

FIGURE 15.30 Distribution of Option Prices

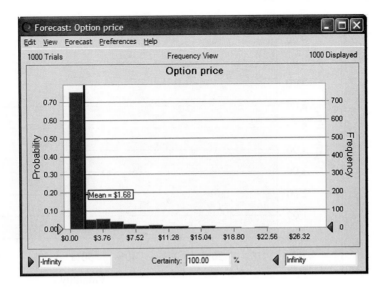

value of the option (cell G7). The average of these 1,000 values becomes our estimate of the fair market value for this option.

Figure 15.30 shows the distribution of option values. Here, we observe that about 70 percent of the time, the option has no value. In these cases, the price of the stock has not risen above the strike price ($40.00) at the end of six months, so the option is not exercised. In the other 30 percent of the cases, the stock price is above the strike price, and the option does have value. In the extreme case, the price rises to about $70.00, giving an intrinsic value of about $30.00. On average, in our sample of 1,000, the discounted value is $1.68, which is an estimate of the fair market value for this option. Note the extreme asymmetry of the distribution of option prices. As we mentioned, options are used to hedge risk. In our example, however, roughly 70 percent of the time, the option has no value. But when the stock price rises sharply, an owner of this option can make significant profits. At the extreme, for an investment of $1.68, the owner can make a profit of $30.00 in just six months' time. No wonder many investors are tempted to invest in options!

15.5.4 Sensitivity to Volatility

We can get some additional insight into the forces behind the value of options by considering the impact of variability in the stock price. We assumed that the underlying stock has an annual standard deviation of 30 percent. Would the option be worth more or less if the stock price were more volatile? To answer this question in the abstract, recall our two-price model for price uncertainty, where prices could go up to $45.00 or down to $35.00 with equal probabilities. We found that the option under these assumptions had a value of $2.41. But what if the stock price was more variable and could be $50.00 or $30.00 with equal probabilities? When the price is low, we still make nothing, but when the price is high, we make $10.00 instead of $5.00. In this case, the option is worth more than in the original case: its value is $9.66(= 10/1.035). It follows that increasing the standard deviation of a stock price increases the value of an option, because the gains increase while the losses never go below zero.

Figure 15.31 shows the results of varying the standard deviation in our option price model from 10 to 90 percent. Once again, we use the CB Sensitivity tool to carry out this set of simulations. We can see that option prices are worth very little when the underlying stock has little volatility, but they can be worth a great deal when the stock is highly volatile. Of course, the exact value is also influenced by the strike price and the time to expiration.

FIGURE 15.31 Sensitivity
of Option Price to Volatility

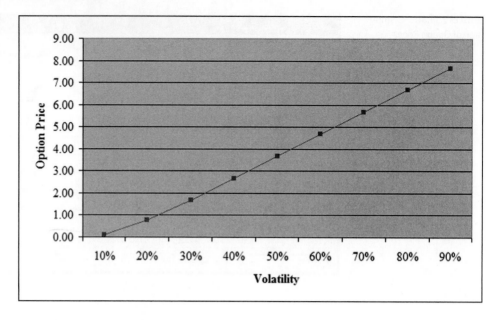

15.5.5 Simulation Accuracy

We mentioned previously that our option prices were estimates, based on a simulation of 1,000 stock prices six months out. How accurate are these estimates? One simple way to answer this question is to take repeated samples of 1,000 prices and compare estimates of the mean values. The following table shows the results of 10 simulations, each with 1,000 trials:

Run	Option price
1	$1.52
2	$1.72
3	$1.70
4	$1.65
5	$1.79
6	$1.67
7	$1.63
8	$1.81
9	$1.77
10	$1.84

Our original estimate of $1.68 is certainly in the right ballpark, but these estimates range from a low of $1.52 to a high of $1.84. We would have to take a much larger sample than 1,000 trials if we needed to determine the option price to within $0.05 or $0.01. Later, we discuss more formal methods of achieving acceptable levels of precision with simulation estimates.

15.6 SELECTING UNCERTAIN PARAMETERS

With few exceptions, there is some degree of uncertainty surrounding the true value of *every* parameter in a model. Nevertheless, it would be a mistake to treat every parameter as uncertain in a simulation analysis. As we know from our discussion of sensitivity analysis in Chapter 6, variations in many parameters have little effect on the outcomes. Therefore, randomness in these parameters will likely generate negligible randomness in the outcomes. It takes time and effort to develop an appropriate probability distribution for a parameter; this time and effort can be better used elsewhere if that parameter has little impact on the outcome.

Selecting which parameters to treat as uncertain is more an art than a science. However, some guidelines are useful. First, it is essential to carry out a deterministic analysis with the model *before* considering simulation. This involves establishing a base-case set of inputs and calculating the base-case outputs. Some thought should be given, even at this early stage, to where the base-case inputs lie within their ranges of uncertainty. In the Advertising Budget example, if we assume that the price next year is $40, we should ask whether this is the *average* price or the *minimum* price?

The next step is to perform sensitivity analysis, not only to test the model and learn about the range of possible outcomes, but also to get a sense of whether simulation is needed. In the Advertising Budget example, we might test prices as low as $30 and as high as $50. If profit does not vary significantly within this range, we have a good indication that uncertainty in price is not a central concern. (We can think of the range from $30 to $50 as a crude first attempt at defining a probability distribution for the price. In this context, we should test values at or near the extremes rather than values near the mean.)

A tornado chart is a useful way to determine which parameters have a significant impact on the outcome. In Chapter 6, we illustrated the use of tornado charts in the Advertising Budget example. We first varied each of 13 input parameters within 10 percent of its base-case value, using the Constant Percentage option in the Tornado Chart tool. The results suggested that four parameters have a significant impact on profits. For the remaining nine parameters, the impact was negligible. At this point, we could conclude that none of these nine parameters needs to be modeled as random, unless its true range of variability is much larger than ±10 percent. Hereafter, we concentrate on the top four parameters.

We also pointed out in Chapter 6 that using a single uncertainty range for all the parameters could lead to false conclusions. A 10 percent range may be realistic for one parameter, while 20 percent is realistic for another and 5 percent for a third. The critical factor is the size of the forecast error for each parameter. If these ranges are significantly different, we should assign different percentages to different inputs using the Variable Percentage option in the Tornado Chart tool. In the Advertising Budget model, consider the four parameters that appear to have the biggest impact on profits: price, cost, overhead rate, and the first sales parameter. Based on our knowledge of the situation, suppose we knew that price could vary by 5 percent around its base-case value and that cost could vary 15 percent. Similarly, suppose we knew that the sales parameter and overhead rate could both vary by 10 percent. Using these facts as the basis for a tornado chart, we generate the results shown in Figure 15.32. With these

FIGURE 15.32 Tornado Chart with Variable Percentages

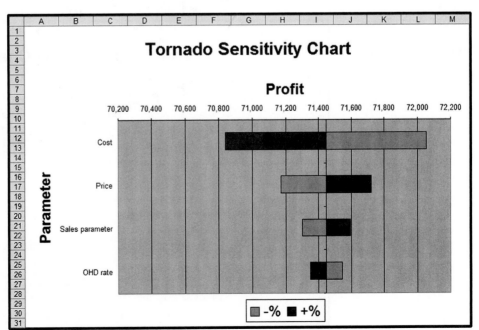

more carefully chosen ranges of variation, we conclude that uncertainty in cost has the biggest impact on profits, followed by price, the sales parameter, and overhead rate.

To this point in our sensitivity analysis, we have not associated probabilities with any of the variations we have considered. We have assigned ranges to each input, but we have not addressed the likelihood that the parameter will take on specific values within this range. Of course, if we ultimately decide to perform a simulation, we have to assign a specific probability distribution to each uncertain input. Creating these distributions can be time consuming. Therefore, it is useful to have the option to perform a deterministic sensitivity analysis, but with parameter variations that carry probabilistic interpretations. This is the purpose of the Percentiles option within the Tornado Chart tool.

The idea behind this method is to use the 10th and 90th **percentiles** of the distribution for each uncertain parameter as the endpoints of a deterministic sensitivity analysis. The 10th percentile is the number *below* which the outcome falls with probability 10 percent; the 90th percentile is the number *above* which it falls with probability 10 percent. One virtue of using this approach is that these values are not restricted to being symmetric about the base-case value. For example, when we specified a 5 percent range for price (around the $40 base-case value), we allowed it to vary from $38 to $42. This might represent a rough estimate of one standard deviation about the base-case value. But the 10th percentile value could be $33, and the 90th percentile $52, if we believe that extremely high values are more likely than extremely low ones.

Figure 15.33 illustrates the results of this approach using the Advertising Budget model. We assume the following values for the critical four parameters:

Parameter	10th Percentile	Base Case	90th Percentile
Price	33	40	52
Cost	19	25	31
Sales Parameter	30	35	40
Overhead Percentage	0.12	0.15	0.19

Price and cost continue to appear to be the most sensitive inputs, but this analysis provides additional insights over the earlier approaches. Figure 15.33 suggests that the uncertainty in cost can lead to a profit as low as −$26,000 and as high as $194,000. But the uncertainty in price leads to even greater asymmetry, from −$25,000 to $236,000.

FIGURE 15.33 Tornado Chart with Percentiles Option

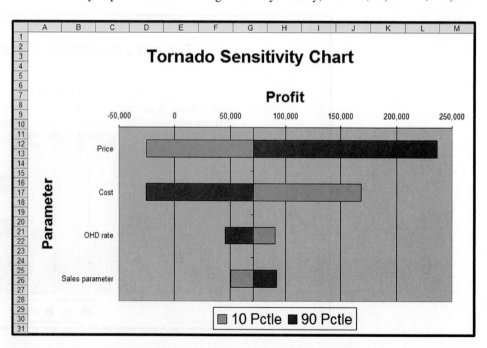

The upside potential caused by the likelihood of an extremely high price (or low cost) is an important factor that can be uncovered by using this method of analysis.

To summarize, uncertain parameters should be selected only after a thorough sensitivity analysis. The purpose of this sensitivity testing should be to discover which parameters have a significant impact on the results, and what the likely range of uncertainty is for each parameter. The process begins with simple what-if testing of high and low values. The Data Sensitivity tool can also be used to test a range of inputs and to determine whether the model is linear in the given parameter. The Tornado Chart tool can then be used to test the impact of entire sets of parameters. The easiest approach, though not the most revealing, is to vary each parameter by the same percentage (the Constant Percentage option). More information is required to assign a separate range of variation to each parameter (the Variable Percentage option), but the results are more meaningful. Finally, we can assess the extreme values of the distribution of each parameter (with the Percentiles option), to show how carefully selected extreme (and possibly asymmetric) inputs affect the outputs. While none of these methods requires us to develop a complete probability distribution, the Variable Percentage and Percentiles options do require us to think carefully about uncertainty.

15.7   SELECTING PROBABILITY DISTRIBUTIONS

Once we have selected a set of uncertain parameters, the next step is to choose a probability distribution for each one. But which type of distribution should we choose: discrete, uniform, normal, triangular, or perhaps something else? And once we have chosen a type of distribution, how do we choose its specific parameters (such as the mean and standard deviation for the normal distribution)? While Crystal Ball provides a menu of 21 types of distributions, most business analysts use only a small handful of them.

15.7.1   Empirical Data and Judgmental Data

In considering how to choose probability distributions, it is important to distinguish between **empirical data** and **judgmental data**. Empirical data consists of numerical observations from experience, such as monthly sales for the past four years or daily stock returns over the previous year. It is often assumed, especially in textbooks, that empirical data are available and are directly relevant to the problem at hand. That is often not the case in problems encountered by the business analyst. Where, for example, could we hope to get relevant empirical data on the sales of an entirely new kind of product or service, such as the sales of an Internet company a year or two after its founding?

There is, however, another source of highly relevant data for the business analyst—one that is often overlooked or devalued. This is judgmental data, such as estimates made by experts in the field or by the decision makers most closely involved in the analysis. While the marketing department may not have empirical data on new product sales, its senior members probably have many years of experience in marketing new products. This experience is legitimate knowledge, and when a group of experts such as these are carefully queried for their judgment on a particular question, that judgment should be taken seriously. With a little prior training, we can learn to ask decision makers for probability estimates such as the mean, the minimum, or the 10th and 90th percentiles needed for tornado chart analysis. As we will discuss, some probability distributions are especially suited for fitting to judgmental data, because their parameters correspond to probability questions that business experts find relatively easy to answer.

In Chapter 1, we noted that expert modelers focus more on the structure of the model and less on collection of empirical data, while novices do the reverse. Novice modelers tend to be naive about empirical data, while experts know that most data contain hidden biases and errors. By the same token, experts are typically far more aware of the benefits of using judgmental data, and are more willing to use it, than are novices. Judgmental data can often be gathered very quickly, sometimes just with a few phone calls. Within the prototyping process, early use of judgmental data can help test and debug an initial model. If sensitivity testing suggests that more accurate information is needed about a particular parameter, then the time and effort to acquire empirical data may be justified.

The traditional answer to the question of which distribution to choose is to select the distribution that provides the "best fit to the data," where the reference is usually to empirical data. However, at least four aspects of this advice can be misleading:

- In most cases, unless we are doing scientific research, no empirical data at all will be available. (Judgmental data, on the other hand, are usually available.)
- Even if empirical data are available, the information may be biased or otherwise inappropriate for the purposes at hand.
- Even if appropriate empirical data are available, it requires judgment to determine whether the distribution that provides the best fit to the given empirical data is appropriate in the model.
- In many cases, the results of interest depend on the mean and variance of an uncertain parameter, but not on the specific form of the probability distribution.

For all these reasons, we believe that empirical data alone are seldom sufficient. Even when empirical data are available, it takes careful judgment to decide whether some or all of that data should be used. Often, we also have some judgmental data at hand, if only the opinions of the decision makers, and these data should be combined with the empirical data when choosing a probability distribution. Effectively using data requires good judgment, not merely good statistical technique.

15.7.2 Six Essential Distributions

While Crystal Ball provides 21 types of probability distributions, many of these are specialized and rarely used. In business analysis, six families of distributions are used most heavily: the Yes/No, discrete uniform, binomial, continuous uniform, triangular, and normal.

The **Yes/No** distribution is used in situations where an uncertain parameter can take on one of only two possible values. For example, a competitor can either enter the market next year or not. This uncertain event can be described by a Yes/No distribution having the outcome 1 (for entry) and 0 (for no entry), with suitable probabilities. Figure 15.34 shows a Yes/No distribution with a probability of Yes of 0.8.

FIGURE 15.34 A Yes/No Distribution

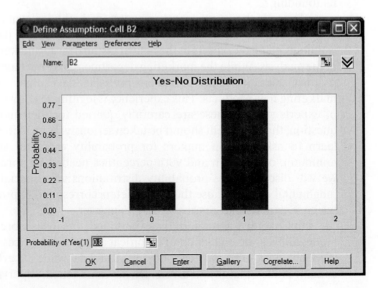

FIGURE 15.35 A Discrete
Uniform Distribution

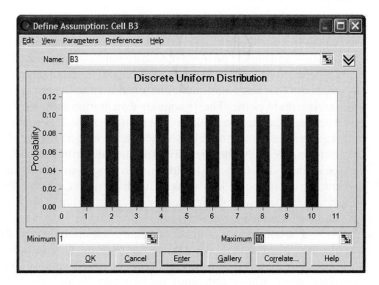

We often wish to model a random outcome that takes on a small number of discrete values. For example, the lifetime of a customer might be random between 1 and 10 years, with fractional values having no meaning. In this case, the **discrete uniform** distribution can be used, as shown in Figure 15.35. For another example, we might represent future market share as being High, Medium, or Low with equal probabilities. If we used the number 3 for High, 2 for Medium, and 1 for Low, the states would be numerically valued. A discrete uniform distribution from 1 to 3 would represent this situation well. (On the other hand, if we assumed the probability of High share were 0.25, Medium share 0.50, and Low share 0.25, then we would use the Custom distribution instead.)

The **binomial** distribution is used for the number of outcomes on repeated trials. For example, if a drug is successful in treating a disease in an individual 70 percent of the time and it is tested on 10 patients, the binomial distribution gives the probability of the number of successful treatments. The binomial distribution is specified by two parameters: the number of trials and the probability of success on each trial. In our example these parameters are 10 and 0.7. Figure 15.36 shows the binomial distribution for the number of successes in 10 trials where the probability of success on each trial is 70 percent.

Three continuous distributions provide a good deal of flexibility in capturing the kind of variability encountered in decision problems. The **continuous uniform** distribution (called simply the Uniform distribution in Crystal Ball) describes an

FIGURE 15.36 A Binomial
Distribution

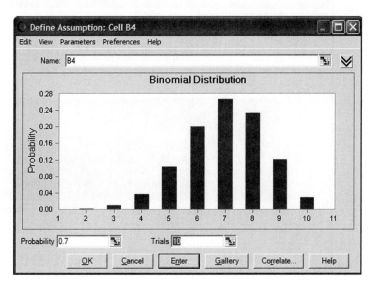

outcome that is equally likely to fall anywhere between a minimum and a maximum value. It is particularly appropriate when we can make a reasonable guess about the smallest and largest possible outcomes but have no reason to suspect that any values in between are more likely than others. The **triangular** distribution describes an outcome that has a minimum and maximum value but is most likely to occur at an intermediate point. The triangular distribution is more flexible than the uniform because it can have a peak anywhere in its range. It is well suited to situations where we can identify a most likely outcome as well as the smallest and largest possible outcomes. Finally, the **normal** distribution describes an outcome that is most likely to be in the middle of the distribution, with progressively smaller likelihoods as we move away from its most likely value. This distribution, which is familiar to many analysts, can describe a symmetric uncertain quantity using only two parameters (the mean and the standard deviation).

The continuous uniform distribution is often the first distribution we use when prototyping a model. We choose the uniform distribution because it is so easy to specify, requiring only a minimum and maximum value. Figure 15.37 shows a uniform distribution whose outcomes lie between 50 and 150. The mean for a uniform distribution is midway between the minimum and maximum values (100 in this case). The critical property that defines the uniform distribution is that every outcome between the minimum and the maximum is equally likely. Often, this is a reasonable assumption, especially when first testing the effects of uncertainty in a model and when no empirical data or other kinds of information are available to suggest different likelihoods.

The triangular distribution is a more flexible family of continuous distributions. These distributions are specified by three parameters: the minimum, maximum, and most likely values. Figure 15.38 shows a triangular distribution from 50 to 150, with a most likely value of 125. Triangular distributions are particularly useful for representing judgmental estimates. Very few managers can specify offhand a probability distribution for an uncertain quantity, but most can give reasonable estimates for the minimum, maximum, and most likely values.

The normal distribution is a symmetric distribution, usually specified by its mean and standard deviation. The normal distribution shown in Figure 15.39 has a mean of 100 and a standard deviation of 25. The normal is often appropriate for representing uncertain quantities that are influenced by a large number of independent factors, such as the heights of a group of people or the physical measurements of a manufactured product. But the normal is often overused, perhaps because it is prominent in statistics, where it plays a central role. The normal should not be used

FIGURE 15.37   A Continuous Uniform Distribution

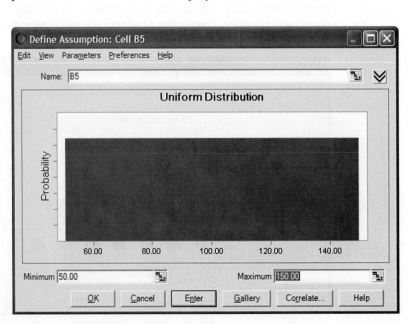

FIGURE 15.38   A Triangular Distribution

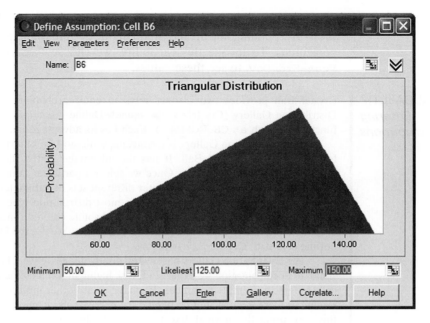

unless there is reason to believe the distribution is symmetric. It also has the sometimes problematic property that negative outcomes are possible, especially if the standard deviation is large relative to the mean. Thus, the normal would not be an appropriate probability model for demand or price, unless the standard deviation were small relative to the mean (say, 25 percent of the mean or less).

Most commonly, the normal distribution is defined in terms of its mean and standard deviation, but Crystal Ball provides the option to use alternative input parameters. (This option is also available for many other continuous distributions.) For example, when we choose `Parameters` from the menu options for the normal distribution, Crystal Ball offers these options: 10th and 90th percentile, 5th and 95th percentile, mean and 90th percentile, mean and 95th percentile, or `Custom` (with the `Custom` option, we can define the distribution using any two percentile values). It is particularly handy to use the 10th and 90th percentiles if they have already been determined for a tornado chart analysis. Then, if a normal distribution seems indicated, it is not necessary to determine the mean and standard deviation, since

FIGURE 15.39   A Normal Distribution

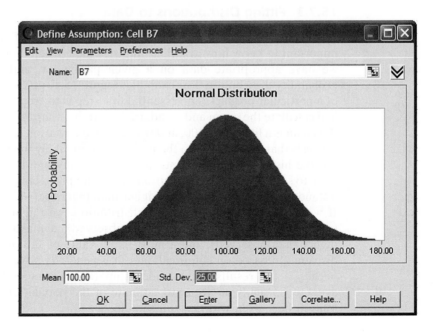

the 10th and 90th percentiles can be entered directly. Crystal Ball calculates the corresponding mean and standard deviation when given the 10th and 90th percentiles. To invoke this capability, we choose `Parameters` again and select `Mean-Std.Dev.` to see these values.

<table>
<tr>
<td>

CRYSTAL BALL TIP

Entering

Distributions

</td>
<td>

Crystal Ball provides two distinct ways to enter probability distributions: through the Distribution Gallery (Crystal Ball▶Define▶Define Assumption) or through Crystal Ball functions (such as `CB.NORMAL`). Each has its advantages and disadvantages.

The Distribution Gallery is a convenient method for entering distributions, especially for new users of Crystal Ball. It has the advantage that it displays all of the available distributions in a visual format. Once we select a particular family of distributions, such as the uniform or triangular, we can enter different sets of parameter values and see how they change the shape of the distribution. For most distribution types, we can enter parameter values either directly or through relative or absolute cell references. In addition, the color-coding of assumption cells occurs automatically when we use the Distribution Gallery; this is not the case with Crystal Ball functions.

The Distribution Gallery has several disadvantages as well. First, it does not provide the standard documentation we expect in Excel: highlight a cell defined as a distribution, and the cell contents are simply a number. We have to use other methods, such as color-coding, to remind us there is a distribution behind the cell. We also cannot copy and paste cells defined this way using the normal Excel commands. Instead, we must use the Crystal Ball▶Define▶Copy and Crystal Ball▶Define▶Paste options within Crystal Ball. Confusing these two ways of copying is a common source of errors in building simulation models. Finally, a distribution entered this way cannot be embedded into an Excel function.

The alternative to using the Distribution Gallery is to use Crystal Ball functions for distributions, such as `CB.NORMAL` or `CB.TRIANGULAR`. Crystal Ball provides a function for every distribution available in the Distribution Gallery. These functions act just like any other Excel functions, so they can be embedded in other functions, are self-documenting, and can take inputs from other cells. They can also be copied using the standard Excel Copy and Paste commands. Many users of Crystal Ball eventually gravitate toward using these functions instead of using the Distribution Gallery.

Using the Crystal Ball functions for distributions also has some drawbacks. One is that the user must learn the required inputs and their order. Another is that the shape of the distribution is not visible. Finally, Crystal Ball does not recognize a distribution function as an Assumption cell. Because certain specialized tasks in Crystal Ball itself require the use of Assumption cells, it is still sometimes necessary to enter distributions using the Distribution Gallery. ■

</td>
</tr>
</table>

15.7.3 Fitting Distributions to Data

Although it is important to understand the limitations of empirical data, it is also important to know how to utilize empirical data when they are available. Assume we have appropriate data on a given parameter, and we wish to choose a probability distribution. For example, Figure 15.40 gives 50 observations on sales of a particular product. The essential first step is to create a histogram of the data and calculate the mean and standard deviation, as shown in the figure. We see that the mean is a little over 100, and the standard deviation is about 24. The histogram suggests that values close to the mean are more likely than values at the extremes, but the histogram does not strongly suggest any one type of distribution. If we were to select a normal distribution, we would probably choose a mean of 100 and a standard deviation somewhat higher than that observed in the data, say 30 or 35. If we were to select a triangular distribution, we might pick a minimum of 40 (somewhat below the lowest value observed), a maximum of 170 (somewhat higher than observed), and a most likely value of 110 or 120. When choosing a distribution based on empirical data, it is generally advisable to widen the range because actual results tend to underestimate the extremes. By contrast, the sample average is usually an accurate estimate of the population mean, and there is no built-in bias, even with a small sample.

FIGURE 15.40 Using Data to Choose a Distribution

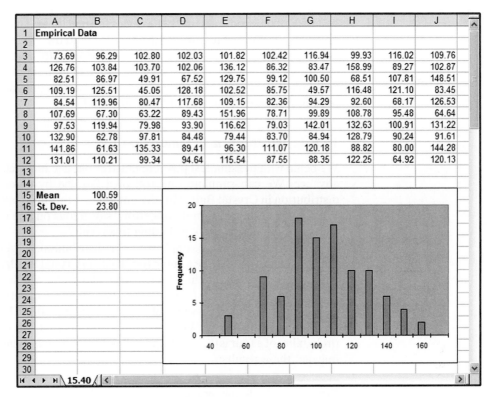

Crystal Ball provides several formal methods for fitting a distribution to a set of empirical data. One alternative, which is useful for fitting one distribution at a time, is to use the Fit option in the Distribution Gallery. If we need to fit a number of distributions, the Batch Fit tool (Crystal Ball▶Run▶Tools ▶Batch Fit) is the preferred approach. More details about how to use these tools can be found in Appendix 15.2.

Summarizing this section, we recommend tackling the problem of choosing probability distributions with a liberal amount of judgment supported by judicious use of data analysis. In our experience, it is often the mere recognition of variability in the critical parameters that gives rise to the vital business insights, not the specific form of the probability distributions chosen to represent that variability. For example, it would be a rare case in which the essential decisions would change if we replaced a triangular distribution with a similar normal distribution in the analysis. This can happen, but it is unusual unless there are major benefits or costs corresponding to outcomes in the tails of the probability distribution. Thus, time spent trying to identify the best probability distribution for a parameter is probably not time well spent.

15.8 ENSURING PRECISION IN OUTPUTS

Every time we run a simulation, we are performing an experiment. The purpose of this experiment is to estimate some quantity, such as the expected value of profit or the probability of a loss. With any simulation result, there is some difference, or error, between our estimate and the true value we are after. Thus, our estimate of the mean profit and the true value of the mean profit differ by some amount of **simulation error**. As with any good experiment, a well-planned simulation study requires effort to measure this error. More specifically, we must ensure that whatever conclusions we draw from the simulation study are not seriously compromised by simulation error.

Simulation error is not the only source of error in our modeling efforts. It may not even be the most important source of error. All models are abstractions of the real situation they mimic, and for that reason, they differ in their behavior from the real thing. We can use the term **model error** to refer to this divergence between the behavior of the model and the behavior of the real thing. The essence of modeling is to abstract the essential features of the problem and then to interpret the model results in order to gain useful insights about the behavior of the real system. In most practical situations, model error is a much larger problem than simulation error. Nonetheless, simulation error itself can cause problems in interpreting model results, and for that reason, it should be measured and controlled.

15.8.1 Illustrations of Simulation Error

We begin with the simplest possible illustration, one in which we know the answer in advance. We can simulate one roll of a fair die by entering a discrete uniform distribution in Crystal Ball, with the outcomes 1 through 6 all having probability 1/6. We know that the probability of getting, say, a four on one roll is 1/6 or 0.1667; how well does simulation work at finding this result?

Each time we take a sample from this distribution, we get one outcome of rolling the die. When we draw one sample (or "trial" in Crystal Ball language), we may get the value three. Based on this information alone, we would have to conclude the probability of getting a four is zero. The difference between the true value of 0.1667 and the estimated value of zero is very large: 0.1667. This is the error in our simulation at this point. When we run a second trial, we may get a one. Still, the probability of a four is $0 (= 0/2)$, and still the error is high. When we run 10 samples, we may get these results:

Trial	Result for Die
1	3
2	1
3	5
4	4
5	3
6	2
7	5
8	5
9	4
10	3

In these 10 trials, we find that four appears twice, so our estimate of the probability of getting a four is now $0.20 (= 2/10)$. The simulation error is now $0.0333 (= 0.2 - 0.1667)$, which is much smaller than it was with one or two trials. If we run 100 trials, we get 16 fours. Our estimate now is 0.16 with an error of 0.0067. Finally, if we run 1,000 trials, we get 161 fours, and our estimate of the probability of a four is 0.161 with an error of 0.0057.

This example illustrates several important points. To begin with, small samples can lead to large errors. However, even a sample of 1,000 trials is insufficient to determine the answer perfectly. We do, however, tend to get closer and closer to the right answer as the number of trials increases. We exploit this fact in developing methods for estimating simulation outcomes with acceptable precision.

Let's take a closer look at simulation error in a realistic application before we suggest strategies for dealing with it. Refer again to the Advertising Budget example. We know that profit is $71,447 when the price is $40 for certain. The mean profit remains $71,447 even when price is uniformly distributed between $30 and $50. Now let's see how the number of trials of a simulation affects our estimate of the mean profit.

For dramatic effect, we start with one trial: Choosing Step from the Run group creates a single sample from the distribution for price and displays a single sample for profit. In our run, we found that price is $42.05 and profit is $99,617. (In other trials, we would get different results.) Since we have only one sample for profit, it becomes our best estimate for the mean, but the simulation error is huge: $\$99,617 - \$71,447 = \$28,170$ (or 39 percent above the true mean). Of course, no one would seriously suggest taking only a single sample in a simulation. How much closer to the true value would we get if we took, say, 10 samples and averaged them? The following table shows typical results.

Trial	Result for Profit
1	$99,617
2	−2,246
3	84,813
4	189,680
5	−206
6	10,663
7	66,730
8	185,044
9	83,019
10	201,057

The average of these 10 trials is $78,579, with a simulation error of $7,132 (10 percent). This is still a significant error, but we see that the larger sample has brought us considerably closer to the true mean of $71,447. Would 100 samples be good enough? When we run 100 trials, we get an average of $73,911, or an error of only $2,464 (3 percent). Now we're getting close. With 1,000 trials, we get an average of $71,444, which is indistinguishable from the true mean profit.

What have we learned? Clearly, a sample of 1 or even 10 is not nearly enough in this situation. But a sample of size 1,000 is probably close enough for even the most demanding client. In fact, 1,000 trials may be overkill for practical purposes. As we should expect, the precision of any simulation estimate increases as the run length increases.

15.8.2 Precision Versus Accuracy

It is important to develop some terminology before we address simulation error from a technical point of view. We assume there is a probability distribution for the outcome of interest—profit in our example—although we do not know what that distribution is. Our interest is in particular aspects of this distribution, such as its expected value or the probability of a particular range of profit outcomes. Because of the complexity of our model, we cannot determine these quantities exactly but must resort to simulation. Using simulation, we create a set of sample outcomes for profit from which we can estimate features of the probability distribution for profit. If our goal is to determine the expected value of profit, we compute the average of all the simulation outcomes. For clarity, we refer to this average as the **sample average**, to distinguish it from the true mean profit.

The sample average is an estimate of the true mean. (The sample average of the 10 trials for the Advertising Budget example was $78,579.) Likewise, if we wish to determine the probability of a loss in our simulation, we compute the percentage of outcomes in which a loss occurs. This percentage is the **sample proportion**, an estimate of the true probability of a loss. Whether we are interested in a mean value or a tail probability, our simulation produces an estimate of the true quantity. Our goal here is to understand and control the error in this estimate.

It is important to distinguish between *precision* and *accuracy*. A single sample gives us a perfectly accurate estimate of the true mean profit, as long as there is no bias in the process. Technically, we are saying that the expected outcome of a single sample is the true mean. In this sense, a sample average from a large sample is no more *accurate* than a sample average from a sample of size one. But an estimate based on the larger sample is more *precise* than an estimate based on a sample of one, because the *variance* of the sample average declines with the sample size. In other words, a second sample of size one will most likely be very different from the first, whereas another sample of size 1,000 will most likely *not* be very different from the first, at least for the purposes of estimating the true mean. Repeated batches of samples are more like each other (that is, they show less variability) as the sample size increases, and they are therefore more precise.

While it is important to ensure an appropriate level of precision in our results, there is a trade-off between the *precision* of the results and the *time* it takes to get them. We know that time is valuable for practical modelers, and time spent doing simulation runs may come at the expense of time spent formulating the model, testing, collecting data, or carrying out some other aspect of the modeling process. Thus, an effective modeler does not waste time on long simulation runs unless the additional precision has more value than the next best use of that time.

On a contemporary desktop computer, it takes about three seconds to run 1,000 trials for the Advertising Budget model and only about seven seconds to run 100,000 trials. This suggests that we can easily afford the time for the precision we get at 1,000 trials, and we might even think about increasing the run length if more precision is valuable. But this is a very simple simulation model, so the trade-off between time and precision favors precision. However, it is not difficult to construct a spreadsheet model for which 1,000 trials would take hours. In such a case, it is worthwhile to investigate more carefully how much precision is really needed and to choose a run length that provides sufficient precision without taking too much time.

15.8.3 An Experimental Method

The simplest approach to determining the precision of a simulation estimate is to experiment with multiple independent runs. (More formal methods are covered in Appendix 15.2.) To do this, we must ensure that different random numbers are used each time we run a simulation. In Crystal Ball, we select Run▶Run Preferences, select the Sampling tab, and make sure the Use same sequence of random numbers box is *not* checked. Now we pick an initial sample size—say, 100. We perform 5 to 10 simulations using this run length and compare the estimates of the outcome measure. Are they close to each other or far apart? If they are too far apart for our purposes, we have not achieved sufficient precision in our estimates, and so we cannot rely on any single run at the current run length. We therefore increase the run length, possibly to 500 or 1,000. We make another 5 or 10 runs at this new run length and again compare the results. When the set of results has a sufficiently small range, we have an appropriate sample size.

We can illustrate this procedure with the Advertising Budget model. We set the run length to 100 trials and carry out five runs. The five successive estimates of profit are given in the following table:

Trial	Result for Profit
1	$64,766
2	70,017
3	69,759
4	64,441
5	71,046

If we didn't know that the true profit was $71,447, so that we had only these five observations to work with, we might conclude that there was too much variability in these results to rely on any one of them. If we increase the run length to 500 trials and run 5 runs, we get the following results:

Trial	Result
1	$71,453
2	71,452
3	71,450
4	71,438
5	71,455

Whereas the range from lowest to highest was $6,280 with 100 trials, with 500 trials, it is only $17, quite possibly enough precision for our purposes. Just to be sure, we can perform five runs at 1,000 trials. Here, the results range from $71,442 to $71,449, a difference of only $7. The range of results on independent runs gets narrower as the number of trials increases.

CRYSTAL BALL TIP
Setting Run Length

Use independent random seeds.

Select a low run length.

Perform a small number of independent samples and compare results.

If the range of results is too wide, increase the run length and repeat the process from the start.

Stop when the range of results among independent samples is small enough, given the precision needed in the problem.

15.8.4 Simulation Error in a Decision Context

We offer one final word on the subject of simulation error. Sometimes, because they have lost sight of the broader context, analysts devote excessive effort to ensuring that individual simulation runs are highly precise. But the ultimate goal of a simulation study is usually not to estimate a single number. The broader goal is to provide help in making a decision. The ultimate test of our efforts is whether we have made a good *decision*, not whether our simulation results are highly precise. True, simulation error can lead to bad decisions, but it is only one source of error. As we have pointed out, the modeling process itself introduces errors by the very nature of the abstraction process; the model is not the real world. So the model we use to represent the world itself contains errors, and increasing the simulation run length cannot in any way reduce those errors. In addition, extreme precision may not be necessary if our goal is to make the best decision. (We return to this issue in the next chapter, when we discuss optimization in simulation.)

For example, imagine we are estimating the NPV of a single project in which the choices are simply to accept the project or reject it. Our decision criterion is to accept the project if the NPV is positive and otherwise to reject it. Our simulation model, using a run length of 100, shows an NPV of $12.7 million and repeated runs range from $9 to $15 million. Now this is not a very precise estimate of the NPV. But the chances are slim that the NPV is *negative*, so the decision to accept is pretty clear. In this case, a run length of 100 trials seems fully justified. If we were choosing *between* two projects, however, this level of precision might not be sufficient. If the competing project were to show an estimated NPV of 13.9 million and a range from $10 million to $14 million in repeated runs, we could not be confident that the second project was actually better than the first. In this case, a longer run length would be needed to correctly identify which of these two projects has the higher expected NPV.

15.9 INTERPRETING SIMULATION OUTCOMES

When we run a simulation with, say, 1,000 trials, the raw result is simply a file of 1,000 values for each outcome, or Forecast cell. Fortunately, we rarely have to work with the raw data directly. Instead, we use Crystal Ball to display and summarize the results for us. Most often that summary takes the form of a histogram, or frequency

FIGURE 15.41   The
Forecast Preferences
Window

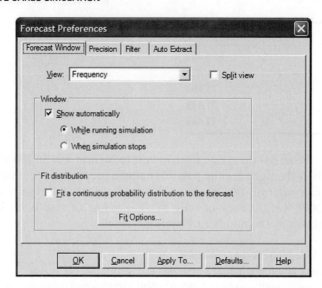

chart, but there are other ways of summarizing output data. We first discuss how to use the Forecast chart and then the Statistics and Percentiles views.

15.9.1   Forecast Charts

In the Advertising Budget example, our outcome cell is Profit, and the Forecast window is shown in Figure 15.4. Normally, the Forecast window displays the histogram in the form of a frequency distribution, but options are available (under View in the Forecast window) to display it as a cumulative or reverse cumulative distribution. We can modify the appearance of this chart in various ways by selecting Preferences▶Forecast or Preferences▶Chart.

The Forecast Preferences window (Figure 15.41) has four tabs whose functions are as follows.

- `Forecast Window`: Select the view of the data, determine whether it will be displayed automatically while running or when stopped, and fit a distribution to the results.
- `Precision`: Set the parameters for Precision Control (see Appendix 15.2).
- `Filter`: Include or exclude specified values.
- `Auto Extract`: Automatically display the mean or other statistics on the spreadsheet.

The Chart Preferences window (Figure 15.42) has three tabs whose functions are:

- `General`: Set chart title, number of bins for histogram, and special effects.
- `Chart Type`: Set chart type and marker lines, such as the mean.
- `Axis`: Set axis label, scale, and format.

One particular feature of the Forecast window is worth highlighting. The number of trials that have been *run* is shown near the top of the window on the left, while the number of trials actually *displayed* is shown on the right. In many cases, the number displayed is less than the number run. (Crystal Ball does not usually display extreme outliers unless explicitly commanded to do so.) To ensure that all the trials are displayed, select Preferences▶Chart▶Axis and under `Scale`, select `Fixed`.

Figure 15.5 illustrates the use of the **certainty sliders**, the small black triangles at the extreme right and left of the histogram. These triangles can be moved to select a range of outcomes. Crystal Ball displays the percentage of trials that lie in the highlighted range in the Certainty window at the bottom of the chart. This is one way

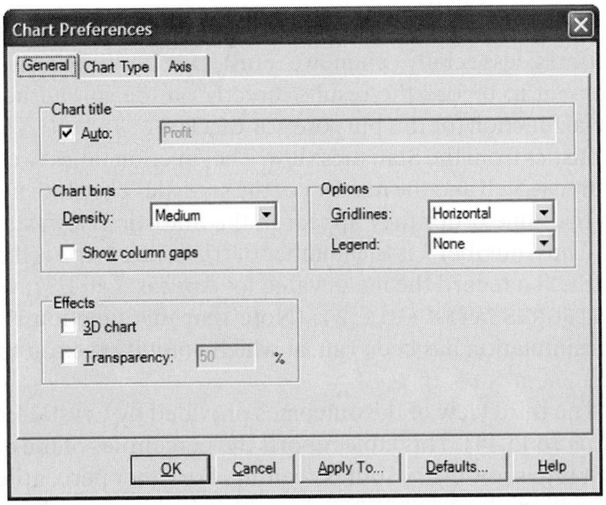

FIGURE 15.42 The Chart
Preferences Window

to determine a tail probability. As an alternative, we can enter numbers directly in the boxes at the bottom of the window; when we press Enter, Crystal Ball uses these limits to calculate the Certainty value.

Although it can be very convenient to use the Forecast window to estimate tail probabilities, this method can sometimes be quite inaccurate. Crystal Ball does not calculate the estimates from the underlying simulation data, but rather from the histogram itself. Because the histogram is only a summary of the underlying data, the required estimate can be quite rough. A more precise alternative is to define a Forecast cell in the model that takes on the value 1 when the event in question occurs (such as NPV > 0) and 0 otherwise. When the Forecast window for this cell is displayed, it shows the probability estimate without any error due to summarizing the data.

15.9.2 Statistics and Percentiles

More detailed information on the outcome distribution can be found by choosing View▶Statistics in the Forecast window (see Figure 15.43). This table shows the number of `Trials`, the `Mean`, and a host of other summary measures. The most useful of these are the `Minimum`, `Maximum`, and the `Mean Std. Error`. The minimum and maximum are simply the extreme values encountered during the simulation run. They correspond to the best and worst cases, which are often of special interest. The mean standard error, discussed in Appendix 15.2, is a useful tool for determining the precision of the estimate of the mean.

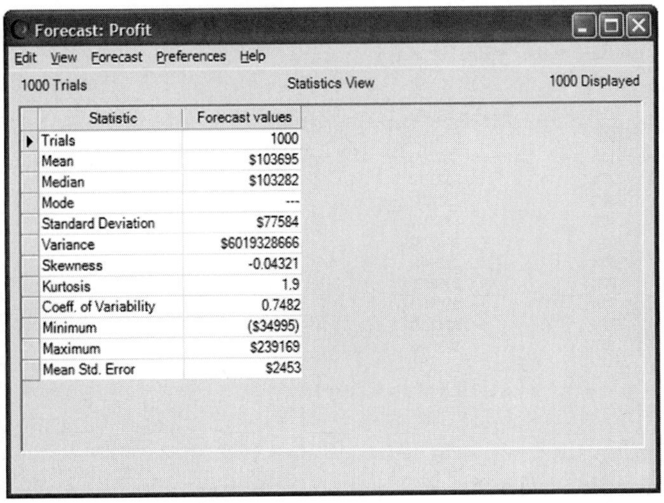

FIGURE 15.43 The
Statistics View

In most cases, we refer to the Forecast window to find the results of a simulation. Sometimes, especially when we must run a simulation many times, it is more convenient to record the results directly on the spreadsheet. Crystal Ball provides a special function for this purpose: CB.GETFORESTATFN. This function records any of the statistics from the Statistics view. The function takes two inputs: the cell address of the Forecast cell and the number of the statistic. The statistics are numbered from 1 to 12, in the same order they appear in the Statistics view, starting with the number of trials. Thus, number 1 is the number of trials, number 2 is the mean, and number 12 is the MSE. To record the mean value for forecast cell E11, we would use the function CB.GETFORESTATFN (E11,2). (Note that this function returns the result #VALUE until a simulation has been run, at which point it takes on the appropriate numerical value.)

The third view of the outcomes provided by Crystal Ball is the Percentiles view (see Figure 15.44). This table reports the percentiles of the outcome distribution. The default is to show every 10th percentile. For other percentiles, we can use the Crystal Ball function CB.GETFOREPERCENTFN, which returns the given percentile value of a Forecast cell. For example, CB.GETFOREPERCENTFN(E11,25) returns the 25th percentile of the Forecast cell E11.

In some circumstances, it is useful to work directly with the simulation data itself and not with the various Crystal Ball Forecast windows. The option Analyze ▶ Extract Data allows the user to create a spreadsheet containing the raw results for each Forecast cell. This is particularly useful if custom graphs are desired. A related option is Analyze ▶ Create Report, which allows the user to create a spreadsheet with both the input assumptions and the outputs. This is a handy means of documenting multiple runs of the same model. More details on these options are available in Appendix 15.2.

While most of this discussion has been devoted to the details of finding specific summary measures for simulation results, there is more to the art of interpreting simulations. First, we must take care in defining outcome variables. Unless we capture the essential aspects of the model, our interpretations will be handicapped. Having done this, we must then ensure that our estimates are sufficiently precise to support meaningful interpretation. Finally, we come to the results themselves. In most simulations, we are interested in both the expected outcome and the variability in outcomes. These two aspects of the situation are captured in the mean value, in the variance (or standard deviation), and in tail probabilities. Often, the value of simulation comes from providing insight into the trade-off between the expected outcome and the associated risks. This trade-off is illustrated well in the Netscape IPO example discussed earlier, where a deterministic analysis supported a high value for the company, whereas the simulation analysis revealed some extreme risks associated with the IPO.

FIGURE 15.44 The Percentiles View

Percentile	Forecast values
0%	($34995)
10%	($8461)
20%	$23207
30%	$57317
40%	$82142
50%	$103282
60%	$129444
70%	$152799
80%	$183141
90%	$212222
100%	$239169

Forecast: Profit

Edit View Forecast Preferences Help

1000 Trials   Percentiles View   1000 Displayed

CRYSTAL BALL TIP
Viewing and
Recording
Forecasts

There are four ways to view and record the outputs of Forecast cells in Crystal Ball.

1. Forecast display.

When defining a Forecast cell, the `Forecast Window` tab offers the option to show the Forecast window during the simulation run or at the end. To run simulations at the fastest possible speed, do not check `Show automatically`.

2. Analyze Forecast Charts.

If one or more Forecast windows are not displayed after a simulation run, they can be opened by choosing Crystal Ball▶Analyze▶View Charts▶Forecast Charts.

3. Auto extract.

The `Auto Extract` tab on the Define Forecast window offers the option to record simulation results directly on the spreadsheet. One can choose to record the forecast name, the number of trials, and any of 12 statistics (mean, MSE, and so on).

4. GETFORESTATFN.

The function `CB.GETFORESTATFN` can also be used to record any statistic of a Forecast cell directly in the spreadsheet. This approach is somewhat more transparent than the Auto Extract option and is therefore preferred.   ■

15.10* WHEN NOT TO SIMULATE

Sometimes it is *not* necessary to carry out a simulation in order to understand the effects of uncertainty. Recall that the optimal profit in the Advertising Budget example was $71,447 when we assumed no uncertainty and a price of $40. If we now assume that price is the only uncertain input and that it has a uniform distribution between $30 and $50, we find that the mean profit (with 10,000 trials) is $71,118, only half a percent different from the original value. In fact, if we were to increase the number of trials, we would eventually find that the simulated mean was identical to the deterministic mean. In other words, replacing an input with a distribution *can* leave the expected result essentially unchanged. There is a general principle at work here that is important to understand.

The impact that uncertainty in an input parameter (such as price) has on the output (such as profit) depends on the form of the relationship between the two. If that relationship is *linear*, then the expected value of the output is related by the same linear relationship to the expected value of the input. Thus, if we replace an input by a distribution without changing the expected value, then the expected value of the output does not change, and simulation is not needed. An analogous relationship holds for tail probabilities when the relationship between input and output is linear.

As a simple example, consider a firm's profit as affected by uncertainty about sales revenue. We might think of profit as described by the equation

$$Profit = Margin \times Revenue - Fixed\,cost$$

where Margin is stated as a proportion. For example:

$$Profit = 0.4 \times Revenue - 100$$

This equation takes the linear form $Z = aX + b$, with Z in the role of *Profit* and X in the role of *Revenue*. Clearly, *Profit* becomes uncertain when we treat *Revenue* as uncertain. We might want to estimate the expected value of *Profit*, or perhaps the probability that *Profit* is positive. Because the relationship is linear, it follows that

$$Expected\,Profit = Margin \times (Expected\,Revenue) - Fixed\,cost$$

Also:

$$P(Profit > 0) = P(Margin \times Revenue - Fixed\,cost > 0)$$
$$= P(Revenue > Fixed\,cost/Margin)$$

In the Advertising Budget case, the uniform distribution for price translates directly into a comparable distribution for profit. The reason is the linear relation between profit and price. If we express the model in algebraic terms, we have the following equation for profit:

$$Profit = Sales \times (1 - Overhead\ Rate) \times Price - Unit\ cost \times Sales - Fixed\ Cost$$

Now, if Price is the only input that we treat as uncertain, this expression is linear, so that we can write:

$$Expected\ Profit = Sales \times (1 - Overhead\ Rate) \times (Expected\ Price) - Unit\ cost$$
$$\times Sales - Fixed\ cost$$
$$= 16,160 \times (1 - 0.15) \times 40 - 478,019$$
$$= 71,447$$

Similarly, with respect to the probability of breaking even:

$$P(Profit > 0) = P(13,737 \times Price - 478,019 > 0) = P(Price > 34.8) = 0.24$$

Inputs and outputs are not always related in a linear fashion. To illustrate, we examine the impact of uncertainty on another parameter in this model. Cell C13 contains the parameter from the sales-response function that determines the base level of sales when advertising is zero. In the original analysis, this parameter took on the value 3,000. To illustrate the effect of uncertainty in this parameter, we replace this single value with a uniform distribution having the same mean value but a minimum of −5,000 and a maximum of 11,000. (To make the comparison clearer, we also assume for the moment that price is $40 for sure.) When we run a simulation under these assumptions, we see that uncertainty *reduces* mean profit, from $71,447 in the no-uncertainty case to $70,141 under uncertainty (Figure 15.45). We also see that the shape of the profit distribution is no longer uniform. In fact, values toward the upper end of the range are less likely than lower ones. Because the relationship here is not linear, the expected profit is not linear in the expected value of the input parameter.

To summarize these two cases: Uncertainty in *price* gives us no new information about the expected profit or about the probability of breaking even, but uncertainty in the *sales parameter* shifts the mean profit and changes the shape of the profit distribution. Why are these two cases different? The explanation lies in the relationship between the outcome variable and the uncertain parameters: Profit is linear in

FIGURE 15.45 Distribution of Profit with Random Sales Parameter

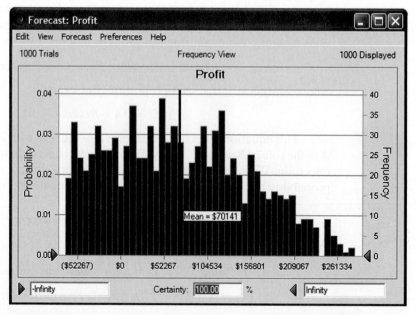

price but nonlinear in the sales parameter. (Recall that, in this model, sales are related to the square root of the product of advertising and the sales parameter.)

There are other cases in which it is possible to determine the expected value of the output without using simulation. Occasionally we may go to the trouble of conducting a simulation only to discover that the effort could have been avoided. However, in complex models with many uncertain parameters, it is often difficult to determine whether simulation can be avoided. Moreover, we do not often know in advance exactly which outputs we want to analyze. Thus, unless our model is particularly simple and we suspect that linearity holds, simulation remains our general-purpose tool for analyzing uncertain situations.

15.11 SUMMARY

We introduced simulation in Chapter 6 as one phase in a general analytic procedure for spreadsheet models. Simulation answers the question, "What are the risks?"—showing us how uncertainty in the inputs influences the outputs of our analysis. Like optimization, simulation can be seen as a sophisticated form of sensitivity analysis.

In Excel, simulation can be carried out conveniently using Crystal Ball. Crystal Ball provides all the probability models needed to express the uncertainties in our assumptions, and it automates the repetitive process of sampling from these distributions. Finally, it provides extensive methods for displaying and analyzing the results.

Simulation is a powerful tool when used appropriately, but it should never be used *before* an appropriate sensitivity analysis is carried out on a deterministic version of the model. What-if analysis, involving use of Data Sensitivity and the Tornado Chart tool, uncovers those input parameters that have the biggest impact on the outcomes. These should be the focus of any uncertainty analysis. We have designed the Tornado Chart tool to support a sequence of analyses that can help focus the simulation analysis on the critical parameters.

Every simulation analysis involves four major activities:

- Selecting uncertain parameters
- Selecting probability distributions
- Ensuring precision in the outcomes
- Interpreting outcome distributions

The parameters that are treated as uncertain in a simulation analysis should be those that are subject to substantial uncertainty and have a significant impact on the outcome. Selecting uncertain parameters is a natural outgrowth of sensitivity analysis. Although many probability models are available, only a few are used routinely by business analysts. We have described these models (the Yes/No, uniform, binomial, triangular, normal, and discrete distributions), and we have indicated the most appropriate applications for each. Ensuring that our simulation results are sufficiently precise is primarily a matter of choosing a suitable run length. However, we have stressed the importance of determining how much precision is really needed in a given analysis before making this decision. Finally, simulations produce probability distributions as outcomes, which are by their nature complex. We have emphasized the importance of summarizing and simplifying these results, in order to make them useful to managers.

While simulation is more sophisticated than simple spreadsheet modeling, it is one of the most widely used of the advanced management science tools. It is relatively easy for business analysts to learn, and it provides a means for expressing and understanding the uncertainty that is so prevalent in business. It does require some familiarity with probability, the language of uncertainty, but many analysts have this familiarity, and most can acquire what they need. Often, the bigger challenge with simulation is translating the results into a form that managers can understand and act upon.

SUGGESTED READINGS

Evans, J. R., and D. L. Olson. 2002. *Introduction to Simulation and Risk Analysis.* 2d ed. Upper Saddle River, NJ: Prentice Hall.

This is the only full-length text devoted to simulation using Crystal Ball. The coverage of Crystal Ball is somewhat less detailed than in this chapter, but there are many examples and applications. Discrete event simulation using *ProModel* is also covered.

Seila, A. F., V. Ceric, and P. Tadikamalla. 2003. *Applied Simulation Modeling.* Belmont, CA: Brooks/Cole.

This book covers simulation from the business and engineering points of view. It uses *@Risk* and the discrete event simulation language *Arena.* @Risk is Crystal Ball's main competitor in the marketplace. It is not difficult to learn how to use @Risk after

working with Crystal Ball for a while. The following books are also based on @Risk, although it would not be difficult to read the material and translate the exercises and examples into Crystal Ball.

Winston, W. 1999. *Financial Models Using Simulation and Optimization.* Newfield, NY: Palisade.

Winston, W. 2001. *Simulation Modeling with @Risk.* Pacific Grove, CA: Duxbury.

Financial Models contains 63 examples of simulation applications, most with a financial flavor. *Simulation Modeling* is more like a textbook, with some introductory chapters on simulation in general. The body of this book consists of a large number of worked examples from planning, marketing, finance, and operations.

EXERCISES

1. *Profit Analysis.* A consumer electronics firm produces a line of battery rechargers for cell phones. The following distributions apply:

Unit price	triangular with a minimum of $18.95, most likely value of $24.95, and maximum of $26.95
Unit cost	uniform with a minimum of $12.00 and a maximum of $15.00
Quantity sold	10,000 − 250*Unit price, plus a random term given by a normal distribution with a mean of 0 and a standard deviation of 10
Fixed costs	normal with a mean of $30,000 and a standard deviation of $5,000

a. What is the expected profit?

b. What is the probability of a loss?

c. What is the maximum loss?

2. *R&D Planning.* A firm is in the process of assessing the economic prospects for a new bottling machine it is developing. Future research and development expenses could range from $4 million to $9 million, with a most likely value of around $7 million. The life of the product will be anywhere from 3 to 10 years. Yearly unit sales will range from 100 to 500, with a most likely value of around 300. The machines will sell for between $20,000 and $25,000 each. The production cost of the machine is expected to be $13,000 but could be as low as $11,000 or as high as $15,000. The firm's discount rate is 10 percent.

a. What is the expected NPV for this new machine over 10 years?

b. What is the probability of a positive NPV?

3. *Door-to-door Marketing.* A small nonprofit organization is planning a door-to-door marketing campaign to sell Christmas wrapping and gifts. They plan to visit 100 homes. Consultants have estimated that they should expect to find someone home 80 percent of the time. When someone is home, 65 percent of the time it is a female. Thirty percent of females make a purchase, and when they do so the dollar value of their purchase is normally distributed with a mean of $22 and a standard deviation of $5. Males purchase 20 percent of the time, and the dollar value of their purchase is normally distributed with a mean of $28 and a standard deviation of $3.

a. What is the total amount they can expect to generate in revenues from these 100 visits?

b. What is the standard deviation of total revenues over 100 visits?

c. What is the probability they will make more than $750?

4. *Facility Design.* This firm operates a docking facility for container ships in Singapore. At present, the facility consists of two identical docks. Ships typically arrive during the night. The number of ships that arrive during a single night varies from night to night, as given in the following distribution. Each dock can unload one ship during the day. Ships unable to unload must wait until the following day. The cost of delaying a ship (called a *demurrage* charge) is $10,000 per day. A new dock will cost $5 million a year, including amortized construction costs, maintenance, and operating costs.

Nightly Arrivals	Frequency
0	0.30
1	0.30
2	0.20
3	0.10
4	0.05
5	0.05

a. With the current system, what is the average demurrage charge *per year*?

b. Can you justify adding one or more additional docks?

c. How sensitive are your results to the assumption you make about the number of ships waiting at the beginning of the simulation?

5. *Retirement Planning.* A recent MBA would like your assistance in determining how much to save for retirement. He is planning to invest $3,000 in a tax-sheltered retirement fund at the end of each year (i.e., appreciation of the fund is not taxed). The rate of return each year can be modeled as a normally distributed random variable with a mean of 12 percent and a standard deviation of 2 percent.

a. If he is 30 years old now, how much money should he expect to have in his retirement fund at age 60?

b. What is the probability that he will have more than $1 million in his retirement fund when he reaches age 60?

c. How much should he invest each year if he wants the mean value of his portfolio to be at least $1 million at age 60?

d. How much should he invest each year if he wants there to be a 90 percent chance of having at least $1 million in his retirement fund at age 60?

6. *Health Claims.* A large manufacturing company self-insures its employee health insurance claims. That is, it collects a fixed amount each month from every employee for healthcare costs, and then it pays the entire claim amount using its own funds to make up the difference. It would like to estimate its total healthcare payments for the coming year.

The total number of employees at the start of the year is 11,124. The firm expects the number of employees to change each month over the coming year by a percentage that is uniformly distributed between −2 and 5 percent. Employees contribute $125 each per month toward their healthcare costs, while the average claim is $250 per month. The average claim itself is expected to grow by an amount given by a normal distribution with a mean of 1 percent and a standard deviation of 2 percent.

a. What is the expected cost to the company of covering employee healthcare costs in the coming year?

b. What is the maximum cost to the company of covering employee healthcare costs in the coming year?

c. What is the probability that costs will not exceed $20 million?

7. *New Product Forecasting.* Kardjian Brothers, Inc. has invented a fundamentally new way to control the photo-lithography process used in manufacturing computer chips. Before they sell or license this technological breakthrough, they would like to have some idea of how rapidly it might gain market share. Their analysis is based on the Bass diffusion model, which rests on three assumptions:

> There is a fixed population of potential users, all of whom will eventually adopt.
>
> Adoptions from *innovators* are proportional to the current number of potential adopters.
>
> Adoptions from *imitators* are proportional to the product of the current number of adopters and the remaining potential adopters.

While there are many interpretations of this general model, it is common to attribute the innovation effect to marketing efforts such as advertising, which convert some percentage of potential adopters every time period. The imitation effect is thought to operate through word of mouth, in which every contact between an adopter and a potential adopter results in a new adoption with some probability.

The following model is consistent with these assumptions:

$$n(t) = pN_0 + (q - p) \times N(t) - (q/N_0) \times N(t)^2$$

where

$n(t) =$ customers adopting at time t

$N_0 =$ total number of potential adopters

$N(t) =$ cumulative adopters at time t

$p =$ propensity to innovate (percentage of potentials per time period)

$q =$ propensity to imitate (percentage of potentials times adopters per time period)

Assume an initial population of 1,000 and parameter values of 0.03 for p and 0.38 for q. (These are the average values found over dozens of new products and technologies ranging from toasters to CT scanners.)

a. Build a deterministic model for the number of adopters over time. In what year will the cumulative numbers of adopters *first* exceed half the original population?

b. Build a simulation model for the number of adopters over time, assuming the following uniform distributions for the parameters: p lies between 0 and 0.5; q lies between 0.28 and 0.48. What is the average number of *years* it takes for the cumulative number of adopters to reach 50 percent of the initial population?

c. What is the probability that it will take more than 10 years for the cumulative number of adopters to reach 50 percent of the initial population?

8. *Drug Development.* A pharmaceutical company has a new drug under development and would like to know how much profit it might expect to make. The drug has to be tested to pass FDA approval. One hundred subjects will be tested, and the company estimates that the probability that each subject will pass the test is 25 percent. The FDA will approve the drug if at least 20 out of the 100 subjects pass. Future R&D costs will be between $3 million and $5 million (uniformly distributed). Advertising costs will run between $12 million and $18 million, with $16 million the most likely amount. The total population of potential users of the drug is 40 million. The company expects to gain 8 percent of this market if its drug is successful. (Assume a normal distribution for market share with a standard deviation of 2 percent). There is a one-in-four chance of a competitor entering this market, and if it does, the monopoly share will be reduced by 5 to 15 percent (uniformly distributed). The profit per customer is expected to be $12.

a. What is the mean profit?

b. What is the probability the company makes no profit at all?

c. What is the maximum profit they can make?

9. *IPO Valuation.* A small private company is contemplating an initial public offering (IPO) in which it will sell 40,000 shares of stock. The price of the stock at the IPO is uncertain, with the following distribution:

Price	Probability
10	0.10
11	0.20
12	0.30
13	0.20
14	0.10
15	0.10

In each of the next five years there is a 30 percent chance the company will fail. If it does not fail, its stock value will increase by an amount given by a lognormal distribution with a mean of 1.5 percent and a standard deviation of 0.5 percent.

a. What is the mean value of the stock at the end of five years, assuming the company does not fail in the interim?

b. What is the probability that the company will still be in existence after five years?

10. *New Product Profitability.* A new product will sell for $8. The company expects to sell around 900,000 units. (Use a normal distribution with a mean of 900,000 and a standard deviation of 300,000.) Fixed costs are normally distributed with a mean of $700,000 and a standard deviation of $50,000. Unit variable costs are also normally distributed with a mean of $3 and a standard deviation of $0.25. Selling expenses are lognormally distributed with a mean of $900,000 and a standard deviation of $50,000.

a. What is the expected value of profit for this product?

b. What is the probability that profit will exceed $3 million?

11. *Software System Evaluation.* A new software system will cost $2 million initially and take around two years to install. (The actual time to complete installation will be lognormally distributed with a mean of two years and a standard deviation of 0.5 year.) Development costs each year will be normally distributed with a mean of $1 million and a standard deviation of $0.25 million. (Each year is an independent sample.) The system will cost $5 million per year to operate in the first year. Thereafter, the growth rate will be normally distributed with a mean of 10 percent and a standard deviation of 3 percent.

The system will generate benefits in the first year given by a normal distribution, with a mean of $6 million and a standard deviation of $0.5 million. (Benefits start accruing only after the system is complete.) After the first year, benefits will increase at a rate given by a normal distribution with a mean and standard deviation of 30 percent.

Determine the present value of net benefits for this software over the next five years at a discount rate of 10 percent.

a. What is the expected present value of net benefits over a five-year period?

b. What is the probability that net benefits will be positive?

12. *NPV Analysis.* You have been asked to evaluate the following investment opportunity. A small firm is available for purchase at an initial cost of $150,000, to be paid to the current owner in equal installments over the next five years. The firm has been generating annual revenues of $100,000. Operating costs are 65 percent of revenues. For tax purposes, the firm's earnings would appear on your personal income tax return, and the applicable tax rate would be about 36 percent. Your investment would be deductible when calculating taxes. Under these assumptions, the NPV (at a discount rate of 10 percent) for this project is $12,131.

In light of the fact that most of your information about this firm comes from the current owner, you are concerned that some of your assumptions may be inaccurate. After some research, you have determined the following about the key inputs to this problem:

Actual revenues could be as low as $60,000 or as high as $125,000. The most likely amount is $100,000. Revenues in successive years are independent.

Operating costs could be as low as 55 percent of revenues or as high as 75 percent, with any values in between being equally likely. Costs in successive years are independent.

The tax rate in any year will be 36 percent with probability 0.4 and 40 percent with probability 0.6, depending on factors outside your control and independent from year to year.

In the case of negative taxable income, you will have other income, so the tax effects represented in the model will still hold.

a. What probability distributions are appropriate for the three uncertain quantities in this analysis?

b. What is the mean NPV under the assumptions given?

c. What is the probability that the NPV will be negative?

d. What is the probability that the cash flow will be positive in all five years?

13. *Value of a Customer.* As the manager of credit card services at Bank of Hanover (BOH), you're aware that the average profitability of a credit card customer grows with the number of years they have used the credit card. Two probabilistic factors affect actual profitability. The mean profitability function is given in the following table, which has been gathered from data on BOH customers. The actual profit in a given year follows a normal distribution, with a standard deviation equal to 25 percent of the mean profit.

In addition, there is a probability less than one that a customer will continue to use the card during year t. This probability is sometimes called the *retention rate*. For instance, an 80 percent retention rate means that, during any year, there is a 20 percent chance that the customer will cancel the credit card. Assume that if a customer cancels during year t, then the cancellation occurs at the end of the year, and BOH still gets profits from year t. The current retention rate has been estimated at 80 percent.

BOH uses a discount rate of 10 percent for calculating net present values.

Year	Mean Profit	Year	Mean Profit
1	−40	11	111
2	66	12	116
3	72	13	120
4	79	14	124
5	87	15	130
6	92	16	137
7	96	17	142
8	99	18	148
9	103	19	155
10	106	20	161

a. When the retention rate is 80 percent, what is the average NPV from a customer?

b. When the retention rate is 80 percent, what is the probability that the NPV for a given customer will exceed $100?

c. Determine the average NPV from a customer when the retention rate is 85 percent, 90 percent, and 95 percent. Sketch a graph that describes how the average NPV varies with the retention rate, for retention rates above 75 percent; then, interpret the sketch.

14. *Production Scheduling.* A simple model is sometimes used in order to illustrate the production-scheduling maxim, "balance flow, not capacity." Consider a factory that consists of three workstations where each customer order must proceed through the workstations in sequence. Next, suppose that the workloads are balanced, which means that, *on average*, each order requires equal amounts of work at each of the three stations. Assume that the average operation time is 60 minutes.

Now suppose that six orders are to be scheduled tomorrow. Using average times, we would expect that completion times would look like the following:

	Order					
	1	**2**	**3**	**4**	**5**	**6**
Complete Station 1	60	120	180	240	300	360
Complete Station 2	120	180	240	300	360	420
Complete Station 3	180	240	300	360	420	480

and we would expect that the schedule length would be 480 minutes.

Suppose that actual operation times are random and follow a triangular distribution with a minimum of 30 minutes and a maximum of 90 minutes. *Note*: No order can start at a station until the previous order has finished.

a. What is the mean schedule length?

b. What is the probability that the schedule length will exceed 480 minutes?

c. Change the range of the distribution from 60 to 40 and to 20, and then repeat (a) and (b). What is the mean schedule length in each case? What do you conclude from these observations?

15. *Competitive Bidding.* Two partners have decided to sell the manufacturing business they have been running. They have lined up five prospective buyers and have hired a consultant to help them with the bidding and the sale. The consultant, an expert in assessments of this sort, has told the partners that the business is worth $10 million.

The consultant has obtained indications that the prospective buyers would be willing to participate in a sealed-bid auction to determine who will buy the business and at what price. Under the rules of the auction, the sale price would be the highest bid.

Because of their limited information about the business, the bidders may overestimate or underestimate what the business is actually worth. After listening to some of their preliminary thoughts, the consultant concludes that limited information will lead each of them to value the business at a minimum of $8 million and a maximum of $15 million. Their most likely value is $10 million. (We interpret this to mean that a suitable model for an individual value will be a triangular distribution.) The bidders, however, have an instinct about the Winner's Curse, and they each plan to bid only 75 percent of their estimated value for the business. (The Winner's Curse is a phenomenon in competitive bidding where the winner is generally the one who most overestimates the value of the prize.)

a. What is the expected price that the partners will receive for their business?

b. What is the probability that the partners will receive more than $10 million for the business?

c. Suppose the consultant asks for a fee in order to identify five more bidders to participate in the auction. How large a fee should the partners be willing to pay for this service?

16. *Equilibrium in Competitive Bidding.* A sealed-bid auction is going to be held in the near future for Medex Pharmaceuticals. You represent one of two companies expected to enter bids. The basic data available to your firm consist of an estimate of the value of Medex and some

MEMO

TO: Susan Morganstern
FROM: Vaughn Newman
RE: Bidding for Medex

As promised, I am following up our conversation of a few days ago with more information. You mentioned that your staff group might be able to help us prepare our bid for Medex Pharmaceuticals. Here are some of the details you asked about.

First of all, I don't want you to get the impression that our primary objective is simply to win the bid. We'd like to own Medex, of course, but only if the net effect is to increase our shareholder value. One of my big concerns is that we might win the bid but overestimate the value of Medex. That would not be a success.

Second, I'm confident that my Valuation Committee is doing its best to determine how much Medex is worth, but, as you said, we have to recognize the uncertainty we're dealing with. Medex might be worth a lot more or a lot less than our estimate—it really depends on how their R&D division does and on what happens to the market for the new drug they just got approved. I looked back at some of our previous work, and it looks like we've been high or low in our assessment by as much as 50 percent. That's a lot of uncer-

tainty, but it just seems to be the nature of the situations we've been in.

Third, I am pretty sure that the only other bidder for Medex will be National, in which case we'll have only one rival to worry about. Somehow, this ought to make things simpler than if there were several bidders out there.

Finally, as a corporation, National resembles us closely, and whichever one of us gets Medex should be able to extract the same value from the assets. National's access to information is about the same as ours, so their level of uncertainty should be the same. In addition, National has had some experience in this sort of bidding, and they're not naive about bidding strategy. Judging from their track record, they'll want to avoid overbidding, too. In essence, I guess I'm saying that they are likely to analyze the deal pretty much the way we are.

Any insight you could give us on how we should approach the bidding would be appreciated. The sealed bid is due at Morgan Stanley next Friday.

information on the uncertainty surrounding that value. Your task is to prepare a quantitative bidding strategy for this auction. The attached letter (box) from your boss explains his thinking about the problem and offers some suggestions for your approach.

Here are some guidelines for your analysis.

Your boss has provided an estimate, based on his past experience, of the range of errors that are likely to be made in valuing companies such as Medex. Errors up to 50 percent above and below the true value are possible. If we assume that the true value is $100 million, we could represent the range of possible estimates by a uniform probability distribution with a minimum value of $50 million and a maximum value of $150 million. Other probability models would also be plausible.

We know that our competitor, National, is similar to our company in all important ways. Thus, we may assume that their probability distribution for the value of Medex is the same as ours.

Bidding theory suggests that we should bid less than our estimated value in a common-value auction such as this. Formulate your strategy in terms of a *bid level*, which is the percentage of our estimated value we will bid.

We clearly cannot know for certain what bid level National will choose. But we can determine what our bid level *should* be for any given bid level they might choose.

While your boss has specified the problem rather precisely, you should explore the sensitivity of your results to your assumptions, including the range of uncertainty, the form of the probability distribution, and the number of bidders.

17. *Pricing Exotic Options*. A given stock currently is priced at $100. Historically, its annual return has been 12 percent with a standard deviation of 15 percent. Build a spreadsheet simulation model for the stock price, using the option pricing model described in the text. Build the model to simulate the stock price over 126 days. Assume that the risk-free rate of return is 6 percent.

a. A particular European call option gives the owner the right to purchase this stock after six months at a strike price of $105. What is the price of the option?

b. Create a graph of the option price as a function of the strike price, for strike prices from $100 to $110 in increments of $1.

c. A particular *European put option* gives the owner the right to sell this stock after six months at a strike price of $95. What is the price of the put?

d. A *lookback call option* on this stock has an exercise price given by the minimum price observed over its six-month term. What is the price of the lookback option?

e. An *Asian option* on this stock has a strike price set by the average value of the stock during its term. What is the price of the Asian option?

f. A *knockout call option* on this stock terminates if the stock price reaches or exceeds $125 (that is, the option cannot be exercised). Otherwise, it has the same structure as the normal call option. What is the price of the knockout option?

APPENDIX 15.1 CHOOSING CRYSTAL BALL SETTINGS

Crystal Ball provides a number of choices under Run Preferences for tailoring the simulation. Many of these options are important only for advanced users, but all users must understand a few of them. In this appendix we describe the most important options and provide guidelines for making wise choices. This section is organized in the same order as the option tabs are organized in the Run Preferences window.

TRIALS

In the text we discussed the question of how to choose an appropriate run length for a particular analysis. In the Run Preferences▶Trials window (Figure 15A1), this parameter is entered next to `Number of trials to run`. Below that are two check boxes. If we check `Stop on calculation errors`, the simulation stops and issues a warning when Excel encounters an error, such as trying to divide by zero. It is a good idea to keep this box checked since it can help reveal bugs in the model. If we check `Stop when precision control limits are reached`, the simulation stops either when the maximum number of trials is reached or when the output measure has been estimated with sufficient precision, whichever comes first. The `Confidence level` parameter entered into this window sets the target level of precision in the forecast cell at which Crystal Ball stops the run. (For more detail on using Precision Control, see Appendix 15.2.)

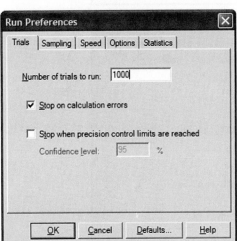

FIGURE 15A1　Trials Tab under Run Preferences

SAMPLING

This tab (Figure 15A2) gives the user several options for controlling the process of generating random inputs. To fix the random number sequence and use the same values on each simulation run, check `Use same sequence of random numbers` under `Random number generation`. The `Initial seed value` specifies the starting point for the sampling process within Crystal Ball. A unique set of random numbers will be drawn for any positive integer specified in this window. If this option is checked, Crystal Ball chooses the same samples from the input distributions on each run, and the outputs are thus identical. If this option is *not* checked, Crystal Ball chooses different samples from the input distributions on each run, and the outcomes are different as well. Use the same sequence of random numbers when comparing alternatives but different sequences when determining run length.

The other option in this panel is `Sampling Method: Monte Carlo` or `Latin Hypercube`. As a general rule, we recommend using Latin Hypercube sampling (a form of stratified sampling) over Monte Carlo sampling because it achieves the same precision with fewer

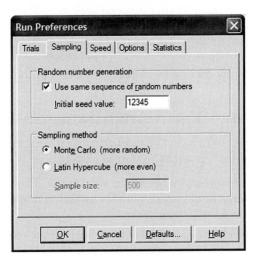

FIGURE 15A2　Sampling Tab under Run Preferences

FIGURE 15A3 Speed Tab under Run Preferences

FIGURE 15A4 Options Tab under Run Preferences

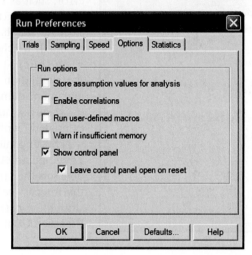

trials. It does, however, require more computer memory, so problems may arise if computer memory is limited.

The final option here is `Sample Size`. The technical issues here can be complex. Our advice is to set this parameter to an even fraction of the run length. For example, when the run length is 1,000 trials, set this parameter to 500.

SPEED

Crystal Ball has several different run speed options available under *Run mode* (Figure 15A3). `Demo speed` is useful if we are demonstrating Crystal Ball to novices. Check `Extreme speed` to run a simulation as fast as possible. We can further improve the run speed by choosing `Suppress chart windows (fastest)`. With this option, Crystal Ball does not redraw each of the forecast windows as the sampling proceeds.

OPTIONS

This tab (Figure 15A4) allows the user to control five aspects of Crystal Ball. Most of these options can be left unchecked until needed.

> `Store assumption values for analysis`. Check this box if we need to examine the random outcomes for assumption cells on a given run. Normally this box can be left unchecked.

> `Enable correlations`. Leave this box unchecked unless we have specified correlations between assumption cells.

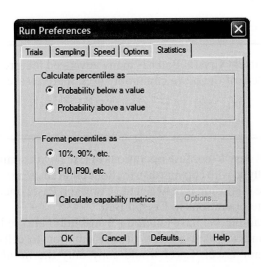

FIGURE 15A5 Statistics Tab Under Run Preferences

Run user-defined macros. Leave this box unchecked unless we are running macros within Crystal Ball.

Warn if insufficient memory. Normally this box can be left unchecked.

Show control panel. If checked, this option displays the Crystal Ball control panel on the screen.

Leave control panel open on reset. If checked, this option will leave the control panel visible when you reset a Crystal Ball model to begin a new simulation.

STATISTICS

This panel (Figure 15A5) controls the calculation of percentiles. Depending on which option is selected, a given percentile, say the 45th, will be calculated as the value below or above which 45 percent of the outcomes lie. The usual choice is "below." The second option allows the user to display percentiles either as 90 percent or P90.

APPENDIX 15.2 ADDITIONAL FEATURES OF CRYSTAL BALL

As with Excel itself, Crystal Ball has many advanced features that a typical user will rarely use. A few of the more commonly used features are described here.

EDITING IN CRYSTAL BALL

It is sometimes easy to confuse operations in Excel with similar ones in Crystal Ball. This is especially so with copying distributions entered using the Distribution Gallery. In this case, the confusion is between the Copy and Paste operations in Excel and the Copy and Paste operations in Crystal Ball.

If, for example, we have entered a distribution into cell B2 using the Distribution Gallery and we want to copy that distribution to cells B3:B10, we must use Crystal Ball, not Excel. Excel would copy only the *number* in cell B2, not the *distribution*. To copy the distribution, we first need to enter a number in each cell in the paste range B3:B10. Then we highlight B2 and choose Crystal Ball▶Define▶Copy. Then, highlight B3:B10 and choose Crystal Ball▶Define▶Paste. We should then see the same *distribution* that was in cell B2 copied to the cells in B3:B10. (Check by moving the cursor over one of these cells and selecting Crystal Ball▶Define▶Assumption.) When we recalculate the spreadsheet, we get independent samples from this distribution in all the cells B2:B10.

It is sometimes necessary to locate all the Assumption cells in a spreadsheet. This can be accomplished by choosing Crystal Ball▶Define▶Select▶Select All Assumptions. Crystal Ball then highlights with a red border all the Assumption cells—that is, those cells that contain distributions entered through the Distribution Gallery. (Unfortunately, this does not work to highlight distributions entered using Crystal Ball functions.) Similar options exist in the Define group for locating Forecast and Decision cells.

Occasionally one can run into a bug in Crystal Ball that has its origins in an Assumption or Forecast cell that has been misplaced during revision of the spreadsheet. The solution is to first locate those cells using Crystal Ball▶Define▶Select▶Select All Assumptions or Crystal Ball▶Define▶Select▶Select All Forecasts. Then, if necessary, one can delete unneeded Assumptions or Forecasts using Crystal Ball▶Define▶Clear.

CRYSTAL BALL FUNCTIONS

In our examples, we have often used the Distribution Gallery to input probability distributions. This feature is one of our favorite aspects of Crystal Ball, not only because it is easy to use, but also because it reinforces the idea that the choice of a probability distribution for an uncertain parameter is just another modeling choice requiring judgment. However, the Distribution Gallery has several drawbacks. One is that the distribution is not visible as a formula in the spreadsheet. Another is that we cannot embed these distributions in other formulas. Finally, copying distributions entered this way is somewhat clumsy. Fortunately, Crystal Ball provides an alternative method.

Crystal Ball provides 21 special functions for taking samples from probability distributions. For example, if we enter the formula

```
CB.Normal (100,25)
```

in a cell, Crystal Ball interprets that formula just as if we had entered a normal distribution with mean of 100 and standard distribution of 25 from the Distribution Gallery. This formula returns a random sample from this distribution each time the spreadsheet is recalculated. Since Excel interprets this function as a standard Excel function, we can copy and paste it just as we would any other function (using

Excel, *not* Crystal Ball), and we can embed it in a more complex formula, for example:

$$IF((D20 \geq B7), CB.NORMAL(100, 25), 0).$$

The formulas for the other major types of distributions take a similar form, for example:

```
CB.YESNO(probability)
CB.BINOMIAL(probability, number of trials)
CB.UNIFORM(minimum, maximum)
CB.TRIANGULAR(minimum, most likely, maximum)
CB.CUSTOM(I1:J4)
```

In the last example, we enter a discrete distribution using the CB.CUSTOM function and specify the cell range where the outcomes and probabilities are located. More details on these functions and their arguments are available by choosing Insert Function and selecting the Crystal Ball category.

Crystal Ball provides a number of other specialized functions besides probability distributions. One particularly useful function records any of the statistics from the Statistics view of the Forecast window in the spreadsheet. This is particularly useful when a model has a large number of Forecast cells. For example, if we enter the formula

```
CB.GETFORESTATFN(E11, 2)
```

in a cell, Crystal Ball records the mean value of the forecast cell in E11 after a simulation is run. (Note that this function returns the result #VALUE until a simulation has been run, at which point it takes on the appropriate numerical value.)

The first input in this function is the cell address of the Forecast cell; the second is the number of the statistic. The statistics are numbered from 1 to 12, in the same order they appear in the Statistics view in the Forecast window (see Figure 15.43), starting with the number of trials. Thus, number 1 is the number of trials, number 2 is the mean, number 10 is the minimum, number 11 is the maximum, and number 12 the MSE (mean standard error).

USING THE MEAN STANDARD ERROR

An important measure of precision in a simulation estimate is the **mean standard error** (MSE). In statistics, this metric is also called the standard error of the mean. In a simulation experiment, we are essentially estimating the mean value of a population, and an interval estimate describes the precision associated with our estimate. The following statements are all true of the MSE:

A 68 percent confidence interval for the true mean extends to one MSE on either side of the sample average.

A 90 percent confidence interval for the true mean extends to 1.645 MSEs on either side of the sample average.

A 95 percent confidence interval for the true mean extends to 1.960 MSEs on either side of the sample average.

A 99 percent confidence interval for the true mean extends to 2.576 MSEs on either side of the sample average.

In the Advertising Budget simulation model, for example, a run length of 1,000 trials generates an MSE of 2,484. This is reported in the Statistics view on the Forecast window, as shown in Figure 15.43. (Results may vary slightly due to simulation error when this experiment is repeated.) Thus, a 68 percent confidence interval for the mean is $103,271 \pm 2,484$, or from 100,787 to 105,755. In other words, in repeated experiments, the true mean falls within this interval 68 percent of the time.

If we want a confidence level higher than 68 percent, we have to widen the range. For example, a 95 percent confidence level corresponds to $103,271 \pm 1.96(2,484)$, or from 98,402 to 108,140. In repeated experiments, the true mean falls within this interval 95 percent of the time.

With a smaller sample size, we would expect the simulation error, and therefore the MSE, to be larger. For an experiment consisting of 100 trials, the sample average is $88,897, and the MSE is 8,387, or about 9 percent. Thus, we would expect the true mean to lie within the range from 80,510 to 97,284 about 68 percent of the time. Notice that in this case, a range of one MSE on either side of the sample average does *not* include the true mean (which is roughly 101,600). This should be sobering, if not startling. There is, after all, no *guarantee* that a range of even 1.96 MSEs around the sample mean contains the true mean. All we can say is that the probability of this outcome is 95 percent in repeated experiments.

The MSE declines with the square root of the sample size, so as we increase the sample size, we increase the precision of our estimates but not in a linear fashion. In fact, if we want to cut the MSE in half, we have to *quadruple* the sample size, owing to the square root relationship. More samples are always better, but successive samples of a given size contribute less and less additional precision.

A good way to use the MSE is to determine the acceptable error before running a simulation. In the Advertising Budget model, we might be willing to accept an MSE that is roughly 5 percent of the mean, or about 3,600. Suppose we run 100 trials and find that the MSE is about 15 percent of the mean. We could then increase the sample size, on a trial-and-error basis, until the MSE is sufficiently small. Or, drawing on the square root relationship in the formula, we could increase the sample size by a factor of about 9. Note that this approach always requires us to run at least a small simulation experiment, in order to estimate the MSE.

USING PRECISION CONTROL

Crystal Ball provides another approach to the problem of controlling simulation error, known as Precision Control. With this feature, we can specify, in advance, the required precision in any outcome. Crystal Ball will then run trials until the desired precision is reached. To use this capability, we must enter the appropriate parameters when we define a Forecast cell and under Run Preferences.

First, consider the Forecast cell for which the required precision is specified. Highlight this cell and select Define▶Define Forecast from the Crystal Ball menu. Then follow these steps (see Figure 15A6):

1. Click on the More button (double down arrows).

2. Select the Precision tab.

FIGURE 15A6   Setting Precision Control

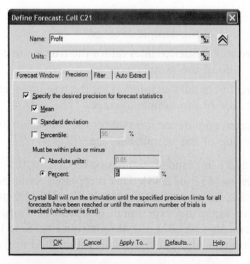

3. Check the box Specify the desired precision for forecast statistics.

4. Choose Mean, Standard deviation, or Percentile as the statistic to apply Precision Control to.

5. Choose Absolute units or Percent under Must be within plus or minus, and enter the appropriate parameter. This parameter sets the half-width of the desired confidence interval. For example, if we enter 100 for Absolute units, Crystal Ball will run until the half-width of the confidence interval is 100 units.

The second set of arrangements must be made under Run▶Run Preferences, on the Trials tab (see Figure 15A1). Check the box Stop when precision control limits are reached and enter the percentage for the desired confidence interval. For example, if we select a confidence interval of 95 percent, then Crystal Ball runs until the half-width of a 95 percent confidence interval is 100. At this time, we should also make sure that the number of trials is a large number, since Crystal Ball stops the simulation when the number of trials is reached or the precision is reached, whichever comes first.

When we run a simulation using Precision Control, Crystal Ball periodically calculates the confidence interval for the Forecast cell we have specified, and it stops the simulation when the required precision is reached. In other words, Precision Control allows us to set the maximum acceptable width of a confidence interval around the result.

CONTROLLING PRECISION IN TAIL PROBABILITIES

The MSE can also be used when we are estimating a probability related to the outcome. We know that we can estimate a probability from a single simulation run by calculating the percentage of trials in which the event occurred. But, just as with the sample average, this estimate of the probability differs from the true probability by some unknown amount. To determine the precision in such an estimate, we add a cell to the spreadsheet that shows the value 1 when the event occurs and a 0 otherwise. For example, the statement IF(Profit > 0,1,0) returns the value 1 when profit is positive and the value 0 otherwise. We define the new cell as a Forecast cell. Since this cell takes on only the values 1 and 0, the Forecast window reports under the Mean the percentage of times a 1 appeared. The MSE then represents the standard error of the estimate of this proportion.

Here is an illustration. We created a simple model with one Assumption cell containing a normal distribution with a mean of 100 and a standard deviation of 25. Then, we added an IF statement to determine whether each sample was above or below 100. We know, because the normal distribution is symmetrical, that precisely 50 percent of such samples in the long run should be above 100. Let's experiment to see how close we get to this known value for different sample sizes. The results are shown in the table below:

Trials	Sample Mean for Percent Over 100	MSE
10	0.30	0.15
100	0.47	0.05
1,000	0.50	0.02

With 10 trials, three exceed 100, so our estimate of the probability is 0.3. The MSE is understandably high, at 0.15, or one-half the estimate. At 100 trials, our estimate of 0.47 is much closer to the true value of 0.5, and the MSE has dropped to 0.05, or 11 percent of the estimate. With 1,000 trials, the sample mean is right on target, and the MSE has fallen to around 4 percent of the estimate.

FILTERING OUTPUT VALUES

Occasionally we want a Forecast report involving only certain selected values from a Forecast cell. Here's an example: We are studying the inventory situation at a warehouse. Each week, we are either able to meet all orders for a given item, or we are short some number of items. Using a simple IF statement, we can determine the percentage of weeks in which we are unable to fill all orders. But we also want to know

FIGURE 15A7 Filtering
Options in the Define
Forecast Window

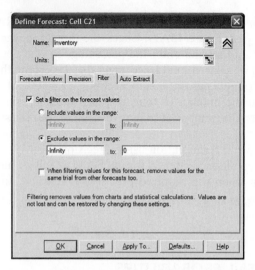

the expected number of units we fall short of demand in those weeks in which we are not able to meet all demand. In a simulation of 1,000 weeks, we might completely meet demand 80 percent of the time. If we examine a Forecast window for the cell representing unmet demand, it takes on the value zero 80 percent of the time and a positive value the remaining 20 percent of the time. The reported expected value combines these two types of outcomes and reports the overall number of units short, rather than the units short in just those weeks in which we are short, which is what we want to know.

A Crystal Ball option comes in handy here. When we define a Forecast cell, we normally enter just its name and appropriate units. But if we select More (double-down arrows), we are given additional options for controlling the Forecast cell. Under the Filter tab (Figure 15A7), we can filter out of the Forecast Window values that fall inside or outside defined ranges. In the preceeding example, we would filter out all zero values for unmet demand by entering 0 in the field under Exclude values in the range. This window also provides the option to apply the filter on one forecast to other forecasts (check Apply To . . .). So we could also use this approach to calculate the mean profit for those weeks in which unmet demand was positive.

OVERLAY CHART

Crystal Ball produces a Forecast window for every Forecast cell in a model. Because each of these windows contains so much information, it is often difficult to compare results across several forecasts. The Overlay Chart can help here by displaying two or more distributions superimposed in the same graph.

We will use the option pricing model from the text to illustrate. We are interested in displaying two distributions: the stock price at the expiration date

FIGURE 15A8 Overlay
Chart

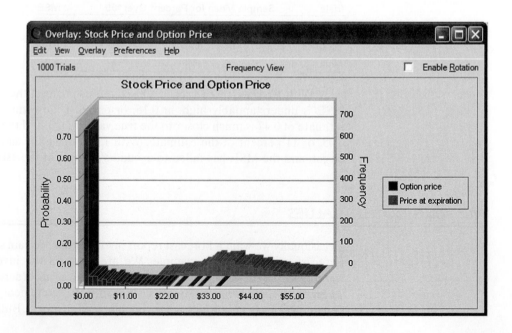

and the price of the option. To display both Forecast windows in an Overlay Chart, we select Crystal Ball▶Analyze▶View Charts▶Overlay Charts, after the simulation is finished. This window allows us to select the particular Forecasts we wish to include in the Overlay Chart, and to tailor the display to our preferences. The results are shown in Figure 15A8. As the chart shows, the distribution for the stock price at expiration is lognormally distributed, while the distribution of the option price has a large spike at zero. This reflects the large number of simulation trials on which the stock price is below the strike price and the option is not exercised.

SENSITIVITY CHART

Throughout this book, we have emphasized the importance of sensitivity analysis. In Chapter 6, we discussed using Data Sensitivity to determine the relationship between a single parameter or decision variable and the outcome. We also introduced the concept of a tornado chart, which provides a ranking of parameters in terms of the impact they have on the outcome. Recall that in a tornado chart, we assume each parameter takes on its high and low values one at a time, with all other parameters fixed. While a tornado chart can help determine which variables have the strongest impact on the outcome, it cannot take into account the probability distribution behind a parameter, nor can it vary all parameters simultaneously.

Crystal Ball's Sensitivity Chart feature does precisely this: It takes into account both the uncertainty in a parameter and the mathematical relationship between that parameter and the outcome. In a nutshell, this feature determines the extent to which each Assumption cell is correlated with the Forecast cell. If large values of one Assumption tend to occur in the same trial as large values of the Forecast (regardless of the values of other Assumptions) and vice versa, then the sensitivity of the Forecast to this Assumption is high.

To illustrate this feature, we use the Advertising Budget example. We use three Assumption cells for this illustration: Price has a uniform distribution between 30 and 50; cost has a uniform distribution between 20 and 30; and overhead percentage has a triangular distribution with a minimum of 10 percent, a maximum of 20 percent, and a

FIGURE 15A9 Sensitivity Chart for Advertising Budget Simulation

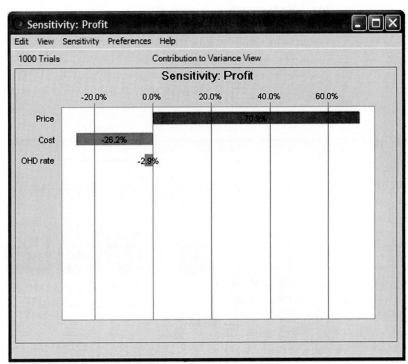

most likely value of 15 percent. After the simulation run, we can select Crystal Ball▶ Analyze▶View Charts▶ Sensitivity Charts. The result is shown in Figure 15A9.

This chart shows that price is most strongly correlated with profit: the higher the price, the higher the profit. Cost is next most strongly correlated, and the relationship is negative, as we would expect (low costs lead to high profits and vice versa). The overhead percentage ranks third in terms of impact.

FITTING DISTRIBUTIONS TO DATA

In this chapter we discussed how to select a particular probability distribution for an uncertain parameter. We advocate using a high degree of judgment in this process, since data are usually not available or are biased. However, there are formal methods for determining which family of distributions (for example, normal or triangular) fits a given set of data most closely. Crystal Ball provides the Batch Fit tool to help carry out this process. (*Warning*: The Batch Fit tool should be used only after determining that the data are appropriate for the parameter in question and have been adjusted for any biases.)

To implement the Batch Fit tool, we place data in a row or a column (as in Figure 15A10) and select Crystal Ball▶Run▶Tools▶Batch Fit. In the first stage, we have the option to fit some or all of the continuous distributions on the standard list provided. Suppose we select all of the distribution options. In the second stage (which we reach by clicking Next), we specify the range in which the data can be found. In this example, there are a hundred data points, in the range A2:A101. At the second stage, the Batch Fit tool offers three different tests of "goodness-of-fit": the Anderson-Darling (A-D), Chi-squared, and Kolmogorov-Smirnov (K-S). (More information on these tests is available in the Crystal Ball user manual.) We select the Chi-squared test initially. Finally, we choose to place the results in the current worksheet.

The result for the example data set is shown in Figure 15A11, in columns D and E. The values of the Chi-squared statistic are shown in E6:E18 for the 13 distributions tested. The best results are shown in E2:E4. For the Chi-squared test, a Weibull distribution is selected as providing the best fit among the distributions tested. In columns G and H we show the parallel results for the K-S test, and in columns J and K we show the results for the A-D test. The logistic distribution provides the closest fit for these two tests.

One final comment on this example is in order. We created the data in this example by simulating 100 independent trials from a *normal* distribution with a mean of 100 and a standard deviation of 25. The sample data clearly reflect the distribution that created them: the sample mean is 100.3, the sample standard deviation is 22.7, and the histogram looks approximately normal. However, the normal distribution

FIGURE 15A10 Data for Fitting Probability Distributions

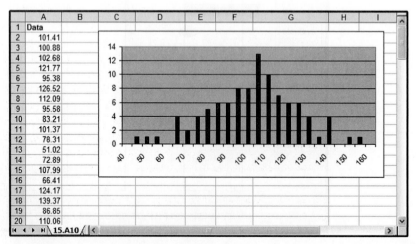

FIGURE 15A11 Results of
Batch Fit on Normally
Distributed Data

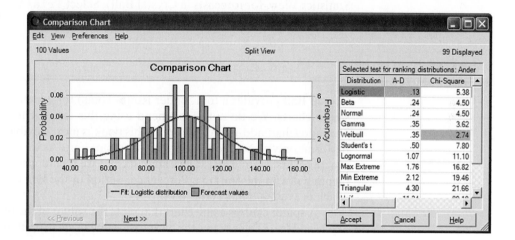

	A	B	C	D	E	F	G	H	I	J	K
1	**Data**			Data Series:	Data		Data Series:	Data		Data Series:	Data
2	101.41			**Chi-Square:**	2.740		**Kolmogorov-Smirno**	0.045		**Anderson-Darling**	0.127
3	100.88			Distribution:	0		Distribution:	0		Distribution:	0
4	102.68			Best fit:	Weibull		Best fit:	Logistic		Best fit:	Logistic
5	121.77										
6	95.38			Normal	34.400		Normal	0.051		Normal	0.244
7	126.52			Triangular	21.660		Triangular	0.172		Triangular	4.303
8	112.09			Lognormal	11.100		Lognormal	0.094		Lognormal	1.074
9	95.58			Uniform	80.180		Uniform	0.276		Uniform	11.344
10	83.21			Exponential	236.600		Exponential	0.421		Exponential	27.688
11	101.37			Weibull	2.740		Weibull	0.066		Weibull	0.353
12	78.31			Beta	4.500		Beta	0.051		Beta	0.242
13	51.02			Gamma	3.620		Gamma	0.063		Gamma	0.346
14	72.89			Logistic	5.380		Logistic	0.045		Logistic	0.127
15	107.99			Pareto	215.920		Pareto	0.393		Pareto	23.989
16	66.41			Max Extreme	16.820		Max Extreme	0.103		Max Extreme	1.758
17	124.17			Min Extreme	19.460		Min Extreme	0.111		Min Extreme	2.123
18	139.37			Student's t	7.800		Student's t	0.065		Student's t	0.498
19	86.85										
20	110.06										

⊮ ◂ ▸ ⊮ \ 15.A11 / ◂

FIGURE 15A12 Results
of Using the Fit . . . Option
Within the Distribution
Gallery

was not the closest fitting or even the second closest fitting distribution in the three cases we tested. The lesson is that if there is this much difference between a data sample and the distribution that generated it, we should be very skeptical that actual empirical data accurately reveal the *shape* of the underlying probability distribution. Judgment in this matter, as always, is required.

Crystal Ball also provides the option to fit a distribution to data using the Distribution Gallery. Suppose we wish to input one Assumption cell using the Distribution Gallery. We select Fit from among the buttons at the bottom of the Distribution Gallery. This selection implements a variant of the Batch Fit tool. If we specify the same 100 data points (Figure 15A10) as input data, then we obtain the same information in a slightly different format. Here, the candidate distributions are presented graphically, one at a time, in order of goodness-of-fit. The first distribution displayed for the Chi-squared test is the Weibull distribution, as shown in Figure 15A12, in which the best-fitting distribution and the histogram of sample data can be compared. The buttons for Next Distribution and Prev Distribution allow us to examine this comparison for any of the fitted distributions, and the button for Accept allows us to select one of the candidates to serve as the distribution in our Assumption cell.

CREATING REPORTS

Consistent documentation of simulation results is difficult because each run contains so much data. Crystal Ball provides a Report option that creates a separate spreadsheet in which we can store all the necessary information from a simulation. After running a simulation, we simply select Crystal Ball▶Analyze▶Create Report, and a window appears that permits us to save selected results. This can include the distributions of Assumption cells and all aspects of Forecast cells. We can also select Overlay Charts or Sensitivity Charts. This is a handy feature when we use a simulation model in production mode and need to save the essential features of our results in a single place.

EXTRACTING DATA

Occasionally the data-analysis and graphing capabilities of Crystal Ball may not be adequate for our purposes. In these cases, it is helpful to create a file of the raw output data. This can be accomplished using Analyze ▶ Extract Data. This command creates a new spreadsheet containing the results of the simulation in one of six different forms. These six choices are provided in the Data section of the Extract Data window. The statistics form follows the standard Excel statistical summary (also used in the Statistics View, for forecasts in Crystal Ball). Select Trial Values to extract all the raw simulation results for the Forecast cells.

TORNADO CHARTS

Crystal Ball provides a tool (under Run▶Tools) for generating tornado charts and spider charts. We do not recommend using this tool for tornado charts, since the Tornado Chart add-in provided with this book is more flexible. The Crystal Ball tool performs only a Common Percentage tornado chart. As we explain in Chapter 6, this is a quick first step in sensitivity analysis, but we would usually recommend supplementing it with the Variable Percentage option or the Percentiles option, neither of which is available in Crystal Ball.

A spider chart is a line chart that plots the values of the objective for two values above and two values below the base-case value of each input. It is similar to a tornado chart in that the sensitivity to multiple inputs can be tested at one pass. It is different in that it tests *two* values on each side of the base case rather than one, so any nonlinearities in the response can be uncovered. Spider charts can be useful and we recommend them, especially when there is reason to think the model is nonlinear.

CORRELATED SAMPLING

Crystal Ball provides several methods for creating correlations between various probability distributions. The simplest approach is to enter correlations between Assumption cells in the Distribution Gallery. To do this, we enter the distribution for the first Assumption cell as usual. Then we enter the distribution for the second, correlated Assumption, and choose Correlate . . . to enter the correlation parameter. This method is straightforward but can become tedious if many correlated distributions are needed.

The Correlation Matrix option (under Run▶Tools) provides a more powerful method for entering correlations among Assumptions. With this tool, we can select all or just some of the Assumption cells in a model. It then creates a matrix into which we can enter the correlation parameters directly. When Crystal Ball comes to taking samples from the Assumption cells during a simulation, it uses this matrix of correlations to relate the random samples as required.

BOOTSTRAPPING

Sometimes we wish to analyze unusual output statistics, such as the minimum, maximum, or the ratio of the mean to the standard deviation. To determine how accurate our estimates of these statistics are, we need to know their sampling distributions. We can use the MSE to determine an appropriate sample size for the mean because we know its sampling distribution is normal. However, the sampling distributions for unusual statistics are not necessarily normal. The bootstrap is a statistical tool for determining these sampling distributions. It works by taking repeated samples from the model and constructing the sampling distribution empirically. Crystal Ball provides the Bootstrap tool (under Run▶Tools) for bootstrap estimation. Refer to the user manual for more details.

Optimization in Simulation

16.1 INTRODUCTION

In the simplest terms, simulation is a method for describing the probability distribution of an outcome variable given a set of input variables. Sometimes those input variables include one or more decision variables, and the ultimate goal is to determine the best values for those inputs. But simulation, by itself, offers no assistance in identifying an *optimal,* or even good, set of decisions.

Ideally, we would like to marry the power of optimization to identify the best decision variables with the power of simulation to describe outcome distributions. Unfortunately, the optimization approaches using Solver that we covered in Chapters 10–13 are all based on the premise that the objective function can be measured deterministically. But in simulation models the objective function is the expected value or some other function of a random variable. Solver cannot be used to optimize these models. However, as we will show in this chapter, there are a number of practical approaches to optimizing simulation models.

We begin with a simple but common example of a problem with a single decision variable, and we illustrate several approaches to optimization when the problem has one or two decision variables. Then we move on to more complex problems, which involve three or more decision variables and possibly constraints as well. Finally, we discuss models in which some decisions can be made after some of the uncertainties are resolved. These so-called embedded decision problems require linking Solver and Crystal Ball.

16.2 OPTIMIZATION WITH ONE OR TWO DECISION VARIABLES

We begin our study of optimization in simulation models with a simple but common example that involves choosing a supply quantity before demand is known for certain.

EXAMPLE
Hastings Sportswear

In November, Jeff Hastings of the fashion skiwear manufacturer Hastings Sportswear, Inc., faces the task of committing to specific production quantities for each skiwear item the company will offer in the coming year's line. Commitments are needed immediately in order to reserve space in production facilities located throughout Asia. Actual demand for these products will not become known for at least six months.

Production costs for a typical parka run about 75 percent of the wholesale price, which in this case is $110. Unsold parkas can be sold at salvage for around 8 percent of the wholesale price.

Jeff has asked six of his most knowledgeable people to make forecasts of demand for the various models of parkas. Forecasts for one product are given in the following table, along with the average and standard deviation of the forecasts. (Experience suggests that the actual standard deviation in demand is roughly twice that of the standard deviation in the forecasts.) Based on this information, Jeff must decide on an order quantity for this model of parka.

Forecaster 1	900 units
Forecaster 2	1,000
Forecaster 3	900
Forecaster 4	1,300
Forecaster 5	800
Forecaster 6	1,200
Average	1,017
Standard deviation	194

■

16.2.1 Base-case Model

Our first model for this situation is shown in Figure 16.1*. This model has one decision variable—the number of parkas ordered. We have arbitrarily set it equal to the mean forecast of 1,017 (cell C13). We have also assumed a normal distribution for demand, with a mean of 1,017 units and a standard deviation of 388, or twice the standard deviation of the six forecasts. Random samples from this distribution are created in cell C16 using the Crystal Ball function `CB.NORMAL(C8,C10*C9)`. However, a normal distribution with a standard deviation nearly 40 percent of the mean can produce negative results, so we truncate the normal sample with the maximum function (MAX) to ensure that demand is nonnegative. A complete description of the model follows.

Data

Cells C4:C9: Given data.

Cell C10: A parameter representing the amount by which we inflate the actual standard deviation of the demand estimates. The problem statement suggests the value 2.

Decision

Cell C13: The order quantity.

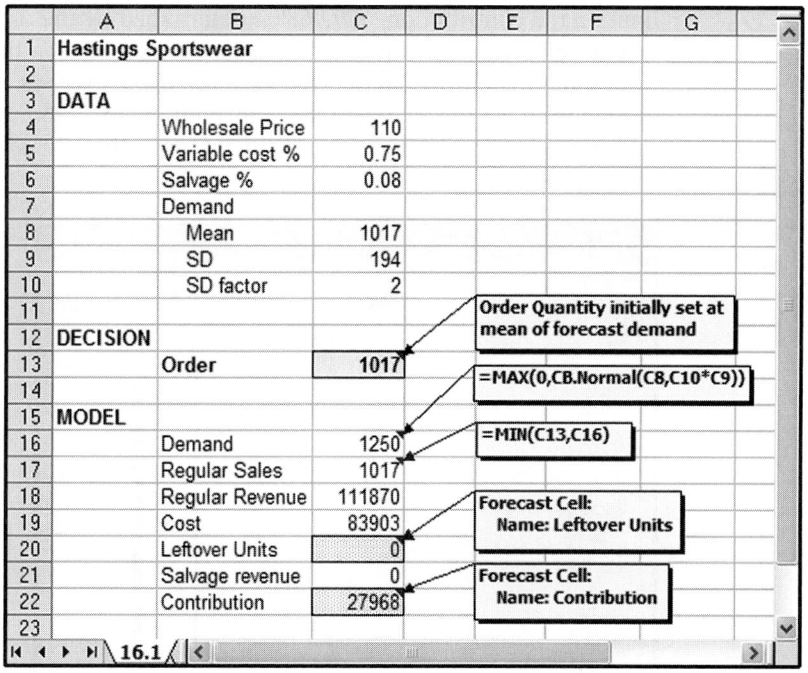

FIGURE 16.1 Hastings Sportswear Spreadsheet

*To download spreadsheets for this chapter, go to the Student Companion Site at www.wiley.com/college/powell.

Model

Cell C16: The actual demand is calculated using a normal distribution with mean given in cell C8 and standard deviation calculated from the given standard deviation (cell C9) multiplied by the SD factor (cell C10), truncated to be nonnegative.

Cell C17: Regular sales is calculated as the smaller of demand (C16) and the quantity ordered (C13).

Cell C18: Regular revenue is regular sales (C17) times the wholesale price (C4).

Cell C19: The cost is the number of units ordered (C13) times the wholesale price (C4) times the variable cost percent (C5).

Cell C20: Leftover units is calculated as the difference between the order quantity and demand, or zero if demand exceeds the order quantity.

Cell C21: Salvage revenue is leftover units (C20) times wholesale price (C4) times the salvage percent (C6).

Cell C22: Profit contribution is the sum of regular revenue (C18) and salvage revenue (C21), less cost (C19).

Two outcomes of this model are of particular interest: the profit contribution and the number of leftover units. Accordingly, we have designated two Forecast cells: Contribution in cell C22 and Leftover Units in cell C20. Hastings Sportswear would like to determine an order quantity that leads to a large profit contribution, but without running the risk of having too many parkas left unsold. Since we cannot optimize two objective functions, we take contribution as our objective to be maximized, but we impose a constraint on the number of leftover units.

The results of running this model, using 1,000 trials, are shown in Figures 16.2 and 16.3. Figure 16.2 shows that the average contribution from this product is about $12,661 if we order 1,017 units. (The Mean Standard Error (MSE) is $725, or about 5.7 percent of the mean. MSE is a measure of the precision in the estimate of the mean. The concept is covered in Appendix 15.2.) Contribution cannot exceed $27,968, but it can fall as low as −$74,953. Evidently, there is considerable financial risk associated with this decision, in addition to the risk of having leftover units. The upper limit on the contribution ($27,968) is determined by the order quantity. Because we cannot sell more than we order, revenues cannot exceed the value of the wholesale price times the order quantity. Whenever demand exceeds the order quantity, we sell exactly what we ordered, and the contribution is $27,968. According to Figure 16.2, this occurs about 50 percent of the time. One of the interesting aspects of this case is

FIGURE 16.2 Distribution of Profit Contribution for Hastings Sportswear

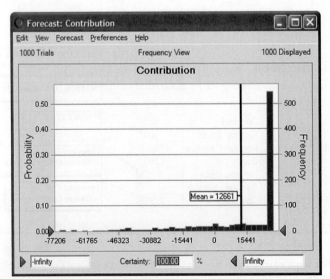

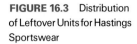

FIGURE 16.3 Distribution of Leftover Units for Hastings Sportswear

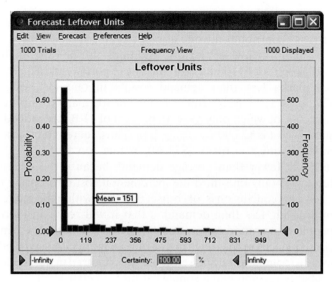

how the normal distribution for demand is transformed by the structure of the model into the highly skewed distribution of profit contribution shown in Figure 16.2.

Figure 16.3 shows the distribution of leftover units associated with ordering 1,017 parkas. On average, we can expect to have 151 units left over (with an MSE of 7 units, or 4.6 percent of the mean), but this amount could range from zero to 1,017. In about half the cases simulated, demand exceeds supply, so no units are left over. But there is also a small chance that demand will be zero and then the entire stock will be left over.

We remarked earlier that simulation should be used only in situations where uncertainty is an essential feature of the problem. This is one of those situations. If there were no uncertainty in demand, and we knew demand would be exactly 1,017, we would simply order 1,017 and be guaranteed to make $27,968 with no units left over. Without uncertainty, the decision is obvious, and the results are entirely predictable. But if we ignore uncertainty we miss the essential challenge of the problem—that when demand is uncertain, we must strike a balance between two kinds of risks. In one direction, there is the risk of ordering too many and having costly leftovers; in the other, there is the risk of ordering too few and having unmet demand. With uncertainty, moreover, our expected profit is only $12,661.

Simulation analysis allows us to measure the risks associated with ordering mean demand, but to this point, it does not suggest an optimal order quantity. The next question is: Can we improve on our initial decision to order 1,017 parkas?

16.2.2 Grid Search

Our goal in this problem is not merely to estimate the contribution we would receive for a particular order quantity, but to determine the best order quantity. The term *best* implies the largest possible expected contribution, but it might also involve ensuring that the risk of a low contribution is not too great and that the number of parkas left over is acceptable. At this stage of our analysis, we have determined only that we would make $12,661 on average if we were to order 1,017 parkas. We also observed that we would have an average surplus of 151 parkas. These results might suggest that we consider ordering fewer than 1,017 parkas, since having so many units left over seems to be a waste of resources.

It is straightforward to change the number of parkas ordered (cell C13) and rerun the simulation to determine a new expected contribution. The results are as follows: When we order 900, we make $14,223 on average, which is better than when we order 1,017. The average number of unsold parkas declines, as we would expect, to 97. If we reduce the order quantity still further, to 800, average contribution rises to $14,764, and the average number unsold drops to 64. If we order 700, we make $14,480 with an average of 40 unsold; at 600, we make $13,496 with an average of 25 unsold.

It appears that, up to a point, ordering fewer parkas than average demand can increase contribution while also decreasing the leftover stock.

It is worthwhile to pause and think through the implications of these results. Parkas sell for $110 and cost Hastings Sportswear $82.50 (= 0.75 × 110). Ordering one parka less than demand results in one lost sale. The forgone profit is $27.50 (= 110 − 82.5). But ordering one too many results in $82.50 of excess production cost, of which only $8.80 (8 percent of 110) is recouped in salvage revenue. The surplus cost is $73.80 (= 82.5 − 8.8). Thus, there is a basic asymmetry in the costs of ordering one too many ($73.80) or one too few ($27.50). The economics favor ordering fewer than average demand, because the incremental cost of ordering too few is only one-third the incremental cost of ordering too many.

This conclusion is, of course, true only within the model world. One implication of ordering less than demand is that it will result in more unsatisfied customers, people who wanted our product but found it out of stock. This result can have serious consequences in the long run for our company, if unsatisfied customers tend to drift away to competitors. Such costs are not captured in our model. If they were, we would probably recommend a somewhat higher order level.

The procedure we have illustrated here is a form of **grid search**. In a grid search, we select a series of values we wish to test for a decision variable, and we run the simulation at each of these values. Our grid in this case consists of the order levels 600, 700, 800, and 900. We show the results of an expanded grid search in the following table.

Parkas Ordered	Expected Contribution	Expected Leftovers
600	$13,496	25
650	14,070	32
700	14,480	40
750	14,726	51
800	14,764	64
850	14,617	79
900	14,223	97
950	13,609	117
1,000	12,766	139
1,050	11,639	165
1,100	10,195	193
1,150	8,468	224
1,200	6,525	257

These results suggest that contribution is highest in the vicinity of 800 units, with an average of about 64 units unsold. (For more precision in our estimate of the best order quantity, we could refine the grid search by using a step size smaller than the 50 used in this table.)

16.2.3 Replicating the Model

When our model is particularly simple, we can use another, more efficient approach to grid search. The trick is to replicate the model for each value of the decision variable we wish to test. This is illustrated in Figure 16.4, in which we have taken the one-column model from Figure 16.1 and essentially copied it 13 times, for order levels between 600 and 1,200. These alternatives for the order level appear in cells D13:P13. For each different order level, there may be different outcomes in the cells below. However, the parameters in the range C4:C10 are used in the calculations for each alternative.

Several aspects of this model are noteworthy. One is that we have simulated demand only once, in cell C16, and then used this random value for all the other

FIGURE 16.4 Hastings Sportswear Spreadsheet with Replications

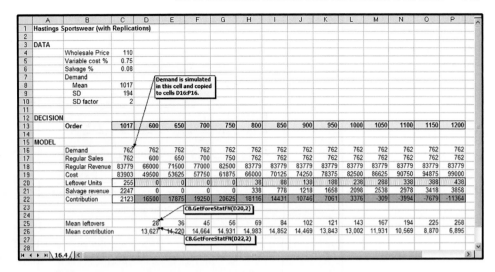

values of the decision variable. In other words, the cells to the right of C16 all reference the contents of C16. The alternative would be to sample from a different distribution for each decision variable. However, in that design, there would be two possible sources of variability in the profit contribution—the randomness in demand and the choice of an order quantity. Sampling once not only cuts down on simulation run time, but it also removes one of these sources of variability. Thus, the only source of difference between one profit outcome and another is the choice of order quantity.

Because we are interested both in contribution and in the number of leftover units as the order level changes, we must create a Forecast cell for each result for each order quantity. First, we remove the Forecast status of cell C22 by selecting this cell and choosing Crystal Ball▶Define▶Clear, clicking OK to confirm our intention. Next, we define cells D22:P22 as Forecast cells. Although it's a little tedious, it helps to give each of these cells a descriptive name. Since we are searching among order levels, we might name the cells according to the corresponding order level, "Contribution at 600" for cell D22, "Contribution at 650" for E22, and so on. We repeat this procedure for the leftover units in cells D20:P20, using appropriate names. This gives us a total of 26 forecasts. When we run the simulation, 26 Forecast windows open on the screen. If the windows seem distracting, we can send them to the background by clicking on the spreadsheet itself. Alternatively, when the simulation is completed, we can choose Analyze▶Close All on the Control Panel. To turn off the display of Forecast windows during a simulation, choose Crystal Ball▶Run▶Run Preferences▶Speed, and under Chart windows select Suppress chart windows (fastest).

One convenient way to record the results on the spreadsheet itself is to use the Crystal Ball function CB.GETFORESTATFN, which we described briefly in Chapter 15. In the Results section of Figure 16.4, we have used this function to record the mean values for both the leftover units (in row 25) and the contribution (in row 26) for each order level. For example, the formula for cell D25 is CB.GETFORESTATFN(D20, 2). Once the simulation has been completed, this cell displays the mean value of the forecast for leftover units in cell D20.

In Figure 16.5, we show graphs of these results as the order level varies from 600 to 1,200. The graph for mean contribution shows that the maximum occurs at an order level of about 750 or 800. It also suggests that any order level between about 700 and 850 may be acceptable, since mean contribution is within 1 percent of the optimum in this range. Over this same range, the mean number of leftover units varies from 40 to 80. If we wish to take the risk of low profits into account, we can choose an order level anywhere in this range and be sure we are not giving up too much in mean contribution. Moreover, we can select an order level at the lower end to save about 40 leftover units, on average, at a cost of only 1 percent of contribution.

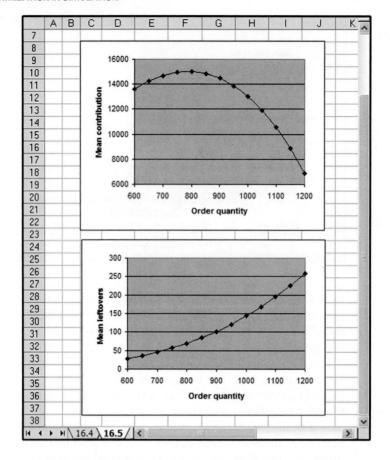

Crystal Ball provides a specialized chart called a **trend chart**, which can be used to depict the sensitivity of Forecast cells to decision variables or other inputs. After the simulation run is finished, we select Analyze▶Trend Charts on the Control Panel (or Crystal Ball▶Analyze▶View Charts▶Trend Charts). Under Choose Forecasts, we select the 13 outputs for contribution (D22:P22). Figure 16.6 shows a 10 percent Certainty Band around the median level of contribution for each of the 13 order quantities from 600 to 1,200 units. Recall that the median of a distribution divides the outcomes in half. Referring back to Figure 16.2, we can see that the median lies above the mean in this case because the outcomes are skewed to the left. Figure 16.6 shows that

FIGURE 16.6 Trend Chart
for Median Contribution

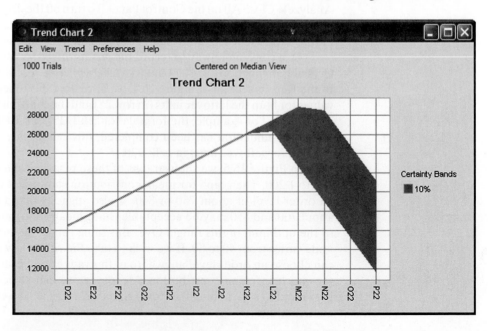

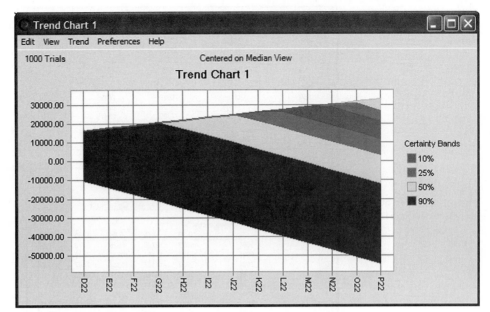

FIGURE 16.7 Trend Chart for Median Contribution with Uncertainty Bands

if we wanted to optimize the median contribution (rather than the mean), we would choose an order level around 1,000 units, close to mean demand.

Figure 16.7 displays another trend chart for the same data. This version gives an indication of the range of outcomes, or the risks, associated with the alternative order quantities. To produce this display, we chose 10, 25, 50, and 90 percent Certainty Bands. This chart shows that the risk, or range of outcomes, increases as the order quantity increases. Most important, the *downside* risk increases, because the upside profit is limited by the order quantity. Again, if we wish to reduce downside risk, we might want to order fewer than 1,000 parkas, although we lower the median contribution by doing so.

The Crystal Ball trend chart is a handy way to display the sensitivity of an output variable to any input that ranges over multiple values. It is a natural way to perform optimization in simple simulation models with a single decision variable, provided that the median outcome is a reasonable objective. It also provides a convenient device for displaying the trade-off between the median outcome and the risks of extreme outcomes.

16.2.4 Using CB Sensitivity

The CB Sensitivity tool, which we introduced in Chapter 15 in the context of sensitivity analysis, can also be used for optimization. It is particularly useful for models that are too complex for the replication approach, or when we want to vary two inputs (either decision variables or other parameters). We illustrate using the original Hastings Sportswear model of Figure 16.1. When we call up CB Sensitivity (Add-ins▶Sensitivity Toolkit▶Crystal Ball Sensitivity), we find that the two Forecast cells are already identified. We choose to record not only the mean values, but also the minimum and maximum values for each Forecast. To find the optimal value for the order level, we vary it from 600 to 1,200 in steps of 50. The results are shown in Figure 16.8. As we have already determined, the optimal order level for maximizing mean profit is around 800. However, the *range* of outcomes from minimum to maximum increases as we increase the order quantity, so it might be advantageous to order fewer than 800 if we want to limit the downside risk. Also shown in Figure 16.8 are the mean, minimum, and maximum values for units left over. Here, we can see that the maximum number of units left over is always the order quantity, so this measure increases linearly with the order quantity. The mean number left over, however, increases at an increasing rate.

FIGURE 16.8 CB Sensitivity Table for Order Level

	A	B	C	D	E	F	G
1	Order	Contribution: Mean	Contribution: Min	Contribution: Max	Leftover Units: Mean	Leftover Units: Min	Leftover Units: Max
2	600	14171	-44220	16500	23	0	600
3	650	14799	-47905	17875	30	0	650
4	700	15234	-51590	19250	40	0	700
5	750	15488	-55275	20625	51	0	750
6	800	15533	-58960	22000	64	0	800
7	850	15332	-62645	23375	79	0	850
8	900	14887	-66330	24750	97	0	900
9	950	14155	-70015	26125	118	0	950
10	1000	13200	-73700	27500	141	0	1000
11	1050	11964	-77385	28875	167	0	1050
12	1100	10464	-81070	30250	196	0	1100
13	1150	8687	-84755	31625	227	0	1150
14	1200	6638	-88440	33000	260	0	1200
15							

16.2 and 16.3 ╲ 16.8

FIGURE 16.9 CB Sensitivity Table for Order Level and Price

	A	B	C	D	E	F
1	Contribution: Mean					
2		Variable cost %				
3	Order	0.70	0.75	0.80	0.85	0.90
4	500	15028	12778	9528	6778	4028
5	600	17417	14117	10817	**7517**	**4217**
6	700	19047	15197	**11347**	7497	3647
7	800	**19818**	**15418**	11018	6618	2218
8	900	19791	14841	9891	4941	-9
9	1000	18726	13226	7726	2226	-3274
10	1100	16481	10431	4381	-1669	-7719
11	1200	13169	6569	-31	-6631	-13231
12						

In this model, the only true decision variable is the number of parkas ordered, cell C13. We would like to optimize this variable, but we might also like to know how sensitive the results are to the cost of parkas (cell C5). Using the CB Sensitivity tool, we can run a simulation and record the expected contribution for each combination of input values for order quantity and unit cost. We let the order level range from 500 to 1,200 in increments of 100, and we let the cost range from 0.70 to 0.90 in increments of 0.05.

For these settings, CB Sensitivity runs Crystal Ball 40 times (eight values for the order level times five values for costs) and builds the table shown in Figure 16.9. For a fixed order level, we can see how sensitive the mean contribution is to the cost by reading across the rows. For a given cost, we can determine how sensitive the mean contribution is to the order level by reading down the columns. The optimal expected contribution for each value of the cost parameter is highlighted in bold. One interesting message emerging from this table is that the optimal number of parkas drops from around 800 to around 600 as costs increase from 70 to 90 percent.

16.3 COMPLEX OPTIMIZATION PROBLEMS

The Hastings Sportswear example represents a simple optimization problem in the sense that it has only one decision variable. In general, grid search is a practical approach to optimization when we have one or two decision variables. The CB Sensitivity tool automates a grid search, but it, too, is limited to one or two variables. When the problem involves three or more decision variables, and possibly constraints as well, these approaches have limited usefulness. In such cases, we turn to a sophisticated Crystal Ball tool called **OptQuest**, which optimizes the choice of decision variables when the objective function is based on simulation outcomes.

Optimizing decision variables based on simulation outcomes can be an extremely challenging task. We saw in Chapter 10 that optimizing deterministic models requires some attention to model structure so that the optimization algorithm matches the problem at hand. Simulation models make the problem even more complex because we cannot measure the objective function precisely. Instead, we can only estimate it within the limits of precision achieved by our simulation. This "fuzziness" in the objective function rules out the possibility of directly adapting the deterministic optimization approaches (such as hill climbing) to problems involving randomness. OptQuest takes a novel approach to this problem, which we describe in general terms later.

16.3.1 OptQuest Concepts

Most of the concepts needed to use OptQuest should be familiar from our study of deterministic optimization in Chapters 10–13. OptQuest attempts to maximize or minimize an **objective function**, by changing the values of **decision variables**, possibly subject to **constraints**. OptQuest also introduces a new concept, that of a **requirement**, which is a restriction on the distribution of forecast values, such as the mean or 10th percentile.

The objective function in OptQuest can be any summary measure of a Forecast cell. Typically, we would maximize or minimize the mean value of the forecast. However, in some circumstances we might wish to minimize the variance, minimize the probability of a loss, or maximize the 5th percentile of the distribution of forecast values.

Decision variables in OptQuest, just as in Solver, are cells in the spreadsheet that the optimization software varies in order to optimize the objective function. Decision variables are specified directly in Crystal Ball in the same way as Assumption or Forecast cells. When we specify a Decision variable, we also choose whether it is to be discrete or continuous. With the discrete option, we can specify the number of evenly spaced discrete alternatives between a minimum and maximum value. In the case of continuous decision variables, fractional values are allowed.

Constraints, or relationships among decision variables, are a common feature of optimization problems. OptQuest allows the user to specify only *linear* constraints among the decision variables. For example, in a portfolio problem, the total amount invested must add up to the amount available. OptQuest does not consider candidate solutions that violate any of the constraints.

Sometimes, we wish to impose a constraint on the distribution of a Forecast cell. For example, we might wish to maximize the mean return from a portfolio, subject to a ceiling on the standard deviation of the return (a measure of risk). The objective here is to maximize mean return. The constraint, or *requirement* in Crystal Ball language, is that the standard deviation must not be too large. In this case, the objective function and the requirement apply to different measures of the distribution of the same Forecast. In other cases, the objective function and the requirement could apply to different Forecasts. Requirements are different from constraints because they cannot be imposed before a simulation is run, only afterward.

CRYSTAL BALL TIP
OptQuest Concepts

Objective: Forecast cell to be maximized or minimized. OptQuest allows the user to optimize any one of various summary measures of the objective—for example, mean, standard deviation, or 10th percentile.

Decision variables: Spreadsheet parameters OptQuest uses to optimize the objective. These must be defined as Decision cells in Crystal Ball.

Constraint: OptQuest allows any number of linear constraints among the decision variables. Solutions that violate these constraints are not considered feasible and are not reported.

Requirement: A constraint on a summary measure of a Forecast. For example, we could require that the standard deviation not exceed a set limit. Requirements can be evaluated only after a simulation run; thus, OptQuest may report a solution that violates a requirement, but it will label the solution as infeasible. ∎

The algorithms used by OptQuest are complex and beyond the scope of this book, so we only sketch them here.[1] OptQuest takes a **heuristic** approach to optimization, by which we mean that it searches intelligently for better and better solutions, but OptQuest cannot guarantee that it finds the global optimum. As a

---

[1]A more complete description can be found at the website http://www.crystalball.com/support/optimization/optimization_home.html.

consequence, we must take extra care to ensure that the results OptQuest gives us are sensible.

OptQuest uses three distinct heuristics in its search for optimal solutions: scatter search, tabu search, and neural networks. **Scatter search** generates an initial population of candidate solutions and uses simulation to estimate the objective for each one. It then creates the next generation of solutions by taking combinations of the previous solutions. At each generation, the best solutions are saved and the worst discarded. In this fashion, the general quality (by which we mean the value of the objective function) of the population of solutions improves over time. **Tabu search** is superimposed on the scatter search to control and direct the generation of solutions. Tabu search uses computer memory in various ways to ensure that the search does not reinvestigate solutions that have already been evaluated (such solutions are "tabu") and to ensure that the population remains sufficiently diverse over time. Finally, neural networks can be used (at the option of the user) to quickly screen out candidate solutions that are likely to result in poor values of the objective. A **neural network** is a predictive model that, in this case, predicts the objective function value for a candidate solution based on all the past solutions that have been evaluated. Using these heuristics, OptQuest can evaluate hundreds or thousands of candidates, depending on the time it is given and the complexity of the model, and it often finds optimal or near optimal solutions to quite complex problems. We now illustrate how to use OptQuest with examples from production planning, investment management, and cash management.

16.3.2 A Production Planning Problem

In Chapter 11, we discussed the allocation problem facing Veerman Furniture, which was to choose how much of three products (chairs, desks, and tables) need to be produced to maximize profits, without using more production time than is available in three departments (fabrication, assembly, and shipping) and without exceeding demand. We solved this problem as a deterministic linear program, and we found that maximum profits of $8,400 were achieved by making 275 desks, 100 tables, and 0 chairs (see Figure 11.5).

Although this solution is unambiguously optimal for the problem as we stated it, it may not be directly applicable in the real world. For one thing, demands are usually forecasts, and those forecasts are somewhat uncertain. If the actual demands turn out to be higher or lower than forecasts, the optimal solution to the deterministic problem may no longer be optimal, or even feasible. For example, in the optimal solution, we make 100 tables, which meets the demand exactly. If actual demand is 110, we might wish we had made more tables. At the same time, if demand is 90, we will have 10 tables in surplus and would probably have done better to reallocate our resources. For simplicity, we assume that solutions in which demand is less than production for at least one product are considered infeasible. That is, Veerman Furniture wants to avoid a surplus.

Our first step in introducing uncertainty into this model is to analyze the performance of the optimal deterministic solution when demand is uncertain. We assume that demand for each product is normally distributed, with a mean equal to our point forecast and a standard deviation equal to 10 percent of the mean. Similarly, we assume that the profit contributions from each product are normally distributed, with a mean given by our point forecasts and a standard deviation equal to 10 percent of the mean. We modify the original spreadsheet by introducing normal distributions (using the Distribution Gallery) for the profit contributions in cells B8:D8 and demands in cells G15:G17 (see Figure 16.10). We also determine whether the solution is feasible by adding IF functions in cells H15:H17 that test whether demand for the given product exceeds production. The formula in H19 takes on the value 1 when demands for *all* the products exceed production (i.e., there is no surplus), and the value 0 otherwise. The Forecast cells are Total Profit in E8 (our original objective function) and Feasibility in cell H19.

FIGURE 16.10 Veerman Furniture Spreadsheet Prepared for OptQuest

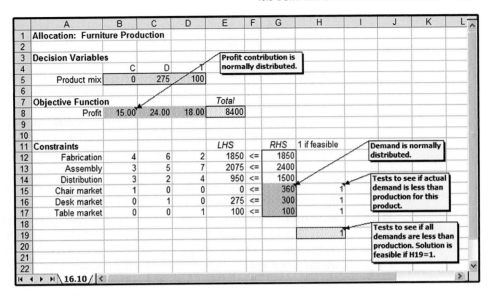

When we run a simulation using the optimal deterministic solution, we find that the mean profit is \$8,365, essentially unchanged from the deterministic solution. However, that solution results in surplus production, and is thereby infeasible, 62 percent of the time. (We obtain this estimate as the mean value of the Feasibility Forecast cell.) Note that because the demand constraint on tables was binding in the original model, half the time the simulated demand falls below the mean and makes the solution infeasible. The constraint on desk demand was not binding, but the excess demand was small enough that an additional 12 percent of the time in the simulation, this constraint was violated when table demand was not binding.

A solution that is infeasible 62 percent of the time is unlikely to be attractive to management. But we cannot simply impose a constraint that our solution must be feasible, because we do not know demand in advance. The best we can do is find a set of decisions that offers high average profit and is highly *likely* to be feasible. This is a task for OptQuest.

To set up the spreadsheet for OptQuest, we must define the decision variables, the constraints (if any), the objective function, and any requirements. Uncertain parameters (Assumption cells), outputs (Forecast cells), and decision variables (Decision cells) are all defined before opening the OptQuest program; the remaining inputs are defined within OptQuest itself.

We define the decision variables in cells B5:D5 one at a time, using the Crystal Ball command Define▶Define Decision (Figure 16.11). This is an opportunity to assign a name to the decision variable, for clarity in the steps that follow. Initially, we specify that each decision variable is discrete, with a step size of 10 units, a lower bound of zero, and an upper bound equal to mean demand. (Since our goal is to limit the percentage of time the solution is infeasible, we can anticipate that the optimal values of the decision variables lie below mean demand.)

Finally, it is necessary to determine an appropriate run length before opening OptQuest because it uses the simulation run length that has been specified in Run Preferences. Again, recall from Chapter 15 that results differ somewhat in different runs because of the variability in random samples. Recall also that we can control such differences by selecting the simulation run length. A preliminary simulation run with 1,000 trials yields an MSE for profit of \$21, or about 0.2 percent ($= 21/8,400$). A separate run with 100 trials yields an MSE of \$74, or about 1 percent. Since 1 percent accuracy is probably sufficient

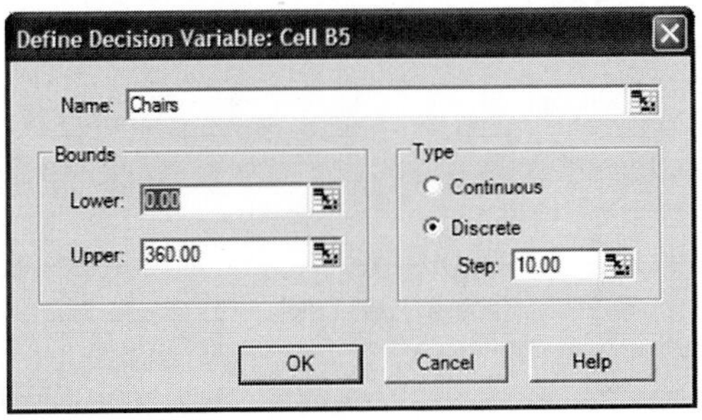

FIGURE 16.11 The Decision Variable Window in Crystal Ball

for our purposes, and the shorter run length allows OptQuest to examine more alternatives, we specify a run length of 100 trials. It is also important to set the random number seed (in Crystal Ball, check Use same sequence of random numbers under Crystal Ball▶Run▶Run Preferences▶Sampling) so that the same random outcomes are used on every OptQuest run. This reduces the variance between runs and makes the search for an optimum more efficient.

We open OptQuest by choosing Crystal Ball▶Run▶Tools▶OptQuest. (It is a good idea to have only one spreadsheet open in Crystal Ball when running OptQuest.) Within OptQuest, we click on the New button, and OptQuest opens the OptQuest Wizard. This Wizard brings up four windows in turn: Decision Variable Selection, Constraints, Forecast Selection, and Options. We can edit the default information in these windows, or click OK to accept them as given. We can also return to any of these windows by making a selection from the OptQuest Tools menu or its Window menu.

The Decision Variable Selection window in this case simply confirms the definitions of the variables specified earlier in Crystal Ball. In the Constraints window, we enter the three production constraints (Fabrication, Assembly, and Distribution). The easiest way to do this is to click on Sum all Variables and edit the text as necessary. When all three constraints have been entered, we click OK. The next window is Forecast Selection. Here, we see two rows, one for each Forecast cell (Profit and Feasibility). Profit is our objective, so we specify Select▶Maximize Objective and then Forecast Statistic▶Mean. Our requirement is that the solution be feasible at least 90 percent of the time, so for the Feasibility Forecast, we choose Select▶Requirement, Forecast Statistic▶Mean, and in the Lower Bound column, we enter 0.9. This ensures that cell H19, which takes on the value 1 when the solution is feasible and value 0 otherwise, will be 1 on at least 90 percent of the trials. In other words, the solution will be feasible at least 90 percent of the time.

These three windows can be resized so that they are displayed simultaneously, as shown in Figure 16.12. The last window that OptQuest opens automatically is the Options window. Run-time options are shown on a drop-down list under the Time tab. However, the user can override the options given. (Five minutes represents the shortest run time on the drop-down list of times, but shorter run times are useful during debugging and preliminary testing, while longer run times ensure higher quality solutions.) We enter three minutes as a run time and click on OK. Then, we select Run▶Start.

When OptQuest begins a run, it opens a Status and Solutions window. This window shows the values of the Decision cells and the Forecast cells for the current

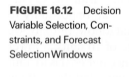

FIGURE 16.12 Decision Variable Selection, Constraints, and Forecast Selection Windows

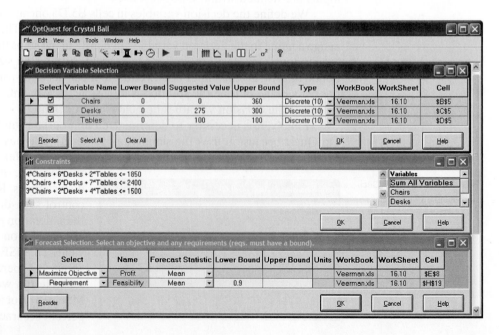

run, the best run so far, and a number of previous runs. Two other useful windows can be opened from the OptQuest menu: the Performance Graph and the Current Decision Variables bar graph. The Performance Graph shows the value of the objective for the best alternative found so far during the search. This graph shows the best value of the objective generally increasing (for maximization) or decreasing (for minimization) as the search progresses. In most cases, it changes quickly early in the run, as improvements are being found frequently, and then it changes more slowly as better solutions become harder to find. It is a good idea to watch this graph during an OptQuest run, as it gives a good overall indication of how the search is progressing. The Current Decision Variables window, which shows the values of the decision cells being tested on the current run, may also be helpful by providing a visual sense of which combinations of decision variables are being tested.

The results of this first run are shown in Figure 16.13. The best solution found was to produce 60 chairs, 240 desks, and 80 tables. This solution has an estimated profit of $8,023 and is feasible 93 percent of the time. The Performance Graph shows that the best alternative was found rather early in the search and could not be improved with further testing. We can learn more about the search by choosing Run▶Solution Analysis from the OptQuest menu, selecting the top 10 percent of the runs, and then selecting Analyze. The results are shown in Figure 16.14. Among the top 10 percent of the cases tested, the average value of profit was $7,513, and the average values of the decision variables were 137 for chairs, 193 for desks, and 50 for tables. It appears that the optimal solution involves production of all three products, with a higher number of desks and chairs and fewer tables. However, we also notice in Figure 16.14 that in the top 10 solutions, the optimal values of the decision variables are not consistent. The number of chairs, for example, varies from 60 to 140. This suggests that a more refined search might be valuable.

One way to improve the search would be to allow the decision variables to vary by 1 unit rather than 10. This can be done by selecting Tools▶Decision Variables,

FIGURE 16.13 OptQuest Results for Step Size 10

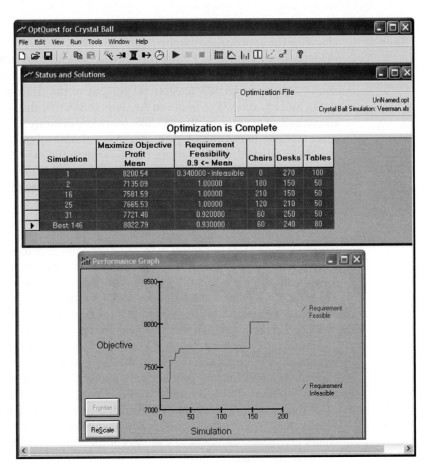

FIGURE 16.14 OptQuest
Solution Analysis

Analysis					
Name	Best	Minimum	Average	Maximum	Standard Deviation
▶ Profit	8022.79	7223.50	7512.79	8022.79	181.539
Chairs	60	30	137.143	320	72.3089
Desks	240	80	192.653	250	47.0248
Tables	80	10	50.2041	80	13.0133

Solutions (* Indicates that a solution falls outside the confidence

Solution	Objective Profit	Chairs	Desks	Tables
▶ 1	8022.79	60	240	80
2	7903.70	80	230	70
3	7875.72	110	210	70
4	7785.55	60	230	80
5	7784.61	100	220	60
6	7721.48	60	250	50
7	7698.91	130	190	70
8	7693.50	90	230	50
9	7668.23	140	190	60
10	7665.53	120	210	50
11	7637.55	150	190	50
12	7633.08	70	240	50
13	7616.74	280	100	60
14	7609.57	180	170	50
15	7605.10	100	220	50
16	7602.40	80	240	40
17	7581.59	210	150	50
18	7577.12	130	200	50
19	7572.65	50	250	50
20	7549.14	160	180	50

changing the appropriate parameters, and clicking OK. A 10-minute run of OptQuest gives the results shown in Figure 16.15. With OptQuest searching over a finer grid, we would expect the solution to improve, and it does. The best solution found in this run shows a profit of $8,060, feasible 90 percent of the time, producing 64 chairs, 237 desks, and 86 tables. The Solution Analysis shows that the top 10 percent of the cases tested had an average profit of $7,848. More importantly, the top 10 cases show much more stability in the values of the decision variables. For chairs, the solution values vary from 60 to 79, a much smaller range than in the previous run. We might expect the percentage of time the solution is feasible to decline as profit increases. This is confirmed in this case: The OptQuest run with a step size of 1 achieves the minimum feasibility of 90 percent, while with a step size of 10 we were only able to achieve 93 percent feasibility.

The solution found above is probably good enough for practical purposes. But it is a good idea to test this solution by redefining the decision variables again, this time as continuous. The optimal solution shows no improvement in a short run, but with longer runs, we have encountered a profit of $8,380, feasible 90 percent of the time, producing 54.8 chairs, 243.6 desks, and 84.3 tables. The Solution Analysis shows a limited range of variation in the values of the decision variables. The number of chairs produced in near-optimal solutions ranges from 54.5 to 95.6, desks from 216.1 to 243.9, and tables from 84.1 to 85.9. The continuous runs of OptQuest confirm what we found earlier using a discrete search. We can construct a solution in which production exceeds demand for any product only about 10 percent of the time by producing around 50 chairs, 240 desks, and 85 tables. The profit from this plan is not quite as high as in the deterministic formulation of the problem, but it is not radically lower. Finally, there is some degree of freedom in our choice of production levels, at least for chairs and desks, since these can vary somewhat from the optimal levels without significantly impacting profit.

FIGURE 16.15 OptQuest
Results for Step Size 1

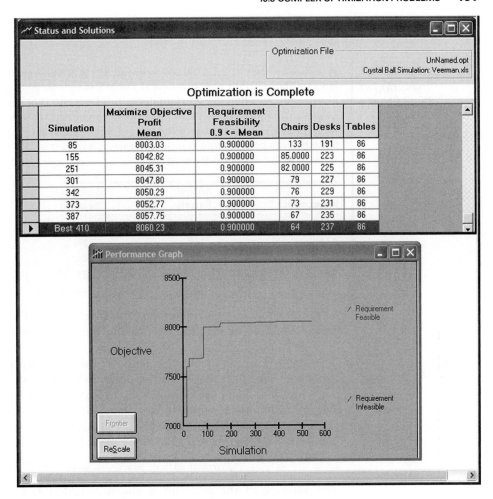

This set of decision variables is quite different from the deterministic solution— not only quantitatively but qualitatively as well. In the deterministic formulation of the problem, we produce no chairs at all, and the binding constraints are fabrication capacity and tables demand. In the current version of the problem, we find it advantageous to produce some of all three products, although we continue to produce more desks than either chairs or tables. From a deterministic point of view, *none* of the constraints is binding under this solution. We actually have unused production resources in all three departments. While this makes no sense from the point of view of linear programming, it does make sense when we take uncertainty into account, along with the desire to maintain a high probability of feasibility in demand.

16.3.3 A Portfolio Optimization Problem

In Chapter 10 we introduced the problem of determining the best allocation of a pool of money to a set of investments. Each investment vehicle has its own characteristics for return and risk. Some, such as government bonds, have low returns and low risk. Others, such as technology stocks, have high returns and high risk. The objective is to formulate an investment portfolio that has an attractive overall return with low risk. In general, these goals conflict: high return is usually associated with high risk.

Risk and return can be defined in many ways in the context of investments. Return is usually defined as the average or *mean return* on an individual asset or portfolio. Risk is measured by the variability of the asset or portfolio. The most common measure of variability is the *standard deviation of returns*, so we initially focus on choosing a portfolio that has a high mean return with a low standard deviation. But there are other, perhaps better, measures of risk for a portfolio, and we subsequently develop methods for choosing a portfolio with low values of these other measures of risk.

EXAMPLE
Investing in
Four Stocks

A particular investor has $100,000 to invest. She is considering investing her money in four stocks: Microsoft, GM, GE, and AT&T. The following table gives the average returns on these investments as well as the standard deviation of returns. (For simplicity in this example, we assume that returns among these assets are uncorrelated.) We want to determine how much to invest in each stock to maximize the average return, while keeping risk at an acceptable level. Since risk can be measured in different ways, it is important to explore the sensitivity of the solution to the risk measure used.

Investment	Annual Return	Standard Deviation
MSFT	40%	28%
AT&T	16%	22%
GM	20%	24%
GE	30%	18%

Our initial spreadsheet for this problem is shown in Figure 16.16. The given data are the mean and standard deviation of the return for each of the four stocks. The four decision variables represent the proportion of the portfolio allocated to each investment. The total amount invested is calculated by adding the four decision variables. We require that the entire portfolio be invested in these alternatives. The mean return of the portfolio, which serves as our objective function, is the weighted average of the mean returns of the individual stocks, with the weights being the proportions invested. In other words, if we label the returns r_i and the proportions w_i, the mean is calculated as follows:

$$Portfolio\ Mean = w_1 r_1 + w_2 r_2 + w_3 r_3 + w_4 r_4$$

The variance of the portfolio is also a weighted sum of the variances of the individual assets (assuming no correlation). However, the weights are the squared proportions invested:

$$Portfolio\ Variance = w_1^2 \sigma_1^2 + w_2^2 \sigma_2^2 + w_3^2 \sigma_3^2 + w_4^2 \sigma_4^2$$

A detailed description of the model follows.

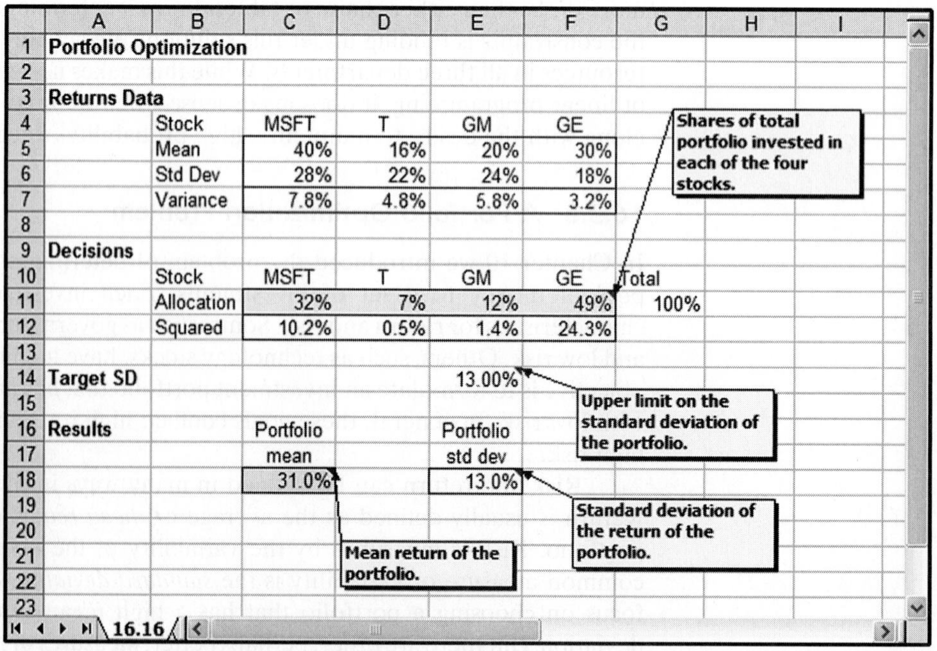

FIGURE 16.16 Spreadsheet for the Portfolio Allocation Problem

Returns Data

Cells C5:F5: Annual stock returns.

Cells C6:F6: Annual standard deviations of stock returns.

Cells C7:F7: Variances of stock returns, calculated by squaring the standard deviations (C6:F6); for future use.

Decisions

Cells C11:F11: Proportions of the portfolio allocated to each asset.

Cell G11: The total amount invested is the sum of the proportions (C11:F11). This total must equal 1.0.

Cells C12:F12: Squared decision variables (C11:F11); for future use.

Target SD

Cell E14: This parameter represents the maximum standard deviation for the portfolio.

Results

C18: The mean of the overall portfolio. Calculated as the SUMPRODUCT of the individual stock means (C5:F5) and the investment proportions (C11:F11).

E18: The standard deviation of the overall portfolio. Calculated as the square root of the SUMPRODUCT of the individual stock variances (C7:F7) and the squared investment proportions (C12:F12).

The investor's primary objective is to make the portfolio mean return as high as possible. This could be achieved by investing the entire portfolio in Microsoft, because it has the highest mean return of the four stocks. However, the portfolio would then have a very high risk, as measured by the standard deviation of 28 percent. One way to control the risk would be to maximize the mean return subject to a constraint on the portfolio standard deviation. This can be accomplished using Solver. The objective is the portfolio mean return in cell C18. The decision variables are the portfolio weights in cells C11:F11. There are two constraints: One is that the weights must sum to one; the other is that the portfolio standard deviation in cell E18 must be less than or equal to the target given in cell E14 (in this case, 13 percent). The objective function is linear in the decision variables, as is the first constraint. However, the second constraint is nonlinear because it involves the squared values of the decision variables. Thus, the entire problem is nonlinear, and we must use the nonlinear solver to find an optimal solution.

The solution to this problem is displayed in Figure 16.16. The mean return for the optimal portfolio is 31 percent, with the standard deviation at its ceiling of 13 percent. The optimal portfolio weights are 32 percent in Microsoft, 7 percent in AT&T, 12 percent in GM, and 49 percent in GE. This portfolio achieves the highest possible mean return while limiting risk (as measured by the standard deviation) to an acceptable level.

We can gain additional insight into this problem by varying the investor's tolerance for risk, as expressed by the limit on the standard deviation of the portfolio return. Figure 16.17 shows the results of running Solver Sensitivity on this model for values of the standard deviation target from 12 to 30 percent (no feasible portfolios have lower levels of risk). Several interesting observations can be made based on these results. First, as we increase the allowable risk, the portfolio mean increases but at a decreasing rate. Above a standard deviation of 28 percent, no improvement is possible because the entire portfolio is invested in Microsoft. When the allowable risk is low, the optimal plan involves investing in all four stocks—most heavily in Microsoft and GE. As the allowable risk increases, the optimal plan invests more in Microsoft and less in both AT&T and GM. The proportion invested in GE first increases, reaching a maximum of 55 percent, and then decreases to zero.

FIGURE 16.17 Sensitivity of the Optimal Solution to Risk Tolerance

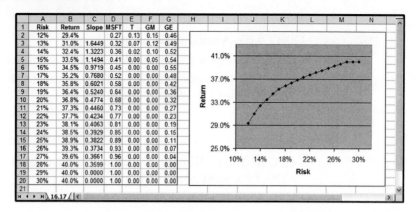

	A	B	C	D	E	F	G
1	Risk	Return	Slope	MSFT	T	GM	GE
2	12%	29.4%		0.27	0.13	0.15	0.46
3	13%	31.0%	1.6449	0.32	0.07	0.12	0.49
4	14%	32.4%	1.3223	0.36	0.02	0.10	0.52
5	15%	33.5%	1.1494	0.41	0.00	0.05	0.54
6	16%	34.5%	0.9719	0.45	0.00	0.00	0.55
7	17%	35.2%	0.7680	0.52	0.00	0.00	0.48
8	18%	35.8%	0.6021	0.58	0.00	0.00	0.42
9	19%	36.4%	0.5240	0.64	0.00	0.00	0.36
10	20%	36.8%	0.4774	0.68	0.00	0.00	0.32
11	21%	37.3%	0.4460	0.73	0.00	0.00	0.27
12	22%	37.7%	0.4234	0.77	0.00	0.00	0.23
13	23%	38.1%	0.4063	0.81	0.00	0.00	0.19
14	24%	38.5%	0.3929	0.85	0.00	0.00	0.15
15	25%	38.9%	0.3822	0.89	0.00	0.00	0.11
16	26%	39.3%	0.3734	0.93	0.00	0.00	0.07
17	27%	39.6%	0.3661	0.96	0.00	0.00	0.04
18	28%	40.0%	0.3599	1.00	0.00	0.00	0.00
19	29%	40.0%	0.0000	1.00	0.00	0.00	0.00
20	30%	40.0%	0.0000	1.00	0.00	0.00	0.00

The analysis to this point is technically deterministic because we have calculated the mean and standard deviation of the portfolio with formulas and not through simulation. This approach gives us some important information about the distribution of returns for any allocation, specifically the mean and variance, but it does not give us the *entire* distribution of returns. To generate this distribution and to prepare for using OptQuest, we modify our model to simulate actual returns from each stock and to determine the resulting distribution of portfolio returns. Figure 16.18 shows the modified model. In cells C8:F8, we have entered normal distributions for each stock, using the given means and standard deviations. Then, in cell C21, we have calculated the simulated portfolio return as the weighted average of the simulated stock returns, with the proportions in cells C12:F12 as weights. (Cell D21 is a duplicate of cell C21, for later use.)

A simulation of 1,000 trials gives the distribution of returns shown in Figure 16.19. The mean return is 31.3 percent, with a standard deviation of 13.1 percent. These results confirm the earlier deterministic analysis. However, the frequency distribution shows that the portfolio return is itself slightly skewed to the right—with a maximum return above 90 percent and a minimum of about −9 percent. More indicative of the distribution, perhaps, are the 10th and 90th percentiles, which are 13 percent and 49 percent, respectively.

We illustrate two different uses of OptQuest in this problem. First, as a test of OptQuest, we resolve the problem we previously analyzed with Solver: maximize the mean return while ensuring that the standard deviation does not exceed a limit. Then,

FIGURE 16.18 Simulation Model for the Portfolio Problem

	A	B	C	D	E	F	G	H	I
1	Portfolio Optimization								
2									
3	Returns Data								
4		Stock	MSFT	T	GM	GE			
5		Mean	40%	16%	20%	30%	Cells C8:F8 simulate returns on the stocks using the normal distribution.		
6		Std Dev	28%	22%	24%	18%			
7		Variance	7.8%	4.8%	5.8%	3.2%			
8		Simulated	75.0%	-0.1%	55.5%	17.3%			
9									
10	Decisions								
11		Stock	MSFT	T	GM	GE	Total		
12		Allocation	47.7%	0.0%	0.0%	52.3%	100.00%		
13		Squared	22.8%	0.0%	0.0%	27.4%			
14									
15	Target SD				13.00%				
16							Portfolio mean calculated using the actual returns on the four stocks.		
17	Results		Portfolio		Portfolio				
18			mean		std dev				
19			34.8%		16.3%				
20									
21		Simulated	44.8%	44.8%			Forecast: Return2		
22									
23							Portfolio mean calculated using the simulated returns in cells C8:F8.		
24									
25							Forecast: Return		
26									

FIGURE 16.19 Simulation Results for the Portfolio Problem

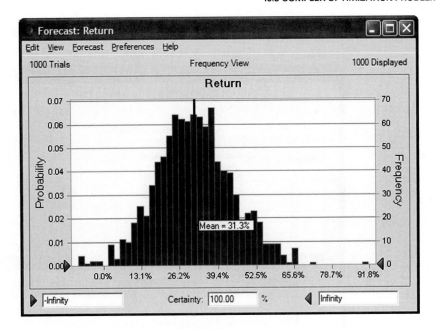

we change our measure of risk to the 10th percentile of the return distribution, to determine how the results change under a more realistic measure of risk.

The model shown in Figure 16.18 is almost ready for using OptQuest. The four proportions invested are the Decision variables, defined in Crystal Ball as continuous variables between zero and one. The Forecast cell is the total return in cell C21. The random inputs are the returns on the stocks, defined using the Crystal Ball function CB.NORMAL(mean, standard deviation). We choose a run length of 1,000 trials, with an MSE of 0.4 percent on a mean return of about 30 percent. The only additional input is needed because of a peculiar feature—we might even call it a bug—of OptQuest. OptQuest does not operate correctly unless the model includes at least one random input defined using the Distribution Gallery. We have four random inputs in cells C8:F8, but all use Crystal Ball functions, not the Distribution Gallery. To get around this problem, we add a random input in cell K21 (out of view), defined as a uniform distribution using the Distribution Gallery. This cell has no influence on the results; it simply tricks OptQuest into running correctly. (If none of the random inputs is entered using the Distribution Gallery, OptQuest attempts to find an optimal solution without taking any random samples. One way to detect the error is to observe that each run takes only a second or two. Alternatively, we can check the Options window to see if the Deterministic (no assumptions) option is checked. In either case, the work-around is to enter into the spreadsheet at least one random variable using the Distribution Gallery.)

When we open OptQuest, it recognizes the four decision variables as continuous between zero and one. We set the initial allocation at 25 percent in each stock in order to test OptQuest's ability to find the known optimal solution from an arbitrary starting point. In general, we would choose starting values for the decision variables as close to the optimum as we could. There is one constraint to add: that the four proportions add to 1.0. The Forecast window in OptQuest devotes one row to the return (cell C21). We can use this to define the objective as maximizing mean return. To impose the requirement that the standard deviation not exceed 13 percent, we must first duplicate the Forecast cell (Edit▶Duplicate), then specify that Return2 (the name given to the duplicate value in cell D21) is a requirement with an upper bound on the standard deviation of 0.13. Finally, we set the time limit to five minutes and run OptQuest. The results are shown in Figure 16.20.

The optimal portfolio has a mean return of 30.5 percent with a standard deviation of 12.6 percent. The proportions to invest in each stock are as follows: 32 percent in Microsoft, 23 percent in AT&T, 0 percent in GM, and 45 percent in GE.

FIGURE 16.20 OptQuest
Results for the Portfolio
Problem

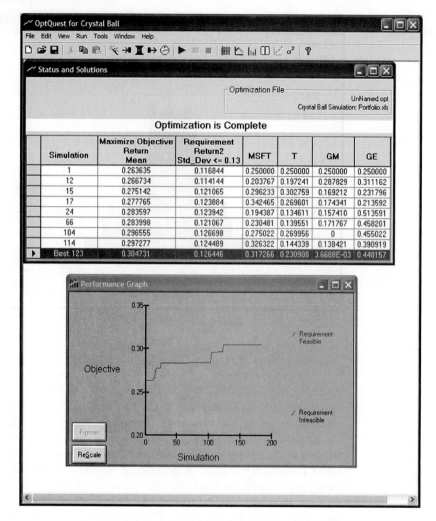

This solution closely resembles the one we found by using Solver. The objective function value is a little lower, and the constraint on the standard deviation is not quite binding, but the stock proportions are similar (except for GM). If we isolate the top 20 solutions using Solution Analysis (see Figure 16.21), we can see that many solutions give a mean return of 29 percent or higher. Among these solutions, most invest about 30 percent in Microsoft and 40 percent in GE; the remainder can be split between AT&T and GM in various proportions.

The standard deviation of the return distribution is just one of many ways to measure risk. One shortcoming of the standard deviation is that it penalizes deviations *above* the mean as much as those *below*, whereas when it comes to returns on a portfolio, deviations above the mean are actually good, not bad. A better approach to limiting risk is to limit the *downside* outcomes. One way to accomplish this is to limit the 10th percentile of the distribution. In OptQuest, this requires only that we change the requirement from an *upper bound* on the standard deviation to a *lower bound* on the 10th percentile.

Figure 16.22 shows the results of an OptQuest run in which we have maximized the mean return while requiring the 10th percentile to exceed 15 percent. The resulting solution has a mean return of 36.1 percent, with a 10th percentile of 15.1 percent. The proportions invested are about 48 percent in Microsoft, 0 percent in AT&T, 0 percent in GM, and 52 percent in GE. This is a rather different investment strategy from the one that resulted from the earlier problem formulation in which we imposed a ceiling on the standard deviation of returns. Higher proportions are invested in Microsoft and GE, with nothing invested in AT&T or GM. The result is a higher mean—36 percent versus 31 percent in the case of the standard deviation constraint. Of course, the standard deviation is also higher (16.8 versus 12.6).

FIGURE 16.21   Solution Analysis for the Portfolio Problem

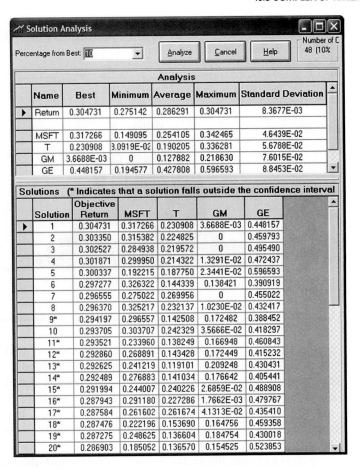

FIGURE 16.22   Solution to the Portfolio Problem with 10th Percentile Requirement

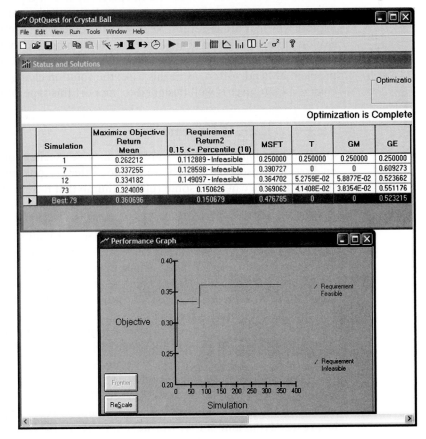

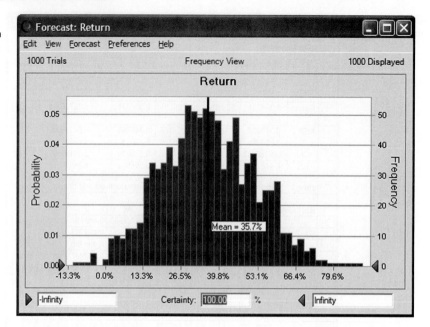

Figure 16.23 shows the distribution of returns for a simulation of this solution (this result differs slightly from the OptQuest run due to simulation error). This distribution should be contrasted with the corresponding distribution for the standard deviation-constrained solution in Figure 16.19. When we control risk by controlling the 10th percentile, the result is a distribution that has higher variance and a somewhat higher mean, but a higher 10th percentile (or probability of a very low return) as well.

This example illustrates a number of practical ideas for using OptQuest. It is always helpful to solve a deterministic version of the problem first, to produce a baseline against which to measure the performance of OptQuest. Then compare the OptQuest solution to the deterministic solution; if they are significantly different, explore why they are different. Next, vary the objective function and requirements to explore how the solution changes. When performing risk analysis, recognize that risk can be measured in different ways and that the method must be tailored to the problem at hand. Often, as in this case, the solution changes as the measure of risk changes. OptQuest is well designed to support this type of model exploration.

16.3.4 A Cash-Management Problem

OptQuest is sophisticated software that can give excellent or poor results depending on how it is used. Although we cannot offer a cookbook for using OptQuest successfully, we can offer some rules of thumb that have proven helpful in a variety of problems. We illustrate the application of these rules using the following example.

Cash management is a common problem for banks and other businesses that experience uncertain cash inflows and outflows. On the one hand, if a bank keeps too little cash on hand, it can run out, which makes it very unpopular with customers and regulators alike. On the other hand, if it holds too much cash, it forgoes the opportunity to earn a return on the money, which makes it unpopular with its shareholders. If a bank adjusts its cash levels too frequently in order to avoid these extremes, it can pay too much in transactions costs. An optimal cash-management policy must determine *when* to adjust the cash balance and *how much* to adjust it so as to maximize net interest earned less transactions costs.

One approach to this problem is to set three parameters to control cash movements. One parameter is the Target: This is the amount we would like to have in the cash account at all times. A second parameter is the Upper Limit: When cash on hand exceeds this amount, we transfer enough from the cash account to an investment account to bring the cash account back to the Target level. The third parameter is the Lower Limit: When cash on hand falls below this amount, we transfer enough money from the investment account into the cash account to bring it up to the Target level.

EXAMPLE
Cash Management

Bank of New Hampshire has set a Target level of $30,000, with an Upper Limit of $70,000 and a Lower Limit of $15,000. It currently has $28,000 in the cash account and $100,000 in an investment account. The investment account earns interest of 9 percent per year or about 0.025 percent per day. The bank must pay a fee of $100 each time it transfers money either way between these accounts. Finally, daily net cash flows (cash inflows less cash outflows) are distributed according to a normal distribution with a mean of $0 and a standard deviation of $10,000. ∎

Our model for this problem is shown in Figure 16.24. We track the inventory of cash (and the value of the investment account) for 30 days, starting with Day 0 in row 16. The cash balance at the beginning of the day is calculated in column D. In columns E and F we use IF statements to test whether cash should be transferred out of the account because it is above the Upper Limit, or into the account because it is below the Lower Limit. If either of these conditions occurs, a transactions cost is paid as determined in column G. In column H, we use the CB.NORMAL function to simulate the daily random cash inflow or outflow. Then in column I, we calculate the net cash transfer, if any. Finally, in column J, we calculate the end-of-day balance.

Columns K–M are used to track the investment account. The beginning balance is calculated in column K, the ending balance in column L, and the interest earned each day in column M.

A detailed description of the model follows:

Data

Cells D5:D12: Given data.

Model

Cells D17:D46: Beginning Cash is the Ending Cash from the previous day (column J).

Cells E17:E46: Tests to see if the Beginning Cash (column D) is above the Upper Limit (cell D8).

Cells F17:F46: Tests to see if the Beginning Cash (column D) is below the Lower Limit (cell D7).

FIGURE 16.24 Spreadsheet Model for Cash Management Example

	A	B	C	D	E	F	G	H	I	J	K	L	M	N
1	Cash Management													
2	1-Jan-06								Total interest earned					
3	SGP								less total transactions				OptQuest Bug cell	
4			Data (000)			Results	Total interest	0.793	cost.				1.02611	
5			Initial cash	28			Total Cost	0.300						
6			Initial savings	100			Net ($000)	493.356						
7			LOWER LIMIT	15			Mean Net	359.537						
8			UPPER LIMIT	70					CB.GETFORESTATFN(H6,2)					
9			TARGET	30										
10			Demand SD	10										
11			Transaction cost	0										
12			Interest rate	0.00025										
13														
14		Model		Beginning	Transfer	Transfer	Transactions		Change in	Ending	Beginning	Ending		
15			Day	cash	out?	in?	Cost	Cash flow	cash	cash	savings	savings	Interest	
16			0	28	No	No	0	-15	0	13	100	100	0.03	
17			1	13	No	Yes	0.1	17	17	47	100	83	0.03	
18			2	47	No	No	0	6	0	53	83	83	0.02	
19			3	53	No	No	0	1	0	55	83	83	0.02	
20			4	55	No	No	0	3	0	58	83	83	0.02	
21			5	58	No	No	0	-8	0	50	83	83	0.02	
22			6	50	No	No	0	10	0	60	83	83	0.02	
23			7	60	No	No	0	-2	0	58	83	83	0.02	
24			8	58	No	No	0	4	0	62	83	83	0.02	
25			9	62	No	No	0	5	0	67	83	83	0.02	
26			10	67	No	No	0	1	0	68	83	83	0.02	
27			11	68	No	No	0	4	0	72	83	83	0.02	
28			12	72	Yes	No	0.1	14	-42	44	83	125	0.02	
29			13	44	No	No	0	4	0	48	125	125	0.03	
30			14	48	No	No	0	-4	0	44	125	125	0.03	
31			15	44	No	No	0	11	0	55	125	125	0.03	
32			16	55	No	No	0	-10	0	45	125	125	0.03	
33			17	45	No	No	0	-2	0	43	125	125	0.03	
34			18	43	No	No	0	16	0	59	125	125	0.03	
35			19	59	No	No	0	-4	0	55	125	125	0.03	
36			20	55	No	No	0	0	0	55	125	125	0.03	

H ◀ ▶ H \ 16.24 / | ◀

Cells G17:G46: Calculates the transactions costs for transfers in or out.

Cells H17:H46: Simulates the daily cash flow using CB.NORMAL with a mean of zero and the given standard deviation (D10).

Cells I17:I46: When money is transferred into or out of the cash account, the amount is the difference between the Beginning Cash (column D) and the Target Level (D9). The sign of the difference depends on whether the transfer is in or out.

Cells J17:J46: The Ending Cash is the Beginning Cash (column D) plus the Cash Flow (Column H) plus the Change in Cash (column I).

Cells K17:K46: The Beginning Savings is the Ending Savings from the previous day (column L).

Cells L17:L46: The Ending Savings is the Beginning Savings from the current day (column K) less the Change in Cash (column I).

Cells M17:M46: The Interest earned on the savings account is the Beginning Savings (column K) times the daily interest rate (D12).

Results

Cell H4: Total Interest earned is the sum of the daily Interest (column M).

Cell H5: Total Cost is the sum of Transactions Costs (column G).

Cell H6: Net Cost is Total Interest (H4) minus Total Cost (H5).

Cell H7: This cell records the mean for Net Cost over a simulation run, using the CB.GETFORESTATFN function.

This model has three decision variables: the Upper Limit, the Lower Limit, and the Target. When set at base-case values, the mean Net Interest earned over 30 days is $370 (Figure 16.25).

An important rule of thumb for running OptQuest is to experiment with different values of the decision variables to make sure the objective function responds to each decision variable in the way we expect. If our goal is to maximize the objective, we expect the objective function to be *concave* in each decision variable—that is, increasing at first and then decreasing.

A natural way to test these relationships is with CB Sensitivity. Figure 16.26 shows the results of a CB Sensitivity experiment in which we varied the Target from 15,000 to 70,000. (Remember that all other parameters remain fixed during this experiment. In particular, the Lower Limit is fixed at 15,000 and the Upper Limit at 70,000.) This graph has just the shape we want: increasing, then decreasing. OptQuest should have little trouble finding the optimal value for the Target given this relationship.

Figure 16.27 shows the corresponding graph for a CB Sensitivity run in which we varied the Upper Limit from 30,000 to 150,000. This graph shows that Net Interest does increase as we increase the Upper Limit, but at a decreasing rate, and around 100,000 changes in the Upper Limit have no impact on Net Interest. What is behind

FIGURE 16.25 Distribution of Net Interest

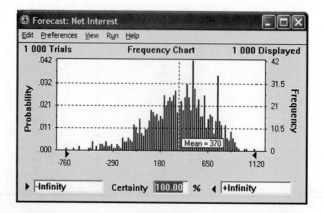

FIGURE 16.26 Sensitivity of Mean Net Interest to Target

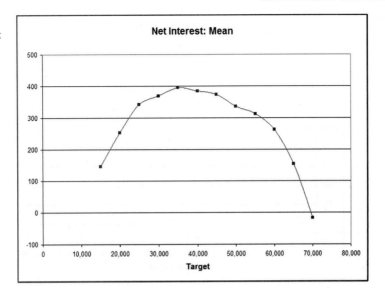

this result? Some exploration with the model will suggest that once the Upper Limit is set very high, the likelihood of a transfer out of the cash account (within 30 days) approaches zero. Therefore, it makes little difference to Net Interest what the value of the Upper Limit is, once it is high. This suggests that we should be careful when using OptQuest to limit the range over which to search for the optimal value of the Upper Limit, and not to take as meaningful precise values at the upper end of the range. In other words, if OptQuest reports an optimal value for the Upper Limit of 114,569, we should realize that any value between 90,000 and 150,000 may be just as good.

Figure 16.28 shows the CB Sensitivity results for the third decision variable: the Lower Limit. Net Interest declines steadily as we increase the Lower Limit from zero. This suggests that the optimal Lower Limit is zero or even perhaps negative. Unless we have thought hard about the problem and have excellent intuition, this relationship probably comes as a surprise. What is behind it? Again, some exploration with the model will suggest that there is no penalty for reducing the Lower Limit toward zero. Reducing this floor reduces the number of times money is transferred into the cash account and thereby reduces transactions costs. There is an implicit constraint in this problem that the cash account should not be allowed to get too low, but this constraint (or an appropriate cost penalty) is not explicitly represented in the model. This suggests that we should either eliminate the Lower Limit as a decision variable when running OptQuest (since we already know its optimal value), or we should change the model to reflect the real costs of low cash balances.

FIGURE 16.27 Sensitivity of Mean Net Interest to Upper Limit

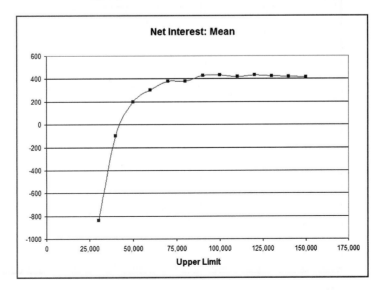

FIGURE 16.28 Sensitivity of Mean Net Interest to Lower Limit

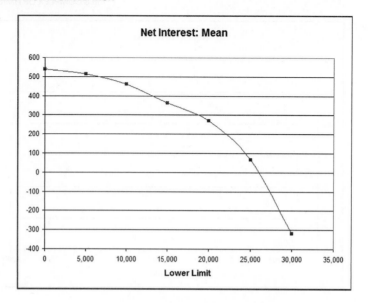

One way to modify the model to incorporate the desire to avoid low cash balances is to include an explicit cost whenever the cash balance falls too low. The model shown in Figure 16.29 is identical to our earlier model (Figure 16.24) except for cells J4:J9. In cell J5 we enter a new parameter (500), which represents the cost for a negative cash balance. In cell J7 we modify the Net Interest objective (H6) by adding the function IF(MIN(D16:D46)<0,-J5,0). This IF statement adds the cost from J5 if the lowest value for the cash account during a simulation is less than 0. In cell J9, we record the mean of this new Forecast cell using CB.GETFORESTATFN.

Before we proceed to running OptQuest, we should check that this new objective is concave in the Lower Limit. This is confirmed in Figure 16.30, where a CB Sensitivity run shows that the new objective reaches a maximum value for a Lower Limit around 15,000.

A second rule of thumb for running OptQuest is to start the search for an optimal solution with a small number of trials in Crystal Ball, a coarse grid for the Decision variables, and a short OptQuest run time. Seldom can the optimal solution be identified reliably in a single run of OptQuest. The search for an optimal solution requires both patience and time to learn about the problem. One way to learn about the problem is to run OptQuest through a sequence of increasingly refined

FIGURE 16.29 Cash-Management Model with Cost Penalty

	A	B	C	D	E	F	G	H	I	J	K	L	M
1	Cash Management												
2	1-Jan-06												
3	SGP												
4		Data (000)					Total interest	0.754		Penalty		Bogus cell	0.8843
5			Initial cash	28			Total Cost	0.300		0.5			
6			Initial savings	100			Net	0.454		Penalty Objective			
7			LOWER LIMIT	15						454.204			
8			UPPER LIMIT	70						Mean Penalty			
9			TARGET	30						309.711			
10			Demand SD	10									
11			Transaction cost	0.1						CB.GETFORESTATFN(J7,2)			
12			Interest rate	0.00025									
13													
14		Model		Beginning	Invest	Sell	Transactions		Change in	Ending	Beginning	Ending	
15			Day	cash	more?	securities?	Cost	Cash flow	cash	cash	savings	savings	Interest
16			0	28	No	No	0	6	0	34	100	100	0.03
17			1	34	No	No	0	-3	0	31	100	100	0.03
18			2	31	No	No	0	5	0	36	100	100	0.03
19			3	36	No	No	0	8	0	44	100	100	0.03
20			4	44	No	No	0	-5	0	39	100	100	0.03
21			5	39	No	No	0	0	0	39	100	100	0.03
22			6	39	No	No	0	14	0	53	100	100	0.03
23			7	53	No	No	0	-9	0	44	100	100	0.03
24			8	44	No	No	0	6	0	50	100	100	0.03
25			9	50	No	No	0	-2	0	47	100	100	0.03
26			10	47	No	No	0	-16	0	32	100	100	0.03
27			11	32	No	No	0	8	0	39	100	100	0.03
28			12	39	No	No	0	10	0	49	100	100	0.03
29			13	49	No	No	0	-13	0	36	100	100	0.03
30			14	36	No	No	0	-10	0	26	100	100	0.03
31			15	26	No	No	0	-13	0	13	100	100	0.03
32			16	13	No	Yes	0.1	5	17	35	100	83	0.03
33			17	35	No	No	0	2	0	38	83	83	0.02
34			18	38	No	No	0	-3	0	34	83	83	0.02
35			19	34	No	No	0	17	0	51	83	83	0.02
36			20	51	No	No	0	1	0	52	83	83	0.02

Penalty for cash balance falling below zero.

Total interest less total transactions cost less penalty.

16.29 / Base Case Results / Penalty Objective / Optquest results-discrete DV / Optquest results-continuous DV

FIGURE 16.30 Sensitivity of Revised Model to Lower Limit

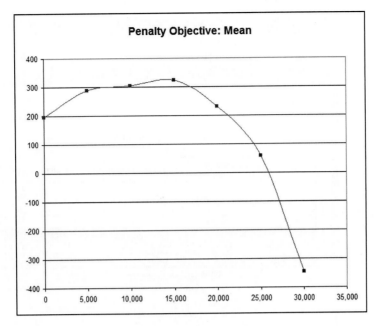

FIGURE 16.30 Sensitivity of Revised Model to Lower Limit

experiments. In the initial runs, it is useful to set the number of trials in Crystal Ball to a small value so that OptQuest has time to examine a reasonably large number of solutions. (If the number of trials is too small and the simulation error is too high, OptQuest could settle on a solution that appears optimal only because simulation error leads to a high value of the objective.) It is also good practice to set wide limits on the range for the Decision variables so as not to miss the true optimal value, but also to define the Decision variables as discrete with a large step size. This specification gives OptQuest fewer alternatives to examine. Finally, initial OptQuest runs should be fairly short (say two to five minutes) so that bugs are found quickly and the learning process is efficient. Often, a near-optimal solution can be identified even in these early OptQuest runs. In later runs, we can always refine the search if more accuracy is needed.

Figure 16.31 shows the results of an exploratory OptQuest run in which the number of trials was set at 500 (with an MSE of about 6 percent of the mean), the step size for all three Decision variables was set at 1,000, and OptQuest ran for two minutes. In those two minutes, OptQuest examined only 38 alternative sets of Decision variables, but it found an optimal solution that improved the base-case objective by 7.3 percent (397 versus 370), with a Lower Limit of 13,000, a Target of 51,000, and an Upper Limit of 124,000. These values for the decision variables seem plausible given the sensitivity analysis we carried out before. The question now is whether we can improve on these results by refining the search.

A third rule of thumb is to refine the search for the optimal solution by increasing the number of trials in Crystal Ball, refining the grid for the Decision variables, or increasing the OptQuest run time. Which of these alterations is most effective depends on the model. However, all three should be pursued at some point, so that the final solution is the result of accurate Crystal Ball runs (with a low MSE), a search over a fine grid of values of the Decision variables, and sufficiently long OptQuest runs.

Figure 16.32 shows the results of an OptQuest run in which the number of trials is 1000, the Decision variables are defined as continuous (that is, fractional values are allowed), and OptQuest ran for 10 minutes. This run gives us an objective function value of 409.2, with a Lower Limit of 12,206, a Target of 45,527, and an Upper Limit of 115,043. In this experiment, OptQuest examined 143 different possible solutions. The new optimal solution improves the objective an additional 3.2 percent over the previous best solution.

A fourth rule of thumb is to use OptQuest's Solution Analysis procedure to examine the best 5 or 10 percent of all the solutions. Several lessons can be learned from this report. First, we can determine whether the optimal solution is rare, or whether many different values of the Decision variables give approximately the same

FIGURE 16.31 Preliminary
OptQuest Run for Cash
Management

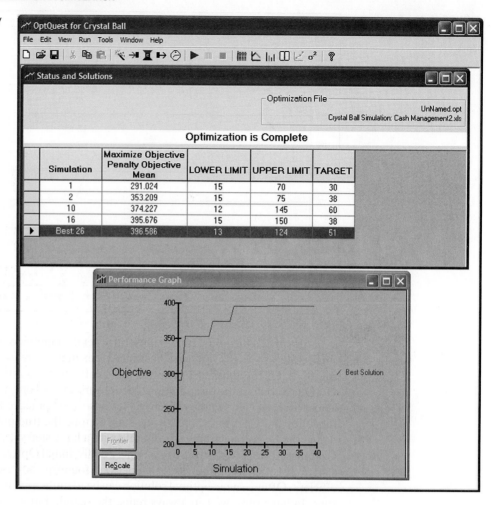

value of the objective. Sometimes, suboptimal solutions are preferred to the optimal solution, for reasons outside the model. Second, we can see how much variation there is in the optimal values of the Decision variables. Consistent values of the Decision variables are a sign that the optimal solution is robust.

Figure 16.33 shows the Solution Analysis for the top 20 solutions to the Cash Management example. We see that the objective function ranges from a high of 409.2 to a low of 405.9, a range of only 0.9 percent. The values for the Lower Limit range from 11,800 to 14,300, suggesting that the optimal value for this Decision variable is tightly limited. The Target ranges from 43,500 to 46,400, suggesting that the Target also should be fairly precisely set. Finally, the range for the Upper Limit is from 110,200 to 131,700. As we learned when we did a CB Sensitivity run on the Upper Limit, all values above about 110,000 give essentially the same results.

Our final heuristic is to limit the number of decision variables by the use of decision rules that relate decision variables to other variables in the model. OptQuest performs best when the number of decision variables is small and the impact of each one on the objective is unambiguous. When the number of decision variables is large, OptQuest may fail to find solutions that are clearly close to optimal.

This heuristic can be illustrated by an example. In many so-called real options problems, a number of decisions are to be made over time as uncertainties are revealed. For example, one might shut a copper mine down each year if the price of copper fell below a certain level. The shutdown price level could be taken as an independent decision variable in each year, but we would then have a large number of such variables. A better approach is to assume that the optimal shutdown price changes over time according to a function of a few parameters. For example, we could assume a linear relationship of the form $Shutdown\ Price = ab \times Time$. This approach effectively reduces the number of decision variables to two: the parameters a and b.

FIGURE 16.32 Final
OptQuest Run for Cash
Management

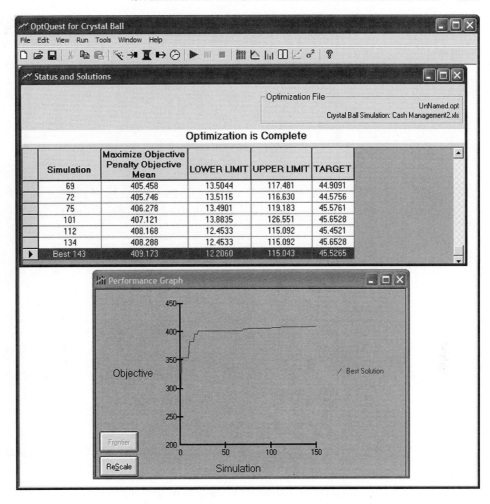

CRYSTAL BALL TIP
Rules of Thumb for OptQuest

Using CB Sensitivity, check that the objective function is concave in each Decision variable.

For initial testing:

- Set the number of trials in Crystal Ball to a small value.
- Define the Decision variables as discrete with a small number of allowable values.
- Set a short OptQuest run length.

In subsequent testing:

- Increase the number of trials in Crystal Ball.
- Increase the number of allowable values for discrete Decision variables and/or convert them to continuous variables.
- Increase the OptQuest run length.

Use Solution Analysis to determine whether the top solutions are consistent, suggesting that a true optimal solution has been identified.

Reduce the number of decision variables by parameterization. ∎

16.4 EMBEDDED OPTIMIZATION: USING SOLVER WITHIN CRYSTAL BALL

In a typical application of simulation, decisions must be made *before* the outcomes of the uncertainties become known. In the Advertising Budget example, next year's price and cost are uncertain at budgeting time, when we commit to our advertising

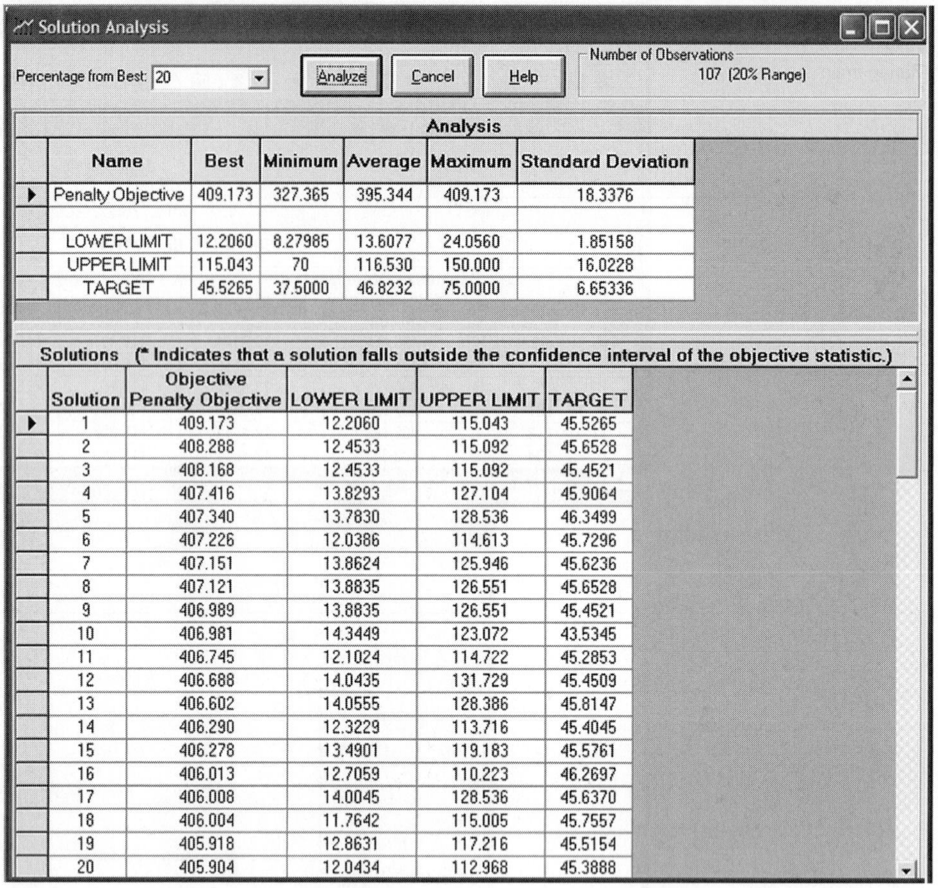

Name	Best	Minimum	Average	Maximum	Standard Deviation
Penalty Objective	409.173	327.365	395.344	409.173	18.3376
LOWER LIMIT	12.2060	8.27985	13.6077	24.0560	1.85158
UPPER LIMIT	115.043	70	116.530	150.000	16.0228
TARGET	45.5265	37.5000	46.8232	75.0000	6.65336

Solutions (* Indicates that a solution falls outside the confidence interval of the objective statistic.)

Solution	Objective Penalty Objective	LOWER LIMIT	UPPER LIMIT	TARGET
1	409.173	12.2060	115.043	45.5265
2	408.288	12.4533	115.092	45.6528
3	408.168	12.4533	115.092	45.4521
4	407.416	13.8293	127.104	45.9064
5	407.340	13.7830	128.536	46.3499
6	407.226	12.0386	114.613	45.7296
7	407.151	13.8624	125.946	45.6236
8	407.121	13.8835	126.551	45.6528
9	406.989	13.8835	126.551	45.4521
10	406.981	14.3449	123.072	43.5345
11	406.745	12.1024	114.722	45.2853
12	406.688	14.0435	131.729	45.4509
13	406.602	14.0555	128.386	45.8147
14	406.290	12.3229	113.716	45.4045
15	406.278	13.4901	119.183	45.5761
16	406.013	12.7059	110.223	46.2697
17	406.008	14.0045	128.536	45.6370
18	406.004	11.7642	115.005	45.7557
19	405.918	12.8631	117.216	45.5154
20	405.904	12.0434	112.968	45.3888

FIGURE 16.33 Solution Analysis for Cash Management

plan for the entire coming year. But it can happen that some of our decisions can be made *after* the uncertainties have been resolved. For example, we might know next year's price either exactly, or with much less uncertainty than at present, by the time we begin the third quarter of the year. In that case, we could choose our advertising expenditures for the third and fourth quarters after we know the price for those quarters.

When decisions can be made after uncertainties are resolved, we are worse off to ignore the fact. If we do ignore the option to act later with more complete knowledge, we must make our plans taking all the uncertainties into account. If, however, we can make our decision after we know the outcome of an uncertain event or parameter, we can match our decision exactly to that outcome and eliminate the risks. In the Hastings Sportswear example, if we must make our production decision before we know demand, we have to balance the risks of producing too many or too few. However, if we already know demand when we decide on production, we simply produce to demand and thereby avoid both leftovers and stockouts. Once we know demand, all risks are removed.

A somewhat more complex example involves a decision to purchase several types of production machinery, each of which has some flexibility to produce different products. Today, we face the decision of how much production capacity of each type to purchase. Future demand for each product is uncertain. In future years, we will know demand fairly accurately each month, and we can assign machines to products so as to minimize costs. This choice of optimal production plan, however, is constrained in the future by the capacity choices we make today. To model this problem realistically, we first need to model the uncertainty in demand. Then, we need to formulate the optimization problem of allocating production capacity to minimize costs, given demand. Finally, we evaluate total costs over a range of choices for the initial capacities, taking into account the uncertainty in demand and the fact that the production plan will be optimized for each demand level.

We call problems of this type, where some decisions are made after uncertainty has been resolved, **embedded-decision problems**. Their main characteristics are the following:

- At the first stage, there is a need to make a set of long-term decisions in the face of uncertainty.

- In the second stage, the uncertainty is resolved; that is, the uncertain factors become known.

- At the third stage, there is a need to make short-term decisions, given the outcomes of the uncertain factors and the constraints imposed by the long-term decisions.

We cannot use Crystal Ball in the usual manner to model these problems, because of the need to optimize and store the solution in the third stage. Instead, we need to call on Solver to carry out the optimization at the appropriate point within each Crystal Ball trial. We first work through an example and then describe the details involved.

16.4.1 A Capacity Planning Example

In a typical embedded-decision problem we make long-term, strategic commitments *before* uncertainty is resolved, and we make short-term, tactical decisions *after* the uncertainty is resolved. In the following example, the long-term decisions involve how much capacity to build at various production facilities. The uncertainties involve the demands for multiple products. The short-term decisions involve where to produce products and what routes to use for delivery. These tactical decisions are made after demand is known, but also after the production capacity decisions are finalized.

EXAMPLE
Long-term Capacity Planning[2]

A producer of industrial chemicals has three manufacturing facilities from which it ships its products to five regions of the country. The chemical company must decide how much capacity to create at each manufacturing site to produce a new product. Because shipping costs are substantial, the profit margin on each unit sold depends on the distance it must be shipped. That is, the unit profit depends on the location of manufacture and the region where the sale takes place. Since industrial chemicals are sold mostly on annual contracts, demand for a given year is quite predictable. Thus, we can choose the optimal production and distribution plan once we know demand. However, at the time the capacity decision must be made, demand is uncertain. ∎

This is an embedded-decision problem because we can choose the amounts to produce and the shipment schedule (short-term decisions) *after* we know demand, but we have to choose capacity (long-term decisions) *before* we know demand. To model this sequence of decisions and random outcomes, we simulate demand using Crystal Ball, and we then optimize the shipments given demand by embedding a macro that will run Solver within Crystal Ball. We then call on OptQuest to search for the optimal capacities, knowing that we can obtain optimal shipments for each random demand.

Our spreadsheet model is shown in Figure 16.34. Product is manufactured in three source locations (Los Angeles, Chicago, New York) and shipped to five destinations (East, South, Southwest, Mountain, West). There are 18 decision variables in all: three long-term capacities (one for each source) and 15 short-term shipment quantities (one from each source to each destination). The objective is to maximize profit, which is calculated by subtracting annual fixed costs on total capacity from the total margin on units sold. There are two sets of constraints: the amounts sold in each region cannot exceed the demands, and the amount produced at each site cannot exceed capacity, which is treated as given.

[2]Wayne Winston, *Decision Making under Uncertainty with RISKOptimizer*, (Newfield, NY: Palisade Corporation, 1999).

FIGURE 16.34 Spread-sheet Model for Capacity Planning Example

	A	B	C	D	E	F	G	H	I
1	Plant Capacity								
2									
3	Profits		East	South	Southwest	Mountain	West		Fixed Cost
4		LA	1.80	2.50	3.00	3.30	4.00		1.50
5		Chicago	2.50	3.30	3.00	3.60	3.40		
6		NY	3.00	3.20	2.60	2.80	2.40		
7									
8	Shipments		East	South	Southwest	Mountain	West	Produced	Capacity
9		LA	0	0	128	0	484	612	612
10		Chicago	0	297	0	603	0	900	900
11		NY	454	15	0	0	0	469	469
12		Sold	454	312	128	603	484		
13		Demand	486	312	362	603	484		
14									
15	Profit	3909		Random demand: CB.NORMAL(C18,C19)					
16									
17	Demands		378	241	439	281	420		
18		Mean	400	300	400	500	380		
19		SD	100	80	90	100	100		
20									

A detailed description of the model follows.

Unit Profit Margins

Cells C4:G6: Profit margins by route (revenue less production and shipping cost).

Fixed Cost

Cell I4: Fixed cost of purchasing one unit of capacity.

Shipments

Cells C9:G11: Shipment quantities by route (short-term decision variables).

Cells H9:H11: Total production by source (row sums).

Cells I9:I11: Capacities for each source (long-term decision variables).

Cells C12:G12: Total shipments by destination (column sums).

Cells C13:G13: Given data: demands by destination.

Profit

Cell B15: Total profit is calculated by taking the SUMPRODUCT of the shipment quantities (C9:G11) and the profit margins (C4:G6) and subtracting total capacity (I9:I11) times the fixed cost of capacity (I4)

Demands

Cells C18:G18: Given mean demands by destination.

Cells C19:G19: Given standard deviations of demand by destination.

Cells C17:G17: Randomly generated demands (using CB.NORMAL) with the given means (C18:G18) and standard deviations (C19:G19).

For a fixed set of capacities (cells I9:I11) and demands (cells C13:G13), we use Solver to determine the optimal shipment schedule (cells C9:G11) subject to the constraints mentioned earlier. The Solver window is shown in Figure 16.35.

To prepare this model for the embedded-optimization process, we create random demands. The means and standard deviations are given in rows 18 and 19, and the actual demands are created in row 17 using the normal distribution CB.NORMAL. We also designate the objective function in cell B15 as a Forecast cell.

The macro we use to run Solver inside the Crystal Ball simulation process copies the random demands in row 17 into row 13 before running Solver. (We describe how to create this macro later.) We can test the macro before proceeding. We run the macro by hitting Ctrl-a (or by choosing Developer▶Code▶Macros▶Run). The macro copies the random samples to the demand cells and calls on Solver to optimize the shipment schedule.

FIGURE 16.35 Solver
Parameters for Capacity
Planning Example

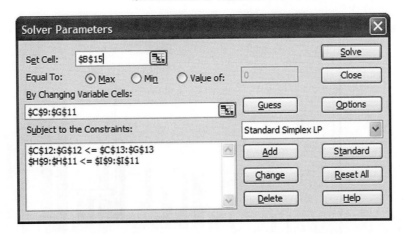

FIGURE 16.35 Solver
Parameters for Capacity
Planning Example

Now we return to Crystal Ball and choose Run▶Run Preferences and set the run length to 100 trials. Under Sampling, we check Use same sequence of random numbers and enter a seed value. On the Speed tab, we check Normal speed under Run Mode (the Extreme Speed option cannot be used when using a macro). On the Options tab, we check the box Run user-defined macros. Figure 16.36 shows the results of a base-case run, in which all three plant capacities are set at 700. The mean profit is $3,419, with a range from about $1,900 to $4,000. To recapitulate, this range of profits represents the combined effects of uncertainty in demand and an optimal shipment schedule for each demand sample, with overall capacity fixed.

Finally, we proceed to the long-term decision problem, where we rely on OptQuest to find an optimal policy. First, we define the capacities as discrete Decision variables, each with a range from 300 to 900. For the purposes of illustration, we use a run length of 100 trials. This run length achieves an MSE of roughly 1 percent, although the actual figure depends somewhat on the capacity choices. As we discussed earlier, the choice of a run length should be determined by the level of precision we wish to maintain in our estimates of the objective function. A single run of 100 trials for this model may take half a minute, even on a very fast computer. Clearly, we cannot expect OptQuest to find a high-quality solution in just a few minutes. This is the kind of application where we should expect to run our computer for a matter of hours, even overnight, to get respectable results. To give an idea of the quality of solutions as the OptQuest run time increases, we ran this model for 10, 30, and 720 minutes (12 hours). The results are summarized in the following table.

Minutes	Simulations	Profit	Optimal Capacities (LA/CHI/NY)
10	30	3,454	591/749/595
30	104	3,459	603/761/584
720	1,445	3,470	612/900/469

The Performance Graph for the 12-hour run suggests that very good solutions were found during the early portion of the run, but the best solution was encountered late in the run. In addition, Solution Analysis confirms that most of the top 20 candidate solutions are very similar to the best solution. This evidence for stability suggests that we are at least very close to the optimal solution.

As a basis for comparison, we can set up a deterministic version of this model that includes the long-term decision variables as well as the short-term decision variables. Taking demands at their mean values, we can optimize this model using Solver. The maximum profit is $3,740, with total capacities of 780 in Los Angeles, 800 in Chicago, and 400 in New York City. (Note that this is not an embedded-optimization problem, because we have suppressed randomness entirely and have substituted mean values.) Interestingly, the total capacity in this solution is almost

FIGURE 16.36 Profit Distribution for the Base-case Solution

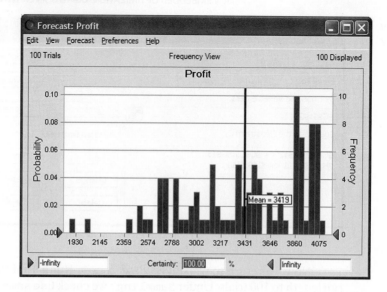

identical to the total capacity in the OptQuest solution, although the distribution across the three locations is different. The fact that the maximum profit is higher than the best value found by OptQuest reflects the fact that there is no uncertainty in the deterministic model. Thus, the plant capacities, however they are chosen, can always be fully utilized. Uncertainty about demand in the embedded-optimization problem makes this virtually impossible to achieve.

Finally, Figure 16.37 shows the distribution of profits in the best solution found by OptQuest (with capacities of 612, 900, and 469). Mean profit increases from the base-case value of $3,419 to $3,475, while the variability of profits decreases somewhat. Still, the wide range of potential profits is remarkable. Even when we can optimize our production decisions after demand is known, profits can vary from about $2,000 to about $4,000. This gives a far more realistic picture of the true uncertainties facing this company than does the deterministic solution.

16.4.2 Creating a Macro to Embed Solver

Optimization within a Crystal Ball simulation requires the use of an Excel macro to invoke Solver. A **macro** is simply a stored series of Excel commands that can be executed automatically, without user intervention (see Chapter 4). Excel has the

FIGURE 16.37 Profit Distribution for the Optquest Solution

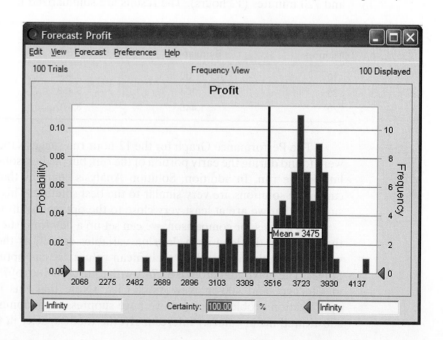

capability of recording the commands entered by a user at the keyboard, so the simplest way to create a macro is to set up the macro recorder and click through the sequence of commands.

The first step is to build a deterministic spreadsheet, treating both decision variables and random inputs as fixed numbers. Next, we reserve a separate part of the spreadsheet for generating the random inputs. (The separation is necessary because we do not want the random inputs to change within a Solver run.) Then, we invoke Solver and define the objective function, decision variables, and constraints in our short-term model. We must actually run Solver once for the overall process to work properly. Finally, we create the random inputs in their reserved location (using Crystal Ball distribution functions or the Distribution Gallery), copy their values into the appropriate cells in the model, and execute Solver. At this point, we are ready to record the macro.

The details of recording the macro are outlined in the accompanying box below.

CRYSTAL BALL TIP *Macro for Embedding Solver in Crystal Ball*

1. Start the macro recorder: Developer▶Code▶Record Macro.

2. Give the macro a name such as EmbedSolver, assign a shortcut key to it, and save it in This Workbook.

3. Click on OK, and the Stop Recording icon appears in the code group.

4. Highlight the random inputs.

5. Choose Edit▶Copy.

6. Highlight the range where the random inputs are needed.

7. Choose Edit▶Paste Special.

8. Check the box for Paste Values. Click on OK.

9. Choose Tools▶Solver. Click on Solve.

10. When Solver finishes, click on OK.

11. Select the objective function cell.

12. Click on the Stop Recording icon in the code group.

Two additional changes are required to the macro as recorded. To edit the macro choose Developer▶Code▶Macros. With the macro name highlighted, choose Edit. This step opens the Visual Basic Editor, as shown in Figure 16.38. First, make sure Solver is linked to the macro by checking Solver.xla under Tools▶References. Second, find the macro in the Project Explorer window on the left of the Visual Basic

FIGURE 16.38 Visual Basic Editor

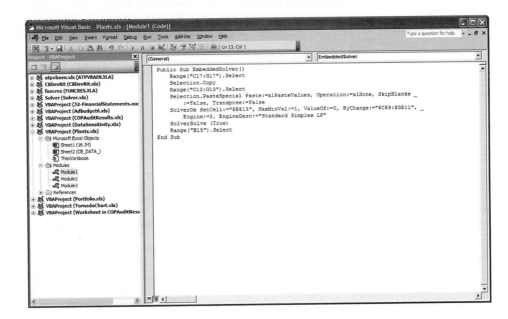

FIGURE 16.39 Function for Calling Macro

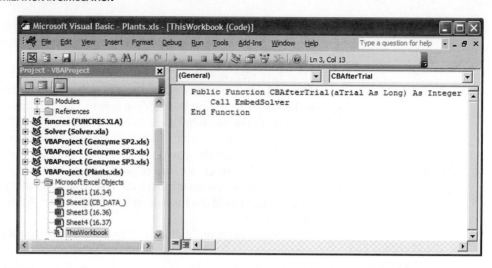

FIGURE 16.40 Macro and Function for Embedding Solver in Crystal Ball

Macro

```
Public Sub EmbedSolver()
    Range("C17:G17").Select
    Selection.Copy
    Range("C13:G13").Select
    Selection.PasteSpecial Paste:=xlPasteValues, Operation:=xlNone, SkipBlanks _
        :=False, Transpose:=False
    SolverOk SetCell:="$B$15", MaxMinVal:=1, ValueOf:=0, ByChange:="$C$9:$G$11", _
        Engine:=2, EngineDesc:="Standard Simplex LP"
    SolverSolve (True)
    Range("B15").Select
End Sub
```

Function

```
Public Function CBAfterTrial(aTrial As Long) As Integer
    Call EmbedSolver
End Function
```

Editor under VBA Projects (Plant.xls)/Modules. Change SolverSOLVE to Solver-SOLVE (True) where it appears in the macro itself. (This command turns off the Solver completion message so that the Crystal Ball run is not interrupted when Solver finishes execution.)

Finally, Crystal Ball requires that we create a function that calls the macro. To accomplish this, open the Visual Basic Editor again (Developer▶Code▶Macros▶ Edit). Double-click on This Workbook under Microsoft Excel Objects in the Project Explorer window on the left. Then enter the following code (see Figure 16.39):

> Public Function CBAfterTrial(aTrial As Long) As Integer
>> Call EmbedSolver
>
> End Function

At this stage, it is a good idea to save the workbook. The final macro and function are shown in Figure 16.40.

16.5 SUMMARY

Simulation is primarily a way to describe the range of uncertainty in the results of a model. It does not automatically provide insight into the question of which values of the decision variables lead to the best possible value of the objective. Thus, optimizing within a simulation analysis is not routine.

The tools of deterministic optimization—Solver with its various algorithms—do not directly apply because, in a simulation model, the objective can only be estimated. However, there are a number of approaches to optimization within simulation, ranging from simple grid search to OptQuest.

Simulation models with one or two variables can be optimized using a variety of techniques. Grid search is the general name for a procedure in which we evaluate the objective over a range of values of the decision variables. Grid search can be automated using the Crystal Ball Sensitivity tool.

To optimize simulation models with three or more decision variables requires the use of OptQuest. OptQuest is a sophisticated add-in to Crystal Ball that uses heuristic search procedures to find the optimal values of decision variables. OptQuest can also deal with the complications of constraints on the decision variables and requirements on the outcome distribution. Because OptQuest uses a heuristic search procedure, we cannot be guaranteed of finding the optimal solution. However, we provide rules of thumb for using OptQuest that substantially improve the quality of its solutions.

Embedded-decision problems are those in which decisions and random outcomes alternate. In these problems, we first make strategic decisions for the long run, then learn about the value of random factors, and finally, make tactical decisions within the constraints imposed by our strategic decisions. These problems can be handled by combining the capabilities of Solver and Crystal Ball. Solver is used to determine the optimal tactical decisions given the values of the uncertain factors. Crystal Ball is used to simulate the uncertain factors and to optimize the strategic decisions (using OptQuest).

SUGGESTED READINGS

Winston, W. 1999. *Decision Making under Uncertainty with RISK-Optimizer*. Newfield, NY: Palisade Corporation.

This handbook contains 34 worked examples for optimization in simulation. It uses @Risk and RISKOptimizer, but the examples can be converted to Crystal Ball and OptQuest quite easily.

EXERCISES

CB SENSITIVITY PROBLEMS

1. *Airline Revenue Management.* Alpha Airlines has ordered a new fleet of DC-717s. At this stage of the contract, Alpha's operations manager must specify the seating configuration on the aircraft that will be used on the Boston–Atlanta–Chicago–Boston circuit. Alpha flies this route once each day.

The configuration decision involves specifying how many rows will be allocated for first class and how many for tourist class. If the aircraft were configured entirely of tourist rows (containing six seats each), there would be 40 rows. First-class seats are wider and afford more legroom, so that, in order to make room for one first-class row (containing four seats), two tourist rows must be removed. Thus, conversion from tourist to first-class seating involves the loss of some seats, but the conversion may be appealing because the revenues are higher for first-class passengers than for tourist passengers (see Exhibit 1).

A perfect match between the configuration and the demand for seats is seldom possible. Historical data suggest a probability distribution of demand for seats on each leg (as detailed in Exhibit 2). There is another distribution for the fraction of demand that corresponds to first-class seats (Exhibit 3), which seems to apply on all legs, although the fraction that occurs in one market on any day is independent of the fraction in the other markets. Finally, there is some chance that all seats in either seating category will be booked on a given leg when demand for that category occurs. Under present management policies, such demand is simply lost to competitors.

Exhibit 1. Revenue per Seat

	First-Class	Tourist
Boston–Atlanta	$400	$175
Atlanta–Chicago	$400	$150
Chicago–Boston	$450	$200

Exhibit 2. Distribution of Total Demand for Seats

	Minimum	Most Likely	Maximum
Boston–Atlanta	160	180	220
Atlanta–Chicago	140	200	240
Chicago–Boston	150	200	225

Exhibit 3. Distribution of Fraction First Class

Fraction	5%	12%	15%
Probability	0.2	0.5	0.3

The fixed cost of operating the full circuit is $100,000 per day. Alpha Airlines is seeking a profit-maximizing configuration.

a. What is the expected profit per day for a configuration of 3 first-class rows and 34 tourist rows? For convenience, you may allow fractional values of demand in your model.

b. With the suggested configuration, what proportion of the days will Alpha at least break even on the Boston–Atlanta–Chicago–Boston circuit?

c. For the demand that Alpha faces, what is the maximum expected profit, and what is the seat configuration that achieves it?

2. *Inventory Planning.* Rowers North, Inc. (RNI) would like to develop an inventory policy that will minimize the total cost associated with the company's inventory of rowing machines, while ensuring that few customers are unable to purchase a machine the day they walk in the store.

The type of inventory policy they prefer involves a fixed reorder point and order quantity. The *reorder point* is the level of inventory at which an order is sent to the supplier. The *order quantity* is the amount ordered each time. These are decision variables, but once chosen, they will not be changed.

Inventory planning at RNI is complicated by several factors. One is uncertainty in demand. Weekly demand can range from zero to five machines. Data covering the past year is given in Exhibit 1. A further complication is that the time it takes for an order to arrive from the manufacturer is variable. This lead time has been as long as four weeks. Exhibit 2 gives the actual lead times for the 20 most recent orders. (Once an order has been placed, the lead time is determined by the supplier and communicated to RNI.)

Some of the relevant cost data are known. For example, it costs $1 per week to hold a rowing machine in inventory, and it costs $50 to place an order (regardless of its size).

One of the central issues for RNI is the cost of being out of stock. Since there are a number of competing retailers in the area, it is common for a customer who doesn't find the preferred machine in stock to leave and look for it elsewhere. Some customers may be loyal enough to wait until the product is back in stock, but even those customers may be displeased by the service they receive. The vice president of marketing has suggested that the cost of an unsatisfied customer is simply the forgone margin on the lost sale (roughly $50 per machine). Others in the company argue that the cost is less, perhaps much less.

Note that if RNI places an order in every week in which final inventory falls below the reorder point, it may find itself with multiple, redundant orders arriving in subsequent weeks. To control this, firms typically track their *order backlog* (i.e., the quantity of units ordered but not yet received). They then take the backlog into account when deciding whether to order in a given week.

a. Estimate the total cost for a reorder point of 1 and a reorder quantity of 5.

b. Determine an appropriate reorder point and order quantity.

c. How sensitive is the optimal solution to the cost of an unsatisfied customer (in the range from $25 to $75)?

Exhibit 1

Week	Demand	Week	Demand	Week	Demand
1	3	21	4	41	1
2	0	22	1	42	0
3	1	23	1	43	1
4	1	24	2	44	0
5	0	25	0	45	1
6	1	26	1	46	4
7	5	27	1	47	1
8	1	28	0	48	1
9	1	29	1	49	1
10	1	30	5	50	1
11	1	31	0	51	0
12	0	32	1	52	2
13	1	33	1		
14	2	34	1		
15	2	35	1		
16	4	36	3		
17	2	37	1		
18	1	38	5		
19	3	39	0		
20	1	40	1		

Exhibit 2

Order	Lead Time (wks.)	Order	Lead Time (wks.)
1	3	11	4
2	1	12	2
3	2	13	3
4	3	14	3
5	1	15	2
6	4	16	3
7	3	17	3
8	3	18	3
9	2	19	3
10	1	20	2

3. *Valuing a Real Option.* You have been hired to estimate the value of the startup company Garcia, Ltd. Garcia has one product, which is expected to sell in the first year for $100. The price will grow in subsequent years by an amount given by a normal distribution, with a mean of 5 percent and a standard deviation of 3 percent. Initial sales will be 5,000 units, expected to grow at 5 percent. The unit cost initially will be $75, and this will grow at a rate given by a normal distribution, with a mean of 10 percent and a standard deviation of 3 percent. The valuation will be based on a time horizon of 10 years. The discount rate is 10 percent.

Garcia wants to investigate an option to decide in year 6 whether to continue in business or go out of business. (This is what is known as a *real option*, as opposed to the *financial options* discussed in the text.) Specifically, management intends to execute the option to go out of business at the end of year 6 if the year 6 contribution is less than some cutoff value. If Garcia opts to go out of business, it will receive zero contribution in years 7–10.

a. Estimate the expected NPV of the business *without* the option to go out of business.

b. What is the *optimal* cutoff value? That is, what cutoff value should Garcia use in year 6 to maximize the expected NPV of the company from the start?

c. The value of this option is the *difference* between the expected NPV *with* the option from part (b) and expected NPV *without* the option from part (a). What is the value of this option?

4. *Production Planning with Returns.* A computer manufacturer sells its laptop model through a Web-based distributor, which buys at a unit cost of $200 and sells at a unit price of $500. The product life cycle is so short that the distributor is given only one opportunity to order stock before the technology becomes obsolete and a new model becomes available. At the beginning of the cycle, the distributor orders a stock level in the face of uncertain retail demand. Based on similar experiences in the past, the distributor believes that a reasonable demand model is a uniform distribution with a minimum of 1,000 and a maximum of 8,000 laptops. The items originally stocked are ultimately sold, returned, or scrapped. Customers place orders on the Web, and the distributor tries to satisfy their orders from stock. If there is a stockout, demands are lost.

The computer manufacturer offers the distributor a returns policy of the following form. It will pay $100 for each returned unit at the end of the product life cycle, but only up to a maximum of 20 percent of the original number of units ordered. Excess stock that cannot be returned to the manufacturer is picked up as scrap material by an electronics recycling center, with no cost or revenue involved. The decision facing the distributor is to choose an appropriate stock level.

a. Suppose there is no ceiling on the return of excess laptops. How many laptops should the distributor stock in order to maximize its expected profit?

b. With the returns ceiling in place, how many laptops should the distributor stock?

c. In part (b), what would be the maximum expected profit for the distributor?

d. What will be the corresponding expected profit for the *manufacturer* if the manufacturing cost is $125 per laptop, and the distributor uses the policy in part (b)?

5. *Overbooking in the Hospitality Industry.* A small hotel has 50 rooms that rent for $105 per night and cost $45 to clean and prepare each night they are used. All rentals are by reservation, and there is a 10 percent chance that an individual reservation will not show up. If a customer arrives at the hotel with a reservation and no room is available due to overbooking, the hotel will rebate the cost of the room and pay on average $150 to put the customer up at another hotel. The hotel would like to determine its *overbooking limit*: the number of rooms to accept reservations for each night in excess of capacity. Its objective is to maximize expected profits.

a. What is the expected profit with an overbooking limit of 50?

b. What is the optimal overbooking limit?

c. Using the optimal overbooking limit, what is the expected number of customers turned away?

d. How sensitive is the optimal overbooking limit to rental prices in the range from $90 to $125 per night?

6. *New Technology.* A firm is trying to decide whether to enter a highly uncertain market now or to wait to decide two years from now, when the size of the market will be less uncertain. If it enters now it must invest $3 billion, while if it waits to invest two years from now the costs will rise to $4 billion. The market size this year will be normally distributed with a mean of $5 million and a standard deviation of $1 million. The growth rate in subsequent years will be normally distributed with a mean of 10 percent and a standard deviation of 5 percent (whatever the growth rate turns out to be, it will be the same in all future years). Unit margins each year are normally distributed with a mean of $50 and a standard deviation of $10. The discount rate is 15 percent and the analysis should cover 15 years.

a. What is the expected NPV if the firm invests now?

b. What is the expected NPV if the firm invests in two years?

c. Modify your model to implement a policy in which the firm will invest after two years only if the market size in year 2 exceeds a cutoff value. What is the optimal cutoff and the resulting expected NPV?

OPTQUEST PROBLEMS

7. *Capacity Planning.* Lang Drug needs to determine the proper capacity level for a new drug, Niagara. Its goal is to maximize the expected NPV earned from the drug during years 0–14, assuming a discount rate of 10 percent per year. It costs $10 to build enough capacity to produce one unit of drug per year. All construction cost is incurred during year 0. It costs $1 per year to maintain a unit of annual production capacity. In year 1, demand will be for 160,000 units of Niagara. The mean annual percentage growth of demand for Niagara is equally likely to assume any value between 10 and 20 percent. The actual growth rate of demand during any year is normally distributed with the given mean and a standard deviation of 6 percent. During year 1, each unit of Niagara sells for $8. The price of Niagara will almost surely grow at 5 percent per year. Unit variable cost is known to be 40 percent of sales price.

Suppose that Lang Drug has the additional opportunity to review demand during year 5 and, if desired, build additional capacity. This means that Lang Drug may not need to build as much capacity during year 1, because it can wait and see whether demand will be high. If demand is high, it can ramp up capacity during year 5 for future years; if not, it can stick with its year 1 capacity. To model this situation, assume that after observing year 5 demand, Lang Drug proceeds as follows. If the ratio of year 5 demand to capacity exceeds some cutoff point C, then Lang Drug will add capacity. If capacity is added, then Lang Drug will add enough capacity to bring total capacity to a multiple M of year 5 demand. We assume it costs $12 to build one unit of capacity at the end of year 5. Thus, Lang Drug's capacity strategy is defined by three decisions:

- Initial capacity (year 1)
- The cutoff value C, which determines whether capacity is added after year 5 (assuming that capacity arrives in time for year 6)
- The multiple M that defines how much capacity is added.

a. Assuming Lang Drug *cannot* build additional capacity in year 5, what capacity level will maximize expected discounted profit? Assume that all building costs are incurred during year 0 and that all cash flows occur at the beginning of the year.

b. With the additional opportunity to review demand and add capacity in year 5, what values would you recommend for the initial capacity, for C, and for M? What is the maximum expected discounted profit when these parameters are optimized?

8. *The Secretary Problem.* You have been asked to interview candidates for an open secretarial position. Each candidate's qualifications for the job can be modeled with a lognormal distribution with a mean of 10 and a standard deviation of 5. Unfortunately, you must decide whether to offer the job to each candidate in turn before being able to interview additional candidates. In other words, you will interview candidate 1 and decide whether to make an offer. If you do not make an offer to candidate 1, you will interview candidate 2 and again make an offer or not. If you pass on candidate 2, you will go on to candidate 3, and so on. If you get to the 10th candidate without having made an offer, you will be forced to accept that candidate regardless of qualifications. Assume all offers are accepted.

Your objective is to hire the candidate with the highest possible rating. To achieve this, you plan to set minimum acceptable scores (MAS) at each interview. For example, you might decide to accept the first candidate with a score over 8. Then your MAS would be 8 at each interview. An alternative policy would be to accept over 8 on the first interview, over 7 on the second, and so on. In general, you have 9 decision variables: one MAS for each interview.

a. What is the expected rating of the candidate hired if all MAS are set at 5?

b. What is the best choice for the MAS if you use the same MAS for all interviews?

c. Using OptQuest and 9 decision variables, determine the best policy. What are the optimal values for the 9 MAS and the resulting expected rating?

d. Using Crystal Ball Sensitivity, determine which of the 9 MAS have the biggest impact on the expected rating of the candidate hired.

e. Assume that a linear relationship applies among the 9 MAS. In other words, parameterize the decisions using the linear equation $MAS(stage\ t) = a + bt$, where t ranges from 1 for the first interview to 9 for the last. What is the optimal policy under this assumption, and what is the resulting expected rating?

9. *Pricing Surplus Inventory*. A large retailer of kitchen appliances has asked you for advice on how much to stock and how to price leftovers of its products. Here's a typical situation.

Demand for espresso machines in the Northeast runs about 2,000 per year (with a standard deviation of 500). They cost the retailer $20 and sell for $40. Since the models change yearly, unsold machines can be hard to sell at the end of the year. Steep markdowns are usually offered, but no real effort has gone into determining what price to set for unsold stock, since the relationship between the price and sales has not been well understood. Management has estimated the following relationship between the price they set for leftovers and demand. *Note*: This represents *mean* demand; actual demand may vary around this mean by a standard deviation of 20 percent of the mean.

Price for Leftover Stock	Mean Demand for Leftovers
$0	1000
$10	600
$15	450
$20	300
$25	150
$30	10

For intermediate values, use linear interpolation. For example, demand at a price of $16 is $450 - (16 - 15)/(20 - 15) * (450 - 300) = 420$.

The retailer needs to know how many machines to order originally, as well as how to set prices on leftover stock. Since the number of units left over is unpredictable, it needs to select recommended price points for its various outlets that will apply regardless of the situation. A typical price schedule is as follows.

Quantity Leftover	Recommended Price
0	$30
10	$25
150	$20
300	$18
450	$16
600	$14
1,000	$12

Again, to determine the recommended price for intermediate values, use linear interpolation.

a. What is the expected profit for an order quantity of 2,000, given that all leftovers are priced at $25 regardless of the quantity leftover?

b. Based on the assumptions in (a), show how expected profit varies for order quantities between 1,000 and 3,000 (with a step size of 100). Also, determine the probability that profits are negative, and show how this varies across the same range of order quantities.

c. Determine the optimal values for the order quantity and the seven recommended price points (as in the second table above).

10. *Project Planning*. An architectural design firm is faced with a decision as to which projects to bid on for the coming year. Ten projects are available for which the firm is qualified. The following table lists the profit it can expect to make from each project, as well as the initial investment it will have to make and the design time required. The firm cannot afford to invest more than $55,000 or use more than a total of 1,000 hours of design time. Its objective is to choose those projects that will maximize its expected profit.

Project	Profit ($000)	Investment ($000)	Design Time (hours)
1	55	6.2	123
2	75	8.8	145
3	98	8.4	164
4	67	5.9	135
5	78	6.9	153
6	82	8.9	122
7	51	6.7	87
8	90	9.2	145
9	76	6.1	137
10	69	6.0	143

a. Assuming *no uncertainty* in profits, investment, or design time, what is the maximum profit the firm can achieve, and which projects should it select? *Note:* This solution must not use more investment capital or design time than is available.

b. Represent the uncertainty in profits, investment, and design time using normal distributions, with standard deviations of 5 percent of the mean for profit, 10 percent for the initial investment, and 15 percent for design time. Determine the maximum expected profit the firm can achieve under these assumptions, and which projects it should select. *Note:* This solution must be such that the investment and design time constraints are violated no more than 5 percent of the time.

11. *Call Center Staffing.* A high-volume call center must determine how many customer service representatives (CSRs) to schedule each day of the week to cover the call volume. CSRs work a five-day week with two days off but can start their week on any day. For example, CSRs who start their week on Wednesday work Wednesday through Sunday with Monday and Tuesday off. Average call volumes (in units of CSRs) are given in the following table. (Actual call volume is normally distributed, with a standard deviation given by 10 percent of the mean.)

Day	Call Volume
Sunday	22
Monday	45
Tuesday	37
Wednesday	33
Thursday	34
Friday	40
Saturday	29

The regular daily wage for a CSR is $400. However, if on a given day volume is such that the regular staff is inadequate, the call center will bring in extra CSRs for all or part of a day. The wage for this emergency work is equivalent to $800 per day. (In other words, if 0.5 CSR units of work are needed on an emergency basis, the cost is $400.)

a. If the call center's objective is to minimize the total cost, including emergency staffing cost, what is the optimal number of CSRs to hire each day and what is the resulting cost?

b. How much emergency staffing will be required under the optimal plan?

c. How would the staffing plan and the minimum cost change if overtime costs were either $600 or $1,000?

d. Working on weekends is unpopular, which leads to higher than normal absenteeism on Saturdays and Sundays. Would it be advantageous for the call center to pay a $100 bonus (a daily wage of $500) for work on Saturdays and Sundays?

12. *Capacity Planning* (*Source*: Winston, *Decision Making under Uncertainty*, p. 123–128). An electric utility currently operates 10 plants. The following table gives the fixed costs, variable costs, and capacities of each of these plants. Daily demand is highly uncertain, given by a normal distribution with a mean of 200,000 kwh and a standard deviation of 40,000 kwh. The utility produces power using the cheapest plants it has to meet the demand each day. If demand exceeds its total capacity, it buys power on the open market at $15/kwh. The utility needs to determine which plants to keep open in the long term, given that it will choose the cost-minimizing plants to use to produce power each day.

Plant	Fixed Cost ($000)	Variable Cost ($/kwh)	Capacity (000 kwh)
1	122	4.3	25
2	185	5.6	34
3	95	6.7	19
4	118	7.8	23
5	121	12.0	14
6	135	4.1	16
7	103	4.9	20
8	188	6.2	21
9	119	5.6	33
10	156	6.9	12

a. If all 10 plants are kept open, what is the total expected cost of meeting demand?

b. If the utility is allowed to close some plants, which ones should it close and what will be the resulting minimum cost?

Modeling Cases

RETIREMENT PLANNING

Bob Davidson is a 46-year-old tenured professor of marketing at a small New England business school. He has a daughter, Sue, age 6, and a wife, Margaret, age 40. Margaret is a potter, a vocation from which she earns no appreciable income. Before she was married and for the first few years of her marriage to Bob (she was married once previously), she worked at a variety of jobs, mostly involving software programming and customer support.

Bob's grandfather died at age 42; Bob's father died in 1980 at the age of 58. Both died from cancer, although unrelated instances of that disease. Bob's health has been excellent; he is an active runner and skier. There are no inherited diseases in the family with the exception of glaucoma. Bob's most recent serum cholesterol count was 190.

Bob's salary from the school where he works consists of a nine-month salary (currently $95,000), on which the school pays an additional 10 percent into a retirement fund. He also regularly receives support for his research, which consists of an additional two-ninths of his regular salary, although the college does not pay retirement benefits on that portion of his income. (Research support is additional income; it is not intended to cover the costs of research.) Over the 12 years he has been at the college his salary has increased by 4 to 15 percent per year, although faculty salaries are subject to severe compression, so he does not expect to receive such generous increases into the future. In addition to his salary, Bob typically earns $10,000 to 20,000 per year from consulting, executive education, and other activities.

In addition to the 10 percent regular contribution the school makes to Bob's retirement savings, Bob also contributes a substantial amount. He is currently setting aside $7,500 per year (before taxes). The maximum tax-deferred amount he can contribute is currently $10,000; this limit rises with inflation. If he were to increase his savings toward retirement above the limit, he would have to invest after-tax dollars. All of Bob's retirement savings are invested with TIAA–CREF (Teachers Insurance and Annuity Association-College Retirement Equities Fund; home page: www.tiaa-cref.org), which provides various retirement, investment, and insurance services to university professors and researchers. Bob has contributed to Social Security for many years as required by law, but in light of the problems with the Social Security trust fund he is uncertain as to the level of benefits that he will actually receive upon retirement. (The Social Security Administration's website is www.ssa.gov.)

Bob's TIAA-CREF holdings currently amount to $137,000. These are invested in the TIAA long-term bond fund (20 percent) and the Global Equity Fund (80 percent). The Global Equity Fund is invested roughly 40 percent in U.S. equities and 60 percent in non-U.S. equities. New contributions are also allocated in these same proportions.

In addition to his retirement assets, Bob's net worth consists of his home (purchase price $140,000 in 1987; Bob's current equity is $40,000), $50,000 in a rainy-day fund (invested in a short-term money market mutual fund with Fidelity Investments), and $24,000 in a Fidelity Growth and Income Fund for his daughter's college tuition. He has a term life insurance policy with a value of $580,000; this policy has no asset value but pays its face value (plus inflation) as long as Bob continues to pay the premiums. He has no outstanding debts in addition to his mortgage, other than monthly credit card charges.

Should Bob die while insured, the proceeds on his life insurance are tax free to his wife. Similarly, if he dies before retirement, his retirement assets go to his wife tax free. Either one of them can convert retirement assets into annuities without any immediate taxation; the monthly income from the annuities is then taxed as ordinary income.

Bob's mother is 72 and in good health. She is retired and living in a co-op apartment in Manhattan. Her net worth is on the order of $300,000. His mother-in-law, who is 70, lives with her second husband. Her husband is 87 and has sufficient assets to pay for nursing home care, if needed, for his likely remaining lifetime. Upon her husband's death, Bob's mother-in-law will receive ownership of their house in Newton, Massachusetts, as well as one-third of his estate (the remaining two-thirds will go to his two children). Her net worth at that point is expected to be in the $300,000–400,000 range.

Bob's goal is to work until he is 60 or 65. He would like to save enough to pay for his daughter's college expenses, but not for her expenses beyond that point. He and his wife would like to travel, and do so now as much as his job and their family responsibilities permit. Upon retirement he would like to be able to travel extensively, although he would be able to live quite modestly otherwise. He does not foresee moving from the small town where he now lives.

Bob has a number of questions about how he should plan for his retirement. Will the amount he is accumulating at his current rate of savings be adequate? How much *should* he be setting aside each year? How much will he have to live on when he retires? How long after retirement will he be able to live comfortably? What are the risks he faces, and how should his retirement planning take these risks into account?

DRAFT TV COMMERCIALS*

Your client directs TV advertising for a large corporation that currently relies on a single outside advertising agency. For years, ads have been created using the same plan: The agency creates a draft commercial and, after getting your client's approval, completes production and arranges for it to be aired.

Your client's budget is divided between creating and airing commercials. Typically, about 5 percent of the budget is devoted to creating commercials and 95 percent to airing them. Lately the client has become dissatisfied with the quality of the ads being created. Along with most advertising people, he believes that the ultimate profitability of an advertising campaign is much more strongly influenced by the content of the advertisement than by the level of expenditure on airing or the media utilized (assuming reasonable levels of expenditure). Thus, he is considering increasing the percentage of his budget devoted to the first, "creative" part of the process.

One way to do this is to commission multiple ad agencies to each independently develop a draft commercial. He would then select the one for completion and airing that he determines would be most effective in promoting sales. Of course, since his budget is essentially fixed, the more money he spends on creating draft commercials the less he has to spend on airing commercials. Note that he will have to pay up front for all of the draft commercials before he has a chance to evaluate them.

The standard technique for evaluating a draft commercial involves showing it to a trial audience and asking what they remembered about it later (this is known as "next day recall"). Ads with higher next day recall are generally those with higher effectiveness in the marketplace, but the correlation is far from perfect. A standard method for assessing the effectiveness of a commercial *after* it has been aired is to survey those who watched the show and estimate "retained impressions." Retained impressions are the number of viewers who can recall the essential features of the ad. Ads with higher retained impressions are usually more effective in generating sales, but again the correlation is not perfect. Both the effectiveness of a commercial (the number of retained impressions it creates) and the exposure it receives (the number of times it is aired) will influence sales.

How would you advise your client on the budget split between creating and airing a commercial?

*Source: O'Conner, G. C., T.R. Willemain, and J. MacLachlau, 1996. "The value of competition among agencies in developing ad compaigns: Revisiting Gross's model." *Journal of Advertising* 25:51–63.

ICEBERGS FOR KUWAIT*

The cost of desalinating seawater using conventional technology in the Persian Gulf is high (around 0.1£ per cubic meter) and requires extensive amounts of oil. Some time ago scientists suggested that it could well prove both practically feasible and less expensive to tow icebergs from the Antarctic, a distance of about 9,600 km. Although some of the ice would undoubtedly melt in transit, it was thought that a significant proportion of the iceberg would remain intact upon arrival in the Gulf. Bear in mind that since water expands upon freezing, 1 cubic meter of ice produces only 0.85 cubic meter of water.

A study was carried out to evaluate the practical problems associated with such a proposal and to quantify the factors that were likely to influence the economics of such a venture. One factor was the difference in rental costs and capacities of towing vessels (summarized in Table 1). Note that each vessel has a maximum iceberg it can tow (measured in cubic meters). It was found that the melting rate of the iceberg depends on both the towing speed and the distance from the South Pole (see Table 2). The data in

TABLE 1 Towing Vessel Data

Ship Size	Small	Medium	Large
Daily rental (£)	400	600	800
Maximum load (cu. meter)	500,000	1,000,000	10,000,000

TABLE 2 Melting Rates (meter/day)

	Distance from Pole (km)			
	1,000	2,000	3,000	≥4,000
Speed				
1 km/hr	0.06	0.12	0.18	0.24
3 km/hr	0.08	0.16	0.24	0.32
5 km/hr	0.10	0.20	0.30	0.40

this table represents the rate at which a hypothetical spherical iceberg shrinks *in radius* over a day at the given distance from the Pole and at the given towing speed. Finally, fuel cost was found to depend on the towing speed and the (current) size of the iceberg (see Table 3).

Determine whether it is economically feasible to produce water from icebergs in the Persian Gulf, and if it is, determine the best means to do so.

*Source: Cross, M. and A.O. Moscardini, 1985. *Learning the Art of Mathematical Modeling*. Ellis Horward Limited, West Sussex.

TABLE 3   Fuel Costs (£/km)

	Current Volume (cu. meter)		
	100,000	1,000,000	10,000,000
Speed			
1 km/hr	8.4	10.5	12.6
3 km/hr	10.8	13.5	16.2
5 km/hr	13.2	16.5	19.8

THE RACQUETBALL RACKET*

It is early in 1999, and a friend of yours has invented a new manufacturing process for producing racquetballs. The resulting high-quality ball has more bounce, but slightly less durability, than the currently popular high-quality ball, which is manufactured by Woodrow, Ltd. The better the players, the more they tend to prefer a lively ball. The primary advantage of the new ball is that it can be manufactured much more inexpensively than the existing ball. Current estimates are that full variable costs for the new ball are $0.52 per ball as compared to $0.95 for the existing ball. (Variable costs include all costs of production, marketing, and distribution that vary with output. It excludes the cost of plant and equipment, overhead, etc.)

Because the new process is unlike well-known production processes, the only reasonable alternative is to build a manufacturing plant specifically for producing these balls. Your friend has calculated that this would require $4–6 million of initial capital. He figures that if he can make a good case to

the bank, he can borrow the capital at about a 10 percent interest rate and start producing racquetballs in a year.

Your friend has offered to make you a partner in the business and has asked you in return to perform a market analysis for him. He has already hired a well-known market research firm, Market Analysis, Ltd., to do some data gathering and preliminary market analysis. The key elements of their final report are given below.

Your problem is to determine how the new balls should be priced, what the resultant market shares will be, and whether the manufacturing plant is a good investment. Your friend is especially concerned about the risks involved and would like some measures of how solid the investment appears to be. He would like you to make a formal presentation of your analysis.

*Adapted from a class assignment developed by Dick Smallwood and Peter Morris

RACQUETBALL MARKET ANALYSIS
Market Analysis, Ltd.
January 20, 2000

a. The market for this type of high-quality ball is currently dominated by a single major competitor, Woodrow, Ltd. Woodrow specializes in manufacturing balls for all types of sports. It has been the only seller of high-quality racquetballs since the late 1970s. Its current price to retail outlets is $1.25 per ball (the retail markup is typically 100 percent, so these balls retail around $2.50 each, or $5.00 for the typical pack of two).

b. Historical data on the number of people playing the sport, the average retail price of balls, and the (estimated) total sales of balls is given in the following table.

Year	Number Players (Thousands)	Retail Price (per ball)	Ball Sold (millions)
1985	600	$1.75	5.932
1986	635	$1.75	6.229
1987	655	$1.80	6.506
1988	700	$1.90	6.820
1989	730	$1.90	7.161
1990	762	$1.90	7.895
1991	812	$2.00	7.895
1992	831	$2.20	8.224
1993	877	$2.45	8.584
1994	931	$2.45	9.026
1995	967	$2.60	9.491
1996	1,020	$2.55	9.996
1997	1,077	$2.50	10.465
1998	1,139	$2.50	10.981

c. According to industry trade association projections, the total number of players will grow about 10 percent a year for the next 10 years and then stabilize at a relatively constant level.

d. In order to assess relative preferences in the marketplace, a concept test was performed. In this test, 200 customers were asked to use both balls over a three-month period, and then specify which ball they would buy at various prices. Many customers indicated they would pay a premium for the Woodrow ball, based on their satisfaction with it and its better durability. Nevertheless, about 11 percent of the customers interviewed indicated a preference for the new bouncier ball at equal prices. The actual observed distribution of price premiums is as follows.

Price Ratio*	Percent Who Would Buy New Ball
0.5	0
1.0	11
1.5	41
2.0	76
2.5	95
3.0	100

*Price of Woodrow ball / Price of new ball.

THE XYZ COMPANY*

The XYZ Company makes widgets and sells to a market that is just about to expand after a period of stability. As the year starts, the widgets are manufactured at a cost of $0.75 and sold at a market price of $1.00. In addition, the firm has 1,000 widgets in finished goods inventory and a cash account of $875 at the beginning of January. During January, sales amount to 1,000 units, which is where they have been in the recent past.

Profitability looks good in January. The 1,000 units of sales provide profits for the month of $250. This amount goes right into the cash account, increasing it to $1,125.

In February, the sales level rises to 1,500 units. For the next several months, it looks like demand will rise by 500 each month, providing a very promising profit outlook.

The XYZ Company keeps an inventory of finished goods on hand. This practice allows it to meet customer demand promptly, without having to worry about delays in the factory. The specific policy is always to hold inventory equal to the previous month's sales level. Thus, the 1,000 units on hand at the start of January are just the right amount to support January demand. When demand rises in February, there is a need to produce for stock as well as for meeting demand, because the policy requires that inventory must rise to 1,500 by March. February production is therefore 2,000 units, providing enough widgets to both meet demand in February and raise inventory to 1,500 by the end of the month.

Your first task is to trace the performance of the XYZ Company on a monthly basis, as demand continues to increase at the rate of 500 units per month. Assume that all revenues are collected in the same month when sales are made, all costs are paid in the same month when production occurs, and profit is equal to the difference between revenues and costs. The cost of producing items for inventory is included in the calculation of monthly profit. Trace profits, inventory, and cash position on a monthly basis, through the month of June. This analysis will give us an initial perspective on the financial health of the XYZ Company. Does the company seem to be successful?

In reality, the XYZ Company behaves like many other firms: it pays its bills promptly, but it collects cash from its customers a little less promptly. In fact, it takes a full month to collect the revenues generated by sales. This means that the firm has receivables every month, which are collected during the following month.

XYZ Company actually starts the year with receivables of $1,000, in addition to inventory worth $750 and a cash account worth $875. (Therefore, its total assets come to $2,625 at the start of the year.) A month later, receivables remain at $1000, inventory value remains at $750, and cash increases to $1,125 (reflecting receivables of $1,000 collected, less production expenses of $750).

When February sales climb to 1,500 units, XYZ Company produces 2,000 widgets. Of this amount, 1,500 units are produced to meet demand and 500 units are produced to augment inventory. This means that a production bill of $1,500 is paid in February. During February, the January receivables of $1,000 are collected, and at the end of February, there are receivables of $1,500, reflecting sales made on account during the month.

For accounting purposes, XYZ Company calculates its net income by recognizing sales (even though it has not yet collected the corresponding revenues) and by recognizing the cost of producing the items sold. The cost of producing items for inventory does not enter into its calculation of net income. In January, net income is therefore calculated as $250, representing the difference between the revenue from January sales of $1,000 and the cost of producing those 1,000 units, or $750.

Refine your initial analysis to trace the performance of the XYZ Company, again with demand increasing at the rate of 500 units per month. Assume that all revenues are collected in the month following the month where sales occur, but that all costs are paid in the same month when they occur. Trace net income, receivables, inventory, and cash on a monthly basis, through the month of June. This will give us another perspective on the financial health of the XYZ Company. What financial difficulty does the model portray?

*Adapted from a homework exercise developed by Clyde Stickney.

MEDICAL SUPPLIES FOR BANJUL[*]

You are the team leader of a unit of a U.S. nonprofit organization based in Banjul, Gambia (capital city). The nonprofit's mission is to ensure that rural populations worldwide have access to health and sanitation-related supplies. Due to the sudden departure of one of your team leaders, you are taking over responsibility for ordering certain medical supplies for three villages. Each village consists of four groups:

- Senior citizens (those over 65)
- Children (population under 12)
- Teens (those aged 13–19)
- The population aged 20–65.

The medical supplies required by each village include bandages (types A, B, and C), medical tape, and hearing aids. Children need type A bandages; teens need type B bandages; and adults (i.e., everyone else), need type C bandages. All members of the population use the same kind of medical tape. Only senior citizens require hearing aids. The former team member explained to you that a good rule of thumb is to ensure that at all times a village should keep in stock two bandages per person and hearing aids for 5 percent of the senior citizen population. Cost and packaging information for the products is as follows:

- Type A bandages come in packages of 30. Each package is $3.00.
- Type B bandages come in packages of 30. Each package is $5.00.
- Type C bandages come in packages of 30. Each package is $6.00.

- Medical tape comes in rolls of 2 feet each. You usually use one roll per package of bandages. One roll is $2.50.
- Hearing aids are sold in single units (1 per package) and are $5.00 each.

Your unit's budget does not enable you to purchase more supplies than you need in a given quarter. At the end of every quarter, one of your team members provides you with the population count by age group for the village and the stocks remaining in each village.

The former team member completed this cumbersome task by hand every quarter. However, owing to your other responsibilities, you will have no more than a few minutes to spend on this task on a quarterly basis—doing it by hand is out of question. In addition, you may be transferred to another post in three to six months, so you may have to pass on the responsibility to a successor before too long.

It is 6:00 A.M. Monday morning. You have three hours left at the city headquarters, until you leave to begin two weeks of fieldwork in the villages without computer access. The initial order must be placed by next Friday, so you will have to take care of procuring a check from the finance officer and placing the order before you leave. Other team members are beginning to arrive, but the office is still quiet. Everything else on your plate can wait until you return. Yet, something else could pop up at any moment, so you have to work quickly. You don't have the latest population or stock figures yet, but the team member who has them will arrive at 8:30 A.M.

[*]Contributed by Manisha Shahane.

REID'S RAISIN COMPANY

Located in wine country, Reid's Raisin Company (RRC) is a food-processing firm that purchases surplus grapes from grape growers, dries them into raisins, applies a layer of sugar, and sells the sugar-coated raisins to major cereal and candy companies. At the beginning of the grape-growing season, RRC has two decisions to make. The first involves how many grapes to buy under contract, and the second involves how much to charge for the sugar-coated raisins it sells.

In the spring, RRC typically contracts with a grower who will supply a given amount of grapes in the autumn at a fixed cost of $0.25 per pound. The balance between RRC's grape requirements and those supplied by the grower must be purchased in the autumn, on the open market, at a price that could vary from a historical low of $0.20 per pound to a high of $0.35 per pound. (RRC cannot, however, sell grapes on the open market in the autumn if it has a surplus in inventory, because it has no distribution system for such purposes.)

The other major decision facing RRC is the price to charge for sugar-coated raisins. RRC has several customers who buy RRC's output in price-dependent quantities. RRC negotiates with these processors as a group to arrive at a price for the sugar-coated raisins and the quantity to be bought at that price. The negotiations take place in the spring, long before the open market price of grapes is known.

Based on prior years' experience, Mary Jo Reid, RRC's general manager, believes that if RRC prices the sugar-coated raisins at $2.20 per pound, the processors' orders will total 750,000 pounds of sugar-coated raisins. Furthermore, this total will increase by 15,000 pounds for each penny reduction in sugar-coated raisin price below $2.20. The same relationship holds in the other direction: demand will drop by 15,000 for each penny increase. The price of $2.20 is a tentative starting point in the negotiations.

Sugar-coated raisins are made by washing and drying grapes into raisins, followed by spraying the raisins with a sugar coating that RRC buys for $0.55 per pound. It takes 2.5 pounds of grapes plus 0.05 pound of coating to make one pound of sugar-coated raisins, the balance being water that evaporates during grape drying. In addition to the raw materials cost for the grapes and the coating, RRC's processing plant incurs a variable cost of $0.20 to process one pound of grapes into raisins, up to its capacity of 1,500,000 pounds of grapes. For volumes above 1,500,000 pounds of grapes, RRC outsources grape processing to another food processor, which charges RRC $0.45 per pound. This price includes just the processing cost, as RRC supplies both the grapes and the coating required. RRC also incurs fixed (overhead) costs in its grape-processing plant of $200,000 per year.

Mary Jo has asked you to analyze the situation in order to guide her in the upcoming negotiations. Her goal is to examine the effect of various "What-if?" scenarios on RRC's profits. As a basis for the analysis, she suggests using a contract purchase price of $0.25, with a supply quantity of 1 million pounds from the grower, along with a selling price of $2.20 for sugar-coated raisins. She is primarily interested in evaluating annual pretax profit as a function of the selling price and the open-market grape price. She believes that the open-market grape price is most likely to be $0.30.

THE BIG RIG TRUCK RENTAL COMPANY

The Big Rig Rental Company, which owns and rents out 50 trucks, is for sale for $400,000. Tom Grossman, the company's owner, wants you to develop a five-year economic analysis to assist buyers in evaluating the company.

The market rate for truck rentals is currently $12,000 per year per truck. At this base rate, an average of 62 percent of the trucks will be rented each year. Tom believes that if the rent were lowered by $1,200 per truck per year, utilization would increase by seven percentage points. He also believes that this relationship would apply to additional reductions in the base rate. For example, at a $7,200 rental rate, 90 percent of the trucks would be rented. This relationship would apply to increases in the base rate as well. Over the next five years, the base rental rate should remain stable.

At the end of five years, it is assumed that the buyer will resell the business for cash. Tom estimates that the selling price will be three times the gross revenue in the final year.

The cost of maintaining the fleet runs about $4,800 per truck per year (independent of utilization), which includes inspection fees, licenses, and normal mainte-

nance. Big Rig has fixed office costs of $60,000 per year and pays property taxes of $35,000 per year. Property taxes are expected to grow at a rate of 3 percent per year, and maintenance costs are expected to grow 9 percent per year due to the age of the fleet. However, office costs are predicted to remain level. Profits are subject to a 30 percent income tax. The tax is zero if profit is negative.

Cash flow in the final year would include cash from the sale of the business. Because the trucks have all been fully depreciated, there are no complicating tax effects: Revenue from the sale of the business will effectively be taxed at the 30 percent rate. Investment profit for the buyer is defined to be the Net Present Value of the annual cash flows, computed at a discount rate of 10 percent. (All operating revenues and expenses are in cash.) The calculation of NPV includes the purchase price, incurred at the beginning of year 1, and net income from operations (including the sale price in year 5) over five years (incurred at the end of the year). There would be no purchases or sales of trucks during the five years.

FLEXIBLE INSURANCE COVERAGE

A company health plan offers four alternatives for coverage, from a low-cost plan with a high deductible to a high-cost plan with a low deductible. The details of coverage are given in the following table. The Human Resources

Department would like to develop a means to help any employee, whether single or married, small family or large, low medical expenses or high, to compare these plan alternatives.

| | | | Plan Options and Costs | | |
| | | | Annual Premium | | |
	Deductible	Co-insurance	1-Person	2-Person	Family
Option 1	$1,500/$2,500	none	$1,825	$3,651	$4,929
Option 2	500/1,000	20%	2,016	4,032	5,444
Option 3	250/500	20%	2,245	4,491	6,063
Option 4	100/200	10%	2,577	5,154	6,959

The deductible amount is paid by the employee. The first figure applies to an individual; the second applies to two-person or family coverage. In the case of Option 1, for example, this means that the insurance coverage takes effect once an individual has paid for $1,500 worth of expenses. (This limit holds for any individual under two-person or family coverage, as well as for an individual with one-person coverage.) In the case of two-person or family coverage, the insurance also takes effect once the household has incurred $2,500 worth of expenses.

The co-insurance is the percentage of expenses that must be paid by the employee when the insurance coverage takes effect. In the case of Option 2, for example, this means that the insurance covers 80 percent of all expenses after the deductible amount has been reached.

The Annual Premium is the cost of the insurance to the employee.

SNOEY SOFTWARE COMPANY

Snoey Software Company is developing a new piece of software that can be tailored to various market segments. At this stage, the developers envision three versions of the software: an Educational version, a Large-Scale version, and a High-Speed version. Each is built around the same basic design, but a number of data-handling and input/output procedures are different in the different versions. By creating these versions, Snoey hopes to extract more value from the marketplace than it could obtain with just one version.

Currently, the developers are close to completing the Educational version, but they have done little more than outline the other two versions. The estimated R&D expenditures required to finish those tasks are $100,000 for the Large-Scale version, and $150,000 for the High-Speed version. The actual variable costs are estimated to be $10 for the Educational version, $20 for the Large-Scale version, and $36 for the High-Speed version.

The marketing director at Snoey Software has identified five market segments that would respond differently to the new software: (1) university students, (2) academic and government laboratories, (3) consultants, (4) small companies, and (5) large companies. The potential sales in each of these markets, together with the cost of advertising in each market, are as follows.

Segment	Market Size	Marketing Costs
Students	400,000	$350,000
Laboratories	1,200	75,000
Consultants	12,000	150,000
Small companies	24,000	200,000
Large companies	6,000	100,000

In a series of surveys and focus groups, the marketing staff has tested the interest of each market segment in the three different versions of the software. The results of the tests have been summarized in a table of values that represent the prices each segment would be willing to pay for each of the versions. This information is shown in the following table.

Segment	Educational	Large-Scale	High-Speed
Students	$25	$40	$75
Laboratories	125	300	1,000
Consultants	100	500	750
Small companies	75	250	500
Large companies	150	1,000	2,500

In order to develop a price structure for the software, the marketing director uses the following logic. For each segment and for each version, the potential customer will calculate the difference between the price and the value. The highest difference will dictate what the customer will purchase. On that basis, it will be possible to estimate the sales volumes of each version in each segment and compute the resulting profits.

You have been hired to build a model that will compute the sales of each version in each market segment and then calculate the resulting profit for Snoey Software. Given the approach they have taken thus far, the company is committed to the Educational version, but it could halt development activities on either or both of the other versions. The question on everybody's mind is: which versions should be brought to market?

COX CABLE AND WIRE COMPANY

Meredith Ceh breathed a sigh of relief. Finally, all the necessary figures seemed to be correctly in place, and her spreadsheet looked complete. She was confident that she could analyze the situation that John Cox had described, but she wondered if there were other concerns she should be addressing in her response.

Mr. Cox, president of Cox Cable and Wire Company, and grandson of the company's founder, had asked Meredith to come up with plans to support the preliminary contract he had worked out with Midwest Telephone Company. The contract called for delivery of 340 reels of cable during the summer. He was leaving the next day to negotiate a final contract with Midwest and wanted to be sure he understood all of the implications.

According to Mr. Cox, he had been looking for a chance to become a supplier to a large company like Midwest, and this seemed to be the right opportunity. Demand from some of Cox Cable's traditional customers had slackened, and as a result there was excess capacity during the summer. Nevertheless, he wanted to be sure that, from the start, his dealings with Midwest would be profitable, and he had told Meredith that he was looking for cash inflows to exceed cash outflows by at least 25 percent. He also wanted her to confirm that there was sufficient capacity to meet the terms of the contract. He had quickly mentioned a number of other items, but those were secondary to profitability and capacity.

Background

The Cox Cable and Wire Company sold a variety of products for the telecommunications industry. At its Indianapolis plant, the company purchased uncoated wire in standard gauges, assembled it into multiwire cables, and then applied various coatings according to customer specification. The plant essentially made products in two basic families—standard plastic and high-quality Teflon. The two coatings came in a variety of colors, but these were changed easily by introducing different dyes into the basic coating liquid.

The production facilities at Indianapolis consisted of two independent process trains (semiautomated production lines), referred to as the General and National trains, after the companies that manufactured them. Both the plastic-coated and the Teflon-coated cable could be produced on either process train; however, Teflon coating was a faster process due to curing requirements. Planning at Cox Cable was usually done on an annual and then a quarterly basis. The labor force was determined by analyzing forecast demand for the coming year, although revisions were possible as the year developed. Then, on a quarterly basis, more specific machine schedules were made up. Each quarter the process trains were usually shut down for planned maintenance, but the maintenance schedules were determined at the last minute, after production plans were in place, and they were often postponed when the schedule was tight.

As a result of recent expansions, there was not much storage space in the plant. Cable could temporarily be stored in the shipping area for the purposes of loading trucks, but there was no space for cable to be stored for future deliveries. Additional inventory space was available at a nearby public warehouse.

Meredith had become familiar with all of this information during her first week as a summer intern. At the end of the week, she had met with Mr. Cox and he had outlined the Midwest contract negotiation.

The Contract

The preliminary contract was straightforward. Midwest had asked for the delivery quantities outlined in Table 1. Prices had also been agreed on, although Mr. Cox had said he wouldn't be surprised to find Midwest seeking to raise the Teflon delivery requirements during the final negotiation.

Meredith had gone first to the production manager, Jeff Knight, for information about capacity. Jeff had provided her with data on production times (Table 2), which he said

TABLE 1 Contract Delivery Schedule and Prices

Month	Plastic	Teflon
June	50	30
July	100	60
August	50	50
Price	$360	$400

TABLE 2 Production Capabilities, in Hours per Reel

Process Train	Plastic	Teflon
General	2.0	1.5
National	2.5	2.0

TABLE 3 Unscheduled Production Hours

Month	General	National
June	140	250
July	60	80
August	150	100

TABLE 4 Accounting Data for Production

Cost Category	General	National
Machine Depreciation	$50.00/hr	$40.00/hr
Direct labor	16.00	16.00
Supervisor	8.00	8.00
Production Overhead	12.00	12.00

were pretty reliable, given the company's extensive experience with the two process trains. He also gave her the existing production commitments for the summer months, showing the available capacity given in Table 3. Not all of these figures were fixed, he said. Apparently, there was a design for a mechanism that could speed up the General process train. Engineers at Cox Cable planned to install this mechanism in September, adding 80 hours per month to capacity. "We could move up our plans, so that the additional 80 hours would be available to the shop in August," he remarked. "But that would probably run about $900 in overtime expenses, and I'm not sure if it would be worth while."

After putting some of this information into her spreadsheet, Meredith spoke with the plant's controller, Donna Malone, who had access to most of the necessary cost data. Meredith learned that the material in the cables cost $160 per reel for the plastic-coated cable and $200 for the Teflon-coated cable. Packaging costs were $40 for either type of cable, and the inventory costs at the public warehouse came to $10 per reel for each month stored. "That's if you can get the space," Donna commented. "It's a good idea to make reservations a few weeks in advance; otherwise we might find they're temporarily out of space." Donna also provided standard accounting data on production costs (Table 4). According to Donna, about half of the production overhead consisted of costs that usually varied with labor charges, while the rest was depreciation for equipment other than the two process trains. The machine depreciation charges on the two process trains were broken out separately, as determined at the time the machinery was purchased. For example, the General process train originally cost $500,000 ten years ago and had an expected life of five years, or about 10,000 hours, hence its depreciation rate of $50 per hour.

The Analysis

Meredith was able to consolidate all of the information she collected into a spreadsheet. Making what she felt were reasonable assumptions about relevant cost factors, she was able to optimize the production plan, and she determined that it should be possible to meet the 25 percent profitability target. Nevertheless, there seemed to be several factors in it that were subject to change—things that had come up in her various conversations, such as maintenance, warehousing, and the possibility of modifying the contract. She expected that Mr. Cox would quiz her about all of these factors, and she knew it would be important for her to be prepared for his questions.

THE BMW COMPANY

Late in the summer of 1989, the government of Germany was seriously considering an innovative policy affecting the treatment of scrapped vehicles. This policy would make auto manufacturers responsible for recycling and disposal of their vehicles at the end of their useful lives. Sometimes referred to as a "Producer Responsibility" policy, this regulation would obligate the manufacturers of automobiles to take back vehicles that were ready to be scrapped.

The auto takeback proposal was actually the first of several initiatives that would also affect the end-of-life (EOL) treatment of such other products as household appliances and consumer electronics. But in 1989, no other industry had faced anything like this new policy. Managers at BMW and other German automakers struggled to understand the implications for their own company. Perhaps the first exercise was to gauge the magnitude of the economic effect. Stated another way, management wanted to know what the cost of the new policy was likely to be, if BMW continued to do business as usual.

Background

A loose network of dismantlers and shredders managed most of the recycling and disposal of German vehicles, accounting for about 95 percent of EOL volume, or roughly 2.1 million vehicles per year. Dismantling was a labor-intensive process that removed auto parts, fluids, and materials that could be re-sold. The hulk that remained was sold to a shredder. Shredding was a capital-intensive business that separated the remaining materials into distinct streams. Ferrous metals were sold to steel producers, nonferrous metals were sold to specialized metal companies, and the remaining material was typically sent to landfills or incinerators. The material headed for disposal was known as Automobile Shredder Residue (ASR) and consisted of plastic, rubber, foam, glass, and dirt. ASR was virtually impossible to separate into portions with any economic value, so shredders paid for its removal and disposal. As of 1989, the annual volume of ASR came to about 400,000 tons. On average, an automobile stayed in service for about 10 years.

Although dismantlers and shredders were unaffiliated, private businesses in 1989, it was conceivable that, under the new government policy, they would be taken over by the auto companies. Even if they remained independently owned businesses, the costs of dismantling and shredding would ultimately be borne by the auto companies, since the policy made them legally responsible for the waste.

Economics of disposal

The costs in this system had been increasing and, in fact, were about to increase more quickly due to two major trends, one involving disposal costs and the other involving material composition. On the material side, automobiles were being designed with less metal each year and more plastics. In the 1960s, a typical car was made up of more than 80 percent metal, but the new models of 1990 were only about 75 percent metal. This meant that more of the vehicle was destined to end up as ASR. Averaged across the market, autos weighed an average of about 1,000 kg each. See Exhibit 1 for some representative figures.

Exhbit 1. Material Trends in Automobile Composition

Material	1965	1985	1995(est.)
Iron and Steel	76.0%	68.0%	63.0%
Lead, Copper, and Zinc	4.0%	4.0%	3.0%
Aluminum	2.0%	4.5%	6.5%
Plastics	2.0%	9.0%	13.0%
Fabric, Rubber, and Glass	16.0%	14.5%	14.5%

BMW 1989 Models	Weight (kg)	Plastics Content
3 series	1150	11.3%
5 series	1400	10.9%
7 series	1650	10.3%

On the disposal side, a much more significant trend was in progress. As in most of Europe, landfill options were disappearing in Germany. In 1989, about half of the waste stream found its way to landfills, with 35 percent going to waste-to-energy incinerators, and the remaining 15 percent to recycling of some kind. But the number of landfills was declining, and it looked like this trend would continue, so that by 1999 landfill and incineration would handle approximately equal shares. The effects of supply and demand were visible in the costs of disposal at landfills. Exhibit 2 summarizes recent and projected costs.

Exhbit 2. Recent and Projected (*) Landfill Costs

Year	Cost (DM/ton)
1987	30
1988	40
1989	60
1990	120
1991*	200
1993*	500 ± 100
1995*	1200 ± 600

Many landfills were of older designs, and public concern about their environmental risks had grown. Recent environmental regulations were beginning to restrict the materials that could be taken to landfills, and there was a good chance that ASR would be prohibited. Specially designed hazardous waste landfills were an alternative, but they tended to be three or four times as costly as the typical solid-waste landfill.

Meanwhile, the number of incinerators had grown from a handful in the early 1960s to nearly 50 by 1989, with prospects for another 25 or more in the coming decade. However, incinerators were expensive to build, and awareness of their environmental impacts was growing. In particular, the incineration of plastics had come under special scrutiny. The net effect was that incineration was about twice as costly as landfill disposal in 1989, and it was uncertain how the relative cost of incineration would evolve in the years to come.

Trends in the Market

Prior to the 1980s, BMW cars were known for their reliability and quality. Only during the 80s did BMW acquire a reputation for performance and begin to compete in the high-end market. As a result, its domestic market share had risen from about 5.6 percent at the start of the decade to 6.7 percent in 1989. Some details of financial and market performance for BMW are summarized in Exhibits 3 and 4.

In 1989, BMW seemed poised to benefit from its successes over the previous several years, having consolidated its position in the marketplace. Long-range forecasts predicted that the economy would grow by about 2 percent in the coming decade, with inflation at no more than 4 percent. However, the proposed takeback policy raised questions about whether the company's profitability could endure. Assuming that, in the new regulatory regime, automakers bear the cost of disposal, the task is to estimate how much of the firm's net income will be devoted to EOL vehicles 10 years into the future.

Exhbit 3. Selected Companywide Financial Data for BMW

	1989	1988	1987	1986	1985
Net Sales (DM millions)	20,960	19,880	17,660	15,000	14,240
Sales (Vehicles)	511,000	486,600	459,500	446,100	445,233
Production (Vehicles)	511,500	484,100	461,300	446,400	445,200
Net Income (DM millions)	386.0	375.0	375.0	337.5	300.0

Exhbit 4. Selected Market Data for BMW Automobiles

Cases	1989 Sales	1989 Share	1988 Sales	1988 Share
Germany	191,000	6.7%	180,200	6.4%
Europe (rest)	163,200	1.7%	153,100	1.9%
N. America	69,200	6.4%	78,800	6.8%
Other	57,300	1.1%	47,700	1.1%

THE ERP DECISION*

During the 1990s, many large companies began to realize that lack of integration among their information systems was leading to serious operational inefficiencies. Furthermore, these inefficiencies were beginning to cause many companies to lose ground to other, better-organized firms. At the same time, enterprise resource planning (ERP) software, especially SAP R/3 (http://www.sap.com/), was reaching a high state of maturity as its penetration rate among the Fortune 1000 rose. The decision whether to convert to SAP (or a competing product) was a strategic one for many companies at this time, both because of the high costs and risks of cost overruns (many SAP implementations had failed or been far more costly than expected) and because of the high risks of *not* implementing integrated software. This case will allow you to explore the analysis done by one typical company for this decision.

What is ERP software? An ERP system is companywide software that links all operations to a central database. ERP software is organized by module, one for each functional area such as Finance, Accounting, Manufacturing, Payroll, Human Resources, and so on. Each of these modules has a common software design, and it shares information as needed with the central database. While converting old systems to ERP is a massive undertaking, once it is accomplished the firm has one common database, one common definition of business concepts, one central warehouse in which all information resides, and individual modules for each functional area that are compatible but can be upgraded independently.

The Situation at Mega Corporation

Mega Corporation has for many years been a dominant manufacturer in its industry. As a worldwide firm, it has four main manufacturing sites and sales offices spread across the world. Since most of the growth in the firm occurred in the 1970s and 1980s, before integrated firm-wide software was available, few of the company's information systems can communicate with each other. This lack of information integration is becoming an increasing burden on the firm. Each of the manufacturing sites has its own hardware and software, and none are linked electronically. As a consequence, much of the sharing of information that goes on among the manufacturing sites is done by telephone, fax, or memo. Each of the main sales offices has purchased and developed its own information systems, and these do not communicate with each other or with manufacturing. Again, this forces the sales offices to use telephone and faxes to share data. The accounting department is centralized at headquarters, but its software system does not interface with the others. Much of their time is spent manually transferring accounting data from the field into their central system. Purchasing is done by each of the manufacturing sites independently, and since their systems do not communicate, the firm cannot keep track of its purchases from single vendors and thus misses out on many discounts. This is just a sample of the problems that Mega suffers from due to a lack of information integration.

As these problems deepened, and the need for some centralized solution became more and more apparent, a conflict arose between the chief information officer (CIO) and the chief financial officer (CFO). The CIO wanted to install an integrated system immediately despite the costs and risks; the CFO wanted to kill any attempt to install this software. Here is a summary of the pros and cons of this decision, as expressed by the two executives.

The Case for ERP

The CIO argued that partial fixes to the company's current information systems were becoming more expensive and less effective every year. The conversion to ERP was inevitable, so why not do it now? Once the system was up and running, the firm could expect to see lower inventories both of finished goods and raw materials. Finished goods inventories would be lower because Marketing and Manufacturing would be able to share common forecasts; raw materials inventories would be lower because Manufacturing would communicate its needs better to Purchasing, which would not have to maintain large stocks of raw materials to cover unexpected orders. In addition, Purchasing would be able to obtain quantity discounts from more vendors by pooling its orders from the various manufacturing sites. Sales would increase because, with better communication between

Marketing and Manufacturing, there would be fewer canceled orders, fewer late shipments, and more satisfied customers. Software maintenance costs would go down because the company would not have to maintain the old, nonintegrated software, much of which existed simply to allow one system to communicate with another. Decisionmaking would also improve with the ERP system, because such basic information as current production costs at the product level would be available for the first time. Finally, once the basic ERP system was in place it would become possible to install more sophisticated software such as a customer relationship management or CRM system. A CRM system sits on top of the ERP system, using its database to help answer questions such as "Are we making money selling products to our customers in the Northeast?" and "Is our sales force in East Asia fully productive?"

The Case against ERP

The case against ERP was made forcefully by the CFO. ERP hardware and software costs are high and must be paid in full before any benefits come in. ERP systems change almost everyone's job, so the retraining costs are enormous. Some people will even leave the company rather than retrain on the new systems. No one within the company has any experience with ERP, so an expensive group of consultants must be hired over many years. Even after the consultants are gone, the company will have to hire a substantial number of highly trained and highly paid systems people to maintain the ERP system. Improved decisionmaking sounds valuable, but it is hard to quantify, and besides, if the company has as much difficulty as some firms have had implementing ERP, the "benefits" may well be negative!

The only rational way to develop an understanding of the likely costs and benefits of implementing ERP, and perhaps to settle this argument, is to develop a model. You have been asked by the Board to do just that. Your model should be *complete* in that it accounts for all the possible costs and benefits from both an ERP system and from installing a CRM system on top of the ERP system. The model should be *flexible*, so that alternative assumptions can easily be tested. It should be *robust*, in that nonsensical inputs should be rejected. It should also provide *insights*, so that the Board can use it effectively to decide under what circumstances the ERP/CRM project would make sense. Some of the initial assumptions on which the Board would like the model to be built are described next.

Assumptions

First, the model should cover 20 years, from 2005–2024. Second, it should account for changes in sales (and revenues) from the ERP and CRM systems, as well as changes in inventories. Finally, it should include the costs of hardware, software, consultants, permanent employees, training of nonprogramming staff, and maintenance of old systems. Specific numerical assumptions follow:

- Without ERP, sales are expected to hold steady at about $5 million per year over the next 15 years.
- Sales can be expected to grow about 1 percent/year once an ERP system is fully operational, which will take two years.

- If a CRM system is installed, sales growth will become 2 percent/year. (The CRM system would be installed in year 4 and become operational beginning in year 5.)
- The company currently spends $5 million per year maintaining its old systems, and this cost will grow by $100,000 per year. All of this maintenance cost will be avoided if an ERP system is installed.
- ERP hardware will cost $5 million in the first year of installation and $1 million in the second.
- ERP software will cost $10 million in the first year of installation and $1 million in the second.
- CRM hardware and software will each cost $1 million in the year of installation (year 4). The CRM installation cannot occur before three years after the ERP installation is begun.
- Consultants work 225 days per year.
- The accompanying table gives:
  - The number of ERP and CRM consultants required, along with their daily rate
  - The number of additional programmers required, as well as their yearly salary
  - The costs of training nonprogramming staff
- Without ERP, inventory turns over 11 times per year. Thus, the average level of inventory (in dollars) is annual sales divided by 11. With the ERP system, turns are expected to increase to 13. To hold a dollar of finished goods inventory for one year costs $3.50.
- Variable costs (excluding the costs of inventory) are 75 percent of sales revenues.

a significantly higher rate should be used given the risks of this project.

- Efficiency gains from ERP systems have varied widely from firm to firm. Some managers within this firm are optimistic and would estimate these gains at $7 million per year. Others are pessimistic and would see a loss of $5 million per year due to cost overruns and unexpected retraining expenses. Finally, there is a neutral camp that would prefer to assume no efficiency gains or losses from ERP.

Analysis

Using the assumptions already given and whatever additional assumptions you feel are warranted, build a model to project the Net Present Value of the gains from the ERP and CRM decisions. Remember that your model should be complete, flexible, robust, and capable of providing insight.

Establish a base case. Perform what-if analysis. Over what ranges for critical parameters does the project look attractive? Which assumptions appear to be especially critical in determining the gains from ERP? Where are the breakeven values for critical parameters at which the project changes from attractive to unattractive?

Synthesize what you have learned from this analysis into a short PowerPoint presentation to the Board. Your presentation should use graphical means wherever possible to convey your insights. Do not repeat anything the Board already knows—get right to the point.

Year	Number of ERP Consultants	Number of CRM Consultants	Cost of Consultants/Day	Number of Added Programmers	Cost of Added Programmers/Year	Training Costs
2005	10	0	1,500	10	100,000	3,000,000
2006	8	0	1,515	8	105,000	2,000,000
2007	6	0	1,530	6	110,250	1,000,000
2008	4	2	1,545	4	115,762	500,000
2009	2	1	1,560	2	121,550	200,000
2010	1	1	1,575	1	127,627	100,000
2011	0	0	1,590	1	134,008	0
2012	0	0	1,605	0	140,708	0
2013	0	0	1,621	0	147,708	0
2014	0	0	1,637	0	155,130	0
2015	0	0	1,653	0	162,886	0
2016	0	0	1,669	0	171,030	0
2017	0	0	1,685	0	179,581	0
2018	0	0	1,701	0	188,560	0
2019	0	0	1,717	0	197,254	0
2020	0	0	1,733	0	206,019	0
2021	0	0	1,749	0	214,784	0
2022	0	0	1,765	0	223,549	0
2023	0	0	1,781	0	232,314	0
2024	0	0	1,797	0	241,079	0

- The hurdle rates normally used in the company to evaluate capital investments range from 10 to 15 percent. However, an argument has been made that

*This case was adapted by Steve Powell and Jeff Camm from "The Mega Corporation's ERP Decision," Case 10 in *Problem-Solving Cases* by Joseph A. Brady and Ellen F. Monk, Course Technology, 2003.

*NATIONAL LEASING, INC.**

Background

New-vehicle leasing has grown to the point that it represents a major factor in new-car sales. Consumers who would otherwise have purchased a new car every few years are now attracted by monthly lease payments lower than those for financing a new-car purchase. Such consumers can thereby drive a nicer vehicle than they could afford to buy or finance. The most popular leases are for expensive or midrange vehicles and carry a term of 24 or 36 months.

The majority of leases are sold via "captive" leasing companies, run by a vehicle manufacturer. About 40 percent of leases are sold by independent leasing companies, primarily banks and other financial firms. Among the independents, six are major national players, competing against a host of smaller regional companies.

Increasing competition among leasing companies and online pricing information have made vehicle leasing nearly a commodity. Consumers care most about getting the lowest monthly payment, other factors being equal. Online information sources at dealers readily report the lowest lease payments for a given vehicle.

Demand for any one lease is highly unpredictable. However, it is generally accepted that demand is sensitive to the gap between the monthly payments of a given leasing company and the going rate in the market for that car model, which is usually set by the lease with the lowest monthly payments. Other factors, such as the contract residual value, appear to be secondary in the consumer's mind.

The most common form of leasing is the *closed-end lease*, in which the monthly payment is computed based on three factors:

- *Capitalized Cost*: The purchase price for the car, net of trade-ins, fees, discounts, and dealer-installed options.
- *Residual Value*: The value of the vehicle at the end of the lease, specified by the leasing company in the lease contract. The consumer has the right to purchase the vehicle at this price upon lease termination (this is known as the "purchase option").
- *Money Factor, or Rate*: The implicit interest rate the leasing company (the "lessor") charges in the monthly payments.

A typical leasing company gets its money at a very low interest rate and finances the purchase of the cars it will lease. Thus, the leasing company is essentially making a monthly payment to its bank on the full price of the vehicle, while getting a monthly lease payment from its customer based on the difference between the full price and the contract residual price.

For a given vehicle, a lower residual value implies a greater drop in value over the term of the lease, prompting higher monthly payments. Therefore, a leasing company offering the highest residual value usually has the lowest, and most competitive, monthly payment. Such a high residual value, relative to competitors, is likely to sell a lot of leases. However, one need only consider what happens at

the end of the lease term to understand how this can be a time bomb. If the *actual* end-of-lease market value is lower than the contract residual value, the consumer is likely to return the car to the lessor. The lessor then typically sells the vehicle, usually at auction, and realizes a "residual loss."

If a leasing company sets a low, "conservative," residual value, then the corresponding monthly payments are higher. This reduces the number of leases sold in this competitive market. And at the end of these leases, if the actual market value is greater than the contract residual, the consumer is more likely to exercise their purchase option. By then selling the vehicle for the prevailing market value, the consumer in essence receives a rebate for the higher monthly payments during the term of the lease. (Of course, the consumer may also decide to keep the car.) When consumers exercise their purchase option, the lessor loses the opportunity to realize "residual gains."

The economically rational thing for the lease owner to do at the end of the lease is to purchase the car when the actual market value exceeds the contract residual (and resell at the higher price) and to leave the car to the leasing company when the actual market value falls below the contract residual. However, not all consumers are rational at the end of the lease. Some percentage will buy the vehicle regardless of the actual market value, presumably because they have become attached to the vehicle or because the transactions costs of acquiring a new vehicle are too high. Some will not purchase even when the actual market value is well above the contract residual. By the same token, some will purchase even when the actual market value is below the contract residual.

The primary challenge, then, for companies offering a closed-end lease, is to intelligently select the contract residual value of the vehicle 24, 36, 48, or even 60 months into the future. Intelligent selection means that the leasing company must offer competitive monthly payments on the front end while not ignoring the risk of being left with residual losses on the back end. To cushion financial performance against this risk, auto lessors set aside a reserve against residual losses in order to report income accurately. This practice is similar to insurance companies' reserves against future claims.

During the period 1990–1995, used car prices rose faster than inflation (5 to 6 percent per year on average in nominal terms). This price rise was driven by the higher quality of used cars (itself a result of higher manufacturing quality standards in new cars), high new-car prices making used vehicles more attractive, and a shift in consumer perceptions making it less unfashionable to own a used vehicle.

In this environment, lessors realized very few residual losses because they were generally conservative in setting residuals, forecasting low used-vehicle prices. They admittedly missed some opportunity to capture the upside "hidden" in residual gains, but this trend caught all players off guard and therefore no single leasing company was able to take advantage of the trend by offering lower monthly payments.

In 1996–1997, used-vehicle prices first leveled off, then dramatically dropped. This shift was driven largely by the oversupply of nearly new used vehicles returned at the end of their leases. The oversupply and attendant price drops were particularly evident for the popular sport-utility vehicles and light trucks. Suddenly, lessors found themselves with mounting residual losses on their books, in some cases as much as $2,500 per vehicle. These losses greatly exceeded reserves.

Company Profile: A Leader in Trouble

National Leasing, Inc. is a major independent provider of auto leases, with $10 billion in vehicle assets on its books. National sold just over 100,000 leases in 1997. Buoyed by the general used-vehicle price strength described above, the company experienced very fast growth and excellent profitability from 1990 to 1994. Competition has driven down share dramatically in the past few years, slowing growth and reducing profitability.

From 1995 to 1997, National Leasing's portfolio became concentrated in less than 20 vehicles, those in which the company offered a competitive (high residual) monthly payment. Six vehicles accounted for about half the total volume. One sport-utility vehicle in particular accounted for nearly 20 percent of total units in the portfolio. These concentrations arose from a "winner's curse" or adverse selection phenomenon, in which National sold large volumes of leases for which it set the highest residual compared to the competition. Such competitive rates were the keys to success in a period of generally rising used-car prices.

But in 1997, when used-car prices dropped 8 percent in the first six months of the year, National was left with significant residual losses. Consequently, the company reported a loss of net income of $400 million in fiscal year 1997, prompting an internal audit. The audit revealed that many of the losses were related to operational errors and inefficiencies, including improper data entry, inadequate information systems, and faulty reporting procedures.

The audit also revealed flaws in the current residual-value forecasting process:

- No explicit consideration is given to the risks of setting residual values too high or too low.
- External market information and expertise are ignored, as estimates are made by a small group of internal analysts.
- Current market residual values are relied upon excessively in setting future contract residual values.

Current Situation

During the first half of 1998, National Leasing revamped its operations, thereby correcting most of the problems related to data entry and information technology. At the same time, the internal residual value forecasting group adopted a very conservative posture, setting residuals for new leases at low levels across the board. Rumors suggested that a new manager would be brought in to run residual setting and that a new process would be developed.

In mid-1998, senior management was divided on the question of what new residual forecasting method to use.

Some believed that National should simply use values in the Auto Lease Guide (ALG), a standard industry reference publication. Others strongly disagreed with this approach, on the grounds that using ALG eliminated National's competitive advantage. This faction further supported their opinion with analysis showing that using ALG would not have avoided the 1997 losses.

Despite a general consensus among industry insiders that most other major lessors experienced similar net income losses in 1997, National's major competitors did not follow its lead in setting lower residuals. The higher monthly payments associated with National's low residual values resulted in a 50 percent drop in sales volume in the first six months of 1998. Used-car prices continued to decline in 1998, apparently driven by flat (or falling) new-car prices. National Leasing's senior management, fearing that the industry was entering a period of sustained used-car price deflation, was therefore reluctant to raise residuals to competitive levels. They thought the competition must be "crazy."

Your Challenge

In recent meetings among the senior management, a number of possible solutions to these problems were been discussed, including improving residual-setting techniques, acquiring competitors, entering the downstream used-car business, and even exiting the new-vehicle leasing business. Your modeling talents and general business savvy have caught the attention of an influential senior manager at National. She believes that a modeling approach might assist National in making better decisions on lease terms on individual vehicles. (She has even hinted that she might be interested in your ideas on how to manage the lease portfolio, that is, the entire book of outstanding leases.) In order to give you a forum in which to promulgate your ideas, she has arranged time for you to make a short presentation to the Board in a week's time. In this presentation, your goal will be to convince the Board that your modeling approach will significantly improve their management of the lease business.

You are being asked to build a prototype model to prove a concept—that is, that modeling can help National management to sell more profitable leases. You are not being asked to find the right answer or build a day-to-day decision support system, of course, but only to show what you could do with the appropriate time and resources.

In this context, you would not be expected to have the last word on what the relationships or parameters were for your model, but the relationships should be plausible and you should be able to say where you would get the data to refine your parameters (if needed).

The most effective way to impress this client is to show that a prototype model can be used to generate insights she currently does not have. Such insights are not usually dependent on the precise relationships or parameters in a model, but rather reflect underlying structural properties.

*This case was developed as a class exercise by Peter Regan, Steve Powell and Jay Goldman.

MEGA PHARMA AND MICRO PHARMA*

Background

Mega Pharma is a large pharmaceutical company with sales in the year 2000 of $5 billion per year (all figures are in constant year 2000 dollars). Mega is developing a drug code-named MegaCardia for a particular variety of cardiovascular disease. MegaCardia was expected to reach the market in 2003. Mega learned that a competitor, Micro Pharma, was developing a similar compound called MicroCardia that was also expected to reach the market around the year 2003. Micro Pharma is a small pharmaceutical company with sales of $1 billion per year. These two compounds are instances of a new class of therapy, and no other companies are thought to be developing competitive products. Patent experts at Mega believe Micro's patent position is quite strong in this area, so it stands a good chance of preventing Mega from marketing its own compound. (*Note*: Micro can only sue Mega for patent infringement if it is successful itself in developing a marketable product.)

Executives at Mega are considering making a deal with Micro that will allow both companies to profit from sale of this new drug without getting tied down in litigation or other costly competitive actions.

Product Development Process

A typical pharmaceutical product goes through a predictable series of development phases, as follows:

Preclinical phase: animal trials focusing on safety (typically lasts 13 weeks).

Phase 1: safety studies conducted on 50 to 100 normal healthy male volunteers (typically lasts from three to six months).

Phase 2: efficacy and safety trials on a diseased target population under controlled medical conditions (typically lasts six to nine months).

Phase 3: efficacy and safety trials on the target population under actual conditions of use (typically lasts six to nine months and may involve thousands of patients).

FDA submission: preparation of a new drug application (NDA), involving extensive statistical analysis and report writing (typically takes six months).

FDA review: the FDA evaluates the NDA based on the preclinical and clinical data. This phase takes 17–24 months.

Both MegaCardia and MicroCardia are currently about to start Phase 2.

Mega's Perspective on Its Compound

Mega believes that its compound has a 50 percent chance of success in Phase 2 and an 80 percent chance of success in Phase 3. The chance of rejection by the health authorities in the major markets (United States, Europe, and Japan) is negligible given successful Phase 3 results. Phase 2 studies will cost $10 million and Phase 3 studies will

cost $40 million. Regulatory review support will cost $2 million.

According to Mega's marketing staff, sales of the new therapeutic class represented by MegaCardia and Micro-Cardia are expected to peak at $500 million worldwide five years after launch. Sales should stay near the peak until patent expiration, which for both compounds will occur in 2013. Profits over the product's lifetime are expected to be 75 percent of sales. Mega believes that its market share of the new therapeutic class worldwide will be 50 percent if MicroCardia is also in the market and virtually 100 percent otherwise. Since the products are almost identical, they will very likely succeed or fail together; clinicians estimate that if one product is successfully brought to market, then there is a 90 percent chance that the other will also be successful.

Patent infringement litigation typically commences when a drug is first marketed. Mega believes that Micro will almost certainly sue and has a 50 percent chance of winning the suit and thereby entirely preventing Mega from marketing its product.

The management at Mega Pharma usually evaluates drug development decisions on the basis of a Net Productivity Index (NPI), which is the ratio of the net profit to the development costs. The reason they do not simply evaluate projects on the basis of NPV is that development funds are limited, so there is an opportunity cost (which is not reflected in the NPV) associated with spending money on one project because it cannot be spent on another. The NPI allows them to compare the net returns from various projects to the net development costs each incurs.

The NPI is calculated by first determining the flow of profits that can be expected from the product after launch, discounting this to the present at an appropriate discount rate, and then by taking an expected value over the different possible future scenarios. Similarly, the net development cost is calculated by determining the pattern of development costs over time, discounting to the present, and taking an expected value. Generally speaking, Mega management would like to see the NPI exceed 5, but there is no specific hurdle rate. (The figure below provides a generic illustration of the calculation of NPI.)

Mega's Perspective on Micro

In thinking about the problem from Micro's perspective, Mega's analysts believe the same success probabilities and cost estimates apply since the compounds are so similar. They also use the same market estimates. The profit received by Micro differs slightly, however, from Mega's case in that Micro does not have the marketing strength to sell its product in Japan or Europe. It will need to find a partner in those markets and will likely receive a 10 percent royalty on sales as opposed to a 75 percent margin. Mega anticipates peak sales in each market of $250 million for the United States, $150 million for Europe, and $100 million for Japan.

Initial Negotiations and Next Steps

Several months ago, Mega decided to offer Micro $50 M for the rights to MicroCardia. When the two companies met to discuss the situation, Micro declined Mega's offer. Mega's executives believe the reason was that Micro expects the new therapeutic class to have greater penetration into traditional treatments. One Micro executive suggested that peak sales for the new treatment market would likely be $900 million (rather than $500 million as estimated by Mega's marketing department).

Mega's executives have asked their internal management science group to do some work on this problem and report back in a week when the executive team meets to prepare for the next round of negotiations with Micro. The following issues are of particular interest to them:

1. Is there a dollar amount that Mega would be willing to pay for the rights to Micro's compound that Micro would be likely to accept? (If Mega buys the rights from Micro, Micro will agree not to develop the drug and not to sue.)

2. Rather than buying the rights to the compound outright, is there a possible deal in which Mega purchases a license from Micro to avoid a patent battle? (Under a license agreement, Mega would pay Micro a set percentage of its revenues if it is successful in the market. Micro can still develop its own drug but cannot sue.) This option would allow both companies to market their compounds separately. If so, how much would Mega be willing to pay and Micro be willing to accept?

3. Mega's CEO is interested in the question of whether a co-development deal could be struck where Mega and Micro form a joint effort to share both development costs and commercial returns. Under such an agreement, both development labs could continue to operate in parallel, or could be combined into a single team. Assuming co-development, at what point should the joint team drop one compound and go forward with only the most promising one?

*This case was developed as a class exercise by Steve Powell and Peter Regan.

Expected Profit

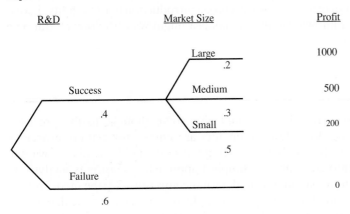

$$EV = 0.4 \times (0.2 \times 1000 + 0.3 \times 500 + 0.5 \times 200) + 0.6 \times 0 = 180$$

Expected Development Costs

Phase 1	Phase 2	Review	Probability	Cost
		Success .9	0.162	10 + 30 + 5
	Success .6			
Success .3		Failure .1	0.018	10 + 30 + 5
	Failure .4		0.120	10 + 30
Failure .7			0.7	10
			1.0	

$$EV = 0.3 \times 0.6 \times 0.9 \times 45 + 0.3 \times 0.6 \times 0.1 \times 45 + 0.3 \times 0.4 \times 40 + 0.7 \times 10 = 8.8$$

NPI

$$NPI = EV\ Profit/EV\ Cost = 180/8.8 = 20.45$$

Appendix:
Basic Probability Concepts

INTRODUCTION

Probability is the *language* of risk and uncertainty. Since risk and uncertainty are essential elements of business life, a basic understanding of this language is essential for the business analyst. In this appendix, we present some of the elements of probability as they are used in business modeling. We begin by describing probability distributions for uncertain parameters; then we discuss expected values, variances, and tail probabilities, describing why they are generally appropriate measures for decision making. Finally, we describe the elements of sampling theory, in order to provide the background for the text's coverage of data analysis and simulation.

This appendix is not oriented toward a broad introduction to probability theory. Instead, the focus is on knowledge that an analyst might want to draw on during a model-building project.

PROBABILITY DISTRIBUTIONS

For any parameter in a model, we should give some thought to the precision associated with its value. Very few parameters are known for certain, especially in models that predict the future. In various chapters of the book, we discuss ways to take this uncertainty into account. The simplest approach is sensitivity analysis, in which we vary one or more parameters to determine how sensitive the model results are to changes in the parameter values. For example, we might determine that if sales are high next year (50 percent above this year's level), our profits will be $5 million, while if sales are low (25 percent below this year's level), our profits will be only $1 million. With just this kind of information—an optimistic alternative and a pessimistic alternative—we have the beginnings of a probability model for the parameter in question. In Chapters 14 and 15, we forge an important link between sensitivity analysis and uncertainty. However, to appreciate this link, we need some basic concepts related to probability distributions.

A **probability distribution** is simply a description of an uncertain event or parameter. A simple and familiar probability distribution is based on tossing two coins and counting the number of heads. The distribution can be described in a table as follows:

Number of Heads	0	1	2
Probability	0.25	0.50	0.25

The same distribution can be described in a chart, as shown in Figure A1. Both the table and the chart depict the **outcomes** of the coin toss and the **probabilities** of each outcome. Any probability distribution must describe these two aspects of an uncertain event.

A **random variable** is a numerically valued outcome of an uncertain event. In the case of tossing two coins, we could have described the outcomes qualitatively (with the list HH, HT, TH, and TT), and we could still associate probabilities with those outcomes. However, when we describe the outcome as the *number* of heads, we are

FIGURE A1 Probability Distribution for Number of Heads

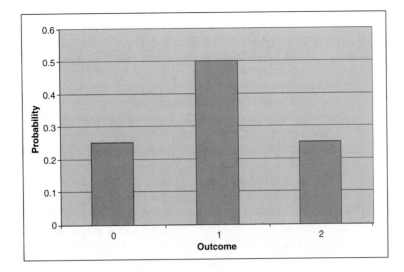

using a numerical value to describe the outcome. In this sense, we can look at a numerical parameter in our models as if it were a random variable. Our three-outcome table is thus the probability distribution for the random variable "number of heads."

When we can conveniently list the possible outcomes of a random variable or identify them with integers, as in the coin-tossing example, we refer to the random variable, and the probability distribution, as **discrete**. We can describe a discrete probability distribution (or, more simply, a discrete distribution) with a table like the one in our example: a list of outcomes together with a list of corresponding probabilities. Since the outcomes are mutually exclusive and exhaustive, the probabilities must sum to 1.

Conceptually, we use a discrete distribution when we are describing a quantity that involves measurement by counting, such as the number of heads or the number of customers or the number of defects. A discrete distribution might not be suitable, however, if we were measuring a time interval or the length of an object. When we deal in intervals, especially where fractions of any size are possible, we refer to the random variable, and its probability distribution, as **continuous**. In such a case, we describe a continuous probability distribution (or, more simply, a continuous distribution) not with a table but rather, with a function—one that we might depict in a graph. The function gives the relative likelihood of various outcomes, and, conceptually, there could be an infinite number of outcomes. For example, how long will it take to drive to the airport? The graph of the function labeled $f(x)$ in Figure A2 shows a continuous distribution for the length of the airport trip. In the graph, x-values for which the function is high are more likely to occur than x-values for which the function is low. In addition, the probability that the length of the trip will lie between two values a and b corresponds to the area under the curve between $x = a$ and $x = b$,

FIGURE A2 Probability Distribution for Time to Airport

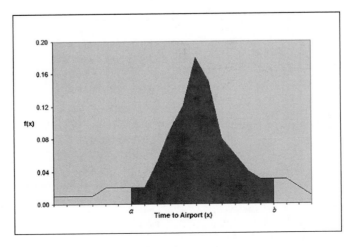

as shown in the figure. Since probabilities correspond to areas, the area under the entire function must be equal to 1.

What if we were dealing with an event that has a vast number of discrete outcomes? Suppose we want to model the number of light bulbs that will be sold in our hardware chain next month. Although we could use a discrete distribution and enumerate the individual possibilities for sales quantity, the list of outcomes could be unmanageably long. It would be more convenient to use a continuous approach, ignoring the fact that fractions are not possible (because we cannot sell a fraction of a lightbulb). Thus, the graph resembling Figure A2 could represent a continuous distribution used as a model for light bulb sales.

Alternatively, we might describe the outcomes with ranges of values. We might classify next year's sales into three outcome ranges: sales below 50,000, sales between 50,000 and 100,000, and sales between 100,000 and 150,000. One way to simplify the ranges is to substitute their midpoints as a single outcome representing the entire range. Thus, the first outcome would be sales of 25,000; the second outcome, sales of 75,000; and the third outcome, sales of 125,000. Figure A3 shows a distribution for these events in which the probability of sales in either the middle or high range is twice that of sales in the low range. This is a discrete distribution with three distinct outcomes and three corresponding probabilities. For some purposes, this model would be a sufficient representation of the possibilities for next year's sales, even though it involves a good deal of simplification.

These two examples show that phenomena in the real world are not intrinsically discrete or continuous. Rather, we can choose to use discrete or continuous models to represent those phenomena. The choice sometimes comes down to what is convenient for modeling purposes and what is plausible for the user.

A frequency distribution, or **histogram**, is a commonly encountered chart that shows how members of a population are distributed according to some criterion. Figure A4 shows how grades are distributed in a certain class of 100 students. Note that the bars depict the number of students whose grades fall in the given ranges (for example, from 86 to 90).

To construct a histogram in Excel, we can use the Histogram function in the Data Analysis tools. We select Tools▶Data Analysis and then select Histogram from the window of options presented. The Histogram tool draws on two types of information: One is an array of raw data; the other is the set of "bins" defining the columns of the histogram. For example, suppose that we have the scores for the 100 students entered in cells B20:K29 and that we list the upper limit for each of the bins in column A of the first worksheet. (The entries in column B are simply used as labels for the x-axis of the chart.) Then, we can invoke the Histogram function in order to produce the result in Figure A4, where we have edited the chart's format.

This histogram can also be interpreted as a probability distribution. For example, the chances are $21/100 = 0.21$ that a randomly selected student's grade

FIGURE A3 Probability Distribution for Sales

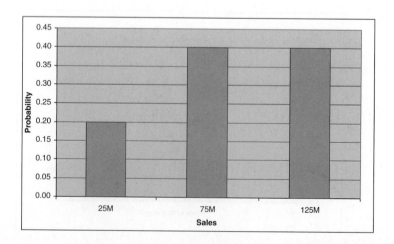

FIGURE A4 A Histogram
for Student Grades

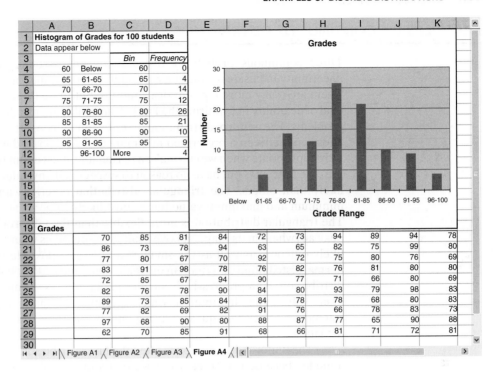

	A	B	C	D	E	F	G	H	I	J	K
1	Histogram of Grades for 100 students										
2	Data appear below										
3			Bin	Frequency							
4	60	Below	60	0							
5	65	61-65	65	4							
6	70	66-70	70	14							
7	75	71-75	75	12							
8	80	76-80	80	26							
9	85	81-85	85	21							
10	90	86-90	90	10							
11	95	91-95	95	9							
12		96-100	More	4							
13											
14											
15											
16											
17											
18											
19	Grades										
20		70	85	81	84	72	73	94	89	94	78
21		86	73	78	94	63	65	82	75	99	80
22		77	80	67	70	92	72	75	80	76	69
23		83	91	98	78	76	82	76	81	80	80
24		72	85	67	94	90	77	71	66	80	69
25		82	76	78	90	84	80	93	79	98	83
26		89	73	85	84	84	78	78	68	80	83
27		77	82	69	82	91	76	66	78	83	73
28		97	68	90	80	88	87	77	65	90	88
29		62	70	85	91	68	66	81	71	72	81
30											

Figure A1 Figure A2 Figure A3 **Figure A4**

will fall in the range 81–85. Similarly, by adding up the heights of the relevant bars, we can determine that the chances are 52 percent that a randomly selected student's grade will fall between 66 and 80.

EXAMPLES OF DISCRETE DISTRIBUTIONS

Although we can specify any discrete distribution by constructing a table of outcomes and probabilities, as we did for the coin-tossing example, there are some specific distributions that correspond to particular real-world phenomena. For example, the **Poisson distribution** describes a random variable that counts the occurrences of random events. In particular, suppose we wish to know the number of times our computer system will break down next week. The possible outcomes are the numbers 0, 1, 2, . . . , and so on. If we know that breakdowns occur at an average rate of 2 per day, then the number that occurs next week (seven days) can be modeled as following a Poisson distribution with a mean of 14. We need only one parameter—the mean value—to specify a Poisson distribution.

Another example is the **binomial distribution**, which describes a random variable that counts the number of successful outcomes in a series of n independent experiments (trials), each with a success probability of p. The possible outcomes are the numbers 0, 1, 2, . . . , n. Suppose we are counting the number of defective chips in a production batch of $n = 100$. (As is often the case in quality control, we can represent a defect as a "success.") If we know that there is a 5 percent chance that an individual chip is defective, then the number of defects in the batch can be modeled as following a binomial distribution with parameters $n = 100$ and $p = 0.05$. We need two parameters—the number of trials and the success rate—to specify a binomial distribution.

A third example is the **geometric distribution**, which describes a random variable that counts the number of experiments needed to generate the first success, in a series of independent experiments like the one we described above, each with a success probability of p. The possible outcomes are the numbers 1, 2, 3, . . . , and so on, without an upper limit. Suppose we are counting the number of days until our computer system will break down. (Here, a "success" is a breakdown.) If we know that there is an 80 percent chance of a breakdown on a given day, then the number of days until a breakdown occurs can be modeled as following a geometric distribution with parameter $p = 0.8$.

EXAMPLES OF CONTINUOUS DISTRIBUTIONS

Three continuous probability distributions are particularly useful in modeling uncertainty in business situations: the uniform, triangular, and normal distributions. There are many more types of distributions, but these three provide us with a good deal of flexibility in capturing the kind of variability we usually encounter in decision problems. The **uniform distribution** describes an outcome that is equally likely to fall anywhere between a prescribed minimum and a prescribed maximum. It is particularly appropriate when we can make a reasonable guess about the smallest and largest possible outcomes but have no reason to suspect that any values in between are more likely than others. The **triangular distribution** describes an outcome that has a minimum and maximum value but is most likely to occur at an intermediate point. The triangular distribution is more flexible than the uniform because it can have a peak anywhere in its range. It is well suited to situations where we can identify a most likely outcome as well as the smallest and largest possible outcomes. Finally, the **normal distribution** describes an outcome that is most likely to be in the middle of the distribution, with progressively smaller likelihoods as we move away from its most likely value. This distribution, which is familiar to many analysts, can describe a symmetrical uncertain quantity using only two parameters (the mean and standard deviation).

The uniform distribution is often the first distribution we use when prototyping a model, because it is so easy to specify, requiring only a minimum and maximum value. Figure A5 shows a uniform distribution whose outcomes lie between 50 and 150. The mean for a uniform distribution is midway between the minimum and maximum values (100 in this case). The critical property that defines the uniform distribution is that every outcome between the minimum and the maximum is equally likely. Often, this is a reasonable assumption, especially when first testing the effects of uncertainty in a model and when no data or other information are available to suggest different likelihoods.

A somewhat more flexible family of continuous distributions is the triangular. These distributions are specified by three parameters: the minimum, maximum, and most likely values. Figure A6 shows a triangular distribution from 50 to 150 with a most likely value of 125. Note that the mean of this distribution is not 100 but somewhat higher, because values above 100 are more likely than those below it. The mean of a triangular distribution is always one-third the sum of the minimum, maximum, and most likely values (108.3 in this case). Triangular distributions are particularly useful for representing subjective uncertainty. Very few managers can specify offhand a probability distribution for an uncertain quantity, but most can give reasonable estimates for the minimum, maximum, and most likely values.

The normal distribution is a symmetrical distribution specified by its mean and standard deviation. The normal distribution shown in Figure A7 has a mean of 100 and a standard deviation of 25. The normal is often appropriate for representing uncertain quantities that are influenced by a large number of independent factors, such as the heights of a group of people or the physical measurements of a manufactured product. But the normal is probably overused, perhaps because it is prominent in statistics, where it plays a central role. The normal should not be used unless there is reason to believe the distribution is symmetrical. It also has the sometimes problematic property that negative

FIGURE A5 A Uniform Distribution

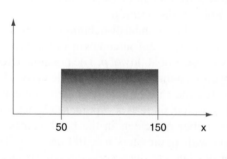

50   150   x

FIGURE A6 A Triangular Distribution

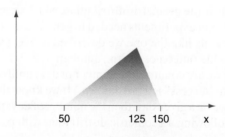

50   125 150   x

FIGURE A7 A Normal
Distribution

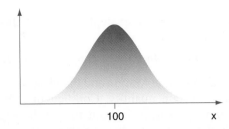

100   x

outcomes are possible, especially if the standard deviation is large relative to the mean. Thus, the normal would not be an appropriate probability model for demand or price, unless the standard deviation were small relative to the mean (say, 25 percent of the mean or less).

EXPECTED VALUES

We use probability distributions in two ways in spreadsheet modeling: first to describe uncertain parameters as inputs and then to describe the resulting outcomes. While distributions are important, they are also quite complex. In particular, many decision makers cannot easily understand the implications of a probability distribution for their situation. Therefore, it is important to be able to capture the essential features of a distribution in a single number. Usually, that number is the expected value. Most often the symbol μ is used to represent the expected value of a distribution.

An **expected value** is simply an average but an average of a somewhat special kind. Recall that Figure A4 depicts the grades of 100 students in a class. One way to summarize this chart is with the average grade, which we calculate simply by adding all 100 grades and dividing by 100. But this procedure does not work as well in calculating the average sales in Figure A3. Here, the outcomes (sales of 25M, 75M, or 125M) do not occur with equal probabilities—the outcome of 25M is half as likely as the other outcomes. Any estimate of the average outcome should take the probabilities into account. The expected value does so by multiplying each outcome by its probability. Thus, the expected value of sales in this distribution is

$$0.2 \times 25M + 0.4 \times 75M + 0.4 \times 125M = 85M$$

If S represents the random variable sales in this example, then we write its expected value as $E[S] = 85\,M$. Note that, as this example illustrates, the expected value is not necessarily one of the actual outcomes of the distribution.

Another way to think about an expected value is as a probability-weighted average. Indeed, someone who has studied mechanics would recognize the expected value as the center of gravity of a one-dimensional object (the random variable), where outcomes play the role of distances and probabilities play the role of weights.

To clarify terminology, we use the terms *expected value* and *mean* interchangeably in this book. However, we reserve the word **average** to refer to the simple (unweighted) average. Thus, we might refer to the expected value of the exam scores in Figure A4 as an average, but the expected value of sales in Figure A3 would be called a mean.

When distributions contain a discrete set of outcomes, it is straightforward to calculate the expected value: We simply multiply each outcome by its probability and add the products. (The calculation can easily be carried out using the SUMPRODUCT function in Excel.) Even if the number of outcomes is infinite, as in the Poisson distribution, there may be a formula that allows us to calculate the required summation. Alternatively, we might be willing to leave out very unlikely outcomes and make an approximate calculation of the expected value. However, in the case of continuous distributions, there is always an infinite number of outcomes, and the procedure for calculating the expected value is more complex. When any distribution is symmetrical, however, the expected value lies at the center of the distribution. Thus, the mean for both the uniform and normal distributions is the center of the distribution. As we pointed out earlier, there also happens to be a simple formula for the expected value of the triangular distribution.

One of the important properties of the expected value is **linearity**. Essentially this means that if an outcome is related in a linear fashion to an uncertain parameter, then the expected value of the outcome is also related in the same linear fashion to the expected value of the parameter. An example will make this clearer. Consider the following simple model for profit:

$$Profit = Margin \times Sales - Fixed\ Cost$$

In this model, we assume that Margin and Fixed Cost are known with certainty. Sales, however, is an uncertain quantity. Consequently, Profit is uncertain. But because the relationship is linear, if we want to find the expected value of Profit, we need to know only the expected value of Sales, that is:

$$E[Profit] = Margin \times E[Sales] - Fixed\ Cost$$

This property of linearity becomes important when we consider the implications of uncertainty in a parameter on the outcomes of a model. We noted earlier that most parameters are uncertain, although we may choose to ignore the fact. Often, the uncertainty present in the situation is not sufficient to justify a full uncertainty analysis. This discussion of linearity points out one such situation: If our model is linear (that is, if the output is related in a linear fashion to uncertain inputs), and if we want to determine the *expected value of the output*, then we can simply use the *expected values of the parameters* as our inputs and not use probability distributions in our evaluation. On the other hand, if either of these requirements is not met, then we will need to take a probabilistic view when analyzing the model.

Why is the expected value of the output a reasonable summary measure of all the possible outcomes? There are several reasons, but the most important one is that the expected value is actually the long-run average outcome if the uncertain situation represented by the model is repeated many times. For example, consider a simple game in which we flip a fair coin and receive $10 for Heads and pay $5 for Tails. Let W represent our winnings when we play the game. The expected winnings can be calculated as a probability-weighted average:

$$E[W] = 0.5 \times 10 - 0.5 \times 5 = 2.5$$

This is not a bad deal, of course: Our *expected* winnings are $2.50 each time we play. If we were to play 1,000 times, we would probably make very close to $2,500, since, in such a large number of repetitions, we would win close to 50 percent of the time. So if we could play this game many times, it would be reasonable to use the expected value of the outcome as a measure of its long-run value. In effect, we can ignore the uncertainty on a single repetition of this game because we are planning to play many times. The general notion here is that a manager facing a series of decisions influenced by uncertainty will maximize profits in the long run by maximizing expected profit on each individual decision.

But what if the outcomes were not in dollars but in *millions* of dollars? The expected outcome is still attractive, at $2.5 million, but we might not be able to ignore the uncertainty we face on each repetition. For example, if we had resources of less than $5 million available, then a loss on the first coin flip would leave us incapable of continuing, and thus incapable of reaching the long run, where our winnings would be great. In this case, the expected value is *not* a sufficient measure of the outcome, even if we can play many times, because it does not recognize the possibility that we could go bankrupt at the first coin flip. Thus, we have to qualify the principle of maximizing long-run profits by acknowledging that the manager can reach the long run only if the firm survives. The risk of an extreme outcome, especially if it jeopardizes the firm's ability to persist, should therefore be considered explicitly.

Throughout this book, we advocate a two-phased approach to summarizing the distribution of outcomes. The first phase is almost always to consider the expected value of the outcome. Even in situations where this is not completely sufficient, it is a necessary first step. But as our simple example shows, sometimes the risks associated with a course of action are so high that the expected outcome is not the only measure to consider. We should then be looking at the probability of extreme outcomes as well.

CUMULATIVE DISTRIBUTION FUNCTIONS

The cumulative distribution function (or **cdf**) gives, for any specified value, the probability that the random variable will be *less than or equal to* that value. For example, suppose we are using a Poisson distribution with a mean of 2 to model the number of breakdowns in a day. The distribution is shown in the following table:

Outcome	0	1	2	3	4	5	6	7	8
Probability	0.135	0.271	0.271	0.180	0.090	0.036	0.012	0.003	0.001

The cdf at a particular value, y, gives the probability that the random variable will be *less than or equal to y*. Thus, the cdf at 1 is equal to 0.406, the sum of the probabilities for outcomes 0 and 1. The cdf at 2 is equal to 0.677, the sum of the probabilities for outcomes 0, 1, and 2. Simple addition allows us to construct a table of cumulative distribution values:

Outcome	0	1	2	3	4	5	6	7	8
Probability	0.135	0.271	0.271	0.180	0.090	0.036	0.012	0.003	0.001
Cumulative	0.135	0.406	0.677	0.857	0.947	0.983	0.995	0.999	1.000

The cdf is usually written as the function $F(y)$, and, mathematically speaking, it is defined for all possible values of y. For instance, in the Poisson example, it follows from the table that $F(4.3) = 0.947$. A graph of this particular cdf is shown in Figure A8.

In the case of continuous random variables, there is also a continuous distribution function. It is again defined by the function $F(y)$, representing the probability that the random variable is less than or equal to y. However, in some cases (such as the normal distribution), this function cannot be expressed algebraically. Therefore, it is common to describe a cdf graphically. In Figures A9 through A11, we show pairs of graphs for the uniform, triangular, and normal distributions, respectively. The first graph of the pair is the probability distribution, and the second graph is the cdf. Mathematically, the cdf $F(y)$ gives the area under the probability distribution graph to the left of y.

TAIL PROBABILITIES

While the expected value is a useful summary of the long-run average value of an uncertain situation, we are sometimes interested in a particular set of outcomes, especially extreme outcomes. An example would be the outcomes that lead to bankruptcy in our coin-flip example discussed earlier. Another example might be

FIGURE A8 A Cumulative Distribution Function for the Poisson Distribution

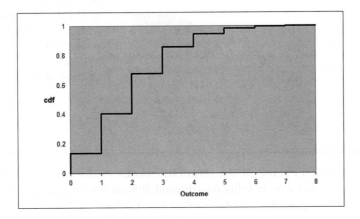

FIGURE A9 Probability Distribution and Cumulative Distribution Functions for the Uniform Distribution

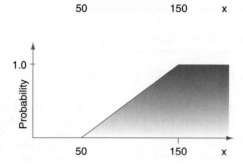

FIGURE A10 Probability Distribution and Cumulative Distribution Functions for the Triangular Distribution

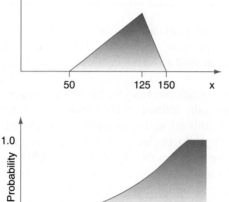

FIGURE A11 Probability Distribution and Cumulative Distribution Functions for the Normal Distribution

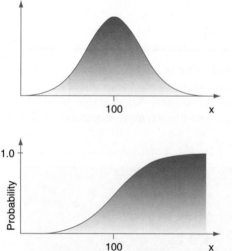

related to our probability distribution of breakdowns, discussed earlier in conjunction with the Poisson distribution. Suppose our system can tolerate only as many as two breakdowns in a day without exhausting our repair capabilities. What is the probability that our repair capabilities will be sufficient on a given day?

Another way to ask this question is: What is the probability that there will be at most two breakdowns in a day, or what is the probability that the number of breakdowns will be less than or equal to 2? The answer is the sum of probabilities on the left-hand side of the Poisson table (see above), or, in terms of the cdf, we want $F(2)$. Referring to our table of Poisson cdf values, we can see that this value is 0.677.

Probabilities relating to a set of outcomes at one side of the distribution are called **tail probabilities**. In some cases, we might be interested in the side of the distribution containing the larger values. For example, in our breakdown example, the risk is that our repair capabilities will be outstripped. The probability of this event is the probability of an outcome larger than 2, which we may write as the complement of the cdf: $1 - F(2) = 0.323$. The probability represented by a cdf value is a tail probability, or, more precisely, a **left-hand** tail probability, since it involves probabilities of outcomes to the "left" of a given value in the table or distribution. The probability represented by the complement of a cdf value is a **right-hand** tail probability. Such tail probabilities are often helpful in assessing risk.

In this context, risk is measured as the probability of some undesirable event, such as running out of funds or losing money on an investment. The probability of such events is often easy to describe as a tail probability. Thus, tail probabilities give us a means of quantifying the extent of particular risks.

VARIABILITY

Another sense of the term *risk* relates to the unpredictability of an outcome. In terms of a probability distribution, this means considering the variance. In particular, for a quantity X that is subject to a probability distribution, we define the **variance** as follows:

$$\sigma^2 = \mathrm{E}[(X - \mu)^2]$$

In words, the variance is the expected value of the squared deviation from the mean. In the case of our Poisson distribution, we can illustrate the calculation of the variance as follows. Recall that the mean is known to be $\mu = 2$.

Outcome (X)	0	1	2	3	4	5	6	7	8
Probability	0.135	0.271	0.271	0.180	0.090	0.036	0.012	0.003	0.001
($X - \mu$)	−2	−1	0	1	2	3	4	5	6
($X - \mu$)^2	4	1	0	1	4	9	16	25	36

Taking the SUMPRODUCT of the last row and the probabilities, we obtain a value for the variance of $\sigma^2 = 1.99$. This calculation is only approximate, because we were using Poisson outcomes up to 8. In fact, there are small probabilities of outcomes larger than 8. If we were to use four decimal places and extend the list of outcomes to 9, we would find that the variance is essentially 2.00.

In the case of continuous probability distributions, the calculation of a variance is complicated, as in the case of calculating the mean itself, although in some cases relatively simple formulas exist. A normal distribution is usually specified by supplying the mean (μ) and the variance (σ^2), so there is rarely a need to compute the variance if the normal distribution has already been specified.

The variance is an important feature of a probability distribution because it measures dispersion—that is, the extent of the unpredictability in the outcome. In some settings, the extent of unpredictability is a reasonable measure of risk, and therefore the variance is sometimes used to assess the level of risk. The variance and tail probabilities are two types of features associated with probability distributions, but they have special importance in business modeling because of their use as measures of risk.

SAMPLING THEORY

One important application of basic probability concepts helps lay the groundwork for statistical analysis. In this application, we take a set of n independent numerical observations (or samples) from an unknown population, and then we compute the average of the observations. We are interested in the nature of this computed average.

We refer to the value of the jth observation as X_j, and we treat it as a random variable, with unknown mean μ and unknown variance σ^2. When we compute the average of the sample observations, we use the following standard formula, giving rise to another random variable:

$$M = \Sigma_j X_j / n$$

When we compute the variance in the sample observations, we use another standard formula, as follows:

$$S = \Sigma_j (X_j - M)^2 / (n - 1)$$

Next, we wish to know the probability distribution of the random variable M. It turns out that the distribution is approximately normal if n is reasonably large, due to the formal result known as the Central Limit Theorem. Since this result allows us to deal with a normal distribution, we need a mean and variance in order to specify the distribution completely, and for this purpose, we use the observed values of M and S. In particular, the linearity property of expected values leads to the following result:

$$\mathrm{E}[M] = \mu$$

FIGURE A12 Distribution of the Sample Mean

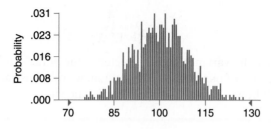

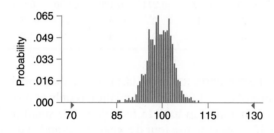

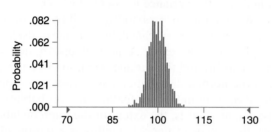

This result means that when we treat the sample average as a random variable, its mean value is μ, identical to the mean of the unknown distribution for X_j.

A companion result states that the variance of the random variable M is equal to σ^2/n. Thus, when we treat the sample average as a random variable, its variance is equal to the variance of the unknown distribution for X_j, divided by the sample size. It follows that in a large sample, the variance of M is small. Figure A12 reinforces these results by showing the distribution of the sample average when sampling from a uniform distribution with a minimum of 50 and a maximum of 100 for three sample sizes: 10, 50, and 100. The charts show that the variability in the sample average declines as the sample size increases.

Index

A

Absolute addressing, 63, 110
Abstract variables, 13
Accuracy *vs.* precision, 409–410
Additive decisions, 246
Adjusted R^2, 178
Algorithms
  GRG, 224–225, 232
  model classification and, 223–225
  optimization and, 214
  in OptQuest, 445–446
  simplex, 247–248
Allocation models, 248–252
  formulation, 249
  optimization, 251–252
  spreadsheet model, 249–251
Analysis
  base-case, 124
  breakeven, 133–135
  data, 140–159
  decision, 342–365
  in model formulation process, 9–10
  optimization, 135–136
  regression, 162–186
  sample data, 151–152
  sensitivity. *See* Sensitivity analysis
  simulation, 388–389
  spreadsheet, 123–137
  what-if analysis, 124–135
Analysis Toolpak, 182
Arcs, 285
Array function, 184
Assignment models, 294–297
  formulation, 294–295
  optimization, 296
  sensitivity analysis, 296–297
  spreadsheet models, 295–296
Assortment model, 335–336
Assortment problems, 335
Assumption cells, 376–379
Assumptions, regression, 181–182
Auditing software, 116–121. *See also*
  Spreadsheet Professional
Auditing tools, 114
Averages
  in expected values, 499
  in Monte Carlo simulation, 370
  sample, 153

B

Background knowledge, 8–9
Balance equations, 298
Base-case analysis, 124
Base value, 190, 199, 202
Basic formulas in Excel, 62–63
Basic functions in Excel, 63–67
Benchmarking, 126
Binary variables
  binary choice models, 320–324
  capital budgeting problems and,
    320–322
  linking constraints and fixed costs,
    326–329
  logical relationships and, 324–330
  relationships among projects,
    324–326
  set covering problem, 322–324
  threshold levels and quantity
    discounts, 329–330
Binding constraints, 223, 250
Binomial distributions, 497
Blending models, 255–260
  blending constraints, 256–257
  formulation, 257–258
  rescaling the models, 260
  spreadsheet models, 258–260
Bootstrapping, 434–435
Brainstorming, 13, 20, 46
Breakeven analysis, 133–135
Budgeting
  capital budgeting, 320–322
  constraints, 218
Building tools, in Spreadsheet
  Professional, 117
Business analysts, 2, 67
  charting skill, 67
Business education, models used
  in, 2–3
Business models, 2–4

C

Calculator use, in workbook
  testing, 112
Capacitated problem, 331–334
Capacity planning problem, 467–470
Capital budgeting problems, 320–322
Cash-management problem, 458–465

Categorical information, 154
CB Predictor, 205–209
  single exponential smoothing
    and, 207–209
  single moving averages and,
    205–207
CB sensitivity, 390–392, 443–444
Cells
  comments in Excel, 77–78
  editing in Excel, 60–61
  naming in Excel, 78–81
  reference checks in workbook
    testing, 113
  selection in Excel, 59
Certainty equivalent, 364
Certainty sliders, 413
Chance mode, 346
Charting in Excel, 67–70
  line charts, 67–68
  scatter charts, 67
Charts
  forecast charts, 412–413
  influence charts, 27–34
  line charts, 67–68
  overlay charts, 430–431
  scatter charts, 67
  sensitivity charts, 431–432
  Tornado charts. *See* Tornado charts
  trend charts, 442–443
Circular references, 56
Code inspection, 6
Code window in Excel, 91
Coefficient of determination (R^2),
  169–173
Coefficient of multiple determina-
  tion, 178
Coefficients, objective function,
  261–262
Communication, spreadsheet design
  for, 101
Complexity, spreadsheet,
  99–100
Computer systems, models
  embedded in, 2–3
Confidence levels, 155–156
Configuration in Excel, 55–57
Conservation law of flows in
  networks, 297